Symphony Orchestras of the United States

 SELECTED PROFILES

Edited by
ROBERT R. CRAVEN

Greenwood Press
New York
Westport, Connecticut
London

Library of Congress Cataloging in Publication Data
Main entry under title:

Symphony orchestras of the United States.

 Bibliography: p.
 Includes index.
 1. Symphony orchestras—United States.   1. Craven,
Robert R.
ML1211.S95   1986   785'.06'610973   85–7637
ISBN 0–313–24072–8 (lib. bdg. : alk. paper)

Library of Congress Catalog Card Number: 85–7637
ISBN: 0–313–24072–8

First published in 1986

Greenwood Press, Inc.
88 Post Road West
Westport, Connecticut 06881

Printed in the United States of America

10 9 8 7 6 5 4 3 2 1

The paper used in this book complies with the
Permanent Paper Standard issued by the National
Information Standards Organization (Z39.48-1984).

Copyright Acknowledgments

For permission to use materials, we are indebted to the following:

From The *San Francisco Symphony: Music, Maestros, and Musicians* by David Schneider.
Reprinted by permission of Presidio Press, © 1983.

From the *New Schwann* catalogs for use of discographies, used with permission of *Schwann
Record and Tape Catalogs*.

Contents _____

Acknowledgments _____

So much correspondence has gone into this volume that it would be impossible to acknowledge all the help that was given by so many kind individuals around the United States. With the certain knowledge, then, that a great many more contributed than can be mentioned, I'll try to enumerate some who have been of special assistance, giving my thanks to:

First and foremost, Marilyn Brownstein, acquisitions editor of Greenwood Press, who had the idea to compile this volume and its forthcoming companion, *Orchestras of the World* (exclusive of the United States). Cynthia Harris, reference book editor at Greenwood Press, who guided my efforts and always answered questions with care and precision.

Dean Charles Ehl and the Leave Committee at New Hampshire College, who awarded the sabbatical that made this project a practical possibility, along with the the staffs of the New Hampshire College Shapiro Library and the New Hampshire College Computer Center.

Music Directors Sergiu Comissiona, James DePreist, Sidney Rothstein, and Lawrence Leighton Smith, all of whom were kind enough to comment on my preliminary list of orchestras. Andrew Stiller and Fred Hauptman, contributors to the volume, for reading some of my manuscript work. Bob Olmstead, director of research and analysis of the American Symphony Orchestra League, who provided raw materials upon which I based the criteria for including orchestras. The editors of the *Horn Call*, the *Sonneck Society Newsletter*, the *AMS Newsletter*, the *Music Educators Journal*, and the other journals that carried announcements of the project. Lawrence Tamburri, manager of the New Hampshire Symphony, and Kay George Roberts, music director of the New Hampshire Philharmonic, both of whom answered questions and otherwise provided information.

Those who contributed articles. All who made recommendations of various kinds. By name, the individuals whose recommendations led directly to article assignments—my sincere apologies to any whose names I've missed. Prof. Otto E. Albrecht, University of Pennsylvania; Prof. James R. Anthony, University of Arizona; Maestro Uri Barnea, Billings Symphony; Prof. James Coover, Library Director, State University of New York at Buffalo; Prof. Ronald Crutcher, University of North Carolina/Greensboro; Prof. Emma Lou Diemer, University of California/Santa Barbara; Prof. Laurel Fay, Ohio State University; Prof. Gerald Fischback, University of Wisconsin/Milwaukee; Ms. Nancy Hafner, San Diego Symphony; Mr. Robert Henke, Akron Symphony; Prof. Barton Hudson, West Virginia University; Prof. Stephen Kelly, Carleton College; Ms. Irene Klug, Fresno Symphony; Prof. Douglas A. Lee, Wichita State University; Mrs. Flori Lorr, Orchestra Da Camera; Mr. Horace Maddux, Florida Orchestra; Prof. John Mohler, University of Michigan/Ann Arbor; Mr. Douglas Patti, Charlotte Symphony; Mr. Robert R. Palmer, Madison Symphony; Ms. Sally Preate, Northeastern Pennsylvania Philharmonic; Prof. David D. Roberts, Eastman School of Music; Prof. Kay George Roberts, University of Lowell; Prof. Harold C. Schmidt, Stanford University; Prof. Albert Seay, The Colorado College; Dean David Shrader, University of Nebraska/Omaha; Mr. Kenneth Steiger, Syracuse Symphony; Prof. Robert Weaver, University of Louisville.

I don't know how to acknowledge properly here the patience of my family during the past years' work on this volume (or the ongoing work on *Orchestras of the World*); I can only try to do so day by day.

ROBERT R. CRAVEN

Introduction ──────────────────

SCOPE AND PURPOSE

The following profiles are intended to present the general reader with introductions to leading symphony orchestras in the United States. They are not intended to expose house secrets behind the public facade, nor do they purport to offer definitive critical assessments. They offer historical précis, describe orchestras' seasonal activities, outline their budget and administration, and describe their cultural impact. The articles' authors are musicologists, composers, music educators, conductors, librarians, historians, humanists, social scientists, music critics, orchestra personnel, and orchestra administrators. Therefore, despite an overriding conformity in scope and coverage, the articles are somewhat diverse in viewpoint, and some stress certain aspects of orchestral development or activity more than others.

The orchestras profiled in the volume were chosen by the editor according to the following criteria: The preliminary group for inclusion comprised all American Symphony Orchestra League (ASOL) 1981–1982 Major and Regional orchestras (so designated primarily according to budget size), as well as the 55 highest-budget ASOL Metropolitan orchestras as of the 1981–1982 season (the most recent data ASOL could furnish in 1983, when the decision was made). To this group were added a prominent orchestra from each state not thereby included. A few Metropolitan orchestras were added that were known for their unusual programming or other activities by which they transcended their budget classifications (the American Composers Orchestra is an example). The Kansas City Symphony, not then a member of ASOL, was also included. A sincere effort was made to obtain profiles of all the orchestras meeting the above criteria. A few could not be profiled, however, because administrators or others connected with several orchestras expressed either directly or indirectly (by not responding to correspondence and phone calls, for example) their disinclination to be included in the volume.

SOURCES

The articles are based on a multitude of sources. Miscellaneous, orchestra-generated materials such as press books, news releases, brochures, and programs were used by nearly all authors. However, they are routinely excluded from articles' selective bibliographies (which nevertheless are collectively a very extensive compilation). Most authors verified the factual content of their articles with orchestra administrators. Further secondary materials were considered whenever they were available. Nearly all the writers conducted interviews with musicians, conductors, and/or administrators; many used orchestra archives (when available) and oral history archives. In several cases, the profiles were first steps toward otherwise uncompiled orchestra histories. Selected examples are William Brown's profile of the Jacksonville Symphony, Joseph Little's of the Charlotte Symphony, Ralph Verrastro's of the Savannah Symphony, and Dale Hall's of the Honolulu Symphony (research for which formed the basis for an upcoming book on that orchestra). Original material in David Schneider's book *The San Francisco Symphony* (1983) is also used in his article here.

DEFINITIONS

In the chronology of music directors following each article, the "present" reflects the situation as of October 1984, unless otherwise indicated by later dates, which are based upon information made public since October 1984. In many cases, orchestras did not use the title "music director" until recent years. Nevertheless, unless it is indicated separately, the term "music director" in each chronology refers to the orchestra's principal conductor, who in practicality is also usually given the responsibility for the musical well-being of the ensemble.

A brief "Recording History and Selective Discography" follows each article when appropriate. The discography lists selected, currently available recordings (the criterion for current availability was generally construed as inclusion in the July 1984 *New Schwann* catalog). Authors were asked to select recordings exemplifying the recorded legacy of the orchestras and their principal conductors. Non-commercial or unavailable recordings are occasionally mentioned in the brief "Recording History" section.

Each orchestra is listed according to the city in which its administrative office receives mail. Following the city entry is the population of the city's 1980 Standard Metropolitan Statistical Area (SMSA). This is followed by the name of the SMSA, if different from that of the city. In cases where the city of residence is subsumed in a larger SMSA, the 1980 U.S. Census city population is given first, then the SMSA and its designation.

In the headings, each orchestra's name is followed (in parentheses) by its ASOL classification, keyed to the December 1984 ASOL directory, and indicated by the following abbreviations:

Mj:	Major (budget of over $3.4 million)
Rg:	Regional (budget of $950,000 to $3.4 million)
Mt:	Metropolitan (budget of $265,000 to $950,000)
Ur:	Urban (budget of $125,000 to $265,000)
NA:	Not applicable or non-member

The adjectives "Major" and "Regional," when capitalized and applied to orchestras, refer specifically to the ASOL classifications noted here. The first reference in each article to an orchestra profiled elsewhere in the volume is indicated by an asterisk (*) for the sake of cross reference.

The term "professional orchestra" in the articles refers to an orchestra in which all musicians are at least minimally paid for their services. The use of the term "fully professional orchestra" (which in the orchestra world is used in different ways) was discouraged in this volume because of its ambiguity, but in those cases in which it does appear, it designates at the minimum an orchestra whose musicians all make their livings primarily through the performance of music. Although there are variations, "per-service" contracts between musicians and orchestras generally specify that the musicians perform a specified number of services (rehearsals and concerts), each remunerated individually. "Full-time" contracts vary widely, and the term should be taken advisedly. It designates a contract entered into on a long-term (at least monthly or seasonal) basis for a salary; however, even though the musicians are full-time from the orchestra's (not necessarily the musicians') viewpoint, many "full-time" orchestra musicians derive only a fraction of their livelihoods from orchestra rehearsals and performance.

ABBREVIATIONS

The following abbreviations are used throughout the articles:

AFM	American Federation of Musicians
ASOL	American Symphony Orchestra League
ASCAP	American Society of Composers, Authors, and Publishers
BMI	Broadcast Music, Inc.
NEA	National Endowment for the Arts

NPR   National Public Radio
PBS   Public Broadcasting System

Orchestra names are routinely condensed to initials in their respective articles (example: New Hampshire Symphony = NHS).

BRIEF BIBLIOGRAPHIC GUIDE

The reader seeking a comprehensive treatment of the history of American orchestras may consult two important books. John Mueller's *The American Symphony Orchestra* (1951) examines the aesthetic/social context of music as performance and the growth of the orchestra as an artistic institution. This volume presents a series of historical profiles of the major orchestras of the day, with detailed discussions of their repertoire. Although now dated, this groundbreaking work is especially useful for its examination of the aesthetic issues surrounding programming and audience development.

A lively and more up-to-date exposition of American orchestral history is found in Philip Hart's *Orpheus in the New World*, the most comprehensive book available on the past and present workings of the orchestral world, with an intimate portrait of the business side of the enterprise, including candid discussions of internal politics, labor relations, and the complexities of meshing artistic goals with financial exigencies. Hart provides penetrating, detailed profiles of six orchestras to illustrate principles developed in surrounding chapters.

For more thorough information on earlier orchestral activity in the United States, one may turn to Charles Edward Russell's *The American Orchestra and Theodore Thomas* (1927); earlier and parallel European orchestral history is accessible in Henry Raynor's *The Orchestra* (1978), although his approach to the subject is rather more musicological. A collection of articles on many aspects of the orchestra and its constituencies in America is provided by George Seltzer in *The Professional Symphony Orchestra in the United States* (1975). Kate Mueller's *Twenty-Seven Major American Orchestras* (1973) provides an analysis of repertoire, while Henry Swoboda's *The American Symphony Orchestra* (1967) transcribes a series of radio interviews with orchestral figures.

The individual orchestras have a long historiography, dating back at least to Krehbiel's *The Philharmonic Society of New York* (1892) and reflecting continual changes in social attitudes toward the orchestra's role in American society. Pre-eminent among the individual histories is Howard Shanet's *Philharmonic: The History of New York's Orchestra* (1975). Other important entries of recent decades are those by Kupferberg (Philadelphia Orchestra, 1969), Marsh (Cleveland Orchestra, 1967), Northcutt (Los Angeles Philharmonic, 1963), Roussel (Houston Symphony, 1977), Schneider (San Francisco Symphony, 1983), Wells (St. Louis Symphony, 1980), and Willis (Chicago Symphony, 1974). A selected bibliography of books concerning the American symphony orchestra generally and individually follows the profiles.

PRIMER OF HISTORICAL COMMONALITIES

Following are a few broad strokes delineating the general bounds of an exceptionally complex subject. With the advent of "jet-set" music directors with international conducting responsibilities, with increased orchestral touring, and with the brisk business in international recordings, there has been over the past decades a muting of what were once considered national or individual characteristics of orchestral sound. Institutionally, however, the professional symphony orchestra is quite different in the United States from its counterparts elsewhere in the world. Many orchestras outside the United States are government subsidized or cooperatively run, and proportionately few support extended, orchestra-only seasons independent of opera, broadcasting, or the recording studio.

Mueller's book treated the history of American symphonies as a gradual breaking away from European sources, first in organization (in the early twentieth century), then in personnel, repertoire, and conductors. Mueller found three main forms of origination among American orchestras—the cooperative society (as in the Philharmonic Society of New York), the proprietary orchestra (as with Theodore Thomas's independent orchestra), and the philanthropists' protégé (as with the Boston Symphony), all evolving in time to the widespread organizational structure in place today (a non-profit organization with an independent Board of Directors and funding from earned income, contributions, and government subsidy). However, other Major (and a great many smaller) ensembles emerged fully formed or developed from university orchestras, from amateur/community ensembles, or in later years from civic organizations at the urging of business leaders, from festival orchestras, or in other ways.

Professionalism has grown steadily since the early days and has accelerated in recent years, especially among the smaller-budget ensembles. This happy situation was in part caused by the orchestras themselves through their ongoing educational programs (which in many communities include one or more youth ensembles). And so while we still look to the Major orchestras as conservators of the art, many smaller-budget groups meet exacting standards of performance and, in proportion to their budgets, more than pull their weight in broadening and enriching the symphonic repertoire. Many also exhibit a dedication to educational functions and audience outreach that their smaller budgets might not suggest.

The movement toward professionalism has also brought new standards of fairness in auditioning, with consequent increases in the numbers of women and minority players, new schemes of collegial evaluation, and a general emancipation from the "dictators of the baton"—often with musicians evaluating conductors in a variety of plans having more or less the force of authority. With a few exceptions (most prominently in the Buffalo Philharmonic and the American Symphony), however, musicians have yet to gain a substantial say in Board-level decision making. The search for economic and job security among musicians of Major (and some Regional) orchestras led to a period of labor disputes that interrupted many seasons, starting in the 1960s and accelerating through the early 1970s. The *New York Times* reported in 1975 that there had been 16 strikes in five years among the Major orchestras. Among the foremost orchestras the issues were often those of parity with similar organizations; among the smaller, the issues were more a matter of "full-time" musicians demanding expanded seasons that would allow them to make their living largely through orchestral playing.

New orchestras have been founded with regularity ever since the era of cooperatives and philanthropists, as indicated in the chronology of foundings following the profiles. An upwelling of civic pride found expression in municipal support of many of them in the 1920s, as did the pragmatic notion, still current today, that the arts are good for business. With the Great Depression came not only bankruptcies, but a significant number of new foundings as well, as many musicians sought refuge after losing positions in movie theater orchestras when the silent film era ended. Recordings, radio broadcasts, and the stardom of the great conductors—Toscanini especially—helped popularize the institution, as did the establishment and widespread imitation of educational programs among the orchestras. The institution also found strength in the accelerating consolidation of symphony musicians through the American Federation of Musicians, and, especially for smaller ensembles, in the support of the Works Progress Administration.

By the 1950s a new spurt of orchestra foundings was under way. The single most important internal development in the post-war years was undoubtedly the growth of the American Symphony Orchestra League. The League estimates that there are today more than 1,500 North American orchestras, more than half of which are ASOL members. Through its management training, research, conferences, public relations work, government liaisons, and publications (*Symphony Magazine*, *Principles of Orchestra Management*, and numerous statistical reports), the League has been a powerful force in regularizing—even standardizing—the orchestras' institutional organization and functions.

Of great importance as well during the past three decades has been the growing sophistication of musical education (the orchestras' part therein already has been alluded to), affecting both musicians and audience. The broadcasting, recording, and electronics industries play important roles in the (broadly defined) educational process by enlarging the symphony audience and raising the expectations of the already-initiated. As to the newer generations of symphony musicians produced in the last decades, one need only cite the outpouring of highly qualified applicants for auditions on instruments for which—in the memory of many older orchestra members—there were once precious few competent players.

The search for organizational and financial stability has also seen important milestones in the past few decades. The Ford Foundation grants initiated in 1966 provided endowments and expendable funds—pending matching monies from the communities—for some 60 ensembles and have had lasting impact on many of them. According to the 1982–1983 ASOL *Annual Report*, orchestras earned a total of 37% of their 1981–1982 budgets through performances and fees, with investments and "other earned income" supplying another 21% and the remaining 42% coming from private and government support. Orchestras, looking to smaller donations from more contributors, have broadened their bases of support over the decades, often with the help of local radio marathons and other public relations projects. Many orchestras today stress in their public communications a businesslike approach to budgeting and marketing; modern marketing procedures have had a financially beneficial (though debatable artistic) effect on many. Innovative arrangements for funding through local businesses have also been developed. An increasing number of already-established mid-sized ensembles have acquired their own concert halls (often renovated movie houses or stage theaters) and act as local impresarios. The short-term financial exposure, however, has not always proven a worthwhile risk.

One answer to financial pressure has been to establish within an otherwise per-service organization a core of full-time musicians—principal strings, principal winds, and/or chamber orchestra—to provide musical and organizational stability while allowing for an otherwise flexible and cost-efficient approach to programming. The practice has coincided with the public's growing appreciation for chamber music, and core groups often have public recognition in their own right, as in Fort Worth, Texas. Independent chamber orchestras have also become well established in the last 20 years or so. Among them are some of the nation's most polished ensembles—in Los Angeles, Minneapolis/St. Paul, Philadelphia, Cleveland, New York, and elsewhere—flourishing despite the proximity of leading Major symphony orchestras.

Public funds for symphony orchestras, while a barely visible part of government budgeting, comprise a significant chunk (generally 10% to 15%) of orchestral income, directly through state or local offices, directly from the National Endowment for the Arts (since 1966) or in NEA regrants via state arts councils. Although severe NEA budget cuts proposed by the Executive branch annually since 1981 have not as yet materialized (having been blocked in Congress), their threat has invigorated corporate sponsorship of the arts and forced orchestras to seek ways of increasing and diversifying even more their grass-roots support. Corporate funding has grown slightly in recent years, though its overall financial impact has probably been less than the flurry of publicity in the early 1980s had predicted. Among the most publicly noticeable national corporate programs for orchestras are Exxon's support for broadcast concerts, its support of the Meet the Composer/Orchestra Residencies program (which places composers-in-residence with Major and Regional orchestras), and the Exxon/Arts Endowment Conductors Program and Xerox Pianists (both administered from New York by Affiliate Artists). Local initiatives also receive much corporate support.

Nevertheless, despite the general advances of the near past, orchestras do have their woes, both financially and artistically. Writing in the June 1980 issue of *High Fidelity*, Gunther Schuller catalogued some of them: Boards composed of non-musicians; music directors who divide their attention among several orchestras; short-sighted, materialistic union goals; and a resultant cynicism among professional musicians—which is thoroughly discussed in Edward Arian's *Bach, Beethoven, and Bureaucracy* (1971). Furthermore, orchestras do continue to fail—more in some geographical areas than others (southern Florida, for example, has had a tumultuous orchestral history, as has New York's Long Island).

In addition to issues of survival and growth, there are other current arenas of debate regarding the orchestra as a musical, social, economic, educational, and theatrical enterprise. Among them is the question of "elitism," as it affects funding, programming, and education. In a pluralistic society, whom should the symphony orchestra serve? One practical expression of this issue is the debate concerning the proliferation of pops programming. Other related issues are also current. Should public funds support organizations that serve mainly an already-affluent segment of the population? What (often invisible) strings attach to such funding? Is public funding of the arts an inescapably political activity?

With so many orchestras in unique social and economic environments, there is considerable variation among them regarding philosophical and practical approaches to programming. Many of the profiled orchestras present recent compositions on a regular basis, and some have banded together for the purpose, as in the Northeast Orchestral Consortium. But in most communities the biggest audience-pleasers, beyond the ubiquitous *Nutcracker* and *Messiah* performances, are still the romantic and late-romantic showpieces, particularly those requiring soloists. The issues surrounding repertoire are implicit in the profiles, as music directors, managers, Boards, and musicians must decide if it is the orchestra's role to follow or to try to form the tastes of its public. Related questions arise. What is the proper balance between artistic and financial responsibility? What local factors should determine the extent of an orchestra's museum function as opposed to its advocacy of the new? These questions, of course, have been debated throughout the history of American music. Some are eternal—we are reminded of Aristotle's *Poetics*: to delight or to educate? And in what proportions?

Despite the many areas of debate surrounding the orchestra as an institution, and despite the precarious financial situations of many of the individual ensembles, it is evident in the profiles that, whatever their state of development, American orchestras remain, as both Mueller and Hart found them, sources of intense civic pride to their communities. It is hoped that the following profiles will make them, in their similarities and diversity, better known to their collective constituencies.

Alabama _____

BIRMINGHAM (847,487)

Alabama Symphony Orchestra (Rg)

The Alabama Symphony is the only fully professional orchestra in the state of Alabama and the only one to tour the state on a regular basis. Each season thousands of people throughout the state hear the orchestra in their hometowns, and thousands more hear it in the Civic Center in Birmingham.

In the Birmingham area, performances are given to suit a broad diversity of musical tastes. The Master Series of 16 concerts and the Pops Series of 16 concerts are the backbone of the ASO's 34-week season. In addition, the orchestra frequently performs with the Civic Opera, the State of Alabama Ballet, the Summerfest Musical Theater, and other groups. Other special performances in the Birmingham area include numerous youth concerts, scholarship concerts, and broadcasts. At its home concerts, the orchestra often performs with leading soloists.

The Birmingham-Jefferson County Civic Center, the ASO's home, is the site of both the Master Series and the Pops Series. Each season the orchestra also performs across the state on college lawns, in high school gymnasiums, and in various other locations. Additionally, a series of outdoor summer concerts is presented in parks around the Birmingham area.

The ASO is governed by a Board of Trustees consisting of leading business, educational, and cultural members of the community. Its Executive Committee of 20, which includes all Board officers, meets at least once every month. The professional staff includes the general manager and nine other persons. A core of approximately 50 musicians is contracted annually, while additional performers are hired by audition according to seasonal requirements.

The orchestra's current budget of about $1.9 million is funded by contributions from individuals and corporations, benefits sponsored by volunteer auxiliary groups, and grants by such sources as city, county, and state governments as well as the NEA. Approximately 50% of the total budget comprises earned income from ticket sales and fees.

The history of the Alabama Symphony may be traced back to 1921, when a 52-piece orchestra was formed of volunteer musicians. Advertised as the Birmingham Music Festival, the initial concert was given on Friday, April 29, and was followed the next day by matinee and evening performances. Friday was billed as "Symphony Night," Saturday afternoon as "Popular Concert," and Saturday evening as "Choral Night." After this limited beginning, it was not until the fall of 1932 that the core of the Birmingham Civic Symphony Orchestra was formed. The first performance of the new orchestra was in November of that year, when it presented a Haydn symphony as background for a Community Chest rally. The following February, the Birmingham Music Club presented the orchestra in its first formal concert, under the direction of pianist and pedagogue Dorsey Whittington.

The Birmingham Civic Symphony Association was incorporated on October 23, 1933, and four concerts were planned for the new season on a budget of $7,000. On October 21, an editorial in the *Birmingham News* stated the following about the new orchestra: "The challenge is to the spirit of Birmingham, which is bidden to go forward with an enterprise which has been so valiantly begun. The challenge is also to the community's appreciation of cultural values, which can only prove itself by the manner in which our people support the venture which has been launched."

The adverse conditions brought on by the United States entry into World War II forced the orchestra to close in 1942. Following the end of the war and during several years of readjustment thereafter, community interest in a revival of the dormant Civic Symphony Association continued to persist. On September 18, 1948, an editorial in the *Age-Herald* noted: "Birmingham needs a symphony orchestra. A city of this size, with a stirring musical life, needs an orchestra of symphonic size as a crown to its efforts. . . . A community's cultural life is always in danger of atrophy, as is any part of its existence. It cannot be guilty of functional curtailment in any part without disturbing the whole."

Shortly thereafter, the Civic Symphony Association was reactivated, and with the assistance of its Women's Committee, began in earnest the task of rebuilding the orchestra. During the autumn of 1948, Arthur Bennett Lipkin was invited to speak to a large organizational gathering; he was at that time conductor of the suburban orchestras of Philadelphia's Germantown and Main Line, as well as a violinist in the Philadelphia Orchestra.* Eugene Ormandy wrote that Lipkin was "a good leader, an excellent musician, a wonderful mixer and an enthusiastic salesman." The following April, Lipkin arrived in Birmingham as the newly engaged conductor. A drive had just begun to raise $35,000, which was needed to supplement the $20,000 expected to be raised from ticket sales.

The first concert under Lipkin's baton was on November 1, 1949, and was followed by four others during the 1949–1950 season. The orchestra's pre-war conductor, Dorsey Whittington, appeared on the fourth concert as soloist in the Beethoven Third Piano Concerto. During the ensuing years, the orchestra was fortunate in obtaining world-renowned soloists. In 1956 the orchestra changed its name to the Birmingham Symphony Orchestra and during that season was established on a professional financial basis. Prior to this time, some of its musicians were paid weekly salaries, others were paid by the rehearsal or concert, and still others were amateurs performing for pleasure.

By 1957, the operating budget had risen to $129,775, as the number of performances and the number of ticket subscribers increased. Growth in membership and concerts across the state continued throughout the later 1950s under Lipkin's leadership. During this time the Birmingham Youth Orchestra was founded under the direction of Herbert Levinson, Symphony concertmaster, and shortly thereafter a training orchestra of young players from the elementary and junior high groups was begun as a feeder for the Youth Orchestra. Robert Montgomery, principal cellist of the Symphony, was chosen as its leader. These years also saw the establishment of several support groups, including the Vanguards, the Symphony League, and the Junior Women's Committee.

Lipkin retired in 1960 and was succeeded by Arthur Winograd, who led the Symphony over the next four years. Winograd had studied at the New England Conservatory and Eastman School of Music before joining the faculty of the Juilliard School of Music, where he served for nine years. Before coming to Birmingham, Winograd had conducted several orchestras in both the United States and Europe, with some 30 recordings to his credit. The 60- to 65-member Birmingham Symphony met increasingly demanding professional standards under Winograd's direction. After 1960, this membership began to reflect a significantly larger percentage of musicians from areas beyond Alabama, primarily as a result of Winograd's increased emphasis upon national recruitment. Winograd left Birmingham in 1964 to accept the post of conductor of the Hartford Symphony.

After a number of auditions and careful screening of applicants for the vacancy resulting from Winograd's departure, Amerigo Marino was appointed conductor. Marino had been associated with the CBS Radio and Television Orchestra (composer and conductor), the Glendale Symphony* (music director), the Los Angeles Philharmonic* (violinist), and, as a winner of the Ford Foundation Conductors Project in 1963, the Baltimore Symphony.*

In 1966 the Birmingham Symphony absorbed the Alabama Pops Orchestra, with Walter Moeck as conductor. During the same year, the Symphony was awarded a Ford Foundation grant of $600,000, to be received over a ten-year period. Subsequent to the formation of the Alabama Symphony Chorus, the Association in 1979 approved a change in name from the Birmingham Symphony Orchestra to the Alabama Symphony Orchestra, in recognition of the growing financial support and interest shown in the organization throughout the state.

During its existence, this orchestra has performed a wide variety of music. In general, programming has focused primarily on the standard literature of the eighteenth and nineteenth centuries, although the Alabama Symphony twice won the national ASCAP Award for the presentation of contemporary American music. Under Marino's leadership, the orchestra currently is devoting a somewhat larger share of its programming to the performance of newly composed scores. "The familiar repertoire of the symphony orchestra," Marino declared early in 1984, "does provide us with great music, but if we are to take our place with the other fine orchestras in this country, we must start introducing new music." Thus the state's largest symphonic organization has charted a new course to traverse fresh and experimental elements in music, along with the traditional masterpieces.

CHRONOLOGY OF MUSIC DIRECTORS: Dorsey Whittington, 1933–1942. (Operations suspended, 1942–1949.) Arthur Bennett Lipkin, 1949–1960. Arthur Winograd, 1960–1964. Amerigo Marino, 1964–present.

BIBLIOGRAPHY: Interview with Edward S. Wolff, ASO General Manager, 1984. "Birmingham's Own Orchestra: A Challenge and a Promise," *The Birmingham News*, 21 Oct. 1933. Joseph M. Ganster, "The Alabama Symphony Orchestra: The First Fifty Years," *The Fiftieth Anniversary Concert Program* (Birmingham: Alabama Symphony Association, 2 Oct. 1983). Amerigo Marino, "Plans for a New Season," *Highnotes* (published by the Alabama Symphony Association), Jan./Mar. 1984. "Reviving the Symphony," *The Birmingham Age Herald*, 18 Sept. 1948.

ACCESS: The Alabama Symphony Association, 2114 First Avenue North, P.O. Box 2125, Birmingham, AL 35201. (205) 326–0100. Edward S. Wolff, General Manager.

JAMES P. FAIRLEIGH

Arizona

PHOENIX (1,509,052)

Phoenix Symphony Orchestra (Rg)

The successor to a number of short-lived community orchestras dating back to 1902, the Phoenix Symphony Orchestra was organized in the spring of 1947 by a Symphony Association, a group of volunteers led by Dr. Howell Randolph. The first conductor was John Barnett, who had studied with Bruno Walter, Felix Weingartner, and Georges Enesco. Barnett led the 77-member ensemble in its inaugural concert on September 18, 1947. Scheduled in this and the following season were four concerts, all held in the auditorium of Phoenix Union High School, which was long to serve as the orchestra's home. During the first four seasons the ensemble included as many as 14 players from the Los Angeles Philharmonic,* where Barnett continued to serve as associate conductor. Most notable in his programming was the frequent inclusion of works by American composers.

In addition to a Symphony Board as a governing body, there was created in 1947 a Symphony Guild, a fund-raising agency for the orchestra until 1982. In addition, the Guild promoted educational organizations such as the Phoenix Youth Orchestra.

Robert Lawrence, a professor at Arizona State College, became conductor after Barnett left in 1949. Although the size of the orchestra had increased to a maximum of 88 players, only six subscription concerts a season were offered in this and ensuing years, the last concert of each season being dedicated to pops material. The budget remained modest ($45,485 in 1951–1952) and the programming conservative.

After Lawrence's resignation early in 1952, Leslie Hodges, also a professor of music at ASC, became the orchestra's conductor and music director.

Ambitious and unusual programming, higher performance standards, and controversy marked his tenure, culminating in his departure in 1959. A major figure in orchestra politics at this time was Lewis Ruskin, who until his resignation from the Board in 1979 continued to have enormous influence in the artistic and financial life of the orchestra, becoming Board president in 1962 and later Board chairman.

Guy Taylor was the next conductor and music director, a position he held for 10 years. During this time the orchestra's annual subscription concert series grew to 10, and a full-time orchestra manager was hired. The orchestra began a series of appearances in local high schools, became involved in concert performances of opera, and in 1964 moved to Grady Gammage Auditorium on the campus of Arizona State University in nearby Tempe. This 3,000-seat structure was one of the late designs of Frank Lloyd Wright. Subscription concert pairs were split for the next eight years between the new hall and the orchestra's original home.

Enthusiasm, growth, and ambition marked the 1960s. Awards were won, the most significant an $850,000 grant from the Ford Foundation in 1966, of which $50,000 was available for each of the next five years, though the remaining $600,000, available on a matching funds basis, was not received until 1976. Metropolitan Phoenix was beginning a period of rapid growth, from 663,510 in 1960 to 914,000 in 1968. Orchestra income from the 1959–1960 season was $84,117, rising to $420,751 by 1968–1969; only minor budget deficits were experienced during the period. The orchestra's first union contract season was 1965. A minimum of $60 per week over a minimum of 26 weeks was called for, and 60 musicians of the ensemble played on a contract basis. A few players, though, found it impossible to continue with the orchestra due to other commitments.

Taylor left at the end of the 1968–1969 season. He had been popular with many of the musicians and had improved the programming. In the mid–1960s several world premieres of commissioned works were presented, among them compositions by Paul Creston, Robert Ward, Carlos Surinach, and John Vincent.

The Board appointed Phillip Spurgeon as resident conductor for the 1969–1971 seasons. During this time guest conductors appeared with the orchestra, many of them evidently candidates for the permanent conductorship. Eduardo Mata was chosen and became principal conductor and music advisor in 1971, then conductor and music director in 1976. During his first years, guest conductors continued to appear frequently; Mata himself conducted no more than six of the annual 12 subscription concert pairs during his seasons with the orchestra. In 1974 Gerald Thatcher, until then Mata's associate conductor of La Orquesta de la Universidad Nacional de Mexico, came to Phoenix in the same capacity, a position he held until the end of the 1977–1978 season. His duties included the preparation of the orchestra for Mata and guest conductors and the direction of the young people's concerts and a few subscription concerts each season. In addition, Thatcher generally conducted the contract orchestra in concerts held locally and in several outlying Arizona communities.

Mata's musicianship and conducting skill were much admired by the orchestra. The composers he selected ranged mostly from post-Beethoven through early twentieth-century conservatives, with a tendency toward their more flamboyant works. In part this may have been in response to the tastes of the audience, portions of which might depart before or during the performance of music by, say, Hindemith.

However, Mata did program several works by Mexican composers during his years in Phoenix, not all of them conservative in character, although none of his own compositions were performed. During his first year one of the subscription concerts consisted of a fully staged production of *Tosca*, the first of several full-scale opera productions in the 1970s undertaken in conjunction with opera companies of Seattle and San Diego. The productions were largely responsible for substantial budget deficits during the 1973–1976 period. The Phoenix Symphony Endowment Trust, established in 1976 after receipt of the matching-funds grant from the Ford Foundation, ensured financial stability for several years following, however.

In the second year of Mata's directorship the home of the orchestra shifted to the 2,557-seat Symphony Hall, constructed as part of a downtown renovation project called Phoenix Civic Plaza. The acoustics of the Hall were designed by Dr. Vernon Knudsen, but due to construction compromises, the results were widely variable and generally disappointing, unlike Dr. Knudsen's work on Gammage Auditorium, hailed for its suitability for orchestral performance since its inaugural concert by Eugene Ormandy and the Philadelphia Orchestra.* Symphony Hall is difficult for the performers, with very short reverberation time and a strong resistance to anything resembling dynamic climax. The move to the Hall for the 1972–1973 season led to the near abandonment by the orchestra of Gammage Auditorium as a performance site.

Mata's departure in 1978 led to the appointment of Theo Alcantara as principal director and musical advisor and to a more conservative fiscal stance. The orchestra's income had grown in 1977–1978 to $1.15 million, reflecting in part the continued population increase in metropolitan Phoenix to 1.41 million by that time.

Alcantara has stressed a more balanced repertoire, programming more music of the classical era and lesser known works by major composers. As were his predecessors, he is solely responsible for programming decisions and the selection of guest artists. The character of the orchestra now emphasizes a dark, rich brass sound with lush strings. Philip Greenberg was associate conductor during the 1981–1983 seasons. Some twenty-one double orchestral concerts, of which three were pops and light classic, were scheduled annually, together with six double concerts of the newly formed

(1980) Phoenix Symphony Chamber Orchestra held in the nearby Scottsdale Center for the Arts. In addition, some orchestra concerts were repeated in outlying cities, including suburban Sun City.

The 1983–1984 season was marked by the beginning of an ambitious three-season effort, the ultimate goal of which was to achieve ASOL Major orchestra status. A three-year contract, lengthening the first season to 38 weeks, to be extended by 1985–1986 to a minimum of 41, was negotiated with the musician's union. The contract had the effect of forcing players to choose between the orchestra, which would now be in daily rehearsals, and other jobs or positions they had held concurrently. Many opted for retirement from the orchestra, allowing for selection of several new members. The number of full-time musicians was determined by contract to be a minimum of 81 to 85.

The need for increased funding led to the creation of a New Dimensions Fund, an elaborate system of contributor categories, and a more ambitious campaign for seeking corporate donations. By May of 1984, corporate pledges totalled $1.1 million of the three-year goal of $1.6 million. A projected orchestra budget of $1.88 million for 1983–1984 was expected to grow to $2.39 million in 1985–1986, the final year of the development plan. Considerable risk has been undertaken in this drive, symbolized by the objection by some in the community to the gift of $650,000 from the City of Phoenix (May 1984), money to come from its Civic Plaza Fund.

Efforts to increase ticket sales were in part responsible for the appointment of Doc Severinsen as the orchestra's first principal pops conductor in the 1983–1984 season. The five pops concert pairs were repeated in Sun City. In all there were 28 concerts by the orchestra, plus six by the Chamber Orchestra. The String Orchestra, whose personnel is separate from the Chamber Orchestra's, was formed in 1980 to perform in schools and for other services. Associate Conductor Clark E. Suttle is responsible for, among other things, a new Discovery Series, an additional set of four concerts designed to attract young listeners. Volunteer supporting organizations now consist of the Phoenix Symphony Auxiliary, whose main function is fundraising, the Phoenix Symphony Council, and the newly founded Phoenix Symphony Pops.

RECORDING HISTORY: No recordings have been made by the full orchestra up to the present time. An ad hoc ensemble was created to record *The Phoenix Symphony Ragtime Ensemble*: World Jazz Records WJLP-S12 (1977).

CHRONOLOGY OF MUSIC DIRECTORS: John Barnett, 1947–1949. Robert Lawrence, 1949–1952. Leslie Hodges, 1952–1959. Guy Taylor, 1959–1969. Phillip Spurgeon, 1969–1971. Eduardo Mata, 1971–1978. Theo Alcantara, 1978–present.

BIBLIOGRAPHY: Interviews with Theo Alcantara, and present and former staff members of the Phoenix Symphony Association. David Scoular, *The First Decade: A History of Events at Grady Gammage Memorial Auditorium, 1964–1974* (Tempe: Arizona State University, 1976). Bryan Carrol Stoneburner, "The Phoenix Symphony

Orchestra, 1947–1978: Leadership, Criticism and Selective Commentary," Masters thesis, Arizona State University, 1981 (contains extensive bibliography to 1978 and includes letters from and transcripts with orchestra supporters, players, concert reviewers, and conductors).

ACCESS: Phoenix Symphony Orchestra, 6328 North Seventh Street, Phoenix, AZ 85014. (602) 277–7738. Robert Gross, General Manager.

WALLACE RAVE

TUCSON (531,443)

Tucson Symphony Orchestra (Mt)

Tucson, Arizona, long known for its extraordinary desert climate and resort attractions, was in its formative years an unlikely area to produce a symphony orchestra. In the 1920s, Tucson was a remote sanctuary for many impoverished tubercular patients and home to rugged pioneer types who had to face the full force of desert sun and summer humidity without the benefit of modern air conditioning. However, despite desert heat and geographic isolation, Tucson developed its cultural as well as its commercial life, including an orchestra, in just the same way as many other cities—by the vision, dedication, and tenacity of certain individuals who served as leaders and catalysts.

It was in 1928 that Italian-born local attorney and music enthusiast Harry Juliani assembled in his offices most of the city's known instrumentalists and proposed the formation of an orchestra. An enthusiastic response from the 50 persons assembled led to the selection of a leader by secret ballot that same evening. Belgian composer-organist Camil van Hulse, perhaps the only truly professional classical musician in town, became the orchestra's first conductor. He concluded the evening by rehearsing Schubert's *Rosamunde* Overture, which the orchestra subsequently performed in its first concert on January 13, 1929.

Despite the enthusiastic response from both players and city—then numbering about 45,000—the fledgling 57-piece amateur orchestra soon fell victim to the difficulties of the times. Predictably, the problem was lack of an adequate base of financial support. Thus by the 1938–1939 season the Symphony faced a crisis: find a sponsor or disband the orchestra. This dilemma was resolved the following year by an uneasy alliance with the University of Arizona, itself a fledgling institution with only recently initiated degree programs in music and only about six music faculty members. Nevertheless, this arrangement made it possible for the orchestra to survive the lean years of the late 1930s and the war years that followed. The Symphony regained its autonomy in 1950 as a result of a confrontation with the musicians' union in which Conductor Samuel Fain, who was a member of both the university faculty and the union, joined with 19 key players in refusing to continue without being paid. This bold move paved the way for the professional status that was to follow. Since 1952, the orchestra's musicians have been compensated without interruption.

The first big step away from provincialism was introduced by Frederic Balazs (Music Director, 1951–1966), who began the practice of importing major guest artists as soloists, thus ending the established practice of featuring only local talent. This in turn brought about greater interest and support from the community. The three conductors who followed Balazs have all been orchestra builders and have had the benefit of a rapidly growing city, an expanding university from which many key players are derived, and a sounder financial base.

Along the way the Tucson Symphony has had the benefit of good halls in which to play. By its third season, the Temple of Music and Art, a 900-seat hall with good acoustics and space enough for an orchestra, had been built. This served for a number of years, as did University Auditorium and Palo Verde High School. At last, in 1971, the Tucson Symphony moved into a new and permanent home in the Tucson Community Center with seating for 2,277 listeners in a facility that its founders could hardly have imagined.

Today, the Tucson Symphony operates under bylaws and articles of incorporation, with a Board of Directors, to whom the music director and general manager report. Over half of the orchestra's $875,000 budget (as of 1983–1984) was derived from earned income (primarily ticket sales), with the remainder from grants and contributions. The dedicated work of the Women's Association (organized in 1952) provides 5% to 7% of the total budget.

Playing to an audience best described as conservative and somewhat older than the national average, Music Director William McGlaughlin is seeking to enlarge and broaden the traditional standard repertoire with new works and works new to Tucson audiences and to increase performances of music by southwestern composers. Recordings and large regional tours have not yet been undertaken nor are they planned for the immediate future.

The goal of the Tucson Symphony is to reach out to a broad spectrum of the public in Tucson and southern Arizona. Presently, the orchestra plans eight pairs of classical programs with major soloists and guest conductors and three pairs of pops concerts, also with guest conductors. In addition, the orchestra is extending its offerings to the surrounding area with a chamber-sized traveling orchestra and with still smaller ensembles: a string quartet, woodwind quintet, and brass quintet performing regularly in schools and other locales where a larger ensemble would not be feasible.

CHRONOLOGY OF MUSIC DIRECTORS: Camil van Hulse, 1928–1929. Joseph de Luca, 1929–1935. Henry Johnson, 1935–1937. Iver Coleman, 1937–1938. William X. Foerster, 1938–1939. George C. Wilson, 1939–1946. Samuel Fain, 1946–1950. Stanley Schultz, 1950–1951. Frederic Balazs, 1951–1966. Gregory Millar, 1966–

1977. George Trautwein, 1977–1981. (Guest conductors, 1981–1982.) William McGlaughlin, 1982–present.

BIBLIOGRAPHY: Joseph Cordeiro, "A Century of Musical Development in Tucson, Arizona, 1867–1967," Ph.D. Diss., University of Arizona, 1968. John Bret Harte, *Tucson: Portrait of a Desert Pueblo* (Woodland Hills, Calif.: Windsor, 1980). Dan Pavillard, *Tucson Symphony: A History in 7 Parts* in the *50th Anniversary Season Program* (Tucson: Tucson Symphony, 1978–1979). C. L. Sonnichsen, *Tucson: The Life and Times of an American City* (Norman: University of Oklahoma, 1982). *Tucson Citizen*, 1 June 1928.

ACCESS: Tucson Symphony Orchestra, 443 S. Stone Avenue, Tucson, AZ 85701. (602) 792–9155. Eric G. Meyer, General Manager.

CHARLES W. KING

California ─────────────────

BAKERSFIELD (403,089)

Bakersfield Symphony Orchestra (Mt)

The Bakersfield Symphony Orchestra was founded in the fall of 1946. Originally known as the Kern Philharmonic, the orchestra gave its first performance in Bakersfield, California on January 20, 1947. For the first few years of its existence, the Bakersfield Symphony was under the auspices of the Kern County Recreation and Cultural Commission. In the beginning, the BSO imported about 20 professional musicians from the Los Angeles area, about 100 miles south of Bakersfield. These artists filled first-chair positions and helped with coaching and with sectional rehearsals in the community ensemble. Over the years the orchestra began to employ more local musicians. The BSO thus evolved from a community orchestra with many amateur players to its present status as a virtually professional ensemble with most of the performers coming from the Bakersfield area.

The BSO presents a season of six subscription concerts along with several additional programs featuring guest soloists or conductors. The orchestra also performs between six and 10 young people's concerts throughout Kern County. An annual Benefit Pops Concert is held to support several local charities and musical organizations. The Civic Auditorium, which seats about 3,500, has been the home of the BSO since 1974. It is a multi-purpose facility used for sports events and conventions in addition to concerts. Average attendance for the Bakersfield Symphony is about 1,500 per concert. During the 1983–1984 season more than 20,000 persons heard the orchestra perform.

The Bakersfield Symphony is governed by a Board of Directors and maintains several affiliated organizations, including the Friends of the Bakersfield

Symphony, the Symphony Associates, and the Kern Philharmonic Association. The annual budget for the orchestra is about $250,000. The administrative staff includes two full-time management positions: operations manager and director of development. Ticket sales account for about 25% of the funds, the remainder provided by corporate and private donations, along with some government support. The majority of the 80 musicians who regularly perform with the orchestra live in the Bakersfield area and are hired on a per-service basis. The current concertmaster, Rebecca L. Brooks, and several other first-chair players are Bakersfield residents. Special program needs are filled by freelance musicians from Los Angeles.

Current Music Director John Farrer has held that position since 1975. He is entirely responsible for artistic decisions and program selection although input from members of the orchestra is also considered. The performance repertoire is mostly drawn from eighteenth- and nineteenth-centurymasterworks, although during the last several seasons the BSO under John Farrer has performed some of the more accessible works by twentieth-century American composers such as Barber, Copland, Piston, and Schuman.

Many of the orchestra members participate in other musical activities in Bakersfield and Kern County. There are several chamber groups, both formal and informal, within the orchestra. Among these is the Bakersfield Symphony Wind Quintet, which was formed by the principal wind players: bassoonist John Campbell, clarinetist Mary Moore, oboist Robert Stewart, and John Reynolds, horn. Members of the BSO also participate in the Beethoven Festival held each summer in Tehachapi, a small community located in the mountains about 50 miles northeast of Bakersfield.

CHRONOLOGY OF MUSIC DIRECTORS: Wendell Hoss, 1947. Edouard Hurlimann, 1947–1970. Alberto Bolet, 1970–1975. John Farrer, 1975–present.

BIBLIOGRAPHY: "A Short History of the Kern Philharmonic Society," (typescript, BSO, 1973).

ACCESS: Bakersfield Symphony Orchestra, 400 Truxton Avenue, Suite 104, Bakersfield, CA 93301. (805) 323–7928. Wesley O. Moore, Operations Manager.

JOHN CLARK

CARMEL (290,444—Salinas/Seaside/Monterey)

Monterey County Symphony Orchestra (Mt)

Founded in 1946 as a county-oriented community orchestra, the Monterey County Symphony's original group was begun in Salinas by Lorell McCann, the first professor of music at Hartnell College. In April 1947, the first concert was presented at Fort Ord, followed by a second performance at Sunset Center, Carmel, in May of 1947.

Gregory Millar, the first professional conductor, was secured for the 1954–

1955 season. John Gosling, appointed for the 1961–1962 season, served six years, and during his tenure the orchestra attained ASOL Urban classification. Gosling resigned in 1967 to take the post of music director of the Erie Philharmonic.

In 1968 the orchestra pushed toward full professional status. Haymo Taeuber was chosen as music director from a world-spanning field of 100 applicants. An experienced orchestra builder with lofty credentials, Taeuber has led the orchestra through a period of musical and organizational growth.

Today a core of professional musicians from Monterey County remain, but many orchestra players are drawn from the Santa Cruz, San Jose, and Oakland* Symphonies to make up the 75-member orchestra. The concert-master comes from the San Francisco Symphony* or the San Francisco Opera Company, as scheduling constraints allow. This import system has necessitated working within schedules of other orchestras; presenting a regular series of concerts has therefore been a minor miracle. Under Taeuber's leadership union scale wages increased, payment for mileage traveled was added, and musicians were put under the Social Security system.

A paired concert series presented in Carmel and Salinas during Gregory Millar's tenure was expanded by Taeuber to include a Monterey concert for a total of 18 evening performances, with six programs, each presented in Monterey on Sunday (following dress rehearsal), in Carmel on Monday, and in Salinas on Tuesday. The Monterey concerts are held at King Hall of the Naval Postgraduate School, where ideal acoustics must be sacrificed for comfortable seating for approximately 1,100 persons in a hall designed for lectures. Carmel's 733-seat Sunset Center Auditorium (sold out well in advance) has a beautiful vaulted ceiling and a fore-stage built by the Symphony to hold most of the string section. The Salinas concerts are held at Sherwood Hall, which seats 1,625. The Symphony opened this new hall (which has excellent acoustics and other amenities) during the 1975–1976 season with a concert filling it to overflowing. The Symphony arranges bus service to concerts from retirement complexes.

To complete the season the annual pops concert is held on a Sunday afternoon in late May on the grounds of the Naval Postgraduate School, formerly the elite Del Monte Hotel. Listeners bring picnic lunches to enjoy before the free concert. Early in 1970 broadcasts of taped concerts were begun, and for a time a series of concerts was also performed in King City, 65 miles to the south.

The orchestra has a large educational function. A series of In-school Demonstration Tours initiated in 1973 (originally totalling 216 per season; now 160) brings a few musicians from the four instrumental sections of the orchestra to fourth and fifth graders in area schools. Two concerts for youth on Monterey Peninsula and two in Salinas bring the same fourth and fifth grade students by bus to hear the full orchestra. A scholarship program awards $500 to one or two worthy student players, and four prior scholarship winners now play with the orchestra. One is principal second violin.

The orchestra has benefitted through the years from strong Boards of Directors working closely with the music director. The general manager is assisted by an administrative staff of four, as well as orchestra personnel functioning as personnel manager and librarian. Two chapters of the Symphony Guild (in Monterey and Salinas) comprise more than 1,000 members. Their many fund-raising and other events such as tournaments, shows, and regular Preview Teas have enabled the Guild to contribute substantially ($50,000 toward the $400,000, 1983–1984 budget). The orchestra is funded by individual contributors, corporations, foundations, the NEA, local governing bodies, business and industry, the County Office of Education, and military institutions. Earned income accounts for about 23% of the budget. Its cultural impact on the community is attested to by the many organizations involved.

Taeuber's choice of repertoire has been traditional, but he has also performed many modern works including the West Coast premiere of Andrew Imbrie's Second Piano Concerto commissioned by solo artist Gita Karasik. Taeuber's previews have been an important part of acquainting Guild members with works to be performed. From 1962, when Symphony Conductor John Gosling founded the Monterey Peninsula Choral Society, a major choral work was performed with the orchestra each season through 1980–1981. Under Haymo Taeuber, who had rebuilt the Vienna Boys Choir after World War II and conducted them for more than 2,000 performances, the chorus also performs Christmas concerts at Carmel Mission Basilica, bringing listeners from all parts of California.

The 1983–1984 season brought two guest conductors, Carter Nice and Thomas Conlin. The 1984–1985 season featured five more during the search for a replacement for Taeuber, who after 16 years with the Monterey County Symphony wished to be free to accept guest conducting in the future. The Symphony Board has asked Taeuber to assist as advisor during the search for his successor.

CHRONOLOGY OF MUSIC DIRECTORS: Lorell McCann, 1946–1954. Gregory Millar, 1954–1959. Earl Bernard Murray, 1959–1960. Ronald Ondrejka, 1960–1961. John Gosling, 1961–1967. Jan deJong, 1967–1968. Haymo Taeuber, 1968–1983. (Guest conductors, 1983–1985.)

BIBLIOGRAPHY: *Monterey County Symphony: 1983–1984* (Carmel, Calif.: MCSO, 1983).

ACCESS: Monterey County Symphony Orchestra, Box 3965, Carmel, CA 93921. (408) 624–8511. Elizabeth Pasquinelli, General Manager.

VIOLET C. BEAHAN AND MARJORIE OREN

FRESNO (514,621)

Fresno Philharmonic Orchestra (Mt)

The Fresno Philharmonic Orchestra played its first concert in May 1954, about two weeks after the 25th anniversary concert of the Fresno State College Orchestra, a college/community orchestra directed by Arthur Berdahl. After Haig Yaghjian, Stanley Keith, and Clarence Heagy called a meeting to organize a symphony orchestra, almost all the musicians in the college orchestra joined the new Fresno Philharmonic conducted by Yaghjian. In a sense the Philharmonic, nurtured in the college setting, graduated from it to become a separate community orchestra while the college music department continued to thrive.

Thirty years after its community orchestra origins, the Philharmonic has a budget of $500,000, an ambitious schedule, and plans for growth. Located in the central San Joaquin Valley of California, in a productive agri-business area almost midway between San Francisco and Los Angeles, the orchestra still retains its community spirit. The 75 professional and semi-professional musicians live in Fresno and other Valley towns. Many have been associated with the local university, colleges, and other schools. Of the musicians playing during the 1983–1984 season, 11 had played in that first 1954 concert.

More than 33,000 attended concerts in 1982–1983, and the orchestra has joined the community in events like the opening of the downtown Fulton Mall (1965), a "Concert of the Armenian Spirit" sponsored by the large Armenian community (1976), and a July "American Celebration" with the Fresno Arts Center (1984). The orchestra works with schools in presenting children's concerts, includes the Community Chorus and choirs from California State University (Fresno) and Pacific College in concerts presenting large orchestral and choral works, and cooperates with Rotary and the Women's Symphony League in the annual Rotary Young Artists Award Competition, which provides a prize and performances with the orchestra for the winners. Runouts made possible by grants from the NEA bring the Philharmonic to new audiences in other San Joaquin Valley communities.

The orchestra season consists of seven pairs of subscription concerts, four pairs of children's concerts, four to seven tour concerts, and several pops concerts or performances for special occasions. String ensembles and wind and brass quintets from the orchestra perform occasionally. The spacious and comfortable William Saroyan Theatre, with continental-style seating for about 2,360, has been the setting for subscription concerts since 1966 when the theater, part of the Fresno Convention Center, opened.

The repertoire, based on traditional programming for orchestra, has also included contemporary composers such as Toru Takemitsu and Heuwell

Tircuit, among many others. Music for pops concerts goes from marches and show tunes to familiar classics, while children's concerts present a variety ranging from program music to compositions written by children in the audience and arranged by orchestra members.

Private and corporate funding, grants, and season ticket sales provide the primary support for the orchestra. A campaign for long-term stability, erasing the deficit of the last few years and providing for future growth, is successfully under way. The Fresno Philharmonic Association is incorporated to oversee the activities of the Philharmonic and two student orchestras (the Junior Philharmonic and Youth Orchestra). The 25 members of the Board of Directors make decisions based on recommendations from the Executive Committee, which consists of eight members of the Board. New members of the Board of Directors, except for the orchestra member (whom the orchestra elects) are suggested by current members of the Board of Directors and approved by the Board of Trustees, an advisory group. The music director and conductor is responsible for selection of music and soloists, programming, concert preparation, and performances. A director of development and an orchestra manager head the administrative staff. Orchestra musicians elect an Orchestra Committee to represent them with management and in general problem solving. Most orchestra musicians are union members; the first union contract for the orchestra was in 1976. The 1982 negotiations resulted in a three-year contract that included putting an orchestra member on the Board of Directors.

Haig Yaghjian was the orchestra's first music director. He was a man of vision, a poetic conductor whose drive, enthusiasm, fine musicianship, and willingness to undertake the business of starting an orchestra were essential to its success. Yaghjian was succeeded by Paul Vermel, a thoroughly professional musician and disciplined conductor who, according to musicians who played under his leadership, "tightened up the orchestra" and "enlarged our understanding." The next music director, Thomas Griswold, very skilled in community relations, saw an increased concert schedule, the first Sierra Music Camp for young musicians (under the supervision of Malcolm Davison), and two outdoor concerts in Yosemite National Park. His successor, Guy Taylor, led the orchestra toward excellence through careful preparation, disciplined musicianship, and an understanding of how music makes sense. His dedication to contemporary music as well as to the standard repertoire led to five premieres of new works with the orchestra and an ASCAP award for Adventuresome Programming of Contemporary Music for 1976–1977. Philip Greenberg, of Grand Rapids, Michigan, became the fifth music director of the Fresno Philharmonic, beginning with the 1984–1985 season. His experience as assistant conductor with the Detroit Symphony* and more recently as resident conductor of the Phoenix Symphony,* his energy, and his musicianship should help the orchestra grow toward ASOL Regional class standing.

Fresno Philharmonic concerts have been recorded for broadcast on local radio, most recently public radio station KVPR, and occasionally have been presented live or on tape over local television.

CHRONOLOGY OF MUSIC DIRECTORS: Haig Yaghjian, 1954–1959. Paul Vermel, 1959–1965. Thomas Griswold, 1965–1969. Guy Taylor, 1969–1984. Philip Greenberg, 1984–present.

BIBLIOGRAPHY: Interviews with Malcolm Davison, Beatrice Fleming, J. Robert Fulton, Irene Klug, Guy Taylor, and James Winter, 1984. David Hale, "Golden Memories at Silver Anniversary of Philharmonic," *The Fresno Bee*, 13 May 1979.

ACCESS: Fresno Philharmonic Orchestra, 1300 North Fresno, Suite 201B, Fresno, CA 93703. (209) 485–3020. Irene Klug, Acting General Manager.

BETTY E. HIGDON

GLENDALE (132,664; 7,477,503—Los Angeles/Long Beach)

Glendale Symphony Orchestra (Mt)

The Glendale Symphony Orchestra provides seven concerts per season, including a repeated Christmas concert. Its educational activities, mostly administered under the supervision of the Women's Committee, include scholarships, music teacher aides, and sectional-ensemble concerts in the schools. Its musicians are engaged on a per-service basis and are all professionals drawn largely from the motion picture, television, and recording studios in southern California. The orchestra presents the standard classical and romantic repertoire, extended with light classical and pops programs as well as traditional holiday fare. Although new music is rarely performed, each season includes American music, and plans for annual all-American programs are under way.

In 1980 the Glendale Symphony Orchestra Association published a thorough history of the organization, *The Glendale Symphony Orchestra, 1924–1980* by Blanche G. Bobbitt, upon which the following account is based.

Community sings had become popular events in the Los Angeles area in the early 1920s, as indicated by the turnout of 15,000 people to hear and participate in the Easter sunrise service presented at Barnsdall Park by the Los Angeles Philharmonic* in 1921. The Glendale Community Service organization in 1923 created a Choral Club, and following a series of well-attended church and community sing-alongs, the Club presented its own massive Easter sunrise service concert at Forest Lawn cemetery in 1924, for which the Glendale Symphony Orchestra was formed under the direction of J. Arthur Myers. The attendance of 7,000 made clear that the orchestra would become a permanent fixture, and further outdoor concerts led to the establishment in 1925 of the Glendale Symphony Orchestra Association, which would organize concerts to be held at the auditorium of the Glendale Tuesday Afternoon Club.

In 1926 Myers took the role of orchestra manager, relinquishing the baton to Modest Altschuler, who had been a guest conductor in the opening season of the Hollywood Bowl. By the 1928–1929 season the orchestra, though still officially non-professional, had attained enough polish to present an Easter concert at the Hollywood Bowl, a production of Tchaikovsky's *Eugene Onegin* and Liszt's Piano Concerto No. 1.

The orchestra continued despite the depression, a period that saw a rapid turnover in conductors and a brief alliance with Glendale Junior College (during which the ensemble was known as the Glendale College Symphony Orchestra). In 1935 the orchestra selected a new music director, William Ulrich, who led it (under the name of the Glendale Community Symphony Orchestra) through 10 years of relative stability, despite the difficulties of World War II. In 1944 the ensemble name was returned to its original title, the Glendale Symphony Orchestra.

Through the late 1940s negotiations with the musicians' union resulted in a semi-professional status for the orchestra, which (as most such organizations do) had for some time used union personnel in its ostensibly community organization.

By the mid–1950s, however, the community-orchestra pattern was no longer drawing audiences as large as it had, and the Association once again reorganized, this time to support a unionized orchestra. Amerigo Marino (then music director for the CBS organization) was hired as resident conductor, and financial backing was provided by Mr. J. E. Hoeft, president of the Glendale Federal Savings and Loan Association. The orchestra from then on was managed as a professional organization. In 1965 the orchestra began giving concerts at the new Dorothy Chandler Pavilion of the Music Center in Los Angeles. Music Director Carmen Dragon, who had conducted many of the concerts during 1963 and 1964, began his long and successful tenure, which lasted until his death in 1984. He is credited with bringing the orchestra to its present state of prominence.

The Glendale Symphony Orchestra Association comprises all subscribers to the Orchestra. It is administered by a 21-member Board of Directors, a full-time volunteer staff of three, and two part-time paid employees. Ticket sales account for 51% of the $300,000 (1983–1984) budget, the remainder deriving from county and city grants, individual contributions, Women's Committee contributions, and corporate contributions. The Association hopes to institute a series of summer pops concerts in parks and other accessible areas as well as free runout concerts in and around Glendale.

CHRONOLOGY OF MUSIC DIRECTORS: J. Arthur Myers, 1924–1926. Modest Altschuler, 1926–1931. D. C. Cianfoni, 1931. Adolf Tandler, 1931–1932. Liborius Hauptmann, 1932–1935. William Ulrich, 1935–1945. Scipione Guidi, 1945–1955. (Guest conductors, 1955–1956.) Amerigo Marino (Resident Conductor, with guest conductors), 1956–1963. Carmen Dragon, 1965–1984. Daniel Lewis (Music Advisor), 1984–1985.

BIBLIOGRAPHY: Blanche G. Bobbitt, *The Glendale Symphony Orchestra, 1924–1980* (Glendale: GSOA, 1980). Glendale Symphony Orchestra, "Five Year Plan," typescript, 1984. Mrs. George J. Seeley, Vice President/Administration, correspondence with author, 1984.

ACCESS: Glendale Symphony Association, 401 North Brand Boulevard, Suite 520, Glendale, CA 91203. (818) 500–8720. Mrs. George J. Seeley, Vice President/Administration.

ROBERT R. CRAVEN

LONG BEACH (361,334; 7,477,503—Los Angeles/Long Beach)

Long Beach Symphony Orchestra (Rg)

Currently the second largest symphony orchestra in Los Angeles County, the Long Beach Symphony Orchestra has emerged in recent years as a major performing organization. From the late 1920s to the 1960s, however, the LBSO was primarily a community orchestra—one of the oldest in southern California.

Long Beach in the 1920s was the fourth largest city in California. The first successful oil drilling in 1921 created an industry there overnight. Plans of the Port of Long Beach were already in progress with federal funding approved. Shipping, fishing, produce canning, and general construction were major industries. Long Beach was a city that took an interest in its musical growth as well. The most significant musical organization, the Long Beach Municipal Band, was organized through subscriptions in 1909. However, all aspects of music were championed by at least one organization and, with the increase in patronage, the climate was right for the founding of the Long Beach Symphony Orchestra.

The LBSO had a rather halting start. Between 1925 and 1928 a group of local Long Beach musicians had been rehearsing informally under the direction donated freely by Leonard J. Walker, who was well regarded in the local music community, particularly because of his association as a performer under such conductors as Toscanini, Stokowski, and Beecham. On October 23, 1928, the first formal concert of the LBSO under Walker's direction was given at the Municipal Auditorium. The 1928–1929 season's eight concerts emphasized local talent, and the policy of encouraging community talent and creating interest among local students was established. The 1929–1930 season offered five concerts, and while eight performances were scheduled for 1930–1931, only one (May 26, 1931) was given.

With the sponsorship of the City of Long Beach Recreation Department, the orchestra was reorganized in 1935. On February 16, 1935, the newly named Long Beach Philharmonic under the direction of Robert Resta, a retired military band leader, gave its first performance in a season of four concerts. Despite favorable public reaction, however, performances ceased after this initial season. The Long Beach Symphony Association continued to work toward the development of an orchestra and, in 1940, with its incorporation, the orchestra once again began operation.

Resta returned as conductor and remained until his resignation at the start of the 1955–1956 season. Most Long Beach Philharmonic members were area teachers; others were gifted students and amateurs. Performances were free and were given in the Municipal Auditorium. Concerts continued through the war years with such soloists as Percy Grainger and Ruggiero Ricci. The orchestra's programming, however, was mostly dictated by circumstances. There were limitations on the difficulty of the music, and for the most part the orchestra played short pieces, excerpts, and marches, with operatic selections also being popular.

During the 1956–1957 season the orchestra found a new conductor in Lauris Jones, a new name—the Long Beach Symphony Orchestra—and a new hall in the Long Beach City College Auditorium. It was during Jones's tenure (1956–1966) that the community began to support its orchestra fully. Until Jones took the podium, there had been four concerts a season. Jones added special concerts to the usual four, differentiating between "regular" season concerts and special occasions. In 1962 began one of the oldest and largest special projects of the LBSO, the "Starlight Serenades." These free concerts in the parks met with great success.

With the resignation of Lauris Jones, an interim period followed in which Akira Endo was appointed conductor for the 1966–1967 season. A succession of guest conductors led to the appointment in 1968 of the Cuban-born, European-trained Alberto Bolet. During Bolet's tenure the LBSO played in a variety of halls, beginning in 1969 with a return to the Municipal Auditorium. During the 1971–1972 season, renovations there forced concerts to shift from one high school auditorium to another. The LBSO returned to the City College Auditorium in late 1974. In January of 1978 the 3,056-seat, acoustically impressive Terrace Theater was inaugurated. Part of the Long Beach Convention Center, it became the LBSO's permanent home.

Bolet's contract expired with the 1977–1978 season. Following two seasons of guest conductors, the Board of Directors appointed Murry Sidlin, who began a process of revitalization that brought the orchestra national prominence. Under Sidlin the LBSO had added several concert series, resulting in a total of 28 performances in the 1983–1984 season. A pops series introduced in 1978 has been continued. A baroque ensemble series with performances in the historic First Congregational Church of Long Beach as well as a "Cabaret Pops" series with performances in the Long Beach Arena were added during the 1983–1984 season.

Under Murry Sidlin's direction the LBSO's personnel has solidified (the orchestra has been unionized since 1979). Most musicians are from the southern California area and are contractually committed to the orchestra for the season. Diversification of repertoire is a hallmark of the LBSO under

Sidlin. The Baroque Ensemble Series, the Pops, and the Cabaret Pops along with the Classics Series have all attracted wide and growing audiences. For the 1984–1985 season the LBSO scheduled the West Coast premiere of Ned Rorem's *Lions (A Dream)* as well as the premiere of a new work by Dave Brubeck.

Recently operating with a $1.1 million budget, the LBSO has come a long way since its early years as a community orchestra. A budget of just over $10,000 in 1955 had reached six figures by 1968; by 1977 it had leapt to $400,000. With the passage of Proposition 13 in June of 1978, the orchestra was directly affected by cuts in financial aid from the city and county. With a reportedly small percentage of its budget furnished by corporate sponsors, the Symphony had by January of 1983 accumulated a $500,000 debt, and it announced that it would have to cut short its season unless it could raise that amount. The city of Long Beach responded with a $175,000 interest-free loan on the condition that the Symphony raise a matching amount, that it reduce its operating expenses, and that it allow the city to review orchestra finances every month. In an emergency fund-raising drive the LBSO received about $800,000 in cash and pledges. Further, the City of Long Beach has recently added a "bedroom tax" on occupied hotel and motel rooms with proceeds going to arts organizations. This, in essence, made a statement about the city's support of the arts. Nevertheless, the orchestra's finances remained critical, and when a $100,000 emergency fund-raising drive netted a mere $9,000 (according to the *Los Angeles Times*), the Board announced that the 1984–1985 season's remaining 19 concerts would be canceled. A series of concerts under the direction of Murry Sidlin has been scheduled for the 1985–1986 season.

CHRONOLOGY OF MUSIC DIRECTORS: Leonard J. Walker, 1928–1931. Robert Resta, 1935; 1940–1955. Lauris Jones, 1956–1966. Akira Endo, 1966–1967. Alberto Bolet, 1968–1978. (Guest conductors, 1978–1980.) Murry Sidlin, 1980–present.

BIBLIOGRAPHY: Nancy Kay Arnold, "The Long Beach Symphony Orchestra," Masters thesis, California State University, Long Beach, 1979. Patricia E. Bowles, "A Financial History of the Long Beach Symphony Orchestra," Masters thesis, California State University, Long Beach, 1984. Steven R. Churm and Maria L. LaGanga, "Symphony's Season to Be Unfinished," *Los Angeles Times*, 15 Nov. 1984. Kenneth F. Delene, "History of the Long Beach Symphony," *Spotlight*, Long Beach Symphony Association [program], 28/29 Jan. 1978. "The Long Beach Story," *Long Beach Review*, Feb. 1978.

ACCESS: Long Beach Symphony Orchestra, 121 Linden Avenue, Long Beach, CA 90802. (213) 436–3203. James Feichtmann, General Manager.

STUART M. ERWIN

LOS ANGELES (7,477,503—Los Angeles/Long Beach)

Los Angeles Philharmonic (Mj)

In any given season, the 105-member Los Angeles Philharmonic performs about 90 concerts at its home in Los Angeles's Music Center. In 1984–1985 the figure was 85 subscription concerts, five youth concerts, and one Pension Concert. In addition, there are about 15 subscription concerts in other southern California communities, including Santa Ana, San Diego, Santa Barbara, and Palm Springs. The orchestra tours at least once a year, either in the United States or overseas, generally giving 15 to 20 concerts during the tour.

The Philharmonic has a 35-member New Music Group that gives a series of concerts each winter season. A collaboration with Pierre Boulez began in 1984 and will continue in 1987 and 1989. During the summer of 1984 the orchestra presented a special week of concerts at the Hollywood Bowl in conjunction with the Olympic Arts Festival.

The audience at the Music Center is a generally affluent segment of the population. It does not demand new music. A subscription season usually includes a week devoted to the music of a contemporary composer who conducts the orchestra in his own music. The Bowl, however, draws a more diverse mix of local residents and out-of-town visitors. Its summer operation tends to give the concerts a pops atmosphere, but not necessarily a pops quality. Lighter fare characterizes the Friday/Saturday programs, while the Tuesday/Thursday concerts are more serious. Also, single-composer programs are given more frequently at the Bowl than at the Center.

The following historical account is especially indebted to the informative studies by I. M. Jones, J. O. Northcutt, and C. E. Smith. For anyone but a Californian, it might be hard to believe that a city which around the time of the Civil War had no daily newspaper, no railroad connecting it to the outside, and no theater for drama or music, would boast a major symphony orchestra 50 years later, one which today ranks among the finest in the United States. Statehood came to California in 1852. Within 35 years, Los Angeles had four concert halls, an oratorio society, the Conservatory of Music and the Arts, an organ factory, and institutions of higher learning offering advanced degrees in music.

Any number of orchestral ensembles—a lute orchestra, for instance—preceded the Philharmonic's founding in 1919. Among them were the Philharmonic Society and Chorus, which disbanded in 1889; the Women's Symphony Orchestra of 1893; the Philharmonic Orchestra, also of 1893; the Los Angeles Symphony Orchestra of 1897, which, under the same Harley Hamilton who founded the Women's Symphony, brought many important works to southern California; and the People's Orchestra, made up of music teachers, which in 1913 was able to perform Verdi's Manzoni *Requiem.*

The Los Angeles Symphony, in particular, backed by staunch supporters and under the baton of the dapper young Viennese Adolph Tandler, survived ups and downs for 23 years, doing much for the city's cultural life. Much but not enough for William Andrews Clark, Jr., a 42-year-old amateur musician, lawyer, and art patron. He set out to establish a grander orchestra (drawing on personnel already with the Symphony) to keep up with the

rapid growth of the Western metropolis. As Henry Higginson had contributed his own wealth to found the Boston Symphony Orchestra* in 1881,
so did Clark for the Los Angeles Philharmonic in 1919. For him, it has been
said, the act was the "incarnation of an ideal and not a display of wealth"
(Northcutt, p. 11). Various persons were contacted for the post of conductor: Henry Schoenfeld, who had been associated with the Women's Symphony Orchestra; Sergei Rachmaninoff, the Russian pianist-composer; Alfred
Hertz of San Francisco*; Emil Oberhoffer of Minneapolis*; and finally Walter
Henry Rothwell of St. Paul, who accepted. Rothwell was a competent conductor (especially with Brahms), but not a great one. Fortunately, he was
a disciplinarian while still a humane man, and one wholly dedicated to
music—which was exactly what the fledgling orchestra needed in its formative years.

Looking to the East for his key musicians, Rothwell assembled an ensemble
of 94 instrumentalists, began rehearsals on October 13, 1919, and lured a
capacity audience to Trinity Auditorium 11 days later (Friday, October 24)
for the opening concert: Dvořák's Symphony No. 5—with its appropriate
New World title—Liszt's Les Préludes, Weber's Oberon Overture, and Chabrier's España. Gala it was, and it was hailed as a triumph. The competing
Symphony folded in 1920.

Needless to say, the organizing Board of the Philharmonic took great
pride in its accomplishment, for it was clear that, thanks to all the groundwork done by Clark and encouraged by the quality and discipline of Rothwell's musicianship, Los Angeles might now think not only of a permanent
symphony but also of a notable one. Of course, the organization enjoyed
the backing of many more prominent Los Angelinos, including Mrs. Artie
Mason Carter, who as president of the Community Sing of Hollywood,
borrowed the new orchestra in 1921 for an Easter sunrise service on Olive
Hill in Barnsdall Park. Attended by 15,000 people, this event began the
illustrious history of the "Symphonies under the Stars," today known as the
Hollywood Bowl concerts (which began an institution under the baton of
Alfred Hertz in 1922).

But back in the heart of the city, the Philharmonic still needed a suitable
hall to do justice to its mission. In the purchase of the Hazard Pavilion—
the home of flower, poultry, and farm exhibits; opera; politicians; sports
groups; and evangelists—the Philharmonic found some breathing space. The
Pavilion was later razed to erect the Temple Baptist Church's Auditorium,
which became known as the Philharmonic Auditorium.

Georg Leonard Schnéevoigt, a childhood friend of Sibelius (whom he
interpreted well), took over the podium in 1927. Following his brief two
years with the orchestra came Artur Rodzinski in 1929. Young (at age 35),
dynamic, and imaginative, he expanded the orchestra's repertoire immensely. Despite his well-known idiosyncrasies, he possessed extraordinary
albeit not well-rounded gifts and enjoyed grandiose projects, and under him

the orchestra "performed." His stint in Los Angeles made him a reputed "orchestra builder."

By the early 1930s the orchestra had established an aura of permanence, despite the real peril of extinction. In time, Clark complained about public apathy in supporting the organization (his own estate had dwindled from $100 million to $4 million in sustaining it); no endowment having been created, he disinherited the orchestra in 1934, the year he died. It was then that the Community Development Association, founded years before by civic leaders and newspaper publishers, asked Harvey S. Mudd to save the organization, which could no longer survive on the generosity of one person alone. Articles of incorporation for the Southern California Symphony Association, now the orchestra's non-profit civic sponsor, were signed on May 31, 1934. A Board of Trustees was set up, the first president being Allan C. Balch, followed by Harvey Mudd, whose quiet leadership proved very effective.

Psychologically renewed, the orchestra saw its Association decide four things: to hire Otto Klemperer as conductor, engage 85 musicians, lease the Hollywood Bowl for summer concerts, and implement every type of fund raising available. Klemperer did much to expand the orchestra's effectiveness and viability as a coherent unit. Bach, Beethoven, Brahms, Mahler (who in Europe had encouraged him in his career), the Italian masters, Franck, Tchaikovsky, contemporary music—all flourished under his baton, not only in the Philharmonic Auditorium but also at the Hollywood Bowl.

When partial paralysis forced him to relinquish full-time conducting in 1939, Klemperer maintained his ties with the orchestra by appearing as one of the many guest conductors in the ensuing three seasons. Walter, Beecham, Barbirolli, Szell, Stokowski, Wallenstein, and others brought new faces to the podium but broke a continuity the ensemble had enjoyed for two decades, especially during the 1930s. The depression had raised stern obstacles, but with the dedication of such new friends as Fund-Campaign Manager Henry C. Cartlidge and Volunteer Committee Chair Mrs. John Crombie Niven, the hope for broader-based support and a genuine sense of permanency materialized.

Revenues from the Hollywood Bowl, abetted by record attendances to hear or see Lily Pons or Fred Astaire or Bruno Walter, even during World War II, helped greatly. Leopold Stokowski took over as Bowl director in 1945. Eight members formed the Executive Council to determine policy concerning the interrelationship of the two organizations: four from the Symphony Association and four from the Bowl Association. These efforts eventually yielded an untitled managerial post to coordinate the administrations. A scare that nearly sent the Hollywood Bowl season into bankruptcy in 1951 inspired the formation of an Orchestra Committee not only to plan that season but also to convince great artists to donate their services in order to save the organization. From then on, and with expanded responsibilities, the Committee played an increasingly important role as a liaison between the union and the Association.

Meanwhile, Alfred Wallenstein had been chosen from among the guest conductors to assume leadership. The first American-born conductor to lead a major American orchestra, he was 45 years old at the time of his accession in 1943. A cellist with the Chicago Symphony,* San Francisco Symphony,* and New York Philharmonic* (under Toscanini, who had urged him to become a conductor), Wallenstein devoted all his energies to his post. He extended the orchestra's activities even more, performing 100 concerts in a 52-week season, traveling to more neighboring communities, assisting in all ways the Bowl (whose music director he became in 1952), bringing the Symphonies for Youth (as he labeled them) to a nationwide radio network, showing a flair for large choral works (he brought the Roger Wagner Chorale to the Philharmonic), and bringing to his audiences truly balanced programs, though with the laudable tendency to recognize modern American composers (for which he received the Ditson Award in 1947).

Wallenstein was succeeded in 1956 by Eduard Van Beinum, who became the idol of the organization and its city. Simultaneously music director of the Concertgebouw Orchestra in his native Holland, he was granted great freedom of movement by the Symphony Association Board. His consummate musicianship and totally humane and unassuming manner in working with an orchestra, not to mention his broad range of sympathies among composers and styles, jammed the concert halls and evinced no negative comments from his musicians or his public. Upon his sudden death in 1959 another series of guest conductors provided variety but loosened the fabric of the orchestral unit.

By this point in its history the Philharmonic had behind it a respectable number of achievements. One was the Symphonies for Youth, begun by Rothwell in 1919—some 30 concerts a year, ubiquitously given, that encouraged the nearly 400 school orchestras in the area and that inspired any number of young artists (such as Alfred Wallenstein himself) to pursue musical careers. The finest conductors took part. The Philharmonic was the first major orchestra in the country to broadcast an entire concert on radio (January 24, 1925). It was the first major western orchestra to be sent abroad by the State Department on an International Cultural Exchange tour (April 25, 1956). Wallenstein conducted the 60 concerts (including youth concerts) in 18 cities of the Orient. Indeed, performances away from home became normal fare for the Philharmonic, having begun in 1920 with a trip to Santa Barbara.

Many of the places where the orchestra performed enjoyed better facilities than Los Angeles, not just for music but for all the performing arts. The time had come for bold action to dignify the arts in the area with appropriate halls, and the woman of the hour was Mrs. Norman (Dorothy Buffum) Chandler—the very lady who in 1951, as head of the Emergency

Committee of the Hollywood Bowl Board of Directors, had helped save the bowl concerts from extinction. A fund-raising plan began in 1955; one affair, the legendary Eldorado Party, netted $400,000. With the enlistment of many prominent citizens, the fund-raising accomplishment was to be described as "the most remarkable and extraordinary feat of its kind ever accomplished in the field of culture in the United States—indeed, the world" (Northcutt, p. 75). The orchestra moved into its new winter home, the 3,197-seat Chandler Pavilion, which along with the Ahmanson Theater and the Mark Taper Forum, comprises the Music Center of the Performing Arts.

The move came at the outset of a period of stability and maturity for the orchestra under the direction of Zubin Mehta, who began his tenure in 1962. The Bombay-born Parsee and graduate of the Vienna State Academy of Music became, at 26, the youngest permanent conductor in the Philharmonic's history. A polyglot, he conducted—and continued to conduct— ubiquitously in Europe and other parts of the world. In Los Angeles, he aroused enthusiasm, conducting most of the time without a score and displaying enormous energy as well as versatility in his musical choices. He showed great understanding of both the symphonic and operatic repertoire—especially Italian—and this has endeared him to many. His performance of Verdi's Manzoni *Requiem* at the outset of his Los Angeles stay remains memorable, and his equal facility with large contemporary scores and elegant Mozart pieces elicited numerous comments about his broad mastery of the art. Basically, however, he concentrated on the post-romantic period and the twentieth-century masters. When he left for New York, he went with some regret, for like his predecessor, he was very well liked. It was under him that the Los Angeles Philharmonic reached the pinnacle of proficiency that enabled Mrs. Chandler, as president of the Symphony Association, to think in the highest terms for a replacement.

Carlo Maria Giulini, an established conductor of international fame, was this successor. In 1978 he was 64. One of the veritably great conductors of the contemporary age, Giulini flourished in his Philharmonic music directorship for the first half of his six-year tenure, bringing the orchestra and himself to new heights of acclaim. However, the serious illness of his wife and then his own bout of poor health resulted in his decision to resign from the Philharmonic post at the end of the 1983–1984 season and to return to Los Angeles only as a guest conductor. Through that combination of lyrical depth and ferric energy, together with his highly personal interpretations that left his signature on many performances, the distinguished maestro did some memorable things with the orchestra—the initial "Los Angeles' Tribute to the World" performance of Beethoven's Ninth, for instance, or the special and much-discussed rendering of Brahms's First. His emphasis was on Beethoven, Brahms, Bruckner, and Mahler and on the large choral/ orchestral works such as the Verdi and Mozart *Requiems* or Beethoven's *Missa Solemnis*.

As of this writing, the baton of the Los Angeles Philharmonic has been placed in the capable hands of André Previn, who in 1986 (with guest conductors until then) will begin his first season with the noted ensemble.

Today, the Philharmonic and the Music Center hold an exalted cultural station in the community. The orchestra has had an ongoing but irregular association with the University of California at Los Angeles and to a lesser degree with the University of Southern California and the California Arts Institute. The orchestra is sponsored by the Los Angeles Philharmonic Association, a volunteer Board of Directors joined by those who contribute to The Music Center Unified Fund of the Performing Arts Council. In addition, there continue to be Affiliate Committees to support its activities (about a score of them, some begun during Clark's tenure, from San Diego to Santa Barbara to Riverside), not to mention diverse sponsorships like the NEA, the California Arts Council, the Los Angeles County Board of Supervisors, the Los Angeles County Music and Performing Arts Commission, and the Cultural Affairs Department of the City of Los Angeles.

Three separate committees work closely with management as the orchestra's representatives. Through direct representation in a system that covers each instrumental section, the orchestra is engaged in the decision-making process that affects both the ensemble's quality and its working conditions. It maintains a five-member Orchestra Committee (dealing with contract negotiation and enforcement as well as internal disputes), a five-member Artistic Liaison Committee (conveying musicians' opinions regarding the choice of guest conductors), and a seven-member Auditions and Renewals Committee (advising the music director regarding auditioning, hiring, and non-renewals). The Philharmonic was the first major orchestra in the United States to develop a confidential conductor evaluation system. The opinions of orchestra members are thus considered in the overall assessment of the conductor.

For the 1984–1985 fiscal year, the Philharmonic Association's budget is approximately $19 million. Ticket sales and other earned income represent about 80% of the budget. The orchestra owns a number of very valuable instruments, including two Stradivarius violins, each valued at over a quarter of a million dollars, a Guarnerius cello, and two violins dating from the mid–1500s.

RECORDING HISTORY AND SELECTIVE DISCOGRAPHY: The Los Angeles Philharmonic has made some 80 recordings, ranging from baroque music to modern film sound-tracks, nearly half of which were under the baton of Zubin Mehta. Most feature romantic and modern music. Recording companies include CBS Masterworks, Decca/London, Deutsche Grammophon, New World Records, Sheffield Lab Records, and Twentieth Century Fox.

Beethoven, Symphony No. 3, Op. 55 (Giulini): DG 2531123. Debussy, *La Mer*; Ravel, *Ma Mère l'Oye* and *Rhapsodie espagnole* (Giulini): DG 2531264 & 3301264. Holst, *The Planets* (Stokowski): Seraphim S–60175. Respighi, *Roman Festivals* and

R. Strauss, *Don Juan* (Mehta): RCA AGL1–1276. Stravinsky, *The Rite of Spring* and *Eight Instrumental Miniatures* (Mehta): London: 41002. Tchaikovsky, *Complete Symphonies* (Mehta): London CSP–10 (6 records). Verdi, *Falstaff* (Giulini): DG2741020.

CHRONOLOGY OF MUSIC DIRECTORS: Walter Henry Rothwell (Principal Conductor), 1919–1927. Georg Leonard Schnéevoigt, 1927–1929. Artur Rodzinski, 1929–1933. Otto Klemperer, 1933–1939. (Guest conductors, 1939–1943.) Alfred Wallenstein, 1943–1956. Eduard Van Beinum, 1956–1959. (Guest conductors, 1959–1962.) Zubin Mehta, 1962–1978. Carlos Maria Giulini, 1978–1984. (Guest conductors, 1984–1986.)

BIBLIOGRAPHY: Special thanks to Mr. Orrin Howard, Director of Publications and Archives at the Los Angeles Music Center, who graciously provided some of the information contained in this essay. *BMI Orchestral Programs Survey* Annual (New York: BMI, 1960–). Philip Hart, *Orpheus in the New World* (New York: Norton, 1973). Isabel Morse Jones, *Hollywood Bowl* (New York: G.Schirmer, 1936). John Mueller, *The American Symphony Orchestra* (1951; reprint, Westport, Conn.: Greenwood Press, 1976). Kate H. Mueller, *Twenty-Seven American Orchestras* (Bloomington: Indiana University Press, 1973). John Orlando Northcutt, *The Story of the Los Angeles Philharmonic Orchestra* (Los Angeles: Southern California Symphony Association, 1963). Harold C. Schonberg, *The Great Conductors* (New York: Simon & Schuster, 1967). George Seltzer, comp. *The Professional Symphony Orchestra in the United States* (Metuchen, N.J.: Scarecrow Press, 1975). Caroline Estes Smith, *The Philharmonic Orchestra of Los Angeles: The First Decade, 1919–1929* (Los Angeles: United Printing Co., 1930). Henry Swoboda, comp. *The American Symphony Orchestra* (New York: Basic Books, 1967).

ACCESS: Los Angeles Philharmonic, 135 North Grand Avenue, Los Angeles, CA 90012. (213) 972-7300. Ernest Fleischmann, Executive Director. Orrin Howard, Director of Publications.

JEAN-PIERRE BARRICELLI

OAKLAND (361,561; 3,250,630—San Francisco/Oakland)

Oakland Symphony Orchestra (Rg)

The San Francisco Bay Area is unusually rich in musical sophistication— a seat of musical education, experimentation, and conservation, it is served by many musical ensembles in addition to the dominant San Francisco Symphony.* With its wide variety of concert series and many ancillary activities, the Oakland Symphony is among the best-known Regional orchestras in the country. Four classical series (including a "Favorite Classics" series) are the mainstay of the season, providing a total of some 30 concerts per year. Six pops concerts, three young people's concerts, six open dress rehearsals, and special programs round out the year's performances at the Paramount Theatre, the orchestra's main concert hall. The ensemble also provides about a dozen concerts away from the Paramount, primarily at

Zellerbach Auditorium of the University of California, Berkeley, and provides additional runouts to other area communities. Further runouts by the core chamber orchestra and ensembles are frequent. Tours and runouts are expected to play an increasingly large role in the orchestra's activities.

Three historical accounts chronicle the Oakland Symphony's development. The most current—and the principal source for the following summary—is an article by Frank Wootten published in the Symphony's 50th anniversary viewbook. It was based on a thesis by Marjorie W. Remington. The orchestra's 1980 five-year plan contains a frank account of the organization's financial downturns and subsequent renaissance.

Although the Oakland Symphony dates its founding to 1933, its musicians and conductor had worked together previously in the YMCA Symphony Orchestra, founded in 1925 under conductor Edward Leslie. Leslie remained until 1933, when Orley See, a previous guest conductor, assumed leadership. With financial backing from Edwin W. Ehmann, See reorganized the group as the Oakland Symphony Orchestra. Chartered as a community orchestra, it would remain so until 1958, with See at the podium and a rule requiring amateur status for at least three-quarters of the playing members. Nevertheless, the orchestra flourished within its self-imposed restraints, offering classical, young people's, and free outdoor concert series. See had been honored by the community on many occasions for his long dedication to the orchestra, but with his death in 1957 the orchestra was clearly at a turning point. Oakland had grown in many ways and was ready for a professional Symphony.

With the leadership of Board President Harry R. Lange, the reorganization began. Piero Bellugi was engaged as music director/conductor, current orchestra members were auditioned (and many dropped), a public relations campaign was begun, funds raised, union cooperation secured, and operations were generally professionalized.

After a year in Oakland, Bellugi left to take over the Portland (Oregon) Symphony,* and upon his recommendation Gerhard Samuel was engaged as his replacement. In the ensuing years the season and organization both grew, a young artists competition was initiated, the Oakland Chamber Orchestra created, and educational activities increased. It was in Samuel's tenure, too, that the orchestra's activities with newer music began to grow, and premiere performances became part of each season's offerings. Two Rockefeller Foundation grants (1965 and 1969) provided funds for campus performances of new music and for a composer-in-residence. It is significant that this period of activity with new music was also accompanied by ever-increasing audience support.

When Samuel left in 1971 to join the conducting staff of the Los Angeles Philharmonic,* the post went to Harold Farberman, a former Boston Symphony* percussionist with much guest-conducting experience. In 1972 the orchestra purchased Oakland's 1931 Paramount Theatre, and a year later a thorough and authentic restoration had been completed, renewing its intricate, dazzling, art deco appointments to their original state. With a capacity of 3,000, the theater is less stunning acoustically than visually, however, and despite a shell brought from its old home Oakland Symphony musicians have professed a hard time hearing one another—a new shell, at a cost of $250,000, is planned for installation in January of 1985.

The tide of artistic and popular success enjoyed by the orchestra in the early 1970s had not been matched by fiscal stability, and by the decade's end a poor ratio of earned income to expenses, exacerbated by declining ticket sales and fund-raising, forced the organization to face a financial crisis. Although it disburdened itself in 1975 of the Paramount (in exchange for rent-free use), the orchestra remained in a serious position. Some Board members even proposed merger with the San Francisco Symphony. After rejecting that idea, the Board engaged consultant George Alan Smith, who advised establishing a professional position of president/manager and instituting five-year plans to allow the orchestra to capitalize on what he perceived as its considerable potential for a viable future. Under President and General Manager Harold Lawrence, a new administrative structure was devised, fund-raising efforts redoubled, minority outreach instituted both in terms of players and audience, and a new public relations drive effected.

When Farberman announced his departure effective in 1979, the music directorship went to the dynamic and highly promising young conductor Calvin Simmons, who did much to raise once again the orchestra's recently diminished profile. Simmon's career, however, was tragically ended in a fatal boating accident in the summer of 1982, and the orchestra once again faced a momentous decision. It chose as its new music director Richard Buckley, also young and rising, a member of the conducting staff of the Seattle Symphony.* He was warmly received.

The Oakland Symphony derived about 38% of its approximately $2.6 million 1983–1984 budget from ticket sales and contractual fees, with a wide diversity of other funding sources providing the balance. A program to solicit first-chair endowments is planned, and there are clear plans as well to develop funding in many other areas. The organization is administered by a 12-member Board of Trustees drawn from a 96-member, regionally organized Board of Directors. The administrative staff of 15 full-time and two part-time employees reports to the president. The Oakland Symphony Guild (founded 1959), with a membership of about 200 women, undertakes fund-raising and educational activities. Its achievements include an in-school docent program and a series of concerts for young children.

The orchestra has made a determined effort to involve itself in the cultural affairs of the community. In addition to the outreach programs alluded to, it maintains ties with the Oakland Ballet and the Oakland Museum, with which it presents collaborative programs. It also collaborates with various theater, mime, gospel, and other arts organizations. Its musicians teach in the many Bay Area universities as well as in private studios. The Oakland Symphony

Youth Orchestra has an international reputation for its high level of perform-ance. Under the direction of Kent Nagano, it has available to it a rich selec-tion of talented young musicians from the Bay Area, and its undertakings have consequently been most ambitious; it is seen as an adjunct to the Oakland Symphony (rather than simply a training orchestra), and one of its functions is to expand the overall repertoire, presenting commissioned works as well as works not easily programmed by the professional group.

The Symphony's repertoire in recent years, although grounded in the traditional favorites, has had a generous share of contemporary music as well as works previously unperformed in Oakland. Most programs contain at least one unusual work, and each season sees several premieres. According to the Symphony office, 60% of the 1984–1985 season programming has never before been performed by the Symphony on the subscription series.

RECORDING HISTORY AND SELECTIVE DISCOGRAPHY: The Oakland Symphony's first commercial recording (music of Henry Brant, listed below) was made in 1970 in conjunction with the Oakland Youth Orchestra, which has made several com-mercial recordings in its own right. The Oakland Symphony recently participated in a Grammy-winning recording with Edwin Hawkins and the Love Center Choir entitled *Gospel at the Symphony*.

Henry Brant, *Kingdom Come* (Brant/Samuel): Desto 7108. Henri Lazarof, Concerto for Cello (Lesser/Samuel): Desto 7109. Ned Rorem, *Water Music* (Oakland Youth Symphony/Hughes): Desto 6462.

CHRONOLOGY OF MUSIC DIRECTORS: Orley See, 1933–1957. Piero Bellugi, 1958–1959. Gerhard Samuel, 1959–1971. Harold Farberman, 1971–1979. Calvin Simmons, 1979–1982. (Guest conductors, 1982–1983.) Richard Buckley, 1983–present.

BIBLIOGRAPHY: Edward A. Gargan, "Calvin Simmons," *New York Times*, 24 Aug. 1982. George Heymont, "Oakland's New Maestro Takes a Bow," *Symphony Mag-azine*, Apr./May 1984. Oakland Symphony Orchestra Association *Five Year Plan* (OSOA, 1980). John Westbrook Ostrom, OSO Director of Promotion, correspond-ence with author, 1984. Andrew Porter, "Musical Events: Bay Laurels," *New Yorker*, 10 Aug. 1981. Marjorie W. Remington, "History of the Oakland Symphony Or-chestra," Masters thesis, California State University, Hayward, 1973. Frank Wootten, "A History of the Oakland Symphony," in *The Oakland Symphony: The Golden Season* (OSOA, 1983).

ACCESS: Oakland Symphony, Paramount Theater, 2025 Broadway, Oakland, CA 94612. (415) 444–3531. Arthur Jacobus, President and General Manager. Mary Maehl, Director of Public Relations.

ROBERT R. CRAVEN

PASADENA (118,072; 7,477,503—Los Angeles/Long Beach)

Los Angeles Chamber Orchestra (Rg)

The Los Angeles Chamber Orchestra is generally considered by critics to be one of the finest contemporary ensembles in the United States. An indication of this stature is the impressive number of recordings (about 30) made by the orchestra since its founding in 1968. Although the LACO's principal concert activity takes place currently at Pasadena's 1,200-seat Ambassador Auditorium, where it offers 15 concerts through the season from October to June, its subscription series are also offered at the University of California, Los Angeles (seven concerts), the Embassy Theater in downtown Los Angeles (six concerts), and the Bridges Hall of Music, Claremont (six concerts). In addition, the LACO regularly gives other series of single concerts at locations in southern California such as El Cajon, La Jolla, Santa Ana, Santa Barbara, Palm Springs, and Ventura. Thus, while the orchestra's principal concert auditorium and administrative offices are in Pasadena, it draws upon a broad base of audience support throughout southern California.

The LACO was founded in October 1968 by members of the Los Angeles Chamber Music Society who invited Neville Marriner to take up the position of music director and to begin recruiting orchestra personnel, the intention being to provide the communities of southern California with a first-rate professional chamber ensemble. The debut of the orchestra took place at the Mark Taper Forum of the Music Center, Los Angeles, in October of 1969. Neville Marriner conducted the first three concerts of that season and Sir John Barbirolli the fourth. After playing regular Monday concerts at the Mark Taper Forum, the orchestra's growing success was consolidated through its first European tour in 1974 when, led by Marriner, it opened the Bath Festival in England and performed in Geneva, London, Madrid, and Paris.

The orchestra's present music director, Gerard Schwarz, took up his responsibilities in 1978 when Marriner left to become conductor of the Minnesota Orchestra.* Schwarz, who had been first co-principal trumpet in the New York Philharmonic Orchestra,* gave up this position in 1976 to concentrate on full-time conducting. In his tenure with the LACO, Schwarz has begun to introduce new American works into the orchestra's repertoire, and a number of these have been recorded by the orchestra. In 1978, the same year it acquired its new music director, the orchestra moved its main concert location from the Mark Taper Forum to Ambassador Auditorium and found permanent quarters for its administrative offices in Pasadena.

In June 1983 the LACO was invited to perform at the Casals Festival in Puerto Rico, the conductors on that occasion being Schwarz and Jorge Mester. For the 1983–1984 season the orchestra made a tour of 13 cities in the United States, going on later to perform at the Colón Theater in Buenos Aires under the guest conductorship of the well-known German specialist in music of the baroque, Helmuth Rilling.

Management of the orchestra is effected through a Board of Directors and the music director, Gerard Schwarz, as well as an administrative staff of nine. The orchestra's 1983–1984 budget was approximately $1.2 million, with a slight increase projected for 1984–1985. Funding has been supplied by the NEA, the Ambassador Foundation, the California Arts Council, the Los Angeles County Board of Supervisors, the Los Angeles County Arts Commission, the Los Angeles City Council, the Irvine Foundation, and the Atlantic Richfield Company.

The repertoire of the LACO features, in addition to standard baroque favorites, new works by American composers. In the 1983–1984 season, for example, the orchestra introduced Robert Starer's *Concert a Quattro* and Joseph Schwantner's *Distant Runes and Incantations for Piano and Chamber Orchestra*; many other new works have been presented in the regular concert season. The programming of the LACO is normally determined by the music director in consultation with members of the orchestra and the administrative staff.

The consistency and polish of the orchestra's sound is due in large part to the small turnover in personnel from season to season. The LACO wind section in particular comprises players who are virtuosi in their own right. Several, such as David Shostac, David Shifrin, and Allan Vogel, are featured soloists in the orchestra's recordings. These and others of the LACO's regular personnel also perform within the orchestra's smaller ensembles such as the Bach Soloists, who are responsible for an annual performance, offered at several locations, of the complete Brandenburg Concertos. Occasionally, a wind quintet or octet from within the orchestra will play under the name of the Los Angeles Chamber Orchestra Soloists. While under normal circumstances it is comparatively rare for antique or restored instruments to be used in the performance of older works in order to simulate authenticity, such instruments as the viola da gamba or viola d'amore will be employed where called for. A modern harpsichord supplies the continuo in baroque works.

RECORDING HISTORY AND SELECTIVE DISCOGRAPHY: Among the companies for which the LACO has made recordings are Angel, Argo, Delos, Nonesuch, and Varese.

Ernst Křenek, *Static and Ecstatic* and *Kitharaulos*(Křenek): Varese VR 81200. Mozart, Symphony No. 40, K. 550 and Symphony No. 41, K. 551 (Schwarz): Delos 3012. Respighi, Three Suites of *Ancient Airs and Dances* (Marriner): Angel S–37301. Prokofiev, Symphony No. 1 (*Classical*) (Schwarz): Delos DMS 3008. Stravinsky, *Concertino in E-Flat ("Dumbarton Oaks")*, Concerto in D for String Orchestra, and *Danses Concertantes* (Marriner): Angel S–37801. Virgil Thomson, Concertino for Harp, Strings and Percussion (Marriner): Angel S–37300. Vivaldi, *Four Seasons* (Elmar Oliveira/Schwarz): Delos DMS 3007.

CHRONOLOGY OF MUSIC DIRECTORS: Neville Marriner, 1969–1978. Gerard Schwarz, 1978–present.

BIBLIOGRAPHY: Frequent articles and reviews appear in the *Los Angeles Herald Examiner* and *Los Angeles Times*.

ACCESS: Los Angeles Chamber Orchestra, 285 West Green Street, Pasadena, CA 91105. (818) 796–2200. Stanley F. Kaminsky, Marketing Director.

JAMES PORTER

Pasadena Symphony Orchestra (Mt)

Originally a function of Pasadena's Tuesday Musicale group, the Pasadena Civic Orchestra Association was founded in 1928. Its 75-member orchestra was first conducted by Reginald Bland (whose students comprised its core), and it was funded by the city of Pasadena. The Association was incorporated in 1932.

In 1936, Dr. Richard Lert was appointed music director and conductor of the Pasadena Civic Orchestra. An experienced European conductor and Hollywood Bowl guest artist, Lert led the Pasadena Symphony for 36 years. Among his many achievements is the PSO's still-active apprenticeship program.

Two years following its 1954 name change to the Pasadena Symphony Association, the organization became a founding member of the Los Angeles County Symphony League, whose members are now funded in part by the Los Angeles County Music and Performing Arts Commission.

Under Music Director Daniel Lewis, who assumed the podium in 1972, the orchestra won four ASCAP awards for adventuresome programming. Lewis expanded the PSO's repertoire by adding less-often performed works of the common-practice period as well as a wide-ranging mixture of twentieth-century works in many styles. Such works accounted for about 40% of the repertoire. According to the Pasadena Symphony's typescript history, "Lewis reinforced his own conviction that we should not be in a sonic museum."

In May of 1984, Jorge Mester was appointed music director. Currently music director of both the Aspen Music Festival and Festival Casals, as well as conductor and chairman of Conducting Studies at the Juilliard School of Music, Mester will lead the orchestra in three of the season's five subscription concerts. He is well known for his recordings and premiere productions of contemporary music during his tenure as music director of the Louisville Orchestra* from 1967 to 1979. Another eminent musician, Los Angeles Philharmonic* Composer-In-Residence William Kraft, has also been associated with the orchestra, recently conducting his own composition in four young people's concerts.

The orchestra's home is the Pasadena Civic Auditorium, constructed in 1931–1932. It is Italian Renaissance in design, with a seating capacity of approximately 3,000, and is the work of three eminent architects, Edwin Gergstrom, Cyril Bennett, and Fitch H. Haskell. Of special interest is the grandeur of the interior, with decor consisting of a series of panels on the walls, containing drawings by Raphael and friezes by the world-renowned artist, John B. Smeraldi.

The Pasadena Symphony is administered by a 45-member Board of Directors. The professional staff includes an executive director, public relations director, business manager, and administrative assistant. The artistic staff includes the music director, personnel manager, and orchestra librarian. Funding for the Symphony's $490,000 (1983–1984) budget comes from a variety of sources, including the county of Los Angeles, the California Arts Council and NEA; individual, foundation, and corporate contributions, endowment funds, and benefits presented by support groups. Earned income, including ticket sales, accounts for 63% of the total. The musicians are from the greater Los Angeles area, and although they are hired on a per-service basis, the roster—particularly a core of regulars—remains generally the same from year to year.

In addition to its five regular subscription concerts, the orchestra presents three Sunday afternoon repeats, four youth concerts, 13 performances of the *Nutcracker* contracted by the Los Angeles Ballet, a specially contracted Armenian concert, and in-school performances by smaller ensembles. Two youth orchestras are sponsored by the Pasadena Symphony Association: the Pasadena Young Musicians Orchestra (an ensemble of 80 high school and junior college students) and the Pasadena Youth Symphony Orchestra (composed of 80 students of junior high school age). Other educational programs include docent lectures, young artist awards, and a Student Apprentice Program in which students perform in the Symphony itself. The Association lists 34 southern California communities serviced by its educational programs.

The programming philosophy stated by the Pasadena Symphony Association calls for balance between standard and contemporary repertoire, with plans for growth in programming leading to commissions. Commercial recordings and tours are also envisioned.

CHRONOLOGY OF MUSIC DIRECTORS: Reginald Bland, 1928–1936. Dr. Richard Lert, 1936–1972. Daniel Lewis, 1972–1983. Jorge Mester, 1984–present.

BIBLIOGRAPHY: "History of the Pasadena Symphony Orchestra," typescript [PSOA, 1984].

ACCESS: Pasadena Symphony Orchestra Association, 300 East Green Street, Pasadena, CA 91101. (818) 793–7172 or (213) 681–6070. Dori Barnes, Acting Manager.

STENNIS WALDON

SACRAMENTO (1,014,002)

Sacramento Symphony Orchestra (Rg)

The Sacramento Symphony is a fully professional, 88-member orchestra serving the greater Sacramento Valley, a large geographic area bounded by Stockton, California, in the south, Chico to the north, the foothills of the Sierra Nevada to the east, and the Sacramento River delta and Napa hills to the west. The populace served by the Symphony is, however, considerably greater than that of metropolitan Sacramento, given the proximity of a large citizenry in the foothills and in numerous smaller cities of the region.

Sacramento has had a civic orchestra since a public meeting was called on October 7, 1910, at the Sacramento High School to create a symphony orchestra "for those that take an interest in that class of music." An inaugural concert was presented on June 30, 1911, in the Theater Diepenbrock; Harry Olsen conducted. In October 1911 a Sacramento Symphony and Oratorio Society was organized to sponsor the first formal season, which began on January 23, 1912. The program for opening night included the overture to *Zampa*, works of Haydn, Luigini, and Grieg, the *Invitationà la Valse* of Weber/Berlioz, and selections from Victor Herbert's *Natoma*. Vice president of the society was the pianist Bertha Elkus, wife of the civic leader Albert Elkus and mother of the noted educator and composer Albert I. Elkus.

Political and financial turmoil caused the first orchestra to disband between 1913 and 1916; a more permanent ensemble, the Sacramento Municipal Symphony Orchestra, was reorganized in 1923 and gave concerts in the Masonic Temple, later inaugurating the Memorial Auditorium (1927). Radio broadcasts began on February 23, 1930, over KFBK, the station of the Sacramento *Bee* newspaper. In January 1934 a Sacramento Symphony Foundation presented its incorporation papers as a non-profit society to the secretary of state. Fourteen-year-old Isaac Stern appeared with the orchestra on December 10, 1935; in 1936 and again in 1937, 70-year-old Alfred Hertz, recently retired from the San Francisco Symphony,* conducted significant concerts. After a wartime hiatus from 1942 to 1944, the municipal orchestra was reactivated by George Barr, supervisor of music for the city schools, and supported by the Junior Chamber of Commerce and the American Federation of Musicians, Local 12.

The modern Sacramento Symphony (at first called the Sacramento Philharmonic Orchestra) was reincorporated in 1948. In the same year Fritz Berens (b. Vienna, 1907), musical director of the San Francisco Ballet, was engaged as first permanent conductor. The orchestra prospered through the 1950s and early 1960s. By 1962 the season consisted of five pairs of subscription concerts, chamber concerts, young people's concerts, and performances by a youth orchestra (established in 1956). Harry Newstone (b. Winnipeg, 1921) first appeared with the orchestra in 1964, during a "season of discovery" (i.e. to discover a new conductor). This British conductor of Canadian birth had enjoyed great success in England for his performances of the works of Haydn; his favored repertoire with the Sacramento Symphony extended past the classical masters to the Scandinavian and British composers of the late nineteenth and early twentieth centuries. Newstone presided over the next major period of growth. By 1973, 53 musicians were under formal contract (in comparison with none a decade before), the number of concerts had nearly doubled, and the budget had tripled (to $290,913). In 1967, the Symphony first collaborated with the Sacramento Civic Ballet in a Christmas production of Tchaikovsky's *Nutcracker*; this annual tradition has now been extended to 17 performances and remains the most popular ticketed event of the region.

The mid and late 1970s witnessed a profound growth of the Sacramento Symphony—in budget, number of concert services, audience, and community prestige. With the appointment of Carter Nice (b. Jacksonville, Fla., 1940) as musical director in 1979 and David M. Wax as general manager at the end of the following season, the orchestra began to achieve its present identity as a fully professional ensemble of regional significance.

The 1984–1985 season was planned to comprise 10 subscription concerts from September to April (four pairs, Saturday evening and Sunday matinee; six triples, including Monday evening; but see the remarks on the University of California, Davis, in this entry); five formal Sacramento concerts of the smaller chamber orchestra (established 1979); five pairs of pops concerts; and, especially for the chamber orchestra, a long list of engagements in theater productions, concerts in public schools and outlying communities, outdoor concerts on a mobile stage, gala concerts, and even a day at the horse-racing track. Michael Neumann serves as assistant conductor and as conductor of the Sacramento Youth Symphony. In 1983–1984 a Sacramento Symphony Chorus was established, directed by Bruce Lamott, a Californian scholar-performer specializing in the baroque repertoire. Subscription performances and most other events take place in the Sacramento Community Center Theater, a handsome house of some 2,400 seats constructed in 1974 along the mall behind the state capitol.

The Sacramento Symphony Association is the parent organization of the Sacramento Symphony Orchestra, Sacramento Symphony Chamber Orchestra, Sacramento Symphony Chorus, and the Sacramento Youth Symphony. The enterprise is governed by a 54-member Board of Directors (from whom an executive committee of 18 is elected) and administered by a full-time staff of 11. The music director chooses the repertoire and makes most artistic decisions. Musicians of the orchestra are represented by a union steward and an Orchestra Committee, who collaborate in national auditions and certain decisions regarding tenure of employment.

The 1983–1984 budget was $1.86 million; the 1984–1985 budget was announced as $2.25 million. This amount is raised by ticket sales ($862,000 in 1983–1984), government grants, proceeds from a $1 million endowment established in 1966 through a Ford Foundation matching grant, and by annual fund raising ($622,000 in 1983–1984). In addition to major corporate and foundation grants, donations from local businesses as well as the venerable newspapers (The *Bee* and *Union* have supported the Symphony in a variety of fashions for many decades). The major volunteer support group is the Symphony League, a descendant of the original Women's Committee of 1952, now made up of three sections: Sacramento, Davis-Dixon (suburban cities to the west), and EnCorps, a group formed in 1981 of younger business and professional men and women.

The orchestra enjoys a close if informal relationship with the Davis campus of the University of California, some 15 miles distant. The music faculty serve as program annotators; several of the players teach orchestral instruments on campus. The orchestra and university have collaborated in publishing a guide to concert-going, and the university offers extension courses to introduce each season's repertoire. Relations with the other nearby university campuses, in Sacramento, Chico, and Stockton, are likewise cordial.

The astonishing growth of the Sacramento Symphony in the last decade has not been without discomforts. Many long-term and devoted members of the ensemble were unwilling or unable to manage the increased commitment of nearly 200 public concerts; a large percentage of the current membership, therefore, has tenure of less than five years. The vastly increased number of services has proved more grueling than envisaged, though it has been the key to providing considerably expanded opportunities of employment. Such unforeseen results of rapid growth have required adjustments, usually reached speedily and with good will by the Board, the musical administration, and the musicians alike. The Board of Directors currently predicts an annual budgetary growth of 15%.

The repertoire of the Sacramento Symphony is typical of a youthful orchestra with wide-ranging commitments and with an enormous constituency to please. Programming for the full orchestra comes largely from the familiar corpus of nineteenth- and early-twentieth-century masterworks; the smaller orchestra has lately offered a good deal of Bach, well played and with the sort of authenticity appropriate to a modern ensemble. The technical proficiency of the Symphony places it clearly among the nation's fine regional orchestras; there is a long tradition of elegant solo woodwind playing, a flamboyant percussion section, and a growing warmth of tone and polish of ensemble within the strings. The musicians now find themselves in a position to strive for mature sophistication and above all unity of interpretive concept, further growth in the richness of sound, and the kind of inner fire and élan that comes from an established, institutional self-confidence and pride of tradition.

Carter Nice and the Sacramento Symphony have indicated a growing interest in performing new music by American composers. In November 1983, the members of the chamber orchestra participated in a day-long reading and public performance of recent works by northern California composers. In January 1984, W. Jay Sydeman's *Study for Orchestra No. IV* was given its world premiere, to be followed in the 1984–1985 season by the first performance of Elie Siegmeister's Sixth Symphony. Harry Newstone was also a strong supporter of the better Sacramento-area composers. His first performances included Ben Glovinsky's *Variation-Fantasy on a Pioneer Theme* (1969); Gaylon Hatton's *Jeu-Partie* (1968) and *Prelusion* (1974); Daniel Kingman's First Symphony (1965) and *Earthscapes with Birds* (1972); Stanley Lunetta's *Unseen Force* (1973); and Jerome Rosen's

Concerto for Saxophone and Orchestra (1958), *Sounds and Movements for Orchestra* (1963), and Concerto for Clarinet and Orchestra (1976, with the composer as soloist).

CHRONOLOGY OF MUSIC DIRECTORS: Original Sacramento Symphony and Oratorio Society and Sacramento Municipal Symphony Orchestra: Harry Olsen, 1911–1913. Arthur Heft, 1916. Franz Dicks, 1924–1928. Arthur Heft, 1929–1934. David Lincoln Burnam, 1934–1938. William van den Burg, 1938–1942. George Barr, 1945–1947.

Sacramento Symphony: Fritz Berens, 1949–1964. Harry Newstone, 1965–1978. Carter Nice, 1979–present.

BIBLIOGRAPHY: Interviews with Thomas Derthick, SSO Union Steward, and Alzka K. Forbes, SSO Director of Marketing and Public Relations, 1984. Adrian Gaster, ed., "Fritz Berens" and "Carter Nice," in *International Who's Who in Music and Musicians' Directory*, 8th ed. (Cambridge, England: International Who's Who in Music, 1977). Sue Gilmore, "Symphony Closes Books on Another Successful Season," Sacramento *Union*, 9 May 1984. Stanley Sadie, "Harry Newstone," *The New Grove Dictionary of Music and Musicians* (London: Macmillan, 1980). David M. Wax (General Manager, 1981–1984), "The Sacramento Symphony: A Study in Responsible Growth," (report to the Board of Directors, 1983). John N. Wilson, "Evolution of a Symphony: The Story of the Sacramento Symphony [1911–1941]" (manuscript monograph).

ACCESS: Sacramento Symphony Association, 2848 Arden Way, Suite 210, Sacramento, CA 95825. (916) 973–0300. Benjamin Greene, General Manager.

D. KERN HOLOMAN

SAN DIEGO (1,861,846)

San Diego Symphony Orchestra (Mj)

The example of the San Diego Symphony is illustrative of some of the problems besetting symphony orchestras in the recently burgeoning cities of the Sunbelt. These cities, frequently without established physical centers, often have no central, long-established, dominant industrial bases. The problem is further compounded by the continual influx of new industries that constantly change the face of the economic landscape. This in turn leads to constant changes in the makeup of the power elite and constant shifts in the influence and potential contributions of prospective orchestra Board members.

Although San Diego ranks seventh in population among American cities according to most recent population estimates, its orchestra has yet to achieve a status commensurate with that ranking. Over the past decade, in fact, the orchestra has grappled with economic and organizational problems and barely escaped collapse in 1978 and again in 1981. Having weathered these crises and having undergone major organizational changes, the orchestra is now embarked on a development program with the goal of ensuring its continued stability.

San Diego is at the same time one of the oldest and one of the newest cities in the country. The city was founded in 1769, but only in recent years has it emerged as a major metropolitan center. For years the city languished in the shadow of Los Angeles, a mere 100 miles to the north. Frequent appearances by the Los Angeles Philharmonic* have been cited by some persons as an inhibiting factor in the development of the local orchestra. Additionally, even supporters of the San Diego Symphony have projected ambiguity regarding an appropriate status for the orchestra, with some wanting to raise its profile and others wishing to retain the orchestra in a more modest ASOL Major capacity.

In 1927, Nino Marcelli, music instructor at San Diego High School, augmented the student orchestra with professional musicians to present a series of summer concerts under the name of the Philharmonic Orchestra of San Diego. In 1928 the name was changed to the Civic Orchestra of San Diego and in 1931 to the San Diego Symphony Orchestra. Musicians at first participated on a cooperative basis, accepting a portion of the proceeds of ticket sales rather than the minimum scale wages established by the local musicians' union.

The Symphony continued in its part-time capacity, with several interruptions, through 1957. In 1958, after several years of attempts by various groups to institute a winter series, the San Diego Symphony Orchestra Association began a similar effort and undertook the production of a winter as well as a summer series for the orchestra.

Unfortunately, as the orchestra's level of activities continually expanded, especially through the 1970s, there was no similar increase in the level of support available from the Board. Even with the signing of the first master agreement between the Symphony and the musicians of the orchestra in 1974, the Board failed to make adequate changes in the ad hoc character of the organization. Nor was the Board, through the 1970s, able to generate adequate support in the community to sustain the orchestra's expanded activities. Earlier studies have shown that the Symphony's Board of Directors during this period consisted largely of persons without the economic, social, and political influence necessary to develop adequate linkages to the surrounding community.

But beginning in the 1980s the Board began to undergo changes that would allow it to support a larger role for the orchestra. Members of the local Jewish community became more involved in the leadership of the orchestra, bringing with them increased support from a group traditionally very committed to music and the arts. Influential leaders in many of San Diego's emerging high tech industries were suddenly more visible within the organization, with leaders from that group assuming more influential roles within the Symphony. Also present in larger numbers than before are leaders of major San Diego financial institutions, a change that has aided the Symphony with an infusion of business acumen sometimes lacking in past years.

Currently the orchestra performs through a 45-week season, including a 10-week summer pops series and six weeks with the San Diego Opera. Winter concerts are performed in San Diego's Civic Theater and at other regional theaters located in San Diego County. The summer series is performed at a newly constructed outdoor shell at Hospitality Point along San Diego's world-famous Mission Bay.

The Symphony also presents an extensive series of educational programs. Children's concerts and young people's concerts each year reach an audience of more than 20,000. A new series, Family Concerts, has been added for 1984–1985. Another innovation is the "Overture" educational program series, through which groups may receive concert previews, guided tours of the Civic Theater's backstage areas, and the opportunity to meet orchestra members. The Composer's Forum, a series of pre-concert lectures, allows audiences to meet composers and performers in informal discussions. Winners of the orchestra's annual Young Artists' competition perform at a young people's concert.

Symbolic of the orchestra's search for higher status are recently announced plans for the acquisition of the Fox Theater as a permanent home for the orchestra. The 2,400-seat theater has been judged by several nationally prominent experts to have exceptional potential for concert-hall acoustics. Part of the building also houses office space that would be used by the orchestra's administrative staff, with the excess space to be leased to local businesses.

The Fox Theater acquisition serves as the centerpiece of an ambitious $12 million fund-raising campaign. Purchase of the theater will require $7.5 million, renovations will cost $1.5 million, $1 million will be set aside as a reserve contingency fund, and $2 million will be used for the beginning of a permanent endowment fund.

Impetus for this fund drive comes from a group of Board members who have joined the orchestra since 1981. Chief among them is Louis F. Cumming, Board president from 1981 to 1984. When faced with a possible bankruptcy in 1981, Cumming and three other Board members, Ben Borevitz, Jack Larsen, and Barry McComack, took over day-to-day operations of the Symphony and helped to steer the organization back to a more viable financial position. During the summer of that year, the orchestra's pops series was cancelled, and musicians were not paid for several weeks. As the financial pressures on the musicians began to mount, an emergency loan fund was created, and each Board member was asked to contribute $3,000 of their own resources to aid the musicians. Those Board members who were unable or unwilling to do so were asked to resign, and their places were taken by others in the community with the resources and the commitment to help support the orchestra. For the 1984–1985 season, the minimum contribution for each Board member has been increased to $7,000, an amount that the Board member must give or solicit.

What is remarkable about these changes is the quickness with which they have been achieved. Of the 63 Board members serving in 1976–1977, only 10 remained by the 1983–1984 season. By that time, 41 new members populated the Board, representing a veritable cross section of San Diego's emerging economic, social, and political leadership.

In a similar manner, the administrative staff of the orchestra has also seen rapid changes. During the financial crisis of 1981, the staff was reduced from 22 to nine members in a effort to reduce expenses. While the staff has been increased to larger levels and has increased in professionalism, turnover remains a problem. Richard Bass, who left during the 1978 financial crisis, has returned as managing director. Clearly, professional staff development is required, for the projected 1985–1986 budget for the orchestra is $5.5 million, which will move the orchestra closer to the enhanced status its supporters hope to achieve.

The goals of all this development are, of course, music making and the support of the orchestra itself. The major achievement in this regard has certainly been the appointment of David Atherton as music director (1980). During his tenure the orchestra has increased in professionalism to a degree that has brought admiration even from the most jaded critics. In addition to his musical talents, recognized throughout the world, David Atherton brings to the orchestra a remarkable ability to teach. He has trained a relatively young orchestra often to outdo itself in terms of musical nuance and expression. Despite his busy schedule—Atherton is concurrently principal guest conductor of the Royal Liverpool Philharmonic and the BBC Symphony Orchestra in addition to appearing as a guest conductor all over the world—he is in San Diego more than six months a year.

For the 1984–1985 season the orchestra also announced the appointment of Pulitzer Prize-winning composer Bernard Rands as composer-in-residence. Rands, who has received a profusion of eminent awards, has been commissioned by the Symphony to write a large work for full orchestra. The work, *Suite: Le Tambourin*, will be premiered by the orchestra during the 1984–1985 season.

Even with all these developments, however, accumulated debt is higher now than ever before, attendance at regular subscription concerts still lags below levels necessary to provide adequate earned revenues, the season is still short of full-time status, and regular recordings have yet to be initiated. Undoubtedly progress has been made—the orchestra has survived and has begun to seek new directions—but the San Diego Symphony remains an orchestra in search of an identity.

CHRONOLOGY OF MUSIC DIRECTORS: Nino Marcelli, 1927–1938. Nikolai Sokoloff, 1938–1942. (Operations suspended, 1942–1949). Fabien Sevitzky, 1949–1953. Robert Shaw, 1953–1958. John Barnett, 1958–1960. Earl Bernard Murray, 1960–1967. Zoltan Rozsnyai, 1967–1972. Peter Eros, 1972–1980. David Atherton, 1980–present.

BIBLIOGRAPHY: Interviews with San Diego Symphony administration and staff. David Estes and Robert Stock, *The San Diego Symphony: Problems of Institution Building* (Institute of Public and Urban Affairs, San Diego State University, 1978). David Estes and Robert Stock, "The San Diego Symphony: Problems of Institution Building," *Performing Arts Review* 8, no. 2 (1978). Peter W. Mehren, "The WPA Federal Music Projects and Curriculum Projects in San Diego," Master's thesis, University of California, Davis, 1972. Mildred Tracy, "Development of the San Diego Symphony," Master's thesis, San Diego State College, 1961. San Diego Symphony Orchestra Association, Minutes.

ACCESS: San Diego Symphony Orchestra, P.O. Box 3175, San Diego, CA 92103. (714) 239–9721. Richard Bass, Managing Director.

DAVID ESTES AND ROBERT STOCK

SAN FRANCISCO (3,250,630)

San Francisco Symphony (Mj)

From its humble beginnings almost three-quarters of a century ago, the San Francisco Symphony has risen to extraordinary heights. The climb was neither easy nor smooth, but a struggle against both external and internal obstacles.

The earliest record of any orchestral events in San Francisco was in 1881 when the San Francisco Philharmonic Society presented a series of concerts under the direction of Gustav Henrich. The programs presented were mainly of a pops variety with an occasional Mozart or Haydn symphony thrown in to add substance. In 1894 a new series of sacred concerts were given by the Imperial Vienna Orchestra. History does not show whether all the musicians were imported from Austria or if some local talent was used. The programs were adorned with a picture of conductor Fritz Scheel in full uniform, complete with medals across his chest. The strong gaze from those steely eyes and the six-inch mustache gave the impression that his directorship was one of immense authority.

In 1896, Henrich resumed his concert series, this time adding the name of his concertmaster to the orchestra, now the Henrich-Beel Symphony Orchestra. It died and another sprang up in 1904 under the batons of Paul Steindorf and Henry Holmes. However, the famous San Francisco Earthquake and Fire of 1906 not only wiped out this orchestra but almost all cultural activities in the city for a number of years.

By 1911 San Francisco had sufficiently recovered to begin thinking about starting another symphony orchestra. Social and business leaders formed the Musical Association of San Francisco, which was determined to present a series of concerts given by the San Francisco Orchestra, as it was then called. Thus, by December 8, 1911, the first official concert of the organization later to be known as the San Francisco Symphony had been performed. The first conductor was Henry Hadley, who came with an excellent reputation both as a conductor and composer. He is also the only director in the orchestra's history who was an American. Hadley must have been a fine conductor and organizer since from the very beginning glowing reviews appeared in the newspapers. Harvey Wickham wrote, "It isn't fair to middling—it's gilt-edged." Of the 62 musicians in that first season, 61 were male, the exception being a Mrs. Von Gzyki, harpist.

Hadley conducted the orchestra from 1911 to 1915, when the podium was taken over by Alfred Hertz, a German whose programs were mainly from the Austrian-Germanic school. Much emphasis was placed upon Wagner and Brahms, and since the orchestra had played the latter's symphonies so often, they became commonplace. However, the audiences didn't object since they were most comfortable with the music of this period.

Between the 1930–1931 season and the 1933–1934 season, the orchestra was alternately under the direction of the English conductor Basil Cameron, and a Russian, Issay Dobrowen. The Musical Association, conductors, and general public all tried vainly to keep the orchestra going through these depression years. However, there were only six pairs of concerts in 1933–1934, and the 1934–1935 season was cancelled entirely.

Nevertheless, hope was rekindled shortly. A group of public-spirited people led by Leonora Wood Armsby persuaded Pierre Monteux to come to San Francisco and begin to rebuild the San Francisco Symphony. In the late fall of 1935 Monteux began the arduous task of recreating a symphony orchestra out of 85 musicians who had played together very sketchily in the preceding few years. He was the man to do this, since his conducting was based on a solid knowledge of the fundamentals of music, musicians, and orchestral organization. He remained in San Francisco for 17 years. His repertoire consisted of the classics and both old and new French music. He surprised his San Francisco audiences by also introducing a great deal of modern music. Famous for conducting the premieres of many of Stravinsky's compositions, Monteux was instrumental in having the composer guest conduct in San Francisco several times. The transcontinental tour of 1947 served to enhance the orchestra's reputation. The San Francisco Symphony travelled by private train on this tour and performed 51 concerts in 56 days. Monteux continued conducting in San Francisco for another five years, and from 1952 to 1954 an intense search was instituted to find his successor.

Among the aspirants for the position of director of the San Francisco Symphony was Enrique Jordá, a young Spanish conductor. He brought with him a great intensity and a deep love of music. His knowledge of Spanish music was vast, so that San Francisco audiences had an opportunity to hear unusual works from this repertoire. Aiding him in presenting these compositions were the Spanish soloists Pablo Casals and Andrés Segovia. Jordá also had an affinity for the larger choral works, and many of these were heard for the first time in San Francisco under his direction. But both the orchestra and the general public were soon to realize that this young man's potential was not going to be fulfilled, and the consensus was that performance standards began to deteriorate.

When Jordá left in 1963, there was a fortunate replacement in Josef Krips. Krips expected much from the orchestra, and with his knowledge of the classics, indications were that his goal of excellence would be reached. Management gave Krips a free hand in accomplishing his purpose. However, he sometimes was so high-handed in his approach to the orchestra and in his hirings and firings that a revolt began to brew among the orchestral personnel. This, along with the need for the orchestra to improve its working conditions (length of season, wages, vacation, pension, and other fringe benefits), led to bitter contract negotiations. A strike, the first in the orchestra's history, occurred in 1967. The season did not start on time that year, and it took a great deal of persuasion before the Board of Governors understood the musicians' position regarding not only material benefits, but a say in the artistic control of the orchestra—even to the hiring and firing of personnel. Although this was shocking to those Board members who felt that the conductor was the supreme commander, persuasion did take place, and this stride turned out to be a very successful one for all concerned. The fortunes of the orchestra started to rise from this point on and have not faltered since.

Krips took the orchestra on its first—and successful—overseas tour to Japan. It did much to widen the orchestra's exposure. At this time it would have been advantageous for the orchestra to resume recording, but Krips, forever "rebuilding," never finished his work to his own satisfaction. Thus were lost to the world some of the finest performances of the great works in the Austro-Germanic repertoire. At the end of Krips's seven-year tenure, one more task remained—to announce his successor, Seiji Ozawa.

It would be impossible to imagine a conductor more dramatically different from Krips than Ozawa. Krips, the last of the great Titans, was completely steeped in the classics; his performances would all be good and predictable. As for Ozawa, young and with a mercurial temperament, the only thing predictable about him and his performances were their unpredictability. Perhaps the most talented of the young generation of conductors, Ozawa had a charismatic personality that attracted audiences visually as well as aurally. Possessor of one of the most phenomenal memories extant, Ozawa learned scores almost overnight. His most effective conducting achievements were in works that used large forces in which he acted as a grand general of the united armies. Also, he utilized his conducting technique, which was abetted by the tutelage of his mentor, Leonard Bernstein, to present modern and unusual compositions to his San Francisco public. Whatever he did, the audiences were enthralled, and under his direction the San Francisco Symphony registered some of its greatest successes.

An extended tour to Western Europe and the Soviet Union took place in 1973. Two years later Ozawa brought his San Francisco Symphony back to Japan for its second tour of the Orient. It seemed that the orchestra was riding the crest of a new wave and would remain there, but a story in *Newsweek* broke the euphoria. Ozawa had accepted a position with the Boston Symphony.* The next day, Ozawa cancelled a rehearsal in the East to confront his San Francisco orchestra. He assured the musicians that he would still conduct as much in San Francisco as he always had; all protestations to the contrary, however, Mr. Ozawa, at the beginning of the 1975–1976 season announced his resignation, to take place a year later. Among the musical cognoscenti this was no surprise, but there was some concern about who his replacement would be.

Edo de Waart, young Dutch maestro, had conducted the orchestra in 1974 and made a good impression. He was hired to be principal guest conductor of the 1976–1977 season. There was some speculation about his taking over the conductor's chores after Ozawa left. Although he professed a reluctance to assume this position along with the similar one he held in Rotterdam, he was persuaded to accept, starting with the 1977–1978 season. Since the *Newsweek* story broke, the orchestra's morale began to go down, and the audiences were tapering off.

It was an unpropitious time for de Waart to enter the arena. He had his work cut out for him. It was necessary that de Waart inspire confidence in the musicians and the public alike in his ability to bring together all the factors that would make the orchestra successful again, even though his personality was diametrically the opposite of Ozawa's. His interviews with the press contained phrases that spoke of making the San Francisco Symphony the primary interest of the city's audiences rather than the conductor himself. Thus his tenure here began rather tentatively. He wanted to rebuild the orchestra's repertoire on the classics, from which musical and tonal values could be established. He also used all his influence to have a hall built in San Francisco strictly for Symphony concerts. During de Waart's first year the orchestra used the War Memorial Opera House except for four months of the year, when it housed the San Francisco Opera Company; it was not an ideal place to hear or play symphony concerts.

Through private donors and official encouragement in funds and sanctions the new hall was completed in 1980. Foremost among the private donors was Louise M. Davies, whose gracious generosity led to the hall being named for her. When the Louise M. Davies Symphony Hall became the permanent home of the San Francisco Symphony, musicians who were in both the San Francisco Symphony and the Opera Orchestras had to choose between them. Most chose the Symphony, but several went the other way, and positions became vacant in the orchestra. That, along with natural attrition and the encouragement of the management for early retirement for some older musicians, allowed de Waart over a period of three years to change about 30% of the personnel. The replacements came generally from the best of the nation's youthful talent, making the Symphony's musicians today among the youngest and most vital in the country.

Although the transcontinental tour of 1980 did not receive very favorable reviews from the critics, the orchestra made significant upward strides. When it went on tour in 1983, critical and public response indicated that the San Francisco Symphony had reached an unprecedented degree of excellence in its performance. Its recordings confirmed that approbation.

At the end of the 1982–1983 season de Waart announced his resignation to take place at the end of the 1984–1985 season. An in-depth search was instituted to find a worthy successor, and for the first time orchestra members, through the Artistic Advisory Committee, were consulted before a decision was made. After an extremely felicitous two-week conducting stint in San Francisco, Herbert Blomstedt, director of the Dresden Staatskapelle, was selected as the next conductor and musical director of the San Francisco Symphony, effective in the fall of 1985.

San Franciscans have always had a very special affinity with their Symphony. The Symphony's first program listed the initial sponsors that launched the orchestra: it included the names of the most prominent people in the fields of industry and banking of San Francisco. Among these were the families of Crocker, Tobin, Sloss, and Sigmund Stern, names still prominent in the cultural life of the city. As time went on others joined, among them Agnes Albert and the aforementioned Louise M. Davies. However, in the 1930s it became evident that the Symphony could not continue to exist from the donations of a few generous donors. The base had to be broadened. A first step was a charter amendment to give a percentage of the taxes collected from the citizens of San Francisco to a symphony orchestra. This, along with a generous contribution of the hotel tax, has put the city of San Francisco solidly behind its symphony orchestra. The management also went to a wider range of private and corporate donors to fill out its budgetary needs. Today, over 60% of the Symphony's budget is derived from earned income (concerts, broadcasts, paid rehearsals, and recordings). During a recent subscription season 77.5% of the capacity of the Louise M. Davies Symphony Hall was taken by season ticket holders. Advance single ticket sales brought this amount up to 94% of capacity.

The San Francisco Symphony gives an average of four concerts a week throughout the year. Besides the regular subscription season there are annual Beethoven and Mostly Mozart Festivals, the New and Unusual Music Series (supervised by the composer-in-residence, John Adams), the Joffrey Ballet season, and several youth concert series. Altogether for the 1983–1984 season the San Francisco Symphony played 250 concerts to an audience of 600,000. The projected budget for the 1984–1985 season is $16 million.

A Youth Orchestra started during the 1980–1981 season under San Francisco Symphony Associate Conductor Yahja Ling is now a thriving organization that gives an annual series of concerts in the Symphony Hall and one concert a year along with the parent San Francisco Symphony. It is an aspiration of many young Bay Area musicians to become members of this fine ensemble. In the 1984–1985 season David Milnes has taken over its directorship.

With the generous help of many private donors, foremost of whom was Frank Tack, a Ruffati organ was installed in Davies Hall in 1984. The largest concert organ in the United States, it has been the final addition to the Symphony Hall that has helped to bring the San Francisco Symphony to its current prominence in the cultural life of the United States.

RECORDING HISTORY AND SELECTIVE DISCOGRAPHY: Between 1925 and 1930, under the baton of Alfred Hertz, the San Francisco Symphony recorded for RCA and its European counterpart HMV. Although the orchestra made quite a few recordings, most were in a very light vein. During Monteux's regime the Symphony began to record again for RCA Victor. The orchestra's reputation grew because of these recordings, some of which won awards. Under Ozawa, recording was again resumed, this time for Deutsche Grammophon and Philips. In 1981 the Philips Company signed a contract with the San Francisco Symphony to make a series of records over the next four years, a number of which have already been successfully produced.

Debussy, *La Damoiselle élue*; Duparc, Songs; Ravel, *Sheherezade* (Elly Ameling, Soprano/de Waart): Philips 6514199. De Falla, *Nights in the Gardens of Spain* (Artur Rubenstein/Jorda): RCA LSC–2430. Gershwin, *An American in Paris* and Bernstein, Ballet Music from *West Side Story* (Ozawa): Deutsche Grammophon 2531355. Grieg, *Music from Peer Gynt* (de Waart): Philips 6514378. Mahler, Symphony No. 4 (Margaret Price, Soprano/de Waart): Philips 6514201. Rachmaninoff, Piano Concerti and Paganini Variations (Zoltan Kocsis, Piano/de Waart): Philips 6514377. Respighi, *Fountains of Rome, Festivals of Rome*, and *Birds* (de Waart): Philips 6514202. Wagner, *Siegfried Idyll* and Strauss, *Death and Transfiguration* (Monteux): Victrola ALK1–4972.

CHRONOLOGY OF MUSIC DIRECTORS: Henry Hadley, 1911–1915. Alfred Hertz, 1915–1930. Basil Cameron and Issay Dobrowen, 1930–1934. (Operations suspended, 1934–1935). Pierre Monteux, 1935–1952. (Guest conductors, 1952–1954.) Enrique Jordá, 1952–1963. Josef Krips, 1963–1970. Seiji Ozawa, 1970–1976. (Guest conductors, 1976–1977.) Edo de Waart, 1977–1985. Herbert Blomstedt, 1985–present).

BIBLIOGRAPHY: Archive of the Performing Arts. San Francisco Symphony, Archives. David Schneider, *The San Francisco Symphony: Music, Maestros and Musicians* (Novato, Calif.: Presidio Press, 1983). Library of Harry Strauss.

ACCESS: San Francisco Symphony, Louise M. Davies Symphony Hall, San Francisco, CA 94102. (415) 552–8000. Peter Pastreich, Executive Director. Deborah Borda, Orchestra Manager.

DAVID SCHNEIDER

SAN RAFAEL (44,700; 3,250,630—San Francisco)

Marin Symphony (Mt)

The Marin Symphony Association was founded in 1951 by a group of musicians who made it their mission to make well-performed classical music available to the community and to provide successive generations of Marin County children with an incentive for musical study and accomplishment.

The first concert, given in a high school gymnasium, was performed by 64 musicians before an audience of 900. Today, the Marin Symphony performs a 13-concert season, including a free pops concert in September and two holiday concerts presented at an intimate, 100-year-old chapel. The remaining 10 concerts (five pairs) form the subscription series and are performed at the Frank Lloyd Wright designed Marin Veterans' Memorial Theater at the Marin Center, which seats 2,000. Both series are extremely well attended by both subscription and single-ticket buyers.

The Marin Symphony Youth Orchestra was formed in 1954 and today maintains an exciting and varied repertoire. It has commissioned new music, for which it won the 1980 ASCAP Award for its "Adventuresome Overall Programming" and a 1981 citation from the American League of Contemporary Composers. In 1957, the Workshop for Strings was created to train the beginning string player for eventual graduation into the Youth Orchestra. Orchestra Piccola (a chamber group) was formed in 1970 in order to give additional training, as well as solo and ensemble opportunities, to the more advanced Youth Orchestra members. The Association also offers a family concert series comprising three concerts designed especially for young children and their families, and including an orchestra sit-in and hands-on demonstration. In addition, music education classes are offered for children between four and 12 years of age.

The Marin Symphony Association is governed by a Board of 38 and administered by a professional staff of eight. The music director and conductor, Sandor Salgo, who recently celebrated his 25th anniversary with the orchestra, is solely responsible for artistic decisions. Approximately 70 musicians are contracted annually, and the remaining 20 to 30 are hired on a per-service basis or are non-union players. Hugo Rinaldi, founder of the MSYO, continues to serve as music director for the youth programs and conductor for the Youth Orchestra and Orchestra Piccola.

As the premier arts organization in Marin County, the Marin Symphony Association has a $689,000 budget and is funded by federal and state government grants, as well as corporate, individual, and foundation gifts. In 1984 the Marin Symphony Association's programs will reach over 30,000 persons.

The Association prides itself on its adventuresome programming, and in addition to its traditional symphonic repertoire presents each year three to four contemporary works. During the 1983–1984 season, with funding from the NEA, the Marin Symphony presented the world premiere of *Ceyx and Alcyone* by Mark Volkert, the Symphony's assistant concertmaster. The performance received excellent reviews in all the local and San Francisco papers. In addition, the Symphony has premiered works by Heuwell Tircuit, Darius Milhaud, and Grant Beglarian and has performed the West Coast premieres of works by Szymanowski, Panufnik, and Dutilleux.

CHRONOLOGY OF MUSIC DIRECTORS: Gaston Usigli, 1951–1953. (Guest conductors, 1953–1956.) Sandor Salgo, 1956–present.

ACCESS: Marin Symphony, 4172 Redwood Highway, San Rafael, CA 94903. (415) 479–8100. Betty Mulryan, General Manager.

ELLIE MEDNICK

SANTA BARBARA (298,694)

Santa Barbara Symphony Orchestra (Mt)

Since its founding in 1953, the Santa Barbara Symphony has had a dominant emphasis on music for youth. When statewide budget cuts in the arts in education affected the local schools, the Symphony continued to provide whatever exposure to symphonic music young people were to have.

The concert season extends from October through May, with seven Tuesday evening (soon to become Saturday evening) and seven Sunday matinee concerts, two performances of the *Nutcracker*, five concerts for elementary school children, and two for tiny tots, in addition to a special concert.

Santa Barbara's size and geographic location between the Pacific Ocean and the Santa Lucia Mountains is a drawback to economic and industrial growth; educational and research institutions have been the main sources of local employment. Despite the consequent lack of major industrial or local governmental support and the seasonal visits of the Los Angeles Philharmonic,* the Symphony Association has seen its budget grow from $10,000 when it was incorporated in 1954 to more than $500,000 in the 1980s.

Adolf Frezin, a community resident, directed the Symphony for its first (1953–1954) season; serving as catalyst was Stefan Krayk, founder and concertmaster until 1983. In the beginning, all musicians were paid largely from contributions since few tickets were sold. This continued for five years until deficits, meager audiences, and even a bank loan made it prudent to discontinue all payments to musicians and to pay only the expenses of the part-time conductor. With the loyal consent of the playing musicians, the plan resulted in greater community support and larger audiences. After two years it was possible to resume reimbursements to musicians on a small scale.

Ernest Gold was conductor in 1957–1958 and was hired for 1958–1959.

However, when Gold was called to write the score of *Exodus* after the first concert of that second season, Amerigo Marino (conductor of the Glendale Symphony*) and Erno Daniel (music director of the Wichita Falls Symphony) acted as guest conductors, until the beginning of the eighth season, when an important milestone in the Symphony's history was reached. The Board of Directors employed Daniel, then a member of the faculty of the University of California at Santa Barbara, as the orchestra's regular, paid, resident music director; Stefan Krayk became concertmaster; and other UCSB faculty assumed first-chair positions. A full-time manager, Terry C. Schwarz, was also hired to replace the volunteers who had been carrying on the administrative work. The musicians received a slight raise in salary, and two performances were given for each of the season's four concerts. The changes brought tremendous growth in audience, requiring a move from the 660-seat Lobero Theatre to the Granada Theatre, with nearly three times the seating capacity.

Five years later, Ronald Ondrejka became music director. Formerly assistant conductor of the Pittsburgh Symphony,* Ondrejka had been hired the previous year as conductor of the University Symphony Orchestra and instructor in conducting. This harmonious relationship of sharing a conductor between the Symphony Association and the University would last for over 20 years.

As the 1967–1968 season with Ondrejka opened, a new full-time managing director, Genevieve S. Fisher, was engaged, and the budget reached $61,000. Following several seasons of increasing activity and budgets, the orchestra moved to the Arlington Theatre, where concerts are still performed. The Arlington, a landmark of attractive Spanish design built in the 1920s, lacks acoustical and visual efficiency as a concert hall, and so the need for an appropriate performance hall remains. In 1984 Fisher retired after 17 years, having brought the Symphony through some lean years and some spectacular ones, but all sound in management. Peter Garnick assumed the post of managing director in July of 1984.

When Ondrejka accepted a post with the Fort Wayne (Indiana) Philharmonic* in 1979, Frank Collura, formerly associate conductor of the Kansas City Phiharmonic Orchestra, became the next conductor/music director. He also assumed Ondrejka's post with the University. Although Collura will retain his title with the Symphony Association through the 1984–1985 season, Serge Zehnacker of France was hired for the University post from 1982 to 1984, when it was decided to resume the close cultural ties between the Symphony Association and the University's music department. A joint Search Committee reviewed over 200 applicants, and the 1984–1985 season will see three guest conductors—Robert Bernhardt, Varujan Kojian, and Evan Whallon—one of whom may be invited to become permanent conductor. An improved program of joint positions with the University is expected to provide a stronger financial and cultural base for the Association.

The orchestra is administered by the managing director working in conjunction with the Administration Committee of the Board of Directors, who, along with an Orchestra Committee and personnel manager from the orchestra are responsible for negotiations with the AFM local. Other committees of the Board are headed by vice presidents. An active Women's Association, later named the Symphony League, was organized in 1960 and has assisted the Association in meeting the annual operating budget, plus assuming responsibility for ticket sales and producing two editions of a *Symphony Cook Book*.

In addition to ticket sales and minor local and national grants, a sustaining-fund campaign is the major source of income. An endowment fund was created through a large primary gift and is expected to be expanded into a major program in coming years. The extremely high cost of living in Santa Barbara makes it prohibitive for musicians to earn a living in this community. Consequently many of the best musicians leave, thus necessitating imports who require travel costs and thereby add to the Symphony's expenditures.

Musical programs are arranged by the conductor, but the budget and selection of soloists and the year's repertoire are planned in consultation with the Artistic Advisory Committee. The Board's current philosophy, in line with the need to curtail costs, is to look for quality among young, promising talents who do not demand high fees and to look within the orchestra itself for talented soloists. Joint symphony-choral programming often involves choral groups from the three major educational institutions (UCSB, Westmont College, and Santa Barbara City College), along with the outstanding Santa Barbara Choral Society.

Among the Symphony's educational programs are "Informances"—45-minute previews for handicapped and older persons. These are conducted by a sight-impaired docent from the Braille Institute and two Symphony musicians for eight organizations of senior and disabled citizens who receive free passes to the Symphony's Sunday matinee concerts.

The early goal of providing fine music for children has blossomed into the current Music Outreach Program, which reaches a total of some 26,000 children. It comprises three free children's concerts, an in-school docent program, runout concerts for children, and an annual essay contest whose three winners each direct a number at the children's concerts. Ballet dancers from a local dance school perform as well. A Young Soloist Competition is held each year for musicians under 18 who reside in the tri-county area. Three winners are chosen, each to perform a concerto with the orchestra at one of the children's concerts. A young artist competition, begun in 1960–1961 and open to all musicians ages 18 to 35, presents the winner with a $1,000 cash award and two solo appearances with the orchestra; other finalists receive honoraria. Three ensemble groups from the Symphony—brass, string, and woodwind—visit schools, offering demonstrations, lecture/performances, and/or master classes. Two concerts for tiny tots feature audience involvement, and an attractive music van is designed especially for third graders. This is a hands-on introduction to the instruments and sounds of the orchestra. A minimum of 40 schools are visited each year, with volunteers driving and presenting the programs. Funding for the Music Outreach Program, which involves a total of some 26,000 children, has been provided by Music Performance Trust Funds of the Recording Industries, the Santa Barbara Foundation, the California Arts Council, the city of Santa Barbara, local corporations, and private individuals.

CHRONOLOGY OF MUSIC DIRECTORS: Adolf Frezin, 1953–1954. Lauris Jones, 1954–1956. Herbert Weiskopf, 1956–1957. Ernest Gold, 1957–1958. (Guest conductors, 1958–1959.) Erno Daniel, 1959–1966. (Guest conductors, 1966–1967.) Ronald Ondrejka, 1967–1979. (Guest conductors, 1978–1979.) Frank Collura, 1979–1985. (Guest conductors, 1984–1985.)

BIBLIOGRAPHY: Interviews with Retired SBSO General Manager Genevieve Fisher and Concertmaster Emeritus/Founder Stefan Krayk. *Santa Barbara New Press*. Santa Barbara Symphony Orchestra Association "Historical Summary, 1953–1964."

ACCESS: Santa Barbara Symphony Orchestra Association, 3 West Carrillo, Santa Barbara, CA 93101. (805) 965–6596. Peter Garnick, General Manager.

ARDIS O. HIGGINS

Colorado _____

BOULDER

Colorado Music Festival Orchestra (Mt)

Founded in 1978, two years after the festival in which it participates, the Colorado Music Festival Orchestra comprises 80 musicians from leading orchestras around the world including the New York Philharmonic,* San Francisco Symphony,* Concertgebouworkest, and others of like stature. About a quarter of the players are from Colorado, some from the Denver Symphony.* There is general continuity in the playing membership, with a small turnover in personnel making for an orchestra that has considerable cohesiveness in its playing.

The orchestra presents full-scale symphonic programs as well as chamber works over a period of six weeks, with some 20 concerts in Boulder, including three regular subscription series, a benefit concert series, preview concerts, and an additional series of runouts to Denver, Fort Collins, and other localities. An outdoor July 4th concert is presented at Chautauqua Park. The season's audience generally totals 26,000. Symphonic concerts in Boulder are presented at the Chautauqua Auditorium (1898), a national landmark located in Boulder's Chautauqua Park. Its shallow depth, wood construction, and exposed beam-work make for brilliant acoustics.

Although the fare for the 1984 concert series was largely from the standard romantic repertoire (with a good deal of Mozart as well), in past years an additional week's programming (the "Special Project") centered around musical, geographical, or period themes has provided an outlet for much new music as well. In 1979 and 1980, for example, "Music of the '60s" and "Music of the '70s" attracted composers, scholars, and others to its concerts and corollary symposia, lectures, and exhibits. In a more widely humanistic vein was 1981's "Between Two World Wars," sponsored in part by the Colorado Humanities Program.

Operating on an annual budget of about $500,000, the Festival relies largely on ticket sales and individual contributions (67%), with additional funding from the Friends of the CMF group, corporations, local businesses, foundations, and government support. It is administered by a professional staff of four (year around) and additional seasonal staff reporting through the general manager to a 34-member Board of Trustees.

The Music Festival was founded in 1976 by its current music director, Giora Bernstein, who with a group of interested community leaders pre-sented a chamber-orchestra summer festival in 1977 at Boulder's First Pres-byterian Church. The full symphony orchestra began in 1978, when the group moved to Chautauqua Park. The next years saw the growth of the Special Projects and the group's first national radio broadcast (in 1981 on NPR). The Festival's budget and reputation have grown steadily since its formation, with positive reviews both locally and in such far-off cities as San Francisco.

CHRONOLOGY OF MUSIC DIRECTORS: Giora Bernstein, 1976–present.

BIBLIOGRAPHY: *Colorado Music Festival* (Boulder: CMF, [1984]). "History of the CMF," *Colorado Music Festival Summer Nights of Great Music* (CMF 1984 Program Book).

ACCESS: Colorado Music Festival, 1728 Sixteenth Street, Suite 3, Boulder, CO 80302. (303) 449–1397. Marcia Schirmer, General Manager.

ROBERT R. CRAVEN

COLORADO SPRINGS (317,458)

Colorado Springs Symphony (Rg)

Colorado Springs was originally a wealthy community supported by the fortunes of successful gold miners and transplanted easterners seeking relief from tuberculosis in the refined, high-altitude atmosphere. Because of its very appealing physical and cultural environment, it has provided fertile soil for the growth of the Colorado Springs Symphony.

In May of 1927, Colorado Springs music teacher Edwin Dietrich assem-bled a 30-piece orchestra that performed one concert in Perkins Hall on the Colorado College Campus. Heralded as the event of the season, the concert prompted Frederick Boothroyd, organist at Grace Episcopal Church, to form the Colorado Springs Symphony Ensemble of 27 players. After five successful years and a favorable write-up in the *New York Times*, the or-chestra was enlarged to 80 players and gave its first performance as a full symphony in November 1933 in the city auditorium.

After minor setbacks during the depression, the Symphony found revived interest and a new home with completion of the Colorado Springs Fine Arts Center in 1936 and its elegant, 450-seat theater. Further encouraged by the completion of Colorado Springs High School's new 1,400-seat auditorium in 1941, a grant from the El Pomar Foundation, and incorporation as the Colorado Springs Symphony Association with an enlarged Board of Directors, the orchestra continued to flourish. Well-known guest artists such as Joseph Szigeti in 1943 and Rudolf Firkusny in 1944 increased the orchestra's fame and fortune. Again the CSS was cited in the *New York Times*, now hailed for its growth, increased ticket sales, and ability to attract feature artists of high calibre. After yet another successful decade, the then 75-year-old Boothroyd retired, closing the first great age—and 26 years—of his orchestra.

The 1954–1955 season opened under a new conductor, Walter Eisenberg, whose reputation as concertmaster and assistant conductor of the Denver Symphony* and conductor of the Pueblo Symphony preceded him. Among other projects, he began a series of summer pops concerts performed in the local geological landmark known as the Garden of the Gods and, in 1958 in conjunction with the Colorado College Dance Department, inaugurated Christmas performances of the *Nutcracker*. Invited by Boston University to join their full-time faculty, Eisenberg resigned in 1966. Under his leadership, it was reported in Denver's *Rocky Mountain News*, the city's support of the orchestra "increased 1,000 percent in five years."

During the following three years, the Symphony was led by an interim conductor, Harold Farberman. He challenged orchestra and audience alike by programming more modern music, including some of his own works that had already been played by major orchestras. He also assisted in the search for a new music director.

In 1970, the orchestra opened its season under Charles Ansbacher and simultaneously entered another phase of extraordinary growth. Within two years the subscription series, then consisting of five concerts, was expanded to 10. In 1983–1984 there were 36 subscription concerts by the CSS (nine concerts, each presented four times) in the winter series, performed in a substantially larger hall. In addition, Ansbacher has taken an active role in community and regional affairs; among other things, he has served on the Colorado Council on the Arts and Humanities and chaired the Design and Construction Subcommittee of the new Pikes Peak Center.

The Center, for which the CSS took leadership in fund raising and design, was constructed with $7.3 million contributed by the private sector toward a $13.4 million building subsequently owned by El Paso County. Now home of the CSS, the Center's El Pomar Great Hall seats 1,835. With acoustics that have received national attention (Isaac Stern called it "a superb piece of work, certainly one of the finest new halls that I have been in recently"), the Center has afforded great opportunities for the Symphony and other regional arts organizations.

The orchestra's 32-member Board of Directors meets monthly and participates actively in planning and development. The orchestra is managed by Beatrice Vradenburg and a full-time staff of 14. Originally the founder of the Symphony Guild in 1955, Mrs. Vradenburg has frequently been honored by the ASOL; her community leadership and appointments to directorships on corporate, civic, and charitable boards have proven invaluable to the success of the CSS. Within the CSS organization, she has been instrumental in establishing numerous important operational procedures. The Orchestra Liaison Committee, with members from the Board and orchestra, has successfully worked out all governance relationships between management and musicians, including salaries, benefits, and general future planning of the CSS. There exists an open, healthy, and trusting relationship between players, management, and Board.

Under Vradenburg's management, the budget and programs of the CSS have grown dramatically in size and number. The 1984 budget of $1.8 million nearly quadrupled the 1978 budget of $483,000, while the current Sustaining Fund of $275,000 (from 2,015 contributors) shows the same growth over the 1978 total of $77,000 (from 900 contributors). Other revenues come from federal and local government grants, foundation grants, corporate gifts, income earned by affiliated concert series and support groups (Symphony Guild and Young Men's Council), and ticket sales.

Numerous unique programs developed in Colorado Springs by the music director and manager have received national attention. In 1977 the first (and now annual) "Broadmoor Christmas Pops on Ice" concert was conducted by Arthur Fiedler and presented in conjunction with the Broadmoor Skating Club featuring world-class skaters. The CSS also initiated the "Classical Splash" with U.S. Olympic synchronized swimmers. Summer Symphony concerts performed in Colorado Springs parks and sponsored by the city were inaugurated in 1973; the orchestra also presents these concerts in other regional cities, including Denver. The 1984 series included 13 concerts and a patriotic July 4th performance that attracted some 60,000 people. The orchestra also presents performances of the *Nutcracker* each December and 12 full-orchestra youth concerts. The CSS Trio, Brass Quintet, and the DaVinci String Quartet, each made up of Symphony players, perform regularly under auspices of the CSS, while other ensembles of orchestra players give numerous concerts in local schools. In the role of impresario, the CSS also presents pops, jazz, and showtime series by visiting, nationally recognized artists, orchestras, and dramatic companies.

The repertoire of the Winter Series is set by the music director. Although he generally centers programs on the standard eighteenth- and nineteenth-century orchestral works, Ansbacher frequently ventures back to the baroque and into the realm of less accessible twentieth-century styles. Concerts are often programmed according to a theme, such as a single composer (Beethoven) or nationality (Russian). Generally, all but one concert of the series has a guest soloist. These include well-established artists as well as gifted lesser-known and younger performers. In order to meet the audience demand for superstars, but not allow the fees to impinge upon the musicians' salary segment of the budget, the orchestra sponsors a self-supporting Great Artist Series of one or two concerts a year.

CSS musicians are selected from a national applicant pool. Although the Symphony's 87 players are part-time, the Colorado Opera Festival, the Colorado Springs Chorale, and numerous other organizations rely upon the CSS for their orchestras. The players also nurture protégés in the Colorado Springs Community Orchestra; this organization, co-sponsored by the CSS, boasts more than 100 members and fosters the careers of young musicians by featuring as soloists the annual winners of Young Artists Auditions.

CHRONOLOGY OF MUSIC DIRECTORS: Edwin Dietrich, 1927. Frederick Boothroyd, 1928–1954. Walter Eisenberg, 1954–1965. Harold Farberman, 1967–1970. Charles Ansbacher, 1970–present.

BIBLIOGRAPHY: Interviews with CSS Music Director Charles Ansbacher and Manager Beatrice W. Vradenburg, 1984. Colorado Springs Symphony, *Fifty Years with the Symphony* (Pamphlet, Colorado Springs, [1977]). *Colorado Springs Sun. Denver Post. Gazette Telegraph. Rocky Mountain News.*

ACCESS: Colorado Springs Symphony, Post Office Box 1692, Colorado Springs, CO 80901. (303) 633–4611. Beatrice W. Vradenburg, Manager.

MICHAEL D. GRACE

DENVER (1,620,902)

Denver Symphony Orchestra (Mj)

Since its inception the Denver Symphony Orchestra has been considered a vital part of the Denver metropolitan area and has enjoyed excellent support from the entire state of Colorado. During the 1983–1984 concert season, the Denver Symphony Orchestra celebrated its 50th anniversary with an impressive season that included first performances for the orchestra of many works, as well as a commissioned work by Ezra Laderman. This particular anniversary was considered an important event in the city's history since the Symphony's achievements have been symbolic of Denver's growth.

Denver was established in 1858 primarily to accommodate the mining trade. During Denver's earliest years efforts to encourage and develop musical talent were evidenced by the numerous music schools that existed in the area. By the turn of the century, many music organizations were active, and a constant hope of Denver music enthusiasts was the establishment of a permanent orchestra. Two salaried symphonies in the early years of the twentieth century preceded the more significant formation of the Denver Philharmonic Orchestra in 1912. This orchestra served Denver until the

World War I years, when many of Denver's musicians entered the military. After the Denver Philharmonic series was discontinued, the excitement associated with symphony concerts in Denver that had prevailed during the pre-war period diminished.

The number of skilled musicians who had acquired their musical training in Denver but had left the city, due in part to the war but also due to the lack of professional musical opportunities, became a concern. This, coupled with a commitment to promote music and an awareness of civic responsibility, were prime factors that led to the formation of what can truly be regarded as the forerunner to the Denver Symphony Orchestra.

The Denver Civic Orchestra was formed in 1922. Its objectives were simple and direct: to develop a high calibre symphony orchestra for Denver by encouraging future symphony musicians, to provide regularly scheduled concerts, and to develop an audience.

The first performance by this orchestra was held on November 6, 1922, with Horace Tureman conducting. Six concerts were planned for the first year, and the second year grew to include six pairs of concerts. Each included a short informative talk by the conductor concerning the works performed. A conservative yet varied repertoire and devoted musicians enabled Tureman to achieve a standard of performance that proved acceptable to both critics and audiences. Inexpensive tickets made the concerts available to all, and Tureman's talks helped develop an appreciation and enjoyment of music in the Mile High City.

The orchestra's success encouraged the Civic Orchestra Society to formulate plans for Denver's first professional orchestra in 1934. With Tureman providing the ideas and leadership, the Civic Symphony Society established what would become a three-division structure. Although separate and non-conflicting, the divisions were also dependent on one another.

The Junior Symphony, established in 1935, was a youth orchestra whose members were all under the age of 18. It was established to develop and prepare instrumentalists for admission into the Civic Orchestra and to link the orchestral training taught in the public schools with the musical activities of the Civic and Denver Symphonies. The Civic Orchestra remained semi-professional; its primary purpose to train instrumentalists for symphonies, not only for Denver, but for other communities that were forming their own orchestras using local or native talent.

The Denver Symphony Orchestra was organized as a completely professional body. Most of its 43 members had been developed through the Civic Orchestra, although a few were imported. During the first season in 1934, the Civic Orchestra Society presented the DSO in a series of three evening concerts featuring world-famous guest artists.

These three musical groups (Civic Orchestra, Junior Symphony, Denver Symphony) were governed by the Civic Symphony Society, consisting of community members led by officers, a Board of Trustees, and Executive

Committee. Conducting duties for all three divisions were held by Horace Tureman, who retained their directorship for 28 years.

The DSO concluded its first season with a budget surplus of $134, and it looked forward to the 1935–1936 season with a projected budget of $25,000 and an additional 20 musicians. This was despite the difficult economic times and the added burden of maintaining two other orchestras. Throughout the DSO's formative years, Tureman's contributions were significant and numerous. A major change in the 1937–1938 season was the addition of wind and percussion players to accommodate the standard instrumentation of the symphony orchestra. The 1940–1941 season saw the DSO increase its concert series to five concerts. A ballet program was added to the concert series during the 1941–1942 season, as were a children's program and a major choral work.

The success of all three orchestras was due to a combination of factors. The well-organized and effective Civic Symphony Society had led successful campaigns to educate citizens to appreciate orchestral music. The DSO provided the community with the best available musicians performing concerts of high calibre at a price the vast majority of citizens could afford. The city provided free hall use, the musicians' union allowed its professional players to perform with amateurs, and many individuals donated time, money, and talent.

Tureman's ill health forced him to retire at the close of the 1943–1944 season, the same time his plans were announced to develop the DSO into a full-fledged, 85-member ensemble with increased seasonal offerings, a nationally known conductor, and a budget five times the current $10,000. After a season of guest conductors, Saul Caston became musical director and conductor at the beginning of the 1945–1946 season and was the DSO's first professional conductor. Prior to his arrival in Denver, Caston had served as principal trumpet and later as assistant conductor of the Philadelphia Orchestra.*

Under Caston the DSO grew in size and stature, and during the years that he served as conductor the orchestra became the center focus for the city's musical life. Its activities increased to include over 60 performances per season by 1964, including Tuesday night subscription concerts, free family concerts, four intimate concerts featuring informal discussion between audience and guest composers, and free concerts for over 60,000 students in the Denver Public Schools. In addition to the Denver Symphony Society, other support associations that organized during the Caston era included the Junior Guild, Business Women's Guild, Men's Guild, and Symphony Debutantes. These organizations held concerts and social events that financially benefited the orchestra.

The orchestra's appearances grew to include out-of-town concerts for the major cities and towns of Colorado and Wyoming. In 1956 a DSO concert sponsored by the Prudential Life Insurance Company, was telecast by NBC, giving the orchestra national exposure. In the late 1950s the orchestra also took part in a film featuring lesser-known U.S. symphony orchestras, which was shown in 88 countries. An important series of concerts that gave the DSO national recognition was the "Red Rocks Music Festival," a seven-concert series held 15 consecutive summers at the Red Rocks amphitheater (located in the foothills west of Denver), until two summers of unseasonably bad weather in 1960 and 1961 forced its cancellation.

Nevertheless, during the late 1950s the quantity and quality of Caston's work came under fire, and amidst considerable controversy he resigned at the close of the 1961–1962 season. Another year of auditioning conductors began with the 1963–1964 season. The 1964–1965 season began with a proposed budget of $375,000, eight new string players (bringing total membership to 81), a new business manager, and a new conductor, Vladimir Golschmann.

The Golschmann era was ushered in with predictions of high musical achievement and significant institutional advancement. He had been a world-famous conductor before the existence of the DSO, had risen to musical prominence conducting throughout Europe, and as music director of the St. Louis Symphony* had achieved a reputation for superior performance evident by that ensemble's many recordings. With the DSO's financial position more secure than it had been in years, the stage was set for the Golschmann era, and hopes surfaced that the orchestra would regain the popularity it had once enjoyed.

Under Golschmann the DSO began to expand operations that would extend beyond his tenure. By the mid–1960s the number of subscription concerts had increased from 16 to 36, a Monday night concert series was added, as were the Wednesday Matinee Phipps Concerts and performances of the *Nutcracker* in cooperation with the Denver Civic Ballet. An opportunity for financial growth came in 1966 from a Ford Foundation grant of $1.75 million, of which $1 million was for endowment, $500,000 was expendable, and $250,000 was for development. The $1 million was to be matched by DSO fund-raising within five years. Denver corporations, businesses, and individuals responded with enthusiasm and met the challenge.

The prosperity enjoyed throughout the 1960s, affected only slightly by rising deficits at each season's end, took a turn for the worse at the end of that politically and socially troubled decade. For six years Golschmann had guided the musical course of the DSO through many triumphant musical moments and had lifted the orchestra out of a somewhat stagnant state to a new plateau of musical excellence. His health, however, was a restricting factor and his age seemed at odds with the youth-conscious 1960s. Golschmann's tenure with the DSO ended at the close of the 1968–1969 season, and he was named Conductor Emeritus.

Despite the financial stability provided by the Ford Foundation, DSO musicians still faced a meager salary schedule. Although the season appeared threatened, a strike was avoided when management met many of the musicians' demands, including a 35-week season and improved health and pension benefits.

During the ensuing season of guest conductors, a highlight was the DSO's being selected to tour under the baton of Arthur Fiedler. The tour lasted four weeks and the orchestra visited towns and cities in Nebraska, Kansas, Oklahoma, Texas, and Colorado. Brian Priestman assumed conducting duties at the start of the 1970–1971 season. Priestman's conducting skills had been nurtured by guest appearances with major orchestras in Europe, Canada, and the United States. He was a founder of a chamber orchestra and opera company, had built the Edmonton Symphony Orchestra to national reputation, and served as acting musical director of the Baltimore Symphony Orchestra.*

After the conclusion of his first season conducting the DSO, Priestman began to make many changes. These included changes in personnel, experiments with the acoustics of the city auditorium, and a change in Monday night concert dress to give the orchestra an informal look. The orchestra's visibility increased through effective public relations and by tours in Colorado and surrounding states. Under Priestman the DSO made two major tours: in 1971 to the Northwest, and in 1972 to the East Coast, with debut performances at Carnegie Hall and the Kennedy Center. Priestman was also responsible for the in-residence program through which orchestra musicians became virtually visiting faculty to all state college and university music programs in the state.

Under Priestman new concert series were added and the season was extended so that by 1977 it included 46 weeks. In order to accommodate the extra services in the extended season, two assistant conductors were named to share conducting duties, including the appointment of Sixten Ehrling in 1977 as musical director and principal guest conductor of the DSO.

Despite the artistic and cultural success that the orchestra enjoyed in the 1970s, finances continued to trouble the Denver Symphony Association. The rising costs of maintaining artistic excellence over increasingly extended seasons created large deficits. Although the Ford Foundation endowment funds had been matched, the Association had borrowed from the endowment throughout the previous decade to meet annual deficits that totalled $300,000 in 1977. The opening of the 1977–1978 season had been delayed due to a breakdown in negotiations between musicians and management, and the situation was resolved only after Governor Richard Lamm served as mediator. An eight-point administrative program was designed, affording more efficient use of a concert hall, more aggressive fund raising, reductions in expenses, an appeal to city and state governments for aid, and a more conservative approach to concert scheduling.

Priestman's greatest contribution to the DSO and to the musical community of Denver may have been his influential role in the construction of the new concert hall that the DSO occupies today. Prior to Priestman's arrival in Denver there had been talk of a new hall or remodeling of the old city auditorium, and Priestman's experiments with the acoustics of the old hall indicated the need to address existing problems. Priestman's artistic improvements, coupled with an artistically aware public, created an appropriate time to promote the construction of a new hall specifically for the orchestra's use. Priestman provided the leadership needed for this achievement through his brilliant ability to promote the Symphony. Behind an effectively orchestrated public relations campaign, the city began construction in 1972 of the new concert hall at an initial cost of $13.2 million. The Boettcher Concert Hall was the first in the United States with a stage enclosed entirely by auditorium seating. Financing came from a bond issue approved by Denver voters and from matching funds from the private sector. Its successful opening on March 4, 1978, had involved citizens from every walk of life and had required imaginative and assertive fund-raising from many organizations, most notably radio station KVOD with its DSO marathon, now an annual event with a fund-raising goal of over $300,000.

Priestman resigned at the end of the 1977–1978 season, having accomplished the three major promises he made when he arrived: to make a recording; to take the orchestra on a national tour; and to move the orchestra into a new concert hall. After a year-long search by a Search Committee that for the first time in the orchestra's history included orchestra members, Gaetano Delogu was named conductor and music director at the beginning of the 1979–1980 season. Delogu has established himself as an artist with extremely high standards and a specific concept of what he expects from an orchestra.

Community support for the DSO remains high. The DSO Association has 17,562 subscribers with over 90% of the house sold for each concert. A bigger box office income is hoped for, to meet the 1984–1985 budget of over $8.5 million. In addition to the over $2.5 million projected from the annual fund drive and $500,000 from various support groups, major funding is expected from such sources as the DSO Endowment Fund, the NEA, and the Andrew W. Mellon Foundation.

The Symphony's outlook for the future is excellent. During the 1984–1985 season the orchestra will expand to 90 musicians contracted for a 41-week season expected to include 21 sets of programs in the subscription series, a pops series of 12 pairs of programs, and concerts for children. Other series will include the tiny tots concert for pre-school age children, youth concerts for Denver and surrounding area schools, free city-wide concerts, "Concerts at the Zoo," "Concerts in the Parks," and the Red Rocks concert series each summer. In total, the DSO will be featured in over 350 performances during the 1984–1985 concert season.

Plans are also being made to include another East Coast tour in addition to regular in-state tours. The in-residence program will continue, and more recording dates have been scheduled. The DSO is featured at professional sports events for promotional efforts and is seen on local PBS stations in concert throughout the year. Symphony performances are also heard weekly on KVOD.

RECORDING HISTORY: The DSO has not been active in commercial recording, and neither of its two records are now in print.

CHRONOLOGY OF MUSIC DIRECTORS: Horace Tureman, 1934–1944. (Guest conductors, 1944–1945.) Saul Caston, 1945–1962. (Guest conductors, 1963–1964.) Vladimir Golschmann, 1964–1969. (Guest conductors, 1969–1970.) Brian Priestman, 1970–1978. (Guest conductors, 1978–1979.) Gaetano Delogu, 1979–present.

BIBLIOGRAPHY: Bill Barker and Jackie Lewin, *Denver* (Garden City, N.Y.: Doubleday, 1972). Bill Brenneman, *Miracle on Cherry Creek* (Denver: World, 1973). Sandra Dallas, *Yesterday's Denver* (Miami: Seeman, 1974). *The Denver Post. Denver Republican. Denver Times.* Lyle W. Dorsett, *The Queen City: A History of Denver* (Boulder: Pruett, 1977). "Encore '84," Bulletin of KVOD Radio Station & Denver Symphony Association, 1984. William Kostake and Association, Inc., *Program to Grand Opening of Boettcher Concert Hall.* (Denver: Al Cohen Construction, 1976.) *Rocky Mountain News.* Malcolm G. Wyler and Edwin J. Stringham, eds., *The Lookout from the Denver Public Library: Music in Denver and Colorado* Vol. 1, No. 1 (Denver: Carson, 1927).

ACCESS: Denver Symphony Orchestra, 910 15th Street, Suite 330, Denver, CO 80202. (303) 572–1151. Jack M. Mills, Executive Director.

DANIEL ALFARO

Connecticut _____

NEW HAVEN (417,592—New Haven/West Haven)

New Haven Symphony Orchestra (Rg)

Founded in 1894, the New Haven Symphony Orchestra is among the oldest symphony orchestras in continuous operation in the United States. During its 40-week season, the 90-member ensemble reaches over 80,000 people through a variety of programs: eight subscription concerts at Yale University's Woolsey Hall, the orchestra's home since it was built in 1903; a pops concert series held on stage at the unique, wide-screen "theater of racing" Teletrack Theater in New Haven; a chamber orchestra series specializing in baroque repertoire at the Palace Performing Arts Center in New Haven's entertainment district; outdoor summer concerts; a series of young people's concerts for elementary school students; Kinder Konzerts for preschoolers; and hospital concerts, as well as other special appearances. All eight of the Symphony's subscription concerts are regularly broadcast on a tape-delayed basis over the stations of Connecticut Public Radio. In conjunction with the securities firm Merrill Lynch Pierce Fenner & Smith, the orchestra sponsors a presenters' series, "Merrill Lynch Great Performers at Woolsey Hall," bringing great artists and orchestras of the world to the hall in a seven-concert subscription season.

Begun by musician, teacher, and scholar Morris Steinert in New Haven as a reading/rehearsal orchestra in 1894, the ensemble soon became inexorably, albeit informally, tied to Yale University and to the Yale School of Music, with many of its musicians and conductors in the early days coming from that institution. Indeed, it was composer and scholar Horatio William Parker, dean of the Yale School of Music, who, during his tenure as music director, developed the orchestra into an ensemble worthy of public performance and who developed the orchestra's tradition that still exists today of performing music by contemporary composers.

Parker was succeeded in 1919 both as dean of the Music School and as conductor of The New Haven Symphony by David Stanley Smith, who, during his 26 years on the podium, restored financial prosperity, in part because of the Symphony's merger with the Civic Orchestra of New Haven in 1936. Two more Yale professors were to conduct New Haven's orchestra. In 1946, succeeding Dean Smith were the former conductor of the Civic Orchestra, Hugo Kortschak (chairman of the violin department) and Richard F. Donovan (Battell Professor of Music). Sharing the podium as associate conductors until 1952, they continued Parker's tradition of performing contemporary music and introduced to New Haven first performances of works by Copland, Hindemith, Mahler, Shostakovich, Stravinsky, and Prokofiev.

In 1952, the tradition of Yale professors succeeding one another as music director ended with the appointment of Frank Brieff, a member of the NBC Symphony under Toscanini. Under his direction, which was to last some 20 years, orchestra quality experienced a renaissance, the orchestra's only significant recording activities took place, new works were commissioned and premiered, and in 1964, the New Haven Symphony became the first visiting orchestra invited to perform at Lincoln Center in New York City.

Erich Kunzel became music director upon Brieff's retirement in 1974; and in 1977 the Board of Directors appointed the orchestra's present music director, Murry Sidlin, who is also music director of the Long Beach (California) Symphony Orchestra* and resident conductor and co-director of the Conducting Studies Program at the Aspen Music Festival.

Under Sidlin's leadership, the orchestra has developed into a professional ensemble and has become a significant artistic and educational resource. Although informal ties still exist with Yale and with its School of Music, only about 30% of the orchestra members now are graduate students at the Music School. Using the Symphony's performance tradition of early romantic and late German repertoire as a cornerstone, Sidlin has during his tenure emphasized his own particular propensity for music composed from 1880 to 1940 and has expanded that repertoire to include twentieth-century American works laced with a significant number of experimental compositions. Of particular note is the on-going relationship with an organization of composers living in Connecticut, Connecticut Composers, Inc., that has also developed during Sidlin's tenure. The orchestra performs works by the organization's members both in special concerts and on the regular subscription series. In addition, during Sidlin's tenure the orchestra joined with the Albany Symphony,* the Hudson Valley Philharmonic,* the Springfield Symphony,* and the Hartford Symphony to form the Northeast Orchestral Consortium for the purpose of commissioning and premiering works by contemporary composers. During the 1983–1984 season, John Harbison's *Ulysses's Raft* was given its world premiere by the New Haven Symphony with Sidlin conducting. Under Sidlin, the sound that pervades all of the Symphony performances, whether standard repertoire or new music, can be described as Viennese—with sustained, warm string sound and an integration of the winds to create an orchestral homogeniety.

The New Haven Symphony is headed by a 65-member Board of Directors, under whom are the music director and general manager. The music director is responsible for artistic decisions, although he is advised by a formal Music Advisory Committee of the Board and by the general manager, as artistic decisions are indeed linked with financial matters. A core of about 70 musicians is contracted, with remaining musicians being hired on a per-service basis. A Liaison Committee made up of musicians, members of the Board of Directors, and management meets monthly; musicians are invited on a regular basis to attend certain Board committee meetings.

The New Haven Symphony's annual operating budget of just over $1 million is funded by income from contractual services; ticket sales; program book advertising; NHSO endowment; a formal Annual Fund and capital drive; government, private, and foundation grants; private and corporate donations; and by The New Haven Symphony Auxiliary, the volunteer fund-raising arm of the orchestra, which among other projects, maintains a full-time consignment shop.

Although New Haven is rich in cultural resources, including a still-developing entertainment district partially financed by the city and many musical organizations centered at Yale University, The New Haven Symphony is the city's only professional, full symphony orchestra. Close cooperation exists between the Symphony and other city-based artistic institutions, including the nationally known Long Wharf Theater. During that theater's 20th anniversary season in 1984–1985, the two organizations collaborated on 56 performances of Benjamin Britten's opera *Albert Herring*, with Murry Sidlin serving as music director and LWT's Arvin Brown as artistic director.

RECORDING HISTORY AND SELECTIVE DISCOGRAPHY: Under Frank Brieff the Symphony recorded Mahler's Symphony No. 1 in D Major, with the newly discovered "Blumine" movement, Columbia Odyssey 32–16–0286.

CHRONOLOGY OF MUSIC DIRECTORS: Horatio William Parker, 1895–1919. David Stanley Smith, 1920–1946. Hugo Kortschak (Associate Conductor), 1936–1951. Richard F. Donovan (Associate Conductor), 1936–1952. Frank Brieff, 1952–1974. Erich Kunzel, 1974–1976. Murry Sidlin, 1977-present.

BIBLIOGRAPHY: Interviews with NHSO General Manager Catherine Lacny and Music Director Murry Sidlin, 1984. Steve Kemper, "Pa Steinert's Band Turns Ninety," *New Haven*, Sept. 1983. Helen H. Roberts and Doris Cousins, *A History of the New Haven Symphony Orchestra Celebrating its Seventy-Fifth Season, 1894–1969* (New York: Yale University Press, 1969).

ACCESS: The New Haven Symphony Orchestra, 33 Whitney Avenue, New Haven, CT 06511. (203) 865–0831. Catherine A. Lacny, General Manager.

NANCY PARKS LOADER

Delaware ————————————————

Delaware Symphony (Mt)

Chartered on April 28, 1971, the Delaware Symphony Association, an organization of some 80 musicians, is the only professional orchestra in Delaware. From its permanent home in the Wilmington Grand Opera House, it provides annually, for the residents of the state and surrounding communities in Pennsylvania, New Jersey, and Maryland, 48 concerts of high quality and great variety. Its main concert hall, the Opera House, built in 1871 and restored in 1976, is acoustically superior and centrally located on Market Street in the heart of downtown Wilmington.

The orchestra's season extends from October to May and is organized around three series of regular concerts on specified Thursdays, Fridays and Saturdays; a three-concert pops series; a children's concert series, and several special concerts.

The administration of the orchestra consists of a Board of Directors of approximately 40 members, a full-time general manager (Jeffrey Ruben), a music director/conductor (Stephen Gunzenhauser) and a Women's Committee of over 100, which incorporates sub-committees for hospitality, membership, publicity, and mailing. Appointed in 1979, this new administrative team has dramatically improved the orchestra's operation, with an increase in audience size from 10,400 to 56,800, an increase in the number of concerts from 14 to 48, an increased number of rehearsals and players, and an increase in the annual budget from $135,000 to $700,000. In 1978–1979, 51% of the orchestra's total income was generated by ticket sales, 28% from contributions, 9% from the State Arts Council, and the remainder from activities of the Women's Committee and miscellaneous sources.

Approximately 50% of the orchestra is drawn from Philadelphia and West Chester and comprises teachers or talented students from the Curtis Institute, Temple University, the Philadelphia College of the Performing Arts, and West Chester State University. The ensemble is fully unionized. When it is necessary to reduce the size of the orchestra for performances in the schools or to accompany Opera Delaware during its 15-performance season, the top players from the orchestra form the Delaware Symphony Chamber Orchestra for these engagements.

In the only published history of the orchestra, *The Delaware Symphony* (1984), Lillian R. Balick traces the origin of the orchestra back to the Tankopanicum Orchestra organized and conducted by Alfred I. du Pont in 1886. This community orchestra (whose players' lessons were underwritten by its conductor) disbanded in 1906 because of du Pont's increasing deafness. Through the efforts of Major Kellogg Kennan Venable Casey and Cyrus Peter Miller Rumford (two Wilmington businessmen) and with financial backing from du Pont, the Wilmington Orchestra succeeded the Tankopanicum Orchestra in 1906. Although its membership soon grew to 80, the orchestra sank into insolvency, and finally, in 1909, a dispute over the protocol of including both his first and second wives on the Ladies Committee caused Alfred du Pont to withdraw his financial support and the orchestra collapsed.

Wilmington was without an orchestra for three years until Harry Stausebach (who was associated with both earlier groups) assembled the Wilmington Symphony Club, which merged in 1929 with the Wilmington Music School Orchestra to become the Wilmington Symphony Orchestra—with Harry Stausebach as conductor. The new orchestra presented its first concert on Sunday, May 4, 1930, at the Schubert Playhouse to a large and responsive audience. The program listed 59 players and was shared with two local choral groups. Despite the considerable number of professional musicians in the group, it remained an amateur orchestra and gave two yearly concerts that were open to the public without charge. By 1947 it had grown to 106 players. When Stausebach retired in 1955 he had given 43 years of service, which greatly enriched his community.

With Stausebach's retirement, the Board decided to appoint Van Lier Lanning and to charge him to develop a fully professional orchestra in Wilmington. During Lanning's tenure of 22 years, he increased the number of regular concerts, established a children's concert series with narration, initiated a subscription plan, elevated the technical level of repertoire, initiated pops concerts, instituted professional performance standards for all players, established a Repertory Orchestra for semi-professionals, and arranged a permanent residence for the Symphony in the Grand Opera House. During the Lanning years, the orchestra's name was changed from the Wilmington Symphony to the Delaware Symphony Association, Inc. When Lanning resigned in 1979, there was broad agreement that he had been most effective in doing the job he was hired to do. Stephen Gunzenhauser, director of the Wilmington Music School, was appointed to succeed him.

Perhaps the most distinguishing characteristic of the Symphony's repertoire, even while an amateur organization, was the frequency with which new music was performed. Each of the last three conductors has felt a responsibility to introduce new music, much of it written by local composers. Each director sought to educate (as well as to entertain) and therefore carefully balanced light and heavy literature. When the orchestra attained professional status, there were few limitations on the work to be performed. Balick's analysis of Delaware Symphony programs from 1965 to 1970 reveals somewhat less Austro-German music and slightly more American music than the national norm.

The Delaware Symphony has always sought to educate the community, a philosophy dating back to du Pont, who purchased better instruments and paid for private lessons for the orchestra members. That philosophy continued to manifest itself through the establishment of a Beginning Orchestra by du Pont; a Youth Orchestra, scholarship project, and rehearsal plan by Stausebach; and a Repertory Orchestra and children's concert series by Lanning. The policy of the orchestra to utilize local talent whenever possible led to collaborations with local soloists, conductors, and ensembles such as the du Pont Chorus, the University of Delaware a Cappella Choir, the Northern Delaware Oratorio Society, and the Brandywiners Chorus.

CHRONOLOGY OF MUSIC DIRECTORS: Harry Stausebach, 1912–1955. Van Lier Lanning, 1955–1979. Stephen Gunzenhauser, 1979-present.

BIBLIOGRAPHY: Interview with Delaware Symphony General Manager Jeffrey Ruben. Lillian R. Balick, *The Delaware Symphony: Origins and the First Fifty Years* (Wilmington: Delaware Symphony Association, 1984). *Who's Who in American Music: Classical* (New York: Bowker, 1983). Toni Young, *The Grand Experience* (New York: American Life Foundation and Study Institute, 1976).

ACCESS: Delaware Symphony Orchestra, P.O. Box 1870, Wilmington, DE 19899. (302) 656–7374. Jeffrey Ruben, General Manager.

EUGENE THAMON SIMPSON

District of Columbia _____

WASHINGTON (3,060,922)

National Symphony Orchestra (Mj)

The presence of the National Symphony Orchestra in Washington, D.C., has given rise to at least two distinctions. First, it has been the official orchestra for every presidential inaugural concert except one since its founding in 1931 and is often referred to as the "Orchestra of the Presidents." Second, it is the only American symphony orchestra in residence at a national monument, the John F. Kennedy Center for the Performing Arts. Despite the fact that the NSO performs at national events such as inaugural concerts and the Fourth of July celebrations at the Capitol, it is not a "national" orchestra in the sense of being operated and funded solely by the federal government.

The NSO performs over 200 concerts in a 52-week season, which includes regular subscription concerts, a NSO pops series, young people's concerts, summer concerts at Wolf Trap Farm Park for the Performing Arts and at the United States Capitol, concerts at New York's Carnegie Hall, and frequent tours. The NSO is known for dynamic performances and a commitment to contemporary and American music, with over 140 world premieres to its credit. The orchestra employs revolving seating in the string section except for the concertmaster and the assistant and associate concertmasters and other principals; the cellos are arranged in the center of the stage instead of the far right.

The NSO has exerted leadership in the Washington, D.C., area's cultural and artistic growth. Orchestra members teach privately and on the faculties of American, Catholic, Howard, Georgetown, George Washington, and Maryland universities and at the Peabody Conservatory of Music in Baltimore. They form the nuclei of many chamber ensembles and also give solo performances in local concert series.

The NSO's educational program is central to its impact on the community. It embraces young people's concerts, initiated in the first NSO season; youth fellowship and young apprentice programs, in which high school students are given scholarships to study with a NSO member and/or attend rehearsals, concerts, and seminars with the musicians and staff; Youth Orchestra Day, when high school performers participate in a NSO rehearsal; and, above all, the Young Soloists Competition, which offers to winners a guest soloist appearance with the NSO and a solo recital appearance on the radio. Other parts of the education program are Career Day, a ticket bank through which teachers may receive free concert tickets, and a docent program. For adults there are regularly scheduled matinee-luncheon, picnic, and dinner lecture series.

The NSO is governed by an 85-member Board of Directors, elected by members of the sustaining organization, incorporated in 1931 as the National Symphony Orchestra Association. The administrative staff is headed by the executive director, finance director, marketing director, orchestra manager, artistic administrator, and development director. The music director and the executive director are assisted in hiring and dismissal procedures and matters relating to repertoire, guest conductors, and soloists by the administrative staff and various committees of orchestra members. A union contract agreement, renewed every three years between the NSO Association and the D.C. Federation of Musicians, insures the minimum wage. Orchestra members are covered by a non-contributing pension fund, established in 1962 by the NSO Association and financed by ticket sales. Support for the orchestra's budget of over $11.5 million comes from the annual fund, endowments, ticket sales, recordings, and grants from the NEA, the Department of the Interior Capital Park Service, and private and corporate donors.

The Women's Committee for the NSO and the Friends Assisting the National Symphony (FANS) contribute services and finance special events. NSO trustees advise the Board of Directors on matters involving national and international activities.

The following historical account is based primarily upon the publication *National Symphony Orchestra 1931-1981* by Richard Freed and articles appearing in the Washington newspapers.

Washington, D.C., was slow to develop its own symphony orchestra. Designed as the seat of federal government, the city had no major industry or large corporate base, and it was dependent upon a predominantly transient population. In the late nineteenth century, orchestras from New York, Boston, and other cities included Washington on their tours. Serious interest in a resident symphony surfaced early in the twentieth century, and by 1920 three attempts, each lasting only two to three years, had been made to establish one. In January of 1930 a new attempt would succeed.

Despite the Great Depression, Washington was home to a large number of professional musicians drawn there by employment opportunities in movie and hotel orchestras. Large orchestras from other cities were visiting Washington less frequently in these years, even though the population of the city had doubled since the turn of the century, and both its wealth and its prestige in cultural matters were on the rise.

The experimental "National Symphony of Washington, D.C.," was formed by a group of 80 musicians. Its first concert (January 1, 1930) was conducted by Rudolph Schueller and occasioned the announcement of a policy of support for American music. Significantly, the program included Edgar Stillman Kelley's *Symphonic Variations on a New England Hymn*. Hans Kindler, who had made his conducting debut in Washington in 1928 and who would become the permanent orchestra's first conductor, led the second and third concerts in 1930 with Gustav Strube, conductor of the Baltimore Symphony,* assisting in the second. Heartened by the public response, Kindler and others crusaded to establish the financial and musical bases for the new orchestra.

The NSO gave its first concert on November 2, 1931, with Kindler as music director. Best known as a solo cellist, Kindler possessed a flair for conducting and programming; in the course of his 18 years of leadership, the orchestra made solid progress. With the NSO Association, a Board, and a manager in place, the orchestra presented a season of eight mid-week symphony concerts, eight children's concerts, and eight Sunday concerts. In the second season the presidential inaugural concerts were begun with the first inaugural of Franklin D. Roosevelt. (The series was broken only in 1973 with President Nixon's invitation to the Philadelphia Orchestra* to play for his second inaugural; in 1977 the Atlanta Symphony* was invited to perform along with the NSO for the inauguration of President Carter.) By the 12th season the NSO was performing over 100 concerts per season and had added a NSO Pops concert series and a series for young adults.

Programming under Kindler, while devoted largely to traditional repertoire, was marked by the generous inclusion of music by American composers and the presentation of world premieres—and of his own orchestral transcriptions. NSO performance of works by Mahler won Kindler the Bruckner Society Medal. The tradition of bringing prominent guest conductors and soloists was initiated. The orchestra grew to 90 members, permitting the performance of larger late-romantic works. The first regular radio broadcasts took place in 1947–1948 on station WMAL. The Watergate concerts, the NSO's first outdoor series, began in 1935 and continued for 30 years. Presented by the NSO on a barge on the Potomac River, they occasionally drew audiences of 20,000. Yet, for all its steady artistic growth, the NSO experienced financial crises in 1937 and in 1939–1940, and the orchestra's inadequate financial base continues to trouble it even today.

Howard Mitchell succeeded Kindler in 1949, becoming one of the few American-born conductors of major orchestras at that time. Like Kindler (and all NSO music directors to follow), he was a cellist; he joined the NSO as principal cellist in 1933 and was named assistant conductor (1941) and later associate conductor (1948). He brought in musicians of greater proficiency and raised technical standards while increasing the size of the orchestra. A newly initiated practice of repeating the subscription concerts, the addition of a summer series at Merriweather Post Pavilion in Columbia, Maryland, the performance of free concerts in various metropolitan communities, and the tiny tots concerts led to a greatly enlarged season. Thus, in 1961 the NSO performed 206 concerts for 440,000 persons. The prestigious Marjorie Merriweather Post competitions were instituted as part of "Music for Young America." The practice of inviting stellar soloists and conductors was continued on a higher level, building local esteem for the NSO and enhancing its reputation nationally. Occasions such as the 25th anniversary celebration and the Inter-American Festivals furnished special opportunities to introduce contemporary music (for which the NSO won a 1966 ASCAP Award).

In addition to a regular series of Sunday afternoon concerts in New York, under Mitchell there were several tours of the United States, a 12-week tour of 19 Latin American countries presenting 68 concerts (1959), and a 1967 tour of 10 European cities. While on tour, Mitchell included a composition by an American composer in each program.

The years between 1962 and 1964 were troubled by financial crises and strikes, one of which was the longest experienced to that date by a symphony orchestra. Mitchell left the orchestra in 1969 and was named Music Director Emeritus.

After a season of eminent guest conductors, Antal Dorati became NSO music director. A distinguished conductor of international standing with an impressive reputation for building and improving orchestras, Dorati seemed ideal for the NSO at this stage. Dorati was a pianist, cellist, composer, and conductor with an immense knowledge of opera, ballet, and orchestral repertoire as well as broad exposure to contemporary music. The orchestra had artistic achievements to its credit and felt ready to move to a position among the world's finest. Dorati stressed the need to assist players to attain higher standards of performance individually, thereby contributing to an improvement in the orchestra's morale as well as its sound.

The crucial move from Constitution Hall, home of the NSO for 40 years, to the newly completed John F. Kennedy Center for the Performing Arts was signaled by a concert there on September 9, 1971. One of the three largest performing arts centers in the United States, the Kennedy Center was built at a cost of $700 million contributed by the federal government and the private sector. This was the first instance of such funding by Congress. The complex includes the 2,750-seat concert hall used by the NSO, an opera house, the Eisenhower Theater, Terrace Theater, Cinema Hall, library, and restaurants. It is the only Washington memorial to John F. Kennedy, who had strongly supported plans for the center. The new home offered an acoustically superior hall; according to Dorati, "the sound was liberated" (*Washington Star*, April 4, 1974). Although the official resident orchestra of the Kennedy Center, the NSO rents the concert hall and remains completely independent.

Dorati began to fill in standard-repertoire gaps of the NSO—works of Haydn, Mozart, Bruckner, and Mahler, for example. The NSO performed more commissioned works and gave NSO premieres of works by Americans such as Ives, Schuman, and Carter and by contemporary European composers such as Krzysztof Penderecki and Olivier Messiaen. Thirteen new works were performed during the U.S. Bicentennial season alone. The NSO enjoyed its first 52-week season in 1974–1975 and made its first visit to the Dominican Republic and Greece in the next year. Many agreed with Dorati's observation, "I think I was instrumental in making a first class orchestra" (*Washington Star*, April 4, 1979).

At the outset, Dorati had announced he would not remain with the NSO longer than 1977 or 1978. After guest appearances by Mstistlav Rostropovich in 1975 as cellist and conductor with the NSO, the decision was made to secure him as music director. Dorati stepped down in 1977; he was principal guest conductor from 1978 to 1980.

Rostropovich continues today as one of the most exciting, challenging, and charismatic conductors in NSO history. Renowned as a leading cellist of the world, he had also conducted opera and symphonic concerts widely in the Soviet Union before his NSO conducting debut of 1975. Although some travel limitations had been imposed on him in 1970 as a result of his aid to Nobel Prize winner Aleksandr Solzhenitsyn, Rostropovich was allowed to leave Russia with his family. He and his wife Vishnevskaya were deprived of Soviet citizenship in 1978 "because of actions inimical to the government" (Freed). Rostropovich immediately dedicated himself to raising NSO performance standards even higher by helping individual members reach the limits of their musical talents—a goal enunciated more than once by Dorati. Rostropovich has developed warm relationships with members of the orchestra and spends much time in conducting master classes and coaching small ensembles. The NSO programs continue to be characterized by many premieres and commissioned music; American composers continue to be favored, but more Russian music than previously performed has been heard by Washington, D.C., audiences.

In 1979 an annual outdoor concert series began under sponsorship of the U.S. Department of the Interior. These free concerts were called "An American Festival/Concerts at the Capitol"; they brought audiences of as many as 240,000 to the Capitol and were carried on national television. Tours under Rostropovich have been numerous: within the United States and to the Far East, South America, and Europe.

With increased exposure and heightened artistic levels, the NSO has reached a status described by Leonard Bernstein as "world class" (*Washington Post*, September 21, 1980). On the other hand, the orchestra's financial situation has become more strained. The cost of celebrated performers is high, and there have been internal reverses such as a major NSO strike in 1978. Beyond these are the basic problems that have always existed: lack of an adequate endowment, the paucity of funds available from the city of Washington, D.C., Arts Commission, and a shortage of investment funds. The NSO has a deficit of $3.7 million, the largest of any major symphony orchestra. A $20 million endowment drive is now underway with the purpose of eliminating the deficit and establishing an endowment comparable to that of other major American symphony orchestras.

RECORDING HISTORY AND SELECTIVE DISCOGRAPHY: The NSO's first recording was of a "Toccata" attributed to Frescobaldi and transcribed by Hans Kindler (RCA, 1941). Under Howard Mitchell the orchestra recorded for Westminster and RCA, adding to its standard repertoire a highly praised series of educational records. Dorati recorded with the NSO for London Records and Turnabout, winning six major international prizes. Under Rostropovich the NSO has recorded for Deutsche Grammophon and Columbia; the first recording for Deutsche Grammophon was conducted by Leonard Bernstein, the single instance of a NSO recording not performed under its music director.

Bernstein, *Songfest* (Bernstein): DG 2531044. Dallapiccola, *Il Prigionero* (Dorati): London 1166. Dorati, Concerto for Piano (Alpenheim/Dorati): Turnabout 34669. Schumann, Piano Concerto (Argerich/Rostropovich): DG 2531042. Tchaikovsky, Violin Concerto (Stern/Rostropovich): CBS XM:35126. Wagner, *Der Ring des Nibelungen* Orchestral Excerpts (Dorati): London 6970.

CHRONOLOGY OF MUSIC DIRECTORS: Hans Kindler, 1931–1949. Howard Mitchell, 1949–1969. (Guest conductors, 1969–1970.) Antal Dorati, 1970–1977. Mstistlav Rostropovich, 1977-present.

BIBLIOGRAPHY: "Briefs on the Arts," *New York Times*, 26 July 1982. "The Dorati Difference," *The Washington Post*, 30 Mar. 1981. Richard Freed, *History of the National Symphony Orchestra, 1931–1981* (Washington, D.C.: NSO, n.d.). Barbara Gamarekian, "For the National Symphony, An Upbeat Tone Is Welcome," *New York Times*, 31 Mar. 1982. Brendan Gill, *John F. Kennedy Center for the Performing Arts* (New York: Henry W. Abrahms, 1982). Paul Hume, "The National Symphony Orchestra at 50," *Washington Post*, 21 Sept. 1982. Barbara Kober, "Antal Dorati Looks Back to the National Symphony," *Washington Star*, 4 April 1979. Alfred T. Marks, "National Symphony Orchestra Formed by Musicians in the Capitol, *Musical America*, 25 Jan. 1930. John Mueller, *The American Symphony Orchestra* (1951; reprint, Westport, Conn.: Greenwood Press, 1976). Nelson Sokolov, "Washington Symphony Orchestras—Past and Present," *The Washington Post*, 20 Nov. 1932.

ACCESS: National Symphony Orchestra, The Kennedy Center for the Performing Arts, Washington, D.C. 20566. (202) 785–8100. Stephen Klein, Executive Director. Joann Steller, Director of Marketing and Public Relations.

DORIS EVANS MCGINTY

Florida

FORT LAUDERDALE (1,018,200)

Philharmonic Orchestra of Florida (Rg)

Originally known as the Fort Lauderdale Symphony Orchestra (founded in 1949), the Philharmonic Orchestra of Florida merged in 1984 with the two-year-old Boca Raton Symphony Orchestra. The Philharmonic presents 10 pairs of subscription concerts led by Music Director/Conductor Dr. Emerson Buckley at Fort Lauderdale's 2,500-seat War Memorial Auditorium, a multipurpose hall with an acoustical shell and adequate acoustics. The Philharmonic plays to near-capacity audiences (about 2,250 per concert) and features international guest artists and conductors. Future plans envision a new concert hall for which 75% of the cost has already been realized. In 1984–1985 the orchestra expanded its services with a youth series, a sub-scription series, and a pops series in communities outside Fort Lauderdale. The merger has allowed the addition of a new subscription series of eight programs in Boca Raton's 2,400-seat auditorium at Florida Atlantic University.

In the 1983–1984 season, two additional programs were presented at Miami's Dade County Auditorium, cosponsored by WSVN-TV and the *Miami Herald*. Overall programming spans the classical to contemporary periods, with a special commitment to American and twentieth-century composers' works. The main series is supplemented by pops concerts, young people's concerts, and 70 to 80 annual in-school programs with sectional ensembles ("Four Families of the Orchestra") or the full orchestra, reaching over 50,000 youngsters. Annually more than 100,000 people of all ages listen to the Symphony's performances. New audiences are attracted through WTMI, Miami's classical radio station, a 13-week TV series on the local cable system, and two nationwide network broadcasts annually on "America in Concert."

Presently, other active orchestras nearby are Fort Lauderdale's South Florida Symphony Orchestra* (formerly the Florida Chamber Orchestra) and the Greater Miami Symphony (formerly the Miami Beach Symphony)—professional organizations—and the Greater Palm Beach Symphony, growing in professional stature.

The Philharmonic's 85 musicians, nearly 50% of whom are women, are augmented to about 100 whenever the repertoire requires. Fundamentally professionally playing musicians and/or teachers, they reside in Fort Lauderdale (Broward County) or the Greater Miami (Dade County) area. Artistic programming is the sole responsibility of the music director, although a five-member Advisory Board also exists. Audience surveys, conducted since 1972, form a basis for programming. They solicit the opinions of concert-goers (who are typically middle-aged) regarding works already performed, requests for program implementation, and preference for guest soloists by instrument. An overwhelming number choose pianists, violinists, cellists, and vocalists, in that order. The Philharmonic's Board of Directors sets policy; an executive vice president/general manager directs fund raising. The annual combined Boca Raton/Fort Lauderdale budget of more than $2 million comes from ticket sales, private and corporate donations, state funds, and the NEA.

Fort Lauderdale in the late 1940s was a small town with only three hotels and no principal concert hall, but with its own particular charm. Its residents were largely former midwesterners, many with substantial wealth, who were attracted to the area's sunshine, beaches, and waterways. In later years the area would become a famous resort and cruise port as well as a diversified metropolitan center. Its Symphony would partake in that growth.

Before the Fort Lauderdale Symphony Orchestra (Ft.LSO), symphonic music was limited to the Fort Lauderdale Civic Music Association's four winter concerts by guest artists and guest orchestras and to the concerts of the University of Miami Symphony Orchestra. The Ft.LSO's first conductor, John Clair Canfield, was a music educator and band director who had been raised, in part, in Fort Lauderdale. In the spring and summer of 1949 he assembled 52 musicians, mostly semi-professionals from the Fort Lauderdale and Miami areas, and after some rehearsals, conducted the orchestra's first concert on December 8, 1949, in South Broward High School Auditorium to a standing-room-only audience. Early in the orchestra's formation community leaders were recruited who immediately pledged their support, forming the Board of Directors and Ladies' Auxiliary. In the orchestra's first season, three concerts were presented, with ticket prices at $1 and $2.

Following Canfield's resignation in the 1950–1951 season, Concertmaster William Reivo became interim conductor through the following concert year. A turning point for the Ft.LSO was the arrival of A. Louis O'Connor, Detroit engineer/inventor and manufacturer, who as the orchestra's business manager in 1952–1953 contacted the charismatic Vasilios Priakos (at that

time in West Palm Beach himself in hopes of founding an orchestra there).
Priakos was appointed Ft.LSO music director in 1952, and he remained until
1958. O'Connor and Priakos were financially and artistically dynamic, and
together they revived community interest and raised artistic standards.
Membership was increased and community needs satisfied with pops concerts, in-school performances, scholarship programs, and benefit concerts
for civic and cultural groups. By 1953 the Ft.LSO had expanded to 65
musicians, whole-hearted community support was a reality, a new outreach
branch, the North Broward Society, was formed, and the orchestra was
running in the black. The *Miami Herald* reported a capacity audience at
the opening concert of the 1953–1954 season at the newly completed War
Memorial Auditorium, noting that 5% of the city's residents were there.

In the spring of 1958 Priakos resigned and nearly one hundred conductors
applied for the position. Following a season of guest conductors, Mario di
Bonaventura was selected from among them—he served until 1962. Bonaventura commissioned a new symphony by Darius Milhaud for the Ft.LSO
and premiered the first of its three movements in 1960. He presented
programs with works by Wagner, Brahms, Ravel, Britten, and Ives. Another
season of guest conductors followed in 1962–1963 (again selected from
over 100 applicants), and 1963–1964 opened with the appointment of Dr.
Emerson Buckley as the new music director.

A new and important chapter now began for the Ft.LSO. Under Buckley's
direction the Ft.LSO developed artistically and operationally, a full-time
general manager was appointed, and within five years it grew from a community orchestra to ASOL Metropolitan status. During his 21-year tenure,
Buckley has expanded the scope of the orchestra's repertoire to include a
special emphasis on twentieth-century works, especially those of Americans.
In 1964 he received the Alice M. Ditson Conductor's Award from Columbia
University in recognition of his work with contemporary American music.
Also in 1964 Buckley and the Ft.LSO premiered Carlos Surinach's Concerto
for Orchestra. Following years saw an expanded season, artistic growth,
ensemble performances in the schools, and the birth of new support branches
such as the West Broward Symphony Guild, the Fort Lauderdale Junior
Symphony Guild, and, in 1971, the Drummers, a fraternal organization by
invitation, with membership limited to 200.

In the 1970–1971 season the Ft.LSO's programs included works by five
twentieth-century composers, including a world premiere of Surinach's *Tres
Cantares*. In 1973, Buckley's tenth season with the orchestra, he was appointed artistic director of the Greater Miami Opera Guild, where for the
past 20 years he has been its conductor and music director. Orchestra
support continued to grow, and by 1973–1974 ticket sales comprised 42%
of the orchestra's budget. Due to the sell-out season in 1974–1975, Monday
afternoon dress rehearsals were opened to the public as a series.

The Boca Raton Symphony Orchestra, formerly the Boca Raton Chamber

Symphony, was formed in 1982 by its artistic director and conductor, Paul Anthony McRae, former principal trumpet of the Fort Lauderdale Symphony Orchestra. After the demise of the Florida Philharmonic Orchestra (Miami), McRae recruited 52 professional musicians, and after eight weeks of rehearsals this ensemble played its premiere concert on November 10, 1982, at Boca Raton's Center Auditorium of Florida Atlantic University to an audience of 1,600. The second season immediately sold out, the budget was raised from $256,000 to $650,000, the orchestra expanded, and its name was changed to reflect its growth. The 1983–1984 season included the U.S. premiere of John Williams's *E. T.* and the Southeastern premiere of Polish composer Andrzej Panufnik's two-movement *Symphoniae Sacrae.*

The newly merged Philharmonic, with Emerson Buckley as music director and Paul Anthony McRae as resident conductor, has planned five major series; both conductors will equally share the Boca Raton series and McRae will lead two of the Fort Lauderdale series. Today's programming is artistically challenging. The 1984–1985 season was notable, with first performances in South Florida of contemporary works by Robert Ward, Paul Creston, David Amram, and others.

CHRONOLOGY OF MUSIC DIRECTORS: John Clair Canfield, 1949–1951. William Reivo, 1951–1952. Vasilios Priakos, 1952–1958. (Guest conductors, 1958–1959). Mario di Bonaventura, 1959–1962. (Guest conductors, 1962–1963.) Dr. Emerson Buckley, 1963-present. Paul Anthony McRae (Resident Conductor), 1984-present.

BIBLIOGRAPHY: Interviews with Dr. Emerson Buckley and Paul Anthony McRae, 1984. *Fort Lauderdale Symphony,* (Ft.LSO 30th Anniversary Book, 1979). Stuart McIver, *Fort Lauderdale and Broward County* (Woodland Hills, Calif.: Windsor, 1983). James Roos, "Provocative Symphony Program," *Miami Herald,* 4 Jan 1984.

ACCESS: Philharmonic Orchestra of Florida, 1430 N. Federal Highway, Fort Lauderdale, FL 33304. (305) 561–2997. Joseph Leavitt, Executive Vice President/General Manager.

VIOLET VAGRAMIAN-NISHANIAN

JACKSONVILLE (737,541)

Jacksonville Symphony Orchestra (Rg)

The circumstances leading to the formation of the Jacksonville Symphony occurred in 1948, when Olin E. Watts, a well-known Jacksonville attorney and president of the Chamber of Commerce, was asked about the quality of the city's symphony orchestra by a visitor. He replied that Jacksonville was not so blessed but much thought had been given to the prospect of having an orchestra. The following year, conductor Van Lier Lanning, organizer of the Arlington (Virginia) Civic Symphony was a guest of the Chamber and he too inquired about the city's orchestra. Their conversation produced the incentive to form the Jacksonville Symphony Orchestra with

Watts becoming the founding president of the Symphony Association Board and Lanning its first music director. Consequently, the Jacksonville Symphony Orchestra was born September 18, 1949. The original objectives for the orchestra were to maintain a symphony orchestra in Jacksonville, to encourage musical appreciation and culture among all the citizens of the community, and to help worthy musicians and young people obtain musical training, education, and experience. Those objectives remain the foundation upon which the JSO operates today.

Lanning's tenure was a notable artistic success. However, maintaining such high quality required expenditures beyond the resources of the Symphony Association. Mr. Lanning and the Board agreed to sever their relationship after three seasons. James Christian Pfohl, founder of the Transylvania Music Camp in Brevard, North Carolina, conductor of the Charlotte (North Carolina) Symphony,* and music director at Davidson College, was appointed music director of the Jacksonville Symphony September 3, 1952. Pfohl's 10 years with the JSO justified the Board's confidence that he would produce a fine orchestra on a businesslike basis without sacrificing its professional quality. Most of the activities he established—youth concerts, televised concerts, pops concerts, and paired subscription concerts—continue today. Another highlight of Pfohl's years with the orchestra was receiving the Ditson Award for work in contemporary music.

On June 1, 1962, John Canarina, former assistant conductor of the New York Philharmonic,* became the JSO's third music director. He continued to build the orchestra's artistic base by imaginative programming. Under his baton the orchestra played its first Mahler symphony. The brief tenure of the next music director, Daniell Revenaugh, began during a period of internal conflicts and deficits, chronicled in a lengthy *New York Times* article headlined, "Was It Murder—Or Suicide." The Symphony Board had dissolved the orchestra, and Revenaugh's epoch concluded without his having conducted a single concert.

A new group of officers and Board members was assembled following the disastrous 1969–1970 season. Ira M. Koger, president of Koger Properties, Inc., and deeply involved with the arts, became president of the Symphony Association. No one has had a more profound effect on the organization since the founding president, Olin Watts. Koger's artistic awareness, foresight, and leadership guided the startling rebirth, which led to his being invited to appear before the United States Congressional Hearing on Federal Assistance in the Arts and to address the American Symphony Orchestra League. These events inspired yet another *New York Times* article on June 27, 1971, whose headline was "A 'Suicide' That Wasn't Fatal."

Willis Page, former member of the Boston Symphony,* conductor of the Des Moines (Iowa) Symphony,* Yomiuri Nippon Symphony in Tokyo, and the Nashville Symphony,* became the fifth music director. Page brought artistic maturity and a mastery of orchestral procedures that made him a favorite with musicians and audience alike. Under Page's tutelage the Symphony witnessed its greatest growth. There were commissions from American composers Carlisle Floyd and Duke Ellington; concerts in Washington's Kennedy Center and New York's Carnegie Hall; sold-out houses in Jacksonville, a feat noted by the ASOL for its rarity; pairs of subscription concerts; a collaboration with the local ballet companies to present an annual *Nutcracker*; the first appearance of black artists on a subscription concert series; the establishment of a core orchestra of musicians hired for the full year, which immensely improved quality; and, under Page's baton, the first JSO performance of Handel's *Messiah*. Page's 12-year tenure was the longest and most significant in the orchestra's history. The 1983–1984 season witnessed a series of guest conductors. Roger Nierenberg, music director of the Stamford [Connecticut] Symphony Orchestra, became the sixth music director for the Jacksonville Symphony during the 1984–1985 season.

The Jacksonville Symphony's annual budget is approximately $1.3 million. Ticket sales account for approximately 39%, while the remaining budget is funded by special concert revenues, grants, and contributions. The orchestra has over 26 full-time contract musicians in addition to 65 part-timers. Its 36-week concert season begins in early September and ends in mid-May. The season's seven pairs of subscription concerts played by the full orchestra are supplemented by a chamber orchestra, string orchestra, brass quintet, string quartet, woodwind quintet, and a pops orchestra, all performing in outlying areas. This array of musical organizations plays over 200 concerts each season, reaching over 250,000 people. The orchestra's repertoire relies heavily on compositions from the romantic era, balanced by some baroque and classical works and an occasional contemporary composition.

The orchestra's educational program is three-fold: over 100,000 students are transported to the Civic Auditorium for full orchestral concerts during the school year; the orchestra's small ensembles travel to approximately 100 elementary schools giving concerts and lecture/demonstrations; and the pops orchestra performs at more than 20 junior and senior high schools throughout the school year.

The organizational structure consists of a Board of 42 members, elected on a staggered year basis, and an administrative staff of eight. The artistic staff consists of the music director, associate conductor, and assistant conductor. The Guild, formerly the Women's Committee and later the Women's Guild, began shortly after the formation of the Symphony Association. This organization has been responsible for a variety of activities to support the development of the orchestra. Their continued importance is demonstrated by the fact that they maintain offices in the same suite as the Symphony Association.

Women have historically played a significant role in the Jacksonville Symphony. Its first concertmaster was, in fact, a concertmistress, Mrs. Alice B.

Sager. Mrs. Sager is presently the associate concertmaster, and her daughter, Susan C. Stein, is the orchestra's general manager. During the 1982–1983 season, Mrs. Constance Steward Green became the first woman to serve as president of the Symphony Association Board.

CHRONOLOGY OF MUSIC DIRECTORS: Van Lier Lanning, 1949–1952. James Christian Pfohl, 1952–1962. John Canarina, 1962–1969. Daniell Revenaugh, 1969–1970. Willis Page, 1971–1983. (Guest conductors, 1983–1984.) Roger Nierenberg, 1984-present.

BIBLIOGRAPHY: Interviews with Willis Page, Helen Frick, Dr. Gerson Yessin, James Christian Pfohl, Dr. Frances Bartlett Kinne, Ira Koger, Alice Sager, and Martha Page Parkhill, Kathy McDaniel, and Lona Bartlett, 1984. *Florida Times Union. New York Times.* "Pronounced Dead, Jacksonville Symphony Comes Back to Life," American Symphony Orchestra League *Newsletter*, April 1971. Olin E. Watts, *The Beginnings of the Jacksonville Symphony Association* (Jacksonville, Fla.: Jacksonville Symphony Association, pamphlet, 20 Oct. 1960). Olin E. Watts, *Jacksonville Symphony Association: Summary of Its Policies, Aims, and Organization* (Jacksonville, Fla.: Jacksonville Symphony Association, pamphlet, 2 June 1955).

ACCESS: Jacksonville Symphony Association, 128 East Forsyth, Suite 300, Jacksonville, FL 32202. (904) 354–5479. Susan Sager Stein, Executive Director.

WILLIAM A. BROWN

PLANTATION (1,018,200—Fort Lauderdale; 576,863—West Palm Beach/Boca Raton)

South Florida Symphony Orchestra (Mt)

Dr. James Brooks, current artistic director and conductor, founded this ensemble in 1978 as the Florida Chamber Orchestra. In 1984 the ensemble changed its name to the present South Florida Symphony Orchestra to reflect its growing size and widening repertoire. The orchestra consists of 49 professional musicians—31 men and 18 women as of 1984—who reside in the greater Fort Lauderdale (Broward County) or Miami (Dade County) areas. Many of the musicians are also involved in other performance groups and in teaching. The immediate area's other main orchestra is the Philharmonic Orchestra of Florida,* formed in 1984 by the merger of the Ft. Lauderdale and Boca Raton Symphonies.

The SFSO presents eight pairs of concerts annually at Broward Community College's Bailey Hall (usually to a typical audience of full capacity—1,150 per concert) and Boca Raton's Florida Atlantic University Center Auditorium, a multipurpose hall with an acoustical shell (to a typical audience of half capacity—1,200 per concert). The 1984–1985 season was planned to include a new four-concert Sunday matinee series and an increased commitment to the community with more outreach concerts at shopping plazas and more pops programs. One such program in March of 1984, with country-western singer Tammy Wynette at Ft. Lauderdale's Lockhart Stadium, attracted an audience of 8,000.

Artistic programming is the sole responsibility of the orchestra's artistic director, who typically selects a very wide range of compositions, classics to new music, with well-known guest artists and conductors, based on audience appeal and budget considerations. A typical SFSO program in 1984 with a guest artist was, for example, Roussel's Concerto for Small Orchestra, Shostakovich's Concerto for Cello and Orchestra No. 1 in E-flat (with Yo-Yo Ma as cello soloist), and Mendelssohn's Symphony No. 1 in C Minor. A more adventurous program, also in 1984, presented Ravel's *Le Tombeau de Couperin*, Devienne's Concerto for Flute and Orchestra No. 7 in E Minor, Griffes's *Poem for Flute and Orchestra*, and Ginastera's *Variaciones Concertantes* (with guest flutist Eugenia Zukerman and guest conductor Thomas Briccetti).

The SFSO's 16-member Board of Directors sets standard policies, decides the number of concerts for the season, and actively organizes fund-raising events. The ensemble's budget is $800,000, and funding comes from the NEA, Florida State Arts Council, Broward County Tourist Development Fund, Broward Community College, private and corporate donations, and ticket sales.

The SFSO Association has a positive impact on area youth. It sponsors the Broward Community College's Youth Symphony, founded by Dr. Brooks in 1973; its present conductor is Charles Noble. The Youth Symphony is a training orchestra of 66, often combined in concert with its counterpart, the Youth Symphony Dancers (Sharon Brooks, director-choreographer), 30 youngsters who present young people's concerts annually. Youth programs are sponsored with area colleges, such as an in-school string program, which reaches over 5,000 elementary school children annually. Other programs reach about 40,000 children through concerts and workshops. The SFSO Association has a scholarship program, which provides full tuition and financial aid for talented young musicians and brings young, musically gifted Latin American students to the United States to study music at South Florida's institutions of higher learning.

During July, the SFSO Association presents the Florida Music Festival and the International Conductor's Symposium, begun in 1979 in Ft. Lauderdale, also by Dr. Brooks. The Festival Orchestra, 68 professional musicians, comprising 20 SFSO members and other players from major American and worldwide orchestras, performs classics to pops. On a budget of $200,000 to $250,000, the Festival programs include international guest artists, master classes, seminars, the advanced Conductor's Symposium, symphony and ballet concerts, and a classic music film festival. Subscription concerts at FAU Auditorium and BCC's Bailey Hall, as well as free outdoor concerts with fireworks, provide summer cultural activities for South Florida's residents and visitors. The overall activities of the SFSO Association reach over

100,000 people annually. The Festival Orchestra has travelled to Honduras and Costa Rica, and there are future plans, under the leadership of Panamanian-born Dr. Brooks, to establish an annual International Latin American Music Festival in different Latin American capitals and in South Florida as a cultural link with the Americas.

CHRONOLOGY OF MUSIC DIRECTORS: Dr. James Brooks, 1978-present.

BIBLIOGRAPHY: Interviews with SFSO Music Director James Brooks and FMF Manager Renée La Bonte. Steven Brown, "Chamber Orchestra Plays Youthful Mozart with Vim," *Miami Herald*, 27 Jan. 1984. Camilo Delgado, "Maestro Brooks," *Aboard*, July 1983.

ACCESS: South Florida Symphony Orchestra, 1822 North University Drive, Plantation, FL. 33322. (305) 474–7660. Renée LaBonte, Florida Music Festival Manager.

VIOLET VAGRAMIAN-NISHANIAN

SARASOTA (202,251)

Florida West Coast Symphony Orchestra (Mt)

Led by music director and conductor Paul Wolfe, the FWCSO serves Sarasota and Manatee Counties on the central west coast of Florida. The organization has had a tremendous cultural impact on the area's young musicians and has consequently received much-deserved national recognition.

The FWCSO plays five sets of three subscription concerts, including one matinee series with guest artists, to sold-out audiences. These concerts are held at Bradenton's Neel Auditorium, at Manatee Junior College (seating capacity 900 with good acoustics) and at Eugenia Van Wezel Performing Arts Hall. The latter is an 1,800-seat auditorium, without center aisles, designed by Frank Lloyd Wright Taliesen Associates and situated on the bayfront of Sarasota's Civic Center. The orchestra also performs four pops concerts per season.

The FWCSO sponsors comprehensive youth programs (with a yearly budget of $150,000) in its $1.5 million Music Center: summer workshops (since 1952), where young people perform and train with Symphony musicians; three youth orchestras—advanced (since 1959), junior (since 1974), and junior high school (since 1984); three preparatory string orchestras (since 1981); wind and brass ensembles (since 1984). The programs include over 300 young people, and nearly one-third of the FWCSO's personnel are graduates of the youth orchestras. The FWCSO claims the distinction of being the nation's only orchestra with such an extraordinary commitment to its area's youth.

The orchestra's $700,000 budget covers both Symphony and youth programs, with funding mainly from ticket sales and private and corporate donations. The organization has an active Board of Directors, an adminis-trative staff, and a Program Advisory Committee. Of the Symphony's 96 musicians—54% of whom are women—80% receive a salary. Most are also involved in teaching and/or business.

In the late 1920s Sarasota became the home of John Ringling, who built his mansion and galleries there. The area quickly attracted artists, writers, and musicians, and by the late 1940s a booming economy and growing interest in cultural activities had been established. At that time, Mrs. Thomas W. Butler of Sarasota, an active music teacher and pianist, decided to or-ganize an orchestra in her home town.

According to Dennis R. Cooper's history of the FWCSO, Mrs. Butler gathered 40 local instrumentalists from the Sarasota-Bradenton area and secured Tampa orchestra conductor Dr. Lyman Wiltse. The success of the first concert on January 2, 1949, led to the push for a permanent ensem-ble. After fewer than two months of rehearsals, a joint benefit concert for the Symphony with the Manatee River Choral Club at the new Sarasota Municipal Auditorium presented 65 mostly amateur musicians to a sold-out audience. A 33-member Board of Directors, with support from the towns of Bradenton, Sarasota, and Venice, planned a concert season of three programs with a budget of $1,200. The new Florida West Coast Symphony Orchestra would hold concerts at Manatee County High School Auditorium in Bradenton (until 1962) and Sarasota's Municipal Audito-rium (until 1970).

Following the successful first season, the distinguished violinist-conductor and teacher Alexander Bloch was named the FWCSO's first permanent con-ductor. At age 68, retired from active musical life, he nevertheless ap-proached the job with vigor and dedication, and the still mostly amateur orchestra attracted large audiences and broadcast concerts on Sarasota's radio station WSPB. Bloch's commitment to the orchestra's development and its prime concern, stimulating musical advancement among the com-munity's young people, began with the establishment of a fund at the end of the 1951 season to aid young orchestra musicians in pursuing continued education and attending music camps. Summer workshops, school outreach programs, in-school workshops, and free children's concerts since 1953 have reached more than 10,000 youngsters annually. By the orchestra's tenth season, national TV feature stories, magazine articles, and an intensive study of the FWCSO (along with eight other orchestras in the country) by the ASOL and the Rockefeller Foundation had brought the orchestra wide recognition.

Women have played an active role in the Symphony's success story. Its founder was a woman, women figure prominently in its committees, and the Symphony Women's Association, formed in 1956, has been responsible for youth programs, education and research activities, the FWCSO's Schol-arship Fund, and the Building Committee for the orchestra's rehearsal hall.

According to ASOL, this is the first hall to be built for the use of an American community orchestra.

When Alexander Bloch resigned in 1961 due to failing health, over 100 persons applied for his position. The appointee, the multitalented, 35-year-old Paul Wolfe, strongly reaffirmed Bloch's musical commitments. He energetically set forth to coordinate all the youth programs, conduct the youth orchestra, and further improve the quality of the FWCSO by adding players (professionals and volunteers) and increasing rehearsal time. During the next 24 years he furthered the community ties between the public schools and the orchestra. In 1965 he received a grant of $188,000 from the U.S. Department of Health, Education and Welfare to promote a three-year Experimental Instructional Performance Clinic, which brought outstanding musicians from throughout the nation to Sarasota to work with local students and teachers for six weeks each summer. Professional affiliation between the orchestra and the area colleges, Manatee Junior College and New College, has brought college music students and faculty within the ranks of the FWCSO. In 1965 Wolfe founded the New College Music Festival of chamber music, which presents June master classes and concerts by guest artists, that are attended by more than 100 young musicians selected by competition from conservatories and universities throughout the United States and the world.

The following years continued to be productive, with deficits only from 1968 through 1970; since then the orchestra's finances have been secure. Its move to acoustically sound halls helped its musical growth, and the orchestra continues to develop new programs; a chamber orchestra concert series, a lecture series, a "Florida Wind Quintet" concert series, teaching and youth programs. As part of its 35th Anniversary celebration the FWCSO commissioned Thomas Svoboda's *Serenade for Orchestra*, which it premiered in March of 1984. The orchestra continues its dedication to providing the best music education for as many youngsters as possible.

CHRONOLOGY OF MUSIC DIRECTORS: Lyman Wiltse, 1949–1950. Alexander Bloch, 1950–1961. Paul Wolfe, 1961-present.

BIBLIOGRAPHY: Interviews with FWCSO General Manager Gretchen Serrie, 1985. Dennis R. Cooper, *The Florida West Coast Symphony Orchestra* (FWCSO, 1974).

ACCESS: Florida West Coast Symphony Orchestra, 709 N. Tamiami Trail, Sarasota, FL 33577. (813) 955–4562. Gretchen Serrie, General Manager. Dorothy Garland, Educational Director. Millicent Fleming, Festival Staff Administrative Director.

VIOLET VAGRAMIAN-NISHANIAN

TAMPA (1,569,134—Tampa/St. Petersburg)

Florida Orchestra (Rg)

As its recent name change implies, the Florida Orchestra has begun promoting itself as the predominant symphony orchestra in this fast-growing state. With concert halls in three home cities—Tampa, St. Petersburg, and Clearwater—the orchestra was for 16 years known as the Florida Gulf Coast Symphony and had achieved a modest regional reputation. Critics at home and in surrounding cities routinely praised its musical offerings. Certainly it enjoyed the highest profile of any fine arts institution in the Tampa Bay area.

January 1984 provided a new beginning. With finances finally in order, and with the concurrent opportunities of a statewide tour and exposure on British television about to occur, management announced intentions to reach ASOL Major status by 1990 and simplified the name. Officers of the rival Florida Symphony Orchestra in Orlando objected to the name change in court; the suit was settled a year later when the Florida Orchestra agreed to add the words, "Tampa, St. Petersburg, Clearwater" to its logo and other identifying materials. But the larger issue was best expressed by reporter Stephen Wigler in *The Orlando Sentinel*: "The Tampa orchestra," he wrote, "which has been growing like crabgrass in recent years, is making its big move."

In its struggle for dominance, the Florida Orchestra's future has not always seemed so secure. It was founded in 1968 through a merger of the old Tampa Philharmonic (organized and conducted since the 1950s by CBS music director Alfredo Antonini) and the St. Petersburg Symphonic Society. In that time the west coast of Florida was culturally naive—prominent classical artists visited occasionally, but geography and temperament combined to make the region an artistic frontier. The potential of inter-city rivalry was so threatening, moreover, that the merger papers were signed on a windswept tugboat in the middle of Tampa Bay.

Among the organizers' first decisions was to hire as music director Irwin Hoffman, whose musical personality has dominated the orchestra ever since. Hoffman was then acting music director of the Chicago Symphony*; he had been associate conductor since 1964 and for a dozen years before that, music director of the Vancouver Symphony. For two years the imperious, urbane, cigar-loving Hoffman divided his time between Florida and Chicago. But when Sir Georg Solti won the permanent appointment in Chicago and offered Hoffman the number two spot, Hoffman decided his days as an assistant were over. Lured by the potential for growth, he chose Florida.

The combined orchestra he inherited was composed of retirees from established northern orchestras, local music teachers, and other musicians best described as dedicated but semi-professional. "The orchestra was able to give some very fine performances, but not consistently from a technical point of view," Hoffman said in a 1983 interview. "That doesn't mean that in 1968 people weren't getting their money's worth. The earmark of a worthwhile evening is that people are touched. A great orchestra can be immaculate and boring; the magic just doesn't happen. But I know we touched people. I remember their reactions."

From the start Hoffman relied heavily on the romantic repertoire of the nineteenth century, finding that audiences here as everywhere responded best to works that they found familiar. Hoffman is also a "big-picture" conductor; his style on the podium is frequently to involve himself in massive swaying, arms outstretched, subordinating the individual beat as he moves large blocks of music around. Despite his proven skills in other musical styles, Hoffman has for these two reasons achieved a reputation as a romantic conductor, a label he tries to resist. But on the west coast of Florida, as Hoffman remarks, "they like Rachmaninoff, Tchaikovsky, and Brahms."

Hoffman's local pigeon-hole label has been abetted also by the orchestra's unusual assortment of concert halls. From the beginning the orchestra has had at least two homes: the old McKay Auditorium on the campus of the University of Tampa (a wide, boomy hall with a large balcony and a stage that spills out beyond the proscenium) and the acoustically dead Bayfront Theatre in St. Petersburg; in 1976 the orchestra began serving the fast-growing North Suncoast from a high school auditorium just north of Clearwater. Tumultuous, emotional music can be positively riveting in McKay; it is about the only thing that works at the Bayfront. In the 1983–1984 season, however, the orchestra began performing in the newly constructed Ruth Eckerd Hall in Clearwater. Its superior acoustics were demonstrated early in the season, when Hoffman conducted a piano concerto transcribed from Johann Sebastian Bach. Hoffman had the reduced orchestra and visiting pianist Oxana Yablonskaya in fluid, delicate balance. The following evening at McKay, Hoffman's interpretation was the same, but the sound was muddy and overwrought. Obviously, existing facilities had not provided an adequate showcase for Hoffman's full range of talents.

Construction began on a new concert hall in Tampa in the spring of 1984; occupancy is expected by late 1986. In St. Petersburg, a committee of interested citizens began meeting in mid–1984 to plan improvements for their 20-year-old hall, but many political and financial obstacles remain.

In recent seasons Hoffman has been pressing his audiences to accept more unfamiliar repertoire, but it is a continuing challenge. The St. Petersburg audience, especially, consists predominantly of older people who fit Hoffman's description of their tastes to a "T." But even in relatively youthful Tampa, a petition was circulated in spring of 1984 complaining of Hoffman's flirtation with Bartók and Prokofiev—not to mention such contemporaries as David Del Tredici and Witold Lutoslawski. Still, Hoffman forged ahead, scheduling works the following season by Alban Berg, Leslie Bassett, and Krzysztof Penderecki (the latter to be conducted by the composer)—leavened by ample helpings of Berlioz, Mendelssohn, Samuel Barber, and an entire evening of Mozart.

In its first dozen years the orchestra saw only moderate growth, the expansion into Clearwater being the most notable occurrence. But in 1981–1982 the foundation was laid for a lively adolescence. Policy-making, which had been divided ambiguously among semi-autonomous Boards of Directors in the various home cities and a Master Board, was centralized in a new 50-member Board of Governors, drawn from the entire area. Local Boards of Directors, now totalling 140 members, were retained for fund-raising and public-relations assistance. A fully professional staff was assembled, including specialists in marketing, development, and accounting. Aggressive new fund-raising schemes were born, focusing on the Tampa Bay corporations that enjoy what several authorities have described as Florida's most lucrative business climate. That same season, the orchestra's budget surpassed $1 million for the first time.

A musicians' strike in the fall of 1982 focused even more attention on the orchestra's future. By now Hoffman had succeeded in stocking his orchestra mostly with bright young musicians from the nation's best conservatories; 81 were on annual contract, paid on a per-service basis. Now they demanded full-time status and a longer season. As the negotiating theatrics continued, three groups of regular season concerts were postponed, and one was eventually cancelled.

After a month the strike was settled. Largely through accelerated fund-raising goals (and partly with the assistance of first-time contracts from opera companies in St. Petersburg and Sarasota) management committed itself to double its budget within the next three years. The season was progressively lengthened, from 19 weeks in 1982–1983 to 28 weeks in 1984–1985.

Musicians agreed to accept full-time status for only 64 of their number; another 24 would be retained part-time. Both sides began working eagerly together on positive public relations and ambitious future plans. By spring 1983, more good news was announced: for the first time in four years the company had ended the season in the black, and, even better, the accumulated debt of many years had been retired.

From $1.2 million in 1981–1982, the orchestra's budget mushroomed to $2.5 million in 1984–1985. The general public sees evidence of this in many ways. To supplement the three standard "Masterworks" series (a sequence of 10 classical concerts in each home city), the orchestra began a pops series in 1983. Free outdoor concerts with corporate sponsors are a frequent occurrence year-round throughout the two-county area; attendance sometimes reaches as high as 20,000. The orchestra gives 40 youth concerts a year, reaching more than 60,000 fourth and fifth graders; small ensembles give another 150 performances in local schools. The company provides the pit orchestra for the Florida Opera (formerly known as Florida Opera West and the St. Petersburg Opera Company) and the Sarasota Opera (formerly known as Asolo Opera), as well as other special occasions such as the 1984 gala grand opening of Ruth Eckerd Hall, in which the celebrated Russian emigré violinist Viktoria Mullova gave her North American orchestral debut.

A television crew from the BBC accompanied Mullova through her first year in the West—hence the Florida Orchestra's debut on British television.

In the last three years private contributions have tripled, and audiences have grown from 170,000 to 375,000. In the spring of 1984, Florida's Secretary of State George Firestone announced prospects for an even wider audience by naming the Florida Orchestra the first such organization ever to receive taxpayer and corporate funds to tour the state. Supporters were overjoyed. The Florida Orchestra, it seemed, was beginning to live up to its name.

RECORDING HISTORY AND SELECTIVE DISCOGRAPHY: In 1979 the orchestra recorded on a private label Respighi's *Pines of Rome* and Tchaikovsky's *Romeo and Juliet* Overture-Fantasy, available through the orchestra.

CHRONOLOGY OF MUSIC DIRECTORS: Irwin Hoffman, 1968-present.

BIBLIOGRAPHY: James Harper, "Composition of a Conductor," a long profile of Irwin Hoffman, *St. Petersburg Times*, 21 Oct. 1983. *St. Petersburg Times*. Stephen Wigler, "Florida's at the Heart of Symphony Feud," *Orlando Sentinel*, 22 Apr. 1984.

ACCESS: The Florida Orchestra, 2709 Rocky Point Drive, Suite 201, Post Office Box 24419, Tampa, FL 33607. (813) 887–5715. Faye Bailey, Executive Director.

JAMES HARPER

Georgia _____

ATLANTA (2,029,710)

Atlanta Symphony Orchestra (Mj)

The Atlanta Symphony Orchestra is one of the youngest major American orchestras, attaining prominence in the last quarter century. From its inception in 1944 as the Atlanta Youth Symphony, the orchestra has matured to its current position of artistic excellence and cultural influence regionally and nationally.

The ASO presents more than 200 programs each year to a live audience of nearly one million. The orchestra is valued as a significant resource contributing to the economic and cultural vitality of the Atlanta metropolitan area, the state of Georgia, and the southeastern region at large. Through recordings and annual tours, the orchestra is well known nationally for its innovative programming and artistic excellence.

Unlike its older counterparts, the ASO has been served by only two music directors: Henry Sopkin, from 1945 to 1966, and Robert Shaw, from 1967 to the present. Shaw was formerly associated with the Cleveland Orchestra* under George Szell and was director of the famed Robert Shaw Chorale. In 1977, Louis Lane joined the ASO as co-conductor and served as such until 1983. For the 1983–1984 season Lane assumed the position of principal guest conductor. Like Shaw, Lane was also associated with the Cleveland Orchestra (1947–1973) and is the featured conductor on 14 recordings of the Cleveland Orchestra issued by Columbia and Epic during this period.

In addition to the conducting staff (conductor, assistant conductor, principal guest conductor), the ASO employs 91 musicians and a management support staff of 25. The string section is made up of 32 violins, 10 violas, 11 cellos, and eight bass violins. The support staff includes a general manager who also serves as the executive vice president of the Atlanta Symphony Orchestra League Board of Directors. The players are represented by the AFM and employed on a full-time, 48-week contract basis. The Atlanta Symphony Orchestra League, a non-profit corporation chartered in the state of Georgia, is responsible for the overall management and operation of the orchestra.

The ASO operates on an annual budget of over $8.5 million. The orchestra's 26-week, 69-concert subscription series is augmented with a winter pops season, special and traditional holiday programming, a series of Saturday morning "Coffee Concerts," and a summer series at Atlanta's Chastain and Piedmont Parks. The orchestra is a feature attraction of the annual Atlanta Arts Festival and presents numerous runout concerts on college campuses and in communities and institutions within the state and region. Program material from the 26-week master season is recorded for a feature program series broadcast by WABE, Atlanta's NPR affiliate. Holiday and special programs are produced for broadcast by local and area teletlvision stations.

The orchestra takes seriously the responsibility of providing concert programs for senior citizens, youth audiences, the handicapped, institutionalized segments of the community, and other non-traditional audiences. The orchestra also schedules a three-week national tour each season. During the 1982–1983 season, for example, the ASO performed in Ohio, Indiana, Illinois, Iowa, New Jersey, New York, Pennsylvania, and Delaware.

The performance home of the ASO is Symphony Hall, the largest auditorium of the Robert W. Woodruff Arts Center, which includes the Memorial Arts Building—completed in 1968 and home of Symphony Hall—and the High Museum of Art, completed in 1983. The Center is named for Atlanta's "anonymous donor," Coca-Cola philanthropist Robert W. Woodruff, who played a major role as benefactor in the construction of the arts complex. Prior to moving to Symphony Hall in 1968, the ASO's programs were presented in the Atlanta Municipal Auditorium and other theater locations in the city. The winter pops series is presented at the restored "Fabulous" Fox Theatre in midtown Atlanta.

The ASO Symphony Hall seats 1,762. A hydraulically operated orchestra pit can be raised to floor level, allowing for an additional 92 seats, or raised to stage level to expand the performance area. The distance from the stage to the last seat row of the auditorium's orchestra section is 95 feet; to the last seat row in the top balcony, 125 feet. Seating in Symphony Hall is thus intimate and comfortable, with excellent visual perspective and acoustical properties.

The history of the Atlanta Symphony Orchestra can be divided into two distinct phases: the Henry Sopkin years from 1945 through 1966, and the Robert Shaw era from 1967 to the present.

The beginning of the ASO can be traced to 1939 and the "In and About

Atlanta High School Orchestra," a festival orchestra drawing young musicians from as far away as Chattanooga, Tennessee. The event's organizer, Anne Grace O'Callaghan (music supervisor in the Atlanta public school system) witnessed Sopkin guest conducting in conjunction with the 1943 meeting of the Southern Division of the Music Educators National Conference and invited him to serve as guest conductor for the "In and About" orchestra concert the following spring. Sopkin accepted the invitation.

Several previous attempts to establish a professional symphony in Atlanta had failed when Josephine Saunders, President of the Atlanta Music Club, heard the spring 1944 "In and About" orchestra concert with Sopkin conducting and was favorably impressed. Viewing the "In and About" orchestra as a possible nucleus for a professional symphony, Mrs. Saunders discussed the idea with Miss O'Callaghan, Frank Harrold, education chairman of the Atlanta Music Club, Ira Jarrel, president of the Atlanta Board of Education, and Marcia Weisgerber, a music teacher at Girl's High School. A plan to start the Atlanta Youth Symphony Orchestra was formulated and presented to the full membership of the Atlanta Music Club for formal consideration. The plan called for establishment of an all-city youth orchestra augmented with available and interested adults to fill out the several sections. The ensemble was to be rehearsed and prepared by Miss Weisgerber for two concert performances conducted by Sopkin during the 1944–1945 season.

In analyzing previous attempts and failures in establishing an orchestra in Atlanta, the group concluded that the community tended not to take local musical effort seriously, favoring instead outside groups visiting the city. The Metropolitan Opera, for example, has included Atlanta as a tour city since 1910, and, as with other touring groups, traditionally receives a warm and enthusiastic community reception. With this realization, Mrs. Dorothy Grove, public relations chairman of the Music Club, was given the task of promoting the new orchestra. News and feature stories were written on every aspect of the new orchestra and appeared frequently and regularly in the print and broadcast media. School Board President Ira Jarrel assumed the major responsibility for fund raising. According to accounts, Jarrel contacted businesses and individuals with a request that they contribute specified amounts in accordance with budget estimates for the orchestra project. In total, 48 contributions were obtained, and the first season of the Atlanta Youth Symphony was launched.

With Henry Sopkin conducting, the Atlanta Youth Symphony gave two concerts in the Atlanta Municipal Auditorium on February 4 and April 15, 1945. For both programs the public was invited at no charge, with sponsors recognized in the printed program given special seating. Following the April 15 program, Sopkin was invited to move from his home in Illinois to Atlanta to build a professional symphony. For a salary of $3,000, considerably less than that earned as an instructor at Woodrow Wilson Junior College in the

Chicago area, the 41-year-old Sopkin surprisingly accepted the offer and challenge.

On September 21, 1945, the Atlanta Youth Symphony Guild was incorporated under Georgia State Statute. Its budget was $5,000, of which $3,000 was to be used for Sopkin's salary. Three regular concert programs were presented during the 1945–1946 season. The addition of 15 part-time professional players was projected for the 1946–1947 season at a cost of $13,000. Funds were obtained for this purpose and for a salary increase to $5,000 for Sopkin. Five concert programs were presented during the 1946–1947 season, each contributing to the orchestra's musical stature and public support. The mixing of amateur and professional players posed problems for the local office of the musicians union. While consenting to the arrangement, the union at first disallowed admission charges to concerts, eliminating an important source of financial support.

The first concert by the Atlanta Youth Symphony outside Atlanta was presented at the University of Georgia in Athens on May 11, 1947, and featured Hugh Hodgson as a piano soloist. At approximately the same time, the "Youth" designation was deleted from the orchestra's name, and the group became known as the Atlanta Symphony Orchestra. Also during the spring of 1947 an understanding was attained with the union local, and subscription tickets were marketed for the 1947–1948 season.

Henry Sopkin proved an effective recruiter and enticed many young musicians to move to Atlanta, often with an arrangement for a teaching position or other supplementary full-time employment opportunity. By 1950 the ASO had 50 players under part-time contract, with an operational budget of $77,000. Interestingly, $34,000 of this amount was derived from ticket sales. The 1950–1951 10-program season featured a soloist and program formula that became somewhat standardized for the remainder of Sopkin's tenure. The program would begin with an overture, followed by a symphony or suite, a concerto or song group if the soloist was a singer, and an appropriate shorter closing selection. By 1951–1952, the entire orchestra was paid on a part-time, per-service, or contract basis and joined the ranks of the 25 major American orchestras by virtue of its $113,000 budget.

In 1962 the lives of 106 Atlantans, most of whom were staunch patrons of the arts, were lost in an airplane crash at Orly Field in Paris. In response to this tragedy and as a memorial to those who died, the Atlanta Arts Alliance was established and planning for the construction of an arts center initiated. With initial gifts from the Callaway Foundation and Robert W. Woodruff, a grass-roots fund campaign was launched resulting in the completion of the Memorial Arts Building in 1968. The pioneering effort of Henry Sopkin, who retired in 1966, brought the ASO to Symphony Hall as a permanent home and to the threshold of becoming one of America's finest orchestras. After a year-long search, Robert Shaw was selected as music director of the orchestra for the 1967–1968 season. He conducted the debut performance in Symphony Hall in 1968.

Under Robert Shaw's musical leadership the orchestra continued to develop. A multi-million dollar challenge grant from the Ford Foundation resulted in the establishment of a permanent endowment and a series of endowed chairs. In 1972 the orchestra under Shaw collaborated with the Afro-American Workshop at Atlanta's Morehouse College in the world premiere of Scott Joplin's *Treemonisha*, leading to a New York production and other performances of this long-neglected opera. In 1974 the Atlanta Symphony Youth Orchestra was founded. The Bernstein *Mass: A Theater Piece for Singers, Players, and Dancers* received its southeastern premiere in Atlanta in 1975. The appointment of Louis Lane as co-conductor and Hiroyuki Iwaki as principal guest conductor in 1977 brought additional strengths and prestige to the conducting staff. During this period Shaw also created the Atlanta Symphony Orchestra Chorus and Chamber Chorus, with a combined membership of 250 singers.

Each year the orchestra adds 15 to 20 works to its repertoire with a non-defined ratio of standard to contemporary works. Works of the twentieth century and those composed since 1950 are systematically included as an important component of programming practices. Capitalizing on Shaw's knowledge of and experience with choral literature and style, a good deal of emphasis is placed on orchestral literature requiring the addition of choral forces. With something of a shifting emphasis, programming over the years maintains an appropriate balance between the standard repertoire, newer works, and compositions of a choral nature. The orchestra only recently has begun to allocate resources to commissioning new works; it plans to expand this activity over the next several years. In October 1983, the ASO premiered a well-received commissioned work, *Desert Forest*, by Henry Brant. During the 1984–1985 season the ASO featured a work by Karel Husa commissioned by the University of Georgia in commemoration of its bicentennial as the nation's first state-chartered university (1785). Several other commissioned projects are currently in the planning or negotiation stage.

Thus, the orchestra's programming can be described as innovative and varied. It is approached with consideration for the audience, a sense of responsibility to twentieth-century composition as a living and dynamic art form, a perspective that capitalizes on the strengths of the players and conductors, and with a focus having the potential of attracting national and international attention.

The ASO is made up of a mixture of seasoned orchestral players and a sizeable group of highly talented younger musicians. The orchestra's sound varies according to the period and style of each work performed. Consistency is achieved through an exceptional sense of rhythm, ensemble, precise articulation, and sectional clarity resulting in a freshness of sound with listener appeal and critical acceptance.

RECORDING HISTORY AND SELECTIVE DISCOGRAPHY: In 1979 the ASO's Telarc Records issue of the *Firebird Suite* and excerpts from *Prince Igor* was the first release of an American orchestra using the Soundstream digital recording process. Within months the recording became a national best seller, receiving the 1979 Audio Excellence Award. A series of other Telarc digital recordings followed. The 1981 two-record set of Orff's *Carmina Burana* and Hindemith's *Metamorphosis* have been critically acclaimed as "definitive musical masterpieces" and "state-of-the-art" examples of the digital recording process.

Stravinsky, *The Firebird Suite*; Borodin, Overture and Polovetsian Dances from *Prince Igor* (Shaw): Telarc DG–10039. Boito, Prologue to *Mefistofele*; Verdi, *Te Deum* (Shaw): Telarc DG–10045. Orff, *Carmina Burana*; Hindemith, *Symphonic Metamorphosis* (Shaw): Telarc DG–10056/57. Poulenc, Organ Concerto, *Gloria* (Shaw): Telarc DG–10077. Copland, *Fanfare for the Common Man, Appalachian Spring*, Four Dance Episodes from *Rodeo* (Lane): Telarc DG–10078. *Nativity* (Shaw): Vox QTU-S 34647/48. *Christmas with Robert Shaw* (Shaw): Turnabout QTU-S 34639.

CHRONOLOGY OF MUSIC DIRECTORS: Henry Sopkin, 1945–1966. Robert Shaw, 1967-present. Louis Lane (co-conductor), 1977–1983; (Principal Guest Conductor), 1983-present.

BIBLIOGRAPHY: *The Atlanta Constitution. The Atlanta Journal.* Atlanta Symphony Board of Directors, *Minutes. The Atlanta Symphony Orchestra* (Atlanta Symphony League, 1983). Anne Arant McFarland, "The Atlanta Symphony: The Sopkin Years," Masters thesis, University of Georgia, 1976.

ACCESS: Atlanta Symphony Orchestra, 1280 Peachtree Street, NE, Atlanta, GA 30309. (404) 898–1182. J. Thomas Bacchetti, Executive Vice President and General Manager. Lynn Varner, Director of Media Relations.

RALPH E. VERRASTRO

SAVANNAH (230,728)

Savannah Symphony Orchestra (Mt)

Founded in 1953 as a community orchestra, the Savannah Symphony and its ensembles today present 140 programs each year reaching a live audience of approximately 100,000 people. The orchestra employs a core of 36 full-time professional musicians and operates over a 34-week season. Additional professional musicians are hired on a per-service basis for specific programs.

The performance home of the SSO since 1971 is Mercer Theater located in the Savannah Civic Center. The theater has a seating capacity of 2,500 and possesses excellent acoustical and physical characteristics for orchestral programs. The orchestra is governed by a 10-person Executive Committee drawn from the Board of Directors of the Savannah Symphony Society, Inc., and is administered by a full-time general manager and eight-person professional staff.

The SSO is under the artistic direction of its music director/conductor, with assistance and continuity provided by a resident conductor. The orchestra operates on a $1 million annual budget, of which ticket sales and concert fees account for 60%. Remaining income is derived from grants (10%), contributions and gifts (27%), and investment and miscellaneous sources (3%). Christian Badea serves as music director and conductor, a position he has held since 1977. Michael Luxner is the SSO's resident conductor.

The SSO's subscription schedule of concert performances includes a Masterworks Series of nine Saturday evening programs with an orchestra of 75 musicians. Its standard symphony orchestra programs regularly include serious works of the twentieth century. Prominent soloists appear regularly on the Masterworks Series as does the Savannah Symphony Chorale. The Sunday Afternoon Series of four programs—also with full symphonic orchestration—focuses on the music of a single composer, a musical theme, American music or that of another nationality, or a program of light classics and/or show music.

The Chamber Orchestra series of eight concerts under the resident conductor with the core orchestra also features a wide variety of literature. A six-program Chamber Music Savannah series presented mid-week at the Temple Mickve Israel features ensembles from the core orchestra and visiting chamber music groups. A series of eight free, public programs at Forsyth Park and the Civic Center are sponsored by the City of Savannah. Special holiday, pops, and benefit concerts and regional touring complete the orchestra's performance schedule.

With a serious commitment to musical education, the SSO began giving concerts to school children in 1954. Paralleling the young people's concerts, the SSO sponsors three training ensembles for young musicians. The Savannah Symphony Youth Orchestra, comprising junior and senior high school students, is the most advanced and well known of these groups and presents two concert programs annually. The Symphony also conducts an annual, national young artists competition.

Another SSO adjunct group is the Savannah Symphony Chorale, an adult volunteer organization that performs with the orchestra on two or three programs each year. All concert programs presented by the SSO are recorded for rebroadcast by WSVH-FM, the NPR affiliate in Savannah.

A telephone call from nearby Hilton Head Island resident and amateur composer Robert Roebling to Dwight J. Bruce in February 1953 marks the beginning of the Savannah Symphony Orchestra. Bruce, then a Savannah radio station manager and active local organist, was contacted for assistance in arranging a performance of Roebling's composition entitled *Live Oak*, for a small orchestra to be accompanied by dancers. As a group of musicians were assembled and the work presented, the need for an orchestra in the Savannah community became apparent.

Savannah is a rather cosmopolitan community characterized by a pattern of in-migration since the end of World War II. In the early 1950s Savannah saw the influence of new residents, increased financial resources, growing community pride, and a striving for an improved quality of cultural life. Both the restoration of the city's historic district (under the Historic Savannah Foundation, 1955) and the development of the SSO were part of this revitalization. With financial support provided by Roebling and other business and community interest groups, the Savannah Concert Association and Savannah Concert Orchestra were founded.

Under the musical direction of Chauncey Kelley, the ensemble launched its first season during the fall of 1953 with performances presented at the Savannah Municipal Auditorium. Dwight Bruce was the first president of the new orchestra association, a position he held through the 1955–1956 season. Part of the $20,000, 1953–1954 budget paid travel and salary expenses for musicians garnered with the assistance of Henry Sopkin in Atlanta and Hugh Hodgson in Athens. Kelley's appointment proved a wise decision. His association with New York's ABC and NBC orchestras (under Toscanini) provided immediate credibility to the new orchestra program in Savannah.

The orchestra association over the next decade became incorporated as the Savannah Symphony Society, with the orchestra's name changing accordingly. By 1967 the Orchestra Society's Women's Guild (with 500 members) had become one of the more prominent social organizations in the community as it assumed an ever-increasing role in promotions and fundraising. Despite pressures from various interest and support groups to lighten musical programming, the orchestra by 1967 (still under the direction of Chauncey Kelley) had developed a reputation for performing the standard orchestral literature at a consistently high quality level.

The SSO's development from 1967 to 1977 was marked by progress and problems. In 1969 Kelley left the orchestra and was replaced by Ronald Stoffel. In 1970 Stoffel was appointed resident conductor and music director, a post he held until 1972. In 1971 the SSO moved into the Mercer Theater located in the new Savannah Civic Center Complex. As the orchestra's role and importance in the community was expanding, however, financial support was not keeping pace. The artistic and musical direction of the orchestra during this period also was in flux as an effort to find a permanent music director continued.

Facing serious debt in 1977, the Savannah Symphony Society (then operating the orchestra on an annual budget of $135,000) contracted the services of Christian Badea as music director and determined to expand all aspects of the orchestra's operation. An experienced conductor, Badea was the 1983–1984 principal guest conductor of the New Orleans Philharmonic,* and is resident conductor of the Spoleto Festivals both in Italy and Charleston, South Carolina.

The 1977 debt has been retired and the budget increased to $1 million for the 1983–1984 season. Other developments since 1977 include an expansion in the size of the core orchestra, lengthening of the symphony season, an increase in the schedule of concert programs, and the addition of a resident conductor to the orchestra staff.

The sound of the SSO is well-disciplined, exciting, and brilliant. Badea recruited a full-time core orchestra made up of young-artist-level professionals, augmented on a need basis by professional musicians from throughout the state and region, all of whom are auditioned. Given the technical standards and energy level that characterized Badea's conducting, it is not surprising that the performance level and musical quality of the SSO is at once technically uncompromised and stylistically inspired. The sound of the SSO has been similar to that of other important orchestras in the country under the baton of Christian Badea. In 1985, Badea left the SSO after previously assuming duties as the music director of the Columbus (Ohio) Symphony.* Philip Greenberg has been appointed as the SSO's new music director.

CHRONOLOGY OF MUSIC DIRECTORS: Chauncey Kelley, 1953–1969. Ronald Stoffel, 1969–1972. Michael Charry, 1973–1974. George Trautwein, 1974–1977. Christian Badea, 1977–1985. Philip Greenberg 1985-present.

BIBLIOGRAPHY: Extensive interviews with the following former and current SSO directors, conductors, and administrators: Dwight J. Bruce, Dorothy W. Courington, Helen Downing, Michael Luxner, Roger A. Malfatti, Marge Mazo, Barbara Page, Dr. Peter Scardino, and Dr. and Mrs. Herbert L. Windom. SSO scrapbooks (Savannah Symphony Orchestra Society).

ACCESS: Savannah Symphony Orchestra, 309 E. York Street, P.O. Box 9505, Savannah, GA 31412. (912) 236–9536. Patricia F. Saseen, General Manager.

RALPH E. VERRASTRO

Hawaii _____

HONOLULU (762,565)

Honolulu Symphony Orchestra (Rg)

A performance season comprising nearly 150 concerts on six of the seven inhabited islands of an ocean archipelago makes the Honolulu Symphony Orchestra unique among American orchestras. In addition to its twenty neighbor-island concerts, it offers a large number of performances on the home island of Oahu: 12 pairs of regular concerts of classical music; a unique series of 10 concerts entitled "Music on the Light Side" including jazz, popular, Hawaiian, and other ethnic music as well as classical music; and a Summer Starlight Festival of four pops concerts. It also presents 10 free community concerts, 58 full orchestral youth concerts, and 240 perform-ances in Hawaii's schools by smaller ensembles of orchestra members. Sev-eral chamber music groups consist primarily of HSO musicians: the Spring Wind Quintet, the Honolulu Brass Quintet, and the Galliard String Quartet. The HSO cooperates in joint performances with other performing groups such as the Hawaii Opera Theater and the Hawaii Youth Symphony.

The HSO is governed by a 35-member Board of Directors and advisory Board of Governors. Reporting to the Board of Directors are the music director, assistant conductor, and executive director, who supervises an administrative staff of 15. The Board hires 57 full-time professional musi-cians, nine of whom belong to minority groups, in part a reflection of Hawaii's multiracial population. It also hires as many as 30 musicians part-time, depending on the program. Full-time players are selected by auditions heard by the music director and an audition committee at the end of the season, first in Honolulu, then in Los Angeles, Chicago, and New York.

During the 1982–1983 season its revenues of about $2.9 million were drawn from ticket sales, grants from the State of Hawaii, the City and County of Honolulu, the National Endowment for the Arts, a number of local foundations, and contributions from corporations, individuals, and various concert presenters. Support organizations include the Women's Association and the Symphony Guild. The Musicians' Union and a Musicians' Committee meet to consider contract negotiations and personnel relations. Both the music director and assistant conductor are responsible for program selection; they are assisted in their decisions by a program committee of two musicians, key staff members, and a Board member.

The HSO traces its beginnings to a men's social club, the Honolulu Symphony Society (HSS), founded in the early twentieth century. The HSS was not, however, the first such organization in Honolulu. Reference to a Honolulu Amateur Musical Society benefit concert for the then newly founded Queen's Hospital is cited in the June 2, 1859, *Pacific Commercial Advertiser*; a "symphony club" consisting of 14 pieces was founded by Auguste J.-B. Marques in 1881, but dissention among its members caused its dissolution in 1884; in 1899 an amateur orchestra of 23 pieces was associated with the YMCA; it played for charitable and other entertainments. These three groups preceded the HSS, which adopted a constitution on August 30, 1902, that aimed "to encourage the cultivation of the art of music and to promote sociability among its members." The emphasis was at first on sociability; many of the approximately 60 early members played no instrument. Gaston J. Boisse, a cornetist in the early days of the HSS, remembered that the members especially looked forward to beer after rehearsals. "We used to put away a good deal 'til they began to charge a nickel a glass for it," he said in a 1941 interview.

On October 11, 1902, the HSS held a musicale and smoker for the captain and officers of the S.M.S. Cormoran, a German cruiser. The heavy representation of German and Austrian composers on the program was no doubt in part due to the nationality of the honored guests, but also probably a reflection of the preferences of the first music director, German-educated Professor F. A. Ballaseyus, instructor of music at Oahu College (later Punahou School). "Good music should be cultivated and find a place of refuge in this desert of musical barbarism and indolence," he is supposed to have said. If he was serious, his pronouncement would not have endeared him to members of the HSS. His resignation in January 1903 directly followed a concert given December 27, 1902, announced in the *Advertiser* as "ladies' night in [the Society's] cosy clubhouse on Punchbowl [an extinct volcano in Honolulu]." Like many early concerts of the HSS, this one was probably not open to the public.

An announcement of the May 2, 1903, concert at the Hawaiian Opera House in the *Advertiser* called it the first concert of the HSS, probably meaning that it was the first one open to the public at large. Early programs of the HSS frequently offered a variety of solo ensemble offerings in addition to symphonic presentations. One extraordinary concert on February 4, 1905, included six orchestral numbers, solos by a guitarist and a cellist, several songs, a recitation, a "burlesque of hypnotism," and a raconteur who regaled the audience with several stories.

In 1903, 1,000 persons attended a lawn concert held on the grounds of the J. B. Castle home in Waikiki, the present location of the Elks Club. In 1904 the HSS moved to more commodious quarters at Haalelea Lawns, located on Hotel Street opposite the Iolani Palace grounds. A rapid turnover in music directors characterized the early years; concerts were given at irregular intervals by performers ranging in number from 20 to 30. Wind and brass players were usually scarce; a pianist or organist is sometimes listed among the personnel in early newspaper accounts of concerts, perhaps to fill out what must have been a rather thin musical texture.

A long period of relative inactivity for the HSS began in 1909. One of the last concerts given before World War I, on May 25, 1914, included 36 orchestra personnel. Members of the Hawaiian Band, later known as the Royal Hawaiian Band, still active today, were present at this concert as guests of the HSS. The Band, which gave frequent concerts, was far better known to the public in Honolulu than the HSS. Its director, Henri Berger, who conducted it from 1875 to 1915, was the outstanding personality in concert life in Honolulu during these years.

Honolulu was not ready for a modern symphony orchestra until 1924, when the HSS, reorganized after 10 years of inactivity, hired a Norwegian composer/conductor, Alf Hurum, as musical director. During 1924–1925 Hurum directed about 60 musicians in six twilight concerts before the regular evening film at the new Princess Theater on Fort Street. According to HSS records, professional players were paid $2.50 a rehearsal and $5.00 a concert. Hurum programmed a considerable number of compositions by Scandinavian composers including himself, Grieg, Sibelius, Johan Svendsen, Ole Olsen, and others.

Rex Dunn, a violist in the 1924–1925 orchestra, was hired to replace Hurum as musical director in 1925. During the 1926–1927 season the HSS offered him $2,000 to conduct the four concerts given. Arthur Brooke, formerly with the Boston Symphony Orchestra,* conducted the orchestra during 1928–1931. Looking forward to an all-Wagner concert in late 1929, he told an interviewer, "Wagner is perhaps the only composer whose music can fill an entire concert without becoming monotonous." He must have changed his mind, since he included compositions of other composers among the three by Wagner on the second concert of the season, given December 11, 1929. During Brooke's tenure youth concerts, later to become the focus of the educational efforts of the HSS, were given for the first time.

In 1932 Fritz B. Hart, a composer, conductor, and colleague of such British composers as Gustav Holst and Ralph Vaughan Williams, took over the directorship of the HSO after several years as director of the Melbourne Conservatory and Melbourne Symphony Orchestra in Australia; he remained director of the HSO until his death in 1949. In his concerts he included compositions by many British composers such as Delius, Edward German, Dame Ethel Smith, Granville Bantock, and Samuel Coleridge-Taylor, as well as his own compositions and those of Holst and Vaughan Williams. The December 7, 1941, attack on Pearl Harbor brought HSO concerts to a halt, but they resumed in 1942. Since 60% of the players were military personnel, it was sometimes necessary to postpone concerts until the musicians were able to leave their posts. Because of the curfew requiring civilians to be off the streets at an early hour, afternoon concerts were the rule; they were given in McKinley High School Auditorium.

During the 1949–1950 season three guest conductors were invited to appear with the HSO, which was selecting a new music director. The HSS chose the Hungarian composer/conductor George Barati. During the same season a full-time manager was hired and a volunteer group, the Women's Association, was organized. During Barati's tenure the season was expanded to include a Neighbor-Island Tour program, a decision which earned the HSO national publicity. In 1964 the concerts were moved to their present location, what is now called the Neal Blaisdell Center Concert Hall, which seats 2,107 persons. Barati stressed scores of progressive twentieth-century composers in his concerts to a greater extent than had been usual before, with compositions by Stravinsky, Bartók, and twentieth-century American composers whose works had not yet been heard live in Honolulu.

Further expansion of services occurred under the directorship of Robert LaMarchina, who followed Barati. A program of free community concerts, the summer Starlight Festival Series, and a pops series were begun. The present music director, Donald Johanos, has provided the HSO with excellent leadership during the difficult economic times of recent years. Under his direction, the HSO has offered a larger variety of concerts to appeal to a broader base of listeners. A unique series of concerts begun during 1982–1983 called "Music on the Light Side" included light classics, ballet, jazz, popular, Hawaiian and other ethnic music, as well as classical music in its offerings. For the 1984–1985 season, unusual stage lighting and decoration, displays of ethnic art, and the serving of ethnic food at intermission were planned as part of this series.

The present assistant conductor, Henry Miyamura, has ably continued the extensive educational program of the HSS that reaches over 100,000 school-age children on Oahu and five neighbor islands. Each spring, elementary- and secondary-school students (140 in 1984) audition for spots as soloists with the HSO in 22 youth concerts. Currently, 26 youth scholarships are offered to enable students to study privately with members of the HSO.

Like many U.S. orchestras, the HSO was plagued by financial problems in the 1970s and 1980s. To meet rising expenses the Board of Directors felt compelled to borrow money and eventually to spend from its endowment, drastically reducing it from $1.5 million in the 1970s to $300,000 in 1980. Recently, sound financial planning, grants, and donations have offset deficits, and the HSO was able to end the 1982–1983 season with a small surplus. The HSO has succeeded in meeting the challenges that faced all U.S. symphony orchestras in the 1970s and 1980s and looks forward to bringing good music to the people of Hawaii in the years to come.

CHRONOLOGY OF MUSIC DIRECTORS: F. A. Ballaseyus, 1902. W. F. Jocher, 1903–1904. Gerard Barton, 1904. Auguste J.-B. Marques, 1904. Carl Busch, 1905. Joseph H. Stockton, 1905–1906. R. Rudland Bode, 1906–1908. W. K. Vincent, 1910. Carl Miltner, 1912–1914. (Disbanded, 1914–1924.) Alf Hurum, 1924–1925. Rex Dunn, 1925–1928. Arthur Brooke, 1928–1931. Fritz Hart, 1932–1949. George Barati, 1950–1967. Robert LaMarchina, 1967–1978. Donald Johanos, 1978-present.

BIBLIOGRAPHY: Interviews with Henry Adams and Henry Miyamura, 1984. Leon H. Burton, "The Honolulu Symphony Orchestra: Its Educational Contributions and Suggestions for the Future," Diss., Columbia University, 1963. *Evening Bulletin*, 1902–1912. *Hawaiian Star*, 1902–1912. *Honolulu Advertiser*, 1921-present. *Honolulu Star Bulletin*, 1912-present. *Pacific Commercial Advertiser*, 1859–1921. Lois Schenck, *A History of the Honolulu Symphony Society* (Honolulu: Honoluluy Symphony Orchestra, c. 1975) (pamphlet). A book about the history of the HSO by Robert E. Potter, Leon H. Burton, and Dale E. Hall is in preparation.

ACCESS: Honolulu Symphony Orchestra, 1000 Bishop Street, Suite 901, Honolulu, HI 96813. (808) 537–6171. Howard W. Grant, Executive Director. Henry Adams, Director of Communications and Marketing.

DALE E. HALL

Idaho ————————————————

BOISE (173,036)

Boise Philharmonic Orchestra (Mt)

The Boise Philharmonic Orchestra has its origin in the old "Boise Orchestra" begun as a sometime musical venture in 1887. Since then it has persevered to become a modern symphony orchestra of 80 performers with a well-established staff and structure. The official organization of the orchestra began with the formation of its Board of Directors in 1953 and the subsequent engagement in 1960 of its first full-time conductor, Jacques Brourman.

The orchestra currently gives six subscription concerts, occasional pops and run-out concerts in Idaho or Eastern Oregon communities, children's concerts, and a large Christmas concert. The conductor, Daniel Stern, is also music director of the Boise Opera Company, and players from the Philharmonic form the orchestra for these productions. A corollary ensemble, the Treasure Valley Youth Orchestra, is conducted by the Philharmonic's principal cellist, Ned Johnson. This orchestra sponsors an annual concerto contest, and the Philharmonic itself has an annual Young Artists Competition. In the 1984–1985 season the orchestra moved to new quarters in the newly completed Morrison Center for the Performing Arts, a hall large enough (2,030 seats) to allow the return to single local performances of each subscription concert. Stern describes it as "ideal in size and acoustics as an orchestral concert hall." Both the shell and the auditorium area are equipped with tunable panels designed by the acoustical planners Paoletti and Lewitz.

The center of a significant but geographically isolated metropolitan area, Boise is a perhaps unique setting for a professional American symphony orchestra. The nearest comparable cities are at least 300 miles away, necessitating that all the orchestra's regularly performing musicians must reside in the immediate area. One result is a strong sense of community involvement among the musicians; another is the orchestra's central position in the community's cultural life.

While most players are engaged on a per-service basis, full-time contracts retain a nucleus of principal performers, who also provide chamber music and solo recitals under Symphony auspices. A chamber orchestra also utilizes this nucleus, augmented by other regular members of the orchestra.

A Board of Directors appoints the general manager and the music director, who jointly conduct the actual business of the orchestra. The 1983–1984 budget was $340,000, 60% of which was raised from subscriptions or other earned income, the rest coming from gifts, grants, or other sources. The Idaho Commission for the Arts has been of significant aid in this respect.

Conductor Daniel Stern has characterized the mission of the BPO's repertoire as follows:

1. Education: To present a logical series of significant music to its audience. Much of this music may be new to many Boise patrons, if not to the concert world as such. For example, Bach's tricentennial in 1984–1985 was observed by programming a different Brandenburg Concerto in each subscription concert.

2. Museum: Our cultural institutions must serve as repositories of the great ideas of the past as well as the present. The bulk of the Philharmonic's repertoire fulfills this function.

3. Entertainment: The Boise Philharmonic activities admittedly serve as a high-level type of entertainment for the community, with emphasis on the "creation" aspect of recreation.

CHRONOLOGY OF MUSIC DIRECTORS: Jacques Brourman, 1960–1967. Mathys Abas, 1967–1974. Daniel Stern, 1974-present.

BIBLIOGRAPHY: Interview with BPO Music Director Daniel Stern. Boise Philharmonic Association, *News*.

ACCESS: Boise Philharmonic Association, 205 N. 10th St., Boise, ID 83702. (208) 344–7849. Michael Winter, General Manager.

FLOYD PETERSON

Illinois _____

CHICAGO (7,103,624)

Chicago Symphony Orchestra (Mj)

It is traditional to divide the history of the Chicago Symphony Orchestra into three periods: the Thomas-Stock era (1891–1942), the middle years (1943–1953), and finally the Reiner-Martinon-Solti period (1953-present). The orchestra was founded and directed by Germans who created a strong German tradition. The middle period was marked by comparative instability (perhaps mirroring the mood of the nation during World War II). Both Reiner and Solti were Hungarian, but with an affinity for German repertoire. Both gained a reputation for insisting on technical perfection. It is during this last period that the CSO came to be internationally known for its virtuosity.

Theodore Thomas, the founder of the orchestra, was acknowledged the leading conductor of his day and was named music director of the Philadelphia centennial of 1876. He was a tireless apostle of symphonic music with a particular regard for the Beethoven symphonies. An ardent supporter of the new music of his day, he championed Richard Strauss, who himself conducted the Chicago Orchestra in 1902.

The Theodore Thomas Orchestra had toured extensively as an ensemble of the highest calibre, but by the end of the century it was a financial failure. In 1889 Charles Norman Fay, the brother of Thomas's second wife, Rose, invited Thomas to direct a permanent orchestra. Thomas gave the famous reply, "I would go to hell if they gave me a permanent orchestra." The first concerts of the Chicago Orchestra were given in the celebrated Auditorium Theater, designed by Louis Sullivan, on October 16 and 17, 1891.

Thomas felt his orchestra would never be secure and never have a full impact on Chicago until it had its own home. In 1902–1903 Thomas gave his ultimatum: either the orchestra would be given a home or he would leave. Orchestra Hall was completed in 1904. Although Thomas's health was failing and the hall incomplete, the opening concert was given on December 14, 1904. Included on the program were Beethoven's Symphony No. 5 and Strauss's *Death and Transfiguration*, works that symbolized Thomas's personal triumph over adversity.

Thomas was responsible for introducing symphonic and choral music of the highest calibre to much of the United States. He burned with a missionary's zeal. He placed the advanced repertoire early in the program, followed by lighter numbers, so that the audience would stay to the end. His conducting style was unobtrusive, disciplined, and clearly in the German tradition. He is said to be the first conductor to insist on unified bowing. In addition, he lowered the pitch standard of the orchestra about 9/16 of a tone. Although as a young man he had the typical romantic practice of doubling and adding voices and instruments to the music written before the romantic era, he later came to realize that the conductor must be faithful to the intentions of the composer, regardless of the style. At various times he programmed historical concerts to show the changes of instrumental outlook. The important musicologist Bernard Ziehn noted that Thomas was the only conductor of the day to interpret correctly baroque ornamentation.

Frederick Stock had played as violinist in the Cologne orchestra under Brahms, Tchaikovsky, and Strauss. In Chicago he worked under Thomas as violist and associate conductor beginning with the 1895–1896 season. After Thomas's death in 1905 Stock was named acting music director while the trustees looked for a permanent successor to Thomas. The candidates included such notables as Felix Mottl, Felix Weingartner, and Arthur Nikisch. However, because of Stock's long association with Thomas and his apparent gifts as conductor, he was chosen permanent conductor on April 11, 1905— a position he held until 1942.

The repertoire of his early concerts was conservative, but gradually he began introducing newer French and German compositions. During the 1907–1908 season Stock gave a performance of Mahler's Symphony No. 5, a work that met with some adverse criticism. In 1909 the young Rachmaninoff conducted his *Isle of the Dead* and acted as soloist in his Piano Concerto No. 2. A few years later Stock gave the 1913 American premiere of Schoenberg's then controversial and difficult *Five Pieces for Orchestra*, Op. 16.

In 1918 Stock, not yet a citizen, took a temporary leave of absence because of the strong, wartime anti-German feelings. When he returned in 1919, he instituted youth concerts that he himself conducted in grandfatherly fashion. Also, he asked the trustees to establish a pension fund for the orchestra players. Stock founded a training orchestra for younger players to train them for participation in the CSO. This last group has come to be known as the Civic Orchestra and presently has a vital season of its own. Another important group, the Women's Association, came into being with the purpose of fostering social and educational activities to benefit the orchestra. During Stock's tenure the question of the CSO's name became a matter of concern, and after several changes it finally became "the Chicago Symphony Orchestra, founded by Theodore Thomas."

During his long term, Stock became a venerable figure to both his public and orchestra. He continued the solid German tradition of Thomas but with the introduction in the middle part of his career of new repertoire. Unlike Thomas, he never changed from an essentially romantic attitude to the score, even allowing some unorthodox changes in Ravel's *Daphnis and Chloé*. By today's standards, Stock's technique would perhaps seem imprecise; the discipline of the CSO suffered, especially in the period just before World War II.

When Stock died unexpectedly in 1942, the trustees were faced with the difficult task of finding a successor to this most stable of conductors. Probably influenced by the anti-German sentiments of the time, they chose a man of Belgian heritage, Désiré Defauw (Music Director, 1943–1947). Like Thomas, he had a career as a solo violinist, and he had won acclaim as a proponent of modern music while director of the New Symphony Orchestra of London. In addition, he had been praised by such masters as Richard Strauss and Ravel.

Decisions and opinions regarding the CSO became at this time increasingly influenced by the brilliant critic of the *Chicago Tribune*, Claudia Cassidy. Cassidy was and is known for her powerful use of the English language. She enjoyed the support of Col. Robert McCormick, the founder of the paper. McCormick had not been consulted about the decision to bring Defauw to the orchestra, and Cassidy's increasingly caustic reviews may have reflected this.

Defauw is probably the most difficult conductor to evaluate in the CSO's history. His ambitions for the CSO were immense, and he had a genuine regard for modern music. He introduced Webern's *Passicaglia* to Chicago and brought Kodály there to conduct his own *Peacock Variations*.Several rather obscure works of Hindemith and Milhaud were also given performances at this time. However, audiences objected to Defauw's programming, and the orchestra felt he was out of touch with the German tradition. Ticket sales began to drop—a clear sign of public disapproval. For these as well as personal reasons, Defauw resigned and returned to Europe.

Several recordings (such as the one with Claudio Arrau of the Strauss *Burleske*), many reviews, as well as reports of some who attended his concerts suggest that Defauw could give dynamic performances. He deserves a better reputation than history has given him.

Artur Rodzinski (music director, 1947–1948), the protégé of Toscanini, had a brief but stormy career with the CSO. He had a reputation as a vital opera conductor. In 1947 he conducted the CSO with Kirsten Flagstad in a landmark performance of *Tristan and Isolde* at the Civic Opera House for the pension fund. Instead of making a profit, the production incurred a $30,000 deficit. This marked the beginning of Rodzinski's troubles with the public. Although he enjoyed the enthusiastic support of Cassidy, relations with the trustees were strained. He was charged with preferring operas to symphonic music, with making last-minute changes in programs, and with having plans that would continue to result in deficits. Although such celebrities as Koussevitzky came to his defense, Rodzinsky left for Europe at the end of his first season.

During the years 1948–1950 a thorough search was conducted for a new director. Although Wilhelm Furtwängler, the great conductor of the Berlin Philharmonic, was a leading contender, his having remained at his post through the war became a barrier to his acceptance. The trustees once again chose a conductor of non-German descent, this time in the person of Rafael Kubelík, who was educated as a violinist and had an impressive career as a conductor, principally in Czechoslovakia. In 1950 he was named the new music director, a post he held only until 1953.

Like Defauw, he was much interested in contemporary music, especially by composers living in America. During his tenure he gave the premieres of such works as Tcherepnin's Symphony No. 2 and Harris's Symphony No. 7. He had an affinity for his compatriot composers and introduced Chicago audiences to many works of Smetana and Dvořák. Kubelík was the first CSO conductor to appreciate fully the modern media and their potential to increase the orchestra's impact. Under his direction the CSO began giving television concerts on WENR-TV. In 1951 he made four historic recordings using a single Telefunken condenser microphone, that are to this day considered sonically brilliant.

At first he enjoyed the support of Cassidy, but later her reviews became increasingly critical. In the opinion of some, he was too young, too inexperienced to be a permanent conductor of the CSO. Nonetheless, he continues to have warm relations with the CSO and frequently acts as a welcomed guest conductor.

The period following 1953 marks the beginning of the CSO's international reputation. It was a time during which the orchestra grew from a local to an international cultural institution, from a fine orchestra to a great one.

The next choice for music director was Fritz Reiner, who had a term of ten years, 1953–1963. Reiner, educated as a virtuoso pianist at the Academy of Music in Budapest, had an early association with the conductor Arthur Nikisch, resulting in an economical conducting style with a special use of the eyes to indicate entrances. He held important posts as conductor of the Cincinnati Symphony* and the Pittsburgh Symphony,* and as professor of conducting at the Curtis Institute, where his students included Leonard Bernstein and Walter Hendl. When he came to Chicago, Reiner set out to create a brilliant orchestra through increased discipline and the addition of key, virtuoso first-chair players, many of whom are still with the orchestra. The results of his work were quickly felt. Subscription sales went up 16.8% and single-ticket sales 11.5%. A recording contract was signed with RCA-Victor, and Reiner gave regular television concerts on WGN-TV.

In 1957 Reiner asked Margaret Hillis, the well-known choral director, to create the Chicago Symphony Chorus, the first choral ensemble in the United States permanently associated with a major orchestra. This ensemble allowed the CSO to feature such masterpieces as Handel's *Israel in Egypt* and Beethoven's *Missa Solemnis*. Hillis still continues her work with the chorus, now considered one of the finest in the country and one that gives the Symphony's season special lustre.

Because of failing health, Reiner vetoed a much-discussed European tour for the summer of 1959. In 1960 he had a heart attack, but returned the following year to lead, from a rehearsal stool, a concert featuring spectacular renditions of Wagner overtures. Many impressive plans, including a Met revival of *Götterdämmerung*, were cut short because of Reiner's death on November 13, 1963.

Reiner was above all a disciplinarian. He was both an orchestra builder and teacher whose style was cutting and laconic. He remained aloof from the orchestra members, who both respected and feared him. His vest-pocket beat was almost imperceptible, and his usual manner, save for the biggest climaxes, was immobile. He could be difficult even with composers whom he had commissioned to write works. For example, he not only asked Alexander Tcherepnin to change the title of a work originally conceived as a symphony to "divertimento," but also suggested a large cut in the coda of the last movement (this work is now known as the Divertimento for Orchestra, Op. 90).

Although he introduced much Hindemith, Prokofiev, and Bartók (for whose music he had special affinity), he shied away from the serialists. After giving single performances of Stravinsky's *Agon* and Webern's *Six Pieces*, Op. 10, he decided he had little understanding of the style.

In general, Reiner emphasized clarity of texture, form, and proportion— qualities that allowed him to give some wonderful interpretations of Haydn and Mozart. He left the Chicago Symphony Orchestra as precise as a surgical instrument.

During the last years of Reiner's tenure, a number of guest conductors shared the podium. Among these was Jean Martinon, who in 1962 conducted his own Symphony No. 3 (*Hymne à la vie*). He was to become the next music director, from 1963 to 1968. Born in Lyon, France, Martinon studied composition with Roussel and conducting with Munch. Brilliantly gifted and prolific, Martinon is the only conductor of the CSO to have been an eminent composer.

Martinon's tenure was marked by bitter difficulties. He was first praised, then criticized by Cassidy. His concept of an orchestra, with a French preference for bright colors, elegance, and subtle connections between the choirs, was at variance with the CSO's German heritage. Despite differences with some members of the orchestra, his manner was gentle; his approach was that of a fine composer rather than an orchestral builder.

In 1963 Martinon brought the CSO on an eastern tour, followed in ensuing years by several further national tours, earning high praise from important critics. He also conducted the CSO in a number of contemporary music concerts at the University of Chicago, sponsored by the Rockefeller Foundation. Further, he organized a series of chamber concerts as well as a June festival of baroque music, featuring reduced ensembles from the CSO. As part of the 75th anniversary season, Martinon conducted a number of premieres, including his own Symphony No. 4 (*Altitudes*).

Despite these accomplishments, he faced increasing opposition to his policies. There was, as is usually the case during conflict, a decrease in ticket sales and a consequent decline in the prestige of the orchestra. In 1968 Martinon resigned to return to Europe. Whenever he was questioned, Martinon spoke of the CSO with the highest praise and always stated that being its conductor was the most important position of his life.

In some ways Martinon's career paralleled that of Defauw. There was not only a striking similarity of appearance but also of interest in French contemporary music and method of handling the orchestra. Perhaps both experienced difficulties for the same reasons. Certainly both contributed more to the CSO than is generally recognized.

With the resignation of Martinon it was apparent that the CSO needed a powerful figure to continue the brilliant Reiner tradition. Sir Georg Solti was chosen to bring the CSO to its full potential. Born in 1912 in Budapest, he early manifested pianistic talent. He later studied at the Liszt Academy under Bartók and Kodály. At 18 he became a coach at the Budapest Opera, where in 1938 he made his debut as a conductor. The development of his career was hindered by the political events of the time. On the very day that Solti was making his Budapest debut, Hitler was marching into Vienna, and Europe stood at the brink of war. In the 1950s Solti conducted several important operas at Chicago's Lyric Opera, including *Die Walküre* and *Salome*. He conducted the CSO for the first time in a Ravinia concert of 1954. Finally, in 1969, Sir Georg was appointed music director to the CSO, with Carlo Maria Giulini as his principal guest conductor.

Like Reiner, Solti is a disciplinarian, though of kinder sort. At rehearsal he is extremely well organized, with a sense of where problems might occur. His conducting is marked by rhythmic drive, dramatic tension, and virtuosity. He uses the score in performance to assure absolute security. Again like Reiner, he is at home with such German masters as Beethoven and Wagner. He has also commissioned many major works, including Tippett's Symphony No. 4 (for the 1976 bicentennial) and, most recently, Lutoslawski's monumental Symphony No. 3 (1983).

In many strange ways, Reiner's and Solti's careers parallel each other. Both were virtuoso pianists educated at the same school in Budapest. Both were major opera conductors who turned later in their careers to symphonic music, conducting with the CSO as their medium. Both had an affinity for the same kind of repertoire. Ultimately, both brought tremendous discipline to the CSO, Reiner, in a sense, having prepared the way for Solti.

The Italian tradition of *Cantabile* used by Carlo Maria Giulini and more recently Claudio Abbado (named principal guest conductor in 1982) has acted as a foil to Solti's energy. For Giulini the long phrase and singing line were more important than clarity of detail. Rhythm was handled vocally rather than instrumentally, with major works having the emotional impact of a great aria.

Under Solti the CSO has come to be Chicago's leading cultural institution. Its popular appeal has grown too. The orchestra has won more Grammy awards than any other orchestra and has been hailed by *Time Magazine* as the world's greatest orchestra. In 1971 Solti and Giulini took the CSO on a six-week European tour, surprisingly its first international visit. European tours have occurred at regular intervals since, most recently during the fall of 1981. A successful Japanese tour was held in 1977. Over 400 stations broadcast the 39 concerts of the CSO here in the United States, with overseas broadcasters receiving a shorter series of 13 concerts.

The dramatic growth of the CSO image is, of course, the work of many, but two men have been particularly responsible: John Edwards, the former manager (who has earned the title, "dean of American orchestral managers"), and Louis Sudler, the important Chicago real estate developer, who was president of the Board of Trustees from 1966 to 1971 and chairman from 1971 to 1976. Sudler had the vision necessary for the economic stability and growth of the CSO and was responsible for bringing Sir Georg and Edwards together.

Orchestra Hall is the permanent home of the CSO and presently seats 2,566 persons. It is difficult to attribute the original design to any one person, though Theodore Thomas and Daniel Burnham, the noted Chicago architect and one of the planners of the city's lake front, seem to have cooperated closely on the venture. Ever since its inaugural performance in 1904, the hall has been the subject of renovations, alterations, and various other schemes to improve its acoustics, most notably the extensive renovations of 1966. None was satisfactory, however, until 1981, when the installation of a new Moeller pipe organ catalyzed new acoustical remodelling and the installation of modern media facilities.

During its regular concert season, which runs from the end of September to the beginning of June, the CSO gives about 100 concerts in 12 different series. In addition, it gives 10 concerts in Milwaukee on Monday evenings. During the summer the CSO is present at the Ravinia Festival as its principal orchestra. The annual budget for the calendar years 1982 and 1983 averaged about $15 million, a large part of which comes from such fund-raising devices as the WFMT marathon (which raised $550,000 in 1984), corporate sources, and individual donors.

The CSO is involved in a number of outreach programs. Six concerts from the regular season are made available to area university students at reduced prices and are preceded by symposia of leading artists and musicologists. Twenty-four youth concerts, under the direction of Henry Mazer, the associate conductor, focus on various sections of the orchestra or on different periods of history. "Kaleidoscope" and "Very Special Promenade" concerts are meant for the very young, while "Music is the Message" concerts are geared for high school students. Many of these programs are presented in area schools. Additionally, there are programs designed for handicapped children and senior citizens. Chamber concerts, the famous Allied Arts Series, and programs by the Civic Orchestra under Gordon Peters further enrich the season.

During its long history the CSO has used different seating arrangements. Photographs taken during the Thomas era show the double basses and cellos across the back in a straight line with the cellos in front of the basses. The first violins were placed in the front, stage left, while the second violins were to the right. At present a more conventional arrangement is used, though some guest conductors, notably Stokowski, have experimented with alternatives.

Because of the orchestra's long acquaintance with the standard literature, Sir Georg sometimes rehearses familiar works by working only on problematic sections. Sectional rehearsals are reserved only for newer, more complex scores. Many composers have remarked how quickly and accurately the CSO has learned even their most difficult works. In general, the sonorous character of the CSO is German with an overall effect of great power and depth. No one who has heard the CSO can forget the overwhelming majesty of the brass section, the precision of its strings, or the clearly defined colors of its winds.

RECORDING HISTORY AND SELECTIVE DISCOGRAPHY: The CSO was the first American orchestra to record under its regular conductor. On May 1 and 2, 1916, Stock recorded 20 orchestra selections at Aeolian Hall in New York for RCA-Victor. Included was a performance of Mendelssohn's Wedding March from his *Midsummer Night's Dream*. The CSO did not record again until 1925, when a substantial number of works, including complete symphonies, were again recorded for Victor. The orchestra has made significant recordings under all of its conductors from Stock on. The orchestra has recorded for RCA-Victor, Angel, Mercury, London-Decca, Philips, CBS, and Deutsche Grammophon. A list of CSO recordings, 1916–1983, is available from the CSO office.

Bartók, Concerto for Orchestra (Solti): London/Decca L-LDR–71036. Bartók, *Hungarian Sketches* and *Music for Strings, Percussion, and Celesta* (Reiner): RCA AGL–4087. Beethoven, Symphony No. 9 (Solti): London/Decca L-CSP–8, 9. Del Tredici, *Final Alice* (Hendricks/Solti): London/Decca L-LDR–71018. Haydn, *The Creation*

(Solti): London/Decca 2L-LDR–72011. Mahler, Symphony No. 4 in G (Della Casa/ Reiner): RCA AGL–1333. Mennin, Symphony No. 7 and *Piano Concerto* (Buketoff/ Martinon): CRI 5–399. Schubert, Symphony No. 9 (Giulini): DGG–2530–882. Strauss, *Also Sprach Zarathustra*, *Don Juan*, and *Till Eulenspiegel* (Solti): London/Decca L-CS–6978.

CHRONOLOGY OF MUSIC DIRECTORS: Theodore Thomas, 1891–1905. Frederick Stock, 1905–1942. (Guest conductors, 1942–1943.) Désiré Defauw, 1943–1947. Artur Rodzinski, 1947–1948. (Guest conductors, 1948–1950.) Rafael Kubelík, 1950–1953. Fritz Reiner, 1953–1963. Jean Martinon, 1963–1968. Sir Georg Solti, 1969-present.

BIBLIOGRAPHY: Chicago Symphony Orchestra, Junior Governing Board (Nancy Abshire, Chairman), Oral History Committee (a large project of collecting oral histories in preparation for the CSO centennial of 1991). William Barry Furlong, *Season with Solti: A Year in the Life of the Chicago Symphony* (New York: MacMillan, 1974). Philip Hart, *Orpheus in the New World* (New York. Norton, 1973). Philo Adams Otis, *The Chicago Symphony Orchestra* (Chicago: Clayton F. Summy, 1924). Helina Rodzinski, *Our Two Lives* (New York: Scribner's, 1976). Rose Fay Thomas, *Memoirs of Theodore Thomas* (New York: Moffat, Yard, 1911). Theodore Thomas, *A Musical Autobiography* (reprint; New York: Da Capo, 1964). Thomas Willis, *The Chicago Symphony Orchestra* (Chicago: Rand McNally, 1974).

ACCESS: Chicago Symphony Orchestra, Orchestra Hall, 220 South Michigan, Chicago, IL 60604. (312) 435–8122. Henry Fogel, General Manager.

ENRIQUE ALBERTO ARIAS

Indiana ———————————————

FORT WAYNE (382,961)

Fort Wayne Philharmonic (Mt)

Located about midway between Indianapolis and Detroit, several hours from any of the major midwestern cultural centers, Fort Wayne has evolved a number of arts organizations. The city supports a Civic Theatre (over 50 years old), a Fine Arts Foundation (the third oldest United Arts Fund in the United States), a ballet company, Historical Society, Cinema Center, Art Museum, and the Philharmonic.

With a subscription series of eight concerts, as well as young people's and pops concerts, the full Fort Wayne Philharmonic runs on a 33-week season. A Philharmonic chamber orchestra also presents children's concerts, and various chamber ensembles—string quartet, brass quintet, woodwind quintet, and harp/percussion trio—travel widely in the region, offering more than 200 performances in schools and similar settings. Philharmonic musicians present other works outside the usual symphonic repertoire in the Philharmonic's recently begun "Spectrum" series. The full-orchestra subscription series (with 2,100 subscribers each year) is performed in the Embassy Theatre, a 2,750-seat 1920s movie palace. The chamber orchestra concerts take place in a Performing Arts Center built in 1971, seating 700 and designed by architect Louis Kahn.

According to the Philharmonic's own typescript history, the first orchestra in Fort Wayne was directed by Emile Bouillet. A pit orchestra at the old Jefferson Theatre, it accompanied vaudeville shows and silent movies. Fort Wayne's Central High School conductor, Gaston Bailhe (also director of the European College of Music), later formed the Fort Wayne Civic Symphony, a community ensemble that provided Fort Wayne's symphonic music until World War II forced it to disband.

The Fort Wayne Philharmonic was formed in 1943 as a professional orchestra and placed under the baton of conductor Hans Schwieger. After leaving his native Germany, Schwieger had served on the music staff of New York's City Center of Music and Art and as conductor of the Southern Symphony Orchestra at Columbia, South Carolina. In the Philharmonic's first, six-program season, radio broadcasts were also initiated.

Schwieger left in 1948 and his replacement, Igor Buketoff, remained for nearly 20 years. Runouts were begun, and educational programs now included both string quartet performances in the schools and youth concerts. Broadcasts on radio and television continued, a new Philharmonic Chorus was founded, and chamber concerts under Buketoff led to the formation of the Fort Wayne Sinfonietta from the parent Philharmonic. Its 26 members concertized in Indiana and neighboring states. When the Ford Foundation grants were awarded in 1966, the Fort Wayne Philharmonic had established sufficient prestige and budget to afford it a $250,000 matching grant soon met by the community. With the receipt of a $1 million gift from the Frank Freimann Charitable Trust in 1984, the endowment fund is now over $2 million.

When Thomas Briccetti, then assistant conductor of the Indianapolis Symphony Orchestra,* began his new appointment as Fort Wayne's music director in 1971, he found an orchestra with enough organizational strength to allow a new period of musical growth. Briccetti resigned at the close of the 1977–1978 season and was succeeded by the orchestra's current music director, Ronald Ondrejka. Ondrejka studied at both the Juilliard and Eastman Schools and has conducted widely in the United States. Before coming to Fort Wayne he was music director of the Santa Barbara Symphony.*

The Fort Wayne Philharmonic is administered by a Board of Directors of 35 persons. The orchestra's 18 full-time musicians and 60 per-service professional musicians are unionized and most reside in the Fort Wayne community. Half the budgeted expenditures for musicians go to the full-timers. The Philharmonic's $700,000 budget for the 1983–1984 season derived from ticket sales, NEA grants, Indiana Arts Commission grants, concert fees, and corporate sponsors. The endowment fund contributes 10–12% of the budget. An active Women's Committee of 350 members raised $40,000 in 1983–1984; they recently gave the orchestra a matched set of Ganter rotary valve trumpets from Germany.

Beginning with Igor Buketoff and continuing with Music Directors Briccetti and Ondrejka, there has been a commitment to modern music. Ondrejka has an affinity for American composers of the 1940s and 1950s and feels responsible to perform them. As a result, the orchestra perceives a growing openness in the audience to music of the twentieth century.

CHRONOLOGY OF MUSIC DIRECTORS: Hans Schwieger, 1944–1948. Igor Buketoff, 1948–1967. James Sample, 1967–1971. Thomas Briccetti, 1971–1978. Ronald Ondrejka, 1978-present.

BIBLIOGRAPHY: Interview with Fort Wayne Philharmonic Managing Director Peter Smith, 1984. "The Fort Wayne Philharmonic" (typescript history), Fort Wayne Philharmonic, 1982–1983.

ACCESS: Fort Wayne Philharmonic Orchestra, 1107 South Harrison Street, Fort Wayne, IN 46802. (219) 424–4134.

MICHAEL J. ESSELSTROM

INDIANAPOLIS (1,160,575)

Indianapolis Symphony Orchestra (Mj)

The Indianapolis Symphony Orchestra, with its home in the capital city of the state of Indiana, played for over 300,000 people in 175 concerts during the 1983–1984 season. The ISO tours Indiana each season and has traveled extensively in the United States. The ISO Great Classics Series comprises various groupings of 18 separate programs offered from October through May on Thursdays, Fridays, and Saturdays. Many are preceded by a free "Words on Music" lecture.

In addition to its traditional concert series, the ISO presents a variety of separate performances: "biergarten" pops concerts, ballets, local festivals, and special events such as "A Classical Splash" with the U.S. Synchronized Swim Team. A series of pairs of pops concerts is offered on Saturday and Sunday evenings under the direction of Pops Music Director Erich Kunzel. The chamber series (the four-concert "Connoisseur Series") is devoted to the works of Bach and Handel in 1984–1985, their 300th birthday year. A new Sunday afternoon series of one-hour family concerts features young soloists and/or programmatic works. A unique aspect of the orchestra's season is a 10-concert sunset "Symphony on the Prairie" summer series at Connor Prairie Pioneer Settlement northeast of Indianapolis. The ISO has an impressive array of educational programs, including, among other things, some 20 informally sited "Lolli-Pop" concerts, more than 30 in-school concerts, eight "Visions" concerts, a young musicians contest, and a young people's art contest in cooperation with the Indianapolis Museum of Fine Arts.

Affiliated musical groups include the 200-member Indianapolis Symphonic Choir, organized in 1937. It is currently directed by John W. Williams, since 1982 a member of the Butler University faculty. Small ensembles including members of the ISO are the Indianapolis Jazz/Rock Ensemble, the Brass Quintet, Sonic Boom (percussion ensemble), Suzuki and Friends (sponsored by Cathedral Arts), the Ronen Chamber Ensemble, and the

Falkner Players (different combinations of instruments organized by Albert Saurini, principal flute).

According to Samuel Siurua's 1961 history of the ISO, the orchestra's formation was hastened by the disbanding of theater orchestras following the development of sound films—a situation compounded by the depression and a local musicians' strike. Dr. Ferdinand Shaefer, a local conductor and violin professor, provided the immediate impetus, rehearsing 60 men and women for their debut as the Indianapolis Symphony Orchestra on November 2, 1930. The musicians, among them both professionals and amateurs, shared in the box office receipts. The orchestra's sustaining organization, the Indiana State Symphony Society, was officially incorporated on May 28, 1931; its funding derived from statewide contributions as well as legislated appropriations, innovative in their day.

By 1936–1937 the orchestra was presenting six concerts with four soloists and two guest conductors, one of whom, Fabien Sevitzky, astonished the critics by demonstrating that the orchestra could play not only with great power but with finesse, subtlety, and fine ensemble as well. After Sevitzky's first concert, ISO supporters felt an increased urgency for a permanent, professional orchestra.

The Russian-born Sevitzky (formerly Koussevitzky) was the nephew of Serge Koussevitzky, who had ordered Fabien's name shortened to avoid confusion between them. After playing in the Warsaw Philharmonic, he joined the Philadelphia Orchestra* in 1923 and by 1925 was organizing and conducting orchestras in the Philadelphia area. In the 1930s he was actively pursuing a conducting career in Boston. Following his coup in Indianapolis, Sevitzky was engaged as the ISO's permanent conductor, and by 1937 the orchestra had an annual budget of $118,000, a reconstituted roster, and professional management.

Now a major orchestra, the ISO presented a 1937 season of 32 concerts at the Murat Theater plus five runouts at state universities. In the same year the orchestra embarked on a series of 10 Mutual Broadcasting System programs, and it would broadcast regularly thereafter. In 1940, Sevitzky became a leader among conductors in aiding the National Sibelius Festival Committee, which was actively soliciting funds to be sent to the composer to help his war-torn compatriots. Meanwhile, the ISO weathered World War II, and by 1946–1947 its season consisted of 36 home concerts and 37 tour concerts in 33 cities.

Sevitzky conducted the orchestra until 1955. From his first season with the ISO, during which he performed music written by 14 American composers, he played an American composition on almost every program. According to discographer Frederick Fellers, Sevitzky's respect for American composers, in this case the New England School (MacDowell, Converse, Foote, and others) was stated in an ISO program book: "It is impossible that we should forget what these men have done." However, according to Siurua, Sevitzky's steadfastness in his support of newer music contributed to disagreements with the Board, and when Sevitzky left in 1955, a season of guest conductors was scheduled in a search for a new music director.

The choice, Izler Solomon, former conductor of the Columbus (Ohio) Philharmonic* and resident conductor of the Buffalo Philharmonic,* was a popular success, and a record-breaking audience heard his first concert in October of 1956. Solomon quickly established a pattern in programming whereby representative works of various periods were juxtaposed. Perhaps with recent ISO history in mind, Solomon limited his programming of contemporary works. In 1963 the orchestra moved from the Murat to the newly completed, 2,182-seat Clowes Memorial Hall at Butler University. Another innovation of Solomon's tenure was programming one "Salute" concert per year. Each was taped under auspices of the Voice of America and broadcast in the country being recognized; a reciprocal "Salute" was then broadcast in Indianapolis.

Following Solomon's retirement in 1975, John Nelson was designated music director of the ISO from a world-spanning field of 14 guest conductors who led the orchestra during the 1974 and 1975 seasons. Internationally recognized since his 1972 Carnegie Hall performance of Berlioz's *Les Troyens*, Nelson went on to debut with major orchestras and opera companies. Prior to his appointment to the ISO, Nelson taught orchestra conducting at the Juilliard School of Music. His years with the ISO have brought it to its present stature among American orchestras, heightened by the critical successes of its recent national tours. The present conducting staff consists of Nelson, Associate Conductor William Henry Curry, Exxon/Arts Endowment Conducting Assistant Stephen Stein, and Sunday Night Pops Music Director Erich Kunzel.

Under Nelson, the Great Classics Series concerts present the traditional literature of the eighteenth through twentieth centuries, with the addition of contemporary and late modern works. The opening composition of the 1984–1985 season was a commissioned work by Ellen Taaffe Zwilich. Other non-traditional works for the same season include *The Great American Symphony* by C. Curtis-Smith, Donald Erb's *Prismatic Variations*, *Music Funebre* by Witold Lutoslowski, *Concertato "Moby-Dick"* by Peter Mennin, and Concerto for Piano and Small Orchestra by William Schuman.

A gift in 1983 by retired ISO horn player Philip Huffman of four Wagner tubas has added to the orchestra's instrument holdings. The matched set of two tenor and two bass instruments was made in Munich, Germany.

In 1984 the ISO moved to its new concert hall, the Circle Theatre (1916) on Monument Circle in downtown Indianapolis. A recent renovation for the ISO's benefit has retained its neoclassical revival interior, which may be unique in Indianapolis. The renovation allows seating for 1,847 and stage accommodations for the entire ISO and full chorus—with a permanent orchestral shell and stage seating for chorus or for additional audience, as conditions require.

There are 60 members on the present Board of Directors of the Indiana State Symphony Society, Inc., and they oversee the operation of the orchestra. The ISO's Women's Committee according to the orchestra, consists of 4,000 members, and is the largest and one of the most active of such groups in the country. The 1983–1984 ISO budget was $5.2 million. Expenses for the musicians' salaries and fringe benefits were 57% of the budget, production was 6%, program and concert expenses 22%, and administration 15%. Ticket sales and concert fees accounted for 27% of the budget, the fund drive 19%, government grants 9%, special grants 19%, and endowment income 26%. A $14.75 million capital gifts campaign for endowments and Circle Theatre renovation was announced on March 30, 1984, including challenge grants of $4 million from the Krannert Charitable Trust and $1 million from the Eli Lilly and Company Foundation.

A four-year contract agreement between the AFM and the Indiana State Symphony Society, Inc., was reached in September of 1982, increasing the 88 full-time ISO musicians' base pay and weeks of employment (to 50 in the fourth year of the contract). Seniority pay differentials as well as improved insurance and pension benefits are also included.

RECORDING HISTORY AND SELECTIVE DISCOGRAPHY: The ISO's first recording was made in 1941 under Sevitzky, and according to Fellers, Sevitzky's own hand operated the press that made the first record. Sevitzky's ISO recorded for Victor and Capitol until 1953. The only commercial recording since is included here. The ISO has donated to the Indianapolis Public Library 118, 78-rpm recordings of its broadcasts from 1939 to 1945.

Indianapolis Symphony Orchestra—Fifty Colorful Years, containing Grieg, *Peer Gynt Suite No. 2* (Sevitzky), Dubensky, *Stephen Foster, Theme Variations and Finale* (Sevitzky), Schubert, Symphony No. 9 in C Major (Solomon), Dvořák, Symphony No. 9 in E Minor *(New World)* (Nelson): RCA Special Products DPL 2–0432 (2 record set).

CHRONOLOGY OF MUSIC DIRECTORS: Ferdinand Schaefer, 1930–1937. Fabien Sevitzky, 1937–1955. Izler Solomon, 1956–1975. John Nelson, 1976-present.

BIBLIOGRAPHY: Interview with ISO Manager of Public Relations Jane Terry, 1984. Frederick Fellers, *The Indianapolis Symphony on Record: A Discography of the Commercial Recordings Conducted by Fabien Sevitzky* (Indianapolis: Indianapolis-Marion County Public Library, 1983). Frederick Fellers, *Radio Broadcasts of the Indianapolis Symphony Orchestra: 1939–1945*. (Indianapolis: Indianapolis-Marion County Public Library, 1982). John Mueller, *The American Symphony Orchestra* (Bloomington: Indiana University Press, 1951). Samuel Wasson Siurua, "History of the Indianapolis Symphony Orchestra," Diss., Indiana University, 1961. Jane Terry, ISO Press Book, 1983–1984.

ACCESS: Indianapolis Symphony Orchestra, 45 Monument Circle, Indianapolis, IN 46204. (317) 635–6355. Robert C. Jones, Executive Director. Jane Terry, Manager of Public Relations.

MICHAEL J. ESSELSTROM

Iowa ───────────────

CEDAR RAPIDS (169,775)

Cedar Rapids Symphony (Mt)

Founded in 1921, the Cedar Rapids Symphony Orchestra has more than 60 years of continuous concert seasons to its credit. The orchestra presents seven pairs of subscription concerts each year as well as pops concerts with popular guest artists and young people's concerts for the area's fourth and seventh grade students. The orchestra also travels throughout Iowa presenting runout concerts sponsored in part by the Iowa Arts Council. More than 25 Iowa communities have been thus served. Concerts have also been sponsored by local organizations for private performances.

In 1976 the orchestra moved into its first permanent home, the elegant Paramount Theatre for the Performing Arts. Built in 1928, the theater is on the National Register of Historical Places and is operated by the Cedar Rapids Performing Arts Commission. The hall seats 1,912 and has been renovated in keeping with its original style. Acoustics and sight lines are excellent. Because the stage is five stories high, a removable acoustical shell is in place for orchestra performances. A recently installed sound system was customized for the theater and a new stage lighting system has been added.

The Cedar Rapids Symphony Orchestra Association, Inc., is made up of 54 directors of whom 47 comprise the Board of Directors and seven the Board of Trustees. The governing body consists of the Board of Directors, 10 of whom make up the Executive Committee. This governing body is responsible for the organization's affairs. A staff of four handles the organization's administrative work.

The Symphony Guild contributes in many ways. As well as cosponsoring with Coe College both a Youth Symphony and a Junior Youth Symphony

Orchestra, the Guild aids in planning children's concerts and holds an annual scholarship competition, granting cash awards to talented students to continue their musical education.

An annual budget in excess of $500,000 enables 83 players to be contractually guaranteed at least 55 rehearsals and concerts per year. Half of the orchestra members reside in the Cedar Rapids-Marion area, with the majority of the others coming from Iowa City.

The 1982–1983 season saw a total of 24,000 subscribers, and 35% of the orchestra's income resulted from ticket sales. The remainder derives from an annual fund campaign, grants, and contributions from the Symphony Guild. Earned income, including grants, accounts for approximately 58% of the total.

The Symphony was founded in the spring of 1922 by its first conductor, Joseph Kitchin. During its first 30 years the Symphony was composed entirely of volunteer musicians and performed concerts free of charge, relying on contributions to cover accumulated expenses. In 1953 Henry Denecke became conductor, and during his 17 year tenure the orchestra grew to a season of five subscription concerts with a budget of $28,000.

During the tenure of Richard William, 1970–1980, the Symphony became professional, and its audience was doubled with a series of six concert pairs growing to eight pairs in 1975. The Symphony moved to its new home and grew to an operating budget of $362,500. In 1972 the Cedar Rapids Symphony became Iowa's first Metropolitan orchestra, a designation that made possible a grant in 1973 from the National Endowment for the Arts for the formation of a professional, resident string quartet comprising orchestra section leaders. The orchestra also supports a woodwind quintet and brass quintet. These three ensembles perform throughout the year in more than 60 area schools.

In 1981 the orchestra worked under four different conductors during a nationwide search for a new music director, a post filled in 1982 by Dr. Christian Tiemeyer, former assistant conductor of the Dallas Symphony.*

While the bulk of the orchestra's repertoire comes from the standard literature, there has been much contemporary music. Between 1971 and 1980 there were seven world premieres and two American premieres. Guest artists of international stature regularly perform with the orchestra.

Recorded concerts and television programs expose the Cedar Rapids Symphony to audiences across the United States. KCCK-FM in Cedar Rapids broadcasts each subscription concert of the season. The Iowa Public Broadcasting Network featured two of the orchestra's ensembles, the woodwind quintet and the string quartet, in its series "Chamber Ensembles." National Public Radio broadcast two separate concerts by the orchestra nationwide on the Parkway series "America in Concert."

CHRONOLOGY OF MUSIC DIRECTORS: Joseph Kitchin, 1922–1953. Henry Denecke, 1953–1970. Richard Williams, 1970–1980. Christian Tiemeyer, 1980-present.

BIBLIOGRAPHY: Interviews with CRS Manager Karla Mason and violinist Marsha La Foss.

ACCESS: Cedar Rapids Symphony Orchestra, 201 Security Building, 201 Second Street, S.E., Cedar Rapids, IA 52401. (319) 366–8203. Karla Mason, Manager.

RAYMOND COMSTOCK

DES MOINES (338,048)

Des Moines Symphony (Mt)

"The Surprising Place" is the descriptive phrase adopted by publicists several years ago for Des Moines, the state capital of Iowa. It has proved to be apt. Visitors are surprised at the undulating beauty of the city's ravine-carved contours. New residents and seasoned settlers are impressed by interest in the city's cultural activity and architectural awareness—in the strong, privately financed renewal of the city's inner core.

When the handsome, gleaming white, downtown Civic Center of Greater Des Moines opened in 1979, it heralded the beginning of a significant new era in the life of the Des Moines Symphony. The Civic Center's musical acoustics proved to be the equal of its visual distinction. In its new home, the orchestra responded with a leap in the quality of its performances. Finally, its musicians could hear each other play, as they could not in the previous hall. The Symphony then became firmly established as one of the major cultural assets in a city long proud of its widely famed Art Center. Des Moines is also the home of the increasingly noted Metro Opera Company as well as a fledgling resident ballet company.

The orchestra was founded by Frank Noyes in 1937 when he came to Drake University to teach violin. The seasons of the Drake-Des Moines Symphony each comprised four free concerts presented in high school auditoriums. After the orchestra's inception, a major development was the creation of an autonomous Des Moines Symphony Board in 1967. Its new conductor, Robert Gutter, started the group with a clean slate by requiring auditions for all members of the orchestra.

Another important development was the 1970 move to the mammoth KRNT Theater. The 4,200-seat hall, which because of its size had long attracted road companies, succumbed to disrepair, however, and closed only two years later. This made it necessary for the Symphony to seek the new home it found in Hoyt Sherman Auditorium, which exuded Victorian charm but seated only 1,300. Perhaps it was a disguised blessing because retention of the newly built audience required expansion to pairs of performances for each subscription concert.

Gutter, Willis Page, and Thomas Griswold each directed the Symphony for two years, paving the way for the third landmark development, the tenure of Music Director Yuri Krasnapolsky, who in 1984 celebrated the completion of ten years with the Des Moines Symphony.

Building on the orchestra's existing strength in the late romantic repertoire, Krasnapolsky believes in programming for the Des Moines Symphony as for a major orchestra. A sampling from recent seasons includes Mahler's Second and Fifth Symphonies, Strauss's *Don Quixote*, and Mozart's *Requiem*. Krasnapolsky strikes a balance between his personal leanings toward contemporary composition and the receptivity he anticipates from his Des Moines audience for newer works. Peter Mennin's Ninth Symphony played to an enthusiastic audience. Other instances of challenging modern and contemporary works presented recently include Bernstein's *Age of Anxiety*, William Schuman's Symphony No. 2, and Stravinsky's *Rite of Spring*.

Yuri Krasnapolsky relishes theatricality as part of orchestral performance. "The audience," he says, "never should be allowed, visually or aurally, to be bored." He used this dramatic flair to stunning effect for the opening concert presented from the new Civic Center stage. The audience for Beethoven's Ninth Symphony was thrilled by the sight in 1979 of the then-new Des Moines Choral Society filing, scarlet-robed, 250-strong, to risers above the orchestra for the "Ode to Joy."

Most of the orchestra's members are professionally employed in music, many at Drake or Iowa State Universities. There are a number of ensembles connected with the orchestra, including string and trombone quartets, brass and woodwind quintets, waltz and chamber orchestras, and a percussion group. Also, Drake's Fine Arts Trio includes Des Moines Symphony concertmaster Wilfred Biel, principal cellist John Ehrlich, and keyboard principal Chiu-Ling Lin. Ensembles pay some 70 visits to schools yearly, reflecting the philosophy of building future interest in fine music. The Symphony Guild's young artists auditions result each year in the college grand prize winner receiving a scholarship for the Aspen Music Festival School.

Evidence of an increasingly hospitable climate for classical music in Des Moines shows in the employment of Symphony musicians for increasing numbers of other cultural, social, and business events. Companies emphasize the presence of the Symphony as a Central Iowa growth attraction, classical music is heard on the radio, and the university hosts the Ames International Orchestra Festival at its renowned C. Y. Stephens Auditorium.

The architectural excitement of the Civic Center attracts audiences. The Civic Center was designed by the award-winning Des Moines firm of Charles Herbert and Associates. Consultant Paul Veneklazen of California based the acoustics on highly reflective surface areas, steeply raking the entire hall, providing wide spacing between seating rows, and eliminating aisles and balconies. An outgrowth of his acoustical theory is an unusually wide seating area with a correspondingly large stage in the 2,742-seat auditorium.

The orchestra's Civic Center season is seven Saturday-Sunday concert pairs, three performances for school children, a family concert, a New Year's

Eve pops, and occasional concerts elsewhere in Iowa, all with guest artists. Steady, orderly growth has occurred under a frequently updated long-range plan. The Association has moved from a budget of about $135,000 in 1974 to $620,000 ten years later. Guild membership has risen from about 250 to nearly 550 in the same period with a 100-fold rise in fund-raising, capped by Decorators' Show House profits of $107,000 in 1984.

The orchestra is governed by a Board of Directors elected by members of the Des Moines Symphony Association. All subscribers for tickets, contributors, Guild members, and players qualify as Association members. Strong Board support has resulted in the funding of the Des Moines String Quartet, the orchestra's first full-time player positions. Its new endowment fund has underwritten the concertmaster's chair, and major corporations have begun giving grants in six figures. The planning process itself has been a model for other orchestras.

CHRONOLOGY OF MUSIC DIRECTORS: Frank Noyes, 1940–1967. Robert Gutter, 1967–1969. Willis Page, 1969–1971. Thomas Griswold, 1971–1973. (Guest conductors, 1973–1974.) Yuri Krasnapolsky, 1974-present.

BIBLIOGRAPHY: Interviews with Music Director Yuri Krasnapolsky, DMS musicians and Guild members. Des Moines Symphony, Archives.

ACCESS: Des Moines Symphony, 411 Shops Building, Des Moines, IA 50309. (515) 244–0819. Patricia Minot, General Manager.

KAY BUCKSBAUM

Kansas ———————————————

WICHITA (411,313)

Wichita Symphony Orchestra (Rg)

More than 40 years have passed since a committee of seven people gathered together to see if there were enough musicians in South Central Kansas to form an orchestra. These representatives of universities, public schools, the union, and the community at large drew together 75 players in October of 1944. Since its first concert on January 21, 1945, the Wichita Symphony Orchestra has not missed a season.

The character of that original symphony reflects the nature of the musicians who populate the orchestra today. Principal players generally teach at Wichita State University. The remainder study or teach at one of the three colleges in the city, teach in the public schools, or earn their primary incomes elsewhere within the city and surrounding area.

For the orchestra's first two years its musicians played without pay under an agreement with Local 297 of the AFM. Union guidelines still allow members and non-members to sit side by side in the Symphony, but now all members receive a stipend. In the mid–1960s the personnel formed an Orchestra Committee to negotiate grievances for all members, and the binding agreement for actions between the orchestra and management requires a majority vote of all the players. Currently without full-time status, orchestra players nevertheless have a heavy time commitment with the orchestra: 10 concert pairs preceded by five rehearsals, at least two sets of children's concerts per year, chamber programs by some of the players, and occasional runout concerts. Surely if a few more services were added some players could make their livelihood exclusively from the Symphony.

The founders of the Wichita Symphony had foresight in hiring from the start a full-time manager, and their choice of Alan Watrous for that position insured a healthy infancy for the group. Under his leadership, which lasted until his resignation in 1957, the Symphony's season grew from two single concerts to six concert pairs. Watrous expanded his responsibilities to include fund-raising projects, pops concerts, a youth symphony, and a young artist audition.

In 1944, the orchestra presented its concerts in two separate locations: one at Wichita University's Commons Auditorium and another at Wichita East High School Auditorium. The audiences gradually favored the more central location of East High for both pairs, and the need for a larger and more acoustically favorable site became more apparent to discerning listeners. The city responded when it constructed a large multipurpose complex in 1968. The new circular structure, Century II, contains a concert hall for the orchestra and other large-scale attractions, a little theater for drama and chamber concerts, and a convention hall that takes up half the structure's volume. In January 1969 the Symphony moved into this new home, which it rents from the city at a nominal fee.

Community support still plays a big part in the success of the Orchestra just as it did in the fledgling days of the ensemble. The aircraft industry boomed in Wichita during World War II, and it shared its success with the town by encouraging cultural endeavors such as the orchestra. Private benefactors, whose successes lie in oil, cattle, grain, and banking, also support the Symphony. The most consistent support, however, issues from the Women's Association, one of the first such groups formed in the United States. Their fund-raising projects not only succeed in supplementing the orchestra's budget, but also keep the Symphony's name in front of the public. A Ford Foundation grant in 1967 and a NEA Challenge grant in 1980 received generous matching donations from local citizens. Backing like this contributes significantly to a healthy subscription sale of over 75%.

The orchestra's $1 million annual budget supports 35 concerts per year, some with such international celebrities as Lili Kraus and Itzhak Perlman. The main subscription season features traditional concert fare given in pairs of concerts to accommodate the crowds who come to the 2,187-seat concert hall in Century II. A Holiday Family Concert (sponsored by the Wichita *Eagle-Beacon*) and a Twilight Pops Concert (sponsored by Koch Industries) are free to an even larger audience.

In 1974 the Wichita Symphony added a chamber series to its offerings. This ensemble, selected from the core of the orchestra, performs in the 600-seat Century II Little Theater and programs a wide-ranging repertoire, from Vivaldi's Trumpet Concerto in C to Stravinsky's *L'Histoire du Soldat* with speakers and dancers. At these "Soirees Musicales" the conductor provides commentary, often illustrated by examples played at the piano.

The Wichita Symphony Society, Inc., governed by a Board of Directors and an Executive Committee, also sponsors two youth symphonies and a graduate string quartet. From its first year, 1947, members of the Wichita Youth Symphony entered the ensemble only by audition, and its prestige today draws some members from more than 100 miles away to attend its weekly Saturday morning rehearsals and perform in two concerts per year. Response to the program grew to such proportions that in 1979 a second group, the Wichita Repertory Orchestra, had to be added. The governing body likewise expanded the Symphony staff with a new position to manage the two groups. The Ford Foundation grant enabled the orchestra to offer scholarships to four graduate string students at Wichita State University. In return for their stipend, the students play in the orchestra and perform as a string quartet at public schools and other civic events.

The Symphony's original conductor, Orien Dalley, provided stability for the orchestra by teaching it and the public the standard literature. His successor, James Robertson, continued the tradition but gradually added twentieth-century music, particularly by Americans. During his tenure Wichita audiences heard the music of William Schuman, Gene Gutche, Samuel Barber, and others. Both Dalley and Robertson held appointments at Wichita State University as conductor of the University Symphony Orchestra. When Robertson retired in 1970 the next university conductors, Theodore Avital (1970–1971) and Jay Decker (1972-) held the Wichita Symphony position of associate conductor, with responsibility for one concert pair and one set of children's concerts. The Symphony conductor no longer holds a position at the university.

After a two-year search for Robertson's replacement, the orchestra engaged François Huybrechts, who brought youthful energy and enthusiasm. At first his glamor drew crowds, but after a time ticket sales flagged. In 1977 Michael Palmer came to the Wichita Symphony Orchestra from the Atlanta Symphony,* where he was associate conductor to Robert Shaw. Palmer spent a six-week residency with the National Symphony Orchestra* in the summer of 1976, and that fall he opened the subscription series for the Houston Symphony* and guest-conducted there for that and the following two years. In 1978 he opened the Denver Symphony Orchestra* season and became co-principal guest conductor there. In his years with the Wichita Symphony, Palmer's sound musicianship has been a factor in drawing larger audiences at Century II.

In the past 40 years the Wichita Symphony Orchestra has tried many programming formats, from operas with guest artists such as Anna Moffo to pops concerts featuring Tammy Wynette. Although sell-out crowds invaded Century II for the opera performances from 1968 to 1980, the expense of costumes and scenery outweighed the income from these extra concerts. When the orchestra put on Dollar Concerts from 1962 to 1968, the overwhelming crowds required that performances be held at larger, less acoustically appropriate auditoriums. The current pops concerts, which began in 1973, host good but unpredictable audiences and have an uncertain future.

What does seem to work well with Wichita audiences is the tried and true common-practice literature played on regularly organized subscription series.

CHRONOLOGY OF MUSIC DIRECTORS: Orien Dalley, 1944–1950. James Robertson, 1950–1970. (Guest conductors, 1970–1972.) François Huybrechts, 1972–1977. Michael Palmer, 1977-present.

BIBLIOGRAPHY: "Benny Raises $64,000 for Wichita Symphony," *Variety*, 16 Dec. 1970. "Culture in Kansas," *Time*, 23 Jan. 1956. Judith D. Kelly, *Four Decades of Success*, (Wichita Symphony Society, 1984). *The Podium* (Official organ of the Women's Association of the Wichita Symphony Orchestra). Kathryn A. Slawson and Esterre M. Sevin. *That Musical Wichita* (Wichita: Authors, 1982). "Stringed Performance Grants," *American String Teacher*, 1 Nov. 1961. Wichita Symphony Society, Minutes and Interviews.

ACCESS: Wichita Symphony Orchestra, 225 W. Douglas, Wichita, KS 67202. (316) 267–5259. Mitchell A. Berman, General Manager.

DAVID L. AUSTIN

Kentucky ———————————

Lexington Philharmonic Orchestra (Mt)

The Lexington Philharmonic Orchestra is the principal orchestra serving central and eastern Kentucky. Lexington's rapid growth since the 1950s and the expansion of the educational institutions in central Kentucky have provided the bases of support for a Metropolitan orchestra.

Since 1981, the orchestra's seven annual subscription concerts have been presented in the University of Kentucky's Center for the Arts, a modern hall seating 1,500, built in 1979. There are, in addition, three pops concerts, six young people's concerts (sometimes called "Un-Rock Concerts"), and six to eight visits by the orchestra to other communities each season. Two very successful "Picnic with the Pops" concerts are held each summer at the Kentucky Horse Park near Lexington. Performances for the inaugurations of the last three governors of Kentucky have given the orchestra statewide television exposure.

The LPO is governed by a 39-member Board of Directors with an Executive Committee of eight and is administered by a full-time general manager. The Women's Guild actively supports the orchestra through an annual ball, the Philharmonic auction, and other fund-raising events. The musical director (since 1972, Dr. George Zack) makes artistic decisions in consultation with the first chair players regarding auditions and seating. The programs are selected by the musical director in conjunction with the orchestra's Artistic Advisory Committee and the Fiscal Committee of the Board of Directors.

Most of the orchestra members are drawn from the Lexington area and include faculty and advanced students at the University of Kentucky, local music educators, and faculty at other educational institutions such as Eastern Kentucky or Morehead State Universities. Since 1981 all the performers belong to the American Federation of Musicians; the Board of Directors negotiates the scale and other fees with the Orchestra Committee.

The orchestra's 1983–1984 budget was $430,000. Sources of support are federal, state, and local government grants, corporate gifts, private contributions, and ticket sales. The orchestra also supports a string quartet, woodwind quintet, brass quintet, and the Ashland Trio, all with members drawn from the orchestra's personnel.

Though Lexington has had orchestral activity since the early 1800s (Anthony Philip Heinrich was alleged to have conducted a Beethoven symphony there in 1817), attempts to establish an independent, regularly scheduled orchestra were abortive until 1961, when Dr. Robert King founded the Central Kentucky Philharmonic Orchestra as a community orchestra. After his departure in 1965 the orchestra was reorganized as the Lexington Philharmonic Orchestra, Leo Scheer was engaged as conductor, and a broad base of corporate and community support was established. Because of the demand for tickets, the orchestra's six annual subscription concerts had to be given in pairs, one at the University of Kentucky and one at Transylvania University.

Scheer retired in 1971, and in the following year Dr. George Zack was appointed musical director. Under his leadership the orchestra changed from a community volunteer ensemble to its present status of a paid orchestra under professional discipline and standards. From 1976 until 1982 the orchestra presented concerts at the restored, 1886-vintage Opera House. Beginning in 1982, the LPO ceased giving concerts in pairs, with all performances at the UK Center for the Arts.

The goal of the LPO is to present a comprehensive series of musical programs for the entertainment, education, and enlightenment of the community and region through well-rounded programs from all periods, styles, and countries, with a responsibility to living American composers. All programs are selected with consideration for special performing skills, instrumentation, and extra rehearsal requirements. Five rehearsals are the norm for each subscription concert. The orchestra strives to emphasize phrasemaking, a lush, rich string sound, accurate brass and woodwind ensemble, a balance of choirs, and rhythmic exactness within elastic boundaries. A typical program consists of an overture, a concerto, and a symphony or other large-scale orchestral work, with an overall balance of period and style.

CHRONOLOGY OF MUSIC DIRECTORS: Robert King, 1961–1965. Leo Scheer, 1965–1971. George Zack, 1972-present.

BIBLIOGRAPHY: *Lexington Herald-Leader*.

ACCESS: Lexington Philharmonic Orchestra, ArtsPlace, 161 No. Mill St., Lexington, KY 40507. (606) 233–4226. John D. Barr, President, Board of Directors.

R. M. LONGYEAR

LOUISVILLE (906,152)

Louisville Orchestra (Rg)

The Louisville Orchestra has one outstanding tradition in its nearly 50-year history: its commitment to innovation, change, and expansion. Internationally known for its involvement in new music, the Louisville Orchestra should also be cited for its flexible, market-conscious programming, which was especially noticeable in the 1984–1985 season. Offerings included a formal 10-concert, double-night subscription series entitled the "Whitney Series," eight "Cumberland Coffee" concerts, five "Yellowstone SuperPops" concerts, four Family Series concerts, and two "New Music" concerts, all by subscription. In addition to its regular series, the orchestra provides services to the Louisville Ballet and the Kentucky Opera Association, and the reduced chamber orchestra participates in promotional events.

The city of Louisville, long a cultural crossroad between East and West, adopted a cosmopolitan veneer early in its history, and when industrialization was followed by philanthropy, artistic institutions in the city were seen as bases of economic and social growth. As a pragmatic reason for financial and moral backing for local arts institutions such as the Louisville Orchestra, this philosophy continues to thrive today. In a 1983 poll of Louisville community leaders, "arts and entertainment" ranked as a high first as the area of excellence in the city.

A 36-member Governing Board oversees the development and operations of the Louisville Orchestra, electing its own members, committees, and leadership. Responsible to the Board are a professional manager overseeing a staff of 11, supplemented by orchestra players serving as librarian and personnel manager. Orchestra players participate in several committees and make recommendations to the Board but do not have voting memberships on it. A master contract, which runs for an average of three years, governs all procedures related to the musicians. The Louisville Orchestra has been a union orchestra almost from its start. The 68 full-time players of the Louisville Orchestra are supplemented as needed by per-service extras from a "casual players pool."

The orchestra's expenses and budget have increased significantly since a players' strike in 1981, and in 1983 the organization, despite large increases in funding, carried a major deficit. In 1983 the projected budget for the coming season was $2.7 million, with approximately 61% allocated to artistic expenses, including players' salaries. Ticket sales accounted for 42% of the income, with the remainder coming from endowments, government grants, corporate sponsorships, and fund-raising activities. Louisville was one of the first cities to develop the concept of a community chest for the arts. Former Mayor Charles Farnsley was instrumental in founding this Louisville Fund—now the Greater Louisville Fund for the Arts—in 1948. This umbrella group provides about 15% of the orchestra's budget and now allows the orchestra to make direct donor appeals as well.

Though an orchestra had existed in some form for over 70 years in Louisville, the beginning of the Louisville Orchestra was in 1937. A committee of concerned citizens, seeking to make a cultural contribution to a major rejuvenation taking place city wide, traveled to Chicago to find a conductor who would relocate in Louisville and build an orchestra.

Robert Whitney (b. 1904), a young composer-pianist, left his conducting apprenticeship with a WPA orchestra under Frederick Stock in Chicago to become the first conductor/music director of the Louisville Philharmonic Orchestra, a position he was to hold for 30 years. During his first ten years in Louisville, he and his board, mainly led by businessman J. Alexander Stewart, built a typical small city's symphony orchestra, with a formal double-night subscription series and outdoor summer concerts in the Iroquois Park Amphitheatre and later in Churchill Downs. Programming was conventional: a marked tendency to depend on "name" soloists to draw audiences reflects this. However, soloists' fees far outweighed box office receipts; the orchestra, though improving artistically, accumulated increasing deficits. The Louisville Foundation, a local community chest, granted the $40,000 needed to bail out the orchestra, and it was believed that it would then quietly dissolve. But in 1948 Charles Rowland Peasely Farnsley, president-elect of the Louisville Philharmonic Society, the governing board for the orchestra, was appointed mayor. His aims were—as he told Robert Whitney—to promote the Louisville Free Public Library, the University of Louisville, and the orchestra.

He met with Whitney in the spring of 1948 to discuss his new ideas for putting the orchestra on more solid financial footing. His plans involved the following: ceasing to hire touring concert artists who carried so much money out of the community; drastically cutting the size of the orchestra to classical proportions—no more than 50 players; moving the regular concert season from Freedom Hall (now Memorial Auditorium) to the much smaller Columbia Auditorium at Spaulding College; and commissioning composers to write new works for the smaller orchestra. A lawyer, politician, and Confucian scholar without rigorous musical training, Farnsley was also a neoclassicist fascinated with the 18th century, and he had a strong dislike for romanticism. His charismatic personality held sway with Whitney, and the plan was agreed upon.

For four years, the city-supported commissioning project dominated the orchestra's activities and publicity. Approximately six new works were done each season, one in every subscription concert. Soloists still appeared, though not as frequently, and some commissioned works were even written for soloists and orchestra, most notably Martha Graham's "dance concerti" by William Schuman and Norman Dello Joio. The word "philharmonic" was dropped from the orchestra's name in the 1949–1950 season; the Board remained the Louisville Philharmonic Society until 1977. The orchestra began recording commissioned works in the 1950–1951 season at their new performance hall, Columbia Auditorium.

In April of 1953, the Rockefeller Foundation announced an award of $400,000 to the Louisville Orchestra "toward the composition, performance, and recording of new works by living composers." The grant-funded commissioning project would run concurrently with the city-funded project. In the subsequent three years, over 100 new pieces for orchestra were written for and premiered by the Louisville Orchestra's series of Saturday afternoon concerts. Each concert featured one premiere and three earlier commissions in rotating order. The orchestra recorded most of the pieces on its own label, "First Edition Records," which was manufactured by Columbia Records. The project included the production of several one-act operas, a yearly student composition competition, and prominent participation in radio broadcasts and information centers of the State Department's Voice of America and other agencies.

When the project's cost failed to be supported by record and ticket sales, the Rockefeller Foundation granted another $100,000 so the commissions-in-progress could be honored and the project completed. By 1959 all outstanding commissions had been collected, and the orchestra moved on to recording older, unrecorded commissions, and ultimately, previously composed pieces (not commissions) that had never before been recorded. Composers were solicited to submit already-written works that they wanted to have recorded for the first time.

In 1963, the orchestra moved to the renovated Brown Theatre, which again underwent extensive remodeling in 1972 and was renamed the Macauley Theatre. It remained the orchestra's 1,500-seat home until 1983. Until his retirement in 1967 Robert Whitney continued his activities in new music along with the more traditional functions of his orchestra, his subscription series, and his massive children's concerts, which were held in the larger Memorial Auditorium and were called the "Making Music" series. He remained a notably modest and hard-working conductor who never forgot his personal empathy with composers. In the commissioning part of the new music project alone, he learned over 120 new scores in eleven years (at the rate of one a week for several years). Though only a small amount of the music could be considered avant-garde, much of it was very complex rhythmically and demanded the maximum technique possible from this dedicated part-time orchestra.

Whitney was succeeded by new Music Director and Conductor Jorge Mester, who served from 1967 until 1979. During these years the orchestra struggled with its "new music" image, attempting to become more of a traditional symphony orchestra with a handle on the standard repertoire. The number of players (none full-time) gradually increased to about 80. Mester continued the recording project; the extra funds generated for the musicians remained a strong attraction in an orchestra verging on full-time professional status. As Mester changed the focus of recording from new music to previously unrecorded pieces of earlier centuries, the enthusiasm of the musicians toward new music seemed to decline.

The 1979–1980 season was run by Peter Leonard (conductor-in-residence) and John Nelson, music director of the Indianapolis Symphony,* who served as artistic consultant. They pulled together a season of auditioning guest conductors, which led to the hiring of Akira Endo, previously music director of the Austin Symphony.* An orchestra players' strike in the fall of 1981 led to the orchestra's achievement of full-time status, including daytime rehearsals and substantial salary increases.

Endo was succeeded by Lawrence Leighton Smith, formerly of the San Antonio Symphony,* who guest conducted during the 1981–1982 and 1982–1983 seasons and became music director in 1983–1984. A concert pianist and native of Portland, Oregon, Smith stated his intention of rejuvenating the orchestra's involvement in new music. The new conductor was able to lead the orchestra in its first concert in the Kentucky Center for the Arts on December 2, 1983.

All subscription concerts, with the exception of the pops concert held in the Louisville Gardens, now take place in the 2,400-seat Whitney Hall, the major performing area of the $33.5 million Kentucky Center for the Arts located on the Ohio River at the corner of Sixth and Main Streets. Whitney Hall contains continental seating, a stage curtain in a post-modernist design by Princeton architect Michael Graves and contemporary acoustical devices such as computerized, adjustable, fiberglass ceiling clouds. Reactions to the new hall's acoustics have been mixed and cautious. Extensive modifications in the summer of 1984 have resulted, according to Kentucky Center for the Arts Director Marlow Burt, in an acoustical environment pleasing to both the orchestra and its music director. The orchestra's first concert was sold out. Single-ticket sales and subscriptions both increased dramatically during the remainder of the 1982–1983 season.

Having been through a period of disillusionment with new music, the Louisville Orchestra and its audience as well appear to be realizing their historic debt to contemporary composers. Interest has been gradually building during the last five years; now nearly all subscription series concerts offer at least one work by a living or recently living composer. Additionally, two special concerts billed as the "New Music Series" take place each season. In 1984 the series incorporated a New Music Competition and the revival of the "dance concerto" idea from the commissioning project of the 1950s. The 1984–1985 season saw the orchestra become a participant in the Meet the Composers, Inc., Residencies Program, welcoming Charles Wuorinen to a two-year stint as composer-in-residence with the Louisville Orchestra.

The orchestra's characteristic sound, influenced by its history of being a relatively small ensemble playing much contemporary music in a confined hall, is somewhat aggressive and dry; William Mootz, the music critic who has listened to the orchestra for over 30 years, describes it as "bright, tight and sometimes steely." However, the move to the larger, more traditionally symphonic Whitney Hall, combined with the music director's corresponding wish to build a larger string section, will inevitably lead the orchestra to a more relaxed, full orchestral sound. The influence of new music on the orchestra's accuracy and rhythmic precision will likely continue.

The orchestra has left its impression on the city in two principal ways: in the quality of musical education and in the growth of other performing arts institutions. Many of the musicians attracted to Louisville by its orchestra in the past brought a high level of teaching to the city, particularly to the University of Louisville's School of Music. Over the past ten years, especially since the orchestra became full time, older faculty members have left the orchestra but kept their teaching positions. The orchestra has sponsored educational programs in branch libraries, young artists competitons, and joint activities with the Louisville Youth Orchestra.

The early success of the Louisville Orchestra with its new music project stimulated the adventurous growth of other performing arts institutions in the city, especially the Kentucky Opera Association, the Louisville Ballet, and Actors Theatre. Not only were these groups reassured that the area population (now approximately one million) was able and ready to support fine arts activities, but they were also encouraged to try more innovative, high risk programming. Indeed, the growing international reputation of Actors Theatre is built upon a festival of contemporary plays.

RECORDING HISTORY AND SELECTIVE DISCOGRAPHY: The Louisville Orchestra's initial LP recording was made in the 1950–1951 season for Mercury Records. LO recordings were then released on the Columbia Masterworks Series until 1954, when the independent First Edition Series began. Originally sold by subscription only, they are now also commercially available as single issues. The six-LP-per-year output of the commissioning years subsequently dwindled to two to three per year; plans to increase recording are currently in progress.

Elliott Carter, Variations for Orchestra; Everett Helm, Second Piano Concerto (Whitney): First Edition L583. Karel Husa, *The Trojan Women* (Endo): First Edition LS775. Joseph Joachim, Concerto for Violin and Orchestra in D Minor, Op. 11 *(Hungarian* Concerto) (Mester): First Edition LS705. Otto Luening and Vladimir Ussachevsky, *Rhapsodic Variations for Tape Recorder and Orchestra*; Jacques Ibert, *Louisville Concerto*; Gardner Road, *Toccata Giocoso* (Whitney): First Edition L5455. Bohuslav Martinů, Symphony No. 5; Virgil Thomson, Concerto for Flute (Whitney): First Edition LS663.

CHRONOLOGY OF MUSIC DIRECTORS: Robert S. Whitney, 1937–1967. Jorge Mester, 1967–1979. Peter Leonard (Conductor-in-Residence) and John Nelson (Artistic Consultant), 1979–1980. Akira Endo, 1980–1983. Lawrence Leighton Smith, 1983-present.

BIBLIOGRAPHY: Interviews with LO Assistant Manager Gregory Copenhefer and *Louisville Courier-Journal* Music Critic William Mootz, 1984. Jeanne Belfy, *The*

Louisville Orchestra New Music Project (University of Louisville Publications in Musicology No. 2, 1983). Carole Birkhead, "A History of the Orchestra in Louisville," Masters thesis, University of Louisville, 1979. Philip Hart, *Orpheus in the New World* (New York: Norton, 1973). William Mootz, "Four Composers in Louisville Orchestra's First Competition for New Music," *Louisville Courier-Journal*, 8 Apr. 1984. Oral History, Record Group 60, University Archives and Records Center, University of Louisville. Records of the Louisville Orchestra 1937–1971, Record Group 107, University Archives and Records Center, University of Louisville. F. W. Woolsey, "At the Center of the Center of It All," *The [Louisville] Courier-Journal Magazine*, 15 Apr. 1984. F. W. Woolsey, "Louisville's Classical Victory," *The [Louisville] Courier-Journal Magazine*, 4 Oct. 1970. George Yater *Two Hundred Years at the Falls of the Ohio: A History of Louisville and Jefferson County* (The Heritage Corporation of Louisville and Jefferson County, 1979).

ACCESS: The Louisville Orchestra, 609 West Main Street, Louisville, KY 40202. (502) 587–8681. Karen Dobbs, General Manager.

JEANNE MARIE BELFY

Louisiana ————————————————

BATON ROUGE (494,151)

Baton Rouge Symphony Orchestra (Mt)

The Baton Rouge Symphony Orchestra celebrated its 35th consecutive season during the 1984–1985 concert year. The Symphony performed its first concert in January 1947 under the baton of Frederick Kopp, who served as conductor for two seasons. The civic volunteer ensemble met with such success that, in 1949, it incorporated and began offering regular subscription seasons. The earlier programs usually featured the stand-by and perennial favorites of the classical and romantic periods. More recently, the Symphony has broadened its scope of repertoire, providing its audiences the experience of pieces previously unperformed during a live concert in Baton Rouge. Regular conductors of the Symphony have included David Forrester, Orlando Barera, Richard Korn, Emil Cooper, Peter Paul Fuchs, James Yestadt, and James Paul, who in 1982 was appointed the first full-time music director and conductor.

Early Symphony concerts were held in auditoriums at Baton Rouge High School, Lee High School, and in the Louisiana State University Union Theatre. In the early 1970s, the city-parish government recognized the need for a centrally located, multipurpose theater and voted to create the Centroplex, a complex featuring an arena, government offices, library, parking garages, and theater. Located on the banks of the Mississippi River, the 2,000-seat Centroplex Theatre for the Performing Arts was completed in 1977, and Symphony concerts have since been regularly scheduled there. Although complaints about the theater are numerous during performances featuring vocalists, most Symphony goers find the hall quite satisfactory.

The policies and programs of the BRSO are administered by a 50-member

Board of Directors elected by the membership at annual meetings and serving staggered three-year terms. In addition, other area organizations— the East Baton Rouge Parish School Board, the Junior League of Baton Rouge, the Louisiana State University School of Music, the Southern University School of Music, the Baton Rouge Chamber of Commerce, the East Baton Rouge City-Parish Council, and the East Baton Rouge Parish Office of the Mayor-President—have appointees on the Symphony Board. In 1983 the Board created a Regional Advisory Board, whose members provide advice and counsel with regard to all areas of the Association's activities. Standing committees are responsible for finance, personnel, education, regional development, and other functions.

The BRSO performs in a seven-concert series known as "Tuesdays at Eight." In 1982, an additional subscription series, Lagniappe, was added not only to provide a vehicle of performance for the Chamber Orchestra of the BRSO, but to provide a means of family-oriented concerts such as the *Nutcracker* and *The Mikado*. The Lagniappe series was discontinued in 1984– 1985 to provide a matinee series, Sundays at Two, duplicating the programming of the Tuesday concerts. Occasional runouts were supplemented in 1984 with the Symphony's first concert in New Orleans, a performance of Mendelssohn's *Elijah*.

In addition to the funds provided by its concerts, the BRSO budget of some $700,000 derives from Symphony Auxiliary activities (including sales at La Musique Boutique), federal grants awarded through the Arts and Humanities Council of Greater Baton Rouge, the Division of the Arts of the State of Louisiana, NEA and NEH, the Baton Rouge Area Foundation, the Junior League, and both corporate and private donations.

The BRSO also provides two free concert series, the Symphony at Twilight series of two to three concerts on the lawn of the Old State Capitol, and the Chamber Music in the Gallery series (begun in 1983), which provides solo and ensemble concerts at the Louisiana Art and Sciences Center. Additionally, 12,000 upper elementary students from 95 schools attended the 25th year of youth concerts. The Symphony Auxiliary sponsors annual Youth Performance Concerto Auditions, whose winners perform as soloists with the BRSO during the annual youth concerts. Also, in conjunction with the LSU School of Music, the BRSO annually awards three instrumental music scholarships, granted on the basis of musical proficiency and academic excellence. In return, the recipients are expected to enroll as full-time music majors, maintain a satisfactory grade point average, and meet the schedule of professional services provided by the Symphony Association.

The orchestra employs an average of 75 musicians per concert who are contracted per service. They include students and faculty from LSU and surrounding area universities, private music teachers, and players from Lafayette, Hammond, and New Orleans. The BRSO has no union membership requirement since Louisiana is a "right to work" state. However, the contracts are negotiated through collective bargaining through the local musicians' union. In addition to the per-service players, there are two full-time string quartets, which present over 400 concerts in area schools and for various special clients. The BRSO also sponsors the Original Hyperion Ragtime Orchestra, under direction of BRSO Executive Director Richard H. Mackie, Jr; it performs American vernacular repertoire, 1896 to 1934. The BRSO Brass Quintet and BRSO Woodwind Quintet also perform throughout the community as part of the combined touring effort.

Some national attention has been focused on the orchestra's work with new music, with a 1982 second place ASCAP Metropolitan Orchestra Award for the Programming and Performance of Contemporary Music, annual participation in the Contemporary Music Festival in conjunction with the American Society of University Composers at LSU, and the 1984 performance of a commissioned work by BRSO Concertmaster and Associate Conductor Dinos Constantinides—his Symphony No. 2. BRSO concert excerpts have been broadcast on NPR, and in 1982 the orchestra began broadcasting all its subscription concerts on WRKF, a public radio station in Baton Rouge.

CHRONOLOGY OF MUSIC DIRECTORS: David Forrester, 1948–1949. Orlando Barera, 1949–1950. Richard Korn, 1950–1951. Emil Cooper, 1951–1960. Peter Paul Fuchs, 1960–1976. James Yestadt, 1976–1981. James Yestadt (Musical Advisor), 1981–1982. James Paul, 1982-present.

ACCESS: Baton Rouge Symphony Orchestra, P.O. Box 103, Baton Rouge, LA 70821. (504) 387–6166. Richard H. Mackie, Jr., Executive Director.

ALLISON CHESTNUT

NEW ORLEANS (1,187,073)

New Orleans Symphony Orchestra (Mj)

With a membership of 80 regular players, a total of 100 employees, and an annual budget of approximately $4 million, the New Orleans Symphony is the only ASOL Major orchestra in the immediate region. The orchestra plays for an audience totalling about 250,000 each season (based on ticket sales), in concerts given mainly at the Orpheum Theater in the New Orleans central business district and at the nearby New Orleans Theater for the Performing Arts, but also including frequent engagements elsewhere in Louisiana as well as in other Gulf Coast states and farther afield. The 1983–1984 concert schedule totalled 140 performances. Of these the majority were regular subscription concerts (16 programs, each played two or three times) and youth concerts, but various special events also made important contributions to the Symphony's season.

The Symphony maintains close ties with other musical institutions in New Orleans, most conspicuously by serving as the regular orchestra for the New Orleans Opera Association (13 performances of four operas in 1983–1984).

Symphony members frequently contribute their talents to various independent musical events such as church concerts and the Tulane Summer Lyric Theater and serve as adjunct faculty members at local universities, including Tulane, Loyola, Xavier, and the University of New Orleans.

A significant part of the Symphony's schedule is devoted to attracting audiences outside the ranks of traditional symphony supporters and appealing to cultural sub-groups indigenous to or especially prevalent in New Orleans. The annual pops series has recently featured collaborations with such artists as those of the Ellis Marsalis Trio in a program of jazz arrangements. The "Symphony in Black" series, acknowledging the important cultural contributions of New Orleans's large black population, recently offered a special concert dedicated to the memory of Martin Luther King. At present the Symphony is working on a television series on the nineteenth-century New Orleans composer Louis Moreau Gottschalk, to be aired on PBS during 1985.

The Symphony also recognizes its responsibility to a geographical area much larger than the city of New Orleans. In addition to frequent run-out concerts in neighboring cities, the orchestra maintains a regular six-concert subscription series in Mobile, Alabama, and in 1984 it participated in a festival at Pensacola, Florida. Tour performances concentrate on southern cities, although they have also included New York, Latin America, and Europe.

The orchestra is governed by a 45-member Board of Directors, responsible for all general policy decisions and for hiring the music director and executive manager. Programming decisions and decisions on hiring of players are made by the music director in consultation with management and with members of the orchestra. A Musicians' Advisory Committee, consisting of orchestra members, meets regularly with members of the Board. Funding is derived from local, state, and federal government sources (including an NEA grant of $105,000 for 1983–1984), from ticket sales, and from various fund-raising activities organized by the Women's Committee.

One of the oldest cities in the South (founded in 1718), New Orleans remained through most of the nineteenth century the South's largest, wealthiest, and culturally most important metropolis. Yet during this time, when many northern cities were establishing first-rank orchestras that would survive as potent cultural forces to the present day, New Orleans could boast no permanent symphonic ensemble. All the city's support for the performing arts was concentrated on opera. An obvious reflection of the city's Creole heritage, the French Opera of New Orleans brought much fame to the city as a center of music but had the unfortunate side effect of stifling other forms of musical performance. Just as Paris has always been known more for opera than for orchestral music, so in New Orleans the symphony had to take a back seat.

With time, however, and the gradual dilution of the city's ethnic makeup by non-Creole immigrants, the French operatic establishment was weakened, and opportunities for a more diversified musical life opened up. The first event of lasting importance was the founding in 1906 of the Philharmonic Society of New Orleans, which would eventually become part of the modern Philharmonic Symphony Society, governing the New Orleans Symphony. Conceived by Miss Corinne Mayer, a New Orleans pianist, and led by her for more than four decades, the Philharmonic Society held as one of its chief objectives the establishment of a permanent symphony orchestra in New Orleans. Unfortunately, all of its efforts in this direction proved abortive, and the orchestra eventually was founded independently of the Society. Nevertheless, it played a very important role for many years in stimulating the city's musical interest by importing high-calibre soloists and orchestras from around the world.

Meanwhile the establishment of a permanent symphony in New Orleans proceeded by fits and starts. Significant landmarks along the way were the Crescent City Symphony Orchestra (1917–1919) and the New Orleans Symphony Orchestra Association (1926–1927 and 1930), both directed by Ernest E. Schuyten. These groups enjoyed considerable success temporarily, but neither succeeded in gaining the community's permanent support. It was not until 1936, with the founding of the New Orleans Civic Symphony Orchestra, that the city at last acquired a permanent symphonic ensemble— one that would eventually become the present New Orleans Symphony Orchestra.

The Civic Symphony was organized through the efforts of Mrs. Lucy Benjamin Lehmann and its first music director, the Russian-born Arthur Zack, a mediocre conductor who possessed phenomenal talents for fundraising and administration. Mrs. Lehmann had invited Zack to New Orleans after hearing of his success in founding the Cincinnati Civic Orchestra several years earlier. Working together, they enlisted the support of a broad cross-section of the New Orleans musical community, including the Philharmonic Society and backers of the previous ill-fated orchestras. The result was an all-professional orchestra of 54 musicians that played for 2,500 subscribers in its first full season (1936–1937) and was received warmly by press and public alike.

Regular subscription concerts during each of the orchestra's first few years included six different programs, covering a remarkably wide spectrum of orchestral literature. Works chosen by Zack ranged from Monteverdi and Purcell through the great classics to contemporary works of Ravel and Richard Strauss. A further noteworthy feature of Zack's programming—one that has persisted through various music directors up to the present day— is the high priority given to youth concerts. Zack scheduled six highly imaginative concerts for children during each season (with programs almost entirely different from the adult series) and was widely praised for his success at instilling a love for music in the city's youth.

The end of Zack's directorship came about in a rather unusual manner—

through the brief emergence late in 1939 of a rival ensemble, the New Orleans Orchestra. This latter group appeared from out of the blue, as it were, entirely through the largesse of a wealthy widow, Mrs. Edgar Rogers, who wished to present a series of free concerts in memory of her husband. To lead the group she contracted a Norwegian conductor of some distinction, Ole Windingstad, who seems to have impressed all concerned as a musician of much greater sophistication than Arthur Zack. Most of the musicians in Mrs. Roger's orchestra also played with the Civic Symphony, and it was they who spearheaded the drive to replace Zack with Windingstad. Early in 1940, in the middle of the season, Zack was asked to resign and the change was accomplished.

During the four years of Windingstad's tenure, it was generally agreed that the orchestra made great strides in musical quality matched by concrete signs of expansion in size and scope. Orchestra membership grew from 54 to 70, and for the first time musicians were recruited from outside the New Orleans area. To reflect this more cosmopolitan outlook, the organization's name was changed in 1940 to "The New Orleans Symphony Association." Musicians were now contracted for an entire season rather than on a per-concert basis. Meanwhile, the number of regular subscription concerts per season was expanded to ten, and an entirely new pops series was instituted.

More or less steady expansion continued for the next three decades, which saw several changes in leadership. Massimo Freccia became principal conductor in 1944; he had previously led the Havana Philharmonic. Freccia remained until 1952, when he assumed the directorship of the Baltimore Symphony.* The chief event of his New Orleans tenure was the merger of the Symphony with the venerable Philharmonic Society, whereupon the ensemble became known as the New Orleans Philharmonic Symphony Orchestra. This title was retained until 1984, when the word "Philharmonic"was dropped; the governing body is still called the New Orleans Philharmonic Symphony Society.

The next music director was Alexander Hilsberg, who led the orchestra from 1952 to 1961. Hilsberg had been associate conductor of the Philadelphia Orchestra* under Ormandy for seven years prior to his arrival in New Orleans and maintained strong Philadelphia connections throughout his New Orleans tenure; when he left New Orleans it was to assume directorship of the Orchestra Department of Philadephia's New School of Music. Many felt that during Hilsberg's years in New Orleans the orchestra served as a training ground for the Philadelphia Orchestra, since the membership tended to be quite young and frequently went on to positions with the latter ensemble. Nevertheless, important gains were made. Statewide broadcasts of youth concerts were begun, the orchestra undertook a tour of Latin America, and budget expansion reached the point where for the first time ASOL could classify the organization as a Major orchestra.

A period of very stable leadership followed, with the directorship held from 1963 to 1977 by one man—Werner Torkanowsky. Born in Germany, raised in Israel, and having studied violin in New York with Rafael Bronstein, Torkanowsky was admired for his vitality and excitement, although some players resented his authoritarian approach. During Torkanowsky's tenure the orchestra made its first (and only to date) commercial recordings, including a rendition of the "Star Spangled Banner" with Norman Treigle and local choral groups (intended for use at public events) and a selection of orchestral works by contemporary American composers. The concern that these selections demonstrated for "relevance" to the orchestra's cultural context was also reflected in concert programming, which included such events as the premiere of *A Musical Service for Louis (A Requiem)* by the New Orleans composer Roger Dickerson, written in memory of Louis Armstrong.

In 1973 the orchestra reached an important landmark with its move to a new home. Hitherto, concerts had been given in the Municipal Auditorium—a double hall in which strains of Beethoven frequently had to compete with the sounds of a Mardi Gras ball leaking through from the other side. The new hall—the New Orleans Theater for the Performing Arts—was built specifically to house the Symphony and the New Orleans Opera. The orchestra still plays there for opera performances and youth concerts, although its regular subscription concerts have moved on to the Orpheum Theater.

When Torkanowsky turned in his baton in 1977, the Symphony acquired for the first time a conductor whose name will be familiar to most readers—Leonard Slatkin. Widely respected for his technical precision, Slatkin had already made something of a name for himself as associate conductor of the St. Louis Symphony* before coming to New Orleans. During his New Orleans years he furthered his reputation by serving as principal guest conductor not only for St. Louis but for the Minnesota Orchestra* and Chicago's Grant Park Concerts as well. Perhaps it was inevitable that his New Orleans stay would be brief—in 1979 Slatkin became music director at St. Louis, and soon thereafter resigned his New Orleans position.

Fortunately, another musician was available whose fame was, if anything, greater than Slatkin's. This was Philippe Entremont, who appeared as piano soloist with the orchestra during the 1979–1980 season. Entremont was engaged as music advisor and principal guest conductor for 1980–1982 and has been music director and conductor since. Born in Rheims, France, in 1934, Entremont had achieved worldwide acclaim as a pianist before broadening his activities to include conducting. In 1976 he became director of the Vienna Chamber Orchestra, a post he now holds concurrently with the New Orleans position.

Entremont has received high marks from members of the orchestra for his sympathy with the performer's point of view and for his contagious enthusiasm for music. He has done much to bolster the Symphony's image both at home and on tour. Performances at Carnegie Hall in 1982 and 1984 were well received, and in the fall of 1982 Entremont led the orchestra on its first tour of Europe, receiving rave reviews from Vienna to Paris.

While it is sometimes said that Entremont's strengths lie in the French repertoire, his programming and his critical success as conductor betray no particular national bias. Composers most frequently programmed during Entremont's tenure through the 1984–1985 season have been, in descending order: Mozart (emphasizing the piano concertos with Entremont at the keyboard), Beethoven, Richard Strauss, Ravel, Tchaikovsky, Brahms, Stravinsky, Prokofiev, Schumann, and Dvořák.

There have been a respectable number of performances of new music, especially by British and American composers, due in part to the influence of Associate Conductor Andrew Massey. British-born, himself a composer, and formerly assistant conductor of the Cleveland Orchestra*, Massey came to New Orleans in 1980 (the same year as Entremont) and frequently conducts concerts featuring new works. Also worthy of mention are concerts featuring choral works, with the Philharmonic Chorus prepared by Assistant Conductor Larry Wyatt. In addition to the annual *Messiah* performance, recent concerts have included choral works by Brahms, Haydn, Kodály, Vaughan Williams, and Poulenc.

One of the Symphony's major achievements in recent years has been the renovation of the Orpheum, a 60-year-old beaux arts style theater that had been slated for demolition. Donated to the Symphony in 1980 by All-Right Auto Parts and renovated with the help of a $2 million grant from the State of Louisiana, the theater now stands as an architectural treasure and an official historic landmark. The theater is highly praised for its acoustics and houses all of the Symphony's regular subscription concerts. It is a proud home for what has become one of New Orlean's proudest cultural assets.

RECORDING HISTORY AND SELECTIVE DISCOGRAPHY: During Torkanowsky's tenure the orchestra made its first (and only to date) commercial recordings.

Hovhaness, *Fra Angelico*; Floyd, *Pilgrimage*; Colgrass, *The Earth's a Baked Apple*; Rorem, *Lions* (Torkanowsky): Orion ORS–7268.

CHRONOLOGY OF MUSIC DIRECTORS: Arthur Zack, 1936–1940. Ole Windingstad, 1940–1944. Massimo Freccia, 1944–1952. Alexander Hilsberg, 1952–1960. James Yestadt, 1961–1962. Werner Torkanowsky, 1963–1977. Leonard Slatkin, 1977–1980. Philippe Entremont, 1980-present.

BIBLIOGRAPHY: Interviews with NOSO Business Manager Stanley Weinstein and NOSO Member Stephen Weiss, 1984. Cintra S. Austin, "A History of the New Orleans Philharmonic Symphony to 1944: The Founding of an Orchestra," Master's Thesis, Department of History, University of New Orleans, 1972. Bruce Eggler, "Conductor Entremont Praised," *The States-Item*, 15 Nov. 1979. Margaret Fuller, " 'You Get Hooked,' Says Cellist Who Joined the Symphony in 1954," *The Times Picayune/ States Item*, 6 Mar. 1983. Frank Gagnard, "Crises a Spur to Massey's Career," *The Times Picayune/States-Item*, 19 Sept. 1980. Frank Gagnard, "To Change a City's

Image from Carnival to Culture," *The Times Picayune/States-Item*, 7 Nov. 1982. Frank Gagnard, "N. O. Symphony Wins New Yorkers' Cheers," *The Times Picayune/ States-Item*, 11 Jan. 1982. Bernard Holland, "Concert: New Orleans Philharmonic," *New York Times*, 11 Jan. 1984. John Perkins, "Russell Flagg Proud of Orchestra's Strides," *North Pontchartrain Newspapers*, 11 Nov. 1983.

ACCESS: New Orleans Philharmonic Symphony Society, 203 Carondelet Street, Suite 903, New Orleans, LA 70130. (504) 524–0404. David Levenson, Executive Director.

DAVID BEVERIDGE

SHREVEPORT (376,710)

Shreveport Symphony Orchestra (Mt)

In 1948, Maestro John Shenaut and a group of interested citizens, with a budget of $5,000 and using 50 local musicians, founded the Shreveport Symphony. In the 32 years under Shenaut's direction, the Symphony grew to an annual budget of over $470,000 and an ensemble of 70 qualified musicians.

A highlight of the 1975–1977 seasons was the Shreveport Symphony Bicentennial Trilogy, which gained national and international recognition as one of the most unique and creative products of the U.S. Bicentennial. The project included the commission of three major works: a symphonic composition, an opera, and a ballet by the American composer Elie Siegmeister. Shenaut retired in 1981, earning the title Conductor Emeritus. Following three years under Principal Conductor Paul Strauss and Associate Conductor (later Acting Music Director) Margery Deutsch, Peter Leonard made his debut as music director and conductor during the 1984–1985 season.

Beyond the seven subscription concert pairs in the city's Civic Theatre, the Symphony sponsors several programs serving the Arkansas-Louisiana-Texas region. These include a Chamber Orchestra series, special events, youth concerts, the Shreveport Symphony Nena Plant Wideman Piano Competition for young pianists, and full-orchestra run-out concerts. Summer activity includes the free Expo Pops series, attracting over 11,000, and the 4th of July Celebration, drawing an audience of 35,000 people. In all, the Symphony and its ensembles appear in more than 125 live performances before 90,000 people. The orchestra regularly features soloists of international renown in a largely traditional repertoire.

The Shreveport Symphony is a professional orchestra employing a core of 29 musicians with annual contracts pro-rated over a twelve-month period. This core services the established Music Enrichment Program that provides ensembles to educational institutions and special service organizations for more than 30,000 school children. The balance of the orchestra is employed on a per-service basis, depending on the requirements of programming.

With a budget of $715,000, the Symphony pays over $350,000 in musicians' salaries, making an important contribution to the local economy, since 77% of this amount is spent in the Ark-La-Tex region.

Through the years the Symphony has been the recipient of grants from the Louisiana Council for Music and the Performing Arts, the Louisiana Tourist Development Commission, the Louisiana State Arts Council Division of the Arts, and the NEA. In 1965 it received a $350,000 Ford Foundation grant, which today is part of the orchestra's permanent endowment of over $1 million. In 1975 the Symphony was named "Distinguished Salesman of Shreveport" by the Sales and Marketing Executives of Shreveport, and in 1976 it was honored by the American Revolution Bicentennial Administration for its Bicentennial Trilogy. The 1984–1985 season was the second consecutive one to have all concerts sponsored by corporations or individuals, thereby establishing a new form of financial support.

The Shreveport Symphony Women's Guild has been a vital influence in the growth and development of the organization. This group of more than 585 members operates a used clothing business from three adjoining, Symphony-owned properties which serve as "Encore Shop" outlets. Monies from this endeavor finance their operations and special projects, which have contributed more than $50,000 annually to the Symphony operating fund. In addition, the Women's Guild sponsors the Ark-La-Tex Youth Symphony.

It was the Guild that raised the money in 1957 to restore the Col. Robert H. Lindsey House, a fine example of the transitional style of southern residence between the Greek Revival and Late Victorian periods and the only existing post-Civil War architecture of its type in Shreveport today. The building was moved to a corner lot on the campus of Centenary College and became the first building in the area to be placed on the Register of National Historic Places. Known as Symphony House, it currently houses the administrative offices.

CHRONOLOGY OF MUSIC DIRECTORS: John Shenaut, 1948–1981. Paul Strauss (Principal Guest Conductor), 1982–1984. Margery Deutsch (Associate Conductor), 1981–1983. Margery Deutsch (Acting Music Director), 1983–1984. Peter Leonard, 1984-present.

BIBLIOGRAPHY: An oral history is currently in preparation.

ACCESS: Shreveport Symphony, 2803 Woodlawn Drive, P.O. Box 4057, Shreveport, LA 71134, (318) 869–2559. Sandra Keiser Edwards, General Manager. Clay Edwards, Director of Development.

SANDRA KEISER EDWARDS

Maine _____

PORTLAND (183,625)

Portland Symphony Orchestra (Mt)

The first forerunner of the Portland Symphony Orchestra, the Amateur Strand Symphony Orchestra established in 1923 by Arthur F. Kendall, gave its first concert on February 25, 1924, under his direction in the old Strand Theater on Congress Street, Portland. It was not until 1932, after a number of reorganizations, that it gave a concert under its present title on May 27, directed by Charles Raymond Cronham. Cronham had been the conductor since 1927, during a period of great musical turmoil in Portland. From its inception it considered itself more than a local Portland organization, performing whenever possible in various parts of southern Maine, under different auspices, and with widely varying types of programs.

The Amateur Strand Symphony Orchestra was reorganized in 1924–1925 as the Portland Symphony Society, but in spite of the support of John S. Morris, a local broker and its primary patron, it came to an end in 1926. The Portland Music Commission then fired Kendall and appointed Charles Raymond Cronham, the municipal organist, as conductor of the newly formed Portland Municipal Orchestra. The orchestra grew to 82 members during 1927–1928, about 25 of whom were professionals.

During the 1931–1932 season, as a result of a controversy between Cronham and the Portland Music Commission, the orchestra broke from the Commission, Cronham withdrew from the battlefield, and the Commission itself was dissolved by unanimous vote of the city council.

The 1936–1937 season saw the formation of the Portland Symphony Association for the purpose of supporting the orchestra. During the next 20 years a Women's Committee and a Men's Committee appeared, a series of youth concerts began, a Student Philharmonic Orchestra was formed, and finally the Portland City Hall Auditorium became the home for PSO rehearsals as well as concerts. An endowment fund was established in 1958. In 1959, extensive revision of the bylaws permitted the orchestra to become professional, to enlarge the Board, to hire a permanent manager, and to set a wage scale to be approved by the AFM local, thus finally permitting the orchestra to grow into today's mature, responsible musical organization.

The 1984–1985 Portland season includes seven concerts in its classical series, four in its pops series and seven in its youth concerts and Kinder Konzerts, many of which are repeated elsewhere. In addition, there was a 1984 Summer Starlight series of three concerts at various locations in or near Portland.

The PSO has spawned a number of subsidiary organizations including chamber orchestras of various sizes (since 1928), youth orchestras (begun in 1942–1943 under Clinton W. Graffam, Jr.), the Community Orchestra of the Portland Symphony (COPS: an amateur orchestra currently directed by Graffam, former oboist with the PSO), and the Portland String Quartet (in 1969; now a separate organization). The COPS, selling its own services and raising its own contributions, is self-funded. The PSO has held young artists award competitions since 1959–1960, under various titles.

The PSO has 81 regularly contracted professional personnel, coming in equal proportions from Portland, from nearby areas, and from Boston, all paid per service. Its size changes with the works performed. Its 1984–1985 gross budget of $800,000 is derived from the NEA; the Maine State Commission on the Arts and Humanities; individual, business, and foundation gifts; ticket sales; program advertising; and sale of services and concessions; 72% comes from earned income.

The PSO has operated in the black for at least the past four seasons. Regular concerts are substantially sold out (97% in 1983–1984). The PSO's home is the 2,340-seat Portland City Hall Auditorium, a large reverberant hall with a shallow, high, wide stage also housing the imposing Kotzschmar organ. The orchestra is governed by a 44-person Board of Directors. There is also a 400-member Women's Committee of the PSO with its own Board of 35, and an Advisory Board of 35.

The PSO is an organization whose vigor comes in part from its willingness to experiment with programming, structure, educational activities, seeking new audiences, fulfilling community and state needs, and adapting to new concepts of the public and social functions of music. In November of 1969 it became the first orchestra to tour outside the United States under the sponsorship of the NEA, when it performed in Canada's maritime provinces. It made its first recording in 1939–1940 for study purposes but currently records for subsequent radio broadcasts and occasional television appearances.

In recent years the orchestra has had a wide repertoire ranging from the seventeenth to the twentieth century, together with contemporary American music, including newly commissioned works. While the major portion of its programming comes from the classic, romantic, and late-romantic periods and early twentieth century, approximately 10% is drawn from post-World War II sources and approximately 15% is American. Music written for or commissioned by the PSO in recent years has included works by David Amram, Barbara Kolb, and Ned Rorem, as well as by Maine composers Elliott Schwartz, Jerry Bowder, Norman Cazden, and Walter Piston.

CHRONOLOGY OF MUSIC DIRECTORS: Arthur F. Kendall (Amateur Strand Symphony Orchestra), 1923–1924; (Portland Orchestral Society), 1925–1926. Charles Raymond Cronham (Portland Municipal Orchestra), 1927–1932; (Portland Symphony Orchestra), 1932. Charles A. Warren, 1932–1935. Paul E. Melrose, 1935–1937. Dr. Russell Ames Cook, 1937–1951. Richard Burgin, 1951–1956. (Guest conductors, 1956–1958.) Rouben Gregorian, 1958–1962. Arthur Bennett Lipkin, 1962–1966. Paul Vermel, 1967–1975. (Guest conductors, 1975–1976.) Bruce Hangen, 1976–1985.

BIBILIOGRAPHY: Interview with PSO General Manager Russell I. Burleigh, 1984. Raymond J. Blair, "Fifty-Nine, Going on Sixty," *Down East*, Oct. 1983. Darryl A. Card, "A Brief History of the Portland Symphony Orchestra (1923–1975)," Masters thesis, University of Southern Maine, 1975. George Thornton Edwards, *Music and Musicians of Maine* (Portland: Southworth Press, 1928).

ACCESS: Portland Symphony Orchestra, 30 Myrtle Street, Portland, ME 04101. (207) 773–8191. Russell I. Burleigh, General Manager.

ROBERT K. BECKWITH

Maryland _____

BALTIMORE (2,174,023)

Baltimore Symphony Orchestra (Mj)

Founded in 1916 as a municipal orchestra (America's first), the Baltimore Symphony has achieved a position of importance among the country's Major orchestras, with a 52-week season comprising some 215 concerts (including several subscription series, pops concerts interspersed throughout the season, about 60 youth concerts, 12 Baltimore Opera Company performances, and a variety of summer concerts, as well as runouts and tours). The orchestra's 1984–1985 budget of approximately $8 million is funded through ticket sales, sponsored concerts and hall rentals (50%); a sustaining fund (15%), grants from the NEA, state of Maryland, city of Baltimore and county of Baltimore (14%); special grants (14%); and endowment interest (7%). Since 1983, the BSO has presented the majority of its concerts at the strikingly designed Joseph Meyerhoff Symphony Hall in downtown Baltimore.

Baltimore has a long and varied musical heritage. According to music historian Lubov Keefer, band concerts in the parks had been popular since 1865. Much musical activity also centered around the Peabody Institute after its founding in 1857 by George Peabody, the New Englander who moved to Baltimore and became one of its leading patrons of education and the arts. By the end of the nineteenth century, there were many cultural attractions (theater, dance, musicals, opera, chamber, and symphonic music) to entice the fancy of music lovers, but all were transient, for Baltimore at the time was a way-station—a musical suburb—between New York and Washington. Nevertheless, there had been for a few years in the 1890s a "Baltimore Symphony" under the direction of Ross Jungnickel. This early group developed to the point where it could offer a "Symphony Orchestra School" in 1898, two years before the orchestra's demise.

The City of Baltimore became an entrepreneur of music starting with the mayoralty of James H. Preston (1911–1919), when it began supporting choral and instrumental ensembles under the guidance of a regular music administrator hired by the municipality. Frederick R. Huber, then manager of the Summer School of the Peabody Conservatory of Music, served in the administrative position of municipal director of music from May 16, 1918, to September 1, 1947, with jurisdiction over all the musical activities sponsored by the municipality, including community singing and open-air concerts paid for by City funds.

Finally a permanent orchestra became imminent in 1914, when the City's Board of Estimates appropriated $8,000 for a music group that would give concerts in the various neighborhoods of the rapidly expanding community. The first seasons were immensely successful, and Frederick Huber soon requested and received an additional appropriation of $6,000 (the first by an American municipal government) to create a symphony orchestra. Huber immediately appointed as its conductor the German-trained Gustav Strube, former violinist and assistant conductor of the Boston Symphony* and Head of the Theory Department at Peabody Conservatory. With musicians from the local musician's union (and a few borrowed from the Philadelphia Orchestra*), and with Huber as volunteer manager, the Baltimore Symphony Orchestra made its debut on February 11, 1916, at the Lyric Theatre, featuring as soloist the distinguished Metropolitan Opera soprano Mabel Garrison, a Baltimore native.

The early years of the Strube era, which was to last until 1930, were aimed at establishing a solid foundation for the nascent orchestra: extending the concert season; balancing the need for salary increases against maintaining ticket prices within the financial reach of the entire community (since it was, in the true sense, a people's orchestra); surviving city politics and "blue laws"; and coping with the war and its aftermath. By 1919 concerts had increased to two a month, and the Lyric Theatre was purchased for the orchestra's use. Strube's musical achievements included children's concerts (from 1924), a program presenting famous Europeans (such as Siegfried Wagner) as conductors, a contest to discover the best local performing talent (the prize being an appearance with the orchestra), performance of works by Maryland composers, radio broadcasts, and orchestral concerts directed to Baltimore's black community.

After Strube's resignation in 1930, there ensued an interim period in which four conductors took over the musical reins of the BSO, each for a brief period of time. The first was George Siemonn (1930–1935), a local musician who had previously guest-conducted one of his own compositions. He fought for increased budgets and fended off a movement to eliminate the Municipal Music Department. His BSO also introduced new music to

Baltimore and continued to recognize the city's own music and musicians. Another achievement was the orchestra's first coast-to-coast broadcast over the NBC network.

Among the eminent visiting soloists was Ernest Schelling, who was appointed to follow Siemonn to the podium. Under Schelling's brief stewardship the program for the children's concerts was expanded according to a model he initiated with the New York Philharmonic.* Handel's *Messiah* was presented during Christmas week with the assistance of the newly formed Handel Choir. After Schelling became ill while in Europe, the BSO was led briefly by Werner Janssen (1938) and Harold Barlow (1938–1941). The BSO repertoire under these American conductors continued to feature American compositions, and the BSO organization began exploring means to lengthen the concert season and also encourage wider public (civic-plus-municipal) support.

By the 1940s, however, the road to Baltimore's orchestral maturity had become difficult, and the fortunes of the organization began to fail. Local authorities, having experienced the difficult depression years, were reluctant to supply funds to extend the season, and the frequent changes of podium leadership had taken their toll on the orchestra's musical and organizational foundations. The press complained—often very colorfully—of the "sorry state of affairs" and appealed for restructuring the orchestra so that it might stand comparison with those of comparably populated cities.

It was necessary to find, as quickly as possible, a person with the youthful spirit and enthusiasm to set new directions, redefine objectives, and do it all with an optimism that would permeate the entire organization. That savior turned out to be Reginald Stewart, a musician who was then enjoying a fourfold career as conductor, pianist, musical administrator, and pedagogue, and who was appointed the fifth director of the Peabody Conservatory on September 1, 1941. A native of Scotland who emigrated to Canada in 1933, Stewart had conducted at the Toronto Conservatory of Music, organized the Bach Society of Toronto (which performed Bach works never before heard in Canada), founded the Toronto Philharmonic Orchestra (1934), and inaugurated the Promenade Concerts that presented fine music to the public for a small admission charge.

Soon after assuming the podium in 1942, Stewart wrote a letter to the Board of Municipal Music suggesting the institution of an orchestral association, allowing the orchestra to become an independent, full-time, 90-piece ensemble funded in part by private subscription for an 18-concert, 20-week season. Of the proposed $185,000 budget, $50,000 would comprise the city of Baltimore's subsidy-purchase of both popular and children's concerts. With support from luminaries such as Metropolitan Opera soprano Rosa Ponselle and Eleanor Roosevelt, the plan met with success, and by February 1945—despite the war—$75,000 had been pledged. The popular Sunday-night concerts continued the tradition of municipal support, while the extended mid-week series gave scope for a broadened repertoire and for the introduction to the city of world-renowned artists. All sides were pleased, and the ensemble that existed prior to 1942 was now referred to as the "old orchestra."

Stewart's twin directorial roles with the BSO and Conservatory enriched both institutions, and some of the finest musical artists were attracted by the dual offer of a position on the Conservatory faculty and membership in the orchestra. Stewart further stocked the orchestra with players from premier ensembles. Tours were booked on a more extensive scale and, despite their expense, returned profits in pride and good will. The policy of making the orchestra available for the presentation of contemporary works, both American and European, was expanded, and premieres became more frequent. Special activities and concerts added greatly to the BSO's schedule, among them a complete Brahms cycle, for example, involving as well the Conservatory, Baltimore's major choral organizations, visiting artists, and chamber ensembles. The orchestra's recognition and popularity grew enormously through expanded radio broadcasts, enlarged children's concert activities, and "All-Request" programs.

By the early 1950s, the BSO had become firmly rooted in the cultural life of city and state, and a happy mixture of the more erudite and lighter musical fare was achieved in the programming. Nevertheless, a sizeable deficit had accumulated as fund drives fell short of their goals. "Save the Symphony" editorials appeared, and there was even talk of merging the Baltimore Symphony and National Symphony.* Among other suggestions were salary and season reductions, word of which caused many BSO musicians to take positions elsewhere. In an effort to save the deteriorating situation, Stewart appeared before the City Council on November 23, 1951, to defend his position. The proceedings, however, were sensationally detailed in the press, and Stewart resigned on January 1, 1952. He bade farewell to the orchestra at the final mid-week concert on March 12, 1952. The praise heaped upon the conductor was voluminous. Ironically, a report published by the *Baltimore News-Post* two days before had informed the public that the name of Reginald Stewart was high on the list of those who had made private, voluntary contributions to the orchestra.

Viewed in retrospect, the next two BSO regimes, those of Massimo Freccia and Peter Herman Adler, constitute an interregnum between the influential period of Stewart and the epoch-making Comissiona era, which was to begin some 15 years later. Although activities in every area were continued (and in some cases increased) and matters were handled in a thorough and professional manner, the main difference was that not much of a musical imprint was left on the performance posture of the BSO. Both the Italian-born Freccia and his assistant, Remo Bolognini, were tireless workers in fulfilling the scheduled assignments. In his programming Freccia gave the most attention to music of Austro-German and Russian composers and to producing large-scale orchestral-vocal attractions including concert versions of stage works.

One of the many guest conductors under Freccia was Peter Herman Adler, who was appointed music director beginning with the 1959–1960 season. The Adler years were marked with an increase in the number of concerts per season (to 180 by 1964), as well as an intensified outreach to youth, from pre-grade school through the university levels. With Allan Miller as director of the Youth Education Program and with the help of Paul Freeman and associate conductors Herbert Grossman and Elyakum Shapira, BSO educational activities flourished, with as many as 70 concerts per year directed to youth. "Lolli-pops" concerts and Kinder Konzerts were also instituted, the latter conducted by Harry John Brown.

In 1964 the orchestra began an enduring association with the Baltimore Civic Opera Company (now the Baltimore Opera Company) with a production of Bizet's *Carmen*. Although the Opera had previously utilized BSO musicians, this was the first time the entire orchestra was used in the pit. During the Adler years Baltimore audiences also heard 75 European and 25 American works for the first time, in addition to four U.S. and five world premieres.

The BSO's next music director, Romanian-born Sergiu Comissiona, came onto the Baltimore musical scene during the middle of the 1967–1968 season in quite an unheralded manner, leading the orchestra in a subscription concert and three runouts. His soloist on each occasion was the American pianist Anthony di Bonaventura, an artist with whom he developed an immediate ensemble rapport and who was to make several later appearances with the BSO. Comissiona soon demonstrated a voracious appetite for work, an unrivalled command of the repertoire, an uncanny sense of programming (allowing the mixture of traditional and novel in a blend that would please the listener and challenge the player), not to mention a personal charm and magnetism.

The orchestra soon responded, becoming more formidable and versatile, able to express stronger and more varied symphonic nuances, to assimilate a great amount of the traditional and contemporary repertoire within a more stable ensemble discipline. Accordingly, the Baltimore public was introduced to over 100 different works of Europeans from the baroque through the twentieth century. American music was also emphasized and widely programmed. A yearly commissioning program established in 1970 resulted in world premieres by many leading contemporary American composers. By the end of Comissiona's first decade (1968–1978), the Symphony Association's publication, *Overture*, could report the performance of 600 different works a total of 1,869 times in 544 concerts, representing the creative products of 184 composers, 61 of whom were American. Twelve world and four U.S. premieres were presented during that period.

Touring was continued with renewed interest and vigor during the Comissiona era, with visits within the state, to most of the eastern seaboard states, to Mexico in 1979–1980, and to Germany in 1981 for 15 concerts (making the BSO the first major American orchestra to perform in East Germany).

Back home, the concert season for young audiences was again expanded, with tiny tots concerts and a "Music for Youth" series, soloist and composers competitions, and a program begun in 1977 to permit gifted young players to participate in a full-fledged rehearsal with BSO musicians. The BSO Women's Association (later known as Baltimore Symphony Associates) began sponsoring annual young soloist and conductor competitions, the winners of which received cash prizes and appearances with the BSO. During the July concerts of the 1978–1980 seasons, winners of other performing contests (Piatigorsky Competition, American National Chopin, etc.) were also given featured exposure with the orchestra. In 1983 a new program entitled the Baltimore Symphony Awards was established, its audition winners appearing with the BSO in recital.

In an effort to extend the concert season and provide year-round music, several distinctive summer series were developed in the late 1960s through the 1970s in which the BSO played in city plazas, outlying parks, colleges, and other informal settings. With the completion of the Meyerhoff Symphony Hall before the summer of 1983, however, the thrust of summer programming reverted to the downtown area.

Comissiona had raised the idea of a new concert hall about eight years earlier, but the person who nurtured it to reality in four short years was Joseph Meyerhoff, president of the BSO from 1965 until his death in February 1985. A philanthropist of wide recognition, Meyerhoff led the project both administratively and financially (with a gift of $10.5 million toward the hall's eventual cost of $23 million). The hall's first musical event was a "Hard Hat Concert" attended by all who worked on the project, during which acousticians endeavored to fine-tune the auditorium for the festive inauguration which occurred on September 16, 1982. With excellent acoustical properties, an unobstructed view for an audience of 2,467, interior appointments that bathe the listener in a warm atmosphere of intimate elegance, and a stage that can easily accommodate large orchestral and choral forces, Meyerhoff Symphony Hall is a symbol of Baltimore's continuing cultural renaissance.

Two other of Comissiona's dreams that were fulfilled were the initiation of commercial recordings and the endowment of principal chairs. The endowments began in 1978, and there are to date 13 endowed chairs. Leaving behind a legacy of rich and diversified achievements, Comissiona parted with the orchestra during the summer of 1984, and his successor will be David Zinman, director designate for 1984–1985. Zinman will assume command on a full-time basis in the 1985–1986 season.

RECORDING HISTORY AND BRIEF DISCOGRAPHY: The BSO began commercial recordings in 1973 under Sergiu Comissiona, and has since recorded for Desto, Deutsche Grammophon, Turnabout, Vanguard, and Vox.

Britten, *Diversions on a Theme for Piano Left-Hand*; Laderman, Concerto for Orchestra (Fleisher/Comissiona); Desto 7168. Brahms-Schoenberg, Piano Quartet, op. 25 (Comissiona): Vox Cum Laude D-VCL–9066. Mendelssohn, Symphony No. 4, op. 90, and Symphony No. 5, op. 107 (Comissiona): Turnabout QTV-S–34643. Pettersson, Symphony No. 8 (Comissiona): DG 2531–176. Respighi, *The Pines of Rome* and *Roman Festivals* (Comissiona): Vanguard VA–25004. Saint Saëns, Symphony No. 3 in C-Minor (Comissiona): Vanguard VA–25008.

CHRONOLOGY OF MUSIC DIRECTORS: Gustav Strube, 1916–1930. George Siemonn, 1930–1935. Ernest Schelling, 1935–1937. Werner Janssen, 1937–1938. Harold Barlow, 1938–1942. Reginald Stewart, 1942–1952. Massimo Freccia, 1952–1959. Peter Herman Adler, 1959–1968. Brian Priestman (Resident Conductor), 1968–1969. Sergiu Comissiona, 1969–1984. David Zinman, 1984-present.

BIBLIOGRAPHY: *Baltimore Evening Sun. Baltimore News-Post.* Kenneth S. Clark, *Baltimore—Cradle of Municipal Music* (Baltimore: City of Baltimore, 1941). Lubov Keefer, *Baltimore's Music: The Haven of the American Composer* (Baltimore: Author, 1962). John Mueller, *The American Symphony Orchestra* (1951; Westport, Conn.: Greenwood Press, 1976). *Overture*, Publication of the Baltimore Symphony Association. *Washington Post.*

ACCESS: Baltimore Symphony Orchestra, 1212 Cathedral Street, Baltimore, MD 21201. (301) 727–3700. John Gidwitz, Executive Director. Mark VanOss, Director of Marketing and Public Relations.

SAM DI BONAVENTURA

Massachusetts ———————————

BOSTON (2,763,357)

Boston Symphony Orchestra (Mj)

The Boston Symphony Orchestra is among the busiest, presenting up to 280 concerts per year to a live audience of some 1.5 million. It yearly offers eight subscription series in its regular fall and winter season, nine weeks of Boston Pops concerts, outdoor performances, residence at Tanglewood Music Center, a series of young people's concerts, and frequent tours. The BSO Chamber Players, largely BSO principals, have an additional season. Since 1970 the BSO has been joined in selected concerts by its affiliated Tanglewood Festival Chorus, which also participates in some of the orchestra's approximately 10 recordings per year.

Founded in 1881 and incorporated in 1919, the BSO is headed by a 27-member Board of Trustees and a much larger Board of Overseers. The BSO has some 225 full-time employees (including over 100 playing members) on an annual budget of about $24 million. Committees of musicians, management, and/or Board members consider contract negotiations, dismissals, personnel relations, seating, and to a limited extent, artistic policy. A pension fund, established in 1903, is financed in part by special concerts. Contracts conform to the BSO Trade Agreement governing benefits, working conditions, and base salary; however, about two-thirds of the musical personnel receive payment beyond the minimum. The BSO is funded through its endowments, Rockefeller and Ford grants, public endowment funds, ticket sales, recordings, broadcasts, private and corporate donations, and the Friends of the Boston Symphony Orchestra, founded in 1934. A more aggressive management style has emerged in recent years under BSO Manager Thomas W. Morris, as public fund-raising has become an increasingly important sector of BSO income. Thirty BSO chairs are currently endowed, as are the positions of stage manager and music director.

The BSO string section is enriched by numerous privately owned instruments of the Italian masters. The orchestra maintains an extensive inventory of orchestral instruments in addition to its Casedesus Collection of Ancient Instruments, currently on display at Symphony Hall.

The only Major orchestra in New England, the BSO has an enormous cultural impact. Its musicians teach privately and in neighboring universities, most notably Boston University and the New England Conservatory. BSO members commonly participate as conductors, concertmasters, or soloists in the many smaller orchestras in and around the greater Boston area. The BSO is widely the model in terms of seating, repertoire, and musical desiderata east of the Connecticut River Valley. Its influence extends well beyond the conservatories. Alluding to this fact and with a pun on the high "A" (442 cps) that brightens the BSO sound, there is a familiar maxim among New England musicians that "The farther from Boston, the lower the pitch."

As the subject of about a dozen books and countless articles, the BSO and its affiliated organizations and personnel have probably been written about more thoroughly than any other American orchestra.

Nineteenth-century Boston was a busy port enjoying a steady flow of foreign and home trade, a great university, and a historical heritage second to none. It was capable of supporting a major orchestra—it had wealth, education, and tradition. But unlike cosmopolitan New York (already home to three large orchestras including Theodore Thomas's touring ensemble), Boston had yet to generate its own major ensemble. Symphonic music in Boston before 1881 was provided chiefly by the Philharmonic and the Handel and Haydn Societies,* the latter being Boston's oldest continuously active musical group, still an important institution today. For some years at mid-century the Germania Orchestra resided in Boston, leaving behind the cultural influence of German taste and tradition. The home of other local groups as well, Boston was visited regularly by the Theodore Thomas Orchestra, whose symphonic repertoire and high standards provided an important link to the European musical ideals that would soon be realized in Boston's own Symphony Orchestra.

The story of Henry Lee Higginson's philanthropic founding of the BSO is well known. The son of a prominent and well-established Boston family, young Higginson studied music in Europe, where he was enraptured by the great German and Austrian ensembles in their late romantic splendor. After returning to America, Higginson joined his father's financial firm and resolved to bring to his fellow Bostonians the musical excellence of the Continent. The task would take the rest of his life, wreaking havoc with his personal fortune, but establishing within his lifetime one of the world's finest orchestras.

Higginson's original plan for the BSO included both a winter symphonic season and a summer season of lighter fare; also chamber concerts, open rehearsals, seats set aside at low prices for last-minute sale, the eventual establishment of an associated music school, and—an innovation in Boston—a roster of 72 musicians wholly committed to and employed full-time by the orchestra. In its first, 20-concert season (1881–1882), under the artistic direction of Georg Henschel, the orchestra achieved important immediate goals of sufficient recognition and audience support to enable a second season of 32 performances.

Higginson retained personal proprietary control of the BSO for many years but delegated artistic authority wholly to the music director. In 1885 his became the first American orchestra with a full-time manager, Charles Ellis. Nevertheless, Higginson until 1919 personally negotiated all contracts with BSO employees. His paternalism made the orchestra one of few in which a concert musician could find a degree of financial stability.

Under Georg Henschel the BSO established both its form and a long-standing tradition of being a molder of popular taste in symphonic music, as exemplified by Henschel's penchant for Brahms and Dvořák. However, recognizing the new orchestra's need for an audience, and given the current level of Boston's musical sophistication, Henschel wisely programmed more popularly appealing music in the second half of each program.

His successor in 1884, Wilhelm Gericke, dropped the lighter works, presenting concerts in today's pattern, with major pieces last. Gericke introduced many new works, including Brahms's Third Symphony, which promptly cleared the hall of Bostonians whose tastes were for opposing styles. A disciplinarian, Gericke replaced many local BSO musicians with German instrumentalists securely trained in the rigors of orchestral routine. Gericke also initiated tours, first to Philadelphia in 1885 and then in the 1886–1887 season to New York, an event that made the nation and, just as importantly, the BSO itself, realize how fine and thoroughly established an orchestra it was. Tours continued, and the concert season increased to 112 performances in Gericke's last year (1889).

Following Gericke was the fiery, charismatic Arthur Nikisch—perhaps too fiery for some Bostonians. To him may be attributed the popular perception of Boston as home to an ensemble that could not only attract a Nikisch, but could execute his always unexpected commands with aplomb.

After a brief interregnum by BSO concertmaster Franz Kneisel in 1893, the BSO contracted Emil Paur, whose major addition to the repertoire was his inclusion of Richard Strauss. In 1893 Wilhelm Gericke returned, and he too played Strauss and other contemporaries. By the end of Gericke's second term, the BSO had reached maturity. Its alumni included world-famous conductors; it was recognized internationally as a major ensemble; it toured extensively; its repertoire was wide and ever growing; its management was stable; and it had administrative amenities, such as high salaries, extended seasons, and a pension fund, to make it a most desirable employer.

Moreover, in 1900 the BSO had occupied its permanent home, Symphony Hall. Planned for years under Higginson's personal supervision, it was the first hall built according to principles of acoustical engineering. Project Consultant Wallace C. Sabine studied the BSO's old Music Hall as well as the Leipzig Gewandhaus and other halls to combine their best qualities. Symphony Hall seats some 2,600 during the regular season; with row seats removed for the tables and chairs of Pops season, capacity decreases by about 300.

Gericke's successor in 1906 was Karl (Carl) Muck. From 1908 to 1912 his tenure was interrupted, and the BSO was led by Max Fiedler, who, unlike Muck, courted audience approval through somewhat lighter programs. Muck was a scholar whose first interest was the quality of musical experience. He continued the BSO tradition of premieres by including works of Schoenberg, and he also tried to balance programs for their period and stylistic content. He made shifts in personnel to create a tonal balance he thought most suitable to his varied repertoire. Although the orchestra was still predominantly German and Austrian, French and American musicians gained some in prominence.

The BSO's identification with German conductors, musicians, and composers led the orchestra, and Muck especially, into hard times during World War I. Intense, irrational American sentiment against German culture led to a complex series of misunderstandings resulting in Muck and the BSO being accused of refusing to play the "Star Spangled Banner," an incident taken up as a cause célèbre by antagonistic journalists. Muck, under federal scrutiny as an "enemy alien," departed, and in 1918 both the BSO and Higginson were left in near ruins.

Higginson died soon afterward, unable to provide his intended endowment, and the BSO was to undergo several years of turmoil and change. Ellis, the manager, retired and was replaced by his assistant, William Brennan. Only through the generosity of the newly appointed Board members did the orchestra remain solvent.

Following Muck's last year came a season under Henri Rabaud, who in 1918–1919 filled vacant wind seats with his French compatriots. The French tradition in wind playing was at its height, and the French style, with its lightness and vibrato, must have had a profound impact on the BSO's musical character. He complemented this move with works of already-accepted French and Russian composers, along with German composers who were safely enshrined in the classical past.

The BSO was to be healed by its first towering conductor of the modern period, Pierre Monteux. In the years surrounding the BSO's incorporation and revised administration, salaries had suffered, and in 1920 a cadre of musicians refused to perform. The strike finally lost the BSO 31 players. (Nevertheless, until 1942 the BSO remained unaffiliated with the AFM.)

Once again, vacant seats had to be filled, and the renewal of the BSO as a top orchestra took several years. Monteux continued, as he had in Paris and elsewhere, to introduce new music. Vaughan Williams, Holst, Respighi, Milhaud, Moussorgsky, Honegger, and Griffes all had their moments, but the most dramatic must have been Stravinsky's *Rite of Spring*, which Monteux had conducted in its tumultuous Paris debut, and which he brought in 1924 for the first time to Boston (and, through the BSO tour, to New York as well).

In 1924 came Serge Koussevitzky, still remembered for his idiosyncrasies, autocratic manner, and great musical foresight. Koussevitzky increased by 25% the number of individual pieces played per season, enlarged the ensemble's size, expanded the playing year, encouraged joint choral performances, established the still-current practice of inviting guest conductors to take over at mid-season, and, more than anyone before, he encouraged new music. The most famous and enduring example is probably Bartók's Concerto for Orchestra, composed for the BSO shortly before Bartók's death. Koussevitzky's lasting musical legacy to the BSO, however, according to some orchestra members, was his insistence on perfecting both tone production and ensemble playing, qualities by which the BSO makes its reputation still.

Two years after Koussevitzky's arrival the BSO began regularly scheduled radio broadcasts. Suspended for some years in the late 1930s by union pressure, they were ensured in 1958 by the establishment of the Boston Symphony Transcription Trust, which makes broadcast tapes available around the world.

In 1936 Koussevitzky and the BSO were invited to perform at the music festival at the 210-acre Tanglewood estate at Lenox, Massachusetts. Shortly thereafter, the estate's land and buildings were donated to the BSO, and in 1938 a permanent structure, the Music Shed, was built to accommodate the orchestra's summer season of concerts, open rehearsals, and special events. At Koussevitzky's urging, the BSO founded at Tanglewood in 1940 the Berkshire Music Center for educating individual musicians, fostering ensemble skills, and nurturing new music. The Center (renamed the Tanglewood Music Center in 1984) now enrolls about 500 students annually in a variety of programs. It has been estimated that over 20% of the musicians in major American orchestras are Tanglewood Music Center graduates.

When Charles Munch came in 1949, the BSO was on the verge of its first international tours: in 1952 to 11 European cities; in 1956 to the Soviet Union, the first American orchestra to visit that country; in 1960 to the Far East and Australia. The Boston Symphony Youth Concerts were inaugurated in 1959 at the urging of Harry Ellis Dickson, BSO violinist and Pops assistant conductor. Under Dickson's musical direction, the 15-concert season reaches some 40,000 young people, with an effort to feature compositions and performance by area youth and to encourage audience participation.

With the arrival of Erich Leinsdorf in 1962 came the series of regularly scheduled television broadcasts. When these ended in 1980 they were in joint production with WGBH-TV under the title *Evening at Symphony*. Perhaps through association with the then-popular image of Boston as a reserved and wealthy city, through the BSO's finesse with tone and ensemble, or through Leinsdorf's reserved and aloof stage presence, these telecasts seem to have lent popular credence to the BSO's image as the "aristocrat of American orchestras."

The year 1962 also marked Joseph Silverstein's inauguration as BSO concertmaster. Silverstein emerged as a leader among New England musicians. BSO associate conductor, frequent soloist, and renowned teacher, he left the BSO in 1984 to become music director of the Utah Symphony.* Silverstein retains his faculty position at Tanglewood while the BSO associate conductorship remains vacant as of mid–1985; the position of concertmaster has been awarded to Malcolm Lowe.

In 1964 Leinsdorf organized the Boston Symphony Chamber Players, chiefly BSO principals who perform their eclectic repertoire in concert at Boston's Jordan Hall, on recordings, and on tours throughout the world. The mutual responsiveness among BSO principals in symphonic settings has been attributed in part to sensitivity to tone quality, ensemble, and musical dialogue fostered in their chamber music association.

Following William Steinberg's three-year appointment and the brief stewardship of Assistant Conductor Michael Tilson Thomas, the BSO found its current maestro, Seiji Ozawa. Under Ozawa, whose energies are divided among many conducting duties around the world, the BSO has intensified its tour schedule. The orchestra visited Europe in 1976, Japan in 1978, and in 1979 mainland China, where performances were interspersed with master classes and discussion groups. That tour was chronicled in the Emmy-winning CBS television special "Boston Goes to China." Since then the BSO has visited European music festivals on one tour and both Europe and the Orient on another. In its centennial celebration (1981–1982), the BSO commissioned 12 works, eight of them by Americans, including Roger Sessions's Pulitzer-prize-winning Concerto for Orchestra. When Ozawa left the San Francisco Symphony* for Boston in 1972, he brought a fluidity and rhythmic vitality that gave his conducting a naturalness many found comforting. He has won critical praise for these qualities and for his ability to clarify the most complex scores; yet he has been criticized in the press for allowing the BSO to be (among other things) sometimes too comfortable with its music making, sometimes too restrained or objective.

THE BOSTON POPS: In 1885 the BSO began a 10-week spring season of lighter music to please audiences and fill out the musicians' work year, thereby solidifying their allegiance to the BSO. These "Music Hall Prome-nade Concerts," modeled on a London prototype, were later known as "Popular" or "Pops." In 1930 the Pops secured the services of BSO violinist and violist Arthur Fiedler, who had just founded the outdoor series of Esplanade concerts. Fiedler's first Pops concert ended with Sousa's "Stars and Stripes Forever," now indelibly associated with the Pops and a mainstay of pops programs throughout America. Fiedler supported many emerging American composers and arrangers. Leroy Anderson and Richard Hayman are prominent examples. Upon Fiedler's death in 1979, John Williams was appointed conductor.

Despite the difficulty of following a leader whose public personality ex-uded such magnetism as Fiedler's, Williams proved an apt choice from the audience viewpoint. He has maintained the traditional Pops programming, with generous helpings of his own compositions (among them his popular film scores). He also appears frequently in the capacity of performer/con-ductor. His recent (and inescapably public) disagreement with Pops mu-sicians over orchestra discipline seems to have had little effect on audience loyalty to either Williams or the orchestra.

The Boston Pops comprises regular BSO members, except principals, who instead tour as the BSO Chamber Players. Programs typically consist of three musical sessions and two intermissions. Light classical fare is followed by a soloist, and the evening ends with show tunes or other currently popular music. They are held six nights a week for several weeks in the spring as well as during the Christmas/New Year's week, when the champagne nor-mally served during Pops concerts takes on a more traditional meaning. Since 1969 selected programs have been televised as "Evening at Pops," an annual series of 12 shows.

RECORDING HISTORY AND SELECTIVE DISCOGRAPHY: The BSO's first major re-cording (Tchaikovsky's Fourth Symphony) was made under Muck in 1917 at RCA's facility in Camden, N.J. In 1935 the floor of Symphony Hall was transformed into an on-demand recording studio, for which it is still used today. The BSO recorded exclusively for RCA until 1969, when it became the first American orchestra to record for Deutsche Grammophon, for which it has recorded regularly since. Recent releases on Philips, Telarc, New World, and CBS labels have extended the orchestra's range of recordings. Many BSO members record individually (particularly for North-eastern Records), and some of their discs are collectors' items, especially those on the old "Boston" label. The following record selections were made by BSO Musi-cologist and Program Annotator Steven Ledbetter.

Beethoven, Piano Concerto No. 4, op. 58 (Serkin/Ozawa): Telarc DG–10064. Debussy, *La Mer*; Ibert *Escales* (Munch): RCA ATL–1–4157. *An Evening at Pops* (Fiedler): RCA AGL2–2443 (2 records). Ives, *Three Places in New England*; Ruggles, *Sun-Treader* (Thomas): Deutche Grammophon 2530048. Mahler, Symphony No. 8 (Ozawa): Philips 6769069 (2 records). *Pops around the World—Digital Overtures* (Williams): Philips 6514186. Schoenberg, *Gurrelieder* (Ozawa): Philips 6769038 (2 records). Sibelius, Symphonies and Selected Works (Colin Davis): Philips 6709011

(5 records). Tchaikovsky, Piano Concerto No. 1; Franck, Symphonic Variations (Rubenstein/Leinsdorf): RCA AGL1–5217.

CHRONOLOGY OF MUSIC DIRECTORS: Georg Henschel, 1881–1884. Wilhelm Gericke, 1884–1889. Arthur Nikisch, 1889–1893. Emil Paur, 1893–1898. Wilhelm Gericke, 1898–1906. Karl Muck, 1906–1908. Max Fiedler, 1908–1912. Karl Muck, 1912–1918. Henri Rabaud, 1918–1919. Pierre Monteux, 1919–1924. Serge Koussevitzky, 1924–1949. Charles Munch, 1949–1962. Erich Leinsdorf, 1962–1969. William Steinberg, 1969–1972. Seiji Ozawa, 1972-present.

BIBLIOGRAPHY: Interview with BSO Musicologist and Program Annotator Steven Ledbetter. Janet Baker-Carr, *Evening at Symphony* (Boston: Houghton-Mifflin, 1977). Harry Ellis Dickson, *Arthur Fiedler and the Boston Pops* (Boston: Houghton-Mifflin, 1981). Harry Ellis Dickson, *Gentlemen, More Dolce, Please (Second Movement)* (Boston: Beacon Press, 1974). Philip Hart, *Orpheus in the New World* (New York: Norton, 1973). Mark Anthony DeWolfe Howe, *The Boston Symphony Orchestra, 1881–1931* (Boston, 1931). Hugo Leichtentritt, *Serge Koussevitzky, the Boston Symphony Orchestra, and the New American Music* (Cambridge: Harvard University Press, 1946). John Mueller, *The American Symphony Orchestra* (1951; reprint, Westport, Conn.: Greenwood Press, 1976). Harold C. Schonberg, *The Great Conductors* (New York: Simon & Schuster, 1967). Louis Snyder, *Community of Sound: The Boston Symphony and Its World of Players* (Boston: Beacon Press, 1979). Deborah Trustman, "Ozawa's BSO: The Sound and the Fury," *New York Times Magazine*, 12 Oct. 1980.

ACCESS: Boston Symphony Orchestra, Symphony Hall, 301 Massachusetts Ave., Boston, MA 02115. (617) 266–1492. Thomas W. Morris, General Manager. Caroline Smedvig, Director of Promotion.

                                                        ROBERT R. CRAVEN

Handel and Haydn Society (Mt)

The Handel and Haydn Society is the oldest choral-orchestral organization in America. Founded in Boston in 1815, the Society has presented—without interruption—169 continuous seasons, or nearly 2,000 concerts as of 1984–1985. Presently it offers between six and seven subscription programs in its fall-to-spring season, with each concert repeated once. Recently, one non-subscription concert has been offered to the general public in December, featuring the Society's musical centerpiece, *Messiah*, which has been performed in the subscription series every Christmas season since 1854.

Members of the Handel and Haydn Society chorus and orchestra represent the finest professional talent available throughout the New England area; they qualify only after rigorous auditions. They are contracted on a per-service basis, although many members perform year after year, providing continuity in personnel. Internationally recognized vocalists and instrumentalists regularly appear with the group. The Society's musical influence on Boston and the surrounding region has been considerable, particularly in the area of choral music. Within the last five years the Society has participated in a series of programs sponsored and broadcast by NPR.

Since its beginning the Society has been administered by a president and Board of Governors. The Board is still responsible for the overall management of the Handel and Haydn Society, including fund-raising, administration, and the election of the Society's president, but it no longer fully exercises its mandate in creative areas. In 1967, with the appointment of Conductor Thomas Dunn, the Board added the title of artistic director to that position. The artistic director/conductor is currently responsible for recruiting singers and instrumentalists, planning concert seasons, selecting all musical works, and conducting the ensemble.

With a subscriber base of almost 4,000 members, the Society generates over 60% of its operating expenses through ticket revenues. Additional funding for the 1984–1985 budget of approximately $750,000 is provided by the NEA and the Massachusetts Council for the Arts and Humanities, a state agency whose funds are made available through recommendations proposed by the governor and approved by the State Legislature.

In 1815, a group of prominent musical amateurs organized the Handel and Haydn Society and dedicated it to "introducing into more general use the works of Handel and Haydn and other eminent composers." By selecting Handel, the Society affirmed its interest in the music of the past; its choice of Haydn, who had died only six years earlier, verified a commitment to contemporary music. The Society's first concert was held in Boston's Stone Chapel on Christmas Day, 1815. A chorus of 100, an organist, and an orchestra of 12 performed selections from Handel's *Messiah*, *Israel in Egypt*, and *Judas Maccabaeus*, as well as portions of Haydn's *Creation*. By 1817 the Society was in a position to offer the public complete performances of *Messiah* and the *Creation*, a Boston premiere for the former work and an American premiere for the latter.

The conductor of the orchestra, Gottlieb Graupner (who had played in London under Haydn), was the only professional musician in the ensemble during its early seasons. A founding member, he is thought to be largely responsible for much of the Handel and Haydn Society's early repertoire and its strong commitment to the music of its two namesakes. It may have been he who suggested to the Society that it commission Beethoven to write an oratorio, an offer left unanswered by the composer.

The Society pursued its own music publishing enterprises, which included making available new editions of vocal and choral scores from the standard oratorios of the day. Titled the *Handel and Haydn Collection of Church Music*, the first volume appeared in 1821. These editions had much to do with standardizing sacred music of this type throughout New England.

Ensuing years brought several important developments. The Society moved in 1852 to the Music Hall, considered in its day one of the finest concert halls in the country. It served as home to the Society until 1900, when it moved to the Boston Symphony Orchestra's* new Symphony Hall, where it still performs. When Jonas Chickering (owner of the Chickering piano firm) appointed the Society's first music director in 1847, he was responding to years of critical charges that Society presidents (not always skilled musicians) should not be conductors; Charles E. Horn thus became the organization's first official conductor, although it would be many years before the Board relinquished its full control over the repertoire.

In 1854, the Society appointed as conductor Carl Zerrahn, a former flutist with the famous Germania Society orchestra that had had such an impact on musical taste in the United States. With Zerrahn came other former Germania musicians, and under his direction the Society moved directly into its romantic period, performing works of Beethoven, Berlioz, Brahms, Mendelssohn, and Verdi—without, however, compromising its commitment to perform Handel and Haydn. Zerrahn increased the overall size of the ensemble to heroic dimensions; Boston music lovers were enamored of romantic "bigness." At an 1872 event sponsored by entrepreneur Patrick Gilmore, 20,000 singers and 1,500 musicians were brought together for a single concert. The formation of the Boston Symphony Orchestra in 1881 helped the Handel and Haydn Society re-evaluate the wisdom of performing the larger symphonic works added to the repertoire by Zerrahn. Zerrahn initiated several commissions for the Society, the most interesting of which engaged Robert Franz to reorchestrate Mozart's version of *Messiah* to rid it "of all objectionable passages." Franz's version was to be the Society's most popular until the mid-twentieth century. Zerrahn's 40-year association with the Society also saw American premieres of various other Handel and Bach works, including the *St. Matthew Passion.*

Despite its move to Symphony Hall in 1900, the Handel and Haydn Society began to experience serious difficulties. Still governed by antiquated bylaws and an all-male Board, the Society was able, despite internal struggles, to maintain its stature in the eyes of many Bostonians as the premier ensemble for performing *Messiah, Elijah,* and other classic works of the past. Despite some noble experiments with more modern composers (the all-Wagner program of 1935, for example), the Society and its music continued to be identified with bygone days.

The post-World-War-II era brought reforms to the Society that produced some very positive improvements. In 1965, to celebrate its 150th consecutive season, the Society hosted an international choral festival, inviting choruses from the USSR, England, Hungary, and New Zealand.

Two years later Thomas Dunn was appointed music director and conductor. One of the country's leading Handelians, Dunn had considerable experience with choral and orchestral music. His influence on the Society was immediate and ultimately dramatic. During Dunn's tenure, the Society has modernized its bylaws and administrative procedures. Dunn reduced the size of the chorus to an average of 30 members and that of the orchestra to about 20. In addition, he raised the overall standards of the ensemble to satisfy professional criteria. The old familiar masterpieces were performed with new insights while remaining faithful to the original scores; and the overall repertoire was enriched with new works capable of appealing to a much more diverse and musically sophisticated audience. For example, Dunn's early seasons included works by Schütz, Scriabin, Satie, and Stravinsky; the 159th season was eclectic and innovative, premiering a Haydn symphony with annotations from an eighteenth-century critic-at-large. To celebrate its 170th (1984–1985) season, the Society will recognize the 300th birthdays of Handel and Bach with all-baroque programs including *Messiah*, the *B-Minor Mass*, *Alexander's Feast*, the complete *Brandenburg Concertos*, and the *Suites for Orchestra*.

In 1984, the Society announced that Thomas Dunn would retire as music director in June of 1986. He will continue as Conductor Laureate, principal guest conductor, and artistic advisor and will supervise a two-year search for a successor. There seems every reason to believe that the Society will continue to meet the principal mandate of its founders: to perform the music of the past and present while serving the "highest artistic interests, and these only."

RECORDING HISTORY AND SELECTIVE DISCOGRAPHY: The Handel and Haydn Society produced its first recording in 1955, an abbreviated version of *Messiah*, on the Unicorn label. The most recent recording, now out of print, is a 1979 performance of *Messiah* with Dunn conducting (Sine Qua Non).

CHRONOLOGY OF MUSIC DIRECTORS: President-Conductors: Thomas S. Webb, 1815–1817. Benjamin Holt, 1817–1818. Amasa Winchester, 1818–1826. Lowell Mason, 1827–1832. Samuel Richardson, 1832–1834. Bartholomew Brown, 1836–1837. Charles Zeuner, 1838–1839. George J. Webb, 1839–1842. Jonas Chickering, 1843–1847.

Music Conductors: Charles E. Horn, 1847–1849. J. E. Goodson, 1851–1852. George J.Webb, 1852. Carl Bergmann, 1852–1854. Carl Zerrahn, 1854–1895. Benjamin J. Lang, 1895–1897. Carl Zerrahn, 1897–1898. Reinhold Herman, 1898–1899. Emil Mollenhauer, 1899–1927. Thompson Stone, 1927–1959. Edward F. Gilday, 1959–1967. Thomas Dunn (Artistic Director), 1967–1986.

BIBLIOGRAPHY: Interviews with Handel and Haydn Society Musicologist Joseph Dyer and Director of Marketing and Development Peter Kosewski. William F. Bradbury and Courtenay Guild, *History of the Handel and Haydn Society of Boston*, Vol II (1911–1934; reprint, New York: Da Capo, 1984). Handel and Haydn Society, Archives, Boston Public Library. H. Earle Johnson, *Hallelujah, Amen!: The Story of the Handel and Haydn Society* (Boston: Bruch Humphries, 1965). Charles C. Perkins and John S. Dwight, *History of the Handel and Haydn Society of Boston*, Vol 1 (1883–1893; reprint, New York: Da Capo, 1984).

ACCESS: The Handel and Haydn Society, 158 Newbury Street, Boston, MA 02116. (617) 266–3605. Mary Hall, General Manager.

DON W. SIEKER

SPRINGFIELD (530,668)

Springfield Symphony Orchestra (Rg)

The Springfield Symphony Orchestra, which observed its 40th anniversary during the 1983–1984 season, has emerged as one of the leading and most diversified orchestras of New England. The SSO serves not only the Pioneer Valley area, but also universities, colleges, and public schools throughout New England. The 1983–1984 season included 45 concerts in western Massachusetts, among them 12 classical concerts, 3 pops concerts, 10 summer concerts, 16 educational programs, and 4 special programs.

The orchestra performs in Symphony Hall (originally known as Springfield Municipal Auditorium). The inaugural concert in the auditorium in 1911 was presented by Leopold Stokowski conducting the Philadelphia Orchestra.* In 1972, it was renamed Symphony Hall in recognition of the SSO, its primary tenant. An example of neoclassical revival architecture, the hall was renovated in 1980, making it suitable for ballet and opera productions. The SSO gives three programs regularly at the University of Massachusetts as well, and under the auspices of the New England Promoters, it has performed with Jean Pierre Rampal at the Universities of Connecticut, Massachusetts, New Hampshire and Vermont. The 1984–1985 season included concerts at the University of Maine, Andover Academy, Connecticut College, University of Massachusetts with Peter Serkin, and Fitchburg State College. Of the present 75-member orchestra, 60% are from Boston and New York and 40% are from the Pioneer Valley.

From 1922 to 1933 there had been an orchestra named the Springfield Symphony (conducted by Arthur Turner), and during the depression Milton Aronson led the Works Progress Administration Orchestra of Springfield. Later that group became known as "Aronson's Quadrangle pick-up orchestra." When it was ready to disband, Faye Shapiro (d. Sept. 1984), a violinist who had often played with various ensembles in Springfield, was the prime mover in initiating the SSO as a continuation of the WPA Orchestra. The new leaders invited musicians to join and hired Dr. Alexander Leslie, conductor of the Pioneer Valley Symphony in Greenfield as conductor.

Leslie held his first rehearsals in December of 1943 with an orchestra of 40 to 50 members. Their first program was presented on March 5, 1944, to standing ovations from an audience of 3,400 in the Springfield Municipal Auditorium. The group by then included 85 instrumentalists, 32 of whom were women. During his first two years, Leslie realized that there was no opportunity for young people to perform, and he organized the Springfield Young People's Symphony, as well as a symphony chorus. Civic leaders formed the Springfield Orchestra Association, provided financial support, and a volunteer committee was incorporated in June 1944. With the death of Alexander Leslie in February of 1955, Richard Burgin, Boston Symphony

Orchestra* concertmaster and assistant conductor, completed the 1954–1955 season as guest conductor. Robert Staffanson, conductor of the Billings (Montana) Symphony* was appointed SSO music director in August of 1955, a post he held until he resigned in 1969 to become director of the Center of Western Americana in Cody, Wyoming. In that year Robert Gutter was appointed music director. Gutter recently announced that he will resign after the 1985–1986 season.

The most important administrative event leading the orchestra to its present status was the accession of Wayne Brown as executive director in 1979. It was Brown who extended the influence of the orchestra into the entire Pioneer Valley by scheduling concerts outside Springfield and by initiating formal and informal programs in the region's public schools. The orchestra has also grown under Music Director Robert Gutter. He has developed the SSO into one of the finest ensembles of its kind, winning critical approval from Andrew Porter of *The New Yorker* for the orchestra's role in the international conference on "Music in Paris in the 1830s" at Smith College.

Tours and music festivals have played a major role in the SSO's development. In 1982, the SSO became resident orchestra for the Berkshire Choral Festival, Sheffield, Massachusetts. In 1983, Wayne Brown founded a summer series at Stanley Park in Westfield, during which three programs attracted 9,500 people. In 1984, the audience totalled 19,000 for four programs. The SSO has performed numerous special programs to observe various occasions: bicentennial town celebrations, institutional centennials, a Classical Roots program of music by black composers, and a program of Irish symphonic music. The latter featured works by contemporary composers and a world premiere of Archie Potter's Symphony No. 2, a work commissioned by the Irish American Cultural Institute.

With a grant from the New England Arts Council, the SSO participates in the Northeast Orchestral Consortium with the Hudson Valley Philharmonic,* the Albany Symphony,* the Hartford Symphony, and the New Haven Symphony.* The Consortium has commissioned works by American composers Ned Rorem, Charles Wuorinen, Robert Starer, Earl Kim, and Tobias Picker. Each work will be played twice by each orchestra.

The SSO is organized and administered by the SSO Association, comprising a Board of 50 volunteer members and an administrative staff of 10. The budget for the 1984–1985 season is $1.25 million, funded by the proceeds of ticket sales and underwritten by the Springfield Business Fund for the Arts as well as by individual and corporate contributions. A Women's Symphony League organized under Board member Mary Wallace (Mrs. Douglas) in 1948 has nearly 650 members today. They assist with an annual fund drive and other projects, including an annual Symphony Ball and the Florence Center Life Membership Fund to benefit the SSO youth orchestras: the Western Massachusetts Young People's Symphony (Robert Gutter, conductor) and the Young People's Philharmonia (Michael Greenebaum, conductor). There is a master agreement between AFM Local 171, the musicians, and the SSO Corporation. The SSO is a per-service orchestra, with approximately 90 services per year.

The orchestra performs a broad representation of symphonic literature, especially less familiar works by significant composers. They also observe the anniversaries of well-known composers. Gutter has a profound interest in contemporary works, as evidenced by the Consortium project. After considering recommendations of an Artistic Advisory Committee (of community leaders and Board members) and various orchestra members, the music director selects substantive works for the orchestra, based on the opinion that the orchestra has a responsibility to educate as well as entertain. Programs show a balance between staple works and new literature, while bringing to light compositions unfamiliar to the general audience. For example, in 1985 the orchestra will perform Vaughan Williams's *Flourish for a Coronation* and Handel's *Roman Vespers*, recently discovered by H. C. Robbins Landon, is to receive its American premiere March 16, 1985.

The orchestra plays an important role in Springfield's strong tradition of maintaining the community's cultural life. A "cultural cabinet" includes administrative heads of the SSO, Stage West (Theater), the Springfield Library and Museums Association, and WGBY Public Television. All work cooperatively in exchanging programs. The SSO's educational programs—including in-school ensemble performances—are guided by an administrative coordinator with advice of public school educators.

The SSO's vitality is partly due to its youthful membership, consisting mostly of graduate students at Juilliard or the New England Conservatory. According to Robert Gutter, they are particularly facile in eighteenth- and twentieth-century music. The orchestra's sound is characterized by solidarity in the brass section and homogeneity among brass and woodwinds. Descant horns and rotary-valve trumpets are used where appropriate, and there is attention to historical style.

RECORDING HISTORY AND SELECTIVE DISCOGRAPHY: The SSO has made two recordings, available through Opus One, Box 604, Greenville, Maine 04441. They contain works of contemporary Americans, including premiere recordings.

Lewis Spratlin, *Two Pieces for Orchestra*; Robert Stern, *Carom for Orchestra and Magnetic Tape*; Francis Thorne, *Fanfare, Fugue and Funk* (Gutter): Opus One, No. 19. Charles Fussell, *Three Processionals for Orchestra*; Max Schubel, *Fracture*; Newton Strandberg, *Sea of Tranquility* (Gutter): Opus One, No. 21.

CHRONOLOGY OF MUSIC DIRECTORS: Alexander Leslie, 1943–1955. Richard Burgin (Guest Conductor), 1955. Robert L. Staffanson, 1955–1969. Robert Gutter, 1970–1986.

BIBLIOGRAPHY: Mark G. Auerbach, "Marketing an Orchestra through the Travel Network," *Symphony Magazine*, Aug./Sept. 1984. Byron Belt, "Bright Future Forecast for Symphony Hall," *The [Springfield] Morning Union*, 22 Mar. 1978. Byron

Belt, "A Successful Restoration," *Musical America*, Mar. 1981. Byron Belt, "Symphony Hall Music to Springfield's Ears," *On the Arts*, 5 Oct. 1980 (Newhouse News Service). Richard C. Hammerich, "A Violinist Recalls Symphony's Beginning," *The [Springfield] Sunday Republican*, 9 Oct. 1983. Andrew Porter, "Musical Events," *The New Yorker*, 12 July 1982 and 3 Sept. 1984. Lee Sheriden, "A History of the Springfield Symphony Orchestra," in Mark G. Auerbach and Margaret Lococo, *Springfield Symphony Orchestra 1983—40th Anniversary—1984 Commemorative Book*. Melissa Sutphen, "The Berkshire Choral Institute," *High Fidelity/Musical America*, Sept. 1984.

ACCESS: Springfield Symphony Orchestra, 31 Elm Street, Suite 210, Springfield, MA 01103. (413) 733–2291. Wayne Brown, Executive Director.

CATHERINE DOWER

Michigan ——————————————

DETROIT (4,353,413)

Detroit Symphony Orchestra (Mj)

The Detroit Symphony is Michigan's only Major orchestra and as such both represents and serves the state's musical interests. The DSO performs over 200 concerts each year, including its regular subscription series, a Weekender Pops Series, a Christmas festival (*Nutcracker* and pops), an Educational Concert Series and the Saturday young people's concerts in its home at Ford Auditorium. The DSO also performs a Friday night subscription series, a Chamber Orchestra series, a Christmas *Messiah* series and its annual Classical Roots Concert at Orchestra Hall, its first permanent home; it also performs the Hudson's Tour of Metropolitan Detroit and visits the Detroit public schools and suburban shopping malls.

The orchestra's summer home is the Meadow Brook Music Festival, located on the campus of Oakland University, 30 miles north of Detroit. There it performs 24 concerts in the Baldwin Pavilion, renowned for its excellent acoustics and beautiful, natural setting. The orchestra, acknowledging and earning the support of Michigan's citizens provided through the executive and legislative branches of government, performs annual residencies in three or four of the state's major cities and, in addition, performs concerts in five or 10 other Lower Peninsula cities. In addition, for the past 12 summers the DSO has spent a week performing its Annual Upper Peninsula Festival Tour, visiting eight to 10 cities and Mackinac Island with both classical and pops concerts. The orchestra annually visits Carnegie Hall in New York City and the Kennedy Center in Washington, D.C. In 1979 it made its first European tour to 23 cities in eight countries.

The orchestra is able to maintain such a full schedule and to reach many listeners because it can be divided into two separate orchestras to perform its pops, chamber, educational, young people's, in-school, in-residency, and Upper Peninsula concerts—a feature allowed by the nature of the programming and often necessitated by the size of the performing space. This schedule also reflects an effort to increase the number of the orchestra's listeners and supporters, thereby avoiding the chronic difficulties of the past which have, on more than one occasion, forced the orchestra to interrupt its operations. Those difficulties had their origins in the changing fortunes of Detroit's heavy industrial base, in the national and world economy, and in the need to provide the arsenal of democracy during World War II.

It was at 8:00 on Monday evening, December 19, 1887, at the Detroit Opera House that a Detroit Symphony Orchestra gave the first concert of its first season under the direction of Mr. Rudolph Speil. It continued to give four concerts each season through 1910. Fritz Kalsow, a bugle player who had left a touring Prussian band to settle in Detroit, became the manager; and in 1900, his son Hugo Kalsow, who had studied music and played violin in Dresden, became director of the orchestra until it ceased operations in 1910.

Then, early in 1914, Miss Frances Sibley, the daughter of an old Detroit, music-loving family, assembled a group of Detroit's leading ladies to discuss the possibility of providing the financial and volunteer support for a demonstration concert of a symphony orchestra to be conducted by Weston Gales, a Bostonian. So successful was that first concert on February 25, 1914, at the Detroit Opera House, and so enthusiastic were those assembled, that Weston Gales was appointed music director and a season of concerts was immediately planned for 1914–1915. Mr. Sidney T. Miller, a member of the Executive Committee since that 1887–1888 season, was chosen as first vice president; and the Detroit Symphony Society was incorporated as a nonprofit organization in the state of Michigan on May 4, 1914.

In her history of the Detroit Symphony Orchestra, Edith Rhetts Tilton recounts that upon resigning in 1917 Weston Gales was asked to define the orchestra's greatest need. He replied tersely: "Money." And he continued: "Furthermore, there are only two places where we can hold concerts: one of the theaters which can be had only in the afternoons and the Armory, which is neither suitable nor comfortable. A music hall is a crying need." Of the procession of guest conductors that followed, one was the unanimous choice for music director: Ossip Gabrilowitsch, the world-renowned pianist and conductor. However, Gabrilowitsch refused to return to Detroit as music director unless a concert hall were built. He could not even remain long enough after his last concert with the orchestra in early 1919 to discuss the matter because he was expected in New York and Philadelphia on a solo recital tour. While on that tour he was speaking with Leopold Stokowski in the lobby of his hotel when a boy from Western Union presented him with a telegram. Its message was as terse as Weston Gales's earlier appraisal of the orchestra's problems: "Money pledged. Hall assured."

Orchestra Hall was built in four months and 23 days during the following summer and dedicated by Gabrilowitsch and the orchestra on October 23, 1919. From that date until illness forced his retirement in 1935, Gabrilowitsch presided over what is now referred to as the Detroit Symphony Orchestra's Golden Age. Virtually every great name of music appeared in Orchestra Hall with Gabrilowitsch and the orchestra. They performed 268 Detroit premieres, 18 American premieres, and three world premieres.

Two features of this period are especially distinctive: radio broadcasts and education. In 1922 the DSO was featured on radio station WWJ in the first broadcast of a complete, live symphony concert. Gabrilowitsch conducted and Arthur Schnabel was the soloist. On Sunday, January 4, 1931, Gabrilowitsch and the DSO made the first national broadcast of a program of live, symphonic music. Later in the 1930s the orchestra gained prominence with the weekly national broadcasts of the Ford Sunday Evening Hour. Radio broadcasts continue to be a means of reaching large audiences. During the 1985–1986 season 26 subscription concerts will be broadcast nationally, sponsored in this instance by General Motors Corporation.

To discover new listeners and supporters for the orchestra, Gabrilowitsch also persuaded Edith Rhetts to come to Detroit in 1922 to apply her experience as an educational director for the Victor Record Company and the St. Louis Symphony.* Rhetts inaugurated a very successful series of concerts for school children. After weeks of preparation the students were tested in school and the top finishers won the opportunity to hear at Orchestra Hall the program they had been studying. The remaining students listened to the concert in their classrooms by means of a live radio broadcast. This tradition continues today as the DSO performs 16 educational concerts at Ford Auditorium and in-school concerts in 30 different Detroit schools each year.

Also noteworthy is the fact that on April 16, 1926, Gabrilowitsch and Joseph Maddy brought together on the stage of Orchestra Hall the first National Youth Orchestra, which grew into the National Music Camp and the National Academy of the Arts at Interlochen, Michigan.

Toward the end of the orchestra's Golden Age, during the depression, Gabrilowitsch conducted without a salary and the musicians were on half pay. Following Gabrilowitsch's retirement in 1935 and his death in 1936, the orchestra continued under Franco Ghione and Victor Kolar until 1939, when increasing financial difficulties forced it to move from its heavily mortgaged home to rented quarters in Masonic Auditorium. Ghione left in 1940 and the orchestra continued under Victor Kolar until it was decided to cease operations in 1942.

The orchestra was reborn in 1943 under Detroit industrialist Henry H.

Reichhold, who brought Karl Krueger to Detroit from Kansas City as music director. Reichhold purchased the Wilson Theatre and converted it to Music Hall as the orchestra's own home. Not satisfied with the recordings done with Victor, he took control of the Vox Record Company, and he assembled what he acclaimed as the world's largest orchestra—110 musicians. However, plagued by the prolonged strike against the recording companies, stung by the censures of critics, and led, supported, and attended by too few, the Detroit Symphony Orchestra again ceased operations in 1949 when Reichhold decided he could no longer go it alone. Just as Gabrilowitsch had realized that his orchestra was supported and attended by too few—and therefore had taken steps to change that situation—so, too, did Henry H. Reichhold finally come to the conclusion that his bold, innovative, and singular style had caused his orchestra to be led by too few—namely, himself.

In 1951, John B. Ford, a long-time devotee and supporter of the DSO, reorganized the orchestra and created the oft-imitated Detroit Plan for maintaining it. Modeled on the United Foundation, the Detroit Plan calls for the relatively modest support of a great many contributors. For instance, in response to John B. Ford's initial request, Henry Ford II promptly offered $100,000 but was told that $10,000 would do. The major corporations in Detroit were similarly asked for a $10,000 maximum contribution and each was simultaneously given a seat on the Board of Directors and on the Finance and Policy Committees of the Orchestra. Ford wisely sought broad-based involvement in addition to investment.

From the roster of guest conductors for the 1951–1952 season, Paul Paray was chosen as music director, and, by means of its national tours and its recordings on the Mercury label (two of which won the Grand Prix du Disque), the DSO became nationally and internationally esteemed for its interpretation of the masterpieces of the French repertoire. In 1958 the Detroit Symphony Orchestra succeeded the Philadelphia Orchestra* as the official orchestra of the Worcester Festival, America's oldest music festival; and on December 9, 1959, the orchestra's historic concert at the United Nations established it among the leading ensembles of the world.

Sixten Ehrling succeeded Paul Paray in 1963 and greatly increased the number and diversity of the orchestra's activities. During his 10 years as music director, Ehrling conducted more concerts than any other DSO conductor—732—and the orchestra performed 664 compositions and 24 world premieres. Ehrling also presided over the founding of the Meadow Brook Music Festival in 1964. In 1973 he was succeeded by Aldo Ceccato, who led the orchestra in 46 works previously not performed by the orchestra and four world premieres.

Antal Dorati was appointed the orchestra's ninth music director in September 1977. During his reign the orchestra increased its national and international standing with four annual mid-season festivals: Beethoven, Schubert and Vienna, Brahms, and Bartók. The Beethoven festival was featured in a nine-program PBS television series hosted by Dorati and E. G. Marshall. Each of the festivals attracted performers, patrons, scholars, and critical attention from throughout the world. The orchestra increased its visits to Carnegie Hall and Kennedy Center and returned to the recording studios, this time with London Records. Their recording of Stravinsky's *The Rite of Spring* won the first Grand Prix du Disque for a compact disc recording. In the autumn of 1979 Dorati led the orchestra on its first European tour. The DSO played numerous encores and received standing ovations and rave reviews at 24 concerts in 23 cities. Some 468 newspaper reviews and articles, including 120 from the foreign press, lauded the DSO for its accomplishments.

In November 1980, owing to uncertainties over the financial and, hence, the artistic future of the orchestra, Dorati announced his resignation effective May 31, 1981. He was subsequently named Conductor Laureate, and Gary Bertini was named music advisor for a two-year period. In November 1983 Günther Herbig, the distinguished East German conductor and music director of the (East) Berlin Symphony, was appointed music director designate, becoming music director in September 1984.

During the years of transition from Antal Dorati's resignation to Günther Herbig's appointment, the Detroit Symphony Orchestra was able to draw upon the broad base of support and involvement created by John B. Ford. Five community leaders formed the Office of the Chairman to directly guide the orchestra's destiny during the period when past debts had to be settled and future resources secured. Following a year of carefully guided, necessary austerity, the Board of Directors elected Walter J. McCarthy, Jr., chairman of Detroit Edison, as chairman of the Detroit Symphony Orchestra. Just as John B. Ford increased the involved support of the DSO, McCarthy has increased the involved leadership of the orchestra to define and to achieve its goals of quality music and access; and access to the orchestra for anyone wishing to hear it is being given additional emphasis through the orchestra's programs of education and outreach. During the two years up to 1982–1983 the number of donors to the orchestra increased from 6,000 to 32,000; and the team effort which succeeded in that instance is being applied to increasing attendance and enlarging the endowment.

The Detroit Symphony Orchestra has a Board of Directors of over 175 community leaders and representatives who, through their Executive and Standing Committees, are responsible for the maintenance and operation of the orchestra. This volunteer leadership works closely with the professional staff in the areas of finance, development, marketing, and education/outreach. In addition, various musician committees and representatives serve in an advisory and consultative role in the areas of day-to-day operations, conductor evaluation and selection, auditions, artistic matters, travel, pension, and marketing. Two very active auxiliaries, whose leaders serve on the Board of Directors and Executive Committee, assist greatly in the orchestra's development. They are the Women's Association and the Detroit Symphony Orchestra League. Ever since they first met at the request of Miss Frances Sibley in 1914, the women of Detroit have been indispensable to the maintenance and enhancement of the Detroit Symphony Orchestra.

The budget for the 1985–1986 season is $14 million, with 30% from concert revenue, 36% from contributed income, 7% from endowment income and 27% from government grants for services. A long-range strategic plan has been put in place and is annually reviewed and updated. Its purpose is to protect against repetition of the past difficulties peculiar to Detroit's traditionally boom-or-bust economy, its changing industrial base, and the accompanying demographic shifts. Through all these vicissitudes, however, Detroit's love of music and the desire for an outstanding symphony orchestra have never been extinguished; today's orchestra is proof that it cannot only survive but flourish. The Detroit Symphony Orchestra continues to be noted for the excellence of its performances, its powerful sound, and the unique spirit and feeling that its music conveys.

RECORDING HISTORY AND SELECTIVE DISCOGRAPHY: The DSO first recorded for Victor on April 16–18, 1928. Gabrilowitsch conducted, and Brahms's *Academic Festival Overture* and the Waltz from Tchaikovsky's *Serenade for Strings* were featured. Karl Krueger also recorded with the orchestra on the Victor label. The two series of note are those with Paul Paray on Mercury and with Antal Dorati on London Records.

Debussy, *Iberia, La Mer, Prélude à l'ápres-midi d'un faune* (Paray): Mercury 75053. Dvořák, *Prague Waltzes* and *Czech Suite* (Dorati): London LDR 71024. Strauss, *Also Sprach Zarathustra* and *Macbeth* (Dorati): London LDR 7113. Strauss, *Don Juan, Till Eulenspiegel,* and *Death and Transfiguration* (Dorati): London LDR 71025. Stravinsky, *The Firebird* (Dorati): London 410 109–1 (1984). Stravinsky, *Petrouchka* (Dorati): London LDR 71023. Stravinsky, *The Rite of Spring* (Dorati): London LDR 71048.

CHRONOLOGY OF MUSIC DIRECTORS: Weston Gales, 1914–1917. Ossip Gabrilowitsch, 1918–1936. Franco Ghione, 1936–1940. Victor Kolar, 1940–1942. (Operations suspended, 1942–1943.) Karl Krueger, 1943–1949. Paul Paray, 1951–1963. Sixten Ehrling, 1963–1973. Aldo Ceccato, 1973–1977. Antal Dorati, 1977–1981. Gary Bertini (Music Advisor), 1981–1983. Günther Herbig, 1983-present.

BIBLIOGRAPHY: Detroit Symphony Orchestra, "Report of the Strategic Planning Task Force," 29 July 1982. Paul Ganson, "Detroit's Orchestra Hall," *Bulletin of the Detroit Historical Society*, January 1971. Lynne Marie Mattson, "A History of the Detroit Symphony Orchestra," Masters thesis, The University of Michigan, 1968. John H. Mueller, *The American Symphony Orchestra* (1951; reprint, Westport, Conn.: Greenwood Press, 1976). Theodore G. Seemeyer, Jr., "The Detroit Symphony Orchestra," *Impresario*, 1964/1965. Edith Rhetts Tilton, "The History of the Detroit Symphony Orchestra", *The Detroit Symphony Orchestra Program Books*, 1964/1965.

ACCESS: The Detroit Symphony Orchestra, Ford Auditorium, Auditorium Drive, Detroit MI 48226. (313) 567–9000. Oleg Lobanov, President.

PAUL GANSON

FLINT (521,589)

Flint Symphony Orchestra (Mt)

Whiting Auditorium, the 2,000-seat home of the Flint Symphony Orchestra and the performing arts center for the city of Flint, is located on a half-mile strip known as the Campus-Cultural corridor. This corridor on Kearsley Street is the address for every major cultural institution in the city, including the Planetarium, the Bower Theatre, DeWater Arts Center, the Alfred Sloan Historical Museum, the Flint Public Library, and the University of Michigan-Flint. The Dort Music Center, home of the Flint Institute of Music (FIM) (whose Governing Board controls the Flint Symphony Orchestra, the Dance Repertory Company, and the Community Music School) is also on Kearsley on the site of the former Dort mansion, just a block from the Charles Stewart Mott estate. Kearsley Street was the residence of auto industry pioneers, the industrial giants whose personal fortunes became the good fortune of Flint.

With the completion of Whiting Auditorium in May 1967, just months after the arrival of William C. Byrd, the first permanent conductor of the Flint Symphony Orchestra, the desire for appropriate space and a professional orchestra came together. The same families that founded the automotive industry founded the cultural institutions of Flint. These families initiated cultural activities and opportunities that would provide balance to an industrial city.

Today the Flint Symphony Orchestra has 75 musicians under contract, with 48 services guaranteed (80–85 is an average number of musicians per contract). Many of the FSO's professional musicians live outside the city of Flint, most notably in Ann Arbor and in the greater Detroit area. These musicians arrive for rehearsals and performances by chartered bus. In addition to its eight-concert subscription series, the FSO accompanies the Dance Repertory Company for the annual *Nutcracker* performances. In prior years, musicians from the orchestra accompanied the Flint Festival Chorus for the yearly performance of Handel's *Messiah*. Orchestral activities also included pops and rug concerts as well as children's concerts. These and the professional Flint Arts Chorus maintained by FIM have been discontinued due to lack of funds. The orchestra plays repertoire from the late eighteenth century to the present. Its involvement with new music, while increasing, remains slight. Nationally known guest artists appear at seven of the eight subscription concerts. The eighth concert presents the winner of the annual William C. Byrd Young Artists' Competition sponsored by the St. Cecilia Society. String, wind, piano, and voice competitions rotate annually.

The budget for the FSO is approximately $422,000, the combination of direct and administrative costs. Average attendance per concert is about 1,850. Ticket sales provide one-third of the funding; the remainder is provided through grants and gifts from individuals, businesses, and foundations. Seventy-eight percent of expenditures relate to performance costs, 22% to administration and promotion. The orchestra is under standard union contract. The Flint Institute of Music organizational concept is based on an active 31-member Board of Trustees who meet monthly to deal with its affairs, including the FSO. An executive director reports to the Board.

The antecedents of the FSO date to the first half of the century, when musical activities, entirely by amateur musicians—comprising orchestras, bands, and choruses—abounded. The Community Music Association (CMA) was formed in 1917 "to promote the community interest in Flint by developing a common or general participation in music." Its Board included representatives from the Board of Education, the Manufacturers' Association, and the Board of Commerce. Activity included sponsorship of sings and of a small community orchestra comprised of amateur and professional players. During the 1920s new choral groups replaced the earlier sings, and the community orchestra became the focal point of instrumental activities. Music in the Flint public schools was co-sponsored by the CMA and, in 1930, the CMA director was officially employed and paid by the Flint Board of Education.

Membership in this organization dropped dramatically during the war years, and its financial support was seriously eroded. Despite this, a symphony orchestra (of amateurs and professionals), chorus, and opera survived. In 1963, the professional musicians in the orchestra broke from CMA to form the Flint Philharmonic, the first orchestra in which all members were paid. Two years later, the Musical Performing Arts Association (MPAA) was formed to support the professional orchestra, and the following year William C. Byrd was appointed the first artistic director and conductor of the MPAA. Byrd's accomplishments included bringing the Flint Philharmonic into the MPAA and adding ballet, a symphonic chorus, and other programs relating to the public schools. In 1971, the CMA and MPAA ceased independent operation and merged into the Flint Institute of Music. That same year the Dort Music Center, which houses the FIM, was opened.

Byrd had noteworthy success as an administrator in bringing together divergent musical groups in the area, and the Flint Symphony saw musical growth as well. Two years after Byrd's death in 1974, John Covelli assumed the music directorship, and the orchestra's playing continued to improve as an increasing number of orchestral players from Ann Arbor's School of Music auditioned and were added to local Flint musicians.

The current music director, Isaiah Jackson, is also associate conductor of the Rochester Philharmonic* and has appeared as guest conductor on many of the most distinguished podiums in America and Europe. Solely responsible for artistic decisions, he typically concludes FSO concerts with an encore, often a well-loved work from the non-orchestral repertoire performed in transcription. Prior to performances of new music, Jackson provides verbal explanation from the podium. Jackson uses the old orchestra setup for the strings: basses stage right, second violins stage left, and cellos immediately in front of the conductor.

The FSO is probably the most important musical organization in the city of Flint. It continues to draw near-capacity crowds. In the past three years, under Jackson, there has been a concerted effort to broaden the support for the orchestra and to increase substantially the number of minority individuals who attend Flint Symphony concerts. An active program in which 100 minority children are brought to each concert has been instituted. Programming consciously includes works by black Americans, both composers and guest artists.

The FIM String Quartet, all members of the FSO, performs annually to 35,000 students throughout Genessee County, thus preparing today's youth to become tomorrow's symphony patrons.

CHRONOLOGY OF MUSIC DIRECTORS: William C. Byrd, 1966–1974. John Covelli, 1976–1982. Isaiah Jackson, 1982-present.

BIBLIOGRAPHY: Mrs. J. Dallas Dort, Manuscript notebook from the personal library of David T. Dort, First President of the MPAA. Flint Institute of Music, Archives. "History," brief unsigned document prepared by FIM Executive Director Thomas Gerdom, 1983. *Flint Journal* articles, including those by Arts Editor S. Gordon Gapper and a special section (Nov. 1971) at the opening of the Dort Music Center. "Music in Flint: A Brief History of the Musical Scene in Flint, Michigan from the 1800's to 1976," Flint Institute of Music, Frederick W. Peryer, Managing Director, 1976.

ACCESS: Flint Symphony Orchestra, Flint Institute of Music, 1025 E. Kearsley Street, Flint, MI 48503 (313) 238–9651. Thomas Gerdom, Executive Director.

MARGARETTE F. EBY

KALAMAZOO (279,192)

Kalamazoo Symphony Orchestra (Mt)

The Kalamazoo Symphony Orchestra is a community organization serving, along with the orchestras of Grand Rapids, Battle Creek, and St. Joseph, the musical needs of southwestern Michigan.

Mrs. Leta Snow, having attended a conference in Davenport, Iowa, concerning the administration of this sort of orchestra, established the Symphony in 1921. She served as manager and member of the Board (at first active and then honorary) for more than 50 years. She also founded the American Symphony Orchestra League in 1941 and was its first president. Kalamazoo Symphony historian Dwight Tiefertal reported that upon her return from Iowa in the summer of 1921 she undertook meetings and arrangements so energetically that a first rehearsal was possible on October

19, and a concert was presented in the Masonic Temple on December 18, 1921. The conductor was C. Z. Bronson, formerly associated with circus bands, who led the orchestra of about 25 players, some of whom had prepared themselves on their instruments especially for the occasion; their rendition of Schubert's *Unfinished* Symphony provoked critical comment more encouraging than extravagant.

The succession of conductors in the early years consisted mostly of concertmasters promoted to the podium for several years and retiring, providing the next in turn the opportunity to conduct. Even Herman Felber, Jr., the man with the record tenure of 25 years conducting, had spent his year leading the first violins; however, not all concertmasters took the baton. A number of very colorful sorts played Kalamazoo, surely not for the salary, but probably because they enjoyed working in a small but comfortable orchestra.

It was during Felber's time that many of the traditions of the orchestra and its operation became established. The Kalamazoo Symphony presents seven subscription concerts a season, one of them now an opera and another with the Grand Chorus from Western Michigan University. In addition, there are normally about eight young people's concerts in various area schools and a series of three or four chamber concerts on Sunday afternoons at Kalamazoo College. A popular series of summer outdoor concerts dating from 1962 and sponsored by the Downtown Kalamazoo Association has evolved into a group of four concerts in various area parks, presented through the generosity of the businesses and civic leaders of the cities involved. Christmas usually sees paired performances of *The Nutcracker* and an occasional *Messiah*. Either the whole or a reduced orchestra has also taken part in run-out concerts.

In 1925 the concerts were moved from the Masonic Temple to Central High School (now called Chenery) Auditorium, a splendid room seating about 2,800 and possessing fine natural acoustics. In 1968 the Symphony took part in the dedication concerts of Western Michigan University's newly constructed Miller Auditorium, which it has gradually made its home. This hall is very large, seating 3,600, and this may in part account for a somewhat troublesome lack of reverberation. The appointments are, however, splendidly up to date.

The orchestra is administered by a full-time manager and governed by a 35-member Board of Trustees, including several members of the Players' Committee. Personnel and program decisions are the exclusive right of the music director, but he does informally solicit suggestions. The main source of income has been fund drives, but the orchestra has been supported by grants from foundations and arts councils and gifts from businesses and individuals, as well as ticket sales. The annual budget is $550,000. Aside from the concertmaster, all of the players continue on a per-service basis, and most are from the immediate area. Faculty and students from area colleges have provided a rich source of fine players for the orchestra, especially in the principal chairs.

If there has been a specialty in the orchestra's programming in its long history, it has been the avoidance of having a specialty. Major guests have included the most sought-after artists of their day, and the orchestra has been able to commission and premiere several new works by area composers, such as *Confluences* by Lawrence Rackley, *Windsong* by Ramon Zupko, and *The Great American Symphony* by Curtis Curtis-Smith. In the main, however, the repertoire has followed the changing tastes evident in program selection across the country.

The Kalamazoo Symphony has been especially attentive to youth. Besides the full orchestra's young people's concerts, the orchestra sponsors four small ensembles: string quartet, wind and brass quintets, and percussion ensemble; all tour area schools and present concerts at the Kalamazoo Institute of Arts. The orchestra has a long-standing cooperative scholarship arrangement with Western Michigan University called the Honors String Program, in which students perform in the orchestra in return for grants supporting them in quartets and other ensembles at Western. The Leta Snow Regional Auditions, established in 1971, were among the important competitions for young artists from the entire country.

Since 1961 conductors have included Gregory Millar and Pierre Hetu. Yoshimi Takeda has just completed his ninth excellent season as music director. Along with the professionalism of the directors, there has been an increase in such concomitant professional problems as salary disputes, but it is expected that such difficulties will be overcome to the benefit and continued growth of the orchestra.

CHRONOLOGY OF MUSIC DIRECTORS: C. Z. Bronson, 1921–1924. Henry Eich, 1924–1926. George Buckley, 1926–1928. David Mattern, 1928–1934. Herman Felber, Jr., 1934–1961. Gregory Millar, 1961–1968. Pierre Hetu, 1968–1973. Yoshimi Takeda, 1974-present.

BIBLIOGRAPHY: Dwight Tiefertal, "A History of the Kalamazoo Symphony," unpublished typescript, Kalamazoo, 1943.

ACCESS: Kalamazoo Symphony Orchestra, 426 South Park Street, Kalamazoo, MI 49002. (616) 349–7759. Paul Ferrone, Manager.

JOSEPH T. WORK

Minnesota ──────────────────

DULUTH (226,650—Duluth, Minn./Superior, Wis.)

Duluth-Superior Symphony Orchestra (Mt)

Located at the western end of Lake Superior are the Twin Ports of Duluth, Minnesota and Superior, Wisconsin. They are the hub of economic, educational, and cultural activity for a tri-state region including Northeast Minnesota, northwest Wisconsin, and the Upper Peninsula of Michigan. Foremost among this region's cultural organizations is the 90-member Duluth-SuperiorSymphony Orchestra.

Under the auspices of the Duluth-Superior Symphony Association, the orchestra's October to May season includes seven subscription concerts featuring internationally renowned soloists, a fully staged grand opera production with members of the Metropolitan Opera and New York City Opera heading the cast, an annual Holiday Concert, and run-out concerts in surrounding communities. The orchestra's home hall, the 2,400-seat Duluth Auditorium, opened in 1966. Located on the Duluth waterfront, it ideally suits acoustically and aesthetically the needs of both orchestra and audience.

Responsibility for governance and financing of the DSSO rests with the 30-member Board of Trustees. Funding for its budget, in excess of $450,000, is generated through season ticket sales, government grants, a chair sponsor program, and the fund-raising activities of the Women's Association of the Duluth-Superior Symphony Orchestra and the Saint Louis County Heritage and Arts Center. A full-time general manager oversees day-to-day operations.

The orchestra's influence on the community's cultural life extends beyond the concert hall. A series of annual school concerts, begun in the 1940s, was expanded in the 1970s by sending to area elementary schools small instrument-family ensembles in a program called "People Music." More recently, a chamber orchestra has been organized to present concerts in schools and churches throughout the community. The Junior Symphony (now the Youth Orchestra) was established in 1940, and the Duluth-Superior Sinfonia, a string orchestra for elementary and junior high students, was organized in 1979. The Duluth-Superior Symphony Chorus and Opera Chorus also offer performance outlets for area singers by performing annually in the subscription series and providing the chorus for the yearly opera production.

The origin of professional symphony concerts in the Twin Ports dates back to 1925 and the Duluth Symphony Orchestra, conducted by Fred Bradbury. Sponsored by the Duluth Orchestral Association, it comprised professional Duluth-Superior theater musicians, augmented by Bradbury's students. Because of insufficient financial support, that orchestra disbanded in 1928, the same year that the advent of sound films spelled disaster for the thousands of musicians across the country who earned their livings playing orchestral accompaniments to silent films.

In 1931, despite (or perhaps because of) this event and the concurrent Great Depression, a group of about 35 local musicians, mostly from disbanded theater orchestras, began rehearsing in the loft of an old carriage house in Duluth under the direction of Walter Lange, a well-known trumpet player. In order to remain in Duluth, they would have to develop a formal organization and seek civic support. Thus the Duluth Civic Symphony Association was formed, with attorney James G. Nye as its first president. Abe Miller, one of the violists, was appointed manager and served the orchestra in that capacity until 1969. Paul Lemay, principal violist and assistant conductor of the Minneapolis Symphony* under Eugene Ormandy, was summoned to Duluth to conduct, and the newly formed Duluth Civic Symphony gave its first concert under his direction on December 26, 1932, to a crowd of about 1,500 people in the National Guard Armory, which remained the orchestra's home until 1966.

From 1932 to 1934, Lemay commuted from Minneapolis to conduct three concerts a year, bringing with him about a dozen musicians from the Minneapolis Symphony, which made the resources of its substantial music library available to the Duluth musicians during those early years. By 1934, increased funding allowed hiring Lemay full-time. Under his direction the orchestra grew quickly in funding and stature, hiring soloists such as Kirsten Flagstad, Rudolf Serkin, and Jascha Heifitz. During the late 1930s and early 1940s the orchestra was heard regularly on nationwide radio broadcasts. It also expanded its territory by touring outlying communities. Most notable was its 1939 Port Arthur (now Thunder Bay), Ontario, performance before the king and queen of England, broadcast via shortwave radio throughout the British Empire.

When Lemay enlisted in the U.S. Army Air Corps in 1942, the orchestra engaged Finnish-born Tauno Hannikainen, who was unable to return to his native country because of the hostilities. Lemay was killed in action over Belgium in 1944. A very serious and highly professional musician, Hannikainen is remembered for his disciplined approach. The orchestra continued improving under his direction until 1947, when he resigned to become associate conductor of the Chicago Symphony.*

He was succeeded by Joseph Wagner, composer and former conductor of the Boston Civic Orchestra, who spent three seasons at Duluth before going to Central America. In 1950, the orchestra engaged Hermann Herz, a pianist and conductor with substantial experience in Europe and South Africa. During his 17-year tenure Herz established the Grand Opera tradition in Duluth. (In September of 1983, the Symphony Association celebrated its 25th consecutive year of opera production.) Herz was succeeded in 1967 by Joseph Hawthorne, a former conductor of the Chattanooga* and Toledo Symphonies.* A well-schooled violist and violinist, Hawthorne notably improved the string section. He retired at the end of the 1976–1977 season and remains the orchestra's conductor laureate. During his tenure the substantial contribution of musicians and civic supporters from Superior was recognized, and in 1973 the orchestra was renamed the Duluth-Superior Symphony Orchestra.

Taavo Virkhaus, the orchestra's current music director, is a native Estonian and former faculty member and conductor at the Eastman School of Music. Under his direction the orchestra has continued to improve and expand its repertoire. Citing the fact that the traditional repertoire can be heard on live radio broadcasts by the major orchestras, Virkhaus offers a blend of standard orchestral works and seldom-played works from both the traditional and modern repertoire. During recent years local audiences have heard for the first time live performances of the original version of Schumann's Fourth Symphony, Bruckner's Seventh Symphony, and Stravinsky's *Rite of Spring*.

CHRONOLOGY OF MUSIC DIRECTORS: Paul Lemay, 1932–1942. Tauno Hannikainen, 1942–1947. Joseph Wagner, 1947–1950. Hermann Herz, 1950–1967. Joseph Hawthorne, 1967–1977. Taavo Virkhaus, 1977-present.

BIBLIOGRAPHY: Bob Ashenmacher, "Duluth-Superior Symphony Turns 50," *Duluth News Tribune & Herald: Accent North*, 26 Apr. 1981. Anne Bailey Crooks, "Duluth/Superior Orchestra: 50 Years of Professionalism," *Minnesota Monthly*, March 1982. Walter Eldot, "These Are the Things Bill Helped Build," *Duluth News Tribune & Herald*, 17 Jan. 1984. Adrienne Josephs, "Duluth Symphony Orchestra: From Garage to Auditorium," Unpublished MS, 1966. Mary Matteson, "50 Years Duluth Superior Symphony," *Lake Superior Port Cities*, Vol. 3, No. 3. Herb Palmer, "There was Music in the Air and Duluth Grew Culturally," *Duluth Budgeteer*, 16 Sept. 1981.

ACCESS: Duluth-Superior Symphony Orchestra, 506 West Michigan Street, Duluth MN 55802. (218) 727–7429. Jeffrey E. Prauer, General Manager.

THOMAS A. BUMGARDNER

MINNEAPOLIS (2,113,533—Minneapolis/St. Paul)

Minnesota Orchestra (Mj)

The Minnesota Orchestra, ranked among the top orchestras in the United States today, was founded as the Minneapolis Symphony Orchestra in 1903. Although based on Minneapolis since its founding, the orchestra also performs in neighboring St. Paul and throughout the state as well. The change of name came about in 1968 when the Board of Directors decided the new name would reflect the broader geographical role the orchestra has long fulfilled. The decision accompanied a major expansion of the orchestra's operations. In the years from 1964, when planning began, to 1976, the season expanded from 30 to 50 weeks, operating costs quadrupled, and performances outside the Twin Cities increased.

Currently the Minnesota Orchestra is led by a team of conductors. Neville Marriner, music director since 1979, heads the group, which also includes Charles Dutoit, principal guest conductor (succeeding Klaus Tennstedt in 1983); Leonard Slatkin, Artistic Director of Sommerfest; Henry Charles Smith, resident conductor; and Stanislaw Skrowaczewski, conductor emeritus. In 1985 the orchestra announced the appointment of Edo de Waart as music director, effective in the 1986–1987 season.

The orchestra's concert season extends a full 52 weeks. Its 219 concerts include a 24-week subscription series with performances in four cities, various pops concerts, free concerts in the parks, young people's series, a summer festival, and regional and national tours. Besides Minneapolis, subscription series are offered in St. Paul, Rochester, and St. Joseph (near St. Cloud), where local committees work on promotion and ticket sales. The orchestra performs pops concerts during the season in the Weekender Pops Series, and during the summer in a Night-at-the-Pops series in a cabaret setting with refreshments. Key among the winter holiday events each year are the orchestra's annual performances of Tchaikovksy's *Nutcracker* (with the Minnesota Dance Theatre) and Handel's *Messiah*.

The year 1980 saw the first annual Sommerfest, a varied series of concerts and other events. The series now spans four weeks and features over 30 separate events, most of them concerts of orchestral or chamber music, but including dance, recitals, and master classes as well. Sommerfest is unique in that the orchestra does not repeat works from the season and in that it is presented not in a new location but at its primary home downtown. Many events take place in the Peavey Plaza next to Orchestra Hall, which is transformed into a Viennese Marktplatz. The primary musical emphasis of Sommerfest is composers associated with Vienna, and often new Viennese works are given U.S. premieres.

An important component in the orchestra's impact on the region is its young people's concerts, which have been performed continuously since 1911 (except for the 1929–1930 season). Besides the regular young people's series, there are Kinder Konzerts, which are designed for the youngest children. Recently the orchestra has experimented with televising concerts during the day to make them available to schools where reduced budgets or distance have made transporting students unfeasible. In the young audiences program sponsored by the Women's Association of the orchestra, ensembles of orchestra musicians (and other local musicians) are sent out directly into the schools to perform. By the late 1970s young artists ensembles were logging over 650 such performances per season.

The cultural impact of the Minnesota Orchestra is extended further through radio broadcasts and tours. Nationwide broadcasts of weekly subscription concerts began in May 1980 over National Public Radio, and now the orchestra's concerts are carried by more than 100 stations nationwide. The orchestra's extensive touring began early and earned it the appellation "orchestra on wheels." It launched its first annual spring tour in 1907, and in 1912 a mid-winter tour was added, which in that year brought the orchestra to New York. Over the years it has played in most of the states and in many foreign countries as well. Currently each season contains at least one regional tour into neighboring states and at least one tour to major cities in the eastern United States. An extensive State Department-sponsored tour in 1957 took the orchestra to Central Europe, the Mideast, and India. Plans are now under way for a trip to Australia in 1985 and other foreign destinations in subsequent years.

Orchestra Hall in Minneapolis, the home of the Minnesota Orchestra, was constructed in 1974 at a cost of $10.1 million and opened on October 21 of that year. Designed by the St. Paul architectural firm of Hammel Green and Abrahamson, Inc., in conjunction with Hardy Holzman Pfeiffer Associates of New York and with Dr. Cyril M. Harris of New York as acoustical consultant, the building stands as a model of contemporary design and architectural engineering. The 2,573-seat concert hall is separated from the rest of the building—offices, lobby, and service facilities—by a one-inch gap that isolates the hall from extraneous noise. The rectangular interior of the concert hall features wood floors, which offer good resonance, and a front wall and ceiling that have large, three-dimensional cubical shapes projecting from their surfaces to diffuse the sound. This design offers literally hundreds of reflective surfaces. The orchestra's earliest home was the original Minneapolis Auditorium (later Lyceum Theater), which stood on the site of the present building until it was razed for new construction. From 1930 until 1974 the orchestra performed in the 4,800-seat Northrop Auditorium on the University of Minnesota campus.

The Minnesota Orchestral Association (formerly Orchestral Association of Minneapolis) was incorporated in 1907, four years after the founding of the orchestra. The Association's Board of Directors meets quarterly, the Executive Committee of the Board, monthly. Its function is to chart long-range plans and review administrative decisions.

At the highest level of management there are six officers who oversee day-to-day operations of the orchestra and the hall: the president, general manager, director of development, director of finance and planning, director of marketing, and director of administrative services. They manage a staff of 65, a significant proportion of which is involved in hall operations, including building operation, ushering and security, and hall rental; others carry out the Association's impresario role of bringing quality artists to the area for performances at Orchestra Hall and other local facilities. Although artistic and programming decisions are made primarily by the music director, they are also discussed with members of the administrative staff.

The annual budget of the orchestra for the 1984–1985 season was approximately $12.1 million, its income derived from ticket sales, grants from Dayton Hudson, McKnight, and other foundations, recordings, broadcasts, endowments, private and corporate donations, and gifts from the Women's Association. Ticket sales surpassed $1 million in 1981 for the first time, and in recent seasons typically 90% of all available seats were sold on subscription. The endowment fund, established in 1967, currently stands at $22 million but a special drive under way at the time of this writing will see it rise to $40 million. The endowment provides funds for operating expenses and particularly for endowed chairs of principals and co-principals. Currently 17 chairs are endowed and more will be added in the future.

An important auxiliary supporting organization is the Women's Association of the Minnesota Orchestra (WAMSO), founded in 1949. Having as its goal "to stimulate interest in and encourage support of the orchestra," WAMSO stages an annual symphony ball and other fund-raising projects. It also supports several educational projects: the Young Audiences Programs, a Young Artists Competition, and various music lecture programs.

The Minnesota Orchestra currently numbers 96. That number will expand to 100 during the next few years. Twenty-nine of these orchestra members have 25 years or more experience with the orchestra; over one-fourth are women. A number of the musicians teach in local colleges and universities, and many serve as conductors, concertmasters, or soloists with local orchestras.

The musicians are members of the AFM. Contracts, which come up for renewal every three years, are negotiated by a committee of musicians elected from the orchestra. The administration is represented in contract talks by the general manager, operations manager, director of administrative services, and an advisory committee from the Board. Although the general manager is in charge of artistic positions and signing contracts, the decision to hire a prospective instrumentalist is made by the music director, who also seeks the advice of the musicians' Auditioning Committee.

On June 6, 1872, an 18-piece orchestra sponsored by the Minneapolis Musical Society gave its first concert in Minneapolis. At that time the rapidly growing town's population numbered a mere 20,000. This earliest forerunner of the Minnesota Orchestra, though not successful, was followed by the Minneapolis Orchestral Union, which gave regular concerts for three years. The early 1880s saw the formation of an orchestra by Frank Danz, Sr., leader of the military band at Fort Snelling. Danz lured his son, Frank Danz, Jr., from New York to Minneapolis to lead the 16-piece Danz Orchestra, which, besides making itself available for social occasions, established a regular series of biweekly concerts.

The immediate progenitor of the Minneapolis Symphony, however, was the Philharmonic Club. A mixed chorus that emerged in 1897 from the Filharmonix, a group of musical amateurs that offered their services for entertainment, the Philharmonic Club soon rose to prominence under the direction of Emil Oberhoffer, who took direction in 1900. The ambitious Oberhoffer, a native German who had worked as a church musician after being stranded in Minneapolis by an opera troupe that went broke, hired pick-up orchestras to perform large oratorios with his chorus. He dreamed of and worked for a full-fledged symphony orchestra.

Oberhoffer's dreams were realized in the fall of 1903. On November 5 of that year the new Minneapolis Symphony Orchestra under his direction performed a concert including works of Wagner, Strauss, and Verdi, with Marcella Sembrich as soloist. It was the eighth major orchestra in the United States, though the city ranked 18th in population. The orchestra of 50 included many musicians from the Danz Orchestra, including Frank Danz, Jr., who willingly gave up his baton to become concertmaster. The new orchestra was enthusiastically received. The tall young conductor's dramatic flair and spirited performances caught the attention of audiences and critics wherever the orchestra performed, though it was often criticized for its overpowering brass.

In its third season the fledgling orchestra acquired a new business manager and a Board of Directors headed by lumberman Elbert L. Carpenter, who became president of the Orchestral Association in 1905, when it was incorporated; Carpenter remained in that position until his death in 1945. His untiring efforts to build a financial base and his personal largess were essential to the young orchestra's survival.

In 1905 the MSO began playing its concerts in the new Minneapolis Auditorium. Sunday afternoon pops concerts were initiated in 1906, and touring began the same year with a trip to North Dakota and northern Minnesota. Subsequent tours during the first 15 years carried the orchestra through the southern and Pacific states and four times to the eastern states. New York audiences heard it first in 1912, Boston in 1916.

When the "self-made" and "home-grown" Oberhoffer resigned in 1922, the management turned to Europe for a conductor, as it would for subsequent leaders. The Belgian Henri Verbrugghen, one of five visiting conductors to lead the MSO during the 1922–1923 season, was engaged as the new director. A significant event of that interim season was the first radio broadcast of the orchestra on WLAG under the baton of Bruno Walter.

Verbrugghen had begun his professional career as a violinist in Glasgow, but had established a reputation both there and on the continent as a conductor. A meticulous and methodical classicist, Verbrugghen polished the orchestra technically but gave less-inspired performances than his predecessor. He introduced Twin Cities audiences to the music of Bach (with harpsichord), attempted a cycle of six all-Beethoven concerts, and added chamber music to the orchestra's season. Like most other MSO conductors, he championed new music, programming new works by Schoenberg, Stravinsky, Honegger, and others. Under his leadership the MSO made its first recordings. While in New York in 1924 they produced four records for the Brunswick-Balke-Collender Company. Verbrugghen's term ended after he suffered a cerebral hemorrhage in the fall of 1931. The previous season he had conducted the first concerts in the orchestra's new home, Northrop Auditorium on the University of Minnesota campus.

Upon Verbrugghen's collapse, the promising young Hungarian Eugene Ormandy was brought to fill in. His opening concert before a filled house was so electrifying that an extra performance was immediately scheduled and a contract tendered. Reviewers hailed him as a "young genius" and compared him with Toscanini, Koussevitzky, and Stokowski. The young conductor's innate musicality and driving ambition did much to keep the MSO going during the depression years and to build the orchestra's reputation. Its sound became richer and fuller, especially in the strings. Ormandy designed his programs carefully, balancing his literature between classics and new works. The orchestra was again heard on the air waves; 24 concerts were broadcast in 1933–1934 under Ormandy's direction.

After Ormandy's departure for Philadelphia in 1936, the orchestra again saw a series of guest conductors. Among them the Greek conductor Dmitri Mitropoulos stood out, and he was appointed for the following season. For the next 12 years the orchestra enjoyed the leadership of this inspiring conductor. He offered intensely personal readings that, according to critics, were exciting and uplifting, though occasionally irritating. The MSO went through its most unorthodox period of programming under Mitropoulos, who gave little attention to balance, variety, or audience attitudes. Numerous new works were programmed, and arguments raged between traditional and progressive-minded factions of the audience. The latter appreciated the prominence in MSO programs of the atonal school—Schoenberg, Berg, and Křenek (who then taught at Hamline University in St. Paul) and also the new works by Sessions, Bartók, Shostakovitch, and several local composers. Mitropoulos also showed a fondness for romantics such as Schumann and Mendelssohn. During his tenure the orchestra recorded for Columbia, and from 1939 to 1941 they added 17 titles to the Columbia catalogue. These recordings did much to establish the worldwide reputation of the MSO. Although touring stopped for three years, it was resumed in 1948. On the eastern tour that year the orchestra returned to New York after an absence of 27 years. In 1949 they performed for the last time under Mitropoulos at the Goethe Bicentennial Festival at Aspen. Mitropoulos left that year for the New York Philharmonic.*

Although nearly as flamboyant on the podium as his predecessor, the new director, Antal Dorati, offered less eccentric readings. According to John K. Sherman, "interest shifted from the interpretation of the music to the music itself, which seemed more palatable if occasionally less rousing" (p. 289). Although new music continued as a part of almost every program, its juxtaposition with the familiar made it easier for the audience to accept. The Dorati years witnessed frequent programming of Bartók and an increased use of area choruses for large choral-orchestral works. Important events of the Dorati years were the orchestra's first telecasts in 1949–1951 and the State Department-sponsored tour to Central Europe, the Mideast, and India in 1957.

When Dorati resigned in 1960, Stanislaw Skrowaczewski, then director of the National Philharmonic Orchestra of Warsaw, was appointed music director. During the nearly two decades of his leadership the MSO increased from 85 to 95 members, expanded its season from 30 to 50 weeks, and nearly quadrupled its budget. The controversial decision to change its name to the "Minnesota Orchestra" came in 1968. Noteworthy events of these years were the American premiere of Penderecki's *St. Luke Passion* in 1969, the guest appearance of Igor Stravinsky in 1966, the concert at the United Nations for Human Rights Day in 1965, and the orchestra's debut at the new Kennedy Center in 1972. The tradition of presenting new works continued, and twice the orchestra and its director received ASCAP awards for adventuresome programming of contemporary music.

When Skrowaczewski left in 1979 to devote himself full-time to composing and guest conducting, the Orchestral Association shifted to a team of conductors with Neville Marriner as artistic director and principal conductor. Founder and director of the Academy of St. Martin-in-the-Fields, Marriner has continued in his role with that orchestra and in addition currently holds posts as music director of the South German Radio Orchestra (Stuttgart) and the Strassbourg Philharmonic Orchestra. He also maintains several guest conducting posts and was until 1984 artistic director of the Meadow Brook summer festival in Michigan. Under Marriner the Minnesota Orchestra has recorded extensively on a variety of labels. National weekly radio broadcasts began in 1980, and the orchestra's opening concert for the 1982 international Scandinavia Today festival in the Twin Cities was televised over the Public Broadcasting System. The annual Sommerfest of the Minnesota Orchestra commenced in 1980 under the direction of Leonard Slatkin and has enjoyed increasing popularity. Programming of new works continues. The Minnesota Orchestra is one of seven select orchestras that participate in the Composers-in-Residence project supported by the Rockefeller Foundation, Exxon, and the National Endowment for the Arts and currently has two composers in residence. The orchestra also enjoys a productive collaboration with the Minnesota Composers Forum.

RECORDING HISTORY AND SELECTIVE DISCOGRAPHY: When the Minneapolis Symphony made its 1924 recordings for the Brunswick-Balke-Collender Company it became only the third American orchestra to record (after the Boston Symphony Orchestra* and the New York Philharmonic). Ten years later the MSO cut a number of records for RCA Victor under Ormandy. From 1939, under Mitropoulos, the MSO recorded for Columbia, and during Dorati's tenure for Mercury. Most recording connoisseurs consider these Mercury recordings, five of which have been reissued, to be among the best the orchestra has produced. Since 1960 the MSO (since 1968 as the Minnesota Orchestra) has entered the catalogue on many labels: Vox, Turnabout, Columbia, Philips, Pro Arte, CBS, Telarc, Candide, and EMI.

Dvořák, Symphony No. 8 in G (Marriner): Philips 6514–050. Penderecki, Violin Concerto, premiere recording (Stern/Skrowaczewski): Columbia M–35150. Prokofiev, *Love for Three Oranges Suite* and Stravinsky, *Petroushka* (Skrowaczewski): Candide QCE 31103. Ravel, *Complete Works for Orchestra* (Skrowaczewski): 4-record Vox Box 5133. Tchaikovsky, *Nutcracker Suite* and *Swan Lake Suite* (Slatkin): Pro-Arte PAD 121. Tchaikovsky, *1812 Overture* and *Capriccio Italien* (Dorati): Mercury SRI 75001 (reissue). Wagner, Overtures to *Flying Dutchman, Rienzi*, and *Meistersinger*; *Siegfried's Rhine Journey* (Marriner): Telarc DG–10083.

CHRONOLOGY OF MUSIC DIRECTORS: Emil Oberhoffer, 1903–1922. (Guest conductors, 1922–1923.) Henri Verbrugghen, 1923–1931. Eugene Ormandy, 1931–1936. (Guest conductors, 1936–1937.) Dmitri Mitropoulos, 1937–1949. Antal Dorati, 1949–1960. Stanislaw Skrowaczewski, 1960–1979. Neville Marriner, 1979-1986. Edo de Waart to begin duty in 1986.

BIBLIOGRAPHY: Interviews with Minnesota Orchestra personnel, 1983. Barbara Flanagan, *Ovation* (Minnesota: Minnesota Orchestra, 1978). *Fourscore: A Commemorative Yearbook for the 80th Season of the Minnesota Orchestra* (Minneapolis: Minnesota Orchestral Association, 1983). *The Minneapolis Symphony Orchestra: Complete Record First through Forty-Second Season, 1903–04—1944–45* (Minneapolis: Orchestra Association of Minneapolis, n.d.). John Mueller, *The American Symphony Orchestra* (1951; reprint, Westport, Conn.: Greenwood Press, 1976). George Seltzer, *The Professional Symphony Orchestra* (Metuchen, N.J.: Scarecrow Press, 1975). John K. Sherman, *Music and Maestros: The Story of the Minneapolis Symphony Orchestra* (Minneapolis: University of Minnesota, 1952).

ACCESS: The Minnesota Orchestra, 1111 Nicollet Mall, Minneapolis, MN 55403. (612) 371–5600. Richard W. Cisek, President.

GERALD HOEKSTRA

ST. PAUL (2,113,533—Minneapolis/St. Paul)

St. Paul Chamber Orchestra (Mj)

The 34-member St. Paul Chamber Orchestra is the only chamber orchestra with ASOL Major status. Founded in 1968, it has obtained a worldwide reputation in a strikingly short time.

Under Music Director Pinchas Zukerman, and several guest conductors, the SPCO presents about 85 concerts in its eight series in the Twin Cities (at eight different locations) as well as 50 regional, national, and international concerts. Live concert attendance during its 40-week season approaches 200,000 each year, while regular broadcasts over Minnesota Public Radio and American Public Radio make the orchestra available to many more listeners throughout the country. The orchestra reaches hundreds of talented young musicians every year through its ambitious educational programs. The versatility that has long characterized the SPCO and its practice of breaking down into smaller ensembles make it an ideal group for workshops, lecture-demonstrations, and open rehearsals. In addition, many of the musicians teach at local colleges and universities.

After 16 years of changing locations, the orchestra moves in 1985 into its first permanent home, the stunning new Ordway Music Theatre in downtown St. Paul. Designed by noted architect Ben Thompson to resemble an old European concert hall, the $46 million Ordway includes an 1,800-seat main hall and a small theater seating 300, designed for local and experimental arts groups.

The orchestra is administered by a 24-person professional staff presided over by Vice President and General Manager Richard Contee, who reports to a 70-member Board of Directors chaired by John M. Musser. Contee, formerly president of the Dayton-Hudson Foundation has primary responsibility for all financial and development activities, while musical decisions are left to the music director. The orchestra elects a non-voting member of the Board and maintains a negotiating team for collective bargaining. As specified in its master agreement, the SPCO, like other orchestras, has an Auditioning Committee that helps select finalists from whom the music director chooses the appointee and an Orchestra Committee that insures compliance with the master agreement. The SPCO has a 1984–1985 projected budget of almost $4.5 million. In 1983–1984, 57% was raised from earned income, while 43% came from contributions. The orchestra spends 72% of its budget on performance costs, 12% on marketing, 12% on administration, and 4% on fund-raising.

Although St. Paul is Minnesota's capital, its larger twin, Minneapolis, is home to the University of Minnesota, major league sports teams, the Guthrie Theatre, and the Minnesota Orchestra.* Because of Minneapolis's real or perceived pre-eminence, the growth of the St. Paul Chamber Orchestra can be seen as a reflection of St. Paul's attempt to emerge from the cultural shadow of its sister city.

Even before World War I, St. Paul had its own symphony, founded in 1903, to compete with the Minneapolis Symphony (now the Minnesota Orchestra). The St. Paul Orchestra folded, and despite periodic attempts at revival, it was not until 1959 that a Civic Philharmonic Society was founded and Conductor Leonard Sipe chosen as music director. Sipe gathered together two dozen free-lance musicians, including several first-chair players from the Minneapolis Symphony, for the first season of the St. Paul Philharmonic. By 1966 the orchestra presented a 10-concert season in a local high school auditorium, and in the same year made its New York debut at the Grand Ballroom of the Biltmore Hotel.

Following the New York debut, Sipe and the Society began a determined effort to gain support for a full-time orchestra, and by 1968 had sufficient backing to launch the 22-member St. Paul Chamber Orchestra. For the inaugural 1968–1969 season Sipe and America's first full-time professional chamber orchestra moved their concerts downtown to a hall in the St. Paul Arts and Science Center. Despite its lean roster, which led one player to remark that "no one dared to be sick," the orchestra gave both local concerts and an extensive East Coast tour, including a Carnegie Hall debut on February 21, 1969. This concert, whch included works by Haydn, Mozart, Orff, and the premiere of Hans Werner Henze's *Kammerkonzert*, was warmly received. Critics noted both the "sparkling performances" and St. Paul's conversion from being an artistic appendage of Minneapolis.

The hiring of Stephen Sell in 1969 as the orchestra's first full-time managing director marked a turning point in the early history of the orchestra. Sell, later to become executive director of the Philadelphia Orchestra,* had differences with Sipe over the orchestra's direction. After Sipe left in 1971 Sell announced a season that would feature as guest conductors candidates for the position of music director.

By April 1972, the orchestra and Board announced the unanimous selection of 28-year-old Dennis Russell Davies as the new music director, to preside over a 43-week season. Born in Toledo, Ohio, in 1944, Davies studied piano and conducting at Juilliard. With the Juilliard Ensemble in a 1969 series called "New and Newer Music" at Lincoln Center, Davies began to gain a reputation as one of the most talented young conductors of contemporary music. With his long hair and fondness for motorcycles, Davies represented both a new image and a new musical direction for the SPCO. He substituted stylish blue velvet suits for the traditional black tie and tails and attempted to introduce a less formal atmosphere in his concerts. Grants obtained through the tireless efforts of Sell resulted in the "Music on the Move" program, which brought the orchestra much more fully into the life of the city, state, and region. The small and flexible orchestra performed concerts and workshops in every venue, including concert halls, schools, colleges, churches, and even shopping centers.

In a 1973 *Minneapolis Tribune* interview Davies stated his desire to "build an important professional reputation by making [the SPCO] an orchestra of worldwide importance," and his first year marked a giant step in that direction. The orchestra regularly filled a hall three times the size of its previous location, and Davies began two important new series, one devoted to baroque music, and one, the informal "Perspective Series," devoted primarily to contemporary music, presented at the renowned Walker Art Center.

Inventive programming was also a hallmark of the regular concert season. For three years Davies organized the entire season around two highly contrastable composers: in 1972–1973 they were Archangelo Corelli and Charles Ives; in 1974–1975, Joseph Haydn and John Cage. In a normal concert year half the works performed were from the twentieth century and over one-third by American composers. The inventiveness and style that characterized Davies's early years as conductor continued throughout his eight-year tenure with the then 16-member orchestra. Residencies with dancer Erik Hawkins and composers (such as John Cage, Hans Werner Henze, and Louis Ballard), collaborations with jazz musicians (Keith Jarrett, Dave Brubeck, and Herbie Mann), and many premieres kept contemporary music at the center of the SPCO's activities and the SPCO at the center of American music making. Davies took the orchestra on extensive tours of the United States, Europe, and the Soviet Union, in which it visited over 35 foreign cities as well as 140 American cities. Seasons had expanded to 60 concerts. Davies established the group as one of the leading chamber orchestras in the world.

Recognized as a talented young conductor, Davies was ready to move on. In May of 1978 he announced his decision to leave the SPCO after the 1979–1980 season to become general music director of the Stuttgart Opera and to pursue other conducting opportunities in Europe. Davies regretted leaving the United States, but felt that young American conductors had little chance of advancing their careers without first establishing a reputation in Europe.

During the Davies years, though, the orchestra's growth in reputation and activities were not coupled with equal financial security. In 1975 only a drastic five-week layoff saved a major grant that required a balanced budget, and by 1978 the orchestra was struggling with a $200,000 deficit. The orchestra had won new audiences, but it had failed to inspire St. Paul's business and civic leaders. As a result, the orchestra's new Board chairman, John Myers, issued a challenge to the business community of St. Paul to either support the orchestra or watch it die. Through educational efforts and creative marketing, Myers gained the support needed, and by the time Pinchas Zukerman was chosen to replace Davies, the orchestra was on a much firmer fiscal footing. In choosing Zukerman, the Board had clearly decided to move the SPCO in a new direction. Zukerman, though a brilliant violinist and violist, had limited conducting experience. He had, however, a superstar's charisma, and the Board felt he would be a galvanizing force in attracting big-name soloists and, as a result, new audiences and new support.

Zukerman, one of the great musicians of our time, was born in Israel in 1948. Through the intervention of Pablo Casals and Isaac Stern, the child prodigy was brought to study at Juilliard with Ivan Galamian in 1962. His brilliant career was launched after winning first prize in the Leventritt International Competition in 1967. Citing the orchestra's "music making of the highest level," Zukerman came to St. Paul with the agreement that the orchestra would add five strings and three winds, bringing the total number of players to 34. After his current contract, which runs through the 1985–1986 season, he hopes to expand further to 44 players, enabling the orchestra to play the early romantic repertoire. This proposed expansion has aroused financial and philosophic concerns, and the outcome is uncertain. What is clear is that Zukerman's vision for the SPCO is quite unlike that of Davies.

During Zukerman's first season he firmly established his independence from former practices. The season was expanded to 90 concerts, and three new series were added with a lineup of world-famous soloists such as Isaac Stern, Daniel Barenboim, and Leonard Rose. As if to symbolize the change, gone were the trendy velvet suits and back were the traditional white ties and tails. Zukerman's first season had much less contemporary music and, according to Two Cities critics, an overabundance of the works of Mozart, especially in the major Capital Series. Although he has gradually expanded his repertoire, Zukerman's seasons have had a traditional focus quite different from Davies's more adventurous, if quixotic, seasons. Though he rarely conducts contemporary music himself, Zukerman has not abandoned it. New York composer/performer Mark Neikrug was hired as contemporary music advisor to administer the Perspective/New Music Series as well as other new-music activities.

Not surprisingly, along with the programming changes, the sound and style of the orchestra have changed. To some extent this change is due to the increasing size of the ensemble, but much more reflects Zukerman's concept of instrumental and orchestral sound. The SPCO now has a dark and rich tone like Zukerman's own solo timbre, and the crisp, bright attack and release as well as the transparency of texture of the Davies years have been replaced by a more fluent and lush sound.

Whatever misgivings some had about the changes in the SPCO, from a marketing point of view the advent of Zukerman was a rousing success. Concert fees rose by 64%, ticket revenue by 71%, and there was a 200% increase in Twin Cities ticket sales. Zukerman's talent and name have brought the orchestra recording opportunities with RCA and CBS and television appearances. Tours to South America as well as throughout the United States, residencies at Chicago's Ravinia Festival, and American Public Radio broadcasts continue to spread the reputation of the St. Paul Chamber Orchestra, which now seems firmly established as one of the world's leading orchestras.

RECORDING HISTORY AND SELECTIVE DISCOGRAPHY: The SPCO began its commercial recording history in 1971 with two CRI pressings conducted by composer Sydney Hodkinson. During Davies's years the orchestra was represented on the CRI, Nonesuch, and Sound 80 labels, with a repertoire primarily of twentieth-century music. With the ascendance of Zukerman, the orchestra now records on the CBS and RCA labels.

J. S. Bach/Vivaldi, *Concerti for Two Violins* (Isaac Stern and Richard Killmer/ Zukerman): CBS Masterworks IM37278. William Bolcom, *Open House: Commedia for (Almost) Eighteenth-century Orchestra* (Paul Sperry/Davies): Nonesuch H71324. Copland, *Appalachian Spring*; Ives, *Three Places in New England* (Davies): Sound 80 S80-DLR–101. Mozart, Violin Concerto Nos. 3 and 5, K. 216 and K. 219 (Zukerman/Zukerman): CBS IM37290. Phillip Rhodes, Divertimento for Small Orchestra (Davies): CRI SD361. Schubert, Mass No 5 in A-flat, D. 678 (Carleton College Choir, William Wells, director; Marlee Sabo, Jan DeGaetani, Paul Sperry, Lesie Guinn/Davies): Nonesuch H72335. Vivaldi, *The Four Seasons* (Zukerman): CBS Masterworks IM36710.

CHRONOLOGY OF MUSIC DIRECTORS: Leonard Sipe, 1968–1971. (Guest conductors, 1971–1972.) Dennis Russell Davies, 1972–1980. Pinchas Zukerman, 1980-present.

BIBLIOGRAPHY: Michael Anthony, articles and reviews in the *Minneapolis Star and Tribune*. Roy Close, articles and reviews in the *St. Paul Dispatch and Pioneer Press*. Jennifer Dunning, "Exchanging the Bow for the Baton," *The New York Times Magazine*, 15 Nov. 1981. *The New Grove Dictionary of Music and Musicians* (1980). *St. Paul Chamber Orchestra: A Case Statement* (St. Paul: SPCO, 1983). Nan Tillson Birmingham, "St. Paul: The Other Twin," *Town and Country*, June 1984.

ACCESS: St. Paul Chamber Orchestra, Landmark Center, 75 W. 5th St., St. Paul, MN 55102. (612) 292–3248. Richard Contee, Vice President and Managing Director.

STEPHEN KELLY

Mississippi ─────────────────────

Jackson (320,425)

Jackson Symphony Orchestra (Mt)

Mississippi is still, in many respects, an agricultural state, with more land in forests than in towns. The Jackson Symphony, with an ASOL high Metropolitan-class budget, is the largest orchestra in the state and the only one with touring capabilities. Beyond a radius of 60 miles of the capital city of Jackson, one finds few people in Mississippi—adults or children—who have ever heard a live symphony orchestra.

Annually, from October to May, the JSO performs 46 to 50 concerts, half of which are outside Jackson. The special concerts throughout the state add measurably to the number of persons who hear the orchestra each season and to its income. In a state with just over two million people, more than 400,000 hear the JSO or one of its ensembles each season.

The annual subscription series at the 2,500-seat Jackson Municipal Auditorium offers eight concerts, comprised of five classical, plus three pops or three chamber concerts. (At additional cost, subscribers may attend both pops and chamber concerts.) The contemporary hall, built in 1968, is the cornerstone for an imposing Mississippi Arts Center complex. Additional concerts in Jackson include a free Valentine program for senior citizens, a Zoo Concert, children's programs, and concerts at various parks around the city.

The JSO was founded in 1944 by a group of prominent businessmen and community leaders who felt the need to fill a gap in the city's cultural life. Local musicians were recruited, with tremendous assistance from personnel then stationed at the Veterans Hospital and the Jackson Air Base during that World War II year.

The first rehearsal of the 45-member orchestra was held in September, in preparation for the premiere concert on October 19, 1944, at the Heidelberg Hotel. (Today's JSO comprises almost double that original figure, with 28 musicians being full-time symphony employees.) Admission to the initial concert was by invitation only. Estimates of the audience ranged from 300 to 500. At the first program, an invitation was issued to those present to buy season tickets for the year's remaining four concerts, and about 300 did so. (There are approximately 4,500 ticket holders and members today.) The original budget for the fledgling orchestra was $2,500. Businessmen were asked to underwrite the orchestra with annual contributions of $50 each for a period of two years. This provided only a part-time conductor and made no provisions for paid musicians, guest soloists, or rehearsal space.

Theodore C. Russell, then chairman of the music department of Mississippi State College for Women, was chosen manager and conductor of the new JSO. He held that position until his resignation for personal reasons in August 1965. Also begun in 1944 was the Jackson Symphony Orchestra Association, formed to give the orchestra the stability and backing necessary to insure its success. The Chamber of Commerce facilitated the initial meeting, and a Board of Governors was elected. The present Board of Governors is composed of 52 men and women who serve three-year terms.

The JSO's second and present conductor, Lewis Dalvit, formerly conducted the Beloit (Wisconsin) Symphony Orchestra. When he joined the JSO, its budget was $28,000, and the orchestra began striving for Metropolitan status. Accepting the challenge, Dalvit hired the first full-time musicians, a string quartet functioning as string section-leaders.

The conductor of the JSO is responsible for selecting music and guest artists for all concert performances, as well as selecting musicians, although he may make the decision in consultation with an auditions committee. The manager of the JSO is the chief executive officer, responsible for supervision of all areas of the Association's operation to insure that it functions on a sound financial basis. The staff also includes a public relations director, secretary, bookkeeper, librarian, operations manager, education director, stage manager, and part-time development director. The orchestra's $750,000 budget is funded by major contributions, ticket sales and memberships, special concerts, grants from the school systems, federal and state grants, and the Jackson Symphony League. JSO repertoire is largely romantic, with classical, baroque, and modern works included.

In 1947, the Jackson Symphony began giving concerts for children and young people. Currently, 25% of its budget is allocated to various educational programs. Over 25,000 Mississippi school children annually hear the Symphony perform concerts designed especially for them. Since 1965, the JSO has sponsored free string lessons twice a week in the schools. The JSO absorbs the students' instrument costs in cases where they would pose financial difficulty for the family. Presently, over 700 youngsters participate in the string program, which includes a staff of ten teachers and an education director. The realization that young musicians need orchestral experience both for their own development and to provide future orchestra players resulted in the organization in 1955 of the Jackson Symphony Youth Orchestra. Chosen by yearly auditions, over 90 students, ages 9–17, participate in junior and senior orchestras.

The JSO has three ensemble groups: the Jackson Symphony–Mississippi College String Quartet, the Brass Trio, and the Woodwind Quintet. All three groups are composed of full-time musicians from the orchestra. They perform weekly school concerts in Jackson and also travel the state for special programs.

CHRONOLOGY OF MUSIC DIRECTORS: Theodore C. Russell, 1944–1965. Lewis Dalvit, 1965-present.

BIBLIOGRAPHY: Judy W. Ritter, comp., *JSO Oral History Transcripts*, Archives and History Department, State of Mississippi.

ACCESS: Jackson Symphony, P.O. Box 4584, Jackson, MS 39216. (601) 960–1565. Carolyn S. McLendon, General Manager.

PATRICIA H. EVANS

Missouri _____

KANSAS CITY (1,327,106—Kansas City, Kans./Mo.)

Kansas City Symphony (NA)

The history of professional symphony orchestras in Kansas City records the establishment and demise of several organizations from the 1880s until the present day. The Kansas City Symphony, founded in 1982, was preceded by organizations of longer duration, most notably the Kansas City Philharmonic (1933–1982) and others, including the Kansas City Symphony Orchestra (1896–1905; 1911–1917), directed by John Behr and later by Sir Carl Busch, and the Little Symphony (1922–1927), a chamber orchestra organized and conducted by Nazareno DeRubertis.

Not surprisingly, the present Kansas City Symphony inherited many musicians and supporters from the Kansas City Philharmonic, some of whom were longtime members of the latter orchestra, and the Symphony's concert season and programming decisions closely resemble those of the Philharmonic. Mention of some of the most significant events and personalities in the history of the Philharmonic will explain in part the tradition preceding the present orchestra.

The Kansas City Philharmonic was founded in 1933 by Karl Krueger, a native Kansan of German heritage, who was also its director until he resigned in 1943 to become conductor of the Detroit Symphony.* Unlike many other American conductors of his day, Krueger favored hiring American rather than European musicians for the Philharmonic, particularly midwesterners who had just completed their conservatory training. Under his direction, the orchestra survived the economic challenges of the depression years and earned a place among the important American orchestras of the period.

Krueger's successor in 1943 was Efrem Kurtz, who had made a name for himself as conductor of the Ballet Russe de Monte Carlo. His fondness for the dramatic element in music was well received by Kansas City audiences during the years of his tenure. Kurtz resigned in 1948 to become conductor of the Houston Symphony Orchestra.*

From 1948 to 1971 the Philharmonic was led by Hans Schwieger, who had enjoyed a successful career in his native Germany until Nazi oppression forced him to leave his homeland and, eventually, to settle in the United States. Of particular significance during Schwieger's years with the Philharmonic were the orchestra's recordings and "Connoisseur Concerts" of lesser-known works, which he directed and which received widespread attention. The orchestra's financial difficulties and Schwieger's disagreements with the management during the 1970–1971 season caused him to resign, and Jorge Mester assumed the conductor's post until 1974.

Maurice Peress succeeded Mester in 1974 and was director until 1980, when Peress's differences with musicians and Board members necessitated his withdrawal from the position. Highlights of Peress's term include the Philharmonic's concerts in Washington and New York.

During the following two years, the Philharmonic was under the direction of numerous guest conductors, some of whom were being considered for the permanent post, scheduled to begin with the 1982–1983 season. In 1981, the music director of the New Jersey Symphony,* Thomas Michalak, was appointed music advisor of the Kansas City Philharmonic and was a leading contender for the permanent position. Severe financial difficulties, however, forced the orchestra to disband at the end of the 1981–1982 season.

Financial backing in the form of a $1 million grant for the formation and first season of the new Kansas City Symphony was provided through R. Crosby Kemper, a Kansas City banker, from the Enid and R. Crosby Kemper Foundation. The following year a Board of Directors was formed, whose members jointly underwrote the operating expenses of the Symphony's second season and pledged to assist in raising a $10 million endowment fund for the continued support of the Symphony. The Board also pledged to underwrite the next two seasons of the Symphony to avoid an annual fund drive and to encourage donors to contribute instead to the endowment fund. Currently, financial assistance for the Symphony also comes from ticket sales; projects of the Junior Women's Symphony Alliance, the Symphony Women's Association, Friends of the Symphony, the Symphony League, and the Guild for the Arts, North; the Missouri Arts Council; and performance fees from outreach concerts.

Artistic director of the Symphony during its first years has been Russell Patterson, general manager of the Lyric Opera of Kansas City for over a quarter of a century and former horn player with the Kansas City Philharmonic during Hans Schwieger's tenure. Patterson conducts several of the subscription and other concerts during the year, with guest conductors filling the remaining dates. A search is in progress for a principal guest conductor of international prominence who would spend five to six weeks each year in residence with the Kansas City Symphony to conduct subscription concerts and to help build its reputation as an important orchestra. Guest conductors scheduled for the 1984–1985 season include Hans Schwieger, Berislav Klobucar, Jiri Belohlavek, Reinhard Peters, and Leopold Hager.

The majority of the KCS's 75 musicians were members (including some charter members) of the Philharmonic. Some of them are also faculty members of the Conservatory at the University of Missouri, Kansas City.

Ten pairs of subscription concerts are held during the regular season at the Kansas City Lyric Theater (home of the Lyric Opera), each pair comprising identical Friday and Saturday evening programs. The theater seats 1,700, comfortably accommodating the average audience of some 1,200 per performance. Additional concerts at various locations in Kansas City and in other communities in the state of Missouri supplement the subscription concerts each year. Plans for the 1985–1986 season include concerts in other parts of the Midwest as well. Among those given in the Kansas City area are the Connoisseur Concerts (patterned after those begun during Schwieger's term), a series of pops concerts, an Honors Concert with guest soloists selected from the student body at the Conservatory of the University of Missouri at Kansas City, concerts at the Nelson Art Gallery and Kansas City's Crown Center, many young people's concerts at the Lyric Theater, and a "jeans" concert at the Conservatory (so named for the attire of orchestra members and audience alike). The Symphony also provides pit orchestras for the Lyric Opera and the Kansas City Ballet.

Works from the standard repertoire, from those of Haydn and Mozart through the more traditional of the early twentieth-century works, comprise the major portions of the orchestra's programs to date. Most concerts feature a guest soloist of local, national, and/or international prominence. Decisions regarding program content are made by the artistic director in conjunction with the guest conductors and soloists.

With substantial progress toward establishing an endowment fund, able leadership, increased attendance at concerts, and the resultant improvement in morale among musicians, the future of the Kansas City Symphony looks very promising. The Kansas City area seems well able, and now more willing than ever, to establish a professional symphony orchestra on a solid basis of support.

CHRONOLOGY OF MUSIC DIRECTORS: Russell Patterson (Artistic Director), 1982-present.

BIBLIOGRAPHY: Interviews with KCS Operations Manager Susan Franano and KCP/KCS violist Mary Tuven Hoag, 1984. Jessie Benton, biographical article of Sir Carl Busch, *Kansas City Star*, 17 Nov. 1949. James Milford Crabb, "A History of Music in Kansas City, 1900–1965," Diss., University of Missouri, Kansas City, 1967. N.

DeRubertis, article on the Kansas City Little Symphony, *Kansas City Star*, 7 Aug. 1927. James C. Fitzpatrick, "Russell Patterson: Symphony, Opera Hum under Business-Minded Musician," *Kansas City Times*, 31 Mar. 1984. Charles W. Graham, "All Elements of a Great Symphony in the Life of Hans Schwieger," *Kansas City Star*, 16 May 1948. Harry Haskell, "A Symphony Orchestra Dies at 50," *Musical America*, Dec. 1982. John Haskins, "Keys in Schwieger Decision," *Kansas City Star*, 24 Feb. 1971. Betsey Solberg, "Hans Schwieger Quits," *Kansas City Star*, 24 Feb. 1971.

ACCESS: Kansas City Symphony, Lyric Theater, 1029 Central, Kansas City, MO 64105. (816) 471–4933. Nat Greenberg, Advising Manager. Susan Franano, Operations Manager.

MARTHA D. MINOR

ST. LOUIS (2,356,460)

St. Louis Symphony Orchestra (Mj)

Between the Civil War and World War I, cultural activities in St. Louis were largely in the hands of Germans. It is ironic that the St. Louis Symphony Orchestra is usually described as having been founded as one of the singing societies that flourished among them.

Despite some early ensembles, the primary sources of employment for instrumentalists in nineteenth-century St. Louis were theater orchestras in the winter, including the full spectrum of vaudeville, light opera, opera, and "legitimate" theater; and, in the summer, beer gardens, including those with bands and those offering light opera outdoors. Orchestral music in nineteenth-century St. Louis came from the St. Louis Musical Society Polyhymnia, founded in 1845; the St. Louis Philharmonic, founded in 1860; the visits of the Theodore Thomas Orchestra; the efforts of Hans Balatka and Robert Severin Sauter to raise orchestras locally; and the St. Louis Amateur Orchestra, which was founded in 1893 and took the name Philharmonic in 1923–1924.

The Germans' social activities included forming dozens of singing societies, beginning about 1840. The St. Louis Choral Society was not, in its beginnings, untypical of these Saengerbunds. Joseph Otten, its founder, was a German Catholic organist educated at the Lieger, Holland, conservatory. The new Society rehearsed at Trinity Episcopal Church and first performed March 24, 1881, at Mercantile Library Hall. Organist Edward M. Bowman accompanied the chorus of 50 in Handel's *Dettingen Te Deum*, Gounod's *Psalm 137*, and other music by Handel, Costa, and Lachner.

The second season featured a chorus of 90 and orchestra of 35 in Handel's *Messiah* and other works, *Messiah* being repeated in 24 of the next 25 seasons. During the 1884–1885 season Robert S. Brookings became president of the Society, and finances found their way to more solid footing. Existing histories of the St. Louis Symphony recount its having been founded as a chorus whose growing emphasis on orchestral music led to the absorption in 1890 of the Musical Union Orchestra. The latter deserves closer scrutiny.

The Musical Union Orchestra was founded in 1879 by its conductor, August Waldauer, and Dabney Carr, a prominent amateur flutist. Waldauer is described in *Missouri Music* as "a slender, very short violinist of considerable talent," but more a theater player than a concert artist and notable for his organizational and fund-raising abilities. The Musical Union is credited with introducing Wagner's music to St. Louis, and may have merged at some point with the Grand Orchestra, founded in 1880 at Schnaider's [Beer] Garden. The orchestra contained about 50 players, with double reeds hired from Cincinnati. Waldauer was "compelled by failing health" to sell rights, title, and property of the orchestra to the Choral Society in 1890. Beginning in 1884, the Choral Society hired instrumentalists to accompany its concerts on a regular basis, but neither the players' names nor that of the Musical Union, their purported source, are mentioned in Choral Society programs. The Society paid the instrumentalists $11 per concert and expanded the season to eight concerts.

The Society's shift from choral to orchestral music was gradual. Experiments with instrumental concerts culminated in the 1889–1890 season, when the Choral Society absorbed the Musical Union; the St. Louis Choral-Symphony Society was incorporated in 1893.

At the end of the 14th season the Directors decided to cut the number of concerts per season from seven or eight to six. Krohn said a misunderstanding led to Joseph Otten becoming upset with this turn of events; Otten quit, and the Society accepted his resignation. Otten must nevertheless be credited with bringing his choir to great size, incorporating it with the principal orchestra in the city, keeping the organization together for 14 years, and bridging the gap between choral and orchestral conducting.

Otten's replacement was a 26-year-old German opera conductor named Alfred Ernst. A talented pianist, composer and, in his better moments, conductor, he was also hot tempered. Ernst's greatest achievements include expansion of the season and his role at the 1904 Louisiana Purchase Exposition.

The 1904 World's Fair, commemorating the 1803 Louisiana Purchase, was the most important cultural event in the history of St. Louis. Ernst was granted the great honor of conducting 22 of the 25 orchestral concerts in Festival Hall, while other honors—such as the composition of official exposition music—fell to out-of-towners. According to Katherine Gladney Wells, the chorus and orchestra gained "artistic power and interpretive ability" under Ernst's direction, and this improvement was accompanied by a further turn toward orchestral works. He resigned in 1907 and returned to Germany soon afterward.

In 1907 the chorus was dropped and the St. Louis Symphony Society formed. This was the culmination of long-evolving changes and serves to emphasize the contrast between the greater popularity of choral music in nineteenth-century St. Louis and the greater popularity of orchestral music since the World's Fair. The Symphony has supported adjunct choirs twice since then, but never on an equal footing with the orchestra.

Also in 1907, violist Max Zach was hired away from the Boston Symphony Orchestra* to lead the St. Louis Symphony. Under Ernst the St. Louis orchestra had increased from 52 to 64 players. Between Zach's first concert in 1907 and his last, in 1921, it increased to 82 players. Zach continued modernizing the repertoire, giving first local performances of Tchaikovsky, Strauss, Ravel, Debussy, and Bruckner. He emphasized American composers, and he earned a great reputation as a businesslike orchestra builder in sharp contrast with Ernst's bursts of temper.

Zach died February 3, 1921. The remainder of the season was conducted by Assistant Conductor and bassoonist Frederick Fischer, and by guest conductors Theodore Spiering, Dirk Foch, and Rudolph Ganz.

Ganz succeeded Zach, although he was second choice to Fritz Kreisler. Ganz's fame at this point was based on his prodigious piano playing, and his orchestral conducting experience was mostly limited to his own compositions. His infamous first statement before the orchestra is reputed to have been, "Gentlemen, the orchestra is not my instrument, so please do your best and we will learn together" (Rice, *St. Louis Post-Dispatch*).

Despite criticisms of his musicianship, he must be credited with modernizing the repertoire by directing local premieres of music by Schoenberg, Stravinsky, Mahler, Respighi, and Honegger. He added 25% new personnel, saw Fischer devote full time to being assistant conductor, announced the contents of all 15 pairs of concerts in advance, and inaugurated a series of children's concerts.

Ganz served as conductor in St. Louis from 1921 to 1927. In 1926, the Odeon Theater, long the residence of the Society, burned, and the season was completed at the Scottish Rite Cathedral and Washington University Field House. Fischer inaugurated a new series of 15 post-season pops concerts.

The series of guest conductors following Ganz included George Szell in his U.S. conducting debut. Russian-born Frenchman Vladimir Golschmann was eventually hired, based on the advice of Walter Damrosch and Serge Koussevitzky and on Golschmann's reputation for his *Concerts Golschmann* in Paris.

Golschmann was a "major architect" of the St. Louis Orchestra (Wells, *Symphony and Song*). He exuded sophistication, charm, and elegance, and his appeal was based on his sensitivity to audience feelings. He brought new players, lengthened the season, introduced new literature to the repertoire, and expanded recording and touring activities. The first decade of his tenure was characterized by musical highs and financial lows. Salaries and ticket prices were pared during the depression, and the orchestra was saved from disbanding in 1933 by Society President Oscar Johnson and others.

During the Golschmann period the musical greats of the world began in ever-growing number to appear with the Symphony. In 1934 the Symphony moved into the new Municipal Auditorium (now known as Kiel Auditorium), having performed at the Odeon Theater and previously at the Music Hall of the Exposition Building. The war years also brought financial difficulties, but the orchestra made its first East Coast tour in 1950.

By the 1950s, however, Golschmann seemed to be resting on his laurels, and ultimately the orchestra's financial problems forced him into conductor emeritus status (1955–1958). Guest conductors abounded during this period—among them Solti, Leinsdorf, and Monteux—and much personnel turnover took place. Edouard van Remoortel was given a three-year contract and remained conductor until 1962. For the 1962–1963 season there was no permanent music director, and guest conductors included van Remoortel, Golschmann, and Eleazar De Carvalho.

De Carvalho was appointed music director in March 1963. Wells describes him as a student of Koussevitzky and an experienced professional with a doctorate from the University of Brazil. His programs became notable for modern and avant-garde pieces. In 1967 concertmaster Max Rabinovitsj organized a Symphony String Quartet, which survived until 1976 and inspired the Musical Offering chamber music series. During De Carvalho's tenure, funds were raised, particularly through Oscar Johnson, Walter and Helen Powell, and the Ford Foundation. The St. Louis Theater (erected in 1925) was extensively remodeled into the multi-million-dollar Powell Symphony Hall, which reopened in 1968.

Belabored by complaints that avant-garde music caused box-office problems, De Carvalho resigned effective May 1966. Accomplishments during De Carvalho's tenure included Powell Hall, expansion of the orchestra and its season, acquisition of the first associate conductor who wasn't an orchestra player (George Cleve), and a notable list of first performances. As such, De Carvalho may be the most underrated conductor in the Symphony's history.

Walter Susskind, who was appointed the next music director, commands Wells's respect as the most sophisticated and experienced of all. Susskind led a brilliant career as conductor and pianist, recording extensively and bringing polish to St. Louis. His tenure here was notable for orchestra-building and the Symphony's participation in the Mississippi River Festival. Perhaps most significantly, he brought Leonard Slatkin as assistant and later associate conductor.

Susskind stayed in St. Louis seven years before resigning in 1974. Slatkin removed himself from consideration as Susskind's successor, and Georg ("Jerzy") Semkow became the next conductor. During Semkow's very capable administration the County Pops series was inaugurated, and the St. Louis Symphony Chorus was formed under Thomas Peck. Its auspicious first appearance presented music of Colgrass and Prokofiev. However, Semkow's tenure, like De Carvalho's and Susskind's, was marred by musicians' strikes. Important personnel changes in the 1970s were the ascension of Jacques Israelievitch as concertmaster, Leonard Slatkin as principal guest conductor, and David Hyslop as executive director.

When Semkow resigned in 1979, he was replaced by Leonard Slatkin. A graduate of Juilliard and Aspen, Slatkin had taken a vigorous role with the Symphony, founding the Youth Orchestra, directing frequently, and guest conducting extensively. The city bloomed with automobile bumper-stickers reading "Slatkin's Back." Indeed, Slatkin's return has been triumphant. His popularity is reflected in *Time* magazine's rating the St. Louis Symphony under Slatkin second nationwide; the orchestra has thrived artistically— recently winning a Grammy Award—and the Society has celebrated a centennial.

The orchestra records prolifically, plays over 200 concerts per year, and enjoys the support of an active Women's Association. Finances continue to be a contradictory subject, however. While major grants and endowments have made possible the residencies of composer Joseph Schwantner and assisting conductors, while several chairs in the orchestra have been endowed, and while the Symphony's glamorous residence in Powell Hall contributes to its elite reputation and feeling of permanence, the annual budget and fund-raising remain subjects of concern to the Society.

In recent years Slatkin has begun to carve out a special niche in the repertoire of the twentieth and late nineteenth centuries. Perhaps most notable in Slatkin's modern repertoire have been the world premieres of David Del Tredici's *Final Alice* and Joseph Schwantner's *Magabunda*. Raymond Leppard has recently been named principal guest conductor, and he will emphasize earlier repertoire. In 1984, Peter Susskind, son of the late St. Louis Symphony music director Walter Susskind, was named assistant conductor of the orchestra. He will conduct the youth concerts, educational concerts, regional tours, and other performances with the Symphony.

As the St. Louis Symphony Orchestra enters the 1984–1985 season it enjoys excellent rapport with its music director and a growing worldwide reputation. Slatkin will direct the majority of concert pairs of the orchestra series, and Leppard will be particularly active in the Chamber Orchestra series. Other series include Chamber Music St. Louis and Pops at Powell. Two series for students are offered: young people's concerts for ages nine and up, and Kinder Konzerts for younger children. A special performance of the Christmas portions of Handel's *Messiah* is staged during a school day each December, including the full Symphony and chorus with soloists. For general audiences as well, the Mozart version of *Messiah* keeps its important place in the repertoire. Slatkin's interest in modern music is shown by his scheduling works by Crumb, Reich, Ruggles, Schwantner, and others. In 1985 the orchestra toured the eastern United States and Europe.

The budget for the 1984–1985 season is set at $10.7 million, swelled to that figure by the European tour. The Society's earned and contributed income is derived from concert revenue 31.3%, fund raising, 24.2%, government (3 levels) 12.4%, deficit 9.5%, endowment interest 8.3%, recording and touring fees 6.6%, Women's Association 5.7%, impresario activities (hall rental, etc.) 2%. The Symphony Society itself consists of 11 officers plus a Board of Directors of 108. Members are nominated from within and approved by the membership.

In a city earnestly plying the tourist trade, Slatkin's Symphony is as central an attraction as the zoo, art museum, arch, and Cardinals. And in Slatkin himself one might hope for another "major architect" of the orchestra, who might repeat the brilliance of his mentor, Susskind, and the long tenure of their predecessor, Golschmann.

RECORDING HISTORY AND SELECTIVE DISCOGRAPHY: Rudolph Ganz inaugurated the Symphony's recording career with romantic European music for Victor. Golschmann led recordings of both the romantic and modern repertoire for Capitol, Columbia, Victor, and other companies. Still-current recordings were made mostly under Susskind, Semkow, and Slatkin by Candide, Telarc, Turnabout, Vox, and most recently, Moss Music Group.

Debussy, *La Mer, Danses sacrée et profane, Prélude à l'ápres-midi d'un faun* (Slatkin): Telarc DG 10071. Gershwin, Works for Orchestra, Piano and Orchestra (Slatkin): Vox 3-SVBX–5132 (3 records). Holst, *The Planets* (Susskind): Turnabout 34598. Mahler, Symphony No. 1 (Slatkin): Telarc DG 10066 (Grammy Award). Prokofiev, Symphony No. 5 (Slatkin): RCA Red Seal ARC1–5035 (1985 Grammy winner). Rachmaninoff, Music of Rachmaninoff (Slatkin): Vox C 9013X (4 records). Wagner, *Overtures and Preludes* (Semkow): Turnabout 34719.

CHRONOLOGY OF MUSIC DIRECTORS: August Waldauer (Conductor, St. Louis Musical Union Orchestra), 1879–1890. Joseph Otten (Conductor, St. Louis Choral Society and St. Louis Choral-Symphony Society), 1880–1894. Alfred Ernst (Conductor, St. Louis Choral-Symphony Society and Louisiana Purchase Exhibition Orchestra), 1894–1907. Max Zach (Conductor, St. Louis Symphony Society), 1907–1921. Rudolph Ganz, 1921–1927. (Guest conductors, 1927–1931.) Vladimir Golschmann, 1931–1958. Edouard van Remoortel, 1958–1962. (Guest conductors, 1962–1963). Eleazar De Carvalho, 1963–1968. Walter Susskind, 1968–1975. Jerzy Semkow, 1975–1979. Leonard Slatkin, 1979-present.

BIBLIOGRAPHY: Interviews with Harold Lineback and Frank Peters, 1984. "Gecks, Frank: Scrapbook" Archives of the Missouri Historical Society. John Gecks, "Frank Gecks's Record," typescript in Library of Missouri Historical Society. Ernst C. Krohn, Jr., "The Development of the Symphony Orchestra in St. Louis" and "Some Notes on the Philharmonic," in *Missouri Music* (New York: Da Capo Press, 1971). Richard E. Mueller, *A Century of the Symphony* (St. Louis: Knight, 1979). "St. Louis Symphony Orchestra Scrapbook," Library of the Missouri Historical Society. *St. Louis Globe-Democrat. St. Louis Post-Dispatch.* August Waldauer, "Music in St. Louis," in *Encyclopedia of the History of St. Louis* (New York: Southern History Company, 1899).

Michael Walsh, "Music: Which U.S. Orchestras Are Best?" *Time*, 25 Apr. 1983. Katherine Gladney Wells, *Symphony and Song* (St. Louis: Countryman, 1980).

ACCESS: St. Louis Symphony Orchestra, Powell Symphony Hall, Grand at Delmar, St. Louis, MO 63103 (314) 533–2500 David J. Hyslop, Executive Director. Pam Warford, Director of Public Relations. Kevin Martin, Media Director.

FRED BLUMENTHAL

Montana _____

Billings Symphony Orchestra (Ur)

Though Montana is the nation's fourth largest state in geographic size, it has a population of only 786,000. Billings is the largest city—the commercial, cultural, and entertainment center for roughly 150,000 people.

The Billings Symphony, one of six ASOL orchestras in Montana, was organized in 1950 by its first conductor, Robert Staffanson. The orchestra soon had a Board of Directors, a business manager, a Women's Committee, and a Symphony Chorus that has performed a major work with the orchestra at least once each season. Staffanson established a subscription series consisting of five concerts per season.

When Staffanson left in 1955 to become conductor of the Springfield Symphony (Massachusetts), he was succeeded by George Perkins, who served as the orchestra's conductor for all but one of its next 29 seasons. Perkins, an Eastman graduate, spent two summers studying conducting with Pierre Monteux. During his first four seasons with the orchestra, Perkins retained his teaching position at a Wyoming college and drove 100 miles to conduct weekly orchestra and chorus rehearsals and the five subscription concerts. In 1959, Perkins joined the music faculty at Eastern Montana College in Billings.

An annual children's concert was instituted in 1957, and an annual Young Artist Competition began in 1960. In this competition a young Montana instrumentalist is selected to perform a concerto movement with the orchestra.

The Board's refusal to adopt an orchestra pay scale in 1964 resulted in the formation of a second orchestra, which Perkins conducted for one year.

The Symphony's first pay scale was established in 1965. The Billings Symphony remains the only one of Montana's six orchestras in which all players receive some compensation.

From 1973 to 1981, the orchestra's principal bassoonist, Forest Cornwell, served as business manager. Cornwell was instrumental in increasing the budget, expanding the orchestra's activities, and improving its image in the community. Since 1974, a local bank has sponsored two well-attended pop concerts in the park each summer. From 1978 through 1983, touring ballet companies were engaged to give multiple performances of the *Nutcracker* with the orchestra during the Christmas season. In 1982, the subscription series was expanded to six concerts.

Approximately one-third of the orchestra members are music teachers, and one-quarter are college and high school students. Five musicians commute 50 to 100 miles on a regular basis, and an average of three string players are imported per concert. The Billings Symphony Society's Board of Directors consists of 25 members, including one representative from each of its units—the orchestra, the chorale, and the Women's Association. The Society's budget has grown from $10,000 in 1956–1957 to $136,000 in 1983–1984. Receipts for 1983–1984 actually totalled $141,000, of which 34% was from ticket sales and 66% from contributions, grants, and sponsored concerts.

The orchestra performed in a 500-seat high school auditorium from 1950 through 1962. Since 1963 the concerts have been presented in the Fox Theatre, a 1,500-seat movie theater built in 1931. In 1982 the Fox was purchased by the city of Billings and is now used exclusively for the performing arts. A fund drive is under way to raise money for its renovation; plans include stage enlargement, new seating, and improved acoustics. Attendance at regular concerts averages 650, children's concerts 1,000, and 2,800 for two performances of *The Nutcracker*.

Since 1955 the orchestra has performed about 350 different works (exclusive of operatic arias and pop-concert selections), including 45 symphonies, 60 concertos, 26 works for chorus and orchestra, and 6 operas. About one-third of the total repertoire consisted of twentieth-century music. Among may soloists of similar stature who have appeared with the orchestra are pianist David Bar-Illan (six performances), violinist Young Uck Kim, and cellist Janos Starker.

Beginning with the 1984–1985 season, the orchestra will have its first full-time music director, Israeli-born Uri Barnea, who was chosen from a field of 200 applicants.

CHRONOLOGY OF MUSIC DIRECTORS: Robert Staffanson, 1950–1955. George Perkins, 1955–1984. Uri Barnea, 1984-present.

ACCESS: Billings Symphony and Chorale, P.O. Box 602, Billings, MT 59103. (406) 252–3610. Maxine Philaja, Manager.

GEORGE PERKINS

Nebraska ──────────────────────────

OMAHA (483,053)

Omaha Symphony (Rg)

The Omaha Symphony is one of five symphony orchestras in Nebraska, the others being the Lincoln Symphony, Nebraska Chamber Orchestra, Hastings Orchestra, and Panhandle Orchestra. Of these, the Omaha Symphony is the largest in terms of budget and outreach, with 25 annual subscription concerts, an average audience of 2,500, and an annual budget of approximately $1.6 million.

An early 1900s vaudeville hall, the Orpheum Theater, located in downtown Omaha, has served as the home of the Omaha Symphony since the structure was restored to its original opulent state in 1975. In addition, the Symphony performs regularly in a variety of indoor and outdoor settings throughout the community, state, and region, reaching more than 45,000 people each year. During the 1983–1984 season the Omaha Symphony performed eight subscription series concerts, eight pops concerts, six chamber orchestra concerts, and nine concerts for youth.

The Nebraska Sinfonia, founded in the 1975–1976 season, consists of 38 musicians who serve as the orchestra's nucleus. One of the few full-time professional chamber orchestras in the region, it presents a total of six subscription concerts and has an extensive touring program which, in combination with the subscription series, extends the group to over 20,000 individuals annually. Its primary performance home is the concert hall of the Joslyn Art Museum, built in 1931, which seats some 1,200 in a unique art deco structure. In addition to the Nebraska Sinfonia, the OSA maintains a number of small ensembles, which include the Fontenelle String Quartet, the Omaha String Quartet, the Midlands Woodwind Quintet, the Omaha

Symphony Brass Quintet, and The Trio (consisting of harp, double bass, and xylophone). These groups, performing an average of 200 concerts per year, are heard extensively in Omaha and throughout the region.

The OSA, Nebraska Sinfonia, and its various ensembles are governed by a Board of Directors and administered by a general manager with a staff of nine individuals. Personnel and most artistic decisions are subject to the approval of the music director in consultation with the Orchestra Committee. The members of the Nebraska Sinfonia are appointed on a yearly contract basis, while the non-Sinfonia members of the Omaha Symphony are hired on a per-service basis. Many of the Sinfonia members are members of the faculty at the University of Nebraska at Omaha and/or free-lance musicians. Most funding for the organization is derived from ticket sales and various promotional activities, with additional support coming from state and federal grants as well as charitable and private donations.

Origins of the Omaha Symphony are attributed to an Omaha Symphony that was founded in 1921 under the management of the Business and Professional Women's Division of the Omaha Chamber of Commerce. This organization, however, was preceded by the Omaha Symphony Study Orchestra, which performed from 1911 through 1916 under the direction of Henry Cox. Five years later Cox led the Omaha Symphony in its first performance, which included Schubert's *Unfinished* Symphony and the Piano Concerto in B-flat Minor by Tchaikovsky.

While the Omaha Symphony initially maintained enthusiastic and sustained support, the Great Depression and World War II took their toll on the development of the organization. In 1926 Sandor Harmati conducted his first concert with the OSO with Joseph Szigeti as soloist. Harmati's five-year tenure was highlighted by the appearance of Pablo Casals as guest soloist in 1928 in a performance of the Saint-Saëns's Cello Concerto. In 1930 the Omaha Symphony Orchestra Association assumed management of the orchestra and appointed Joseph Littau as its conductor. Two years later the Association voted to postpone orchestral activities due to the financial uncertainties of the time.

A revival of the OSA took place in 1936 when a group of businessmen formed a new association. Rudolph Ganz was hired to direct the group, which was forced to disband due to financial difficulties after two seasons. In 1940 another attempt was made to re-establish the orchestra under the title of the Omaha Symphonic Strings. It was led by Richard Duncan, a member of the faculty of Omaha University. Because the conductor and so many orchestra members entered the service during World War II, the efforts of the Symphony were again forced to halt.

With the return of Richard Duncan and other players from the war, the Omaha Symphony Association was reorganized and its first concert given in 1947 with pianist Sidney Foster as soloist. Duncan continued to lead the orchestra until his resignation in 1958. Joseph Levine followed as music director and conductor. Under Levine's 11-year tenure, the OSA developed steadily. In 1966 it received a grant from the Ford Foundation providing an $800,000 endowment fund for ongoing support of orchestra operations. A musical highlight of Levine's association with the OSA was the premiere of *I Have a Dream* by Elie Siegmeister, a cantata for solo baritone, narrator, chorus, and orchestra. In 1969 Yuri Krasnapolsky was engaged as music director and conductor. Under his leadership the OSA continued to grow, with diverse programming including several performances of commissioned works.

The year 1975 marked another significant point in the development of the OSA. Thomas Briccetti became music director, and under his leadership the Nebraska Sinfonia was created and the outreach of the OSO expanded significantly. It was at this juncture that the group took on its professional dimensions by developing a full-time core of musicians, a feature of the orchestra that has been maintained to this date. Briccetti's dynamic style led the two ensembles to new artistic levels, championing the cause of twentieth-century music and the lesser-known works of the eighteenth and nineteenth centuries.

After the completion of the 1982–1983 season, Thomas Briccetti resigned his position in order to devote time to compositional activities and guest conducting. The following season was overseen by a series of guest conductors for both the OSA and Nebraska Sinfonia. In 1984 Bruce Hangen, formerly conductor of the Portland (Maine) Symphony Orchestra,* was appointed as music director of the OSA beginning with the 1984–1985 season. Hangen has established a long-range goal of expanding the core of professional musicians as well as continuing the promotion of contemporary American music.

SELECTIVE DISCOGRAPHY: Jan Bach, *The Happy Prince* (Nebraska Sinfonia/Briccetti): Limited Edition Classics: LCI–101 (1980).

CHRONOLOGY OF MUSIC DIRECTORS: Henry Cox, 1921–1923. Ernest Nordin, 1924–1925. Sandor Harmati, 1926–1930. Joseph Littau, 1930–1932. Rudolph Ganz (Guest Conductor), 1933, 1936–1937. Richard Duncan, 1940–1943, 1947–1952. Emmanuel Wishnow, 1952–1954. Richard Duncan, 1954–1958. Joseph Levine, 1958–1969. Yuri Krasnapolsky, 1969–1975. Thomas Briccetti, 1975–1983. (Guest conductors, 1983–1984.) Bruce Hangen, 1984-present.

BIBLIOGRAPHY: Program Notes of the Omaha Symphony Study Orchestra, Omaha Symphony Orchestra, Omaha Symphonic Strings, Omaha Symphony Association.

ACCESS: Omaha Symphony Association, 310 Aquila Court, Omaha NE 68102. (402) 342–3560. William F. Kessler, General Manager.

ROGER E. FOLTZ

Nevada

RENO (193,623)

Reno Philharmonic (Ur)

The Reno Philharmonic offers five subscription concerts per season, plus two children's concerts and one or more extra events. It serves the Truckee Meadows area, including Reno/Sparks/Carson City, Nevada, and Lake Tahoe/Truckee, California, an area with an aggregate population of about 250,000. Most concerts are given in the Pioneer Theater-Auditorium, a county convention authority facility which seats 1,428. Concerts are broadcast on KUNR, local public radio. Since its reorganization in 1979, the orchestra's repertoire has consisted of standard romantic and early twentieth-century literature, selected with the help of an informal Program Committee.

For 1983–1984, the total budget approached $200,000, two-thirds of which derived in approximately equal portions from ticket sales and private contributions, with the remainder coming from foundation support, including grants from the Nevada State Council on the Arts, Young Audiences of Northern Nevada, and the Musicians' Performance Trust Fund. Management services are provided under a contract with a local management firm. The orchestra's Board is active in fund-raising and deals with the musicians indirectly through the music director, who is advised by an elected Players' Committee.

Most of the musicians are hired for the season on a contract basis; a few are imports, and a few play on a per-concert basis. The presence of house orchestras in several local hotel-casinos assures a good local supply of professional musicians. Many Reno Philharmonic musicians also play in the Reno Chamber Orchestra's six-concert season and in the orchestra of the Nevada Opera Association, which presents three to four productions annually.

The population of Reno/Sparks doubled between 1960 and 1980. At the start of this period, only a volunteer University of Nevada-Community Symphony served the area. In 1969, Gregory Stone founded the Reno Philharmonic Symphony Orchestra, which he single-handedly directed and subsidized for 10 years. Stone studied at the Conservatory in Odessa and emigrated in 1923. His background in radio and films as arranger, composer, conductor, and pianist led him toward innovative, showmanship-filled programs. For example, a "Basque Program" from 1969 included Bordes's "Basque Rhapsody," Chabrier's "España Rhapsody" (labeled "From the Basque Country"), some Basque songs in Stone's arrangements, and Prokofiev's *Peter and the Wolf*, narrated in a new Basque translation. "Boliva Festival '77," nominally a celebration of Latin America, consisted primarily of Stone's own music.

The Reno Philharmonic in those years did not draw substantial support from community arts leaders and rarely drew large audiences. But the population continued to grow, and there was at least one attempt to start a rival orchestra. When Stone decided to retire in 1979, reorganization quickly followed. Since then there has been steady growth in attendance, community support, budget, and the quality of the orchestra's performance.

CHRONOLOGY OF MUSIC DIRECTORS: Gregory Stone, 1969–1979. Ron Daniels, 1979-present.

BIBLIOGRAPHY: Interview with RPO Music Director Ron Daniels, 1984. "Gregory Stone," *ASCAP Biographical Dictionary*, 4th ed. (1980). Mark Oliva, "Reno 'Maestro' Transferring Baton to Europe: Gregory Stone Hopes Philharmonic Symphony Will Continue," *Reno Evening Gazette*, 2 Oc. 1978. Nevada Symphony Association archives in UNR Library (8 boxes unsorted papers, 1977–1979).

ACCESS: Reno Philharmonic, P.O. Box 1291, Reno, NV 89510. (702) 329–1324. Manager, Ed Parsons.

CATHERINE PARSONS SMITH

New Hampshire ⸻

MANCHESTER (160,767)

New Hampshire Symphony Orchestra (Mt)

Founded in Manchester in 1974, the New Hampshire Symphony is the state's principal orchestra to perform regularly during the concert season. Symphonic music in Manchester was provided prior to the Symphony's arrival by the New Hampshire Philharmonic, a still-active community orchestra founded in 1959. Foremost among other New Hampshire orchestras are the Nashua Symphony (growing in professionalism and stature), and the New Hampshire Music Festival.

As of the 1984–1985 season, the Symphony's seven annual subscription concerts were presented at Manchester's Palace Theatre, an intimate, 70-year-old hall that well fits the ensemble's average of 55 playing members and typical audience of 750 per concert. With an additional subscription series in Keene and concerts in other communities, the NHS reached an annual audience of over 20,000 through 10 to 12 full concerts and a similar number of school performances. The 1985–1986 season will see the addition of a Sunday matinee series at the Palace, and the annual audience size is expected to grow accordingly.

The NHS is governed by a 21-member Board of Trustees and administered by a full-time general manager. The music director is solely responsible for artistic decisions, although performers' musical interests are considered in programming. A core of about 30 musicians are contracted annually, and several have formed an informal Orchestra Committee to voice the musicians' views. The remaining 20 to 40 musicians (depending on program needs) are hired on a per-service basis after auditions held before the music director and Orchestra Committee. As of 1983, fewer than one-third of the musicians resided in New Hampshire, the rest being drawn mainly from the musically sophisticated freelance market in and around Boston.

The NHS is thus unusual, being a professional-quality ensemble with a relatively low 1983–1984 budget of approximately $260,000. It is funded by federal and local government grants, charitable and arts fund grants (including support from Federated Arts of Manchester), corporate gifts, private donors, and earned income.

The Symphony was founded by its current music director, James Bolle. Bolle, the director of Monadnock Music, a festival in Keene, brought to Manchester in 1974 a brief concert series with some of his Monadnock musicians under the name of the New Hampshire Sinfonietta. With support of influential Manchester music lovers (the core of the first NHS board), concerts were expanded, and in several years the orchestra had attracted enough community support to set more ambitious season goals. An artistic turning point for the orchestra was its 1980 Palace presentation of Mozart's *Don Giovanni* in an avant-garde production by Peter Sellars. It brought critical acclaim locally, as well as from Boston and New York.

One distinguishing feature is the ensemble's performance of several works of contemporary music per season, sometimes to an uncertain local reception, and often with Bolle's verbal note of explanation from the podium. The group presented on PBS the nationally televised American premiere of Bruckner's Fourth Symphony in its original version and has recorded Virgil Thompson's Third Symphony.

In the 1984–1985 season the newly formed New Hampshire Symphony Orchestra Chorus, consisting of auditioned community singers under the direction of Melinda O'Neal, made its first appearance with the orchestra in a performance of Beethoven's Ninth Symphony. The 1984–1985 season also saw the orchestra cooperate with other cultural institutions in New Hampshire by organizing a statewide Scandinavian festival consisting of concerts, cultural fairs, lectures, and other events. The program's success led to plans for a 1985–1986 Hungarian festival along similar lines.

SELECTIVE DISCOGRAPHY: Thompson, Third Symphony (Bolle) in *American Contemporary Symphonies by Virgil Thompson, Robert Helps*: CRI #SD 411.

CHRONOLOGY OF MUSIC DIRECTORS: James Bolle, 1974-present.

BIBLIOGRAPHY: Interview with NHSO General Manager Lawrence Tamburri, 1985. Peter G. Davis, "Opera: 'Don Giovanni,' New Hampshire Style," *New York Times*, 23 Sept. 1980. Richard W. O'Donnell, "An Orchestra on the Rise," *Boston Sunday Globe*, 2 Nov. 1980.

ACCESS: New Hampshire Symphony, 22 Amherst St., P.O. Box 243, Manchester, NH 03105. (603) 669–3559. Lawrence J. Tamburri, General Manager.

ROBERT R. CRAVEN

New Jersey ───────────────

NEWARK (1,965,969)

New Jersey Symphony Orchestra (Rg)

From its beginnings as a community orchestra, the New Jersey Symphony Orchestra grew steadily and in the 1970s attained national prominence under the leadership of Henry Lewis. Since 1968 fully professional, the NJSO has been an important artistic force in the Northeast as the second largest (next to the New York Philharmonic*) orchestra in the tristate metropolitan area. Unlike most orchestras that grew along with a major urban center, the NJSO's growth has been tied to the growth of the New Jersey suburbs. The orchestra continues as a "state" orchestra with a commitment to serving the entire state as much as possible.

In the 1983–1984 season the NJSO's schedule of 145 concerts spanned 18 out of New Jersey's 21 counties and a performance in New York City, to reach a total of approximately 150,000 people. The orchestra's own concerts include approximately 40 subscription concerts in four different halls (in Newark, Englewood, Trenton, and Red Bank); an active educational program with over 60 full orchestra, chamber orchestra, and ensemble concerts; summer pops concerts, and a number of performances with other groups such as the New Jersey Ballet and the June Opera Festival of Princeton. The orchestra's reputation has been enhanced by a number of performances at New York's Carnegie Hall, Philadelphia's Academy of Music, and the Kennedy Center in Washington, D.C., among many others. The NJSO has been exposed nationwide through several TV and radio broadcasts, including the WNET-TV specials "Rhapsody in Song" and "Luciano Pavarotti Live at Madison Square Garden."

The 80-member orchestra includes 64 contracted players, many of whom perform frequently with other metropolitan area groups, including the New York City Ballet, American Symphony,* New York Philharmonic, and the Metropolitan Opera. Since the NJSO's current contract guarantees approximately 20 weeks employment, almost all of the players seek other employment opportunities, which are plentiful in the New York metropolitan area.

The Board of Directors sets policy and directs a full-time professional staff of 16 people. With an annual budget of approximately $3 million, the Board also is engaged in statewide fund-raising campaigns, in which it is assisted by a Board of Regents. A large volunteer organization, the NJSO League, is vital in preserving local contacts for an orchestra with such a wide geographic outreach. The orchestra's largest funding source is the New Jersey State Council on the Arts. Additional funding comes from the NEA, many large corporations and foundations, including the Robert Wood Johnson, Jr., Charitable Trust, which has been extremely important in the development of the orchestra's award-winning educational programs. Individuals also support the orchestra. Other sources of income include, in addition to ticket sales, services of the orchestra sold to outside groups.

Artistically the New Jersey Symphony Orchestra has maintained a conservative profile in terms of repertoire, largely reflecting the tastes of suburban New Jersey audiences. Repertoire ranges generally from baroque to early twentieth century and includes many large orchestral and choral works of the nineteenth century. Internationally renowned soloists are engaged to perform with the orchestra annually, and the roster of guest artists who have appeared with the NJSO over the years includes almost every famous musician from Pablo Casals and Mischa Elman to Itzhak Perlman and Luciano Pavarotti.

Although not incorporated until 1928, the New Jersey Symphony Orchestra gave its debut concert at the Montclair Art Museum in 1922 under Conductor-Music Director Philip James. At the time of its incoporation, the NJSO combined the forces of the Montclair Orchestra and the Haydn Orchestra of East Orange, led by Louis Ehrke, who with other musicians had been associated with the Eintracht Orchestra and Singing Society of Newark, founded in 1846. The early years of the New Jersey Symphony Orchestra included soloists such as Casals, Elman, Joseph Szigeti, and Harold Bauer, and the American premieres of works by Holst and Prokofiev.

The years under Music Director Rene Pollain, retired violinist of the New York Philharmonic, were notable for an improvement in the orchestra's artistic product, brought about partly through the addition of New York Philharmonic players. After Pollain's death, the podium duties were taken over by Dr. Frieder Weissmann (music director, 1940–1947), who increased the number of professionals in the orchestra and expanded the concert schedule.

The tenure of Samuel Antek, a violinist in Toscanini's NBC Symphony, saw the initiation of youth concerts (which remain a major activity of the NJSO), outdoor pops concerts, and geographic expansion. By the 1954–1955 season the schedule had increased to 10 youth concerts in five communities, the volunteer association included people from 15 northern New Jersey communities, and the orchestra ventured into new performing spaces such as the huge Mosque Theater in Newark (now named Symphony Hall). Antek's interest in youth musical education was the inspiration behind the creation of the Samuel Antek Memorial Fund in the 1950s, which supported young conductors. The NJSO continues supporting young talent with a nationally recognized Young Artists Auditions program.

Kenneth Schermerhorn, who took over as music director in 1962 and remained until 1968 (when he became music director of the Milwaukee Symphony*), was responsible for an increased lineup of concerts, an expansion of youth services including the formation of two youth training orchestras, and the creation of a symphony chorus (which later became the world-travelled Newark Boys Chorus). Schermerhorn's interest in contemporary music led to the commissioning of Roger Sessions's Sixth Symphony and works by Ben Weber, Robert Starer, James Yannatos, and Stanley Silverman.

Under Schermerhorn's direction, the orchestra had moved from partly professional to fully professional. The stage was set for the orchestra's leap into major status, which came about within the next few years under the directorship of Henry Lewis, the first black conductor to attain a significant post in American music. Lewis's first concerts were designed to dazzle, not only with repertoire and soloists (Van Cliburn, Marion Anderson, Marilyn Horne), but with geographic spread. Lewis brought concerts into Newark's black ghetto (just months after the devastating riots of 1968), to the Garden State Arts Center, and to the Waterloo Music Festival for its first season.

Under Lewis, the New Jersey Symphony expanded its operations and audiences at a phenomenal rate and in the 1972–1973 season was named one of 35 ASOL Major orchestras. At the peak of its activity, players had a staggering schedule of concerts in over 25 different locations. Almost every soloist of international standing appeared with the orchestra, and Lewis and the group's reputation was firmly established with concerts at Carnegie Hall, Kennedy Center, Wolf Trap Farm Park, and the United Nations.

Unfortunately, rapid growth also led to significant financial and labor problems, both of which have been cured only in the last few years. Lewis resigned in 1976, and the orchestra named Max Rudolf music advisor in the interim. Thomas Michalak, a young Polish conductor with a reputation for fiery performances, took over as music director in 1977. The NJSO continued to play to excellent critical acclaim on both sides of the Hudson, but continued financial problems resulted in the cancellation of the 1980–1981 season. In spite of the season's cancellations, the orchestra was acclaimed nationwide for its "Rhapsody and Song" WNET-TV special, which won guest artist Sarah Vaughan an Emmy Award.

The orchestra resumed performances in 1981–1982 on a reduced schedule and production costs were cut back dramatically by consolidating suburban audiences into bigger halls. It was reclassified ASOL Regional in 1982. The past few seasons have seen a steady increase of performance activity and a continuance of the orchestra's fine reputation.

Following the termination of Thomas Michalak's contract in 1983 podium duties were taken over by Associate Conductor George Manahan and a number of well-known conductors including former music directors Henry Lewis and Kenneth Schermerhorn, Maxim Shostakovich, Sixten Ehrling, Jorge Mester, and others. Hugh Wolff was appointed music director in June of 1985.

RECORDING HISTORY AND SELECTIVE DISCOGRAPHY: Music of Bach, Handel, Vaughan-Williams, Britten, Berlioz, and Mendelssohn in *Christmas with the Westminster Choir* (Joseph Flummerfelt, conductor): Book-of-the-Month Club Records 71–6664.

CHRONOLOGY OF MUSIC DIRECTORS: Philip James, 1922–1929. Rene Pollain, 1929–1940. Dr. Frieder Weissmann, 1940–1947. Samuel Antek, 1947–1958. Mathys Abas, 1958–1960. (Guest conductors, 1960–1962.) Kenneth Schermerhorn, 1962–1968. Henry Lewis, 1968–1976. Max Rudolf (Music Advisor), 1976–1977. Thomas Michalak, 1977–1983. (Guest conductors, 1984–1985.) Hugh Wolff, 1985-present.

BIBLIOGRAPHY: "Jersey Symphony: A Success Story," *New York Times*, 5 Mar. 1971. New Jersey Symphony Archives. "The New Jersey Symphony Story," *Symphony News*, Oct. 1974. Reviews and articles in the *New York Times*, *Newark Star Ledger*, *Philadelphia Inquirer*, and others. Nan Robertson, "Jersey Symphony's Wunderkind," *New York Times*, 4 Aug. 1985.

ACCESS: New Jersey Symphony Orchestra, 213 Washington Street, Newark, NJ 07101. (201) 624–3713. John L. Hyer, Executive Director.

                                                          HELEN SIVE PAXTON

New Mexico ────────────────

ALBUQUERQUE (454,499)

New Mexico Symphony Orchestra (Rg)

The New Mexico Symphony Orchestra serves a metropolitan audience of 29,000 via its nine pairs of subscription concerts played at Popejoy Hall. Two subscription concerts are also played in Sante Fe, as well as runouts and tours to other communities in the state. Three pops concerts, a choral festival, a ballet series, a great artist series, the annual *Nutcracker* perform-ances, and youth concerts round out a season including approximately 60 large orchestral concerts. Smaller ensembles from the NMSO include a chamber orchestra, called the Sinfonietta, conducted by NMSO Associate Conductor Roger Melone, various school ensembles, and the NMSO Wood-wind and Brass Quintets. These ensembles are responsible for the major portion of the additional concerts given.

The organization was founded in 1932 by Grace Thompson Edmister. Then known as the Albuquerque Civic Symphony, it consisted of 61 part-time musicians who gave concerts in a gym to enthusiastic audiences. In 1941, the orchestra was taken over by University of New Mexico faculty member William Kunkel and was kept going during the war years on a reduced basis. In 1945 UNM Orchestra Director Dr. Kurt Frederick was appointed music director. Frederick, born and educated in Austria, was a distinguished conductor and string player, and during his five years with the NMSO great musical improvements were made. Under Frederick's lead-ership, the orchestra premiered a number of important contemporary works, the most noteworthy of which was Arnold Schoenburg's *Survivor From Warsaw*.

Hans Lange succeeded Frederick in 1950, and it was under Lange's tenure that the orchestra became professionalized—at least in the sense that every performer received some remuneration. Lange, of German background, had settled in America in 1923 and held conducting positions with the New York Philharmonic* and Chicago Symphony* prior to arriving in Albuquerque. He retired in 1958 and was succeeded by Maurice Bonny (now Dubonnet). At this time, Ralph Berkowitz became the orchestra's first professional manager, a position he held for 12 years. In 1966 the orchestra moved into its present home, Popejoy Hall. This beautiful facility on the University of New Mexico campus seats 2,200. At that time the orchestra was renamed the Albuquerque Symphony Orchestra. During the 1968–1969 season Dubonnet shared conducting duties with José Iturbi, and the 1969–1970 season saw six guest conductors lead the orchestra. In the summer of 1970, Yoshimi Takeda, then assistant conductor of the Honolulu Symphony,* was engaged as music director, a post he held until the end of the 1983–1984 season. Mrs. Raymond M. Dietrich succeeded Ralph Berkowitz as manager in 1970, and William L. Weinrod was appointed executive administrator in 1974.

Under Takeda and Weinrod the orchestra underwent a tremendous growth. A series of youth concerts was provided for all the third, fourth, and fifth graders in the city. This was initiated in 1973 and has become an annual event. An important grant from McDonald's provided funds enabling an ensemble from the orchestra to perform youth concerts in most of the schools in Albuquerque and Santa Fe. Extra services, such as the *Nutcracker* performances, were added, as well as an expanded statewide touring program. The newly formed Symphony chorus made its debut in 1974 and continues to be featured every season. Free concerts in various city locations, funded by the city, are also very popular. In 1976 the subscription concerts were expanded to include the full series of eight concerts each; in 1984 they were further expanded to nine concerts.

Takeda also expanded the repertoire so that by the end of his tenure many of the great symphonic and symphonic-choral works of the common-practice period had been programmed. It was his policy, wherever possible, not to repeat works during his years as music director. The orchestra won two ASCAP Awards for adventuresome programming of new music. Many internationally renowned soloists—such as Vladimir Ashkenazy and Leontyne Price—appeared with the orchestra during that time.

A major step in the orchestra's growth was the introduction of the statewide touring program in 1973. Reflecting this increased activity, the orchestra was renamed the New Mexico Symphony by the governor in 1976. A series of television broadcasts by station KNME has also expanded the exposure of the NMSO. In 1981 a pops series and a great artists series were both added to the schedule. That year the NMSO was also awarded a challenge grant from the NEA, and the New Mexico State Legislature voted funding for the orchestra in its Major Arts Organization allocation. The year

1981 was also notable for the orchestra's first international tour to Mexico and its 50th anniversary celebration. At a gala concert celebrating this event, former conductors of the NMSO—Edmister (then 90 years old), Frederick, and Dubonnet—shared the podium with Maestro Takeda.

In 1983 the NMSO was raised from ASOL Metropolitan to Regional status. Its current budget of $1.5 million supports an organization headed by a Board of Directors, which sets policy and raises funds and to which the executive administrator and music director are responsible. Currently there are 22 salaried players in the orchestra, and the rest are on a per-service basis. Most players are not able to make a living wage playing in the orchestra, so NMSO musicians hold primary jobs with other employers or augment their orchestra salaries with other work. Current plans call for expansion of the 22-player core of salaried musicians to a full-time professional orchestra.

CHRONOLOGY OF MUSIC DIRECTORS: Grace Thompson Edmister, 1932–1940. William Kunkel, 1941–1944. Kurt Frederick, 1945–1949. Hans Lange, 1950–1959. Maurice Bonney (Dubonnet), 1959–1969. Yoshimi Takeda, 1970–1984.

BIBLIOGRAPHY: Philip Hart, *Orpheus in the New World* (New York: Norton, 1973). New Mexico Symphony Orchestra, Archives.

ACCESS: New Mexico Symphony Orchestra, P.O. Box 769, Albuquerque, NM 87102. (505) 842–8565. William Weinrod, Executive Director.

KARL HINTERBICHLER

New York ─────────────────────

ALBANY (795,019—Albany, Schenectady, Troy)

Albany Symphony Orchestra (Mt)

The Albany Symphony Orchestra performs in the tri-city Capital District of New York State: Albany, Schenectady, and Troy. In addition to these three population centers, there are also significant suburban areas and within an hour's drive are the communities of Saratoga, Glens Falls, Hudson, Williamstown, and Pittsfield.

The Capital District has suffered the urban decline prevalent in the Northeast over the past two decades, but during the past 10 years, due to new arterial expressways and a renewed interest in the downtown urban areas, especially in the building of the Empire State Plaza (an ultra-modern government complex in Albany), the Capital District is developing new and expanded cultural and entertainment activities.

The Albany Symphony Orchestra was founded in 1930 as a semi-professional orchestra by John Carabella, an organist who had trained as an opera conductor. Carabella served as music director until 1939 and was succeeded by Rudolf Thomas, who saw the orchestra through the war years. Ole Windingstad served from 1945 through 1948, during which time he raised the professionalism of the orchestra. Edgar Curtis served from 1948–1966. In 1966, Julius Hegyi, a graduate of Juilliard and former music director of the Chattanooga* and Abiline Symphony Orchestras, was named music director. Under Hegyi it has evolved into a well-polished ensemble.

During its history, the Albany Symphony has performed in many halls in the Capital District, but in 1966 it moved to downtown Albany, first to the Strand Theatre and in 1967 to its current home, the Palace Theatre. Negotiations are currently under way with the city of Albany for the ASO to assume operational responsibility for the Palace and to make it the orchestra's permanent home hall.

The Albany Symphony has a budget of $650,000 for the 1984–1985 season, an increase of nearly 150% over the past five seasons. The orchestra is governed by a 50-person Board of Directors and operated by a professional staff of three. The Board of Directors is responsible for fund raising, subscription ticket sales, and setting artistic and operating policy. Vanguard, founded in 1963, is the orchestra's volunteer guild; it raises funds to support operations and its own educational programs. Earned income (ticket sales, performance fees, and advertising) accounts for 48% of the budget, and the balance is covered by individual, corporate, foundation, and government contributions.

Approximately 75 professional musicians are contracted annually by the orchestra and are paid on a per-service basis. In addition to performing with the Symphony, many perform in other local orchestras including the Northeast Symphonic Band, the Lake George Opera Orchestra, and the Berkshire Symphony Orchestra. Many also teach at local high schools, colleges, and universities.

During its 1984–1985 season the Albany Symphony was scheduled to perform eight pairs of classical concerts at the 1,254-seat Troy Savings Bank Music Hall in Troy (considered by Harold Schonberg as one of the world's finest acoustically) and the 2,811-seat Palace Theatre. The Albany Symphony will also perform several special concerts including a major choral work, Christmas and Mother's Day concerts, four youth concerts, four tiny tots concerts, and several runouts. With the beginning of the 1984–1985 contract years, the orchestra has been able to book ensembles consisting of orchestra musicians for in-school and other types of programs. In July 1984, the Albany Symphony assumed the responsibility for managing and operating the Palace Theatre, under a three-year agreement with the city of Albany and, for the first time in its history, had a permanent home hall. As the operator of the facility, the ASO currently rents the theater to outside promoters, but in the future it may present its own events.

The Albany Symphony is unusual in that over the past ten seasons its repertoire has included, in addition to the typical classical and romantic fare, a significant amount of contemporary music. During the 1983–1984 and 1984–1985 seasons, nearly 50% of the music performed was by American composers. Such programming is a policy arrived at over many years of careful study and thought. Board President Peter Kermani, who has served in this position since 1977, has emphasized adherence to the Symphony's mandate in its bylaws to present "quality performances of classical music, with an emphasis on the contemporary American literature." Over the past ten years, Music Director Hegyi has programmed works by some 25 modern and contemporary Americans; their compatriot predecessors, too, have been featured. The Albany Symphony has joined with four other orchestras (Hudson Valley Philharmonic,* Hartford Symphony, New Haven Symphony,* and Springfield Symphony*) as the Northeast Orchestral Consortium, commissioning music from six composers, including John Harbison and Ned Rorem. The ASO also commissions music on its own and has presented the world premieres of works by John McCabe, Malcolm Arnold, Charles Wuorinen, and Tobias Picker. Future sessions will feature commissioned works by George Lloyd, Lester Trimble, Edmund Rubbra, and Ezra Laderman.

The Symphony's active participation in the world of contemporary music does have its detractors in the Capital District, but subscription tickets are still eagerly sought by local residents. To help audiences understand this unfamiliar music, the composers are asked to visit the area for performances of their works and to speak at preconcert previews, give interviews, and lecture to music classes. The previews are taped for delayed broadcast on a number of local cable television stations. The ASO has won five ASCAP Awards for "adventuresome programming of contemporary music," and its programs have been broadcast in Great Britain by the BBC.

RECORDING HISTORY AND SELECTIVE DISCOGRAPHY: The orchestra's first recording of American music was released in the fall of 1984. All classical concerts are taped for delayed broadcast on WMHT-FM, a local public radio station.

John Alden Carpenter, *Sea Drift*; Daniel Gregory Mason, *Chanticleer: A Festival Overture*; Henry Hadley, *Scherzo Diabolique*; Quincy Porter, *Dance in Three Time* (Hegyi): New World Records NW321.

CHRONOLOGY OF MUSIC DIRECTORS: John Carabella, 1930–1939. Rudolf Thomas, 1939–1945. Ole Windingstad, 1945–1948. Edgar Curtis, 1948–1966. Julius Hegyi, 1966-present.

BIBLIOGRAPHY: "The Albany Symphony Orchestra: Discovering an American Repertoire" Monograph, Washington, D.C.: American Symphony Orchestra League, 1984. "Debuts and Reappearances: Wuorinen Third Piano Concerto, *Musical America*, Sept. 1984. "Merrill Lynch Orchestra Sponsorships: A Breed Apart," *Symphony Magazine*, Dec. 1983. "Musical Events: Roundup," *New Yorker*, 3 Sept. 1984. "Orchestra Thrives by Playing the Music People Didn't Want," *Wall Street Journal*, 19 July 1984.

ACCESS: Albany Symphony Orchestra, 19 Clinton Avenue, Albany, NY 12207. (518) 465–4755. Susan Bush, Manager.

LISA GONZALEZ

BUFFALO (1,242,826)

Buffalo Philharmonic Orchestra (Mj)

The 87-member Buffalo Philharmonic Orchestra performs some 150 concerts a year to an audience of about 325,000 on a budget of a bit more than $4 million. In 1983–1984 the musicians played a 40-week season (scheduled to expand to 44 by 1985–1986).

Its membership still includes most of the musicians who under Lukas Foss and Michael Tilson Thomas brought it international recognition in the 1960s and 1970s as a brilliant and persuasive advocate of the most demanding twentieth-century scores. Perhaps to suit this repertoire, the ensemble's tone is bright, lightweight, and very slightly astringent.

The orchestra is administered by a Board of Directors, most of whom are elected by the membership of the Buffalo Philharmonic Orchestra Society. Since 1978 the Board has included three player representatives chosen by the musicians. Overseeing the Board is a Council of Trustees, which, however, seldom acts. Day-to-day operations are in the hands of a Board-appointed executive director, a post whose title, duties, and occupant have seldom remained constant for more than a few years at a time. Programming is entirely the responsibility of the music director. Under the executive director and the music director is a support staff of 20 people.

The orchestra's home since 1940 has been the architecturally and acoustically magnificent Kleinhans Music Hall, designed by Eliel Saarinen. The fan-shaped main hall (which the Philharmonic is seldom able to completely fill) seats 2,900; across the lobby is an 800-seat auditorium used for chamber music. In addition to the regular season of 16 symphony programs and 12 pops concerts performed in the hall, the orchestra takes numerous runouts to area schools and churches and does a series of summer concerts in the city's parks. The BPO also intermittently serves as the orchestra for the summer opera season at Artpark in Lewiston, 25 miles north of the city, under the baton of Artpark's independently appointed music director.

Except for visiting artists, the Philharmonic totally dominates classical music-making in Buffalo. Its members teach at area colleges (especially the State University of New York at Buffalo, whose history is intimately linked to that of the orchestra) and are individually responsible for a great deal of chamber music activity. An independent spinoff from the BPO is the Ars Nova Musicians, a 13-piece chamber orchestra founded in 1974 and directed by first violinist Marylouise Nanna.

The artistic, administrative, and financial history of the BPO has been exceedingly turbulent. Except for a period of somnolent stability in the 1950s, the orchestra has moved from crisis to crisis, with cliff-hanger rescues from the brink of oblivion in 1939, 1944, 1960, 1969, and 1981—and lesser crises in between.

In order to understand these it is necessary to understand Buffalo: a (until very recently) steel-and-railroad city in which defeatism and overcompensation, the provincial and the cosmopolitan, East and Midwest hold a constant, inconclusive tug of war. The city views its orchestra as a civic asset; its presence is a source of pride, just as the absence of a major-league baseball team is a source of anguish. Thus whenever the orchestra's existence is threatened it is able to draw on extraordinary reserves of public support, even from people who have little interest in music; but it has not been able historically to count on the support on a sustained basis.

The first professional orchestra in the city was the Buffalo Orchestra, which flourished between 1887 and 1898. This orchestra, which grew from a mere 38 members in its first season to 51 in the last, was the joint project of two people: Frederick Lautz, its president (who personally kept it out of the red), and John Lund, its conductor, a German originally brought to the United States to be first assistant to Leopold Damrosch at the Metropolitan Opera.

Lund's orchestra remained green in the memory of Buffalonians for decades after its demise, but attempts to found a successor ensemble proved abortive until, in the depths of the depression, the present BPO was organized. The organizational meeting was held on January 11, 1932, and the first concert given the following May 1. Most of the 78 musicians were unemployed professionals on relief, for whom the new orchestra provided, in the words of a promotional brochure, "an opportunity to practice their art."

The initial concert was very well received, and the fledgling ensemble was invited to participate in the city's centennial festivities later in the season. This generated considerable local support for the orchestra, which from that point on held the status of a civic institution.

The orchestra's first conductor was John Ingram, a Dutch violinist and composer who had played in the New York Philharmonic* under Stransky. He was succeeded in 1934 by the Hungarian Lajos Shuk. Unlike Ingram, Shuk was a professional conductor (he had been a protégé of Weingartner), and an immediate improvement in performance standards was observed under his leadership. With Shuk the orchestra auditioned for the Works Progress Administration, making a highly favorable impression; federal funding for 70 musicians commenced in 1935.

With the advent of WPA funding, the orchestra, which had been variously known as the Buffalo Civic Orchestra, Buffalo Community Orchestra, or Buffalo Symphony, became the Buffalo Federal Symphony Orchestra, retaining this name until the withdrawal of federal funds. Starting in 1935 attempts were made to form a support group capable of maintaining the orchestra independently. Thus the Buffalo Philharmonic Orchestra Society, arranging for the WPA staff conductor Franco Autori to succeed Shuk, was incorporated in 1937.

But until it was forced to take over, the Philharmonic Society provided funds only for 15 players (to bring the orchestra up to 85 members) and for the fees of guest soloists. When the WPA finally did pull out in 1939, the rechristened Buffalo Philharmonic Orchestra was faced with an immediate funding crisis of enormous proportions. This was resolved by a lengthy and dramatic citywide fund-raising drive, which provided a model

for numerous subsequent crisis drives and in which civic pride in the orchestra as a symbol of the city's maturity was strongly emphasized. The
specific donation of money to erect Kleinhans Music Hall (dedicated in
1940) solidified the orchestra's position as a permanent feature of Buffalo
life.

Autori remained as music director until 1944. He was a competent conductor who had gained much experience in Italian opera houses (most
notably under Mascagni) before emigrating to the United States in 1928.
Less conservative than his two immediate successors at the BPO, his programming featured a judicious balance of the traditional and the novel.

But he was unable to sustain public enthusiasm, and ticket sales began
to drop off. As the orchestra slowly slid toward another survival-threatening
monetary crisis, the morale of the musicians deteriorated so badly that just
before the crunch in 1944 Autori and Musicians' Association President
Charles Buffalino nearly came to blows in front of the whole orchestra. A
few months later Autori resigned.

Determined to see the orchestra set on an even keel, a group comprising
some of the wealthiest and most influential families in Buffalo banded together to save it. This group, whose representatives never constituted more
than a minority of the Board of Directors, became the de facto rulers of the
BPO for the next 30 years. The "Buffalo family," as they were called, ran
the orchestra like a private club. They met informally to make decisions
that would then be ratified by the Board. As long as the orchestra remained
essentially a provincial one, this system was quite successful, and there were
no further financial crises until 1960. One key to this success was the
automatic inclusion of the music director within the "family," making him
a "member of the club" and privy to the decision-making process. This was
in sharp contrast to the treatment given to the orchestra manager, who
remained virtually powerless. In return for being accepted as an equal, the
music director was expected to play an active role in Buffalo's social life.
A key figure in the Buffalo family was the extremely wealthy Cameron Baird,
at whose instigation William Steinberg was hired in 1945 to replace Autori.
Baird was equally influential in the choice of Josef Krips to succeed Steinberg
in 1954. Under Steinberg the BPO, drawing on the national talent pool for
new musicians and in 1946–1947 making its first tour, its first broadcast,
and its first recording, took the final steps needed to make it a major orchestra.

The orchestra nevertheless remained basically a provincial one until the
1960s. In 1958, however, the BPO contributed substantially toward the
Buffalo and Erie County Public Library's purchase of the 2,093 sets of orchestra parts that had belonged to Toscanini's defunct NBC Symphony. This
collection remains a major resource not only for the Philharmonic but for
all other area orchestras, professional, amateur, and student.

In 1960, cracks began to appear. In that year financial ruin was averted
only by a bailout from the city and county governments. This inaugurated

a period of increased governmental support of the orchestra, and throughout the 1970s and early 1980s the orchestra received some 30% to 45% of its annual revenues from a combination of federal, state, county, and municipal sources. These funds were relied on in place of an endowment.

The Buffalo family's informal, "clubhouse" management style was inadequate to deal with the orchestra's altered circumstances, and every change in economic conditions (rising player salaries in the 1960s, a temporary decrease in governmental support after 1973, inflation in the late 1970s, recession in the early 1980s) now produced another crisis.

Just two years after the 1960 bailout, the Board threatened to cancel the season if the players did not accept a relatively low salary offer. The Board backed down after the musicians rejected this ultimatum. Krips resigned three months later.

Early in Krips's tenure Baird had a row with him over "the role of Baird's amateur chorus in Philharmonic activities" (Hart, *Orpheus in the New World*, p. 214) and withdrew from his position of leadership. His place was taken by lawyer/businessman Robert Millonzi, through whose vision and diplomatic skills the orchestra was to acquire its two most important music directors.

Steinberg's programming had been both conservative and narrow; Krips's even more so. Under Krips's 1963 successor, Lukas Foss, a composer with no previous conducting appointment, BPO programming immediately became the most radical in the country, and programs from his early season bristle with the asterisks denoting national and local premieres. Among the latter were not only numerous contemporary works, but such twentieth-century classics as *The Rite of Spring* and also some basic repertoire items such as *Ein Heldenleben* and the *Deutsches Requiem*. (A few repertoire gaps—most notably among the Haydn symphonies—remain even today.)

Foss brought a composer's sensibility to the post, and it was not until he was well seasoned in the job that he had much to say in the old standbys. But in twentieth-century music he was superb. The most noteworthy of the contemporary works performed under Foss have been preserved on commercial recordings, except for Stockhausen's *Momente*, which received its U.S. premiere under his baton and was broadcast on National Educational Television.

That Foss was able to succeed in his "radicalization" of the BPO was the result of a unique concatenation of people and circumstances. Millonzi's role has already been alluded to. Foss himself won over many (including the musicians) with his charm and enthusiasm. Another key figure was Allen Sapp, chairman of the Music Department at the State University of New York at Buffalo, where he established a musically radical, composition-oriented program featuring, among other things, a professional, contemporary chamber ensemble called the Center of the Creative and Performing Arts, of which Foss became co-director. The orchestra and the university thus became strongly linked through the person of Foss, each institution serving to legitimize the activities of the other.

A final key figure was John Dwyer, the progressive-minded but courtly and diplomatic music critic for the *Buffalo Evening Post*. Dwyer's articles and reviews did much to educate the taste of Philharmonic audiences while managing to convince many who disliked the new music to tolerate it on a "boys will be boys" or "youth must be served" basis.

Nonetheless a myth (unsupported by the statistics) persisted among Board members that Foss's programming had hurt attendance, and after yet another near-disaster (in 1969; this time a threatened merger with the Rochester Philharmonic), the Board and its music director, mutually fed up, agreed to a parting of the ways.

Foss's successor was in some ways just as startling a choice: 26-year-old Michael Tilson Thomas, in his first major conducting post. Thomas continued the programming tradition started by Foss but was a much finer technician. Under his baton the slight scrappiness in string ensemble that had been evident under Foss (and which returned to plague Rudel) disappeared. The seasons under Thomas in the mid–1970s (particularly those bracketing the U.S. bicentennial in 1976) were the finest in the orchestra's history. The complete works of Ruggles were performed and recorded; those symphonic juggernauts, Ives's Fourth, Mahler's Second, and Messiaen's *Turangalila*, were tackled and conquered; new works were commissioned from Morton Feldman and Lejaren Hiller (both Buffalo residents); Dvořák's *The American Flag* and Heinrich's *The War of the Elements* were rescued from oblivion.

As he had promised the Board, Thomas revived the Buffalo tradition (abandoned by Foss) of participating in the city's social scene, but his youthful lifestyle alienated some on the Board. He tenuously maintained the university connection by briefly teaching a course there and by giving concerts on campus.

The year 1977 was crisis time again. The Board proposed cutting 12 players from the roster and nine weeks from the season; the players rejected this, and the ensuing bitter strike lasted 60 days. The players, desperate to break the power of the Buffalo family, organized a successful insurgence, and in March of 1978 the Board was reorganized along more democratic lines. The old guard nevertheless managed to retain considerable power until as late as 1982.

Meanwhile Thomas, who was catching flak from all sides, left for greener pastures. In somewhat of a panic (Cincinnati* and Houston* were also looking for music directors), the new Board accepted the suggestion of concertmaster Charles Haupt (who had played under him at Caramoor) that Julius Rudel be offered the job.

In an atmosphere now of almost continuous financial crisis, the orchestra under Rudel executed another artistic volte-face. Programs became more conservative than those of Krips a generation earlier and much lighter, sometimes almost popslike. A similar lightening was observed in the pops programs themselves.

The demise of the Center of the Creative and Performing Arts in 1980 and the death of Dwyer shortly thereafter severed the last links between the orchestra and its immediate past. A bright spot in recent BPO history was its 1981 performance at Artpark in the North American premiere of Philip Glass's opera *Satyagraha*.

Later that year the musicians, threatened by the Board with immediate disbandment, reluctantly accepted a shortened season and a renegotiated contract. Currently under strong and stable management, the orchestra has been slowly pulling itself out of the hole, but the economic future remains problematic.

In 1984 Rudel announced his resignation, effective 1985. Semyon Bychkov, associate conductor from 1979, then later principal guest conductor, was announced as his successor amidst plans for a gala 50th-anniversary season and renewal of strong university ties.

RECORDING HISTORY AND SELECTED DISCOGRAPHY: Steinberg's recording with the BPO of the Symphony No. 7 of Shostakovich was for years the only one available. Only local, non-commercial recordings were made under Krips.

Americana (Foss): Turnabout 34398. Cage, *Concerto for Prepared Piano*; Foss, Baroque Variations (Foss): Nonesuch 71202. *The Complete Music of Carl Ruggles* (Thomas): CBS M2–34591. *Gershwin Overtures* (Thomas): CBS M–34542. Sibelius, *Four Legends* (Foss): Nonesuch 71203. Works of Penderecki and Xenakis (Foss): Nonesuch 71201.

CHRONOLOGY OF MUSIC DIRECTORS: John Ingram, 1932–1934. Lajos Shuk, 1934–1937. Franco Autori, 1937–1944. William Steinberg, 1945–1952. Josef Krips, 1954–1963. Lukas Foss, 1963–1970. Michael Tilson Thomas, 1971–1979. Julius Rudel, 1979–1985.

BIBLIOGRAPHY: Interviews with *Buffalo News* Senior Music Critic Herman Trotter, and with the following BPO musicians and staff: Judith Coon, Executive Director Gary L. Good, Donald Miller, and Alan Yanofsky. Buffalo and Erie County Public Library, Buffalo Philharmonic clipping material, 1932—present. Philip Hart, *Orpheus in the New World* (New York: Norton, 1973). Kleinhans Music Hall Management, *Kleinhans Music Hall* (Buffalo, 1942). John Rheinhold Lund, Scrapbook, 1887–1900. *Schwann Artist Issue*, 1955, 1960, 1982.

ACCESS: Buffalo Philharmonic Orchestra, P.O. Box 905–71, Symphony Circle, Buffalo, NY 14222. (716) 885–0331. Gary L. Good, Executive Director. Margaret Schmid, Director of Marketing.

ANDREW STILLER

CHAUTAUQUA (146,925)

Chautauqua Symphony Orchestra (Mt)

Chautauqua Institution began in 1874 as a two-week summer training period for Sunday School teachers, but was intended from the start to include scientific, broadly cultural, and educational subjects. Schools of Music, Lan-guages, and Theology, courses for public school teachers, correspondence courses, a home-reading program and university status were only part of the nineteenth-century accomplishments of this popular mass educational movement that spread through independent Chautauquas across the coun-try, beyond its own location in southwestern New York State. Thus, since the basic emphasis at Chautauqua was and is educational, the arts, including music, are pursued in the context of education. It continues as a private, non-profit corporation within the town and county of Chautauqua.

An Institution orchestra of 21 musicians had been organized in 1903 by Henry B. Vincent, assistant music director at Chautauqua, and a swiftly expanding music program included School of Music artist-teacher recitals and large choral works. Chautauquans welcomed the first visit of Walter Damrosch and his New York Symphony Orchestra in 1909. Subsequent visits became a summer residency—the first for a major American orchestra away from its winter home, according to L. Jeanette Wells in her book *A History of the Music Festival at Chautauqua Institution from 1874 to 1957*. The residency lasted until 1929 when, following the New York Sym-phony's amalgamation with the Philharmonic Orchestra of New York,* the Chautauqua Symphony Orchestra was formed to take its place at the Institution.

Its first director was Albert Stoessel, the young man who had conducted the New York Symphony in most of its Chautauqua appearances. With the opening in 1929 of Norton Hall, a monolithic concrete structure, Chautau-qua now had facilities for opera and dramatic presentations as well as con-certs and recitals. The Chautauqua Symphony Orchestra could now provide a pit orchestra for the new Chautauqua Opera Association. Stoessel made use of former NYS members, some of whom now played with the Philhar-monic, and until his death in 1943 he directed the life of the orchestra, the opera, and the School of Music as well. Under his directorship and despite the effects of the depression on the newly formed group, Stoessel's orchestra grew in stature, with children's concerts, chamber music affiliates, and na-tional radio broadcasts (21 in 1932) to its credit. In keeping with Chau-tauqua's educational and cultural mission, Stoessel's aim was to present the best of modern music, including American works, as well as a liberal amount of the classic repertoire. This pattern has continued.

Upon Stoessel's death, Franco Autori became the second regular con-ductor of the Chautauqua Symphony Orchestra. In nearby Buffalo,* Autori had transformed a Federal Music Project into a community-supported or-chestra, and at Chautauqua he continued Stoessel's policy of programming American works along with the standard repertoire.

Autori was followed in 1953 by Walter Hendl, music director of the Dallas Symphony.* Knowledgeable, painstaking, imaginative, and alert to modern trends, Hendl continued to program monumental works of the symphonic repertoire and contemporary music. He remained with Chautauqua until temporary ill health necessitated his resignation in 1972. In Chautauqua's early years the Juilliard School of Music had exerted considerable influence (through Stoessel's choice of personnel in orchestra, opera, and Music School). Later a significant influence was felt from the Eastman School of Music in Rochester.

Following several years of guest conductors and the brief tenure of Baltimore Symphony* music director Sergiu Comissiona, Varujan Kojian was selected in late 1980 to become Chautauqua's fifth music director. A rising young conductor with an international reputation, Kojian was then music director of the Utah Symphony.* He had also served as conductor of the Stockholm Radio Orchestra and principal guest conductor of the Royal Swedish Opera. He remained at Chautauqua for four years. The Institution expects to announce the selection of a new music director following the 1986 season.

The Chautauqua Symphony Orchestra is composed of 74 to 76 professional musicians from across the country who play a minimum of 21 concerts (52–56 services) over the 51-day period of the contract. Following a two-year probationary period, new musicians (who are chosen by the music director in consultation with the section leader and the business/personnelmanager) become fully tenured.

The music director, appointed by the president of the Institution, sets repertoire, selects soloists and guest conductors, and conducts about 10 concerts each season. All administrative matters and Institution liaison are funneled through the Program Office of the Institution. The orchestra is represented by a committee elected from its membership. The Chautauqua Opera Orchestra, providing a current minimum of 22 services, is drawn from the membership of the Symphony on a rotating basis.

The 1984 Symphony budget of $555,000 is anticipated to rise by approximately 5% to 7% per year over the next few years. Funding is from the operating budget of the Institution. The New York State Council on the Arts and the NEA provide some support, and despite the lack of a formal support group, the orchestra receives widespread support and recognition throughout the Chautauqua community.

The orchestra makes its home in the Amphitheater, Chautauqua's program center. With its 1893 all-wood construction, good acoustics for music are assured. Wooden benches provide seating for approximately 5,000, while its three open sides give a sense of informality and spaciousness. The Amphitheater has recently been restored at a cost of $2.2 million.

Because the season is concentrated into seven weeks and the principal audience is in residence throughout that time, an effort is made to balance the programs to insure that there is something for everyone. The repertoire is principally traditional, and symphonic programs are interlaced with two ballet performances (utilizing the Chautauqua Festival Dance Company), four pops performances, one or two major choral works, one to three evenings focusing on opera. Over the last few years, Rochester's WXXI-FM has been helping to tape five concerts each season for rebroadcast over National Public Radio.

CHRONOLOGY OF MUSIC DIRECTORS: Albert Stoessel, 1929–1943. Franco Autori, 1944–1952. Walter Hendl, 1953–1972. (Guest conductors and special advisors, 1972–1976.) Sergiu Comissiona (with various titles) 1976–1980. Varujan Kojian, 1981–1984.

BIBLIOGRAPHY: *The Chautauquan Daily*. Alfreda L. Irwin, *Three Taps of the Gavel*, 2d ed. (Chautauqua Institution, 1977). Jeanette Wells, *A History of the Music Festival at Chautauqua Institution from 1874–1957* (Washington, D.C.: Catholic University of America Press, 1958).

ACCESS: Chautauqua Symphony Orchestra, Program Office, Chautauqua Institution, Chautauqua, NY 14722. (716) 357–6200. Dr. Daniel L. Bratton, President, Chautauqua Institution. Mary-Therese Mennino, Program Director.

ALFREDA L. IRWIN AND MARY-THERESE MENNINO

MELVILLE (2,605,813—Nassau/Suffolk)

Long Island Philharmonic (Rg)

From its western shore in New York City's boroughs of Brooklyn and Queens to its eastern tip over 100 miles away at Montauk Point, Long Island encompasses an area of extreme variety and contrast. It supports dense urban populations, an enormous expanse of suburban communities with yet more populated centers, and, finally, rural enclaves of farmland and elegant seaside estates. Recognizing and capitalizing upon this area's enormous market for cultural activities, the Long Island Philharmonic has established itself as a leading force in its musical life.

The Philharmonic's season consists of eight subscription concerts presented at Long Island University's 2,242-seat C. W. Post Concert Theatre (opened in 1981), four of which are repeated at Hauppauge High School in Hauppauge and the other four at Huntington's Huntington High School. The orchestra has striven to make itself accessible to its public by offering open rehearsals, young persons' concerts (sponsored by the Islip Arts Council), master classes in Long Island schools, and free outdoor twilight concerts in East Meadow, Huntington, and various towns along the South Shore. Attendance at Long Island Philharmonic concerts is large, with the C. W. Post performances virtually sold out and crowds in the tens of thousands attending outdoor performances.

The orchestra's musicians are top-flight freelancers, about half from Long Island and the remainder from New York; their commitment to the orchestra is per season. The roster of 100 players (of which 95 perform at a typical concert) has remained stable, and the majority of current players have played with the ensemble since its formation.

Filling the gap left by the disbanded Long Island Symphony and Suffolk Symphony, the Long Island Philharmonic was founded in the spring of 1979 according to a carefully conceived plan for its emergence and development as an orchestra of high quality. Its founding Board of 12 businessmen and arts advocates, under the special guidance of Harry Chapin and Board Chairman C. R. Merolla, committed themselves to raise or donate a minimum of $5,000 each on an annual basis; extensive discussions were held with experts in symphony management.

The orchestra's public relations materials emphasize the orchestra's businesslike approach, which allowed it to flourish in a very short time. Within two years, partially with the help of $200,000 appropriated in 1981 by the New York State legislature, the orchestra had largely covered its initial costs. When, after its third season, it faced new debts, it curtailed its season accordingly and today operates soundly on a philosophy of fiscal self-restraint. Approximately 40% of its annual budget (projected for 1984–1985 at $1 million) is derived from ticket sales and concert fees, 45% from the contributions of more than 1,000 businesses and individuals, and 15% from public funds—the NEA, New York State Council on the Arts, Nassau County Office of Cultural Development, and Suffolk County Office of Cultural Affairs. The orchestra presents an annual benefit ball as part of its fund-raising activities, and its Board members (now numbering 42) are individually very active in fund-raising as well.

Having established the group's plan of action, the Board engaged Christopher Keene as the orchestra's first music director in 1979. Keene is also music director of Lincoln Center's New York City Opera and Artpark, a state park for the arts in Lewiston, New York. Keene's conducting style, "extroverted" (in his own appraisal), has been credited with attracting and stimulating Long Island Philharmonic audiences. Prefacing each concert with an informal discussion of the music to come, Keene seeks to involve the audience as thoroughly as possible in the performance.

The orchestra's repertoire stresses the late romantics and their successors, with modern or contemporary works featured in several of each season's concerts. Works of Beethoven and his contemporaries are less frequently performed, along with an occasional work of the baroque or classical period. Each of the past three seasons (beginning 1982–1983) has seen a premiere: the American premiere of British composer George Benjamin's *Ringed by the Flat Horizon*, the world premiere of Jay Reise's Symphony No. 3, and the world premier of David Amram's *Honor Song*, commissioned to celebrate Suffolk County's Tricentennial in July 1983 and performed before a crowd of 25,000 at the County Airport at Westhampton Beach. International soloists such as Janos Starker and Andre-Michel Shub are also featured each season.

The formation of the 170-member Long Island Philharmonic Chorus, which rehearses weekly for ten months of the year, has enabled the orchestra to perform massive orchestral/choral works such as the Verdi *Requiem*. Orchestra members have seen a growth in audience sophistication over the years of the orchestra's operation—evidence of the ensemble's efficacy as a cultural resource. Plans for the future include measured growth in subscription and summer offerings as well as regular radio broadcasts.

CHRONOLOGY OF MUSIC DIRECTORS: Christopher Keene, 1979-present.

BIBLIOGRAPHY: Barbara Delatiner, "Keene's Career on a Fast Track," *New York Times*, 31 Oct. 1982. Barbara Delatiner, "Philharmonic's Approach Pays Off," *New York Times*, 20 Oct. 1983. Michael Walsh, "Five for the Future," *Time*, 19 Apr. 1982.

ACCESS: Long Island Philharmonic, One Huntington Quadrangle, Melville, NY 11747. (516) 293–2222. Laura Maziarz, Director of Development and Marketing/Acting Manager.

MYRNA NACHMAN AND ROBERT R. CRAVEN

NEW YORK CITY (9,120,346)

American Composers Orchestra (Mt)

The American Composers Orchestra devotes itself exclusively to American orchestral repertoire of the twentieth century. Because of this, it assumes a national and international importance despite its New York City sphere of activity and its relatively modest 1985–1986 estimated budget of $375,000 for its five concerts. The ACO has performed works by well over 120 American composers and has commissioned and premiered 35 new works since its founding in 1977. Two of these have won the Pulitzer Prize (Joseph Schwantner's "Aftertones of Infinity" and Ellen Taaffe Zwilich's First Symphony), and another the Friedheim Award (John Harbison's Piano Concerto). Many have been taken up by other orchestras, over a dozen have been recorded by the ACO on Composers Recordings, Inc. (CRI), and a number of composers' careers have been launched.

The ACO was founded as a response to the deplorably low percentage (6%) of American works reported on programs of the Major and Metropolitan orchestras during the bicentennial year. This percentage was found to drop even lower (to 1.6%) when one eliminated works by Ives, Gershwin, Bernstein, Barber, Copland, and Schuman—an indication that *new* works by Americans were not being stimulated or propagated by the nation's orchestras.

The immediate impetus for the establishment of the ACO, however, was provided by the imminent 40th anniversary of the American Composers Alliance. In 1976, ACA President Nicolas Roussakis and his then recently appointed Executive Director, Francis Thorne, composers long involved with presenting contemporary music in the New York area, were searching for ways to mark the ACA anniversary. At the same time, Thorne and the well-known American conductor Dennis Russell Davies discussed the possibility of founding an orchestra to present and stimulate the growth of American works. The target date for the first concert was the 1977 ACA birthday. Funding for this concert was secured from Broadcast Music, Inc. (BMI, with which ACA is affiliated), plus two large grants from foundations with which Thorne had family connections.

The core of the orchestra was assembled by free-lance flutist and conductor Paul Dunkel, who fused a number of new-music ensembles in the New York area. The original 50 players, chosen for their sympathy and expertise in the performance of contemporary music, played works by Dodge, Harrison, Riegger, and Wyner under the direction of Dennis Russell Davies, who remains the ACO's principal conductor. Davies's musical and personal success with the musicians is given significant credit for the venture's subsequent success. That first concert drew tremendous critical and public response.

In order to secure funding from the NEA and the New York State Council on the Arts, the ACO had to sever its ties with ACA. It then planned a season of three concerts of works by American composers regardless of their affiliation. Funding from the NEA and NYSCA came through for that first season despite standing rules that organizations have a three-year history prior to funding. Each successive year has seen growth in budget and season. The 1984–1985 budget of $297,000 derived from foundations (44%), earned income (10.5%), corporations (10.5%), the New York State Council on the Arts (10%), individual contributions (9%), the NEA (8%), and benefits (8%).

The orchestra has performed mostly in the 1,000-seat Alice Tully Hall at Lincoln Center and occasionally with reduced forces at Symphony Space, a renovated movie theater at 96th Street and Broadway. The ACO has appeared in the Great Performers Series at Avery Fisher Hall and at the Kennedy Center in Washington, D.C. It makes occasional runouts. Beginning with the 1985–1986 season, the orchestra will change its performance locations to Carnegie Hall for four concerts in addition to its chamber orchestra appearance at Symphony Space.

The ACO aims to present as wide a cross-section of contemporary American styles as possible. A remarkable policy effected early on provides that a composer not appear on ACO programs again for five years, a rotation system insuring diversity and comprehensiveness. Each concert features one or two carefully chosen orchestral rarities by American masters. About half of the new works are world or New York premieres, and commissions by ACO or other important institutions (NEA, NYSCA, Koussevitzky, or Jerome Foundations) figure prominently. Initially, Thorne himself chose 75% of the repertoire, with additional input from Davies and various guest conductors. Now a Program Committee made up of Thorne, Davies, and a

rotating group of composers meets several times a year. ACO guest conductors are chosen with an eye to assuring that works they conduct will
later be played elsewhere.

In repertoire, mainstream contemporary styles necessarily predominate,
but conservative and radical composers regularly appear. Bows in the direction of popular culture include works by Laurie Anderson, Duke Ellington, Philip Glass, Scott Joplin, and John Philip Sousa, as well as appearances
by Keith Jarrett and Gerry Mulligan. Risk-taking is a policy at ACO, one
almost unheard of among U.S. orchestral institutions today. Not every concert has been judged a complete artistic success, but the group's overall
contribution to the field continues unchallenged.

The cohesiveness of the ensembles is due to the performers, all deft
interpreters of contemporary music, about 80% of whom are constant from
concert to concert. They are said to perform best for Davies, who conducts
at least twice a year and for whom they have enormous respect. Davies says
the ACO is the orchestra that learns quickest from among those with which
he has worked. The orchestra sounds clear, lean, and energetic at Tully Hall
and should sound richer with a few additional strings in Carnegie Hall
(bringing the total number of musicians from 75 to 80). This fuller quality
may be enhanced when Bernstein conducts the ACO in Diamond's Ninth
Symphony in November 1985.

The ACO is a composer-directed orchestra. ACO President Francis Thorne
shares the title "artistic policy co-director" with ACO Board Chairman Charles
Wuorinen. As principal conductor, Davies shares artistic responsibility with
the ACO Artistic Policy Committee, of which he is a member. For six years
Nicolas Roussakis served as manager of the orchestra; only in 1983 did
Lynda Dunn become the ACO's first full-time professional manager. Several
recent long-range planning efforts include student audience development
grants, an NEA challenge grant for a reserve fund, an ambitious commission/
performance/recording plan, and additional endowed chairs.

RECORDING HISTORY AND SELECTIVE DISCOGRAPHY: The ACO has recorded
eight discs for CRI with special additional funding. Every ACO performance has
been taped for subsequent rebroadcast; they may be heard on New York City Public
Radio Station WNYC, nationally on NPR, and internationally on the Voice of America.

Elliott Carter, Symphony No. 1 and other early works (Dunkel): CRI SD 475.
Robert Helps, *Gossamer Noons*; Marc-Antonio Consoli, *Odefonia* (Schuller): CRI
SD 384.

CHRONOLOGY OF MUSIC DIRECTORS: Dennis Russell Davies (principal conductor), 1977-present.

BIBLIOGRAPHY: Interview with Francis Thorne, 1984. Allan Kozinn, "The American
Composers Orchestra," *Symphony Magazine*, June/July1983, *New York Times*.

ACCESS: American Composers Orchestra, 170 West 74th Street, New York, NY
10023. (212) 799–3434. Lynda Dunn, General Manager.

BRUCE SAYLOR

American Symphony Orchestra (Rg)

The American Symphony Orchestra, created by Leopold Stokowski in 1962, is linked to the rebirth of one of the finest halls in America, Carnegie Hall. This was not Stokowski's first attempt at forming a new orchestra. His All-American Youth Orchestra had achieved a certain amount of success and conducted a South American tour before being disbanded during World War II. For his American Symphony, Stokowski had high aims: "to afford opportunity to highly gifted musicians regardless of age, sex, or national origin; to provide a training program for musicians and to show others that such a program will work anywhere." He was also explicit in his desire to give New York City a second major orchestra, mentioning several European cities with more than one great orchestra.

Stokowski threw all his musicianship and magnetism into the project, personally auditioning countless applicants (he heard anyone who wanted to play for him), using his famed charm to raise funds, and actually supplying $50,000 of his own to help defray the costs of the first year. From the podium, his unique and forceful ideas about sound and orchestral technique were immediately communicated to his young musicians. This was mentioned by most reviewers of the successful debut concert, October 15, 1962. The first season comprised only six subscription concerts, but this number gradually increased until 1967–1968, when there were fourteen pairs, and 1970–1971, with eight pairs at Carnegie Hall and eight pairs in a new Philharmonic Hall series.

The Stokowski years at ASO were notable for their challenging repertoire—the cunning blend of glamorous blockbusters and large doses of new music, including much twentieth-century American music, that was associated with the conductor's Philadelphia Orchestra* tenure. Perhaps his greatest coup was the world premiere of the newly reconstructed Ives Fourth Symphony in 1965. The performance of Carl Ruggles's monumental *Sun Treader* in 1967 was also a major event.

However, even Stokowski was unable to secure a firm financial base for the orchestra, and when the maestro moved to England in 1972 after conducting a 90th birthday concert in New York, the next season was cancelled due to lack of funds. At this point the players kept the organization together, paid dues to keep the office open, and raised money to prolong the life of their orchestra. They selected Kazuyoshi Akiyama, who had previously appeared with the orchestra, as their music director and gathered enough resources to have a season of five subscription concerts in 1973–1974, for which all conductors and soloists donated their services.

The orchestra at this stage developed a self-governing structure that it maintains to the present day. Orchestra players comprise about half of the current 31-member Board of Trustees, and membership is decided by an elected Personnel Committee within the orchestra. This arrangement has its analogues in Europe, but is very rare in the United States. The players of the ASO are New York freelancers. Most of the orchestra is made up of members, with the remaining chairs filled on a per-service basis by other available musicians. The personnel is therefore not fixed, but it is estimated that members play about 80% of the services.

Kazuyoshi Akiyama remained music director through 1978. His strength was in the late-nineteenth-century and early-twentieth-century repertoire, and although he lacked Stokowski's flair for eye-catching programming and sponsorship of new music, the subscription series gradually expanded under his leadership and some important works were premiered and recorded, most notably the Corigliano Oboe Concerto in 1976. Akiyama was followed by Sergiu Comissiona, who also had been a frequent guest conductor. Comissiona's more rigorous and disciplined approach led to improvements in the technical skills of the orchestra, but this was not accomplished without the seemingly inevitable increase in friction and tension that such an approach entails.

After the departure of Comissiona in 1982, the ASO was without a music director for two seasons. In 1982 Moshe Atzmon and Giuseppe Patane were named principal conductors, and although Patane had favorably impressed many orchestra members, health problems prevented him from fulfilling any of his engagements with the orchestra in the 1983–1984 season. The 1984–1985 season was slated to be directed by guest conductors as the search continued. In October of 1984, John Mauceri was named music director and principal conductor.

As of 1983–1984 the ASO had an annual budget of approximately $1.5 million. About half of this is earned income, with the rest split between government support and private or corporate donations. The backbone of the orchestra's season is a series of nine Sunday afternoon concerts in Carnegie Hall. The repertoire for these is basically standard, with an admixture of new American music. In addition, the orchestra averages about 20 other concerts a season. It is hired by a wide variety of groups, with recent appearances including a concert of contemporary Japanese music, the Public Television "Gala of Stars," the United Nations Day Concert, and pops performances at resorts in Atlantic City. The ASO provided music for the revival of Abel Gance's silent film *Napoleon* at Radio City Music Hall.

The first extended ASO tour was to Greece in 1980; it was followed by trips to Mexico and the midwestern United States. In cooperation with the Department of Cultural Affairs, the orchestra runs an extensive program in New York City schools, including appearances by small groups of players in classes as well as full orchestral concerts. In addition, the ASO presents children's concerts in Carnegie Hall. The American Symphony offers a yearly award, the Leopold Stokowksi Prize, to a young American conductor. The winner appears with the orchestra at a subscription concert.

In the post-Stokowski era the ASO has tried mightily to establish a stable, recognizable identity. Its Sunday subscription series has been well attended by an audience that the management feels is quite distinct from the weeknight Lincoln Center audience. The position of the ASO in New York's musical life, however, is somewhat anomalous. Without a weekly series of concerts under the baton of a single conductor, the group, despite the excellence and commitment of its personnel, can hardly hope to compete in terms of technique, sound, interpretive force, or knowledge of the repertoire with the world-renowned orchestras that continually pass through New York on tour or with the New York Philharmonic. This accounts for the mixed reviews the orchestra has received in the past decade. Although New York surely has enough musicians to supply two major orchestras, as well as the many excellent opera and ballet orchestras in residence, the financial difficulties have proven insurmountable to this point. Hopefully future circumstances will enable the American Symphony to realize its considerable potential.

RECORDING HISTORY AND SELECTIVE DISCOGRAPHY: Under Stokowski the orchestra made several still-available recordings for major labels. In the past decade there have been some important recordings of new music

Beethoven, Piano Concerto No. 5, op. 73 (Gould/Stokowski): CBS MS–6888. Ives, Symphony No. 4 (Stokowski): CBS MS–6775. Corigliano, Oboe Concerto (Bert Lucarelli/Akiyama): RCA ARLI–2534.

CHRONOLOGY OF MUSIC DIRECTORS: Leopold Stokowski, 1962–1972. Kazuyoshi Akiyama, 1973–1978. Sergiu Comissiona, 1978–1982. Moshe Atzmon and Giuseppe Patane (Principal conductors), 1982–1984. John Mauceri, 1985-present.

BIBLIOGRAPHY: Interviews with ASO musicians and ASO Manager Eugene Carr, 1984. Philip Hart, *Orpheus in the New World* (New York: Norton, 1973). Bernard Holland, "Stokowski's Orchestra is Running Itself," *New York Times*, 3 Oct. 1982. *New York Times*. Leopold Stokowski, "What is the American Symphony," *Music Journal*, 26, No. 5 (May 1968).

ACCESS: American Symphony Orchestra, 161 West 54th Street, Suite 1202, New York, NY 10019. (212) 581–1356. William Brans, Executive Director.

FRED HAUPTMAN

Brooklyn Philharmonic Symphony Orchestra (Mt)

The most populous of the five boroughs of New York City, Brooklyn is in its own right among the very largest communities in the United States. It retains today a nationally acknowledged spirit of independence dating to its earlier days as a separate city with its own mayor and government. It is the home of many cultural and educational facilities—museums, universities, botanical gardens—and various musical and arts organizations, pre-eminent among which is the Brooklyn Philharmonic Orchestra.

The Brooklyn Philharmonic's concert season centers around its Major Concert Series of six subscription programs presented at the Opera House of the Brooklyn Academy of Music (BAM), each performed three times on a weekend, and a second series, Meet the Moderns, consisting of four programs, each usually presented twice (once at BAM, once in the Great Hall of Manhattan's Cooper Union). Both series are conducted by the orchestra's music director, Lukas Foss, who is also music director of the Milwaukee Symphony.* Programs in the main series are less dominated by the late romantic repertoire than are those of many similar-sized orchestras, and they are often dedicated to a single composer (Beethoven and Mozart received such treatment in 1983) or to a period of musical expression (the baroque, for example). Foss, believing that each program should be a coherent whole, plans them very carefully.

The Meet the Moderns Series has received exceptionally good press. It gives Foss, who is internationally known as an advocate of new music and is himself a composer, a forum in which he can illuminate subtle contrasts and similarities among the many contemporary works he presents. The titles of programs in this series reveal a similarity in conception with Foss's other BPSO programming: 1983–1984 saw "Carter, Cage and the New Americans," "Music: Mystic and Meditative," "Tribute to Duke Ellington," and "Berio, Boulez and New Europeans," for a total of nine world premieres and three New York premieres, as well as a remarkable diversity of styles. A similar attitude toward musical vitality informs Foss's approach to the standard repertoire, as indicated by his remark that "I like to conduct Beethoven as if the ink were not yet dry on the score.... Music from whatever period should be played like modern music" (quoted by Arthur Satz in *Musical America*).

An additional series, the Community Concert Series under direction of Tania Leon, presents seven or more concerts—also often arranged thematically ("Dance and Percussion," for example) and aimed at family and/or community audiences. These programs are presented in various Brooklyn and Long Island locations, as are the Summer Park Concerts, free Concerts in the Schools, and a variety of special programs, such as 1984's two concerts with the Dance Theatre of Harlem. An additional series at BAM is the Free Schooltime Series of 10 performances conducted by Youth Program Director David Amram. Their contents are chosen to spark the imagination and capture the interest of their young audiences. The orchestra also travels to summer festivals, an example being the 1983 Pepsico Summerfare Festival at the State University of New York in Purchase, New York. The Brooklyn Philharmonic Chamber Ensemble under Tania Leon has for several years been in residence at the University of Puerto Rico conducting master classes and workshops.

The BPSO was founded in 1954. In its nineteenth-century growth period, Brooklyn had been a vital cultural center, with professional orchestras, including the Philharmonic Society of Brooklyn (founded in 1856), which in that period competed with the New York Philharmonic* and New York

Symphony. Following the demise of that early group, Brooklyn continued to host the New York Philharmonic and other visiting ensembles, but by the end of World War II the borough's musical life had dwindled.

When the Brooklyn Philharmonia (as it was known until 1972) began concertizing with a three-program Beethoven festival in 1955, the event was greeted with warmth by the New York press. Under the musical directorship of Siegfried Landau, the orchestra's activities grew steadily for several years, with an expanded subscription series, a young people's series, the Free Schooltime Concerts at BAM, and workshops in Brooklyn secondary schools, which culminated in joint student/Philharmonic concerts. The orchestra's policy of engaging famous soloists was initiated in the second season.

When Lukas Foss was appointed music director in 1971–1972, he brought with him the innovative spirit that had caused such a stir during his years in the same post with the Buffalo Philharmonic Orchestra* (1963–1970). In an effort to rejuvenate the repertoire, Foss instituted new programming policies, the most surprising of which was a series of concert "marathons," four-hour programs each dedicated to a composer, period, style, or place. This practice, since discontinued due to heavy costs, was mirrored on a smaller scale starting in 1973/1974 in the Major Concert Series, where it continues today. These concerts quickly grew from five to their present number of 18. The Meet the Moderns series began in 1973. In 1977 and 1978 the orchestra visited Mexico, presenting thirteen concerts conducted by Foss and Jorge Velazco. The orchestra was asked back to Mexico for a third tour in 1980. At Foss's suggestion—to assuage those to whom the term "Philharmonia" might connote amateurism—the orchestra changed its name in 1982 to the Brooklyn Philharmonic Symphony Orchestra.

The orchestra's main hall, the Opera House at the Brooklyn Academy of Music, was built in 1901 and seats 2,100. Appointed in the beaux arts style, the hall is known for its scroll work and other embellishments, which were highlighted in gold against a burnt sienna background in a recent restoration project. The 1982–1983 season saw the acquisition of the Stanley H. Kaplan acoustical shell, which has made a pronounced improvement in sound projection.

Approximately 40% of the orchestra's $1.2 million budget for 1984–1985 derives from earned income (including concert fees); the rest is from the Department of Cultural Affairs of the City of New York, the New York State Council on the Arts, the NEA, and corporate and private contributions. Generally, somewhat more than half of BAM's seats are sold on subscription for BPSO concerts, the remainder are available for individual sale; in recent years the orchestra has enjoyed several sell-out performances. The BPSO's governing body is the Brooklyn Philharmonic Symphony Orchestra, Inc., comprising a 46-member independent Board of Directors with a full-time administrative staff of five.

Brooklyn Philharmonic players are first-rate freelancers from New York City, among them some of the best-known chamber music players in the area. Foss has said that the 85-member group is more skilled than some major orchestras whose longer season allows them greater opportunity to polish their ensemble playing. BPSO musicians are generally hired with a year-long commitment to the orchestra, and there has been a welcome continuity in the makeup of the ensemble, some of whose members are tenured and have performed with the orchestra for 10 years or more.

RECORDING HISTORY AND SELECTIVE DISCOGRAPHY: Under Foss the BPSO has made several commercial recordings since 1976 on CRI, Turnabout, and Grammavision labels, including *Lukas Foss and the Brooklyn Philharmonic Symphony Orchestra* (presenting music of Lou Harrison, Vladimir Ussachevsky, John Cage, Henry Cowell, Virgil Thompson, and Leo Shmit). Lukas Foss, *Solo Observed* (works of Lukas Foss, featuring *Night Music*) (Foss): Grammavision GR–7005.

CHRONOLOGY OF MUSIC DIRECTORS: Siegfried Landau, 1955–1971. Lukas Foss, 1971-present.

BIBLIOGRAPHY: Interview with Peggy Friedman, BPO Director of Public Relations, 1984. Corrine Coleman, "A Short History of the Brooklyn Philharmonia," *Twenty-Fifty Anniversary Journal* (Brooklyn Philharmonia, 1979). Joseph Horowitz, "His Orchestra Grows in Brooklyn," *New York Times*, 21 Oct. 1979. Hubert Kupferberg, "Lukas Foss," *Ovation*, Apr. 1984. Barry Laine, "Lukas Foss Still Delights in the Unpredictable," *New York Times*, 21 Nov. 1982. Christopher March, "Lukas Foss as a Conductor and Composer," *The Phoenix*, 3 May 1984. Arthur Satz, "Lukas Foss," *Musical America*, Jan. 1981. David Wright, "Lukas Foss: The Nimble Prankster at 60," *Keynote*, Aug. 1982.

ACCESS: Brooklyn Philharmonic Symphony Orchestra, 30 Lafayette Avenue, Brooklyn, NY 11217. (212) 636–4120. Maurice Edwards, Managing Director.

ROBERT R. CRAVEN AND MYRNA NACHMAN

New York Philharmonic (Mj)

The oldest major orchestra in the United States and among the oldest in the world, the New York Philharmonic has, since its founding in 1842, played more than 10,000 concerts—more than any other orchestra, according to its own accounting. The Philharmonic presents roughly 200 full-orchestra concerts per year. The 1984–1985 subscription season included 36 separate programs comprising 131 performances, 59 conducted by Music Director Zubin Mehta. The Philharmonic has over 33,000 subscribers.

A spring festival series dedicated to one subject evolved into the "Horizons" series inaugurated in 1983—a May/June festival of 10 concerts presenting modern and contemporary music in carefully conceived programs designed to illustrate commonalities and contrasts. Horizons '83 was entitled "Music Since 1968: a New Romanticism?" and its successor in 1984 continued the theme with "The New Romanticism: A Broader View." Symposia and other corollary events are coordinated with the concerts, which take place in conjunction with the national Meet the Composer program.

About a dozen free summer concerts drawing an annual audience of over 500,000 people, are presented in the New York City parks, especially on Central Park's Great Lawn. Domestic and foreign tours account for some 15 concerts, and young people's and educational concerts for another 10. A number of special performances, such as outreach concerts in and around New York City, runouts, the All-City High School Joint Concert and the Pension Fund Concerts, complete the season. Beginning in 1980, selected Philharmonic rehearsals were opened to the public at $3 per seat (free to students). Audiences for these have since grown to the 1983–1984 figure of 35,000. Over a million people hear the orchestra live each year, and many more millions through its year-round broadcasts on the Exxon-Philharmonic Network of 225 stations, "Live from Lincoln Center," and other telecasts over PBS.

The New York Philharmonic's budget fiscal year 1984, in excess of $16.5 million, is funded largely through ticket sales, royalties, performance and other fees (52%). The remainder derives from the annual campaign of the Friends of the Philharmonic (21%), endowment income (20%), and federal, state, and city funding (7%). The Philharmonic sells about 87% of capacity on subscription, 96% including single ticket sales. The annual 60-hour radiothon on WQXR accounted for over $400,000 in 1984.

The orchestra's administrative staff under Managing Director Albert K. Webster numbers over 50 people. The Philharmonic-Symphony Society has a 41-member Board of Directors and officers, as well as five trustees. A volunteer council of over 900 members begun in 1979 comprises some 20 committees to help with publicity, fund raising, staff assistance, and orchestra operations.

Although the orchestra is among the finest, it has always had a dynamic relationship with New York music critics, whose critical teeth have long been honed on the multitude of first-ranked world orchestras carefully groomed for their obligatory New York performances, to which the Philharmonic's are inevitably compared. The press has been an important factor in the orchestra's history and continues to demand no less than the ultimate from the principal orchestra of the nation's music capital.

In the context of histories of other American orchestras, the story of the New York Philharmonic is the only one (except that of Boston's Handel and Haydn Society*) to span the nineteenth-century revolutions in musical composition, conducting, performance, and audience. Its development is chronicled in four books and innumerable articles. In particular, Howard Shanet's *Philharmonic: A History of New York's Orchestra* (1975) details the complex interweaving of Philharmonic history with the city's ever-changing aesthetic environment.

Two earlier "Philharmonic" organizations influenced the New York Philharmonic's formation: the Philharmonic Society (1799–1816), created by the merger of two yet earlier societies; and the short-lived New York Philharmonic Society (1824–1827). The former presented many concerts and played at the funeral of George Washington. In the years before the current Philharmonic's founding, New York was home to or was visited by many musical groups and had a well-established population of local instrumental freelancers and pit musicians. Two foreign influences had also worked conjunctively to make the setting right for the establishment of a permanent symphony in New York: the visitations of Italian opera (which internationalized musical taste and fashion in the city) and the influx of German immigrants, who were becoming increasingly accepted among the city's musicians.

The immediate impetus for the orchestra's birth was a series of large performances beginning in 1839 with the memorial concert for New York musician Daniel Schlesinger and culminating in 1842's Heinrich Music Festival. The "Grand Musical Solemnity" of 1839 drew an audience of 2,000 to hear 60 instrumentalists, an event which, particularly among the newly arrived German population, was in its time an unforgettable achievement in New York.

The New York Philharmonic Society was founded and placed under the leadership of violinist Ureli Corelli Hill on April 2, 1842, at New York's Apollo Rooms. Howard Shanet has shown that the new Philharmonic Society based its constitution and operations on those of New York's two earlier philharmonic societies as well as the London Philharmonic (1813). It was a cooperative, democratic institution, composed (according to its constitution) of "professors of music," in which members and their guests only were admitted to performances, and with provisions for sharing profits. Its members saw it not as a substantial means of earning a living, but rather as a means of supplemental income (to their regular jobs in the pit orchestras) and an artistic outlet through which they could profess and exercise their respect for the masters.

Under direction of Hill and others, the New York Philharmonic Society gave its first performance at the Apollo Rooms on December 7, 1842, in a program of Beethoven, Weber, Hummel, Rossini, Mozart, and Kalliwoda. Like most concerts to follow in that and future seasons, the program comprised a symphony, overtures, vocal solos, and chamber music. The group offered three performances in its first year and by its second had seen social and artistic acceptance in New York. Its greatest artistic achievement in its early years was probably its presentation, with between 300 and 400 performers (in support of a failed 1846 attempt to raise money for a concert hall) of Beethoven's Ninth Symphony.

From 1842 to 1852 the ensemble was led by various of its members and for most of the next 15 years by two per season. Throughout its long history, even after admitting conductors from outside, the Philharmonic would exhibit a far greater turnover and seasonal intermixing of conductors than any of its American counterparts. (It would not have a "musical director" until 1943.)

After its first quarter century, the exclusive, self-sufficient Philharmonic gradually and grudgingly intermixed with the rest of New York's musical scene. Until the 1920s, when it merged with two other ensembles, the society's fortunes peaked and ebbed in response to external economics and the whims of fashion among New York's social elite. Each broadening change was the result of necessity, each an attempt at continued survival in lean times, and each resulted in musical and organizational vitality.

In 1867 by constitutional amendment, Dr. R. Ogden Doremus became the first president who had not been a regular member. With his many social connections and a keen sense of business management, he modernized the orchestra's operation; the rich and influential backed the orchestra, advertising led to increased ticket sales among the general populace (beyond the traditional elite audience), the orchestra reached romantic proportions of some 100 players, and prominent soloists were regularly featured. At the same time, Philharmonic Society member and conductor Carl Bergmann assumed solely the podium he had previously shared with Theodore Eisfeld, and thus the orchestra had for the first time a conductor whose musical sensibility it could share over a period of years. Bergmann championed the newer composers—Brahms, Tchaikovsky, Liszt, Wagner, and others; in keeping with such repertoire, the orchestra kept up too with developments in orchestral sonority and instrumentation. By this period, the Philharmonic had become largely German in its membership, leadership, and repertoire.

By the 1870s though, once again in straits, the Society sought for the first time a conductor from outside its own ranks: the ubiquitous Theodore Thomas, the musical entrepreneur whose touring orchestra had won such fame and brought such musical awareness wherever it performed. Thomas provided the musical and personal impetus for another period of prosperity.

When Thomas left in 1891 to establish the Chicago Symphony Orchestra,* the Society turned to the German-trained Hungarian, Anton Seidl, whose own orchestra worked in New York. By 1892 the Philharmonic had moved through several concert halls to its home-to-be of many years, the Music Hall financed by (and later named after) Andrew Carnegie. Seidl's seven years with the Philharmonic, best remembered today for the orchestra's premiere of Dvořák's *New World* Symphony, ended with his death in 1898. His funeral elicited a massive turnout, significant in Philharmonic history as a sign of the orchestra's station (as Seidl's orchestra) among its rivals in musically bustling New York—this despite its season of only six performances per year. But under Seidl's successor, Emil Paur, the conductor cult dwindled, and by the turn of the century it was apparent that the Society had become antiquated. Its now too-brief season, its aging members with their avocational view of the enterprise, its inward view and lack of subsidy were increasingly out of tune with the New York patrons.

After Andrew Carnegie became president of the Society in 1901, the membership refused his offer of financial backing in return for concessions in their cooperative governance; thus ended also a year under the baton of Carnegie's choice for conductor, Walter Damrosch. Three years of eminent guest conductors temporarily stove off the inevitable, as did three years under the Russian conductor Vassily Safonoff, whose highly interpretive renditions of his compatriots' scores brought notoriety by their novelty and fire. In the 1908–1909 season, however, the Society capitulated to the philanthropists, who, under the leadership of Mr. and Mrs. George Sheldon and backed by J. P. Morgan, Andrew Carnegie, Joseph Pulitzer, and others, made a successful assault. Under the new plan, the orchestra would be underwritten to become a permanent, salaried orchestra governed by a Committee of Guarantors (including three musicians). Youth would succeed age through immediate personnel changes, the season would expand, Safonoff would be replaced, and the orchestra would operate within union rules.

Safonoff's replacement was Gustave Mahler, formerly of the Royal Opera of Vienna and the Metropolitan Opera. Mahler increased the subscription series to 46 concerts, added a Beethoven cycle and others, and established regular tours. The orchestra performed the American premiere of his First Symphony in 1909 to a mixed reception. Mahler's reception personally and as an administrator/conductor was less warm, and within a year or two he had alienated many, including the pre-eminent New York critic, Henry Edward Krehbiel. His death in 1911 left the orchestra once more on the brink of a worrisome future.

A bequest in that same year of nearly $1 million by Joseph Pulitzer was to complete the revolution begun by the 1909 takeover. The bequest required the orchestra to become a membership corporation, secure 1,000 contributing members, offer seats at a generally affordable admission charge, and perform the best-loved music of Wagner, Beethoven, Liszt, and (luckily, for everyone involved) others. Thus the orchestra, in accepting Pulitzer's legacy, increased its popular base and established a wide patronage. Under the musical leadership of Conductor Josef Stransky, the orchestra presented 94 concerts in 1912–1913, of which 31 occurred on tour. Touring increased until the 1920–1921 season, which saw a coast-to-coast tour in addition to the regular season. Under Stransky, standing-room-only crowds heard a widened repertoire, including, according to Shanet, "more performances of American compositions than all his predecessors...put together" (p. 227), a shift only partially attributable to the First World War. The liberalized repertoire would be, in one form or another, a permanent feature of the Philharmonic from then on.

Part of the Philharmonic's troubles in the pre- and immediate post-war years stemmed from its having to compete with other musical organizations in New York. Its greatest rival, an influential orchestra in its own right, was the New York Symphony Society. Founded in 1878 by Leopold Damrosch, it was revived by his son Walter in 1902–1903 after Walter was spurned by the Philharmonic. Befriended by the philanthropists, the Symphony participated (with Tchaikovsky conducting) in the festive performance inaugurating Carnegie Hall. By 1920 its 90 members were providing more than 40 concerts as well as tours, including one to Europe. A second competing orchestra, begun in 1919 by Edgar Varèse as the New Orchestra, evolved into the "National Symphony," conducted by Willem Mengelberg (no connection to Washington, D.C.'s National Symphony Orchestra,* founded in 1931).

As of the 1921–1922 season, the Philharmonic and the National Symphony amalgamated, thereby reducing competition for both audience and funding. Stransky and Mengelberg shared the podium at first, with Mengelberg emerging as the new organization's primary conductor; musicians too were squeezed out. The management changed hands, Philadelphia Orchestra* Manager Arthur Judson taking charge of a new era of change for the Philharmonic. His interest in broadcasting (he would turn his fledgling Columbia Broadcasting System into a multifaceted entertainment empire) was complemented by a dedication to musical growth and education. Henry Hadley was made associate conductor; he would choose American scores to be premiered. Educational concerts in area colleges began, some broadcast (as early as 1922) in coordination with music appreciation courses. The Philharmonic's summer concerts at City College's Lewisohn Stadium began in 1922 as well and lasted for some 40 years with the blessing of the Stadium's donor, Sophie Guggenheim, as the cornerstone of New York's summer musical season. Under Ernest Schelling, the young people's concerts (held since 1913) were expanded to a regular series in 1926.

In February of 1928 a second merger occurred, this time with Walter Damrosch's New York Symphony Society. This created the New York Philharmonic-Symphony Society, with the resources of consolidated finances and the prestige of being (now unquestionably) New York's pre-eminent orchestra. The orchestra, having two years before secured the services of Arturo Toscanini, who shared the podium with many others, was in the beginning of its first golden era. The European tour of 1930, the orchestra's first, did much to secure its identity as an ensemble of the first order. Toscanini's tenure with the Philharmonic left a legacy of rhythmic urgency and steadiness of tempo coupled with an absolute insistence on clarity. To the Philharmonic, however, the lasting value of his association with the orchestra was that he thoroughly popularized the orchestra, bridging—through his charismatic public image—the gap between the subscribers and the ordinary citizens to whom the Philharmonic and its world would otherwise have remained a mystery. When at the age of 70 Toscanini announced his departure, the public reaction was overwhelming.

Wilhelm Furtwängler, who had conducted the Philharmonic during the Toscanini era, was considered as Toscanini's replacement, but his continuing association with the Nazis worked against him. The English-born John Barbirolli was chosen, and his tenure (1936–1941) saw a renewed emphasis on modern composers as well as the standard repertoire (which Toscanini had somewhat truncated in favor of Italian overtures and other personal favorites). Despite a conductor/composer program in which Chavez, Stravinsky, and Enesco participated, the Philharmonic was not at this time in the forefront as a champion of new music. According to Shanet, the Barbirolli and subsequent years were ones of retrenchment following the expansiveness of the 1930s, with cuts in the season from 30 to 24 weeks, in concerts from 122 to 92, and in budget from $725,000 to $534,000.

Following a year of guest conductors, Artur Rodzinski was appointed musical director (the Philharmonic having heretofore not used such a title). Known as an orchestra builder, Rodzinski quickly made personnel changes, carefully planned seasonal activities, and generally improved the orchestra's performance. When Rodzinski left in the middle of the 1946–1947 season, the orchestra secured the services of Bruno Walter as musical advisor. Walter had conducted during the Toscanini years. At age 71 he was not about to embark on a directorship, and until 1949 the Philharmonic saw an eclectic repertoire as guest conductors each emphasized their respective strengths.

Dmitri Mitropoulos became conductor in 1950 and musical director from 1951 to 1957. This was an outwardly stable period, in which the orchestra conducted tours throughout the United States and in 1955 to Europe, the first such tour since Toscanini's in 1930. Radio broadcasts reached some 15 million listeners per month; educational programs were increased; and in 1955–1956 the management committed itself to joining in the plans for a separate Philharmonic concert hall at the proposed Lincoln Center for the Performing Arts.

Nevertheless, there had been for some years a smoldering unhappiness with the Philharmonic and its management, which in 1956 was expressed through the press, particularly in the voice of Howard Taubman of the *New York Times*. He and others found the Philharmonic Symphony Society in need of new management, direction, commitment, and expansion. In what Shanet characterized as a spirit of self-improvement, the Society accepted the criticism, and Arthur Judson (whose ties to Columbia Artists Management were a major bone of contention) stepped down, as did Mitropoulos, in a gradual disengagement that saw him share conducting duties in 1957–1958 with the Philharmonic's former assistant conductor under Rodzinski, Leonard Bernstein. Bernstein had made a front-page sensation in his 1943 debut with the orchestra, and he brought with him in his new role a vigor and audience appeal that would catapult the orchestra to a second great era.

Appointed music director in the 1958–1959 season, Bernstein began systematically revamping the Philharmonic's repertoire, social function, and educational purpose—all to be in tune with his effervescent love of music. Free concerts in the parks brought hundreds of thousands of new listeners (70,000 to the first one alone). In effect, the annual audience tripled. Tours of the Americas, Europe, the Near East, and Far East encouraged a new view of the orchestra both at home and abroad. Television productions began, the best known of which was the series of young people's concerts that did so much to popularize orchestral music throughout the nation. The repertoire was revitalized with much new music, including many American works. In popular eyes the Philharmonic flourished under Bernstein, and today he is a father figure in the minds of countless music lovers who discovered their musical appreciation through his guidance.

Further innovations became possible under Bernstein's leadership by the orchestra's year-round residency in the new Philharmonic Hall. Springtime Promenade Concerts directed by André Kostelanetz and Festival Concerts begun in 1965 under Lukas Foss extended Philharmonic activities, and the orchestra could now run on a 52 week basis. The ensemble had played for many years in Carnegie Hall, a congenial, acoustically pristine auditorium with its own dedicated following and even its own folklore. Philharmonic Hall, despite the best efforts of its designers, was universally proclaimed an acoustical failure, and not until 1976 ("14 years and more than $28 million later," in the words of *New York Times* critic Donal Henahan) would it achieve acoustical excellence. Today known as Avery Fisher Hall, after a chief benefactor of its acoustical reconstruction, the building is part of Lincoln Center, which also houses the Metropolitan Opera, the Juilliard School of Music, the Vivian Beaumont Theatre, and the New York City Ballet, as well as hosting many other groups and events.

Bernstein departed in 1969 (with the title of Laureate Conductor), and George Szell's one-year interregnum followed. The 1971–1972 season saw a deficit of nearly $450,000, and for the first time a public appeal for contributions went out, a campaign that ultimately resulted, through the formation of the volunteer council and WQXR Radiothon, in a much wider base of public support. Wage disputes in following years deepened existing strains between musicians and management, with a prolonged strike occurring in the fall of 1973, during which the musicians took it upon themselves to tour Spain for the benefit of flood victims there and for their own strike fund.

In 1971–1972 the music directorship was again filled, this time by composer/conductor Pierre Boulez. A key figure in the cause of modern music, Boulez created several years of intellectual excitement among the Philharmonic's critics and musicians and brought an unprecedented level of expertise to the performance of the serialists. His short-lived "rug concerts," at which the audience was invited to sit on the floor, drew a somewhat different, though musically aware audience ("flagrantly youthful," wrote Henahan). However, according to Harold C. Schonberg, Boulez had his detractors. Critical opinion was, not suprisingly, that his cerebral approach did not elicit from audiences the enthusiasm accorded his predecessor. When Boulez left to pursue his interest in the avant-garde, the orchestra chose a figure whose attributes were quite the opposite of Boulez's.

Despite his well-publicized comment of earlier years (to the effect that the New York Philharmonic, with its musicians' reputation for intractable orneriness in dealing with conductors, would be a fitting place to send one's enemies), the new music director was warmly greeted by both public and press. Conducting with warmth, emotion, and a modicum of interpretive freedom, Zubin Mehta's greatest repertoire strengths are in the Austrian and German romantics and their successors, although he feels at home throughout the repertoire. Mehta, with a lifetime tenure as music director of the Israel Philharmonic, also received the approbation of the New York Philharmonic management—his contract was renewed through 1990—but he has received mixed reviews from the New York press.

In its brass section, the Philharmonic has evoked comparison to the Viennese school, with a dark, warm tone and graceful slurs in the horns. Rotary-valve trumpets are used when appropriate. Philharmonic principals under Mehta continue their tradition of frequent appearances as soloists with the orchestra.

The orchestra has toured extensively in recent years, including a 1984 tour of Japan and the Far East, with visits to major cities of Mehta's native India. The final park concert of 1984, performed just before the orchestra's departure for Japan, featured an all-American program at Great Lawn before a crowd of 150,000.

RECORDING HISTORY AND SELECTIVE DISCOGRAPHY: The Philharmonic's first recordings were made under Stransky in 1917, and for the next two years it recorded for Columbia records. Following its merger with the National Symphony in 1922, recordings (under Mengelberg for Victor and Brunswick) grew in artistic intention. In 1926 the orchestra recorded acoustically some 60 discs under Hadley, part of a book-and-record music appreciation course under the auspices of Boston publishers Ginn and Company. Toscanini's electrical recordings for Victor, begun in 1929, documented whole symphonies and are today, of course, prime collectibles.

Unfortunately very few of the recordings made under Rodzinski, Stokowski, Mitropoulos, and others are currently available, even as rereleases. Under Bernstein the Philharmonic recorded more than 200 albums for Columbia; by 1969 it was selling some 400,000 annually. Recording continued at a brisk pace under Boulez and Mehta, and the orchestra has to date recorded over 800 discs. It now records for CBS Masterworks, Deutsche Grammophon, London, New World, and RCA, with over 250 discs currently available. Historic recordings (including the first) have been made available in rereleases as premiums to Radiothon contributors.

Beethoven, Complete Symphonies (Bernstein): Columbia D8S–815 (8 records). Berlioz, *Symphonie Fantastique* (Mehta): London LDR–10013. Bernstein, *Candide* Overture, *Fancy Free*, and other works (Bernstein): Columbia MG–32174. Carter, Symphony of Three Orchestras and *A Mirror on Which to Dwell* (Boulez): CBS M–35171. Corigliano, Concerto for Clarinet and Orchestra; Barber, Essay No. 3 for Orchestra (Stanley Drucker/Mehta): New World 309. Mahler, *Das Lied von der Erde* (Mildred Miller and Ernst Halfiger/Walter): CBS MP–39027. Prokofiev, Excerpts from *Romeo and Juliet* (Mitropoulos): Odyssey 32160038. Wagner, Orchestral Music from *Der Ring des Nibelungen* (Mehta): Columbia IM 37795.

CHRONOLOGY OF MUSIC DIRECTORS: The Philharmonic did not establish the office of musical director until 1943. Between 1842 and 1852 the orchestra was led by its members in various combinations each year: Ureli C. Hill, Denis Etienne, Henry C. Timm, W. Alpers, Alfred Boucher, George Loder, Louis Wiegers, Theodore Eisfeld, Max Maretzek.

Theodore Eisfeld and/or Carl Bergmann, 1852–1865. Leopold Damrosch, 1876–1877. Theodore Thomas, 1877–1878. Adolf Neuendorff, 1878–1879. Theodore Thomas, 1879–1891. Anton Seidl, 1891–1898. Emil Paur, 1898–1902. Walter Damrosch, 1902–1903. (Guest conductors, 1903–1906.) Vassily Safonoff, 1906–1909. Gustave Mahler, 1909–1911. Josef Stransky, 1911–1922. Josef Stransky and Willem Mengelberg, 1922–1923. Willem Mengelberg and others, 1923–1929. Arturo Toscanini and others, 1929–1936. John Barbirolli and Artur Rodzinski, 1936–1937. John Barbirolli, 1937–1941. (Guest conductors, 1941–1943.) Artur Rodzinski, 1943–1947. Bruno Walter, 1947–1949. Leopold Stokowski and Dmitri Mitropoulos, 1949–1950. Dmitri Mitropoulos, 1950–1957. Dmitri Mitropoulos and Leonard Bernstein, 1957–1958. Leonard Bernstein, 1958–1969. George Szell, 1969–1970. Pierre Boulez, 1971–1977. Zubin Mehta, 1977-present.

BIBLIOGRAPHY: Samuel Antek, *This Was Toscanini* (New York: Vanguard, 1963). Lee Bracegirdle, "The New York School: Its Development and Its Relationship with the Viennese Style," *The Horn Call*, April 1984. Helen Epstein, "The Philharmonic: A Troubled Giant Facing Change," *New York Times*, 19 Dec. 1976, Sec. 2. John Erskine, *The Philharmonic-Symphony Society of New York: Its First Hundred Years* (New York: Macmillan, 1943). Donal Henahan, "Boulez and His Orchestra Express Pleasure," *New York Times*, 20 Oct. 1976. Donal Henahan, "For Good Listening," *New York Times*, 30 June 1974, Sec. 2. James Gibbons Huneker, *The Philharmonic Society of New York* ([New York], 1917). Henry Edward Krehbiel, *The Philharmonic Society of New York* (New York: Novello, Ewer, 1892). John Mueller, *The American Symphony Orchestra* (1951; reprint, Westport, Conn.: Greenwood Press, 1976). John Rockwell, "Wanted: Leadership for the Philharmonic," *New York Times*, 16 Sept. 1984, Sec. 2. John Rockwell, "Why Isn't the Philharmonic Better," *New York Times Magazine*, 19 Sept. 1982. Charles Edward Russell, *The American Orchestra and Theodore Thomas* (Garden City: Doubleday, 1927). Harold C. Schonberg, *The Great Conductors* (New York: Simon & Schuster, 1967). Harold C. Schonberg, "Zubin Mehta Plans to Go Home Again," *New York Times*, 12 August 1984, Sec. 2. Howard Shanet, *Philharmonic: A History of New York's Orchestra* (Garden City: Doubleday, 1975). Howard Taubman, *The Maestro: The Life of Arturo Toscanini* (New York: Simon & Schuster, 1951). Howard Taubman, "The Philharmonic—What's Wrong with It and Why," *New York Times*, 29 April 1956.

ACCESS: New York Philharmonic, Avery Fisher Hall, Broadway at 65th Street, New York, NY 10023. (212) 580–8700. Albert K. Webster, Managing Director. Francis Little, Director of Advertising and Public Information.

ROBERT R. CRAVEN

Queens Symphony Orchestra (Mt)

For the past decade, the Queens Symphony Orchestra has been recognized as the major musical organization for Queens, the largest (in area) of the five boroughs comprising New York City, with a population of 2.5 million. The QSO's annual concert season consists of the Masterwork Series of five programs featuring renowned guest artists, the chamber series of three programs, and the opera series of usually two grand operas and an operetta, for which the orchestra contracts the services of the Northeast Opera Company and the Manhattan Savoyards, both based in Manhattan. In addition, the QSO offers a pops series of two programs with guest artists, 14 to 20 children's concerts, and a June/July summer concert series (Concerts on the Green) at various parks throughout the borough.

The orchestra was founded by David Katz, its present conductor and music director. In the fall of 1953 he reorganized the then-disbanded Queens Symphonic Society, from which he enlisted mainly amateur musicians. The orchestra's first concert took place at Forest Hills High School on January 22, 1954, before an audience of 400 people. During the ensuing 20 years, Katz worked diligently to upgrade the orchestra's reputation by increasing its professional ranks and by bringing renowned soloists to perform. By the 1974–1975 season, the orchestra became totally professional and thus qualified for support by the New York State Council on the Arts. At this time the QSO established its Board of Directors and hired a full-time manager. In Queens, the orchestra's popularity as a cultural force was assured. After founding the Queens Symphony, Katz, a Juilliard School of Music graduate, assisted Leopold Stokowski in forming the American Symphony Orchestra,* for which he served as associate conductor until 1967. He has also pursued an international career as a guest conductor.

In September of 1979, the QSO was invited to play for President Carter's open town meeting at Queens College. On October 20, 1980, it made its debut at Carnegie Hall to open the series "Salute to New York State Orchestras." Since 1982, the QSO has taken up residence at the 2,100-seat Colden Center for the Performing Arts on the Queens College campus in Flushing, conveniently accessible to Queens and western Long Island residents. The center is an ideal hall for both orchestral and operatic performances. For its inaugural concert at Colden Center, the orchestra featured the Tchaikovsky Violin Concerto with Mischa Elman as soloist.

The QSO is presently governed by a 35-member Board of Directors comprising local business executives, politicians, attorneys, and educators. It is administered by a full-time executive director with a full-time staff of six. Overseeing a budget of $700,000 (as of 1983–1984), the Board meets four or five times annually to discuss such matters as fund-raising, publicity, audience development, and special events accompanying the major programs of the season, including the annual ball. Together with the Board's various committees, there are also an active Women's Auxiliary and a Board of Advisors. The orchestra also works closely with the Borough President's office and the Queens's Arts Council, which help in promoting its concerts. All artistic decisions, however, are the sole responsibility of the music director.

Funding is from ticket sales (about 50%), individual and corporate donations, foundation grants, local, state, and national government agencies, special fund-raising events, and program journal advertising. Additionally, the orchestra has received annual grants from the New York State Council on the Arts, the New York City Department of Cultural Affairs, the Office of the Borough President of Queens, and the NEA.

The orchestra's 75 to 80 instrumentalists are for the most part free-lance musicians from the New York City metropolitan area. They are contracted on a per-service basis, but there has generally been continuity within a core of some 70 members. The QSO also provides contractual services, such as the QSO String Quartet, Brass Quintet, and other chamber ensembles to suit specific needs, as part of its educational and community outreach programs. The programs include series of concerts in elementary schools called Music BAG (for Boys and Girls), the Docent Program of trained volunteers who visit classrooms at teachers' requests to prepare students for the Music BAG programs, young soloist auditions leading to winners' performances with the QSO, open rehearsals for high school and college students, and adult education seminars, wherein David Katz or other qualified representatives of the orchestra present lectures or seminars for groups of twenty or more prior to a Masterwork Series concert. There is also a pre-concert lecture series for the Saturday evening Masterwork concerts.

The QSO tries to reach as many people as possible, and its programs represent a diversity of tastes, particularly in the Masterwork Series, which has also featured a wide variety of internationally famous soloists, such as Itzhak Perlman, Van Cliburn, and Roberta Peters. Katz has been a champion in fostering contemporary American music. The QSO has commissioned works by Morton Gould (*American Ballads* for the bicentennial year) and David Amram (*Elegy for Violin and Orchestra*, 1970).

Among the QSO's most memorable concerts were the evening with the late Count Basie and his orchestra performing with the strings of the QSO (1981), Beethoven's Ninth Symphony (1983), and Mahler's *Resurrection* Symphony (1984), in which three Long Island choral groups participated.

CHRONOLOGY OF MUSIC DIRECTORS: David Katz, 1954-present.

BIBLIOGRAPHY: Irene Stitt, "The QSO: Our Own Symphony," *Queens Tribune* Special Supplement, 14–20 May 1981.

ACCESS: Queens Symphony Orchestra, 99–11 Queens Boulevard, Rego Park, New York, 11374. (212) 275–5000. Joanna Giesek, Executive Director.

ISRAEL J. KATZ

NORTH BABYLON (2,605,813—Nassau/Suffolk)

Orchestra Da Camera of Long Island (Mt)

The Orchestra Da Camera was founded by Flori and Ralph Lorr in 1957 at Farmingdale, New York. From its inception, it utilized the services of only top-rank professional musicians drawn from the major talent pool of the New York City area, many of whom continue to perform. It was thus the first ongoing professional symphony to serve the Long Island community. At the time of its founding, various community orchestras were in existence on Long Island, and several continue to perform. During the long tenure of the Orchestra Da Camera there were six failed attempts to found fully professional orchestras in the area. The Long Island Philharmonic,* founded in 1979, has endured.

The immediate and long-lasting success of the Orchestra Da Camera can be attributed to the dual purpose upon which it was founded: educating young audiences through in-school performances, and providing evening concerts for the general public. Since Long Island has no major concert hall outside of New York City, the orchestra continues to utilize various high school auditoriums for its evening concerts, frequently in conjunction with in-school residencies, though the schools of Long Island have experienced a dramatic decrease in enrollment. With a budget of $283,500 for the 1983–1984 season, the orchestra performed 210 in-school and 6 public evening concerts in various communities on Long Island and in New York City. All concerts were paid for by local sponsors—either school districts or communities—and assisted by support from various grants.

At the time of the orchestra's founding, Long Island was in the midst of major population growth, and school districts were growing at a similar rate. School budgets that were at an all-time high created the perfect opportunity for the performing arts to make an impact on school curriculum. The founders felt that by educating school children, the adult population would ultimately grow in appreciation and professional orchestral music would thus find a solid base in the emerging cultural growth of the community that was to reach some 3 million people.

From an initial assembly program and follow-up evening concert, the orchestra moved through seasons of some 500 performances annually. This was accomplished by utilizing both the full orchestra, and more frequently various units of the orchestra in specially designed programs through careful planning with local school district personnel. As a result of this unique approach, grants were forthcoming from the NEA, New York State Arts

Council, the Musicians Performance Trust Fund, and various local foundations and government grants.

Eventually, the work of the Da Camera was noted by the John D. Rockefeller III Foundation, which provided a major grant for a multiyear residency at the Mineola Public School District. With the security of this seed money, the staff of the Da Camera worked closely with music educators, professional musicians, guest artists, and school administrators in developing curricula for use in the schools. These included programs for students, as well as in-service programs for classroom teachers. This work has received national recognition, and several organizations have sought to develop similar programs based upon their study of the Da Camera's work.

The Orchestra Da Camera is incorporated under the title Music for Long Island, Inc. Its Board of Directors represents the various communities in which it performs. The organization continues to be administered by its founders: Flori Lorr serves as executive director, and Ralph Lorr is artistic director and business manager. They are assisted by a staff which includes orchestral and educational specialists. The orchestra, with a basic roster of 35 musicians, also maintains an Educational Advisory Board of school music educators and school administrators.

Through the years such principal conductors as James Conlon, Gerard Schwarz, Jorge Mester, and Lawrence L. Smith have led the evening series, with Jesse Levine conducting in-school performances. The repertoire has been traditionally devoted to chamber music and has frequently branched out into opera, dance, ethnic music, and special performances with soloists and choruses. The Orchestra Da Camera has commissoned a series of orchestral works especially designed for in-school performances. Over the years the orchestra has performed a wide range of musical styles, from the Renaissance through the avant-garde.

CHRONOLOGY OF MUSIC DIRECTORS: Ralph Lorr (Artistic Director), 1957-present.

BIBLIOGRAPHY: Joseph R. Herbison, "The Orchestra Da Camera of Long Island: An Historical Documentary of a Catalyst for Arts in Education," Diss., University of Arizona, 1984.

ACCESS: Orchestra Da Camera, 5 Jardine Place, North Babylon, NY 11703. (516) 694–3249. Flori Lorr, Executive Director.

JOSEPH R. HERBISON

POUGHKEEPSIE (245,055)

Hudson Valley Philharmonic (Mt)

The roots of the Hudson Valley Philharmonic extend back to the early 1930s when a group of local musicians gathered together to perform for friends and local organizations. This amateur, community ensemble was known as the Dutchess County Philharmonic, and its activities continued for almost three decades. In 1959 Claude Monteux, renowned flutist and conductor, was engaged to form a professional orchestra, and in 1960 the Hudson Valley Philharmonic Society was founded. Its initial objectives were to support a symphony orchestra, to obtain the services of internationally known great artists and ballet and opera companies, to provide musical services for an entire geographical region, and to promote a balanced cultural growth for that region.

The primary concert venues of the HVP are two National Historic Sites: the Bardavon 1869 Opera House, located in Poughkeepsie, New York (Dutchess County), also the main rehearsal hall; and the Ulster County Performing Arts Center in Kingston, New York (Ulster County). During the 1985–1986 season the HVP will extend its concert activities to Middletown, New York (Orange County). Its tri-county volunteer support system and audience made the HVP among the first orchestras in the country to fill a regional role.

The major portion of the HVP season occurs between September and May, although the orchestra performs concerts year-round. The orchestra produces about 150 concerts annually, but its central musical offering is a series of six subscription concerts (with repeats), which most often feature international soloists, a contemporary work (often commissioned), and major works from the standard repertoire. The HVP also has series of pops concerts and young people's concerts and is involved in an opera series. Most programs are repeated at various sites within the region.

A core HVP Chamber Orchestra presents a series of programs at Bard and Vassar Colleges with an emphasis on works by Hudson Valley and other American composers. The HVP is a member of the NEA-funded Northeast Orchestral Consortium, which commissions new compositions for a group of smaller orchestras. In recognition of its unique programming, the HVP received the 1984 ASOL ASCAP Award (third prize, Metropolitan orchestra category) for presenting new music, particularly that of Hudson Valley composers.

The HVP coordinates a chamber music series, which often features small ensembles made up of orchestra members. A wide variety of ensembles fulfills the needs of colleges, choral societies, and ballet companies throughout the region. In addition, the HVP has appeared in major halls in the New York City area on its own and with ballet and opera companies. Currently the HVP reaches almost 130,000 people annually through live performances and at least another 100,000 in a five-state area through broadcasts of concerts by WAMC (Albany) and NPR.

The HVP String Competition is sponsored by the Dutchess County Volunteers and is open to musicians between 18 and 25 years of age. Winners receive a performance with the orchestra in a subscription concert as well as a cash award. The Virtuosi-in-Progress Competition is open to talented local instrumentalists aged 10 to 18. Winners have the opportunity to perform with the orchestra in a special concert.

Under the musical and organizational leadership of Claude Monteux, the HVP grew from three concerts per year and an annual budget of $7,000 to a regional resource with an annual budget of $450,000. Since 1976, when Monteux resigned, the budget has expanded to $900,000 annually. This growth has been marked by the receipt of a number of major awards, including the New York State award in 1968. Further distinction came with a Ford Foundation grant in 1976: an outright gift of $75,000 and a $250,000 sum to be matched by the Society in a five-year period. In addition to establishing an endowment fund, this grant provided support to inaugurate and develop a large-scale educational program including youth and in-school concerts, pre-concert teaching sessions, and a competition for young artists. During its 1982–1983 season the HVP received a NEA Challenge Grant award in recognition of the orchestra's excellent artistic quality, its reliable funding base, and increased audience participation.

The HVP earns almost 50% of its budget through ticket sales, performance fees, and music school tuition. The remainder comes from the support of individuals, the activities of volunteers, support from foundations and corporations, and grants from government organizations such as the NEA and the New York State Council on the Arts. The HVP is governed by a 30-member Board of Trustees that sets policy and has an organizational structure of subcommittees. To aid with diverse fund-raising activities and tickets sales, the HVP has a 300-member volunteer group, the Friends of the Philharmonic, spanning the three home counties. The orchestra is administered by seven full-time and four part-time staff. The general manager is Carla Smith, who, together with a committed Board, worked to bring the orchestra to its present sound financial footing by relieving it of a large deficit.

Since 1976 Imre Pallo has been the orchestra's music director. Pallo is also on the staff of the New York City Opera and guest-conducts worldwide. A Hudson Valley resident, Pallo is in touch with the many talented composers in the area and has strengthened the orchestra by making himself available as a guest speaker for service clubs and the media.

CHRONOLOGY OF MUSIC DIRECTORS: Claude Monteux, 1959–1975. Guest conductors, 1975–1976. Imre Pallo, 1976-present.

BIBLIOGRAPHY: Interview with HVP Director of Public Relations Arlene Gould.

ACCESS: Hudson Valley Philharmonic, Box 191, Poughkeepsie, NY 12602. (914) 454–1280. Carla Smith, General Manager.

                                                                          PETER ALEXANDER

ROCHESTER (971,230)

Rochester Philharmonic Orchestra (Mj)

The Rochester Philharmonic Orchestra is the principal professional orchestra serving Rochester and its suburbs. Within the area are several major industries, eight institutions of higher learning, and many cultural organizations, including the Rochester Oratorio Society, the Opera Theatre, and community instrumental ensembles. The city is noted for its medical, scientific, and industrial research and for its educational opportunities.

Although bands and amateur choruses had existed since Rochester's incorporation as a city in 1834, it was not until 1865 that John Kalbfleish organized a volunteer orchestra, the Rochester Philharmonic (not to be confused with the present Rochester Philharmonic Orchestra), which continued for a dozen years. Among other groups established about the same time was Henri Arpy's Rochester Philharmonic Society, which eventually had 55 members and was active until 1881.

In February 1900, Rochester's first professional orchestra, named for its founder Hermann Dossenbach, gave its inaugural concert. In 1912, reorganized under civic leadership, it became the Rochester Orchestra and began an era of development with such visiting artists as Josef Hofmann and Leopold Godowsky as soloists. It was discontinued in 1919 to make way for the Eastman Theatre Orchestra. In the meanwhile, Ludwig Schenk's Rochester Symphony, begun in 1901 and continuing into the 1920s, existed side by side with the Rochester Orchestra and played an important role in educational concerts for children.

In 1918–1919 George Eastman, public benefactor and founder of Kodak, announced plans to build the Eastman School of Music and Eastman Theatre as a gift to the University of Rochester for the education and enjoyment of the community. The Theatre, a magnificent edifice, would accommodate motion pictures, opera, ballet, and concerts.

Though no musician himself, Eastman was devoted to the arts and maintained his private organist and string quartet. He commissioned Arthur Alexander and Victor Wagner to recruit the finest musicians they could find for the Eastman Theatre Orchestra, whose initial function was to perform between reels of films projected in the 3,200-seat auditorium. At the Theatre's opening (September 4, 1922), the orchestra made its debut accompanying *The Prisoner of Zenda*. Soon thereafter the members of the Theatre Orchestra became the core or nucleus of the larger Rochester Philharmonic Orchestra, formed by the addition of many new performers to present concerts of serious music. With Arthur Alexander conducting and Alf Klingenberg as soloist, the Philharmonic gave its first concert on March 28, 1923.

The RPO's early history was one of a symbiotic relationship to the Eastman School of Music. George Eastman envisioned the Theatre as a complete performing arts center and the school as a complete professional training ground; they were equal parts of a single entity, sharing the extensive building complex for which he was responsible. Eastman supervised the hiring of personnel for both RPO and the school, which resulted in considerable overlapping of duties. Principal players were simultaneously members of the faculty, while artist/teachers were often soloists with the orchestra.

Eugene Goossens opened the initial full season of the RPO on October 17, 1923. In January 1924, Albert Coates arrived to share responsibilities as co-conductor and was daring enough to take the fledgling orchestra to New York for a Carnegie Hall concert in April. Re-engaged for the following season, Goossens and Coates performed not only the standard repertoire but featured as well the music of such contemporaries as Richard Strauss, Holst, Stravinsky, Ravel, and Sibelius. Among Rochester premieres were Bloch's *Two Poems*, Hanson's "Nordic" Symphony, and Palmgren's *Variations for Piano and Orchestra*. But the overwhelming favorites were compositions of Wagner and Tchaikovsky, with entire programs devoted to them.

On May 1, 1925, Howard Hanson, new director of the Eastman School, and the RPO joined forces to initiate the American Composers' Concerts, with the aim to perform new works by native composers. So successful was the venture that Hanson became known as the protagonist of American music, and the joint Eastman School/RPO programs continued until 1931, when the American Composers' Concerts were succeeded by the annual Fetivals of American Music.

After Coates's departure in mid–1925, Goossens remained as conductor until 1931, with Guy Fraser Harrison as his assistant. During his tenure the orchestra's personnel numbered 90–96, and the annual season included 10 concerts. Goossens's inclusion of new American and English works counteracted the predominantly German taste that had prevailed since before World War I. With European reputations behind them, Eastman School faculty soloists added an air of cosmopolitan diversity.

The appointment of José Iturbi as conductor in 1936 after five seasons of guest conductors (1931–1936) began an era of growth during which Spanish music, along with contemporary works from both Europe and the Americas, was added to the repertoire. A conductor beloved by all as a warm personality and brilliant pianist, he often appeared in the dual capacity of conductor-soloist. Until his departure to the West Coast in 1944, he also continued to engage excellent out-of-town soloists as well as local artists. The RPO flourished in spite of war-time restrictions.

Three seasons of guest conductors followed. The RPO continued under the direction of Harrison and out-of-town artists chosen from among the world's finest, but in spite of excellent programs and stable financial support, the interim period was one of uncertainty about the RPO's artistic future.

The 1947–1948 Silver Anniversary Season, expanded to 14 concerts, began auspiciously with Erich Leinsdorf's appointment as music director of the RPO. Performers found him a stern disciplinarian and exacting conductor against whom they rebelled on occasion, but no one could deny his superior musicianship, which earned him the greatest respect. Under his leadership the Philharmonic developed a distinctive sound of its own with strong strings and an overall richness and was raised to its rightful status as a Major symphony orchestra with an outstanding repertoire and a growing reputation for excellence.

When Leinsdorf left in 1956, his presence was sorely missed, especially since Harrison's leadership also ended with his appointment to the Oklahoma City Symphony.* There followed two seasons of guest conductors, after which Theodore Bloomfield arrived in 1958 for a tenure which terminated in 1963.

László Somogyi, who had appeared as guest conductor during the previous season, assumed the directorship in 1964. With hopes of reviving the orchestra and enriching its repertoire, he introduced many compositions by Central European writers, and on nearly every program he included at least one contemporary work. He celebrated important musical occasions with appropriate concerts. He publicized the RPO well and extended his personal greetings to the community. Because of his interest in young musicians, he opened rehearsals to students and visiting organizations whose members might enjoy seeing how an orchestral program was put together.

Somogyi, however, not entirely satisfied with the orchestral personnel, asked for a larger string section to achieve the sonority he desired. Moreover, he wanted players with complete commitment to the RPO and its activities. As much as he respected participation by Eastman faculty and their advanced students, he strove for the RPO's complete independence from the school. In 1969 most faculty players resigned, and the following season began with a host of new performers who required a longer season and increased services in order to realize a viable income. The management, hard put to meet the combined demands of the orchestra and its conductor, cut back on recruitment at the precise time when Somogyi was seeking a larger ensemble. When Somogyi returned to his native Europe in 1970, the relationship between Eastman School and the Philharmonic had come to an end.

Samuel Jones, Somogyi's assistant since 1965, assumed the title of resident conductor for 1970–1972, while the management struggled to re-establish a foundation for future development. Jones left the orchestra in 1972; the management, previously known as the Civic Music Association, was reorganized as the Rochester Philharmonic Orchestra, Inc., and David Zinman was appointed music director-elect.

Zinman, who had been among the guest conductors in 1972–1973, became music director and conductor of the RPO in 1974 with Isaiah Jackson as his associate. With the orchestra responding to his leadership with enthusiasm, his success was almost immediately assured. His programming, including technically difficult compositions for which both performers and audiences were ready, was masterful. In response to growing concert attendance, the season was augmented in 1974 to 15 Thursday evening programs, eight of them repeated on Saturday; in 1978 to 15 symphony pairs; and in 1982 to 16 pairs. A summer Philharmonic Festival series was begun in 1978.

At present the RPO enjoys highly successful seasons with a varied repertoire and outstanding guest artists. Thursday concerts are broadcast, while occasional programs are televised. Recording sessions, tours, and summer festivals are included in the season. While regular symphony concerts are given in Eastman Theatre, the summer programs take place at the Finger Lakes Performing Arts Center in Canandaigua, the orchestra's summer headquarters, where the 1984 schedule includes eight evenings of Saturday classics and 10 of Sunday pops.

THE CORE ORCHESTRA OF THE ROCHESTER PHILHARMONIC: The Eastman Theatre Orchestra, the core or nucleus around which the RPO was developed, was established in 1922 to serve in various capacities at the Theatre, originally in conjunction with motion pictures. As the Theatre's activities expanded, the orchestra also participated under the aegis of the school in dramatic offerings, commemorative programs, and holiday galas, sometimes joining forces with local choruses.

Beginning on December 15, 1925, some 15–20 players from the core orchestra under the direction of Goossens and occasionally of Hanson played in Kilbourn Hall of the Eastman School of Music as the Rochester Little Symphony with music for chamber orchestra constituting the repertoire. When Goossens left in 1931, the group ceased to be called the Little Symphony, but almost immediately assumed a special function as part of the newly established Annual Festivals of American Music of the School. Conducted by Hanson and called the Eastman-Rochester Symphony Orchestra, the ensemble performed featured works at the programs in Kilbourn Hall and the Theatre and participated in a number of festival recordings, some of which were recently reissued as the ERA (i.e. Eastman-Rochester Archive) Records. With the retirement of Hanson as director of the School in 1964, the Eastman-Rochester Symphony terminated its festival appearances.

The Theatre ceased activity as a motion-picture house in 1929 with the advent of sound film. The Theatre Orchestra emerged as the Rochester Civic Orchestra and presented educational programs and participated as the pit ensemble for operettas, ballets, and musicals at both the Theatre and the nearby Masonic Auditorium. From 1934 to 1970 the Civic Orchestra presented Sunday family concerts under the direction of its regular conductor, Paul White, as part of its season.

The present core orchestra of 59 musicians is led by Isaiah Jackson (Associate Conductor, RPO), Erich Kunzel (Principal Pops Conductor), and Enrique Diemecke (Exxon/Arts Endowment Conductor). Its activities include programs at the Theatre, a half-dozen Promenade concerts at the

Dome Arena in suburban Henrietta, summer appearances at Canandaigua, and occasional free performances at Midtown Plaza and Highland Park Bowl. Eastman Kodak Company underwrites noon performances for its employees at Kodak Park.

The core group uses a variety of names because of its many functions. For pops concerts it is called the Rochester Pops; for informal Dome Arena programs it is known as the Promenade Orchestra; and for educational appearances it is known simply as the RPO.

The organization of the RPO appears complicated because of the manner in which it operates. The 59 musicians of the core orchestra participate in the full season of some 46–48 weeks. Augmented by other regularly engaged players, the ensemble, totalling some 90 members, is known as the Rochester Philharmonic Orchestra and performs during the symphony season (October through mid-June). For an extraordinarily large instrumentation, supplementary players are hired on an ad hoc basis after having passed auditions. RPO members render collaborative services to the Rochester Oratorio Society, Opera Theatre of Rochester, and the annual Bach Festivals.

The Rochester Philharmonic Orchestra, Inc., founded in 1923 as the Subscribers' Association and existing for several decades as the Civic Music Association, maintains and operates the Rochester Philharmonic Orchestra. It consists of a volunteer Board of Directors and elected officers and a salaried professional staff for administration, business, development, production, promotion, and sales. A large membership of subscribers and volunteer workers supports the activities of the RPO, including active participation in the annual fund drives. The Rochester Philharmonic League, formerly the Women's Committee of RPO, founded in 1929, is a large volunteer group of women who assist with educational concerts, fund drives, and social activities. Representatives from the orchestra occasionally meet with the governing RPO, Inc., in negotiating contracts and maintaining liaison between the musicians and the management. The RPO's annual budget is $5 million, derived from ticket sales, fund drives, personal and corporate gifts, and grants from the NEA, New York State Council on the Arts, and Monroe County.

RECORDING HISTORY AND SELECTIVE DISCOGRAPHY: Although the RPO recorded infrequently during its early history, David Zinman's tenure has been characterized by considerable recording activity. The orchestra's recordings include representative works from a cross-section of its varied repertoire.

Beethoven, Romance in G Major, op. 40; Romance in F Major, op. 50; Konzertsatz in C Major, WoO 5; Ludwig Spohr, Violin Concerto No. 8, A Minor *In modo d'una scena cantante*), op. 47 (Sergiu Luca/Zinman): Nonesuch 79040. William Bolcom, Piano Concerto (William Bolcom, Piano/Sydney Hodkinson); Samuel Adler, Concerto for Flute and Orchestra (Bonita Boyd/David Effron): Pantheon PFN 2041. Liszt, Concerto No. 1 for Piano and Orchestra, E-flat Major, and Concerto No. 2 for Piano and Orchestra, A Major (Jorge Bolet/Zinman): Vox 9001. Mendelssohn, *Hebrides*

Overture; Symphony No. 3 (*Scotch*); Symphony No. 4 (*Italian*); Symphony No. 5, D Minor (*Reformation*) (Zinman): Vox Cum Laude 2-VCL 9038X. Mozart, Concerto No. 26 for Piano and Orchestra, D Major, K. 537 (Barry Snyder/Zinman); Mass, C Major, K. 316 ("Coronation") (Zinman): Turnabout 34730.

CHRONOLOGY OF MUSIC DIRECTORS: Eugene Goossens, 1923–1931. Albert Coates, 1924–1925. (Guest conductors, 1931–1936.) José Iturbi, 1936–1944. (Guest conductors, 1944–1947.) Erich Leinsdorf, 1947–1956. (Guest conductors, 1956–1958.) Theodore Bloomfield, 1958–1963. (Guest conductors, 1963–1964.) László Somogyi, 1964–1970. Samuel Jones (Resident Conductor), 1970–1972. (Guest conductors, 1972–1973.) David Zinman, 1973-present.

BIBLIOGRAPHY: Vincent Lenti, "Predecessors of the Rochester Philharmonic," Eastman School of Music Community Education Division, *Newsletter*, Spring 1984. Blake McKelvey, *Rochester: An Emerging Metropolis, 1925–1961* (Rochester: Christopher Press, 1961). Blake McKelvey, *Rochester on the Genesee: The Growth of a City* (Syracuse: Syracuse University Press, 1973). Blake McKelvey, *Rochester: The Quest for Quality, 1880–1925* (Cambridge: Harvard University Press, 1950.) John Mueller, *The American Symphony Orchestra* (1951; reprint, Westport, Conn.: Greenwood Press, 1976). Charles Riker, *The Eastman School of Music: Its First Quarter Century, 1921–1946* (Rochester: The University of Rochester, 1948).

ACCESS: Rochester Philharmonic Orchestra, 108 East Avenue, Rochester, NY 14604 (716) 454–2620. Tony H. Dechario, General Manager.

RUTH WATANABE

SYRACUSE (642,971)

Syracuse Symphony Orchestra (Mj)

Although it is one of the younger symphony orchestras in the nation, the Syracuse Symphony has developed an innovative approach to its music making, emulated by other, older orchestras. The SSO is supported by 7,000 subscribers in the Syracuse area and annually presents over 300 orchestral, ensemble, and special programs to an audience of some 400,000 people, 175,000 of whom attend concerts at a reduced ticket price or for free. The orchestra provides 15 pairs of masterwork concerts, eight pairs of pops concerts, five family concerts, five regional series of concerts, plus a Dance Series and the Famous Artist Series. The SSO also accompanies the Syracuse Opera Company, and it produces a summer series of programs, youth and tiny tots concerts, special and runout concerts.

The SSO is overseen by a Board of Directors, two of whom are orchestra members. The orchestra is funded by a combination of federal, corporate, foundation, and individual grants. The annual budget is at the $3.5 million level, and the SSO employs 80 musicians and an administrative staff of 20. Internal affairs for the orchestra are handled by a five-person Orchestra Committee. The SSO is supported by the Syracuse Symphony Guild, which is active in educational, fund-raising, and public relations activities.

Since its inception in 1961, the SSO has had a strong dedication to small ensemble performances. Members of the SSO combine to form 10 smaller touring ensembles: three string quartets, two woodwind quintets, two brass quintets, a baroque ensemble, a percussion ensemble, and, surprisingly, a rock band. These groups travel extensively to small communities throughout the central New York area. Many ensemble concerts are given in schools, hospitals, and nursing homes. Such opportunities demonstrate the orchestra's commitment toward musical flexibility.

The SSO maintains a strong involvement with the area's school children. Members of the SSO play to some 47,000 youngsters yearly in a variety of educational experiences, including tiny tots, youth, and ensemble programs. Between 1978 and 1983 the SSO's resident conductor, Calvin Custer, organized a music education training program for local schools. This "Sound Experience" exposed the children to a wide variety of musical encounters.

Founded in 1969, the Syracuse Symphony Youth Orchestra is an important part of the total SSO organization. The resources of the SSO—conductors, musicians, administrators—are made available to the Youth Orchestra's 80 members, who are chosen through annual auditions. They rehearse weekly under SSO Assistant Conductor Ernest Muzquiz. The Youth Orchestra and the SSO combine forces for one concert each year.

The SSO has always had strong ties with Syracuse University's School of Music, and many SSO members teach at the University. In the fall of 1983, the two institutions, with the cooperation of AFM Local 78, drew together to create a new program of String Fellows. Under this program, ten graduate string students at the University hold positions in the SSO, and they form the nucleus of a University chamber orchestra. To qualify, interested applicants must be admitted to a degree program in the School of Music and pass an audition with the SSO.

During its first 15 years, 1961 to 1975, the SSO had to contend with playing in local high school auditoriums. In January 1976, the SSO took up permanent residency in Syracuse's new, downtown Civic Center of Onondaga County, which also hosts various county services and a theater complex. The SSO performs in the 2,117-seat Crouse-Hinds Concert Theater. This hall was designed in consultation with acoustician Russell Johnson to accommodate all types of musical performances. It includes a wide range of possible acoustical permutations, as well as a sophisticated sound system.

The city of Syracuse has a complex history of symphonic organizations dating from the late 1800s. Before the creation of the present SSO in 1961, there were at least 17 attempts to establish an orchestra in Syracuse. In the 1940s and early 1950s, there were multiple orchestras using basically the same musicians. Such earlier orchestras were formed by and for the musicians, not the community, and their demise usually resulted from a lack of public support.

Dr. William H. Schultze, the first professor of music at Syracuse University, briefly organized an orchestra at the University in 1878. It quickly folded and the city had to wait 12 years for its next symphonic ensemble, the Syracuse Philharmonic Orchestra. A Syracuse Symphony Orchestra Society followed in 1892, and for the next 68 years many other "Syracuse Symphony" orchestras would follow, lasting from a single concert to nine years.

Following several unsuccessful attempts by others at establishing a permanent orchestra in Syracuse, Vladimir Shavitch, a conductor hired from the Eastman School of Music, headed a Syracuse Symphony in 1924 built around a core of players from the Rochester orchestra. Its musicians commuted the 85 miles from Rochester to Syracuse until the orchestra collapsed in 1933, a victim of the depression. Undaunted, 60 members of the now-defunct Syracuse Symphony formed the Syracuse Civil Symphony in the fall of 1933 with Victor Miller as conductor. In 1934 the Civic Symphony went under the auspices of the federal government's Civil Works Administration. Government aid for the orchestra terminated in 1940, and the Civic Symphony ceased to function.

In 1940 Murray Bernthal, a violinist, organized the Syracuse String Sinfonietta, whose 30 players gave three formal concert seasons; they reorganized after World War II and played sporadic concerts until 1956. As a supplemental ensemble filling other needs, the Syracuse Philharmonic was formed in 1941 by Nicolas Gualillo for a series of three concerts and one opera performance. Gualillo reorganized the Philharmonic in 1951 to accompany opera productions in conjunction with his Syracuse-based opera and music conservatory. Two longer-lasting groups, the Syracuse Civil Orchestra and the Civic University Orchestra, were under the direction of Andre Polah from 1940 to 1949, when they were taken over by Alexander Capurso. The Onondaga County Symphony Orchestra, created in 1956 to present concerts for Syracuse area youngsters, was also playing to adults from 1957 until 1960.

Today's SSO was formed in 1961 with the assistance of a $50,000 grant from the Gifford Foundation. The orchestra's creation was due largely to the campaign efforts of harpist Caroline Hopkins and other community members. Karl Kritz was chosen as the orchestra's first music director, remaining at the helm until his death in 1969, and Benson Snyder became the SSO's first manager, guiding the orchestra through the difficult early years. One hundred members of the Syracuse chapter of the AFM auditioned for the ensemble. The first season, 1961–1962, included four subscription concerts and one pops concert. For the second season, the fledgling SSO received a $5,000 grant from the New York State Council on the Arts, while additional funds were raised by the newly formed Syracuse Symphony Guild. The Guild, with more than 400 members, was a major factor in both fundraising and ticket sales until it was phased out of the latter in 1969 and replaced in that capacity by the orchestra's professional staff.

By its third season, the SSO had formed four internal chamber groups (string quartet, woodwind quintet, brass quintet, percussion ensemble). During these early years, performance in the SSO was a part-time job for the 36-member core orchestra. As part of its commitment to a growing audience, typified by numerous concerts throughout central New York, the SSO also promoted new music by regional composers. This objective is still current today.

By 1969 the SSO had expanded its home concert season to 11 pairs of concerts. After Kritz's untimely death, Mihai Brediceanu functioned as the orchestra's principal guest conductor and musical advisor. In 1971, Frederik Prausnitz took over as music director of the SSO. Over the next two years the orchestra raised an endowment fund exceeding $1 million in response to a challenge grant from the Ford Foundation. The SSO was able to expand its regional activities as a result of community support and grants from the New York State Council on the Arts and the National Endowment for the Arts. By 1974 the SSO was providing 250 orchestra and ensemble concerts per year to audiences totalling over 250,000.

Christopher Keene was engaged as music director beginning with the 1975–1976 season, and the orchestra moved into its current prominence as a designated "Major" orchestra after only 15 years of operation. Under Keene, the SSO has demonstrated a firm commitment to new music, and in 1980 the orchestra was cited by ASOL and ASCAP for excellence in programming new music. With Keene, the SSO has performed to critical acclaim in New York City's Carnegie Hall and has made several recordings.

The phenomenal growth of the SSO was not without its growing pains, and the first third of the 1983–1984 season was curtailed due to a players' strike involving the issue of wages. Christopher Keene became music advisor of the SSO for the 1984–1985 season, since he had assumed the role of music director with the New York City Opera Company. After a year-long search, the SSO named Kazuyoshi Akiyama to be the new music director, starting in 1986.

RECORDING HISTORY AND SELECTIVE DISCOGRAPHY: THE SSO's recordings with Christopher Keene are indicative of the ensemble's creative programming policies. Three of these albums are recording premieres: two twentieth-century works (by Burton and Jarrett) and one nineteenth-century American rarity (by Heinrich). The fourth disc is an in-house recording of Handel's *Messiah*.

Stephen Douglas Burton, Symphony No. 2 (*Ariel*) (Keene): Peters International, PLE 128. Anthony Philip Heinrich, *The Ornithological Combat of Kings* (Keene): New World Records, NW 208. Keith Jarrett, *The Celestial Hawk* (Keene): ECM 1–1175.

CHRONOLOGY OF MUSIC DIRECTORS: Karl Dritz, 1961–1969. Mihai Brediceanu (Guest Conductor), 1969–1971. Frederik Prausnitz, 1971–1975. Christopher Keene, 1975–1984. (Guest conductors, 1984–1986.) Kazuyoshi Akiyama to assume duties in 1986.

BIBLIOGRAPHY: Philip Hart, *Orpheus in the New World* (New York: Norton, 1973). Allan Kozinn, "The Syracuse Symphony Has Got a New Conductor, a New Hall," *High Fidelity/Musical America*, Sept. 1976. Susan W. Larson, "A History of Symphony Orchestras in Syracuse, New York, from 1848 to 1969," Masters thesis, Syracuse University, 1970. Bradley G. Morison, "Worse Off in a Better Way: The Syracuse Symphony Orchestra and How It Grew as a Unique Regional Resource," unpublished typescript, Syracuse Symphony Orchestra, 1972. Christopher Pavlakis. *The American Music Handbook* (New York: Free Press, 1974).

ACCESS: Syracuse Symphony Orchestra, Civic Center, Suite 40, 411 Montgomery Street, Syracuse, NY 13202. (315) 424–8222. Donald Roth, Manager.

RONALD N. BUKOFF

North Carolina _____

CHARLOTTE (637,218)

Charlotte Symphony Orchestra (Rg)

The Charlotte Symphony Orchestra, the oldest performing arts organization in the area, played its first concert in 1932. In the 1983–1984 season, the CSO played 209 performances for 185,000 people, 111 concerts being either the full Symphony or a chamber orchestra, and 98 being ensemble performances. Its 41-week season includes five different subscription series and three series of free concerts.

The CSO's primary subscription series of eight week-night concerts is played in Charlotte's Ovens Auditorium, an attractive civic hall of 2,500 seats, located four miles east of uptown Charlotte. The hall's dead acoustics and inadequate facilities have caused much agitation for the construction of a new concert hall and fine arts center. In 1984, it seemed possible that a new hall might be under construction by 1986, probably near Spirit Square, a civic arts center that today includes the CSO's rehearsal hall and business offices.

The orchestra's second series of five Saturday evening concerts began in 1973 and is performed in the modern, 1,000-seat Dana Auditorium on the campus of Queens College, four miles south of uptown. This series usually sells out for the season. A series of four popular Saturday morning "Lollipops" children's concerts was begun in 1981. The Cabaret Concert series, Boston Pops-style concerts with table seating and refreshments, began in 1982 under corporate sponsorship, and in spite of a mediocre location at the all-purpose Park Center civic hall, it has proven exceedingly popular and successful. The fifth and newest of the subscription series was started in 1984, with two concerts of chamber music. This series is being continued and will probably be expanded in the future.

In addition to the subscription series, since 1971 the Symphony has presented each year in early December four very well-attended performances of the *Nutcracker* in conjunction with dancers from Winston-Salem's North Carolina School for the Arts. The CSO also furnishes the orchestras for the Charlotte Opera Association's three or four operas per year, including a two-week tour, and for the two or three annual performances by the Oratorio Singers of Charlotte. The CSO's own concerts away from Charlotte have consisted largely of runouts within a radius of 175 miles of the city.

In 1954 the CSO began its educational program with 36 free in-school concerts. Since then the orchestra has provided educational concerts both through school visits and in Ovens Auditorium with a larger orchestra, and in recent years students have been bused to concerts, usually at the CSO's expense. Many free in-school concerts have also been played by string quartets, woodwind quintets, and brass quartets from the Symphony. The "Sidewalk Concerts," the second free series, are played in such locations as the lobbies of corporation buildings and large shopping malls.

The Summer Pops Concerts, taken over by the CSO in 1983, were begun in 1975 by the independent Charlotte Summer Pops Orchestra, Inc. When the CSO absorbed the Summer Pops, it compressed the summer season into six weeks following its own regular 35-week season, thus expanding its season to 41 weeks.

The CSO is governed by seven officers and 42 directors, with an administrative staff including a manager, assistant manager, and eight other employees. Of the musicians, 54 are full-time employees of the CSO, with 14 per-service players and 18 extra musicians used as needed. An Orchestra Committee represents the musicians to management, and since 1975 the Charlotte Musicians' Association, Local 342 of the AFM, has negotiated contracts with management and Board regarding salaries, working conditions, and benefits.

The orchestra's 1984–1985 budget of $1.7 million is funded by grants from the Charlotte Arts and Science Council, the NEA, the North Carolina Arts Council, local and state governments, by strong financial support from the Charlotte Symphony Women's Association, by individual donations, earned income, corporate sponsorship of several concerts per year, and by special fund-raising projects including the annual Symphony Ball ("Fortissimo"), and an annual Pops Gala Concert.

As of 1984 the orchestra had practically no endowment, as its budget in 1966 was too small to qualify it for a Ford Foundation grant, and yet the Symphony's rapid growth since then has pushed its annual budget beyond the budgets of other orchestras that did receive such grants and consequently now have substantial endowments. Management and Board see an endowment of substantial size as the CSO's greatest need.

The Charlotte Symphony Orchestra was founded during the Great Depression by Guillermo S. deRoxlo (its first music director), J. Spencer Bell (the orchestra's first president and principal flutist), Lonni R. Sides (music supervisor in the city schools), and other Charlotte musicians and civic leaders. The CSO's first performance was a free concert on March 20, 1932, sponsored by the Charlotte Parks and Recreation Commission and played in the Carolina Theatre to a full house. Concerts during the first season were free and were played in several locations. From 1934 to 1939, the orchestra's home was the old 500-seat Alexander Graham Junior High School Auditorium. Audiences in 1934 averaged about 250, when season tickets cost five dollars per couple. In 1939 concerts were moved to the Armory Auditorium as audiences grew larger. DeRoxlo resigned unexpectedly in 1944, and orchestra musician Guy Hutchins took over until 1948.

The 1948–1949 season was directed by Pulitzer Prize winning composer-conductor-flutist Lamar Stringfield, who had founded the North Carolina Symphony.* In September 1949, Stringfield was succeeded by former CSO bassist James Christian Pfohl, then head of the Music Department at nearby Davidson College. Two important changes occurred then: concerts were moved to the 1,000-seat Piedmont School Auditorium, and for the first time the musicians were paid a small honorarium. The Symphony, beginning its in-school educational concerts and for two years playing a weekly half-hour TV program sponsored by a local supermarket chain, expanded its activities rapidly under Pfohl. The CSO's first concert in the new Owens Auditorium in 1955 featured the Beethoven Ninth Symphony with nationally famous soloists.

Following the 25th anniversary season in 1956–1957, a severe financial crisis resulted in the Board's terminating the services of all paid employees. The musicians, playing the 1957–1958 season with guest conductors and without pay, refused to let the CSO die. The CSO's first full-time manager, Esther Waltenberger, offered to remain for one season without salary, and several Board members paid the expenses of guest conductors, one of whom, Henry Janiec, was engaged as part-time music director for the years 1958–1963. The Symphony achieved financial stability enough for the Board to offer Janiec the first full-time music director's position in 1963. He declined, however, and in 1963 Richard Cormier was appointed. A former trombonist with the Kansas City Philharmonic, he had directed the St. Joseph (Missouri) Symphony for several years before moving to Charlotte. Cormier directed from 1963 to 1967, when he resigned to become music director of the Chattanooga Symphony.*

In 1967 auditions for a new music director resulted in the appointment of Jacques Brourman, a Pittsburgh violinist who had directed the Boise (Idaho) Philharmonic* for several years. Brourman programmed more modern music than his predecessors, and many of the contemporary works were not well received by the audience. To his credit, Brourman caused the

Symphony to move ahead by demanding that the Board increase the number of week-night concerts, begin to hire some full-time musicians, and start the Saturday night subscription series. However, disputes between Brourman and local CSO musicians led the Board to recognize the AFM as bargaining agent for the musicians in 1974. Brourman resigned in 1976.

Brourman was succeeded in 1977 by Leo B. Driehuys, a Dutch conductor who was permanent conductor of the Gelders Orkest in Arnhem, Holland, from 1970 to 1977. From his first concert with the CSO, Driehuys was extremely popular with both musicians and audiences; he often received an ovation just for walking on stage. His popularity with the audiences has endured, although some of the musicians' enthusiasm waned after his abortive attempt in 1979 to replace six of the CSO's key wind players, two of whom subsequently resigned.

Under Driehuys's direction, the CSO has improved in quality and stability, beginning the Lollipops, Sidewalk, Cabaret, and chamber music series. The Symphony has also absorbed the former orchestras of the Opera, the Oratorio, and the Summer Pops, actions predictably unpopular with the numerous musicians in those orchestras who were displaced by the Symphony's takeover. Driehuys's early programs leaned toward classical and romantic composers, but he has included in recent years more modern works and compositions by American composers. The CSO has premiered several works, and its assistant conductor, Jordan Tang, a native of Hong Kong, is an accomplished composer. Tang conducts the Educational, Sidewalk, and Lollipops concerts and also the Youth Symphony of the Carolinas, which is sponsored by the CSO and its Women's Association.

Lack of agreement on a new contract caused management to cancel the first three weeks of the 1984–1985 season, but the dispute was settled with a new four-year contract to run through the 1987–1988 season.

RECORDING HISTORY AND SELECTIVE DISCOGRAPHY: The CSO has produced a 50th Anniversary Album (Beethoven: Symphonies No. 1 and 9), Charlotte Symphony Orchestra Records 111082/83X.

CHRONOLOGY OF MUSIC DIRECTORS: Guillermo deRoxlo, 1932–1944. Guy Hutchins, 1944–1948. James Christian Pfohl, 1949–1957. (Guest conductors, 1957–1958.) Henry Janiec, 1958–1963. Richard Cormier, 1963–1967. Jacques Brourman, 1967–1976. Leo Driehuys, 1977-present.

BIBLIOGRAPHY: Interview with CSO Director of Development Sara H. Meanor, 1984. Richard Banks, "It's Our Music and It's Great! Symphony Enters Its 25th Season," *Charlotte Observer*, 25 Apr. 1956. Joseph P. Little, "The Early Years: Conductors and Concert Halls," Charlotte Symphony Program, 12 October 1977.

ACCESS: Charlotte Symphony Orchestra, Spirit Square, 110 East Seventh Street, Charlotte, NC 28202. (704) 332–6136. Douglas A. Patti, General Manager.

JOSEPH P. LITTLE

GREENSBORO (724,129—Greensboro/Winston-Salem/High Point)

Eastern Philharmonic Orchestra (Mt)

The Eastern Philharmonic Orchestra is the resident professional orchestra of the Eastern Music Festival in Greensboro, North Carolina. Founded in 1962 by its current music director and resident conductor, Sheldon Morgenstern, the Eastern Music Festival is the largest festival of its kind in the Southeast. In addition to the professional orchestra, there are also two student orchestras and numerous chamber ensembles. Participants in the Festival are housed on the beautiful campus of Guilford College in northwest Greensboro.

The 85-member Eastern Philharmonic Orchestra comprises musicians from the leading orchestras and music schools in the country: the New York Philharmonic,* Boston Symphony,* Chicago Symphony,* Cleveland Orchestra,* Los Angeles Philharmonic,* Philadelphia Orchestra,* National Symphony,* Juilliard School, Cincinnati College-Conservatory of Music, and Eastman School. In 1983, the orchestra presented nine concerts with eight guest artists within a period of seven weeks. The guest artists also performed six chamber music concerts with members of the Eastern Philharmonic in the Eastern Chamber Players series. Most of the members of the orchestra also serve as teachers for the two hundred students who attend the Eastern Music Festival.

The Festival season extends from mid-June to the end of July. There are six concert series offered to the public—one on each day of the week except Sunday. The Eastern Philharmonic performs on the Saturday evening series and the Eastern Chamber Players on Tuesday evenings. The four other series feature students. Concerts are held in Sternberger Auditorium and Dana Auditorium on the Guilford College campus. In 1983, the audience attending concerts totalled nearly 40,000. Ten concerts of the Philharmonic and the Eastern Chamber Players were broadcast on NPR in 1983.

The Eastern Music Festival had a 1984 operating budget of $770,000. It is funded by federal, state, and local grants, numerous foundation grants, corporate gifts, private donors, and earned income. The multifaceted events and programs of the Festival are administered by a full-time staff of seven and governed by a Board of Directors of approximately 40. There is also a Board of Advisors, consisting of well-known and influential performing artists and civic leaders, and a support group, the Eastern Music Festival Auxiliary. In addition to providing financial support, the Auxiliary sponsors a Kinder Konzert each year designed for and presented free to area children.

The sole responsibility for programming is left to the music director, Sheldon Morgenstern, who has twice won the ASCAP Award for music programming. The Eastern Philharmonic has performed the world premieres of six works and has commissioned several by American composers—most recently, Karel Husa. His *Reflections* (Symphony No. 2 for Chamber Orchestra) was premiered on July 16, 1983.

The Festival has a profound impact on the Triad (Greensboro, Winston-Salem, and High Point). The Eastern Philharmonic is the only professional orchestra in the area with a regular series of concerts during the summer, and the Festival also reaches beyond the concert hall through its community service program, PROJECT: LISTEN. Underwritten by the Ciba-Geigy Corporation, this unique program takes small ensembles into residences, meeting places, and businesses in the community. In 1983, 53 free concerts were presented to handicapped persons, senior citizens, economically disadvantaged groups, and to corporations.

CHRONOLOGY OF MUSIC DIRECTORS: Sheldon Morgenstern, 1962-present.

BIBLIOGRAPHY: "EMF: An Overview," (EMF grant application), 1983.

ACCESS: Eastern Music Festival, 200 North Davie Street, Greensboro, NC 27401. (919) 373–4712. Walter W. Heid, General Manager.

RONALD A. CRUTCHER

Greensboro Symphony Orchestra (Mt)

The Greensboro Symphony Orchestra is one of two ASOL Metropolitan orchestras in the Triad area of North Carolina. Located less than 30 miles from each other, the Greensboro Symphony and the Winston-Salem Symphony* Orchestras have coexisted for more than 25 years. While each orchestra has its own audience, many of the area's musicians perform in both.

The Greensboro Symphony presents an annual subscription series of seven classical concerts in the 2,400-seat Greensboro Memorial Auditorium, a modern facility adjacent to the Greensboro Coliseum. During the 1984–1985 season, the orchestra will present a series of three pops concerts with guest artists and will serve as the orchestra for the Greensboro Opera Company's production of *Tosca*. The orchestra will also perform a series of three children's concerts with such performers as Bob McGrath of "Sesame Street" and several other concerts for young people. Its brass, woodwind, and string ensembles present more than 200 concerts annually to children in Greensboro and in area schools. The full orchestra performs six concerts to more than 15,000 school children each year. In all, the 1984 audience was 20,000.

The original Greensboro Orchestra was organized in 1939 as a joint project of the University of North Carolina Women's College (now the University of North Carolina at Greensboro) and the Greensboro Public Schools. The primary purpose of the orchestra was educational, and most of its activities were related to the Women's College. Concerts were free and the players received no remuneration for their services.

In an attempt to wean the Greensboro Orchestra from its dependence on the university, the Greensboro Symphony Society was formed in 1959. An Advisory Committee was appointed to work closely with UNC-Greensboro in altering the orchestra's college-oriented image and restructuring the organization into one that would be perceived as a community endeavor. In 1963, the Advisory Committee of the Symphony Society was changed to a 13-member Board of Directors. Working toward a budgetary goal that would insure payment of stipends to the conductor, manager, and musicians, this Board oversaw the transition of the orchestra from an amateur to a semi-professional performing organization.

With a 1984 budget of $487,000, the Greensboro Symphony currently employs 80 musicians, two conductors, and an administrative staff of five. The orchestra is governed by a Board of Directors of 35, and its activities are administered by a full-time general manager and operations manager. It is funded by federal, state, and local grants, several foundation grants, corporate gifts, private donors, and earned income.

The primary responsibility for programming is left to the music director, Peter Paul Fuchs. His programs are distinguished by the inclusion of a large number of twentieth-century compositions and other seldom performed works. During the 1984–1985 season, the orchestra will present the world premier of *The Age of Innocence* by Roger Hannay. Another notable feature of the season is being billed as a "North Carolina First": the first joint concert of the Greensboro Symphony Orchestra with the North Carolina Symphony Orchestra.* The two orchestras will perform the Bruckner Symphony No. 9 and Prokofiev *Suite Scythe*.

One of the vital components of the orchestra's support base is the Greensboro Symphony Guild. With more than 650 members, the Guild contributes 5% to 10% of the orchestra's budget annually. In addition to selling tickets and raising funds through various activities and projects, the Guild assists the orchestra with its children's concerts. The Guild also contributes substantially to the Greensboro Symphony Youth Orchestra by awarding scholarships and sponsoring competitions. The Guild's Heartstrings Program serves those in the community who could not otherwise attend a symphony concert. Corporations and individuals purchase tickets that are then given to the handicapped, disadvantaged persons, and senior citizens.

CHRONOLOGY OF MUSIC DIRECTORS: George Dickieson, 1939–1962. M. Thomas Cousins, 1963–1966. Sheldon Morgenstern, 1967–1974. (Guest conductors, 1974–1975.) Peter Paul Fuchs, 1975-present.

BIBLIOGRAPHY: N. Elaine Campbell, "The Marketing Plan and Audit of a Non-Profit Performing Arts Organization," MBA paper, University of North Carolina, 1984. "The Greensboro Symphony Orchestra: A History," GSO, 1971. "History: The Greensboro Symphony Orchestra," GSO, 1973. "Greensboro Symphony Orchestra: Summary of Five Year Artistic and Administrative Development Plan," GSO, 1984.

ACCESS: Greensboro Symphony Orchestra, 200 North Davie Street, Greensboro, NC 27401. (919) 373–4523. Kathy Worrell, Acting General Manager.

RONALD A. CRUTCHER

RALEIGH (531,167)

North Carolina Symphony (Rg)

The North Carolina Symphony is a state-supported orchestra of 69 musicians based in Raleigh, the state capital. Its home is Memorial Auditorium, a 2,300-seat neoclassical hall built in 1932 and extensively renovated for concert use in 1977–1978. The NCS is not the state's only ASOL Regional orchestra, but it avoids direct competition with the Charlotte Symphony* and rarely intrudes on the home turfs of the state's two regular-season Metropolitan orchestras (Greensboro* and Winston-Salem*). Except in these three cities, however, the NCS seems to dominate the orchestral scene within the state.

The orchestra's biggest series are in Raleigh; at present, there are three of these: a classical series of seven programs featuring a mixture of established soloists and less well known artists, a pops series of five concerts involving jazz and popular artists and occasional visiting pops conductors, and a children's series of three Saturday morning events. The 1984–1985 season included 16 series concerts in Raleigh, together with several off-series events including the annual trio of *Nutcracker* ballet performances in conjunction with the North Carolina School of the Arts. In the 1983–1984 season, the orchestra scheduled a total of 67 evening concerts in 38 cities and towns throughout the state. The full orchestra participated in 45 of these; 22 involved reduced forces performing as the North Carolina Symphony Chamber Orchestra. A one-month, four-concert summer season in 1984 extended employment beyond the contractual 36 weeks.

A significant portion of the orchestra's work has historically been—and remains—in education; the state has accordingly provided financial support in ever-increasing amounts since the legislature passed its first appropriations bill for the Symphony in 1943. Tax-supported grants and allocations reached $1.65 million (70%) out of a total budget of $2.37 million in the 1982–1983 season (the latest for which figures were available). In that year the total income from other fund-raising activities exceeded $475,000 (20%); income from performances in the Raleigh metropolitan area reached $168,000 (7%); and income from concerts elsewhere in the state neared $275,000 (11%). In the same year, concert production expenses totalled $483,243. Over two-thirds of the orchestra's services are in the form of free educational concerts given in the state's public schools during school hours; many of these concerts are played by the chamber orchestra. Generally, the month of May is devoted to chamber music, with many small groups touring the state.

The history of the North Carolina Symphony is the story of the efforts of Lamar Stringfield, Joseph Hyde Pratt, and Benjamin F. Swalin. Lamar Stringfield was born in Raleigh on October 10, 1897; after World War I he attended New York's Institute of Musical Art, where he studied flute, composition, and conducting. In 1928 he was awarded the Pulitzer Prize for his orchestral suite, "From the Southern Mountains," which drew upon the folk music of North Carolina. The following year, Stringfield was urged to return permanently to North Carolina; perhaps motivated in part by his interest in collecting folk music, he agreed to do so. His first thought was to get a subsidy to establish a state symphony.

By 1931 a committee had been formed to consider a symphony orchestra for North Carolina. Its chairman was Colonel Joseph Hyde Pratt, professor of Economic Geology at the University of North Carolina. By early 1932, the North Carolina Symphony Society was formed to study, encourage, and promote the establishment of a North Carolina Symphony Orchestra. The first public meeting of the Society was held in Chapel Hill on March 21, 1932; Pratt was elected president, and it was understood that Stringfield would conduct the orchestra. To encourage public support, a "demonstration concert" by 48 volunteer musicians from 16 communities was given in Hill Hall on the campus of the University of North Carolina in Chapel Hill on May 14, 1932. The successful concert led to advertisements for more to come.

But funding was a major problem. During 1934–1935 a grant of $45,000 was received from the Federal Emergency Relief Administration, but this aid was only temporary. In 1935, Stringfield left to accept the post of assistant conductor at Radio City Music Hall. The orchestra broke into small units, some eventually combining with the Federal Music Project Orchestra of Virginia. In 1937 an attempt was made to salvage the Federal Music Project for North Carolina and thus save the orchestra, but this was unsuccessful and the NCS collapsed. In this remarkable though relatively brief experiment, Stringfield and Pratt had assembled an orchestra that gave more than 180 concerts before over 100,000 people throughout the state.

The man who led the attempt to revive the orchestra in 1937 and who was successful in those efforts in 1939 was Dr. Benjamin F. Swalin. Born in Minneapolis in 1901, he joined the Minneapolis Symphony Orchestra* when he finished high school, playing with this group at intervals until he was graduated from Columbia University in 1928. After further study in New York, he received his Ph.D. from the University of Vienna and later became associate professor of Music at the University of North Carolina. In 1939 he, Mrs. Swalin, Pratt, and playwright Paul Green raised enough money to form a new orchestra. They retained the original name and revived the lapsed charter. Under this reorganization Pratt was reappointed president of the Society, Swalin was appointed director, and (according to the North Carolina Symphony Society Papers) a new personnel system was implemented in which "small units of players were organized in each city of the state where musicians of sufficient talent were in residence." The first performance by the reorganized orchestra was on March 16, 1940, in Jones Auditorium on the campus of Meredith College in Raleigh.

From this point forward to Swalin's retirement in 1972, the history of the NCS is "the story of the indomitable spirit and vision of Benjamin Swalin" (NCSS Papers). For the first six years he drew no salary from the orchestra and lived instead on his income as a professor. Working without administrative or clerical help, the Swalins handled everything.

In 1942 the NCSS itself reorganized, this time on a cooperative and truly statewide basis. Committees formed local chapters to finance performances, the orchestra reciprocating with free children's concerts. Swalin's suggestion to Governor J. Melville Broughton led to Senate Bill No. 248, the "Horn Tootin' Bill," whose approval (on March 8, 1943) marked the first time in America that an orchestra was recognized as a state agency and placed under state patronage as an educational institution.

Upon Swalin's retirement in 1972, John Gosling was appointed music director. Under his leadership, the orchestra gave greater emphasis to fundraising, expanded its seasons, added musicians, upgraded its artistic standards, and otherwise embarked on a major period of growth that led to concerts in New York, Washington, and Chicago and to greater concentration on evening programs for paying subscribers within the state. The orchestra relocated to Raleigh from Chapel Hill (Swalin's home), established itself in Memorial Auditorium, and built up its administrative staff.

Gosling's departure at the end of the 1979–1980 season obliged the orchestra to undertake a lengthy search for a replacement. Meanwhile, Lawrence Leighton Smith was engaged as principal guest conductor for 1980–1981 and then Patrick J. Flynn as principal guest conductor for 1981–1982. A strike during this period hurt the orchestra; contributions dwindled, audience support waned, and there were serious questions of whether or not the orchestra would survive to celebrate its 50th anniversary. As a result, there was great political pressure to end the conductor search and to engage an artistic director acceptable to all concerned—including the musicians, whose "mutual agreement" clause allowed them a voice in the selection of their director. Gerhardt Zimmermann was thus appointed music director effective with the 1982–1983 season. Under Zimmerman, big romantic scores from Central Europe have dominated the evening progams, with some excursions into the twentieth century; there is little Haydn or Mozart, almost no French music, and virtually nothing from the baroque. His contract was renewed in 1983 for two additional years. The start of his second season was delayed as a result of contract negotiations with the musicians; as of 1984, relations among the Board, conductor, and orchestra, while outwardly calm, were tenuous.

The NCS is governed by a 34-member Board of Trustees of whom four are appointed by the governor; in addition, a number of state leaders serve in ex-officio capacities, and there are several lifetime and honorary trustees. An Executive Committee makes most of the governing decisions. There is a permanent, paid administrative staff of 13, including an executive director.

NCS concerts have been recorded with regularity by local public radio stations for many years, but broadcasts of the programs have been somewhat sporadic.

CHRONOLOGY OF MUSIC DIRECTORS: Lamar Stringfield, 1932–1935. (Operations suspended, 1935–1939.) Benjamin F. Swalin, 1939–1972. John Gosling, 1972–1980. Lawrence Leighton Smith (Principal Guest Conductor), 1980–1981. Patrick J. Flynn (Principal Guest Conductor), 1981–1982. Gerhardt Zimmermann, 1982-present.

BIBLIOGRAPHY: Lucile K. Byden, "North Carolina's State Symphony," *State Government*, Feb. 1948. Adeline McCall, *Music in America* (Chapel Hill: University of North Carolina Extension Publication X, May 1944). Adeline McCall, "North Carolina Brings Music to Its Children," *Parents Magazine*, March 1946. Adeline McCall, "Symphony Stories" (Chapel Hill: Children's Concert Division, North Carolina Symphony, Spring 1954. etc.). "Music in North Carolina," *InternationalMusician*, Feb. 1954. "Music on the Move," *The Lamp*, Mar. 1953. North Carolina State Archives (Raleigh), "North Carolina Symphony Society, Inc., Papers." "North Carolina Symphony Pioneers in State-Wide Music Appreciation," *Musical America*, 15 Jan. 1948. Howard Turner Pearsall, "The North Carolina Symphony Orchestra from 1932 to 1962," Diss., Indiana University, 1969. John N. Popham, "Suitcase Symphony," *New York Times*, 15 Apr. 1951. Howard Rambeau, "N. C. Orchestra," *The State*, 23 Dec. 1944. Duncan Scott, "The Classics Hit the Road," *New Republic*, 25 Aug. 1947. Madeline Southerland, "North Carolina Symphony," *The State*, 12 Nov. 1949. "Symphony Marks 30th Anniversary," *Chapel Hill Weekly*, 14 Sept. 1961. "Symphony on Wheels," *Pathfinder News Magazine* 31 May 1950.

ACCESS: North Carolina Symphony, P. O. Box 28026, Raleigh, NC 27611. (919) 733–2750. Dr. Banks C. Talley, Jr., Executive Director. Dixie B. O'Connor, Director of Public Relations.

JOHN W. LAMBERT

WINSTON-SALEM (724,129—Greensboro/Winston-Salem/High Point)

Winston-Salem Symphony Orchestra (Mt)

Within 30 miles of each other, Winston-Salem and Greensboro each support an ASOL Metropolitan orchestra with a separate audience, but with considerable overlapping of musical personnel between the two ensembles.

The annual performance schedule of the Winston-Salem Symphony is extremely diverse. Most of its performances are presented in the Joan Hanes Theatre of the beautifully refurbished Roger Stephens Center for the Performing Arts in downtown Winston-Salem. The subscription concerts range from seven pairs of concerts in the Classical Series to three Sunday Afternoon at the Pops concerts. Also included are four outdoor summer concerts at a local park and four Concerts for Kids with such guests as Bob McGrath and the Pickwick Puppet Theatre. In addition, the Winston-Salem Symphony serves as the orchestra for the productions of the Piedmont Opera Company. During the Christmas season, the Symphony accompanies performances of the *Nutcracker* ballet, co-sponsored by the Dance School of the North Carolina School of the Arts. The Symphony presents approximately 85 ensemble programs and two full-orchestra concerts for sixth graders in the Winston-Salem/Forsythe County Schools each year.

Founded in the 1940s, the Winston-Salem Symphony Orchestra began as a community ensemble and eventually became associated with Salem College. Rehearsals took place on the Salem campus, and the conductor, James Lerch, was a music professor at the college. The orchestra's first concert was played to a full house in Memorial Hall on the Salem campus on March 19, 1947, with 39 musicians. Incorporated in 1952 as a non-profit organization, its first professional conductor was Henry Sopkin, conductor of the Atlanta Symphony Orchestra.* After one year, Sopkin recommended that John Iuele, first trumpet and assistant conductor of the Atlanta Symphony, be appointed conductor on a commuting basis; Iuele became the resident conductor in 1955 and remained with the orchestra until 1978.

With a current operating budget of more than $600,000, the Winston-Salem Symphony employs 80 musicians, one conductor, and an administrative staff of six. The orchestra is governed by a 37-member Board of Directors and has a full-time general manager and an operations manager. It receives 21% of its income from the Arts Council, Inc. More than one-third of the principal chairs in the orchestra are corporately or individually endowed. The remainder of its funding comes from earned income, federal and state grants, foundation grants, and private donors.

The current music director, Peter Perret, has the sole responsibility for programming. His programs tend to be fairly traditional, consisting primarily of nineteenth-century orchestral repertoire. One of the interesting aspects of the Winston-Salem Symphony's programs is that it uses principal players, most of whom teach at the North Carolina School of the Arts, as soloists. In addition, there are other distinguished guest artists who perform as soloists.

The Winston-Salem Symphony Guild is a support group primarily responsible for raising funds, selling tickets, and conducting a music education program in the local schools. It is partially through the efforts of the Guild that the Symphony has performed to sold-out houses in recent years. In

1984, the Winston-Salem Symphony Guild collaborated with the Greensboro Symphony Guild in the first televised Triad Symphony Auction; another joint effort is planned for August of 1985.

CHRONOLOGY OF MUSIC DIRECTORS: James Lerch, 1946–1951. Henry Sopkin, 1951–1952. John Iuele, 1952–1978. (Guest conductors, 1978–1979.) Peter Perret, 1979-present.

BIBLIOGRAPHY: Interview with Winston-Salem Symphony General Manager Perry Mixter. Winston-Salem Symphony Orchestra Programs, 1981–1985.

ACCESS: Winston-Salem Symphony Orchestra, 610 Coliseum Drive, Winston-Salem, NC 27106. (919) 725–1035. Perry Mixter, General Manager.

RONALD A. CRUTCHER

North Dakota ――――――――

FARGO (137,574—Fargo, N.D./Moorhead, Minn.)

Fargo-Moorhead Symphony Orchestra (Ur)

Fargo, the largest metropolitan area in North Dakota, is located on the eastern border and is a twin city with Moorhead, Minnesota. The combined communities support a private college, two state universities, the Fargo-Moorhead Symphony, a civic opera, community theater, and two professional dance companies.

After two short-lived earlier attempts to establish a symphony orchestra, the Fargo Civic Orchestra was founded in 1931 with Harry M. Rudd as conductor. Featured on the orchestra's premiere concert was a contemporary work by Eric Coates—and thus the Symphony's commitment to new music was cast. Rudd resigned in 1937, and Sigvald Thompson, who had earlier been principal cellist, assumed the position of music director. That same year the orchestra changed its name to the Fargo-Moorhead Civic Orchestra. Thompson, leading the orchestra from a small struggling civic group to regional prominence as a cultural resource, continued as conductor until 1974. In 1950 the name of the orchestra was changed to the Fargo-Moorhead Symphony Orchestra.

Strong community support through memberships, donations, and government grants allowed the orchestra to present concerts without admission charge until 1980. The Symphony presently has a subscription series with five full-orchestra and two chamber-orchestra performances. Ticket costs range from $2.00 for rush student tickets to $10.00 for reserved seating. The full performances regularly feature professional soloists, including in recent years Janos Starker, Jeffery Seigel, Barry Tuckwell, and guest conductors Karel Husa and Gunther Schuller.

The Symphony has promoted new music actively since its beginning, by encouraging local composers through commissioning new works (since 1960), and by sponsoring the Sigvald Thompson Composition Competition, which started in 1967. Commissions have been extended to numerous composers, including Peter Schickle, Gunther Schuller, and Dominick Argento. In 1976, 1977, 1981, and 1982 the orchestra received awards from ASCAP for adventuresome programming of contemporary literature.

The Symphony presents full-orchestra performances in the Concordia College Memorial Auditorium to an audience averaging 1,400 persons. Chamber concerts are presented at North Dakota State University's 997-seat Reinke Auditorium and on occasion in local churches. Performances are later broadcast over two local NPR stations. The orchestra schedules a series of performances in the public schools of Fargo-Moorhead and an annual children's concert as part of its commitment to music education in the community.

The orchestra is governed by a 26-member Orchestra Association Board including three orchestra members elected by that ensemble. Board members serve a three-year term, which may be renewed for a second consecutive term. A committee of Board members prepares a roster of candidates to fill vacancies, and the entire Board elects new members. A business manager is responsible for administrative, promotional, and production details, while the conductor makes artistic and programming decisions. The orchestra's budget, in excess of $200,000, includes funding from the North Dakota Council on the Arts, the Minnesota State Arts Board, the NEA, Local 382 of the American Federation of Musicians, Performance Trust Funds, and numerous private groups. Approximately 20% of the budget comes from contributions, 20% from a local coordinated Arts Fund Drive, 25% from public and private grants, 10% from subscription series, and the remainder from the Women's Association and miscellaneous special funds.

The Fargo-Moorhead Symphony Orchestra is proud of the continuity of membership and leadership that has provided stability and direction for the ensemble. Numerous family teams (spouses and children) have participated, and many community members have played for more than 20 years. The orchestra has had only three resident conductors in its history; the first business manager served from 1952 to 1967, and the second from 1967 to 1984. Presently, approximately 50% of the orchestra's members are professional musicians, 30% are students, and 20% are community members.

CHRONOLOGY OF MUSIC DIRECTORS: Harry M. Rudd, 1931–1937. Sigvald Thompson, 1937–1974. J. Robert Hanson, 1974-present.

BIBLIOGRAPHY: *Reflections in Gold* (Fargo-Moorhead Symphony Board, 1981). Lois Vogel, "The Fargo-Moorhead Symphony Orchestra, 1931–1981: A Brief History," printed in five segments in the 1980–1981 Symphony Programs.

ACCESS: Fargo-Moorhead Symphony Orchestra, P.O. Box 1753, Fargo, ND 58107. (218) 233–8397. Alice Ackerman, Manager.

ROBERT R. PATTENGALE

Ohio _____

AKRON (660,328)

Akron Symphony Orchestra (Mt)

The 90-member Akron Symphony Orchestra (1984–1985 budget $513,000) was begun from the dream in 1949 of John Barry, then business manager of the Akron *Beacon-Journal*. Barry told civic leader Mabel Graham that Akron needed a symphony and that she was the only one who could get the job done. He gave her $500 to help start the project. For two years Graham worked with community leaders to organize the parent group (the Greater Akron Musical Association, whose Board of Trustees governs the affairs of the organization under state charter), to raise funds and select a conductor to establish the new orchestra.

On February 24, 1953, John F. Farinacci, one of Akron's public school band directors, led the inaugural concert at Central High School auditorium. From 1954 to 1959, Laszlo Krausz, then principal violist of the Cleveland Orchestra* served as conductor. In 1959, the selection of Louis Lane (then assistant conductor of the Cleveland Orchestra) began a period of increasing skill, audience building, and financial support that continued through his 24-year tenure. Current music director/conductor Alan Balter assumed leadership in 1983.

The orchestra offers a seven-concert season plus a holiday concert, a series of Summer Concerts-in-the-Parks, four Young People's Concerts (for grades 3 to 6) and 10 Tiny Tots Concerts (for ages 3 to 6). In its present home in the beautiful E. J. Thomas Performing Arts Hall, a $14 million auditorium built in 1972–1973 on the campus of the University of Akron, the October-through-April concerts draw an average audience of about 2,500 per concert from all segments of the community. A much wider audience is reached through the rebroadcasts of concerts throughout north-eastern Ohio over WKSU-FM (a NPR affiliate station of Kent State University). Additional public service results from video tapes of selected concerts, which are available for public school use.

Symphony musicians are drawn largely from professionals in the greater Akron area, with first-chair players principally music faculty of the University of Akron, Kent State University, and other local area colleges. The orchestra is fully unionized through Local 24, AFM.

A professional staff was established gradually in the 1960s as demands on volunteers became excessive because of the orchestra's growth and out-reach. This greatly enhanced the effectiveness of the organization's opera-tions and sophistication. Funding in the 1983–1984 season drew about 7% from state and national endowments, about 22% from local foundations, and the remainder from ticket sales, private campaigns, and private bequests.

The Greater Akron Musical Association also supports a Youth Orchestra (founded in 1945 by Krausz and since directed by various Akron Symphony concertmasters and other Symphony members such as its current director, violist Marge Henke). Several of its past members have since assumed po-sitions in leading orchestras of the nation.

A Symphony chorus was established in 1957 to perform with the Sym-phony two or three times each year. Its directors have included founder Lenough Anderson (1957–1962), John MacDonald (1962–1982), Kerry Woodward (1982–1983), and Kellie Curtis (1983-present). Its auditioned personnel form a skilled ensemble of 140 members who were invited from 1968 to 1974 to help establish the Cleveland Orchestra's Blossom Festival after the Blossom Music Center was opened in 1968.

The main repertoire of the Symphony and its chorus derives from major works of the seventeenth through the twentieth centuries, newly edited old music, and several commissioned works or world premieres by con-temporary composers such as Carlos Chavez, David Bernstein, and Roger Zahab, among others. Twentieth-century works comprise between 5% and 10% of the orchestra's repertoire. In 1979, the Symphony won an ASCAP Award for adventuresome overall programming of contemporary music. The philosophy of program selection is fundamentally to provide a well-rounded grouping of styles and period representatives. Works indicative of the Sym-phony's capacity in recent years include Strauss's *Ein Heldenleben*, Bartók's Concerto for Orchestra, and Gunther Schuller's *Seven Studies on Themes of Paul Klee*.

Close ties between the Symphony and music faculty of both the University of Akron and Kent State University have been of mutual benefit since the 1960s. A more studied effort to involve the Symphony in faculty searches for the University of Akron's Music Department began in 1976 and has had a marked effect in the improvement of the standards of musical profession-alism in both organizations. Community outreach through small ensembles of the Symphony membership is achieved through the aegis of the University of Akron and Kent State, owing to greater ease of administration in their on-going programs of many years.

CHRONOLOGY OF MUSIC DIRECTORS: John F. Farinacci 1952–1954. Laszlo Krausz, 1954–1959. Louis Lane, 1959–1983. Alan Balter, 1983-present.

BIBLIOGRAPHY: Interview with Robert Henke, Akron Symphony General Manager, 1984.

ACCESS: Akron Symphony Orchestra, E. J. Hall Performing Arts Hall, University of Akron, Akron, OH 44325. (216) 535–8131. Robert Henke, General Manager.

JOHN A. MACDONALD

CANTON (404,421)

Canton Symphony Orchestra (Mt)

The Canton Symphony Orchestra Association was founded as a joint effort between the Canton Junior Chamber of Commerce and a Symphony Committee made up of symphonic music enthusiasts. Although various orchestras known as the "Canton Symphony" had existed in the city as early as 1903, the Canton Symphony Orchestra Association was not begun until 1937; it was incorporated in 1938. Richard Oppenheim of Mount Union College in nearby Alliance, Ohio, was invited to form the new orchestra, which he did by holding an audition/rehearsal and selecting 70 musicians as orchestra members. The first performance was presented on February 16, 1938.

During its first 11 years the Canton Symphony performed four annual concerts, mainly featuring local artists. On the death of Richard Oppenheim in 1948 the Symphony faced both a financial and artistic crisis. While a new music director was being sought, the *Canton Economist* editorialized, "Save the Symphony," and a *Canton Repository* editorial on March 11, 1949, stated, "Canton doesn't want its orchestra to fold up for lack of funds.... It regards the orchestra as a real civic asset."

The financial challenge was met by Board action, to, as the *Economist* put it, "enlarge itself... to seek more contributions from industrial and business firms as well as from individual patrons." The artistic challenge was met by engaging Louis Lane, then apprentice conductor of the Cleveland Orchestra,* as music director. This began a 28-year relationship with the Cleveland Orchestra in which a member of its conducting staff was engaged as CSO music director, a practice that continued until the Cleveland Orchestra restructured its conducting staff after George Szell's death. On Michael Charry's resignation as music director in 1973, no CO conductor was available as a replacement, which forced the CSO to face the future independently of its long-standing tie to Cleveland.

Following a two-year period with Robert Marcellus as music director, the CSO engaged Thomas Michalak, Exxon Arts Endowment Conductor with the Pittsburgh Symphony,* as music director. Michalak made numerous changes in orchestra personnel that, although causing unrest among the musicians, significantly enhanced the quality of the orchestra. Gerhardt Zimmermann, then associate conductor of the St. Louis Symphony,* succeeded Michalak in 1980. Zimmermann continued to enhance the quality of the orchestra both through the calibre of personnel and through selection of guest artists of major stature to the point where "some area musicians rank the Canton Symphony second only to the Cleveland Orchestra in this part of the state" (*Northern Ohio Live*, Dec. 1983).

The full Canton Symphony Orchestra (80 members) performs seven pairs of subscription concerts, eight young people's concerts, and two family concerts at William E. Umstattd Performing Arts Hall, a 1,490-seat auditorium owned by the Board of Education of the Canton City Schools. The hall was constructed in 1976; through development efforts of the CSO trustees, over $600,000 was raised to enhance acoustics and provide more sophisticated stage equipment. Two chamber orchestra concerts, nine concerts for pre-school children, and two outdoor concerts are performed at various other locations throughout the city.

In addition to its orchestral performances reaching an annual audience of 65,000, the CSO has an extensive ensemble program comprising a string quartet, brass quintet, and woodwind quintet, which present 275 performances to 22,500 people annually. String quartet members are salaried; other ensemble and orchestra members are compensated on a per-service basis; all are members of the AFM. The orchestra is unusual in the youth of its members; in addition to residents of Greater Canton, students from the Cleveland Institute of Music, Pittsburgh, Cincinnati, and the Eastman School of Music in Rochester, New York, are contracted orchestra members.

The CSO is governed by a 50-member Board of Trustees. The music director has final decision concerning programming, guest artists, and seating, although programming is discussed with a Music Advisory Committee of the Board. Gerhardt Zimmermann's conviction that American orchestras have a responsibility to American artists and composers is reflected in the practice of opening each season with an American work and including contemporary American compositions and American guest artists each year. Programming also reflects the desire to provide the musicians with the opportunity to expand their knowledge of the full range of symphonic repertoire.

The Canton Symphony's 1983–1984 budget was $515,000. The orchestra is the largest and only fully professional member of the six groups comprising Canton's United Arts Fund. Although the United Arts Drive provides 21.5% of the orchestra's annual income, it places stringent restrictions on the CSO's fund-raising efforts within Stark County. Government funding sources include the NEA, the Ohio Arts Council, the city of Canton, and the Stark County Commissioners.

CHRONOLOGY OF MUSIC DIRECTORS: Richard Oppenheim, 1938–1948. Louis Lane, 1949–1959. Michael Charry, 1960–1974. Robert Marcellus (Music Advisor), 1974–1976. Thomas Michalak, 1976–1980. Gerhardt Zimmermann, 1980-present.

BIBLIOGRAPHY: "Canton's Symphony Orchestra," *Canton Repository*, 11 Mar. 1949. "Classical Music: The Young Maestros," *Northern Ohio Live*, Dec. 1983. "Save the Symphony," *Canton Economist*, 8 March 1949. "Tireless Effort is Key to Symphony Orchestra's Rise Here in 13 Years," *Canton Repository*, 12 Mar. 1950.

ACCESS: Canton Symphony Orchestra Association, 1001 Market Avenue North, Canton, OH 44702. (216) 452–3434. Linda V. Moorhouse, General Manager.

LINDA V. MOORHOUSE

CINCINNATI (1,401,491)

Cincinnati Symphony Orchestra (Mj)

The Cincinnati Symphony Orchestra, founded in 1894, is among the oldest in the country. The CSO's permanent headquarters is Music Hall, built in 1878; a registered historic landmark, its over-3,600-seat capacity makes it the largest hall regularly used by a Major American orchestra. The open-air J. Ralph Corbett Pavilion of the Hulbert Taft, Jr., Center for the Performing Arts or "Riverbend," opened in the summer of 1984, is the orchestra's summer home. The original 10 pairs of subscription concerts in 1895–1896 has grown to the present 24 pairs. Annual regional or eastern tours were begun in the 1897–1898 season. Regular pops concerts, among the first given by a major orchestra, were added in 1910–1911 and young people's concerts in 1919–1920. In 1917 the CSO made its first phonograph recordings and in 1921 its first live radio broadcast. In the summer of 1966 it was the first American orchestra to make an around-the-world tour, and in February 1984 it broadcast a concert direct to Europe via satellite.

The CSO is probably unusual among major orchestras in having been founded by a women's organization. The original Board of Trustees was also composed exclusively of women, with men serving only on an Advisory Board, until the situation was reversed in 1929. In 1936 a Women's Committee was formed to assist in fund-raising and ticket sales, which it continues to do. The administration of the CSO is presided over by the general manager, whose staff comprises four departments, Operations, Development, Financial, and Marketing. The players, who belong to Local One of the American Federation of Musicians, deal with management through two orchestral committees, one in contractual matters and one in noncontractual ones. Players also serve on audition committees.

Although the orchestra was generously supported by benefactors from the beginning, it moved to firmer footing when its ownership passed in

1927 to the newly incorporated Cincinnati Fine Arts Institute. A permanent endowment fund was established the following year by the gift of $1 million by the Charles P. Tafts and the raising of $2.7 million by public subscription. Cincinnatians still help maintain the CSO through the Fine Arts Fund (established in 1949), a united effort that benefits all of the city's major cultural institutions. The orchestra's current budget of approximately $10 million is also supported by city and county funds, local business sponsorship, the Frank Van der Stucken Society (a "friends of the orchestra" organization), and Ohio Arts Council and NEA grants.

The CSO performs between 240 and 280 concerts a year, including those played by fewer than the full complement of players. "Symphony Week," a week of free outdoor concerts on downtown Fountain Square, launches the season every September. Of the subscription concerts, Music Director Michael Gielen conducts 14 pairs, with the remainder divided between guest conductors and Associate Conductor Bernard Rubenstein. (There is also an assistant conductor, who holds solely a training and covering position.) All subscription concerts are rebroadcast over WGUC, a local FM radio station. The orchestra also plays a series of 13 concerts under the name Cincinnati Pops Orchestra (officially established in 1977), conducted by Erich Kunzel. Educational concerts are given during the season: Junior High (grades seven to nine) and young people's (grades three to six) concerts are played in the Music Hall, and the orchestra divides into thirds to play "Lollipop" concerts (for those ages four to eight) elsewhere in the community. Since 1969–1970 the CSO has presented, along with other local performers and ensembles, the Area Artist Series, in which in-school and evening concerts are given in smaller communities within a 150-mile radius. There is also an eastern tour nearly every season as well as runouts and special concerts. In summers there is a concert season at Riverbend in addition to a series of free concerts in city parks. The summer Mini Festival Series also takes the orchestra, divided into halves, to communities within the region for light outdoor afternoon or evening concerts. Finally, the CSO serves as the official orchestra of the annual May Festival, the Cincinnati Opera Company, and the Cincinnati Ballet Company's annual holiday performances of the *Nutcracker*.

With the coming of Michael Gielen in 1980, the proportion of twentieth-century music in subscription concerts notably increased, most dramatically in his first two seasons and thereafter somewhat less so. He continues to believe, however, that music of our time must be heard along with the classics, and his programming clearly reflects this conviction. His own greatest affinity is for the Viennese romantics and moderns, tastes that date from his boyhood in Germany. A special feature of some concerts is the confrontation of old and new music, in which standard and contemporary works are juxtaposed in order to point up similarities or parallels; one such program featured movements of Schubert's *Rosamunde* music alternating with

Webern's *Six Pieces*. Gielen's interpretive approach tends toward crisp tempos and is never sentimental or overtly romantic. His main goals are flexibility and versatility. Rather than there being an identifiable CSO sound, the orchestra must be able to vary its sonority to suit works of different historical periods and styles.

Cincinnati, the "Queen of the West," had by the mid-nineteenth century become the fifth largest city in the country and the chief commercial center west of the Alleghenies. In the 1860s, however, it declined in commerce, population, and prestige, triggering an upsurge of civic pride and development in the next decades. In addition to the building of many important institutions and landmarks during this period, considerable progress was made in the musical life of the city. Attempts had already been made to found resident orchestras, chiefly the Cincinnati Philharmonic Orchestra (1856–1859) and the Carl Barus Orchestra (1866–1869), but the most significant impetus to the city's interest in orchestral music in the 1870s and 1880s was without doubt the frequent visits of the Theodore Thomas Orchestra. Close ties between Thomas and the city's music sprang up; he also conducted the then biennial May Festival from its origin in 1873 to 1904. The persistent desire for a resident orchestra was satisfied only to a degree by the Cincinnati Grand Orchestra, which emphasized pops concerts in its checkered career from 1872 through the 1880s, and by another Philharmonic Orchestra, which lasted only from 1884 to 1889.

Thus in the early 1890s, in spite of hopes and efforts, the Queen City was still without a permanent symphony orchestra. The Ladies' Musical Club, organized in 1891, decided in 1894 to establish one, using the Grand Orchestra players as a nucleus. The necessary $15,000 was raised, and in the following year, 1895, the 48-man Cincinnati Symphony Orchestra was a reality. Frank Van der Stucken, a European-trained American, was chosen as the first music director. After the 1895–1896 season in Pike's Opera House, the concerts were moved to the newly rebuilt Music Hall. Van der Stucken's programs leaned toward such moderns as Wagner, Strauss, Tchaikovsky, and even Americans, and his interpretations were often untraditional, but he was popular with audiences and demanding with his players. The CSO was at first the only orchestra west of the Appalachians besides the Chicago Symphony* to give regular concert seasons. After growing in 1897–1898 to 70 players, the number fell to 60, and by 1907 uncompromising union demands, a $10,000 deficit, and Van der Stucken's resignation dealt a triple blow to the organization, which had to be disbanded until further notice.

Plans for the reconstruction of the orchestra were begun by the Board soon thereafter. By 1909 it had raised a five-year guaranty fund of $50,000 a year and managed to resolve the dispute between union and management. It hired a new music director, Leopold Stokowski, 27 years old, unknown, and inexperienced, but obviously gifted and actively seeking the position.

As the youngest conductor of a major U.S. orchestra, he quickly overcame his limitations, and the CSO, now grown to 77, went from success to success. Stokowski instituted regular pops concerts and experimented with different orchestral seating arrangements. His flamboyancy and unorthodoxy of inter-pretation were already beginning to manifest themselves. Then, early in 1912, just after a move from Music Hall to the new, more intimate Emery Auditorium, he broke his contract and resigned. Despite protestations from orchestra, critics, and community alike, he was determined to leave and did so at the conclusion of the season, amidst general bitterness and disap-pointment; the following season he was engaged by the Philadelphia Orchestra.*

An Austrian conductor, Dr. Ernst Kunwald, was promptly contacted and hired for the following season. A specialist in the German repertoire, con-ducting from memory, he quickly won Cincinnati over with his straight-forward, unaffected, uncontroversial style. Beginning in 1914, the now 83-piece CSO was appointed May Festival Orchestra, and in 1917 it went on its first East Coast tour. When the United States declared war on Germany in April 1917, Kunwald's position was at first little affected, but he, like the Boston Symphony's* Karl Muck, did not escape the increasingly bitter war-time hatred of Germans. When war was declared on Austria-Hungary in December of the same year, he was immediately arrested and imprisoned for alleged unpatriotic remarks and was later deported. The remainder of the CSO's season was divided between guest conductors.

One of them, the Belgian violinist Eugène Ysaÿe, was hired as the new music director. In his four seasons Ysaÿe was extremely popular; in addition to his musical credentials, he was, as a war refugee, a romantic patriotic symbol. His conducting, emotional and spontaneous, never failed to elicit an enthusiastic response, although orchestral discipline was far from what it had been under Kunwald. Ysaÿe's programming was varied, but empha-sized the French School over the German, in keeping with his political sentiments. The orchestra, now numbering 90 players, made notable achievements during his tenure, expanding both home seasons and tours. A summer orchestra, drawn from the main one, began annual festivals (1919) and opera seasons at the zoo (1921). Ysaÿe's unwillingness to keep up the hectic pace of the position, however, led to his subsequent resignation at the end of the 1921–1922 season.

His replacement was the 33-year-old Fritz Reiner, who, already known in Europe, had not yet been to the United States. Reiner came with the aim of making the CSO one of the premier orchestras in the country, and to this end he quickly established high standards and stern discipline. Whole-sale changes in personnel were made (the CSO's first woman player, a violinist, was hired during his tenure). He brought the orchestra to the highest level of accomplishment in its history; it was not long before it was regarded as one of perhaps the top five orchestras in the country. His programming, strongly Germanic, included frequent doses of such moderns as Stravinsky, Bartók, and Hindemith, which were consistently greeted with hostility. But this was no deterrent to Reiner's popularity, which only increased with the growing prestige of the orchestra. At the peak of his success, however, early in 1930, his precipitous divorce and remarriage shocked many in the community and caused some decrease in ticket sales, so the Board chose not to renew his appointment. The Englishman Eugene Goossens was engaged that summer for the 1931–1932 season, but the news of Reiner's departure was kept from the public until December 1930, when it came as a bombshell.

Goossens's arrival in Cincinnati began the longest conductorship in CSO history, lasting until 1947. His courtesy and civility were a welcome relief to the players after the rigors of Reiner's discipline. Goossens's style was restrained, meticulous, and unsensational. His versatility was evidenced in the eclecticism of his programming, which placed almost as much emphasis on the moderns as Reiner had done—and more on American works—but added selections from the ballet repertoire and featured occasional troupes of dancers. For the first time both the regular season and the May Festival were consistently unified under the leadership of one permanent conductor. Both managed to keep going through the depression and World War II, which necessitated the substitution of local music students for players serving in the armed forces. Because of increased ticket sales, in 1937 the orchestra moved back to Music Hall, which has remained its home ever since. The CSO's Golden Jubilee was celebrated throughout the 1944–1945 season.

Goossens's successor was a young American, Thor Johnson, who in his eleven seasons in Cincinnati continued to emphasize both contemporary and American music in his otherwise standard programming—he commissioned 60 works and premiered 60 others. He instituted a series of neighborhood family concerts given throughout the city and significantly increased the number of young people's concerts. His leadership, however, seems not to have had the distinction of that of Goossens or Reiner.

Max Rudolf came from his position at the Metropolitan Opera to take over the leadership of the CSO in the 1958–1959 season. During his 11-year tenure, the orchestra rose again to prominence. The membership grew to 95, the number of subscription concerts was increased from 22 to 24, and two new series—summer Concerts in the Park and Area Artists Concerts—were begun. The most notable event of Rudolf's tenure, however, was the U.S. State Department-sponsored world tour in the summer of 1966, which comprised 42 concerts in 15 countries over a 10-week period and brought the CSO international acclaim. He also took the orchestra on a four-week European tour in 1969. Throughout the Rudolf years the programming carried on the tradition of judiciously featuring contemporary works. In both 1965 and 1966 a Rockefeller Foundation grant made possible the presentation of a week-long Exposition of American Contemporary Music. Rudolf resigned at the close of the 1968–1969 season because of poor health and was named Music Director Emeritus. Erich Kunzel, then associate conductor, was named resident conductor for the next season, in which Rudolf returned for two pairs of concerts. The city's affection for him has been evident at each of his guest appearances since then, most notably at the opening concert of the 1984 May Festival.

The 40-year-old American conductor Thomas Schippers began his tenure as CSO music director in the 1970–1971 season, which was the first to take place in a newly refurbished Music Hall. Schippers brought youthful exuberance, even glamour, to the position. Audiences loved his romantic, uninhibited style of conducting. In his programming, the more forbidding moderns such as the serialists were held to a bare minimum in favor of the standard repertoire and conservative contemporary music, with novelties coming most often from the romantic era. There were a few unorthodox touches, such as concert versions of operas, the featuring of dancers, and the occasional inclusion of chamber music. The orchestra's activities expanded to include summer Mini Festivals and Symphony Week. Schippers's untimely illness and death in 1977 necessitated dividing the remainder of the season between two guest conductors, one of whom, Walter Susskind, was appointed music advisor for the next two seasons.

During the 1978–1979 season Michael Gielen was named music director. He was also artistic director of the Frankfurt Opera. He conducted two pairs of concerts in Cincinnati in 1979–1980 and began his permanent position in 1980–1981. He will step down in 1986, at the end of his current contract, in order to divide his time between Frankfurt and a new position, the conductorship of the Southwest German Radio Orchestra.

RECORDING HISTORY AND SELECTIVE DISCOGRAPHY: The first four recordings of the CSO, under Kunwald, were made by Columbia and released in May and July of 1917; the next ones, under Ysaÿe, appeared in 1920–1921. Under Goossens the orchestra recorded for RCA Victor (1941–1946); under Johnson, Rudolf, and Kunzel, chiefly for Decca (1951–1971); and thereafter, under Schippers, Susskind, and Kunzel, for Turnabout, Vox, and other labels. Current recording contracts are with Vox and Telarc (Gielen and Kunzel).

Berg, Lulu Suite and Lyric Suite (Kathleen Battle/Gielen): Vox Cum Laude 9042. Lutoslawski, Double Concerto for Oboe and Harp; Strauss, Oboe Concerto (Heinz Holliger, Ursula Holliger/Gielen): Vox Cum Laude 9064. Rossini, *Stabat Mater* (Schippers): Turnabout 34634. Schubert, Symphony No. 9 (Schippers): Turnabout 34681. Tchaikovsky, *Capriccio Italien* and *1812* Overture (Kunzel): Telarc 10041.

CHRONOLOGY OF MUSIC DIRECTORS: Frank Van der Stucken, 1895–1907. (Disbanded, 1907–1909.) Leopold Stokowski, 1909–1912. Ernst Kunwald, 1912–1918. Eugène Ysaÿe, 1918-1922. Fritz Reiner, 1922-1931. Eugene Goossens, 1931–1947. Thor Johnson, 1947–1958. Max Rudolf, 1958–1969. Erich Kunzel (Resident Conductor), 1969–1970. Thomas Schippers, 1970–1977. Carmon DeLeone (Resident

Conductor), 1977–1978. Walter Susskind (Music Advisor), 1978–1980. Michael Gielen, 1980–1986.

BIBLIOGRAPHY: James Chute, "Progressive Programming in the Queen City," *Symphony Magazine*, June/July 1982. *Cincinnati Symphony Orchestra: A Tribute to Max Rudolf and Highlights of Its History* (Cincinnati: Cincinnati Symphony Orchestra, 1967). Frederick P. Fellers and Betty Meyers, *Discographies of Commercial Recordings of the Cleveland Orchestra (1924–1977) and the Cincinnati Symphony Orchestra (1917–1977)* (Westport, Conn.: Greenwood Press, 1978). Philip Hart, *Orpheus in the New World* (New York: W. W. Norton, 1973). John H. Mueller, *The American Symphony Orchestra* (1951; reprint, Westport, Conn.: Greenwood Press, 1976). Joseph E. Potts, "The Cincinnati Symphony Orchestra," *The Strad*, July 1966. Henry Swoboda, ed., *The American Symphony Orchestra* (New York: Basic Books, 1967). Louis R. Thomas, "The History of the Cincinnati Symphony Orchestra to 1931," Diss., University of Cincinnati, 1972.

ACCESS: Cincinnati Symphony Orchestra, Music Hall, 1241 Elm Street, Cincinnati, OH 45210. (513) 621–1919. Steven Monder, General Manager.

DONALD H. FOSTER

CLEVELAND (1,898,825)

Cleveland Orchestra (Mj)

For nearly a quarter of a century, the Cleveland Orchestra has for many represented American symphonic music-making at its finest. That an ensemble of such high calibre continues to thrive within their midst is a source of intense pride to Clevelanders, particularly in view of the economic difficulties the city has suffered as the Great Lakes region bowed to the industrialization of the Sunbelt and to other economic pressures.

Ensemble members also take pride in their organization. Several players have attested to an unspoken but nevertheless real and efficient "self-policing" posture that has been extremely important for the sustained maintenance of the group's lofty standards of performance. Unlike some other ensembles, the Cleveland Orchestra will never "sabotage" a guest conductor who fails to win their confidence. Rather, the ensemble has been known to cover readily for both conductors and soloists in public. This quiet self-pride served as one of the orchestra's greatest strengths during the two-year interim (1982–1984 seasons) between the tenures of directors Lorin Maazel and Christoph von Dohnányi, when the orchestra was maintained by a series of guest conductors.

Today the Cleveland Orchestra plays annually to over 10,000 Severance Hall subscribers as well as to many more listeners on tour and at nearly 30 summer programs at Blossom Music Center. Radio broadcasts, a tradition for nearly 20 years, continue throughout North America, Australia, and parts of Europe. Educational concerts, an endeavor the Cleveland Orchestra has long pioneered, continue to attract more than 43,000 children to Severance Hall each year. A docent program provides volunteers who visit school classrooms with 30-minute presentations in order to prepare students for concerts. In the past few years, the educational activities department of the orchestra has added two additional series of programs for children. The "Key" concerts intended for children aged five through nine and held on Saturdays include assorted hands-on musical activities prior to the 50-minute concerts. "Rainbow" programs, added in 1983, bring preschoolers and kindergarteners for 20-minute presentations, often of single instruments.

The orchestra currently operates on a budget exceeding $16 million. Funding is secured through ticket sales, record royalties, tour revenues, broadcasts, endowment monies, and rental of the Severance and Blossom facilities for such events as jazz and rock programs. Grants from government agencies and private foundations continue to be of significant assistance. An annual, three-day fund-raising marathon sponsored by Cleveland's WCLV-FM relies on the assistance of over 300 volunteers who broadcast live each spring from area shopping malls in an effort to broaden the orchestra's base of support through contributions of middle-income individuals. The marathon, imitated recently elsewhere, has provided the orchestra with more than $230,000 in a single year. The radio marathon has also provided the orchestra with extensive publicity. The orchestra's administrative body, the Musical Arts Association of Cleveland, has come to realize the importance of smaller monetary gifts at a time when decreases in government funding have placed progressively heavier burdens on private corporations and foundations.

The Association also acknowledges a commitment toward any efforts that will bring the orchestra to additional segments of the Cleveland community. A survey distributed to patrons at a recent midwinter subscription concert indicated that of 473 respondents, 171 (36%) possessed incomes exceeding $55,000; 229 (nearly 60%) held graduate degrees; and 276 (58%) were 45 years of age or older. Nearly half (220) had subscribed to concerts for over five years. Armed with such knowledge, Kenneth Haas, general manager of the orchestra since 1976, is committed, together with the Musical Arts Association, to the vigorous pursuit of new avenues through which the orchestra can increase its following among the young, members of minority groups, and individuals from lower income levels. The Community Music Project, begun in 1983, has sponsored several programs intended to draw members of Cleveland's sizable black community to Severance Hall. Funded initially through Cleveland and Kulas Foundation grants, the project committee of musicians, clergy, and other community leaders has presented leading black conductors and performers such as Hubert Laws, Isaiah Jackson, and mezzo-soprano Jennifer Jones to enthusiastic audiences.

Not enough time has yet elapsed to determine whether this project and other efforts will be ultimately successful in drawing larger numbers of supporters to the Cleveland Orchestra. Nevertheless, the Musical Arts Association hopes that by eradicating the elitist image of the ensemble, the Cleveland Orchestra will become a cultural resource of personal significance for increasing numbers of citizens.

The founding and development of the Cleveland Orchestra was possible partly because of the city's advantageous location midway on the rail route between New York and Chicago, which permitted Clevelanders to enjoy many of the leading musical superstars of the late nineteenth and early twentieth centuries. In addition, large groups of European immigrants, most notably Germans, Hungarians, and Slavs, promoted their own musical activities within the city, making use of local talents. Numerous attempts were made to establish a symphonic ensemble on behalf of the entire community, but none was permanently successful until the efforts of Adella Prentiss Hughes (1869–1950). A member of one of Cleveland's prominent families, this Vassar graduate was fortunate to possess musical knowledge and sensitivity which, when combined with an indomitable will and strong organizational skills, allowed her to forge various local talents into an orchestra with adequate financial backing to insure long-term survival.

Shortly before the turn of the century, Mrs. Hughes began to establish herself as a sagacious concert promoter and business manager. In 1900 she started what became an annual series of concerts by visiting orchestras, and in 1915 she convinced several area businessmen who had served as guarantors for past events to form the Musical Arts Association of Cleveland. The new association's Board of Directors, with Mrs. Hughes as secretary-treasurer, attempted to coordinate the city's imported musical attractions from a broader base.

By 1918, Hughes had come to feel that the visiting orchestra concerts were no longer sufficient for Cleveland's needs. She became particularly convinced of this after a visit to Cincinnati, where she heard a fine performance by talented high school musicians as well as a children's concert by the Cincinnati Symphony* under their summer conductor, Nikolai Sokoloff. Hughes prevailed upon the Arts Association to hire the youthful Sokoloff to spend a year in Cleveland surveying the town's musical resources in anticipation of developing a strong instrumental music program in the schools and founding a permanent, professional, resident orchestra.

On December 11, 1918, in Gray's Armory, an ensemble of 54 members of the musicians' union made its debut as the Cleveland Orchestra with pieces by Liszt, Bizet, Liadov, Tchaikovsky, and Victor Herbert. The group's first season featured 27 concerts, including performances in nearby Akron, Oberlin, and Pittsburgh. By 1920 the orchestra numbered 85 players, and in 1922 it made its Carnegie Hall debut, receiving positive, if somewhat guarded, reviews. Significantly, female players were included from the outset, an unusual practice in the United States at that time.

By its eighth year, the orchestra's performance season had been extended to 20 weeks. From the start Sokoloff and Hughes sought broadly based support for the orchestra by scheduling concerts for family audiences in various schools and halls throughout Cleveland. Children's concerts were always encouraged, and hundreds of school children studied instruments with orchestra members on Saturdays.

By present-day standards, Sokoloff was probably not a truly great conductor. A violinist who had played under Muck in Boston* at the age of 17, he also spent time observing Nikisch's rehearsals in London. Apparently most comfortable with the late nineteenth-century repertoire, he did little with the classicists and instead stressed Russian and French works. His interpretations were subjective and not suited to the analytical and more objective conceptions that became the hallmark of Toscanini and many others. Much contemporary music failed to interest him. He did attempt to support the efforts of certain American composers, although some of his choices here were, in retrospect, unwise. In fairness to Sokoloff it must be said that he was forced to contend with a public whose musical tastes were extremely circumscribed. His winning personality, organizational skills, and perhaps even his somewhat theatrical podium manner helped to place the orchestra firmly at the center of Cleveland's cultural life.

By 1930 the orchestra had toured throughout the United States, Canada, and Cuba; it had made its first recording (*1812* Overture on the Brunswick label); and it had engaged many of the leading composers of the day (Ravel, Stravinsky, and Respighi among them) to conduct their own works. The orchestra's achievements were fittingly recognized in 1931 with the opening of Severance Hall, the ensemble's present home.

The sum of $1 million was given by J. L. Severance for the hall's construction after $2.5 million had been provided for an orchestra endowment fund. The building sits majestically on Cleveland's University Circle adjacent to Case Western Reserve University, which owns the site on which the five-sided structure is located. (The university "rents" the property to the Musical Arts Association for the annual fee of one dollar.) Inside, the visitor encounters two performance areas: the main hall, which seats 1,996, and a recital hall accommodating 400. The serenity of the Georgian exterior contrasts with the vivid splendor of the interior, which mixes Art Deco, Egyptian Revival, and classical styles with surprising ease. The stage of the main hall was designed to accommodate both orchestral and operatic forces, although a remodeling project in 1958 sacrificed staging flexibility for acoustical improvement. Today Severance Hall boasts one of the most acoustically satisfying performing spaces in the world.

By 1932 it was decided that a change of command was in order, and Sokoloff's contract was not renewed. He was replaced the following year by Artur Rodzinski, who had arrived in the United States in 1926 to serve as Stokowski's assistant in Philadelphia* after successful stints with both the Warsaw Philharmonic and Grand Opera Theatre. From Philadelphia Rodzinski had gone to California, where he made notable progress with the Los Angeles Philharmonic* over a four-year period. Under this intense Polish nationalist, the Cleveland Orchestra was transformed from a fine regional ensemble to one of national significance.

Rodzinski expanded the orchestra's repertoire with additional works by classical composers together with substantial amounts of contemporary literature. His excitable, highly strung temperament was especially well-suited to the works of composers such as Berlioz, Wagner, and Strauss, which rely heavily on brilliance achieved under highly emotionally charged conditions. It was also Rodzinski who brought operatic performances to Severance Hall; during his first four years in Cleveland the orchestra divided its time between symphonic repertoire and staged productions with internationally acclaimed stars. Of special interest was the American premiere of Shostakovich's *Lady Macbeth of Mzensk*, sung by a predominantly Russian cast in the original language. The work, which had been vehemently denounced by Stalin, was well-received at Severance Hall and, a short time later, at the Met with the same conductor and cast.

Unfortunately, Rodzinski grew progressively discontented with his situation in Cleveland after 1936. His beloved operatic productions slowed to a halt in the late 1930s because of financial difficulties, and his personal relations with the Musical Arts Association directors deteriorated. Nevertheless, his star continued to rise nationally, and in 1937 Rodzinski divided his time between Cleveland and New York, where he prepared the new NBC Symphony for Toscanini and made guest appearances with the New York Philharmonic.* He sought to round out the Cleveland ensemble's sound by augmenting the string section but was repeatedly rebuffed by his Board of Directors. Believing that additional growth for the orchestra was unlikely, Rodzinski left in 1943 to lead the New York Philharmonic. Nevertheless, his decade in Cleveland must be viewed as successful.

Rodzinski's successor was 31-year-old Erich Leinsdorf, who had joined the conducting staff at the Met in 1937. Only four months into his first season, however, Leinsdorf was drafted into military service, and the orchestra booked a string of guest conductors as replacements. Although he was able to return for the third year of his contract, he was dismayed to find a number of players missing (also a result of the war effort). George Szell, who had garnered rave reviews during two series of guest appearances with the orchestra, was announced as his successor.

It was under Szell, a Hungarian who had worked under Richard Strauss and Otto Klemperer, that the Cleveland Orchestra stunned audiences the world over with its uncanny precision and sense of ensemble. Szell had made his mark in Europe before Toscanini invited him for a guest appearance with the NBC Symphony. After numerous additional appearances around the United States, Szell joined the Met's conducting staff in 1942. He promised Cleveland that he would transform the city into a capital for orchestral music second to none in the world, provided that the Musical Arts Association gave him the freedom to operate.

Wasting no time, the new maestro dismissed 22 of the 94 musicians at his disposal. He requested and, unlike Rodzinski, received additional string players, bringing the total number of musicians to 106. Many players found Szell's rehearsals terrifying; all found them grueling. Seldom would he address a member of the orchestra directly in rehearsal. Rather, according to old European custom, Szell would relay his concerns to a player through the section's principal. His cool, even imperious demeanor gave special emphasis to the short, sarcastic jabs that he delivered without hesitation when the maestro felt they were warranted. Szell approached every musical composition from a predominantly cerebral point of view and achieved his superior results through relentless attention to detail. Players found their parts covered with the maestro's own instructions prior to the first read-through. One musician once quipped that under Szell even the inspiration was rehearsed.

The constant emphasis on rhythmic precision, uniform rendering of every detail, and absolute blend within sections was reflected in a distinctive tone quality that in time came to be associated with the Cleveland Orchestra alone. The round tone of earlier seasons was gradually replaced by a leaner, more transparent sound often more associated with chamber music. Indeed, Szell often remarked that he required his orchestra to play with the same precision, the same intimacy, and the same unity of conception as the members of a seasoned string quartet.

The world took notice of the Cleveland Orchestra's transformation under its stern taskmaster. The ensemble's annual excursions to Carnegie Hall became highlights of the New York musical seasons. In 1957, at the request of the State Department, the orchestra toured Europe. Critics throughout the tour itinerary were astounded and generally agreed that the Cleveland Orchestra was unlikely to be surpassed for its virtuosity. Similar sentiments were evoked on additional European tours in 1965 and 1967 and on a tour of the Far East in 1970 just prior to the maestro's death. That the Cleveland community was appreciative of their orchestra's efforts was evident in the 5,000 fans who greeted the players as they returned to Cleveland-Hopkins Airport after the second European excursion.

In 1956 Szell brought Robert Shaw on board for the purpose of developing a 250-voice community chorus, capable of meeting the maestro's exacting standards. Although some ranked Szell second only to Toscanini, a few felt that his quest for absolute precision led to results that were too calculated. To be sure, Szell's approach worked more successfully with certain repertoire than others. He was totally at home with the Austro-German repertoire from the Classicists to Strauss as well as with the works of Dvořák and Tchaikovsky. It was with his interpretations of Haydn, Mozart, and Beethoven, however, that Szell established himself as a musical titan. He programmed various contemporary works from time to time, but it cannot be said that he was very enthusiastic about most twentieth-century musical developments. Although he programmed French composers to some extent, the results seldom paralleled his successes with German works. (One former player has recalled that Szell's rigidly controlled interpretation of Debussy's *La Mer* inspired the nickname *"Der Mer"* from some orchestra members.) During the 1960s Szell concentrated with increasing frequency on those works for which he was obviously best suited.

By 1964 the orchestra's performing season had been extended to 48 weeks. The opening in 1968 of the Blossom Music Center provided additional opportunities for summer performances on 500 wooded acres between Cleveland and Akron. A pavilion, accommodating 4,500 seats with adjacent lawn space for up to 10,000 additional listeners, was constructed.

Szell's death in 1970 sent the Musical Arts Association into understandable panic as they searched the world for a credible successor. The Association was fortunate to obtain in 1972 the services of the 41-year-old American, Lorin Maazel. His appointment provoked initial dissatisfaction among the players, but critics cheered his first performances and commented that the orchestra was nevertheless obviously going to cooperate.

Maazel demonstrated a superb baton technique and a sense of intellectual control over his interpretations that in some ways resembled Szell's cerebral approach; however, he refused to dictate every musical nuance and detail, expecting players themselves to attend to such matters as he concentrated upon the structural essence of the work. His manner in rehearsals was aloof, and his decision to replace 18 players with young newcomers rankled some. The orchestra was forced to adjust, however, as it also adjusted to Maazel's frequent departures for guest stints, courtesy of the new jet age.

Maazel divided his time between his duties in Cleveland and those with the Berlin Radio Orchestra, which he continued to conduct until 1975. In an effort to change what he saw as the rather stodgy image of the orchestra, he expanded the ensemble's repertoire extensively with contemporary works and large, complex works of such composers as Berlioz and Mahler. Conducting mostly from memory, Maazel encouraged the type of spontaneity that adds brilliance and tension to a performance. He also stated his opposition to the concept of a "definitive" performance held by some conductors—Szell included—which in his opinion resulted in lifeless, carbon-copy renditions.

Under the new director, the orchestra's tone again took on a rounder, fuller quality, although it never approached the lush sensuousness that at times has characterized both the Boston and Philadelphia sounds. The new sound probably resulted from a combination of new, younger players unmolded by Szell, new repertoire, new freedoms and responsibilities of players under Maazel's approach, and the appearance of several guest conductors, which required musical flexibility. While perhaps some of the almost superhuman precision of Szell's tenure faded a bit during the 1970s, it is generally agreed that under Maazel the orchestra has maintained its technical edge with distinction. Robert Page's presence as choral director assured Maazel of a choir capable of meeting the orchestra's own precision and flexibility. Tours to Latin America, Japan, and Australia allowed the orchestra to show the world that it had not retreated into provincialism with the death of Szell.

The history of the Cleveland Orchestra's labor relations with the Musical Arts Association has been relatively free of trauma; only twice has the orchestra struck in recent memory—in 1970 and in 1980. The latter strike occurred during the summer months and forced the cancellation of musical performances at Blossom Music Center for 14 days.

Maazel's announcement in 1981 of his intention to leave Cleveland to assume the helm at the Vienna State Opera was a blow even to those orchestra members who were never totally won over by his approach. A year later Christoph von Dohnányi, artistic director of the Hamburg State Opera, was named music director designate, with his four-year term to begin in September 1984. Born in Berlin in 1929, Dohnányi received training in conducting under Solti and at Tanglewood. He had won favorable reviews after conducting Europe's premier opera and symphonic orchestras. The grandson of Hungarian composer Ernst von Dohnányi, he is anxious to avoid being associated with a particular school of repertoire at this point. Initial appearances with the Cleveland musicians have left listeners optimistic that under von Dohnányi the orchestra will continue its tradition of music-making at its finest.

RECORDING HISTORY AND SELECTIVE DISCOGRAPHY: Although Sokoloff recorded some pieces with Brunswick in the 1920s, it was Rodzinski who first achieved prominence with the orchestra on disc, recording several works for Columbia. Szell recorded for both Columbia and its affiliate, Epic. Recordings since 1970 have been produced on London, Telarc, Deutsche Grammophon, CBS, and Angel labels and have featured, in addition to Maazel, Pierre Boulez, Neville Marriner, Michael Tilson Thomas, Louis Lane, and Rafael Kubelík as conductors.

Beethoven, Symphony No. 4, op. 60 and Symphony No. 5, op. 67 (Szell): Odyssey Y–34600. Bruckner, Symphony No. 3 (Szell): CBS MS–6897. Gershwin, *Porgy and Bess* (Maazel): London OSA–13116. Mozart, Piano Concerto No. 24 in C Minor, K. 491 (Casadesus/Szell): Columbia M–31814. Prokofiev, *Romeo and Juliet* (Maazel): London CSA–2312 (3 records). Tchaikovsky, Symphony No. 4 (Maazel): Telarc DG10047.

CHRONOLOGY OF MUSIC DIRECTORS: Nikolai Sokoloff, 1918–1933. Artur Rodzinski, 1933–1943. Erich Leinsdorf, 1943–1946. George Szell, 1946–1970. Lorin Maazel, 1972–1982. Christoph von Dohnányi, 1984-present.

BIBLIOGRAPHY: J. Heywood Alexander, *It Must Be Heard: The Musical Life of Cleveland, 1836–1918* (Cleveland: Western Reserve Historical Society, 1981). *Cleveland Orchestra: 1983–1984 Operational Projection*, (Cleveland: Musical Arts Association, 1983). David M. Ewen, ed., *Musicians Since 1900* (New York: Wilson,

1978). *Fortieth Anniversary Book for the Cleveland Orchestra* (Cleveland: Musical Arts Association, 1958). Philip Hart, *Conductors: A New Generation* (New York: Scribner's, 1979). Adella Prentiss Hughes, *Music Is My Life* (Cleveland: World, 1947). Philippa Kiraly, "Youth Concerts Come of Age," *Symphony Magazine*, Feb./Mar. 1984. Robert C. Marsh, *The Cleveland Orchestra* (Cleveland: World, 1967). Helena Matheopoulos, *Maestro: Encounters with Conductors of Today* (New York: Harper & Row, 1982). Musical Arts Association, Archives. Joseph A. Mussulman, *Dear People* ...(Bloomington: Indiana University Press, 1979). Helena Rodzinski, *Our Two Lives* (New York: Scribner's, 1976). Joseph Wechsberg, "The Cleveland Orchestra," in *The Professional Symphony Orchestra in the United States*, ed. George Seltzer (Metuchen, N.J.: Scarecrow Press, 1975).

ACCESS: The Cleveland Orchestra, Musical Arts Association, Severance Hall, 11001 Euclid Avenue, Cleveland, OH 44106. (216) 231–7300. Kenneth Haas, General Manager, Jan C. Snow, Director of Communications and Public Relations.

DAVID G. TOVEY

Ohio Chamber Orchestra (Mt)

Although Cleveland is blessed with a world-class orchestra, the community, over a period of years, voiced a need for an ensemble that could perform the great chamber orchestra literature and was flexible in programming and purpose. Numerous earlier attempts to form such a group had failed, but the Ohio Chamber Orchestra was able to gather and maintain support to fulfill such a need.

The Ohio Chamber Orchestra was founded in 1972 in conjunction with the 75th anniversary of the founding of Baldwin Wallace College. A group of faculty at the College's Conservatory of Music who had performed in various orchestras in the United States sought a forum for the formation of a chamber orchestra in the Cleveland area. When Dwight Oltman joined the faculty, he was requested to form such an orchestra; he remains today as its music director. One of the factors contributing to the orchestra's success was that at its founding two influential supporters of the arts were requested to form a Board of Trustees from among other arts supporters in the community. Having successfully completed this move early on, the orchestra was immediately a credible organization. Its original personnel consisted of both faculty and free-lance musicians.

The purposes of the orchestra are to perform, at the highest artistic level possible, the vast and often neglected body of music for small orchestra; to provide live orchestral music for audiences in institutions and in cities of all sizes; to serve audiences not normally reached by professional orchestras; to function as a flexible organization available for accompanying opera, ballet, and oratorio; to provide a significant performance outlet for artists and professional performers with emphasis on Ohio-trained soloists and composers.

The orchestra is governed by a 30-member Board of Trustees and administered by a full-time general manager and staff. Its 1984–1985 budget was $514,000, 78% of which was earned income. Other income derives from federal and state grants as well as business and private foundations.

In addition to providing five annual subscription concerts, the ensemble also functions as the official orchestra for both the Cleveland Ballet and the Cleveland Opera. The basic orchestra size for the subscription series is 30, although this core is often augmented for ballet and opera productions.

There is no official hall for the Ohio Chamber Orchestra, although the bulk of its rehearsals are held at Baldwin Wallace College in Cleveland's western suburb, Berea. During its subscription season the orchestra performs at the Cleveland Museum of Art, at the refurbished Ohio Theater downtown, and at Baldwin Wallace College. The orchestra still contains musicians from the Conservatory faculty; however, today the majority of its players are professionals accepted by audition from the greater Cleveland area.

Additionally, the orchestra has maintained a high degree of commitment to providing concerts to sectors of the community (particularly inner-city areas) that currently have little or no professional music available. In addition, increasing emphasis is being given to educational projects. Students are offered subscription concert tickets underwritten by private foundations.

The orchestra also appears regularly as part of the Baldwin Wallace Bach Festival, accompanies the choir of Cleveland's historic Old Stone Church, and was the official orchestra of the Fifth Biennial Robert Casadesus International Piano Competition in August of 1983. Occasionally the orchestra has toured beyond Ohio both in concert and on tour with the Cleveland Ballet.

Playing commissioned works by local composers has become an important part of the orchestra's role in the community. In recent years there have been annual commissions and world premieres of works by various composers from the Greater Cleveland area. Over and above this, the orchestra has performed American premieres of works by Matthias Bamert, Bruno Maderna, F. Moreno-Torroba, and Malcom Williamson. The group has also given Cleveland premieres of works by Benjamin Britten, Aaron Copland, Norman Dello Joio, and Walter Mays.

Music Director Dwight Oltman was a student of Nadia Boulanger, Pierre Monteux, Max Rudolf, and Richard Lert. He is principal conductor of the Cleveland Ballet and music director of the Bach Festival at Baldwin Wallace College, where he is professor of music.

Future plans of the Ohio Chamber Orchestra include expansion of the subscription series, development of a three- to seven-day tour of Ohio cities, expansion of outreach and educational programs, and the production of a commercial recording for promotion and publicity purposes.

CHRONOLOGY OF MUSIC DIRECTORS: Dwight Oltman, 1972-present.

BIBLIOGRAPHY: Interviews with OCO Music Director Dwight Oltman and General Manager Randall Rosenbaum.

ACCESS: Ohio Chamber Orchestra, 11125 Magnolia Drive, Cleveland, OH 44106. (216) 229–4144. Randall Rosenbaum, General Manager.

JOHN E. FERRITTO

COLUMBUS (1,093,316)

Columbus Symphony Orchestra (Rg)

The Columbus Symphony Orchestra is at the center of the burgeoning cultural and creative activities in the capital city of Ohio. Well on its way to becoming a full-time professional orchestra, the CSO currently employs roughly half of its normal complement of 95 players on a full-time basis. This core is the nucleus for solo and ensemble activities that the orchestra provides both locally and regionally, in addition to a chamber orchestra series, youth and pops concerts, and two major concert series. In all, the CSO provides the central Ohio community with more than 300 performances, including school concerts, recitals, demonstrations, and clinics.

In the Columbus Symphony Orchestra, the city has finally reached a point of national recognition, although numerous symphonic organizations, professional and amateur, have been offering residents the best in standard repertoire over the past century. The first ongoing effort to maintain professional performance standards was the Columbus Orchestra, founded in 1886 by C. C. Neereamer. Although amateur, it contained full instrumentation and performed the then-current professional repertoire. This orchestra ceased operations with the passing of its conductor/founder. A Columbus Symphony Orchestra and a Columbus Symphony Association held a brief concurrent existence.

Earl Hopkins founded another Columbus Symphony Orchestra in 1924. Although related to neither the present CSO nor the earlier group, Hopkins's ensemble reestablished high-level performances in Columbus. This orchestra was active until 1936 when, with the passing of Hopkins and the weight of the depression, it too ceased activities. The next step was taken in 1941, when Norman Nadel formulated the Columbus Philharmonic Orchestra. With the highly talented Izler Solomon at its helm, this orchestra took great strides musically, while developing a solid basis of community appeal and support. Immediately after World War II, the Columbus Philharmonic was employing 85 musicians on a semi-professional basis and providing a season-long series of major concerts in addition to 20 pops concerts. The Philharmonic was recognized nationally by virtue of appearances on the National Broadcasting Company's "Orchestras of the Nation," which broadcast the orchestra on two occasions, and by the appearance of major concert artists.

Nevertheless, when Solomon moved on and because financial goals were not met, the Philharmonic suspended operations after the 1949–1950 season.

After one season, however, George Hardesty, concertmaster of the now-defunct Philharmonic and conductor of the Ohio State University Symphony, gathered 28 former colleagues into the Columbus Little Symphony Orchestra, from which the present Columbus Symphony developed. The CSO employed as its conductor Henry Mazer, of the Wheeling (W.V.) Symphony.* Even though Mazer was splitting his time, the orchestra moved forward into its first full season of activity (1952–1953). Mazer remained only one season, and steps were taken to obtain the services of a permanent conductor. Claude Monteux, son of the famous French conductor Pierre Monteux, was chosen, and under his direction the orchestra's all-important community base began to grow. In addition to developing a Youth Orchestra, Monteux reestablished the appearance of first-rate guest artists in Columbus and continued in-school, youth, and pops concerts. During his three seasons, a solid coterie of supporters was developed, including some members of the former Philharmonic Association.

As Monteux's replacement, the CSO selected Evan Whallon, winner of the Philadelphia Orchestra's* Young Conductor's Contest. During the Whallon years, the CSO continued its return to its position as a leading Metropolitan orchestra. Professional management helped stabilize the orchestra's finances, both in developing resources and balancing expenditures with the focus on continued artistic growth. The most important aspect of this has been to create financial resources in endowments, fund-raisers, corporate and individual pledges, and earned income. Careful guidance by the CSO Board and management has put the orchestra in a unique position. Its budget has grown from $114,000 in 1960 to $4.4 million in 1985–1986; the organization is debt-free and has never operated in the red.

In addition to gradually increasing the size of the orchestra, Whallon also established the Columbus Symphony Chorus, a 160-voice group of auditioned community vocalists that has given the CSO almost unlimited repertoire selection. While the principal focus in the area has been works from the late eighteenth to the early twentieth centuries, the CSO has performed works from Corelli to Crumb, including both staged and concert performances of numerous operas, and often with world-class soloists. The orchestra was also served well when, during its 25th anniversary year, it moved to the Ohio Theater. This building, a totally restored vaudeville house listed as a National Historical Landmark, is a favorite center-city location for the general audience and is an excellent hall for music.

Following the retirement of Evan Whallon at the end of the 1981–1982 season and after a season of guest conductors, the CSO selected the internationally recognized Romanian conductor Christian Badea as music director and principal conductor. In this brief time, the CSO has continued its growth from Metropolitan to Regional orchestra, progressing apace to full-time professional status.

Excellent repertoire selection in the subscription series, combined with regional tours, local television appearances, and an expanded pops concert series, has served to solidify and broaden community support and interest. As the hub of musical culture for the city, the CSO works in conjunction with Ohio State University (one concert series is located there) and with the public and private schools of the Columbus area. The CSO coordinates with Ballet Met and Opera/Columbus, the majority of whose instrumentalists are its members.

CHRONOLOGY OF MUSIC DIRECTORS: George Hardesty, 1951–1952. Henry Mazer, 1952–1953. Claude Monteux, 1953–1956. Evan Whallon, 1956–1982. (Guest conductors, 1982–1983.) Christian Badea, 1983-present.

BIBLIOGRAPHY: Interview with CSO General Manager Darrell Edwards. CSO Public Relations Office Scrapbook. *A History of the First Fifteen Years of CSO: 1951–1966* (Columbus: Columbus Symphony Women's Association, 1967). George S. Marshall, *A History of Music in Columbus, Ohio 1812–1953* (Columbus: Franklin County Historical Society, 1956).

ACCESS: Columbus Symphony Orchestra, 101 E. Town Street, Columbus, OH 43216. (614) 224–5281. Darrell Edwards, General Manager. Mark Melson, Director of Public Relations.

PETER GANO

DAYTON (830,070)

Dayton Philharmonic Orchestra (Rg)

The 1983–1984 concert season commemorated the fiftieth anniversary of the Dayton Philharmonic Orchestra. The programming for this special season for the first time included compositions by living American composers on five of the nine subscription concerts, and an additional contemporary American composition was premiered on a run-out concert in Piqua.

The inclusion of these new compositions on the regular subscription series of the orchestra represented a break with a long tradition of programs consisting of standard (and popular) nineteenth-century compositions, with an occasional early twentieth-century work and (rarely) a composition from the classical period. The 1983–1984 season programming was consistent with past years in featuring internationally known soloists on all subscription concerts except the traditional Orchestra Night. The Performance of world-class soloists seems to account for the orchestra's sold out (or nearly sold out) concerts.

In addition to offering the nine subscription concerts (four repeated on the following nights) the concert year followed the orchestra's tradition of three pops concerts, four young people's concerts, and run-out concerts in St. Marys, Greenville, and Piqua. A new feature of this 50th anniversary season was a special concert sponsored by the NCR Corporation, at which a gift of $100,000 to the DPO was announced. This gift will endow the NCR Corporation-William S. Anderson Concerts for the next decade. This is a timely replacement for the Mr. and Mrs. Eugene Joffe Patron Concerts, which for the past 10 years have been conducted by Conductor Emeritus Paul Katz. These concerts included both an internationally renowned artist and a soloist who won the annual Dayton Philharmonic Competition for a Musician with Local Ties.

The ASOL classifies the Dayton Philharmonic as a Regional orchestra, based upon its annual budget of approximately $1 million. The orchestra's management evidently perceives the "Regional" status as reflecting a need to service smaller communities near Dayton in the Miami River Valley. With Dayton in close proximity to the Major orchestra of Cincinnati and the soon-to-be Major orchestra of Columbus, future growth in both length of season and outreach seems limited.

The member agencies of the Dayton Performing Arts Fund are the Dayton Ballet, the Dayton Opera, and the DPO, although many other organizations benefit from grants. All three member agencies make their home in Memorial Hall, a 2,500-seat Montgomery County theater dedicated in 1910 (and periodically rejuvenated). The orchestra received $230,000 as a result of the 1983–1984 Arts Fund drive. Additionally, the Philharmonic enjoys the support of the NEA and the Ohio Arts Council, which help fund both the concerts and educational programs. The orchestra supports two string quartets, a woodwind quintet, a brass quintet and a percussion ensemble, all of which perform in schools and community centers. The Dayton Philharmonic Youth Orchestra and the Dayton Philharmonic Junior String Orchestra offer training and experience for young players.

The artistic direction of the Dayton Philharmonic has been in the hands of only two conductors. Conductor Emeritus Paul Katz, who founded the orchestra and guided it for 42 seasons, was succeeded in 1975 by Charles Wendelken-Wilson. From the first performance by 26 musicians in June 1933 to the 88 musicians who performed Beethoven's Ninth Symphony in May 1984, the orchestra has served well the audiences in Dayton and the Miami River Valley.

The Philharmonic still pays its musicians on a per-service basis. There are fewer than 100 services per musician each concert year. The orchestral personnel is drawn largely from Dayton and surrounding localities, although a considerable number of professionals and college and conservatory students come from as far as Cincinnati—about 50 miles away. All told, over 40 players travel to and from orchestra functions from beyond the boundaries of Montgomery County.

In Dayton, as is usually true in other localities, a strong, dedicated musician attracts other musicians to create an orchestra to make music. Managers, Boards of Trustees, and Women's Associations come along to make it possible for the orchestra to continue to make music. Albert D. Epstein, the first manager of the DPO, worked closely with Paul Katz. His successor was Miriam Rosenthal, who served the orchestra from 1933 to 1965. Dr. Katz credits her with making and keeping the Philharmonic a going financial concern. The orchestra has since been ably served by Managers Burdette "Maggie" Thompson (1965–1973), Richard C. McCauley (1973–1977) and David L. Pierson (1977-present).

From the mid–1960s there has been a noticeable change in the conduct and attitude of the Board of Trustees. Recent Boards have asserted more control, and they have been instrumental in shaping the growth of the orchestra's activities as well as broadening and enhancing its financial progress. The Dayton Philharmonic Women's Association, now numbering 600 members, provides necessary fund-raising and artistic support.

CHRONOLOGY OF MUSIC DIRECTORS: Paul Katz, 1933–1974. Charles Wendelken-Wilson, 1975-present.

BIBLIOGRAPHY: ASOL Research and Analysis Department, correspondence with author, 1983–1984. Dayton Performing Arts Center, *The Performer*, Winter 1984. Diane P. DeWall and Charles R. DeWall, *A History of the Dayton Philharmonic Orchestra, 1933–1983* (Dayton Philharmonic Orchestra Association, 1983). Bernard Holland, "Do Concertos Sell?" *New York Times*, 18 Dec. 1983. Paul Katz, personal conversations with the author, 1968-present. George Seltzer, *The Professional Symphony Orchestra in the United States* (Metuchen, N.J.): Scarecrow Press, 1975.

ACCESS: The Dayton Philharmonic Orchestra, Memorial Hall, 125 East First Street, Dayton, OH 45402. (513) 224–3521. David L. Pierson, General Manager.

GEORGE SELTZER

TOLEDO (791,599)

Toledo Symphony (Rg)

Founded in 1943 as the "Friends of Music Orchestra" with only 22 musicians and a three-concert season, the Toledo Symphony stands today as one of our nation's leading Regional orchestras. With a roster of 82 professional musicians, an administrative staff of twelve, and an annual budget of $1.4 million (including $350,000 from community fund-raising), the Toledo Symphony has expanded its concert offerings to include a formal season of nine subscription concerts (performed in pairs) plus a chamber orchestra series, a Mainly Mozart series, a pops series, special concerts for families, and ensemble performances in the schools. The Symphony sponsors a Youth Orchestra program as well as the Toledo Symphony Chorale and administers the popular summer concert band series at the Toledo Zoo. The orchestra performs annually at regional college campuses and schools, where it is estimated to perform for an additional audience of 100,000.

Toledo derives its nickname, "The Glass City," from its famous glass industry (Owens-Illinois, Libbey-Owens Ford, Owens-Corning Fiberglas, and Johns-Manville, etc.), which exports glass products to the world and serves American automobile manufacturing in nearby Detroit. Its strategic location at the western edge of Lake Erie between Cleveland and Chicago also contributes to making Toledo a major transportation center. The successful industry and commerce of the region brought many talented individuals to Toledo who valued and supported its cultural institutions.

For the first half of this century, Toledo's artistic life was dominated by the founding of the renowned Toledo Museum of Art. The museum itself was completed in two stages, 1911 and 1926. A music wing and a School of Art were subsequently added through the generosity of Florence Scott Libbey and a bequest from Edward Drummond Libbey. The music hall, called the Peristyle, was completed in 1933.

The Peristyle is one of America's truly distinctive concert halls. With excellent acoustics and designed in the classical Greek tradition, it is characterized by 28 Ionic columns surrounding the main theater of 1,700 seats. A "sky" canopy utilizing special lighting effects covers the auditorium and produces for the audience the sensation of being seated in an outdoor Greek amphitheater. Leopold Stokowski and the Philadelphia Orchestra* presented the premiere concerts at the Peristyle on January 10 and 11, 1933. This magnificent hall immediately hosted internationally famous performers, but Toledo would wait another 10 years for the founding of its own permanent civic orchestra.

While a Toledo Symphony Orchestra under the direction of Lewis H. Clement existed between 1920 and 1926, it was the Friends of Music Orchestra, founded in 1943 by the Friends of Music, that evolved into the modern Toledo Symphony. Its premiere performance took place on September 28, 1943, at Macomber Vocational High School with Edgar Schenkman conducting. In 1945 concerts were moved to Ursuline Auditorium, and in 1946 Hans Lange became the orchestra's second conductor. The Peristyle became the permanent concert home for the orchestra in 1947, and the orchestra's first performance of a major world premiere occurred on February 18, 1948, featuring Florian Mueller's First Symphony.

The 1949–1950 season brought Wolfgang Stresemann as the orchestra's third conductor, and a youth orchestra was established by Cecile Vashaw. During the 1950–1951 season the Toledo Orchestra Association replaced the Friends of Music and the orchestra was renamed the Toledo Orchestra. In October 1951, Mrs. A. Beverly Barksdale became the first president of the new Toledo Orchestra Women's League, formed to raise funds and plan educational activities.

A $10,000 deficit in 1953 created a serious financial crisis, which threatened the cancellation of the season's final two subscription concerts, but a community fund drive led by William H. Mauk, president of the Orchestra Association, salvaged the season. Mr. Mauk was assisted by $1,000 collected in dime contributions from Toledo's school children.

Joseph Hawthorne became the Toledo Orchestra's fourth conductor in the 1955–1956 season and the following year initiated Toledo's first pops concert. During 1957–1958, the orchestra presented its first regional college concert at Wilberforce College. In 1961 the Toledo Orchestra received the Alice M. Ditson Award "for outstanding programming in the field of contemporary American music."

After a season of guest conductors, Serge Fournier became Toledo's fifth conductor, with his first subscription concert on October 17, 1964. Fournier, demanding high performance levels, is regarded as an influential force in having shaped today's Toledo Symphony. Under Fournier, the Toledo Orchestra grew from a classical orchestra to full symphonic proportions. He led the orchestra to Detroit's Ford Auditorium for a tour performance, founded the Toledo Orchestra Chorale, and added a chamber orchestra series. The orchestra's eight concert season was doubled, repeating Friday's performance on Saturday evening—both at the Peristyle. Also noteworthy under Fournier was the appointment of Darwyn Roy Apple as America's first black concertmaster.

The "Out Music for In People" educational program for teenagers during the 1967–1968 season received first prize at the national American Symphony Orchestra League convention. This 25th anniversary year of the orchestra's founding closed with a budget of $278,600.

The Toledo Orchestra officially became "The Toledo Symphony" during the 1968–1969 season. When the modern, 2,500-seat Masonic Auditorium was completed in suburban Toledo the following year, the Symphony became a two-hall orchestra, with Friday concerts presented at the new hall and Saturday concerts at the Peristyle—a format that continues today.

A series of guest conductors during 1979–1980 led to the appointment of Music Director/Conductor Yuval Zaliouk, who continued the concert season's expansion with the addition of the Ohio Citizen's Family Concerts. In 1982, the orchestra was awarded an ASCAP prize for contemporary American music programming and the following fall expanded the subscription series to nine pairs of concerts. The orchestra also added a Mainly Mozart series at Lourdes College. The close of the 1983–1984 season again brought the Symphony national recognition when, after premiering four commissioned works the orchestra received a 1984 ASCAP award, first prize in the Regional orchestra category. Zaliouk has continued to increase the orchestra's visibility and prominence in Toledo and the region.

The Toledo Symphony is administered by Music Director Yuval Zaliouk and Managing Director Robert Bell, who are assisted by a staff of 11. The president of the Orchestra Association, John Williamson, and the Executive

Committee of the Board of Trustees form a steering committee to review orchestra operations and policies.

The orchestra's musicians are highly visible in the community. They frequently appear in the schools, in opera, musical theater, ballet, concert band, and church performances. Members of the orchestra are selected by nationally announced auditions. Several orchestra performers teach in area colleges and universities as well as in private studios and thus contribute to Toledo's cultural fabric.

CHRONOLOGY OF MUSIC DIRECTORS: Edgar Schenkman, 1943–1946. Hans Lange, 1946–1949. Wolfgang Stresemann, 1949–1955. Joseph Hawthorne, 1955–1963. (Guest conductors, 1963–1964.) Serge Fournier, 1964–1979. (Guest conductors, 1979–1980.) Yuval Zaliouk, 1980-present.

BIBLIOGRAPHY: Interviews with TSO Managing Director Robert Bell, 1984. William Robert Lecklider, "The Toledo Symphony Orchestra," Diss., University of Michigan, 1966. Boris Nelson, "Toledo is Very Rich in Musical Assets," *The Blade*, 12 Feb. 1984. Norma Richards, "History of the Toledo Symphony Orchestra," *40th Anniversary Program* (Toledo Symphony, 1983). Joyce Smar, "The Peristyle—50 Years in Review," *50th Anniversary of the Peristyle Program* (Toledo Symphony, 1983). H. Stoddard, "Music in Ohio," *The International Musician*, April 1954.

ACCESS: The Toledo Symphony, One Stranahan Square, Toledo, OH 43604. (419) 241–1272. Robert Bell, Managing Director.

RICHARD P. KENNELL

YOUNGSTOWN (531,350)

Youngstown Symphony Orchestra (Mt)

The Youngstown Symphony Orchestra has been in existence since 1926, when it was started by brothers/conductors Michael and Carmine Ficocelli. Introduced as the Youngstown Little Symphony, it boasted 12 players, with an average age of 16. This tiny orchestra presented its concerts in school auditoriums for many years, gradually growing in size and stature until World War II, when both its conductors, as well as 25 orchestra members, joined the armed forces.

Following the war, financial difficulties forced the orchestra to disband, but in 1951, a confident new leadership appointed John Krueger as music director/conductor, thereby inaugurating an era of new growth and renewed acceptance in the community. Krueger helped to initiate a number of ancillary services that continue to this day. In 1952, the volunteer Philharmonic Chorus was established; 1954 saw the founding of the Junior Philharmonic Orchestra. Krueger was at the helm of the orchestra throughout the decade of 1957–1967, which was marked by a significant expansion in orchestra size (to 70 members) and competence. In 1967, Franz Bibo was appointed music director/conductor. His broad artistic experience and the Symphony's acquisition of a new home coalesced in the presentation of a gala opening night performance of *Die Fledermaus* on September 20, 1969.

The Symphony is an exception among Metropolitan orchestras by virtue of owning its own home—a former Warner Brothers art deco movie palace purchased in 1968 and donated to the Symphony Society by local philanthropists Edward W. and Alice Powers. The Youngstown Symphony's seven annual subscription concerts are presented in this opulent hall (built as a memorial to the Warner family's Youngstown origins) as well as yearly *Nutcracker* ballet performances and fully staged, locally produced operas (such as *La Traviata*, which was reviewed in *Opera News*). Up to 15,000 children are served annually through the YSO's series of youth and tiny tots concerts; manifold other events—events sponsored by the Symphony Society as well as outside bookings—keep the hall in almost constant use, although the overhead costs outbalance the income realized.

The YSO averages 85 players, with principals drawn mainly from faculty members of the Dana School of Music, a component of Youngstown State University. The musicians are hired on a per-service basis with the exception of the concertmaster, who is under yearly contract. The Society is governed by a 35-member Board of Directors and administered by a full-time general manager with a staff of four. The music director/conductor is completely responsible for artistic decisions and guides all musical programming done by several of the Society's five affiliates—the Junior Orchestra, the Symphony Chorus, and the Women's Committee for Children's Concerts. The Opera Guild and the Women's Symphony Guild are additional affiliates of the Society working actively as fund-raising and ticket-selling units.

The Society operates with an annual budget of $650,000. It is funded by federal and state grants, charitable trusts, corporate and private gifts, as well as an earned income that has fairly consistently provided about 52% of the total, even in the wake of the disastrous steel-mill closings in 1979 and the resultant high unemployment figures (still about 13% in 1984) in the Mahoning Valley.

Subscription ticket sales over the past several years have stayed at a fairly constant figure of 1,600, and single ticket sales have risen steadily, particularly in the past four years, due to the use of adroit marketing techniques by Manager Paul Bunker, who concentrates his efforts on the 18- to 34-year old age group, feeling that they are the people who have the most buying power and are also the most approachable. He uses a great deal of commercial radio time, assuming that listeners to the area's classical stations are already convinced.

Conductor Peter Leonard's carefully constructed programs strike a balance between familiar works and those which challenge both players and audience. Leonard's increasingly popular concert previews, presented immediately before each subscription concert, give insight into the personalities and music to be presented. When appropriate, guest artists also participate in these sessions. Leonard will serve as principal guest conductor and music advisor to the YSO during the 1985–1986 season, after which he will concentrate his efforts as music director of the Shreveport Symphony.*

The YSO's subscription concert series has been heard each season over WYSU-FM, and one concert per season is broadcast on the area's noncommercial TV channels. This exposure has helped make the present orchestra a viable and respected force in the community.

CHRONOLOGY OF MUSIC DIRECTORS: Michael Ficocelli and Carmine Ficocelli, 1926–1951. John Krueger, 1951–1966. Franz Bibo, 1966–1980. Peter Leonard, 1981-present.

BIBLIOGRAPHY: Robert Croan, "News from Youngstown," *Opera News*, June 1983. Adrian Slifka, "City Orchestra to Begin its 50th Season," *Youngstown Vindicator*, 3 Oct. 1976. YSO Commemorative Program, 20 Sept. 1969.

ACCESS: Youngstown Symphony Society, 260 Federal Plaza West, Youngstown, OH 44504. (216) 744–4269.

FRAN GREENBERG

Oklahoma ─────────────────

OKLAHOMA CITY (834,088)

Oklahoma Symphony Orchestra (Rg)

The Oklahoma Symphony Orchestra's roots extend back to frontier Oklahoma Territory, and its history parallels in many ways the growth of its home city. Oklahoma City is a fast-growing metropolis with a stable economy built on energy and aviation industries, agriculture, and health sciences research. The state's capital and largest city, Oklahoma City sprang into being literally overnight with the famous April 22, 1889, Land Run. Within 24 hours, the boom town's population rose from zero to 10,000.

In 1908 a group of Oklahoma City women, hungry for culture amid the raw prairie settlement, formed the Ladies Music Club. Their own string choir entertained club members at each meeting and promoted interest in music. More concerts followed and the increasing stature of the string choir led to the formation of a committee to raise funds for a full orchestra.

A successful fund drive provided money to hire 50 professional and non-professional musicians who agreed to work during the first season. The first of seven monthly concerts of the Oklahoma City Symphony opened on October 27, 1924, to an overflow audience of 1,500. Dean Holmberg conducted the orchestra through its first season and agreed to continue as its director for several more years.

By 1929 this forerunner of the present orchestra had grown to an accomplished group of 65 musicians. But the orchestra's fortunes followed those of the state and nation, and with the coming of the Great Depression it floundered and then collapsed. In 1937 a new orchestra was licensed in Oklahoma City as a Works Progress Administration project. It was officially incorporated under state law as a non-profit educational organization.

The first concert of the Oklahoma Federal Symphony Orchestra was given on January 3, 1938. Ralph Rose, the first conductor, led the orchestra through the winter and summer seasons of 1938. Forty children's concerts were played in Oklahoma City that season, and the first statewide concerts were initiated in Anadarko, Altus, Lawton, Edmond, and other cities. It was a professional orchestra with musicians carefully selected and paid by the government to practice six to eight hours each day. The orchestra opened under a new conductor in the autumn of 1938. Victor Alessandro, a young Texan, was eager to build the orchestra into one of the nation's finest. In what was to be a major step toward national recognition, in 1950 the renamed Oklahoma City Symphony opened a weekly coast-to-coast radio series over the Mutual Broadcasting System, carried by more than 500 stations.

With the departure at the end of the 1950–1951 season of Conductor Alessandro, the Symphony Board invited British-born Guy Fraser Harrison to ascend the podium. Harrison came to Oklahoma from the Rochester Civic Orchestra (now the Rochester Philharmonic).* His appointment reflected the desire of the Board to further develop the children's concerts already begun in Oklahoma. The 22-year tenure of Harrison was one of increasing visibility and recognition of the Oklahoma City Symphony as a major cultural organization in the Southwest. He increased the length of the season, added more concerts (especially children's programming), and was a tireless guest speaker and lecturer on behalf of the Symphony.

Following Harrison's retirement at the conclusion of the 1972–1973 season, Dr. Ray Luke was appointed resident conductor for the next season. Luke, also a prize-winning composer, had been associate conductor for the previous five seasons.

In March 1974, Ainslee Cox, a protégé of Leopold Stokowski with impressive guest conducting credentials, was named the new conductor of the Oklahoma City Symphony. A year later the orchestra's name was changed to the Oklahoma Symphony Orchestra to more accurately reflect the orchestra's activities, presenting concerts to more than 120,000 Oklahomans each year, statewide.

When Cox left in May of 1978, the Search Committee selected as music director Luis Herrera de la Fuente, a Mexican with extensive conducting experience all over the world. Herrera, having committed to memory more than 200 works, generally conducts without a score. His first season, 1978–1979, was programmed with an eye to rebuilding lagging attendance figures and offering a broader appeal. All nine Beethoven symphonies were presented, in addition to other classical favorites. This was a directional change from the preceding conductor's adventuresome programming of modern composers and avant-garde works.

The orchestra's home is the 3,200-seat Civic Center Music Hall in downtown Oklahoma City. Renovations over its 46-year history have improved the acoustics, as did the purchase by the orchestra in 1981 of an acoustical shell. The seating capacity makes this hall one of the largest among performance halls, proportionately even larger considering the population base of the Oklahoma City metropolitan area.

The 32-week season runs from September through April. Twelve classical subscription concert pairs are presented Sunday afternoons and the following Tuesday evenings. Programming is done by the music director with a majority of the works coming from classical and romantic composers, about 20% from the early twentieth century, and 10% from the modern era. At least one major choral work is included each season. Soloists include world-class artists as well as Oklahoma Symphony principals, with pianists and string players predominating.

The Oklahoma Symphony also offers a pops subscription series, the great demand for which has led to its expansion over the past five years. Ten of the fifteen concerts are on Friday nights and five "superstars" each repeat their concert the following Saturday night. A cabaret series of three concerts modeled on the Boston Pops is held in the Great Hall of Oklahoma City's Myriad Convention Center. Table seating for 1,000 is usually sold out well in advance of the dates.

During the 1983–1984 season, the Symphony traveled outside the Oklahoma City area to present run-out concerts in 18 communities statewide. Typical runouts consist of one or two young people's concerts in the schools and an evening classical concert. The number of educational concerts presented in school settings varies from year to year, but the total number establishes the Oklahoma Symphony as a leader among United States orchestras in this field. In 1983–1984, 40,000 children attended 32 metropolitan area, 21 runout, and six Kinder-Konzert performances. One-third of the total Oklahoma Symphony audience is children. Educational concerts have, in recent years, been generously supported by grants from local foundations.

The orchestra accompanies Ballet Oklahoma each season for its series of three or four programs. The orchestra is also available to other arts organizations for special concerts. It regularly accompanies Cimarron Circuit Opera Company, Canterbury Choral Society, and fine arts presentations by area colleges and universities. An annual legislators' Appreciation Concert in the Capitol Rotunda, outdoor concerts in shopping malls and ampitheatres, and benefit concerts are among the special performances built into each season. The 1983–1984 season had a total of 138 performances.

The Symphony occasionally premieres the works of present-day composers. Ray Luke composed his Concerto for Bassoon in 1965 for the Symphony's principal bassoonist, Betty Johnson, who performed it in 1965 and again in 1984. The orchestra also premiered Luke's Concerto for Piano and

Orchestra in 1970 (it later won the gold medal in the Queen Elisabeth of Belgium Competition) and his Symphony No. 4 in the same season. His choral *Plaintes and Dirges* premiered in March 1984.

The 56-member core orchestra is employed full time for 32 weeks. It is supplemented by extra players as demanded by repertoire. Most classical subscription concerts utilize 84 players. Pops concerts and run-out concerts use fewer personnel, with run-out programming tailored to the contract number. All orchestra players are members of the AFM. There are no official sub-groups within the orchestra, but many of the musicians do have positions with other ensembles. They are also active as teachers with area colleges and universities, as private teachers, and with other arts organizations and churches.

A major reorganization occurred in 1979 when severe financial shortfalls and a large accumulated deficit threatened the future of the orchestra. The Board of Directors was re-formed with new and broader responsibilities. The 75 members became responsible for raising money for the orchestra and were assigned to committees on finance, education, orchestra affairs, marketing, development, long-range planning, nominating, and artistic affairs. The Board hires and oversees the music director and general manager and sets policy for the Symphony.

This shakeup led to a revitalized organization. Fund-raising efforts by the Women's Committee auxiliary, the Board of Directors, management, staff, and numerous community volunteers eliminated the deficit and balanced the operating budget. Since then, the orchestra has maintained a break-even budget and has increased efforts to build up an endowment.

A budget of $2.75 million was adopted for 1984–1985. Approximately 50% of the budget is earned income, with the other half coming from federal, state, and local agencies, foundations, grants, corporate sponsorship programs, and individual gifts. The Symphony also benefits from an annual Allied Arts fund drive. By its 50th season (1986–1987) the Oklahoma Symphony hopes to have a substantial endowment, enter into a recording contract, and tour outside the Southwest.

CHRONOLOGY OF MUSIC DIRECTORS: Ralph Rose, Jr. (Conductor), 1937–1938. Victor Alessandro (Conductor), 1938–1951. Guy Fraser Harrison, 1951–1973. Ray Luke (Resident Conductor), 1973-1974. Ainslee Cox, 1974–1978. Luis Herrera de al Fuente, 1978-present.

BIBLIOGRAPHY: Bob L. Blackburn, *Oklahoma City, An Illustrated History* (Woodland Hills, Calif.: Windsor Publications, 1982). Oklahoma City Symphony, Archives. Lucyl Shirk, *Oklahoma City, Capital of Soonerland* (Oklahoma City, Oklahoma City Board of Education: 1957). Roy P. Stewart, *Born Grown: An Oklahoma City History* (Oklahoma City, Fidelity Bank National Association: 1974).

ACCESS: Oklahoma Symphony Orchestra, 512 Civic Center Music Hall, Oklahoma City, OK 73102. (405) 232–4292. Patrick B. Alexander, General Manager.

ANN M. SCHMIDT

TULSA (689,434)

Tulsa Philharmonic (Rg)

Coinciding with the region's development of its abundant natural resources soon after the turn of this century, a forerunner of the Tulsa Philharmonic was developed. The driving force was a small group of Tulsa
music lovers who instituted a series of Starlight Concerts at Skelly Stadium
on the campus of Henry Kendall College, now the University of Tulsa. A
Civic Symphony eventually developed, and although the ensemble was moved
to Oklahoma City during the depression, the desire for a professional orchestra on the part of Tulsa's leading citizens remained. In 1947 the Tulsa
Chamber of Commerce appointed a committee to determine the feasibility
of establishing a permanent orchestra. Results soon followed and the Tulsa
Philharmonic Society incorporated in 1948.

Today's Tulsa Philharmonic occupies a strategic place as the centerpiece
of musical activity in the northeast Oklahoma region. An active schedule is
involved: nine classics concerts, five pops concerts, eight young people's
concerts, and a number of performances throughout Oklahoma and surrounding states. As an important segment of the 39-week season, the Philharmonic personnel can count on engagements with the Tulsa Opera for
its three annual productions and engagements with the Tulsa Ballet Theatre.

The home of the Tulsa Philharmonic is the new Tulsa Performing Arts
Center built in 1977. Chapman Music Hall, the 2,450-seat main auditorium,
is usually full for each of the subscription classics and pops concerts. (Prior
to 1977 the Philharmonic performed at a much smaller facility on West
Brady Street in Tulsa, known affectionately and officially as "The Old Lady
of Brady.") The orchestra often appears outside the Performing Arts Center.
Two of these appearances are now on a regularly scheduled basis and have
become Tulsa traditions: a popular Christmas concert, which literally places
the ensemble "on ice" at the Williams Center Forum (an innovative, mul-
tistoried shopping mall featuring an ice rink at its center), and the Symphony
at Sunset, a pops concert that functions as an autumn kickoff event for the
Philharmonic's upcoming season. The Symphony at Sunset uses the grounds
of the Southern Hills Country Club.

To understand the growth and development of the Tulsa Philharmonic
is to understand the economic and social factors affecting the region it
serves. Tulsa does not have the same ethnic mix that characterizes the
make-up of audiences in larger, older cities; instead, the Philharmonic serves
a clientele, and involves many volunteers who are no more than two generations removed from the oil fields. Three hundred oil-related companies
still have officials or headquarters in Tulsa. While hardly a "boom town"
anymore, its enormous, nearly instantaneous wealth has proven to be a
powerful catalyst for the underwriting of culture.

H. Arthur Brown, founding musical director of the Tulsa Philharmonic, served for 10 years in that position. An active, peripatetic conductor/violinist, he figured in the development of two other orchestras: Louisville* and El Paso.* He was succeeded in 1958 by Vladimir Golschmann, who came to Tulsa from St. Louis* after serving there for over a quarter century. Franco Autori's ten-year reign as music director (1961–1971) brought significant musical development to the ensemble. The fiery Italian championed twentieth-century music and was unrelenting in his pursuit of higher performance standards. Entertainer Skitch Henderson of NBC fame conducted the orchestra next. Henderson's three-year stint was followed by the three-year tenure of Thomas Lewis (1974–1977). Lewis eschewed the twentieth-century programming of Autori and the pops orientation of his immediate predecessor; programs during this period were focused squarely on the romantic era.

Murry Sidlin followed Lewis in 1978 and Joel Lazar in 1980. Sidlin, an attractive, energetic, and articulate music director, balanced the orchestra's repertoire by programming some twentieth-century music. Lazar continued in the same mold during his three-year directorship.

During the 1983–1984 season, no fewer than eight guest conductors competed for the music directorship, and Bernard Rubenstein was named to the post beginning with the 1984–1985 season. Rubenstein comes to Tulsa from the Cincinnati Symphony,* where he was associate conductor. He has a varied background in conducting, including a number of United States premieres, for example, the Ligeti *Requiem* and Sir Michael Tippett's opera, *The Knot Garden*. Rubenstein's work for radio, film, and television includes the musical preparation for the Jean-Marie Straub film of Schoenberg's *Moses and Aaron* and several television operas for the public television station in Chicago. One of the latter productions, *Hansel and Gretel*, was shown nationally over PBS. Rubenstein's recordings with the Northwestern University Orchestra (where he served as conductor from 1968 to 1980) have been broadcast nationally over NPR.

The Tulsa Philharmonic's musical development since 1948 can be characterized as an ensemble growing with maturity each season. This is especially true in the last several years, when a carefully developed master plan has added additional players on both full-time and per-service bases. By continually reducing the number of per-service contract players (the plan runs through the late 1980s), stability has been greatly enhanced. With this stability, the Tulsa Philharmonic's sense of musical ensemble has markedly improved.

The Tulsa Philharmonic programs conservatively and doesn't stray too far from the nineteenth-century traditional fare. To a great degree, geography is the determining factor in this regard; there is no ASOL Regional orchestra closer than 125 miles (Oklahoma City) and no Major orchestra closer than those in St. Louis, Dallas, and Denver. Hence, audiences in Tulsa are more than satisfied to hear live performances from the core of the standard repertoire. There is no viable alternative nor, for that matter, any competition.

The Tulsa Philharmonic's $1.6 million budget is funded by ticket sales, federal, state, and local grants, foundation grants, corporate gifts, private donors, and other earned income. Individuals with wealth derived from the region's natural resources are relied on for much of the support that comes from the private sector. The administrative structure is rather sophisticated and adeptly blends volunteer and professional workers, public and private committee operations, and voting and non-voting interests. Essentially, the president, chairman, and executive director work with a 42-member Board of Directors, a 15-member Executive Committee, and a non-voting Advisory Board composed of 40 individuals. A Volunteer Council that dates back to the Philharmonic's inception now boasts 1,000 members. The newer Junior Division, formed in 1960, has over 150 members who support the Tulsa Youth Symphony and promote various educational activities.

The Tulsa Philharmonic sponsors the Tulsa Youth Symphony, which provides essential orchestra experience for young musicians in grades nine through twelve. It also sponsors the Friends of Strings, an auxiliary organization whose goal is to promote and assist directly in the development of string pedagogy throughout the Tulsa metropolitan area.

When it appears with its full complement, the Tulsa Philharmonic numbers 88 players. From this pool five other ensembles are derived: a 35-piece chamber orchestra, an 18-piece string orchestra, a string quartet, a woodwind quintet, and a brass quintet.

CHRONOLOGY OF MUSIC DIRECTORS: H. Arthur Brown, 1948–1958. Vladimir Golschmann, 1958–1961. Franco Autori, 1961–1971. Skitch Henderson, 1971–1974. Thomas Lewis, 1974–1977. Murry Sidlin, 1978–1980. Joel Lazar, 1980–1983. Bernard Rubenstein, 1984-present.

BIBLIOGRAPHY: Interviews with Nancy Sies, Executive Director of the Tulsa Philharmonic, and John Toms, Music Critic, *Tulsa Tribune*, 1984. "Brown in Last Season with Philharmonic," *Tulsa Tribune*, 20 Mar. 1949. "More Music for Tulsans," *Tulsa Tribune*, 4 Jan. 1957. "Tulsa Philharmonic Begins Under New Director," *Tulsa World*, 23 May 1948.

ACCESS: Tulsa Philharmonic Society, 2210 South Main Street, Tulsa, OK 74114. (918) 584–2533. Nancy Sies, Executive Director.

STEPHEN H. BARNES

Oregon ─────────────────────────

EUGENE (275,226—Eugene/Springfield)

Eugene Symphony Orchestra (Mt)

The Eugene Symphony Orchestra is a direct outgrowth of a group of talented amateur musicians who functioned in the early 1960s under the name of the Emerald Chamber Players. Coordinated by Orvil Etter, the Players were initially brought together for their own enjoyment in the making of music, but as their activity and interest increased, that group decided, in the fall of 1965, to sponsor an expanded ensemble to be known as the Eugene Symphony Orchestra. Lawrence Maves, a professor of violin at the University of Oregon, was appointed conductor, and during the 1965–1966 season the orchestra was initiated. The orchestra continued under the direction of Maves until May of 1981, at which time William Mc-Glaughlin, formerly resident conductor of the St. Paul Chamber Orchestra,* became its first full-time music director and conductor.

The administrative structure for the orchestra was provided by a Board of Directors and a series of part-time managers until March of 1979, when James Reeves was appointed as the orchestra's first full-time manager. His staff has grown to provide full-time responsibilities for personnel, ticket sales, and the usual functions of a symphony administrative headquarters.

For many years the Eugene-Springfield area, with a total population of 175,000, actively supported the orchestra, which presented its six annual concerts in Beall Recital Hall on the University of Oregon campus. The limited seating, for 550 persons, necessitated repeating each concert during the 1970s, and the need for a more appropriate hall became a focus of the orchestra and the community. The orchestra Board became a prime moving force in the search for a new hall, and the support of a large share of the community and other arts organizations led to the construction and opening of the new Hult Center for the Performing Arts in the fall of 1982. The Center is remarkable in many dimensions. Its total cost was 40 million dollars and includes the Performing Arts Center with a 550-seat theater, a 2,550-seat concert hall, parking facilities, a hotel, and a conference center. The complex was constructed entirely with community funds, without any state or federal support. After its opening concert the hall received national acclaim as "the prototype of a concert hall of the future" (Harold C. Schonberg, *New York Times*) and "unquestionably one of the two or three finest performing arts complexes in the world" (Charles Horton, Chapel Hill newspaper).

Moving from a 550-seat hall in which performances, given twice for a total available seating of 1,100, to a new hall with 2,250 seats provided the orchestra with a challenge. The season was increased to eight classical concerts with distinguished soloists, new works were commissioned, and a four-concert season of "Superpops" was programmed. Nine performances of the *Nutcracker* with the Eugene Ballet Company, additional family concerts, and a performance of *Messiah* completed the programming.

Under Conductor McGlaughlin the orchestra has emphasized music of the twentieth century as well, including one such work on each program. Recent performances have included works commissioned and performed by the orchestra. The university brings to its campus each year for workshops several well-known composers, and their works are frequently performed by the Symphony with the composers present at the concert. Within the last year this plan was followed in a performance of "Toccata" by Leon Kirchner and "Island" by Elliott Schwartz.

A comparison of data for 1982–1983 with that of the 1978–1979 series reveals the extent of success achieved by the orchestra and its management. Paid admissions filled 85% of the five-fold increase in seats during 1982–1983. Total audience increased 803% from 1978–1979 to 1982–1983. Operating expenses increased 577%, but patron contributions to the annual fund increased by 1,100% during this same period. Although a controlable accumulated deficit from previous years has still to be met, this season of unparalleled growth ended with a slight cash surplus. The success of the 1982–1983 season is clearly attributable to many people, but chief among these are Conductor McGlaughlin, who enhanced audience appeal, and General Manager Reeves, for thorough management of the available resources.

The Long-Range Planning Committee of the Board has recently stated, "The task for the next five years is to establish a solid foundation that can sustain changes of this magnitude. Once this base is secure we will be able to move in new directions as seen appropriate. . . . We will adapt and temper the examples of major American symphony orchestras to insure that the Eugene Symphony Orchestra can serve its patrons with appropriate excellence."

The presence of a major school of music in the community at the University of Oregon has had an important effect upon the orchestra. Fully 50% of the players are faculty, advanced students, and recent graduates of the school. Orchestra soloists present workshops on campus, libraries and equipment are shared, and beginning with the 1983–1984 season, joint player-faculty positions have been developed, bringing to the community highly qualified artists who are attracted by a career combining professional performance with university teaching. Selection of these players is made by a joint Symphony-University Selection Committee after a national search and requires a personal audition and approval of the president of the university.

The orchestra is the regular pit orchestra for productions of the Eugene Ballet Company. It also works closely with the 50-year-old Eugene Youth Symphony, which feeds players, on graduation, into the Eugene Symphony according to individual proficiency and the needs of the orchestra.

CHRONOLOGY OF MUSIC DIRECTORS: Lawrence Maves, 1965–1981. William McGlaughlin, 1981-present.

BIBLIOGRAPHY: Byron Belt, in *Musical America*, Mar. 1983. Charles Horton, quoted by the *Eugene Register-Guard*, 7 Oct. 1982. Andrew Porter, in *The New Yorker*, 18 Oct. 1982. Harold C. Schonberg, in *New York Times*, 13 June 1982.

ACCESS: Eugene Symphony Orchestra, 1231 Olive St., Eugene, OR 97405. (503) 687–9487. James W. Reeves, General Manager.

MORRETTE RIDER

PORTLAND (1,242,594)

Oregon Symphony Orchestra (Mj)

The Oregon Symphony Orchestra is the oldest on the West Coast and in 1984 became the largest arts organization in the state. Early historical records indicate that Portland's first symphonic concert took place at Oro Fino Hall on June 15, 1866, just 21 years after the city's founding. Ensuing years brought more concerts and several attempts to establish an orchestra; by 1875 the first orchestra society was formed, followed by others over the next two decades.

It was not until 1896 that the Portland Symphony Orchestra was founded. W. H. Kinross conducted the initial concert at the Marquam Grand Theatre on October 30, 1896. By 1899 the orchestra was giving an annual concert series, and in 1902 it embarked on its first tour and gave its first world premiere performance (M. B. Palacio's "Intermezzo," Op. 12, No 1).

In its early years the orchestra was maintained cooperatively by the players, equally sharing ticket sale revenues and electing a conductor from their own personnel. However, in 1911 a major reorganization commenced, which signalled the beginning of the orchestra's modern era and its movement toward professionalism. In the next seven years an office was established, a manager hired, a Board of Directors elected, the earliest contributions were recorded, and the symphony season was expanded to six concerts with tickets being sold by subscription. The reorganization culminated with the orchestra's premiere concert in Portland's new Civic Auditorium and the appointment of its first resident conductor, Carl Denton, in 1918.

The orchestra continued to grow in public esteem and under Willem van Hoogstraten, conductor from 1925 to 1938, became recognized as one of the foremost in America, ranking among the 15 largest orchestras in the nation. However, the depression, the threat of war, and the consequent effect on the sponsoring Symphony Society's ability to carry the orchestra's deficits resulted in the suspension of its support of the orchestra's concerts in 1938.

Portland was without its regular symphonic season for nearly a decade, although the orchestra continued to perform on a limited basis under well-known guest conductors. Concerts during those years included occasional national radio broadcasts and an annual "Stadium Philharmonic" summer series in Multnomah Stadium supported by the federal Works Project Administration (WPA).

Finally, in 1947, with impetus from the local AFM chapter, the Symphony Society was revived and the Portland Symphony Orchestra reorganized as a permanent, professional orchestra. From 1949 to 1962, the Portland Symphony Orchestra was guided by a series of gifted and creative leaders—James Sample, Theodore Bloomfield, Piero Bellugi, and a succession of superb guest conductors.

In 1962, Jacques Singer, former music director of the Dallas Symphony,* the Vancouver Symphony, and Israel's Haifa Orchestra, became music director of the Portland Symphony Orchestra. As the orchestra grew artistically under Singer's guidance, it grew financially as well. In 1966, the Ford Foundation awarded the orchestra a five-year, one million dollar matching grant, giving it the opportunity to begin growth to Major orchestra status. It enabled the orchestra's long-range plans to include a pops series (which began under the direction of Norman Leyden in 1974), a youth concert series (which began in 1963), a longer concert season, and full employment for the orchestra members.

In August 1967, an official change in name to the Oregon Symphony Orchestra reflected the increasing number of concerts played outside Portland and a commitment to serve the larger statewide and regional community.

Norman Leyden, conductor of the orchestra's highly successful pops concerts, was named associate conductor in January 1974. In 1982, two years after current music director and conductor James DePreist took the reins of leadership from the popular Lawrence Leighton Smith, the Oregon Symphony joined the ranks of ASOL Major orchestras.

DePreist, former music director of Canada's L'Orchestre Symphonic de Quebec and associate conductor to Antal Dorati at the National Symphony* in Washington, D.C. is hailed by critics and audiences for his mastery of a vast symphonic repertoire and the ability to inspire orchestras to performances of unprecedented artistic heights.

Under the leadership of Smith and DePreist, the Oregon Symphony has come to be recognized as one of the fastest growing and improving, best attended, and most financially sound of the major orchestras. The orchestra is now playing to 96% capacity in its regular classical series and 99.5% in its pops performances. In the classical series, 86.5% of the house is sold on a subscription basis, and in the pops series, 92% of the seats are subscribed in advance.

The orchestra performs 133 concerts in Portland and surrounding communities in a 42-week season that runs from August through June with a total attendance of approximately 325,000. The season consists of 40 classical-series concerts, 24 pops-series concerts, a six-concert family series, and four sets of youth concerts, as well as various specials, runouts to neighboring cities, and an annual regional tour.

In the 1984–1985 season, the orchestra moved from the Portland Civic Auditorium, a city-managed, 3,000-seat facility where it had played since 1918. The Oregon Symphony Orchestra premiered on September 15, 1984, in the newly renovated Arlene Schnitzer Concert Hall in the Portland Center for the Performing Arts, formerly the Paramount Theatre. The Paramount, a 1927-vintage Rapp and Rapp motion picture palace, is now a magnificent 2,800 seat concert hall complete with orchestra shell and a permanent choir loft. In the fall of 1986, the Performing Arts Center will be complete when a 900-seat theater and a 400-seat "black box" ("empty space") theater are constructed across from the Schnitzer Hall.

The orchestra's move to the new hall has had enormous impact on its artistic quality, concert schedule, and budget size. For many years, due to the limited number of facilities in Portland, the Civic Auditorium was used by virtually every kind of entertainment appearing in the city. This lack of readily available space caused the orchestra to have limited access for performances and on-stage rehearsals. Most of the time the 83 members of the orchestra, their instruments, and their conductor had to rehearse in an uncomfortable, small rehearsal room, which created enormous artistic problems of balance and ensemble. The issue of on-stage rehearsals had no apparent solution until Schnitzer Hall became available.

Now, on-stage rehearsals are held during the morning at the Schnitzer Hall to clear the stage for afternoon move-ins by other users of the hall. Therefore, the daytime jobs previously held by many of the musicians to supplement their incomes have been given up since the move. Dramatic increases in salaries were necessary, and as a result, the orchestra's budget grew from $1.7 million in 1978–1979 to $5.4 million in 1984–1985.

The Oregon Symphony is funded by earned income and corporate, foundation, individual and in-kind donations, grants, and gifts. Earned income accounts for 60% of the orchestra's total income. Performance income is unusually high among orchestras, at 51% of the total. Endowment/investment income is 8% of the total, while fund-raising accounts for 30%.

The Oregon Symphony Association comprises individuals whose voting membership is determined by contributing a sum chosen by the Board of Directors. The Association is governed by the 50-member Board of Directors, elected at the annual membership meeting to staggered three-year terms. The orchestra is managed by a staff of 21, including a general manager, a director of development, a marketing director, an orchestra manager, and a comptroller. Artistically, the music director, who is selected by the Board, is solely responsible for programming on the classical series, while the associate conductor selects programs for the pops series. The orchestra is contracted annually, and extra musicians are hired for individual concerts as needed.

Characteristically, the orchestra's repertoire is, to quote Music Director James DePreist, "the proven formula of the new, compatibly placed alongside the familiar." He continues,

I feel very strongly that audiences and Orchestra alike should have the opportunity to experience the new as well as the familiar in performances that make the former sound compelling and the latter seem fresh. The masterpieces, regardless of century, have been and will continue to be performed more often than less significant works. I have tried to prepare the way for modern music by introducing works non-threatening in their modernity, yet clearly non-conventional, transitional works to lower the threshold of acceptance to the point that tolerance *of* becomes interest *in* and eventually a desire *for* a more varied musical diet.

The OSO has premiered works by Northwest composers, including Aaron Avshalamoff's Symphonic Suite; *The Soul of Kin Sei*; Jacob Avshalamoff's symphonies, *The Oregon* and *Praises from the Corners of the Earth*; Eric Funk's "Emily"; and Tomas Svoboda's *Overture of the Season*, Op. 89 and Symphony No. 4, Op. 69, (*Apocalyptic*). Other OSO world premieres include works by Robert Russell Bennett, Fred Fox, and Darius Milhaud. It has performed several works in their American premieres as well.

In addition to concerts, the Oregon Symphony provides a series of educational programs: youth concerts, performance/discussions with Symphony guest artists (called "Musically Speaking"), "Symphony Sundays" family concerts, a young conductor's program, young artists competitions, and a youth concert poster competition.

CHRONOLOGY OF MUSIC DIRECTORS: Carl Denton, 1918–1925. Willem van Hoogstraten, 1925–1938. (Operations curtailed, 1938–1947.) Werner Janssen, 1947–1949. James Sample, 1949–1953. Theodore Bloomfield, 1955–1959. Piero Bellugi, 1959–1961. (Guest conductors, 1961–1962). Jacques Singer, 1962–1972. (Guest conductors, 1972–1973.) Lawrence Leighton Smith, 1973–1980. James DePreist, 1980-present.

BIBLIOGRAPHY: John E. Graham, "A Report from Portland," *Northwest Arts*, Jan. 1984.

ACCESS: Oregon Symphony Orchestra, 813 SW Alder, Mezzanine Level, Portland, OR 97205. (503) 228–4294. John E. Graham, General Manager.

ELLIE O'HAGAN

Pennsylvania ⸻

AVOCA (640,396—Northeast Pennsylvania)

Northeastern Pennsylvania Philharmonic (Mt)

Scranton and Wilkes-Barre are communities in which music has flourished since the last quarter of the nineteenth century. Over the years many local professional musicians and civic leaders joined together to form various civic orchestras, sinfoniettas, and other such musical groups. However, it was not until 1972 that the Northeastern Pennsylvania Philharmonic came into existence.

But this was not the first time that the two communities had united their orchestral efforts. As early as September 1894 the Symphony Orchestra of Scranton and Wilkes-Barre was formed, an organization was established, and weekly rehearsals of the combined group of musicians from the two cities were begun. The objective, according to Scranton Philharmonic historians Mrs. Yevitz and Mrs. Clark, was to raise "the musical standard in this locality by giving concerts of classical music." Actually, two concerts were given that season: one at the Scranton Academy of Music on November 23, and the other at the Grand Opera House in Wilkes-Barre the following day, all of which indicates early efforts to join the two communities musically.

The Northeastern Pennsylvania Philharmonic was the result of a merger of the Scranton Philharmonic and the Wilkes-Barre Philharmonic Society. Both orchestras before the merger were professional, but with more local musicians in each cadre than after the merger. Problems would be faced in the early days of the merger, both from the local musicians' unions and from certain members of the orchestras. It would not necessarily be an easy time for the first director who took over. Talks leading to the merger were first instituted in April of 1969, when a committee was formed from both communities to assess financial and community ramifications of such a plan. By the end of that year agreement had been reached, and at a meeting on January 14, 1970, the Joint Coordinating Committee concurred on plans for a combined 1970–1971 season.

For two years the two orchestras would continue to operate separately, with Beatrice Brown as music director and conductor of the Scranton Philharmonic Orchestra and Ferdinand Liva continuing in the same capacity with the Wilkes-Barre Philharmonic. For those two years the Philharmonic Society of Northeastern Pennsylvania sponsored a series of concerts, with each orchestra offering two concerts in the two cities. The Joint Coordinating Committee agreed on concert dates, and the two conductors consulted on programs so as to avoid duplication. The announced intention was to launch the newly merged "Philharmonic Orchestra of Northeastern Pennsylvania" by the autumn of 1972. In the meantime the respective Boards of the two orchestras continued to deal with local matters, and the two orchestras continued as separate entities, although there were a number of musicians common to both.

Ultimately came the announcement of the selection of Thomas Michalak as music director of the newly formed orchestra. He took over for the 1972–1973 season and remained in that post until the 1979–1980 season. During this period he was responsible for bringing the various elements together, strengthening the caliber of the orchestra, and developing it into a good ensemble.

When Michalak took over, the season was still limited to four concerts in each city. However, in the 1978–1979 season, a pair of pops concerts were added and a third followed in 1979–1980, the pattern that remains today.

The 1980–1981 season was highlighted by the search for a new conductor. It was considered critical that the orchestra secure an outstanding young conductor who could carry on the work begun by Michalak. In April of 1981 announcement was made that then 28-year-old Hugh Wolff, assistant conductor of the National Symphony Orchestra* (Washington, D.C.), would take over as music director. He was selected from five finalists who auditioned for the post.

The orchestra today comprises an average of 80 players who come from a radius of 120 miles of the two cities. Roughly 20% are local musicians; the others come from Philadelphia, New Jersey, New York, and Northeastern and Central Pennsylvania. More than 70 of the orchestra members are under contract on a per-service basis each season.

The annual budget totals around $500,000, with slightly more than 55% going for the artistic personnel. Roughly 40% of the total comes from subscriptions and ticket sales; the remainder from concert sponsorships, contributions, and grants. This budget has quintupled since the organization was founded.

In addition to the subscription concerts in Scranton and Wilkes-Barre, the orchestra schedules "run-off" concerts in such other communities as Stroudsburg, Honesdale, State College, Bloomsburg, Harrisburg, and Allenstown. These concerts are in keeping with the charge of the Philharmonic's Board when the two orchestras merged: to reach area audiences outside of Scranton/Wilkes-Barre. A number of smaller informal ensembles have grown out of the orchestra itself, most prominently a string quartet, brass quintet, and wind quintet.

By far, most concerts have included guest artists, some of international renown. Over the years the Philharmonic has commissioned a limited number of compositions by Pennsylvania composers. Most significant was the concert opera *The River Flows* by Richard Wargo, a young Scranton composer. It was also significant in the orchestra's development for having been televised statewide on the Pennsylvania Public Television Network. Another of Wargo's compositions, *Celebration* Overture, was commissioned and first performed by the Philharmonic in September 1979. Gerard Levinson, a member of the faculty at Swarthmore College, has likewise been commissioned to write a piece that will in all likelihood premiere in the 1984–1985 season. Other special events have included a locally televised performance of Prokofiev's *Peter and the Wolf*, featuring the Bob Brown Puppets, and a special 1983 gala with cellist Mstislav Rostropovich; another with Metropolitan Opera soloist Paul Plishka, a Northeastern Pennsylvania native, is planned for 1985.

Among the missions of the organization is the desire to encourage and provide an opportunity for growth of young, talented musicians. That was one of the reasons behind the selection of a young music director like Hugh Wolff; a number of guest artists are chosen with that same thought in mind. For some years the Philharmonic sponsored a youth orchestra, but it disbanded, largely because so many of its young members had to travel great distances to reach the orchestra.

The Association has a Board with a maximum of 50 members and the typical cadre of officers. There is a staff of six full-time employees with from a few months' to eight years' service. Sally Preate, general manager, has the longest tenure.

CHRONOLOGY OF MUSIC DIRECTORS: Thomas Michalak, 1972–1980. (Guest conductors, 1981–1982.) Hugh Wolff, 1981-present.

BIBLIOGRAPHY: Interviews with NPP Music Director Hugh Wolff and General Manager Sally Preate. NPP Archives. *Wilkes-Barre Times-Leader*. Mrs. William J. Yevitz and Mrs. George A. Clark, "History of the Scranton Philharmonic Orchestra—1875 to 1954," mimeographed typescript, [1954].

ACCESS: Northeastern Pennsylvania Philharmonic, Box 71, Avoca, PA 18641. (717) 287–1916. Sally Preate, General Manager.

ROY E. MORGAN

PHILADELPHIA (4,716,818)

Concerto Soloists of Philadelphia (Mt)

The distinguished Concerto Soloists of Philadelphia was founded in 1964 by its music director, Marc Mostovoy. Originally playing under the name "16 Concerto Soloists," reflecting the numerical composition of the ensemble, it went through several name changes, including "Mostovoy Soloists" in 1974, before settling permanently on "Concerto Soloists of Philadelphia" in 1977.

The impetus for the group was twofold: to give brilliant young musicians an opportunity to be heard in a concerto format, and to offer to the cultural community works outside the standard symphonic repertoire. Since the demise of the Philadelphia Chamber Orchestra years ago, Concerto Soloists has been the sole permanent alternative to the Philadelphia Orchestra,* and it enjoys an unequalled longevity among similar ensembles in the area. It is now Philadelphia's only professional resident chamber orchestra concentrating essentially on seventeenth- and eighteenth-century music.

A remarkably homogeneous group, its core personnel comprises nine violins, three violas, two cellos, one bass, and a harpsichord. Recently two oboes, two horns, and one bassoon have been added. Other instruments are added as the music requires. All performers but cellos and harpsichord play in standing position. Conceived along the lines of the repertory theater, the ensemble's eminently trained performers might be heard either as soloists or in accompaniment roles. During a concert they often change positions on stage, taking turns leading. Together they perform at a high level of musicianship and artistic integrity.

During the course of a season, the orchestra plays six subscription concerts at the Academy of Music and five subscription concerts at the Church of the Holy Trinity, both in Philadelphia. The latter location features the orchestra in its "Basically Baroque Coffee Concerts" in which orchestra members are soloists. Invited guest soloists appear in the Academy of Music concerts. Additionally, four "Learning through Listening" children's concerts are presented at the Walnut Street Theater. The orchestra has also initiated innovative programs directed to the needs of the community. These include the widely acclaimed Senior Artists Showcase and the Young Artists Competition. Popular, too, have been the "Cushion Concerts," midnight affairs that at one time served as a boon for musical insomniacs.

Concerto Soloists also serves as resident orchestra for such local festivals as Mozart on the Square, Basically Bach Festival, Moravian Music Festival, Innisfree Festival of the Arts, Swarthmore Music Festival, as well as other events in the Mid-Atlantic region. In Philadelphia they are the orchestra for the AVA Opera Theater, the Philadelphia Singers, Singing City, and the Savoy Opera Company. Furthermore, members of the orchestra participate in college residency programs including seminars, master classes and open rehearsals. They also hold lead positions in well-known music festivals around the country.

The orchestra's busy schedule includes statewide, national, and international tours. In 1976 it went to the Middle East with 14 highly successful concerts in Israel. Equally well-received were concerts in Germany in 1981. The orchestra's Carnegie Hall debut in December of 1981 received unstinting praise from the *New York Times*; New York heard the orchestra again in 1985, and a European tour is scheduled for the 1985–1986 season.

The governing body of Concerto Soloists is a Board of Directors, with artistic control in the hands of the music director. The organization also includes a general manager, executive director, personnel manager, and public relations/marketing director. Its 1984–1985 budget is in excess of $1 million, with funding derived from corporate contributions, foundation funds, government and public funds, private sources, ticket sales, and underwritten engagements. In 1982 the core musicians negotiated a salaried contract, which guaranteed a specified number of services within a 40-week season. The 1984–1985 season saw the number of services doubling to approximately 260, putting the ensemble on a sound professional footing.

Music Director Marc Mostovoy is an authority in the performance-practice of the baroque and classical repertoires and personally edits all scores and parts used by the Concerto Soloists. String parts are fingered as well as bowed. All efforts are made to assure that early scores are restored to their presumed original state. The thoroughness of the approach to performance extends to the use of bows specially designed and made by Irwin Groer of Glen Mills. They allow for the better articulation of sound desirable in baroque and classical literature.

Although the orchestra's repertoire is strongest in seventeenth- and eighteenth-century music, it is not unusual to find works from all periods on its programs. Premiere performances of new works by Philadelphia-area composers are regularly programmed with unusual works of the past, including, recently, select masterpieces for chamber orchestra from the romantic period.

Regularly performing sub-groups from the orchestra are a baroque quartet, a string quartet, a baroque sextet, a violin and piano duo, and solo harpsichord.

Affiliated with Concerto Soloists since 1981 has been the internationally distinguished conductor, Max Rudolf. He leads the orchestra in Academy of Music concerts and in the "Basically Baroque Concerts" at the Church of the Holy Trinity. In 1983 Dr. Rudolf was appointed conductor laureate.

CHRONOLOGY OF MUSIC DIRECTORS: Marc Mostovoy, 1964-present.

BIBLIOGRAPHY: Interviews with CSP Music Director Marc Mostovoy, Executive Director Katharine Sokoloff, and Public Relations/Marketing Director D'Arcy Webb, 1984. Bernard Holland, "Music: The Concerto Soloists," *New York Times*, 19 Dec.

1981. Carol Ann Spielman, "Concerto Soloists," *WFLN Philadelphia Guide*, Sept. 1983.

ACCESS: Concerto Soloists of Philadelphia, 338 South 15th Street, Philadelphia, PA 19102. (215) 735–0202. Katharine Sokoloff, Executive Director. D'Arcy Webb, Public Relations/Marketing Director.

GEORGE K. DIEHL

Philadelphia Orchestra (Mj)

One of the country's pre-eminent orchestras, the Philadelphia Orchestra plays between 170 and 180 concerts a year, of which approximately 130 are at home. Almost 100 of these belong to a number of subscription series. Among its non-subscription concerts are an annual Gala season-opener, two *Messiah* performances, a New Year's Eve concert, and an annual Academy of Music Anniversary concert. Interlaced into this busy schedule are 10 concerts for young people.

In the summer the orchestra's 104 musicians play 18 concerts at the Mann Music Center in Philadelphia, a series inaugurated in 1930 at an outdoor amphitheater (Robin Hood Dell) in the city's Fairmont Park section. With the construction in 1976 of the Mann Music Center (an open-sided pavilion with a capacity of 15,000 honoring the tireless efforts of Fredric R. Mann on behalf of music in Philadelphia), the orchestra now gives its Philadelphia summer concerts at the new location over a six-week period in June and July. For three weeks in August it also performs 12 concerts at the Saratoga Performing Arts Center in Saratoga Springs, New York. Its New York City and Washington, D.C., appearances add approximately 14 concerts to the schedule. Three weeks of touring increase the number by another 15 or 20, giving the orchestra a 44-week annual performance schedule. Many orchestra members also perform with numerous chamber ensembles in the Delaware Valley and teach both privately and in local conservatories and universities.

In addition to its playing members, the orchestra has two full-time librarians and a personnel manager. The librarians oversee the detailed operation of the library's holding of about 3,000 scores with parts; the personnel manager provides the important liaison between conductor, orchestra, manager, and union on a variety of operational matters.

A non-profit corporate structure, the Philadelphia Orchestra is maintained and operated by the Philadelphia Orchestra Association. Its officers steer the Association during fairly long tenures and are as conscious of the orchestra's artistic welfare as of its operational needs. Ultimate artistic leadership rests, of course, with the music director. The administrative management is headed by an executive director, a manager, an assistant manager, and directors of development, public relations, finance, marketing, and education.

The current budget of $12 million is derived from endowment income, campaigns, private and corporate donations, ticket sales, recordings, broadcasts, and other avenues emanating from an active development office. Immensely successful radio marathons conducted by WFLN (Philadelphia's classical music station) have added appreciably to the orchestra's revenues—the most visible single fund-raisers, these radio marathons have built a broad and vital base of support.

Among the orchestra's instrument possessions are the usual percussion instruments, an assemblage of winds (including Wagner tubas, Japanese-made rotary-valve "C" trumpets, bass clarinets, basset horns, and alto flute), and a highly prized collection of strings by such distinguished craftsmen as Stradivari, Guarneri, Amati, and Guadagnini.

The Philadelphia Orchestra has an extensive list of published historical accounts, upon which the following is principally based.

Although the orchestra has been playing its concerts in the Academy of Music since its founding in 1900 and has been rehearsing in it since 1912, it was not until 1950 that the Philadelphia Orchestra Association bought controlling stock of the structure, making it the orchestra's official home. The Academy has its own Board of Directors, which partially overlaps with the Orchestra Association's Board.

The cornerstone for the building was laid in the summer of 1855, when Philadelphia had a population approaching 500,000, and the Academy opened with a gala ball on January 26, 1857. It has been a stellar attraction in the cultural life of the city ever since and is now officially designated a national historical landmark. With a seating capacity of 2,929, the Academy was air-conditioned in 1968 and is now in use year-round. In 1971 a massive restoration was undertaken with proceeds from the annual anniversary concerts and balls that celebrate the Academy's birthday. Considered by some to be the "Stradivarius" of concert halls, the Academy's legendary acoustics have become a source of controversy. Not all, including the orchestra's new music director, agree that they are as good as traditional opinion insists. Under serious consideration is the construction of a new theater that can be used for recordings as well as for concerts; it is the Philadelphia Orchestra's wish to record in its own hall. Such a new facility is also seen as enhancing the development of other musical and theatrical undertakings and relieving the pressures on the heavily booked Academy.

The Philadelphia Orchestra was founded in 1900. The scene was ripe for the establishment of an orchestra designed to sustain itself on a broadly based community scale. Even though its founding was beset with difficulties and the prospects of its success were not totally predictable, the financial support for an initial series of six concerts became available. On November 16, 1900, under the direction of Fritz Scheel, the Philadelphia Orchestra gave its first concert in the Academy of Music. The orchestra was chartered in 1903.

Through great efforts by the Philadelphia Orchestra Association and the Women's Committees, the orchestra survived the trying times of its first two decades. The first permanent organizations of their kind in the world, the model for similar groups here and abroad, the Women's Committees promoted the orchestra's earliest out-of-town concerts, established auxiliaries as far away as Baltimore, Washington, and Atlantic City, and became habituées of the perennially favorite Friday afternoon concerts. A recent name change to Volunteer Committees now identifies the 550 members of the seven groups; they traditionally raise the largest amounts of any single component of the orchestra's fund-raising effort.

Fritz Scheel, the orchestra's first conductor, a friend of Brahms, Bülow, Rubinstein, and Tchaikovsky, was an outstanding musical figure and came to the orchestra with an impressive background. Born in Lübeck, Germany, in 1852, he was in Philadelphia in 1899 for a summer series at Woodside Park when he was prevailed upon to assist in the founding of the Philadelphia Orchestra. In preparation for the orchestra's first season, Scheel canvassed the city for the best musicians. In subsequent seasons he made repeated trips to Europe, which he knew well, to recruit the first-class musicians he brought back from principal cities in Germany and the Netherlands. A musician of discrimination, he offered his Philadelphia audiences programs of taste and seriousness. He mounted a Beethoven cycle, gave American premieres of works by major European composers, and invited personalities of the calibre of Richard Strauss to guest conduct. When he died on March 13, 1907, much was still left to be done, but he had set standards for future conductors and laid the all-important groundwork of professionalism.

Succeeding Scheel was another German, Carl Pohlig, born in Teplitz, Bohemia, in 1864. He, too, came with impeccable credentials. Despite initial artistic successes, however, relationships between Pohlig, the orchestra, and the Board became difficult. When he learned that the orchestra was looking for a successor—had indeed signed one—Pohlig tendered his resignation on June 10, 1912, and returned to Germany.

The organizational and artistic accomplishments of Scheel and Pohlig notwithstanding, what the orchestra needed was a figure with striking public appeal who had the ability to move it to progressively higher levels. The answer came in the London-born Leopold Stokowski. It was he who would lead the orchestra to its Parnassus and, one might add, to his own. When Stokowski came to Philadelphia from the Cincinnati Symphony,* he lost no time in displaying his charisma and exercising his strong will. He was 30, tall, and handsome, with an unfailing sense of showmanship. His dynamic style generated new excitement publicly as well as within the ranks of the orchestra. Concert attendance mounted immediately and continued unabated.

In elevating the orchestra's performance, Stokowski retained the best players and changed the rest of the personnel to suit his demanding standard. After nine years at the helm, only a small handful of players remained from the orchestra's early period. To achieve better sonorities and balances, he experimented with unorthodox seating arrangements. And with a particular concept of orchestral sound in mind, as well as for greater freedom in playing, he introduced and continued to prefer free rather than uniform bowing from the string sections.

From Stokowski's first rehearsal on October 7, 1912, it was clear that new leadership was at hand, and new performing standards were going to become a reality. Over the years he transformed a respectable fledgling orchestra into an instrument of tremendous precision and polish.

Under Scheel and Pohlig the orchestra's repertoire was dominated largely by favored works of the great German masters. While Pohlig's particular obsessions were Wagner and Tchaikovsky, Scheel's programs were more balanced. However, with Stokowski the orchestra moved into an era of unusual programming, with an expanding repertoire of contemporary music, balanced with the masterpieces of the past. He clearly favored those composers whose music allowed him to exploit his orchestra's most vivid sounds and most exciting playing. Four years into his tenure he delivered the first American performance of Mahler's Eighth Symphony. The sensational event, using more than one thousand performers, brought the orchestra unprecedented attention. John Mueller (in *The American Symphony Orchestra*, p. 129) attests that it "catapulted the city, the orchestra, and the young conductor into an intoxicating position of notoriety from which each and all distilled the last ounce of profit."

For Stokowski that was just the beginning. His exploring spirit introduced new composers, new works, and new performers to Philadelphia. He kept the orchestra busy reading new material, always in search of novel program content. The sound of Schoenberg, Stravinsky, Cowell, and Bartók—and later Berg, Webern, Varèse and Ives—balanced the classical staples. There were periods during Stokowski's tenure when Philadelphia was viewed as a center for new music. Gradually the orchestra's prominence rose to national and then international recognition.

In 1927 Stokowski began to appear less frequently on the podium, relinquishing the orchestra to noted guest conductors, a format that he continued for the remainder of his stay in Philadelphia. By the early 1930s, polarized factions concerning Stokowski, his programs, and his position with the orchestra developed within the Board of Directors. The reason for his resignation in 1934 remains a source of speculation, although there were, apparently, irreconcilable differences. He continued his ties with the orchestra, and in 1938, after two years of podium-sharing with his successor, he relinquished his orchestra to Eugene Ormandy. He had become a legend. In 1960, on invitation, he returned to Philadelphia to conduct the orchestra. The occasion was in all respects an emotional one. Stokowski's controversiality notwithstanding—and it surrounded practially everything he did— the unshakable truth is that he created a great orchestra.

From 1912 to 1980 the Philadelphia Orchestra's artistic life was in the hands of only two conductors. Leopold Stokowski and Eugene Ormandy afforded the ensemble a continuity and stability not known to any other similar group. They molded its personnel, fashioned its repertoire, and created its distinctive sound. Born in Budapest in 1899, Eugene Ormandy came to the United States in 1921. In 1930 he directed the Philadelphia Orchestra for the first time at Robin Hood Dell. He was invited for the following summer and was later that year engaged to substitute for the indisposed Arturo Toscanini during the orchestra's regular season. While holding the post of music director of the Minneapolis Symphony (now the Minnesota Orchestra*) from 1931 to 1936, Ormandy returned to Philadelphia regularly as a guest conductor, and when it was time to decide on Stokowski's successor, his name was clearly fixed in the minds of those who would make the decision.

In 1936 he was appointed to the orchestra, and although he shared two seasons with Stokowski, he was, in effect, music director. The change of command was achieved without disruption. Ormandy maintained the orchestra's superb performing level and allowed it gradually to take on the opulent sound that became so closely affiliated with him. Under his guidance the Philadelphia Orchestra operated as a beautifully tooled, unusually polished, smoothly running ensemble, designed to deliver great performances.

In the 44 years that Ormandy was music director, he enjoyed an unprecedented length of leadership characterized by a singular devotion to the orchestra. He labored unhurriedly but persistently in striving for the full, rich tone that became a feature of the orchestra's playing. Despite his guest-conducting every major orchestra in the music capitals of the world, he conducted an extraordinary number of concerts with the Philadelphia Orchestra; his commitments there were always his first consideration.

His repertoire strengths when he first came to Philadelphia featured German, Russian, and French composers of the post-romantic and early modern periods, which over the years remained his most successful territory. He played new works but was cautious with contemporary music. His attitude was progressive but not radical in the choice of new repertoire, although in the late 1960s new elements began appearing via an international array of modern composers. This was also a time for the appearance of a galaxy of young but established guest conductors. In the tradition of Stokowski, Ormandy also had to his credit an impressive number of world and American premieres. In 1980, with the appointment of Riccardo Muti as music director, Eugene Ormandy became Conductor Laureate.

Perhaps not unexpectedly—since the operation of a major orchestra is a complex administrative matter—the Philadelphia Orchestra has had its share of internal problems. Power struggles on the Board, confrontations between management and players, union difficulties, and various problems have from time to time resulted in serious impasses, work stoppages, and periods of open hostility. In the long view, however, these may be considered functional appendages in the orchestra's continuing history of musical prominence.

Born in Naples in 1941, Riccardo Muti made his debut with the Philadelphia Orchestra in 1972. He was 31 and his European career was just beginning to solidify. He returned to Philadelphia on a regular basis in successive seasons and in 1977 was designated principal guest conductor, an unprecedented move in the orchestra's history. Three years later he became music director. An appointment not affecting his post in Philadelphia begins with the 1986–1987 season when he becomes music director of Teatro alla Scala in Milan.

Muti's energetic, new leadership has brought changes in programming, repertoire, and performance. More attention is being directed to contemporary music, especially American. To that end the Pulitzer Prize-winning composer Richard Wernick has been engaged as consultant to review and recommend for Muti's consideration twentieth-century scores, particularly of young composers writing since 1960—a repertoire that heretofore has had a low profile on the orchestra's programs. His appointment revitalizes the tradition of commitment to the performance of contemporary music initiated by Stokowski. It is also anticipated that original works will be commissioned for the orchestra on a regular basis.

Muti has, moreover, introduced highly successful concert performances of opera into the repertoire, an undertaking that recalls an earlier phase in the orchestra's history when in 1934 it staged performances of operas in response to the Metropolitan Opera eliminating its regular Philadelphia visits. As a charismatic conductor who is bringing new challenges to his position, Muti has garnered an enthusiastic audience response.

Herbert Kupferberg (in *Those Fabulous Philadelphians*, p. 5) calls the orchestra "Philadelphia's most successful envoy to the world since Benjamin Franklin." In its first season it already ventured outside the city, and its first 25 years saw it traveling extensively in North America. Stokowski took it on its first transcontinental tour in 1936, and during Ormandy's tenure it continued such tours on a regional and national basis. The orchestra has been to Europe many times since 1949. Central and South America have also been visited. Its Oriental tours have taken it to Japan several times (including Korea), and in September 1973 the Philadelphia Orchestra became the first United States orchestra to perform in mainland China.

The history of the Philadelphia Orchestra has had an impact on broadcast media with such events as the first commercially sponsored, nationally broadcast radio concert in October 1929; participation in the making of four Hollywood films, the most famous being *Fantasia*; and the mounting on March 21, 1948, of the first symphonic concert in the history of television, preceding Toscanini and the NBC Symphony by 90 minutes. The orchestra also offers a broadcast transcription service available to radio stations across the country and to the Voice of America for overseas transmission.

The orchestra's concerts for young people constitute the singularly strongest element in its educational policy. Fritz Scheel gave concerts for young people as early as 1902. The now sold-out children's concerts were first presented by Stokowski in 1921. To the Stokowski era also belongs the inauguration of the Senior Student Concerts (1933). The Junior Student Concerts were introduced in 1959 during the Ormandy years. Recently, Muti has opened dress rehearsals to high school and college students.

Associate Conductor William Smith has played an indispensable role in the orchestra's operation since 1952. In addition to acting as standby conductor, he leads the children's, junior, and senior concerts, *Messiah* performances, the New Year's Eve concert, and other non-subscription programs, and conducts on the subscription series as well.

RECORDING HISTORY AND SELECTIVE DISCOGRAPHY: Commencing with its first recording in 1917, the orchestra had an exclusive contract with RCA until 1943, when it moved to Columbia Records. In 1968 it returned to RCA. Between the two companies the orchestra built the largest recorded repertoire of any ensemble (with unsurpassed sales). In 1977 an affiliation began with Angel Records, with the orchestra currently recording for Angel, RCA, Delos, Telarc, and CBS Masterworks Records.

Ormandy's recording activity, principally with the Philadelphia Orchestra, is astounding; he is surely the most-recorded American conductor to date. With a recording career of more than 50 years, even informed estimates of how many recordings he made are difficult to ascertain. Muti's list of recordings with the orchestra increases each year. Numerous albums ranging in repertoire from Beethoven to Stravinsky have already been produced, bringing the orchestra's discography to over 500 recordings.

Chabrier, *España*; Works of De Falla and Ravel (Muti): Angel DS 37742. Dvořák, Symphony No. 8 (Ormandy): RCA ARL–4264. Franck, Symphony in D Minor (Muti): Angel DS–37889. Mendelssohn, Symphony No. 4 (Ormandy): MS–6628. Prokofiev, *Romeo and Juliet* (Muti): Angel DS–37776. Rimsky-Korsakov, *Sheherezade* (Ormandy) RCA ARL1–0028. Stravinsky, *The Rite of Spring* (Muti): Angel SZ–37646. Tchaikovsky, Symphony No. 5 (Ormandy): Delos DMS–3015.

CHRONOLOGY OF MUSIC DIRECTORS: Fritz Scheel, 1900–1907. Carl Pohlig, 1907–1912. Leopold Stokowski, 1912–1936. Leopold Stokowski and Eugene Ormandy, 1936–1938. Eugene Ormandy, 1938–1980. Riccardo Muti, 1980-present.

BIBLIOGRAPHY: Edward Arian, *Bach, Beethoven, and Bureaucracy* (University of Alabama Press, 1971). Abram Chasins, *Leopold Stokowski* (New York: Hawthorn, 1979). Oliver Daniel, *Stokowski* (New York: Dodd, Mead, 1982). Philip Hart, *Conductors: A New Generation* (New York: Scribner's, 1979). Philip Hart, *Orpheus in the New World* (New York: Norton, 1973). Herbert Kupferberg, *Those Fabulous Philadelphians* (New York: Scribner's, 1969). John H. Mueller, *The American Symphony Orchestra* (Bloomington: Indiana University Press, 1951). Paul Robinson *Stokowski* ([New York]: Vanguard, 1977). Harold Schonberg, *The Great Conductors*

(New York: Simon and Schuster, 1967). Frances Wister, *Twenty-five Years of the Philadelphia Orchestra, 1900–1925* (1925; reprint, Freeport, N.Y.: Books for Libraries Press).

ACCESS: The Philadelphia Orchestra, 1420 Locust Street, Philadelphia, PA 19102. (215) 893–1900. Joseph Santarlasci, Manager. Judith Karp, Director of Public Relations.

GEORGE K. DIEHL

PITTSBURGH (2,263,894)

Pittsburgh Symphony Orchestra (Mj)

One of the major orchestras of the world, the Pittsburgh Symphony is a busy one, presenting over 200 concerts per year to an audience of some 600,000 at Heinz Hall, summer outdoor concerts to several hundred thousand more, and conducting several tours. In its 44-week season, the orchestra offers four subscription series (Thursdays through Sundays) in its regular fall and winter season, a series of young people's concerts, a pops series, free outdoor performances at Point State Park and Hartwood Acres, and tours. The PSO produces one or two recordings a year.

Pittsburgh has a long history relating to the music business. Early records from the nineteenth century indicate a violin maker in residence in 1810, eight years before the city was chartered, and a music printer in 1815. Throughout the century there were numerous bands, orchestras, and choral groups. By century's end there seemed to be adequate financial support for a professional orchestra, in addition to support for visiting soloists and other ensembles.

The Pittsburgh Symphony (originally called the Pittsburgh Orchestra) was founded in 1895. Its origin and support came from 25 public-spirited citizens in the Art Society of Pittsburgh (1859–1950). Fifty-two instrumentalists were recruited from several smaller, defunct orchestras. Concerts were given in the newly built Carnegie Music Hall in Oakland under the direction of Frederick Archer, who also served as organist. For the first three years the orchestra played 10 pairs of concerts each season, in addition to special or tour concerts.

When Victor Herbert was appointed conductor in 1898, the orchestra added 15 players and changed the type of programming. Herbert was succeeded in 1904 by Emil Paur, and during the 15 years of their directorships, the orchestra presented almost 1,000 concerts and was classed as third in artistic importance in America, behind Boston and Chicago. In 1906 a Pittsburgh Festival Orchestra, led by Carl Bernthaler, gave concerts throughout Pittsburgh and surrounding communities, providing summer employment for Pittsburgh Orchestra players. By 1907, however, dwindling public support created a severe financial problem. The Art Society withdrew its support in 1910, and, faced with a very large debt, the orchestra disbanded. Sixteen years elapsed before a new orchestra was founded, and it would be 37 years before a permanent conductor of national reputation would take its podium.

In 1910 a Pittsburgh Orchestra Association organized to try to reestablish the orchestra. Another attempt was made in 1916, but little was accomplished. Local music was yielding to the orchestra at nearby Carnegie Institute of Technology (now Carnegie-Mellon University).

A newly formed Pittsburgh Symphony performed on May 2, 1926, in Syria Mosque, also in Oakland. In 1927 nine officers of the Board of Directors were arrested for violating the 1794 Pennsylvania law forbidding ticket sales for Sunday concerts. The law was eventually overturned in 1933, and George Gershwin was given the privilege of selling the first legitimate ticket to businessman Leo Lehman. The orchestra, whose local conductor was Antonio Modarelli, had many guest conductors between 1930 and 1937: Walter Damrosch, Eugene Goossens, and Fritz Reiner, to mention a few. The organization gained in stature during these years, and there was a strong desire to reinstate it to national rank, but the devastating flood of 1936 set back fund-raising activities. The orchestra made its first series of radio broadcasts beginning in 1936 and in 1937 had national radio coverage sponsored by Pittsburgh Plate Glass.

Otto Klemperer, then conductor of the Los Angeles Philharmonic* was employed to audition and select players for the once-again revitalized orchestra. After three weeks of daily auditions and rehearsals, the orchestra debuted on October 21, 1937. Klemperer conducted a few programs before returning to Los Angeles, and other guests completed the year. That season boasted a roster of 101 players; concerts were given on Thursday evenings at Syria Mosque and Friday afternoons at Carnegie Music Hall. In addition, there were several children's concerts.

In 1938 Fritz Reiner was appointed permanent conductor, and during his 10 years in that position he restored the ensemble's former prestige, and it again ranked among the nation's major orchestras. The season too had grown: from 16 pairs of concerts (1938–1943) to the 20 (beginning in 1944) that remained the norm for many years thereafter. In the 1944–1945 season the orchestra performed 107 programs, including a two-month tour, seven popular programs, and concerts for young people. In 1946–1947 the number had risen to 121—and the growth has continued since, to 225 in 1973–1974 and over 200 in 1983–1984. William Edward Benswanger wrote program notes from 1926 to 1945, and Dr. Frederick Dorian from 1945 to the present.

In 1948 financial difficulties reduced the season from 28 to 25 weeks and Reiner resigned. Vladimir Bakaleinikoff (who had previously served as both assistant and associate) became acting musical director. There were also numerous guest conductors, including Leopold Stokowski, Leonard Bernstein, and Charles Munch. In 1952 William Steinberg was hired as permanent conductor; he remained until his retirement in 1976. This was a period of stability for the orchestra, and while there was always a need for more money, there were no financial crises. Touring was a regular feature of PSO activities, and Steinberg took the orchestra to Japan and to Europe as well as to major cities in the United States. His immediate successor was André Previn, who resigned in June 1984. Lorin Maazel is serving as interim music consultant until a new permanent director is hired.

In 1960 Henry J. Heinz II and three other prominent Pittsburghers discussed the possibility of finding a new home for the orchestra, whose needs had outgrown the facilities of the Syria Mosque. The fear of future deficits obviated one ideal location adjacent to the Civic Arena, and a further search in downtown Pittsburgh located the former Loew's Penn Theater, a very opulent 1920s movie house scheduled for demolition. The decision was made in 1968 to purchase and renovate this structure into a multipurpose hall to serve all the performing arts. Work began in May 1970, and the inaugural concert was performed on September 11, 1971. Heinz Hall for the Performing Arts has 2,850 seats and excellent acoustics.

During the next decade Heinz Hall served five organizations: the PSO, the Pittsburgh Opera (1940), the Civic Light Opera Association (1946), the Pittsburgh Youth Symphony Orchestra (1954), and the Pittsburgh Ballet Theatre, Inc. (1969). The success of these latter organizations eventually led their supporters to purchase in 1983 another notable movie house in the immediate vicinity to be remodeled for the needs of opera, ballet, and touring shows. The former Stanley Theater will thus become the Benedum Center for the Performing Arts, named in honor of the $5 million gift from the Claude Worthington Benedum Foundation.

For 10 years (1970–1980) the orchestra had its summer home at Ambler, Pennsylvania, as guest of Temple University. When Point State Park in Pittsburgh was provided with a permanent shell in 1981, the orchestra returned home and now provides a number of free outdoor concerts throughout the summer. The July 4th concerts draw over 100,000 people every year.

During the Steinberg years the PSO's programming emphasized the nineteenth-century Germanic composers; Previn changed the repertoire to include more works by English and Russian masters. While Previn was conductor the orchestra developed cleaner playing, clearer textures, and greater discipline. At least half the players were replaced through retirements and resignations while he was director. The *Pittsburgh Press* quotes Previn as saying that the "Pittsburgh Symphony Orchestra is really one of the best orchestras in the world, but it is also one of the best kept secrets." The orchestra has gained increased recognition, though, through the nationally televised series "Previn and the Pittsburgh."

There have been many works either commissioned for the orchestra or dedicated to it, and the ensemble has been involved with new music since its early years. While the emphasis was on European masters, American composers were frequently featured. During the past several seasons a chamber ensemble performed contemporary works at the neighboring Fulton Theater in a series called "Music Here and Now."

The orchestra's current repertoire is a combination of works that lightly touches the extremes of baroque and contemporary, with a major emphasis on the romantic period, followed by the modern and classical. Program selection is guided by two major factors: popularity of the tried and true masterpieces, and economics. There is a distribution of works featuring soloists, choral ensembles, and guest conductors. The repertoire is very extensive, and even the popular works are rarely repeated within several seasons.

The orchestra is organized and administered by an 80-member Board of Directors elected from among local political, academic, and business leaders, guided by 11 officers and an Executive Committee of 16. Of the 174 employees at Heinz Hall, 101 are PSO performers, all of whom are contracted AFM members. Throughout the years the orchestra players have taught and played at various colleges and universities in Pittsburgh during the regular season and at summer camps locally and at Chautauqua, New York.*

Sixty percent of the PSO's annual budget of $11.5 million derives from ticket sales, the remainder from gifts and grants from the Pennsylvania Council on the Arts, the NEA, Allegheny County, the City of Pittsburgh, corporations, foundations, and individuals throughout the community. The goal for the annual Sustaining Fund in 1983–1984 was $1.34 million.

The 1,700-member Pittsburgh Symphony Association, the orchestra's volunteer auxiliary, was founded in 1946. Their Symphony Ball, held almost annually since 1947, and annual Symphony Fashion Gala, begun in 1964 and co-sponsored by the Joseph Horne Co., enabled them to contribute $246,750 in 1984, the largest single contribution raised in one year. The orchestra had no endowment as recently as 1940. It was not until the 1960s that the fund began to grow, and it now totals over $45 million. In 1984 a special fund was established (with the help of PSA support) for the acquisition of extraordinary instruments.

During the 1983–1984 season there were numerous sub-group activities at different times and places. These include chamber music performances at which the audience sits on stage with the performers, pre-concert chamber music performances in the galleries on the lower level of Heinz Hall, noontime plaza lectures outdoors, demonstrations, and recitals. Another pre-concert activity is the American Composer Forums, which are discussions with the guest composer. A PSO chamber orchestra toured Pennsylvania, and there are also a few ensembles performing independently under professional names.

Pittsburgh is one of the most musical cities in the nation, and its Symphony must be given much credit for creating the musical atmosphere in western Pennsylvania. In 1957–1958, for example, the orchestra began an outreach program, "Gateway to Music," with a string quartet. From its first year of

40 performances it has swelled to more than 500 per year. Although the function of "Gateway" is continuing, it is no longer directly connected to the orchestra. Many players, along with non-symphony players, are still active in it. The groups currently include a string quartet, woodwind quintet, brass quintet, percussion ensemble, jazz quintet, the Pittsburgh Ballet Theatre, and the Pittsburgh Chamber Opera Theater. In addition to the "Gateway" ensembles, there are now at least 45 classical music groups or organizations looking for an audience and recognition in the Pittsburgh area.

RECORDING HISTORY AND SELECTIVE DISCOGRAPHY: The orchestra did not record until after World War II, when Reiner recorded seven works (of Bach, Bartók, Beethoven, Mozart, Shostakovich, and Richard Strauss) on the Columbia label. Steinberg recorded over 20 works for Angel, Command, and other labels. Previn added nine more recordings on the Angel, Columbia, Nonesuch, and Philips labels, with a repertoire ranging from Haydn to Harbison.

Beethoven, Symphony No. 7, Op. 92 and Mendelssohn, Symphony No. 4 (Steinberg): Angel 4XSS–32803. Rimsky-Korsakov, *Le Coq d'or Suite* (Steinberg) Seraphim S–60293. Goldmark, Violin Concerto (Perlman/Previn): Angel S37445. Haydn, Symphonies No. 94 and 104 (Previn): Angel SZ37575. George Rochberg, Violin Concerto (Stern/Previn): Columbia M–35149. John Harbison, *Ulysses's Bow* (Previn): Nonesuch, to-be-released.

CHRONOLOGY OF MUSIC DIRECTORS: Frederick Archer, 1895–1898. Victor Herbert, 1898–1904. Emil Paur, 1904–1910. (Operations suspended, 1910–1926.) (Guest conductors, 1926–1927.) Elias Breeskin and guests, 1927–1930. Antonio Modarelli and guests, 1930–1938. Fritz Reiner, 1938–1948. (Guest conductors, 1948–1952.) William Steinberg, 1952–1976. André Previn, 1976–1984. Lorin Maazel (Interim Music Consultant), 1984-present.

BIBLIOGRAPHY: Edward G. Baynham, *A History of Pittsburgh Music, 1758-1958* (Pittsburgh: Author, 1970). "Opening of Heinz Hall for the Performing Arts and Inaugural Concert by the Pittsburgh Symphony Orchestra," [PSO], 1971. *Pittsburgh Post-Gazette. Pittsburgh Press.* Janet Schlesinger, *Challenge to the Urban Orchestra: The Case of the Pittsburgh Symphony* (Pittsburgh: Author, 1971). William Stark, "Emil Paur and the Pittsburgh Symphony, 1904–1910," 10-page typescript held at Carnegie Library of Pittsburgh, 1935. James Richard Wolfe, "A Short History of the Pittsburgh Orchestra, 1896–1910," MLS thesis, Carnegie Institute of Technology/ Carnegie Library School, 1954.

ACCESS: The Pittsburgh Symphony Society, Heinz Hall for the Performing Arts, 600 Pennsylvania Avenue, Pittsburgh, PA 15222. (412) 281–4800. Marshall W. Turkin, Vice President and Managing Director. Sid Kaplan, Director of Operations.

NORRIS L. STEPHENS

Puerto Rico ————————

SANTURCE (101,103; 1,081,221—San Juan)

Puerto Rico Symphony Orchestra (Rg)

The Caribbean Island of Puerto Rico, located 1,000 miles southeast of Miami and inhabited by some 3 million U.S. citizens of mainly Hispanic extraction, has an orchestral history extending back well over a century. Until transfer of the island's political sovereignty to the United States as a result of the Spanish-American War in 1898, Puerto Rico, economically dominated by a native-born class of merchants and planters, was a generally loyal outpost of the once great Spanish Empire. Island society, especially in the two main towns of San Juan (the capital) and Ponce, developed patterns of leisure and culture that, as elsewhere in the Americas, displayed their indebtedness to European models.

A short-lived Sociedad Filarmónica was formed in San Juan in 1823, to be more successfully revived in 1845. Combining the efforts of music lovers, amateur performers, and professional musicians in a pattern that was to characterize music-making in Puerto Rico for many decades, the Sociedad Filarmónica and its successor organizations established music schools, sponsored orchestras, and presented locally mounted operas and zarzuelas. Ponce and the island's third largest town, Mayagüez, enjoyed orchestral concerts as early as 1831 and 1834, respectively. Also, by the end of the century orchestras existed at three of San Juan's principal churches. Military bands and the pit orchestras for Italian opera and Spanish zarzuela also contributed to a thriving musical life. The island lacked neither a population of able instrumentalists nor the enthusiasm of a receptive public; however, it did lack a commitment by the public to the development of stable musical institutions.

The period 1898–1950 witnessed the creation and rapid disappearance of orchestras bearing such names as Club Armónico, Sociedad de Conciertos, Orquesta Sinfónica de Puerto Rico, and Orquesta Filarmónica de Puerto Rico, as well as anonymous, occasional ensembles. San Juan's Orquesta Filarmónica of 1940, sponsored by the Sociedad Pro Arte Músical and conducted by Ramón Ruiz Cestero, was at the threshold of attaining some stability when World War II intervened.

Post-war orchestral efforts continued in the form of short-lived ensembles. The Communications Authority of the insular government created three musical ensembles, including an Orquesta Sinfónica, reported to have played before audiences of up to 10,000 in open-air concerts, and a Sinfonieta, conducted by popular composer Rafael Hernández. The year 1950 saw a new Orquesta Filarmónica, founded and conducted by popular pianist Arturo Somohano and devoted to light concert music in public parks and through broadcasts. And finally, the University of Puerto Rico Chamber Orchestra came into existence in 1956. Welcoming amateur players and veterans of previous decades' professional orchestral ventures as well as the university students and faculty members who formed its nucleus, this orchestra provided five seasons of concerts devoted to the small orchestra repertoire of all historical periods. It was the immediate predecessor of the present Puerto Rico Symphony Orchestra.

The present PRSO was created by the Legislature of the Commonwealth of Puerto Rico in 1957, and its development was entrusted to the Puerto Rico Casals Festival Corporation, a subsidiary of the Puerto Rico Industrial Development Company (PRIDCO; itself a branch of the insular government). In the same year (1957), the festival agency had sponsored the first of what was to become a series of post-season music festivals in Puerto Rico based on the figure of the great Catalan cellist Pablo Casals and with an orchestra engaged mainly in New York City. It was hoped that the Casals Festival would stimulate tourism and create a favorable image of the island, thus encouraging industrial development by helping to attract off-island venture capital. Festival audiences would be drawn principally from the U.S. mainland, attracted by the type of select programming that had become characteristic of the festivals in Prades, France, with which Casals and his close associate, violinist Alexander Schneider, had been associated since the early 1950s.

The role of the new PRSO, on the other hand, would be to develop a native concert audience by presenting, free of charge, a popular repertoire in parks and other easily accessible locations. In retrospect, and judging from the composition of the new orchestra and the planning of its activities, it is by no means clear that PRIDCO economists and industrial promoters were aware of the island's long orchestral history or of the traditional reception for concert music that had already existed for more than a century.

The new orchestra's brief first season, offering eight concerts in various island locations, took place in November 1958. The orchestra of 46 included nine Puerto Ricans and other established island resident musicians, the remainder having been engaged on the continent by the Casals Festival office in New York City. This general proportion of island versus imported forces was to prevail during the orchestra's first six years, thereby postponing the development of a truly island-based orchestra and paralyzing the length of the orchestra season, as players based in New York could commit only brief periods to playing in Puerto Rico. This situation was to cause considerable criticism directed at the parent Casals Festival Corporation. It frequently called into question that agency's very mission in Puerto Rico.

The first season's concerts were conducted by Pablo Casals, Alexander Schneider, Richard Burgin, and the Argentine composer and conductor Juan José Castro. Under the titular directorship of Casals and Schneider, the repertoire retained a generally pops character, with more serious pieces programmed for the relatively few concerts in large halls and theaters, including those of the University of Puerto Rico in Río Piedras and Inter American University in San German.

The orchestra's fifth season (1962) still offered only eight concerts by a 45-piece ensemble, which included no more than a dozen islanders, mainly in secondary positions. An energetic initiative by these members, advised and represented by Local 468 of the AFM, caused the cancellation of the following season's first concert. The dispute, concerning the length of the season and the ratio of island players to imports, was resolved in time to permit the presentation of an even shorter 1963 series by essentially the same orchestra, but with a commitment by PRIDCO and the Casals Festival Corporation to develop an island-based symphony orchestra beginning in 1964.

Since 1964, the PRSO has taken a steadily greater part in the island's musical life. Auditions were held in Puerto Rico for the first time in six years, the season was expanded to 20 concerts, and more than half of the 60-piece orchestra was comprised of fully resident instrumentalists. Juan José Castro was named musical director. He immediately began to include a greater proportion of symphonic works. Castro took his post very seriously, and (among many other contributions) was the first PRSO conductor to demand that management provide minimum conditions of illumination and acoustic environment for outdoor performances.

Castro resigned in 1965 for reasons of health and was succeeded by Chilean conductor Victor Tevah. Tevah retained his positions as conductor of the Chilean National Ballet and the Chile Symphony Orchestra, while continuing Castro's work in expanding the PRSO's repertoire. His excellent conducting of the Brahms symphonies, as well as his work with French and Russian music and an ample repertoire of Latin American music, is well remembered by many of the present members of the PRSO.

Grants by the Ford Foundation and special appropriations by the government of Puerto Rico, plus the enthusiastic cooperation of host governments, enabled the PRSO to undertake five tours of neighboring Caribbean countries (with a concert in Miami) between 1966 and 1971. In 1972 the orchestra again performed abroad, at an Inter-American Music Festival taking place at Santo Domingo in the Dominican Republic and sponsored by that country's government and a number of other agencies.

The year 1972 also saw a great leap in the length of the season from 17 to 28 weeks due to the direct action of Luis A. Ferré, then governor of Puerto Rico and an avid amateur pianist. A belated but welcome innovation occurred in 1975 with the creation of the post of orchestra manager; until then even the most minute details of the daily management of the orchestra had been handled by executives of PRIDCO or by the Casals Festival staff in New York.

The increasing length of the PRSO season made it difficult for Tevah to satisfy his conducting obligations in both Chile and Puerto Rico. He opted for Chile, and in 1977 was succeeded as musical director of the PRSO by violinist Sidney Harth. During the last years of Victor Tevah's conductorship and throughout Harth's two-year tenure, the PRSO was host to a procession of guest conductors.

John Barnett was named musical director in 1979 as the result of a view that the PRSO's development might now be better guided by a fully resident conductor. An important off-island liaison function was also foreseen for Barnett, in view of his previous activities as a consultant for the NEA. An important innovation of Barnett's tenure was the creation of the post of associate musical director.

In 1980 the PRSO became a subsidiary of the new Administration for the Development of Arts and Culture (ADAC), a government branch created in that year by the insular legislature to relieve the Puerto Rico Industrial Development Company of its complicated responsibilities in the island's musical life. In 1985 another realignment of the government's activities in the arts brought the PRSO under the newly created Corporation of the Musical Arts (CMA). The Puerto Rico Symphony Orchestra Corporation is directly responsible to the parent CMA but its management is also guided by its own five-member Board of Advisors. Administrative duties are exercised by the general director and a small managerial and clerical staff.

The PRSO's early artistic direction paid token attention to the presentation of music by island composers, but later seasons have seen an effort to encourage composition in Puerto Rico by regularly scheduling island works and by commissioning new compositions. Puerto Rican soloists, on the other hand, have been favored from the first season.

The PRSO presently numbers 76 instrumentalists. It offers at least one concert or other activity per week during its 44-week season, with orchestra concerts often taking place in one or another of the two main halls of the Performing Arts Center. The 2,000-seat Festival Hall is used for major events, while the 800-seat Drama Hall is more appropriate for the average size of PRSO audiences. However, its stage is cramped and uncomfortable for the orchestra even without soloists or extra players.

Other orchestra activities include park concerts and educational concerts in the San Juan area and elsewhere, principally at the University of Puerto Rico Theater in Río Piedras, the Theater of the Puerto Rico Conservatory of Music in Hato Rey, and the La Perla Theater in Ponce. In a governmental effort to aid the development of privately sponsored arts ventures, the orchestra is sometimes leased at less than cost to selected island opera companies, concert societies, and ballet groups. In addition, the orchestra occasionally participates in musical activities of another government branch, the Institute of Puerto Rican Culture. Since 1981, the PRSO has been the official resident orchestra for the annual Puerto Rico Casals Festival, now a sister agency under the administration of the CMA.

The 1984–1985 budget of the PRSO is $2.2 million, including appropriations by the Legislature of Puerto Rico, income obtained through ticket sales and the sale of advertising space in program booklets, and donations from industrial firms and other businesses active in Puerto Rico as well as from private donors.

The Associación Pro Orquesta Sinfónica, an organization of music lovers formed in 1976 to aid in the development of the PRSO, regularly sponsors lectures on subjects connected with the PRSO's current activities, sponsors a scholarship fund to help support the further studies of young orchestra members, entertains visiting soloists and guest conductors, and initiates other important liaisons, such as educational and public relations services connected with the PRSO and its programs.

CHRONOLOGY OF MUSIC DIRECTORS: Pablo Casals and Alexander Schneider, 1958–1963. Juan José Castro, 1964–1965. Victor Tevah, 1965–1977. Sidney Harth, 1977–1979. John Barnett, 1979-present.

BIBLIOGRAPHY: Fernando Callejo Ferrer, *Música y músicos portorriqueños* (1915; reprint, ed. Amaury Veray, San Juan: Editorial Coquí, 1971). Héctor Compos-Parsi, *Música, La gran enciclopedia de Puerto Rico* (Madrid: Ediciones R, 1976). Ellen Hawes, "The Sound and the Fury," *The San Juan Star* Magazine Section, 18 Apr. 1982. Elías López Sobá. "Pro Arte Musical y la gestación de una orquesta sinfónica para Puerto Rico," *Pro Arte Musical. Temporada 83–84* (San Juan: Sociedad Pro Arte Musical, 3 Mar. and 21 Apr. 1984). Donald Thompson, "The Collapse of a Festival. Part II: The Puerto Rico Symphony Orchestra and How It Got That Way," *The San Juan Star* Portfolio Section, 30 May 1979. Donald Thompson, "The Puerto Rico Symphony Orchestra: Where Do We Go From Here? *Senza Sordino* 12/5, May 1974. Donald Thompson, "Symphony Orchestra: How to Right a Wrong Note," *The San Juan Star* Portfolio Section, 22 Jul. 1980. Veinticinco (25) Aniversario: La Sinfónica (San Juan: Administración para el Fomento de las Artes y la Cultura, Corporación Orquesta Sinfónica de Puerto Rico, 1983).

ACCESS: Puerto Rico Symphony Orchestra, P.O. Box 41227, Minillas Station, Santurce, Puerto Rico 00940. (809) 727–7070.227

DONALD THOMPSON

Rhode Island _____

Rhode Island Philharmonic Orchestra (Mt)

The Rhode Island Philharmonic Orchestra is the culmination of over a century of effort—at least five attempts—to found a large musical organization in its state. These attempts failed due to a lack of support, coupled with the feeling that the Boston Symphony Orchestra's* five annual concerts in Providence fulfilled Rhode Island's cultural needs.

Luckily, Francis Madeira, a music instructor at Brown University, thought otherwise. In 1945, as a result of his impetus, a Board was incorporated representing the entire state, and the RIPO gave its first concert before 350 persons on November 14, 1945, in Westerly, Rhode Island. This first season set a pattern for future years by including three tours of Rhode Island's five major cities: Providence, Pawtucket, Westerly, Woonsocket, and Newport.

In 1953, the orchestra's eighth season, the tour concerts were discontinued and all performances moved to Veterans Memorial Auditorium in Providence. An office was also opened on Westminster Street, and Ralph Burgard was hired as the first full-time business manager.

The heart and soul of the RIPO was Francis Madeira, who conducted the orchestra from 1945 to 1978. A child prodigy, Madeira began studying the piano at age six: He performed at an early age under the direction of Leopold Stokowski and went on to the Juilliard School, where he won a conducting fellowship under Albert Stoessel. He was also a student of Pierre Monteux.

From the outset, Madeira encouraged native American, and in particular, Rhode Island and New England composers. Despite considerable criticism, Madeira performed works by Hugh MacColl, Mary Howe, Millard Thomson, and Jean Middleton. Works of William Grant Still, Richard Bales, and Quincy

Porter were first played in Rhode Island by the RIPO. Meanwhile, Madeira, appearing as guest conductor with such ensembles as the Philadelphia Orchestra,* the Mozarteum in Salzburg, and the Vienna Symphony, continued to consolidate his reputation as a conductor.

During his 35-year tenure Madeira firmly established the RIPO as Rhode Island's own permanent orchestra and developed a musical organization that included a strong educational program for school children. Madeira led the RIPO in its first concert especially for children (April 1946), thus beginning a tradition of fostering future audiences. So successful were these programs that they were integrated into the school curricula. Then, with Irene Mulick, Madeira founded the Philharmonic Youth Orchestra in 1955 to train young local musicians to fill RIPO vacancies. Joseph Conte, concertmaster of the parent orchestra, was appointed its first conductor. Today, Nedo Pandolfi and Ann Danis direct this ensemble.

A tradition of pops concerts also dates to 1955, with Martin Fischer as conductor. Three pops concerts, under the direction of George Kent, incorporated into the RIPO concert season. Madeira also strove to broaden audiences through radio concerts, and for many years all major concerts were taped for two rebroadcasts. Madeira established other traditions as well. For example, the RIPO presents summer concerts at Narragansett Town Beach, Brown University, and elsewhere around the state.

In 1979, after an extensive search, Alvaro Cassuto was selected as the RIPO's new music director. Cassuto came to Providence with impeccable credentials. Born in Oporto, Portugal, he studied with Karlheinz Stockhausen, Herbert von Karajan, Franco Ferrara, and other luminaries. Cassuto is familiar with both the symphonic and operatic repertoires and enjoys an international reputation as a guest conductor. Presently Cassuto directs both the National Radio Orchestra of Portugal and the National Orchestra of New York. In 1984 he announced that he would not renew his contract for the 1985–1986 season, citing a wish to turn his energies more fully to building the National Orchestra of New York.

During Cassuto's first season the RIPO moved its performances from the Veterans Memorial Auditorium to the Ocean State Performing Arts Center, now called the Providence Performing Arts Center. Despite a net gain of 1,000 seats, the move was opposed by many RIPO musicians on acoustical grounds as well as the necessity to hold many rehearsals away from the new hall; both problems, however, have been solved.

As a conductor of extraordinary talent, taste, and imagination, Cassuto has guided the RIPO to a new artistic level by insisting on more rehearsal time and higher standards. For the first time, a master contract was signed with the Musician's Union, enabling all procedures to be clarified for the musicians, the majority of whom are on part-time status. Cassuto appropriately chose one work—Mahler's Second (*Resurrection*) Symphony—to mark the Philharmonic's 35th anniversary concert in November 1980. In

1981 Cassuto brought the prestigious International Quartet to Providence as regular performing members of the orchestra and as Quartet-in-Residence at Brown University.

The RIPO is financed by grants, earned income, corporate gifts, private donors, and by the work of members of the Conductor's Circle and "Friends Society." A 40th anniversary capital fund drive was opened on February 11, 1984, to raise $1.55 million for its endowment fund and future projects.

The RIPO presents a series of 10 concerts—seven classical and three pops—regularly featuring top international soloists. The orchestra has grown from 31 musicians with a budget of $16,500 to one of nearly 80 musicians and a 1984 budget of approximately $860,000. Its audience averages about 2,800 for each concert, and it is heard in whole or in ensembles by more than 66,000 young people each season. Clearly, the RIPO has a profound impact on the culture of Rhode Island and adjacent areas.

CHRONOLOGY OF MUSIC DIRECTORS: Francis Madeira, 1945–1978. Alvaro Cassuto, 1979–1985.

BIBLIOGRAPHY: Interview with Joseph Conte, 1984. *Musical Courier*, 14 June 1923. *Providence Journal*. RIPO *Program Notes*, 10th Anniversary Concert, Nov. 1955. JoAnn Wooding, "Case Statement," *The Rhode Island Philharmonic Orchestra: 40th Anniversary Capital Campaign*, 1983.

ACCESS: Rhode Island Philharmonic Orchestra, 334 East Westminster Mall, Providence, RI 02903. (401) 831–3123. Mrs. Muriel Port Stevens, Manager.

ARTHUR H. PARÉ, S.J.

South Carolina _____

CHARLESTON (430,462—Charleston/North Charleston)

Charleston Symphony (Mt)

Although there are several recorded instances of small, mostly string, orchestra concerts in Charleston in the early part of this century, the founding of the Charleston String Symphony in 1936 is generally considered the beginning of the ensemble that in 1942 became the Charleston Symphony Orchestra.

The symphony was for many seasons a well regarded community orchestra whose members consisted of the few professionally trained musicians who happened to live in Charleston, enthusiastic amateurs, and music teachers from surrounding public and private schools and colleges. In 1976 Gian Carlo Menotti chose Charleston to be the site of the United State's version of the 22-year-old Italian Spoleto Festival. Since the advent of the yearly Spoleto Festival USA in 1977, there has been a burgeoning of serious professional musical activity in Charleston, providing an impetus toward an expansion in the growth and professionalism of the Charleston Symphony itself.

Most of the orchestra performers had been paid on a per-service basis for several years, but it was in 1977 that the orchestra first employed several full-time conservatory trained musicians—comprising a wind quintet and a string quartet—who performed many run-out services and held the first chair position in each orchestra section. Two years later the CSO became the first (still the only) orchestra in South Carolina to achieve ASOL Metropolitan status.

The retirement of Belgian cellist and conductor Lucien DeGroote in 1982 marked the end of almost 20 years of orchestral stability for the CSO under one conductor. This was followed by a two-year search for a new conductor and an expansion of musical activities under the guidance of Charleston violist/conductor Mark Cedel. Early in 1984 David Stahl was appointed the new music director. Under his leadership the Charleston Symphony Orchestra seems to be in the process of becoming even more active. While still depending to a large extent upon part-time musicians, the emphasis will be toward appointing a full-time chamber core of 21 musicians and developing a more professional musical philosophy.

Since the Spoleto Festival came to town the number of concerts and services has expanded exponentially: from about six to eight concerts each year in the mid-seventies to the 1984–1985 season, which included six subscription concerts, four children's concerts, three pops concerts, frequent performances by reduced ensembles drawn from the orchestra with local opera and dance companies, and a great many appearances of the Charleston Symphony Brass Quintet, Wind Quintet, and String Quartet in local churches, in schools, and generally throughout the state. Also, each orchestra season includes at least five run-out concerts to nearby communities. Additionally, the Charleston Symphony performs several times each year during the Piccolo Spoleto Festival, which is an adjunct to the main Spoleto USA Festival—rather like the Edinburgh Fringe Festival in Scotland.

Subscription and children's concerts take place in Gaillard Municipal Auditorium, a large, multipurpose community hall of about 2,700 seats, named after a former mayor of Charleston. Generally, attendance at each subscription concert averaged about 1,200 in 1983; children's and Christmas concerts have played to considerably larger audiences.

The Manogue International Young Artist's Competition is held annually alternating every other year between string performers and pianists. Though the auditions are held in Charleston, past winners have been from many parts of the country. The winner receives $1,000 and performs with the Symphony in a spring concert.

The CSO is administered by a 36-member Board of Directors, a full-time orchestra manager, and the music director. The 1984 budget of approximately $280,000 was received mainly from federal and local government grants, arts commission grants, corporate gifts, private donors, and earned income. A budget of $400,000 is projected for 1985.

CHRONOLOGY OF MUSIC DIRECTORS: Tony Hadgi, 1936–1942 (Charleston String Symphony). J. Albert Fracht, 1942–1959 (Charleston Symphony Orchestra). Don Mills, 1959–1963. Lucien DeGroote, 1963–1982. Mark Cedel, 1982–1984 (Acting Conductor). David Stahl, 1984-present.

ACCESS: Charleston Symphony Orchestra, #3 Chisolm Street, Charleston, SC 29401. (803) 723–7528. Paul Batchelor, General Manager.

DAVID W. MAVES

South Dakota _____

South Dakota Symphony (Mt)

In its 64th year (1985–1986), the South Dakota Symphony has seen spectacular growth recently by comparison with any other period in its history. The April/May 1984 issue of *Symphony Magazine* featured it as one of the outstanding examples of an orchestra that has successfully capitalized upon the current interest among large corporations in helping develop the cultural institutions in their neighborhoods. For the South Dakota Symphony that interest has been parlayed into a budget of more than $500,000 for fiscal 1985, up from $169,000 seven years earlier.

The beginnings of the orchestra can be traced to Monday, November 13, 1922, when the first group of musicians gathered together at Augustana College in Sioux Falls, under the direction of Miss Isa J. Duncan, to begin rehearsals for the annual Christmas program. There were only nine players, with "a base [*sic*] viol and the usual brass instruments to be added later" (Augustana College *Mirror*).

For the next four years the Augustana College Orchestra was under the direction of Miss Marie Toohey, and although she included members of the Sioux Falls College Orchestra and players from the city, the total number—typically 25—laid severe restrictions on the repertoire that could be performed. In 1927 Professor Richard J. Guderyahn became the conductor, and for 32 years the orchestra grew and changed under his leadership. Guderyahn established a concert season and relied heavily upon musicians among local citizens to build the orchestra to symphonic size. In 1952, in recognition of its community ties, the group changed its name to the Augustana Town and Gown Symphony Orchestra.

Late in the 1958–1959 season, however, Professor Guderyahn died suddenly, and his place was taken for the final concert by Dr. Leo Kucinski, then also the conductor and music director of the Sioux City (Iowa) Symphony Orchestra. For a short time in 1959 Thruston Johnson served as conductor; he was followed by Dr. Kucinski, who was hired by President Lawrence Stavig on a part-time basis. Having the conductor in Sioux Falls only part of the time meant that the college had to hire an additional faculty member to teach strings; for the orchestra it meant a more active Board of Directors. The next year, 1960, the orchestra was renamed the Sioux Falls-Augustana Symphony in recognition of the new state of affairs, and for the 1966–1967 season it became simply the Sioux Falls Symphony, thus cutting all remaining financial ties with the college.

In 1972 Dr. George Trautwein, then associate conductor with the Minnesota Orchestra,* assumed the baton. His four-year term placed new demands on the musicianship of the players and on the fund-raising ability of the 30-member Board of Directors; new attendance records were set almost every year. Under Trautwein the number of regular concerts was increased from four to five and the orchestra, travelling to Brookings and Madison, South Dakota, played outside of Sioux Falls for the first time.

In 1976 James MacInnes took over as conductor, and during his term— in 1977—the orchestra became the South Dakota Symphony. MacInnes was followed in 1978 by Emmanuel Vardi, a well-known violist who had performed several times with the Symphony. Vardi was succeeded in 1983, after a year-long national search that resulted in over 250 applications, by Kenneth Klein, who was for nine years the music director of the Guadalajara Symphony.

The greatest single event in the Symphony's life, next to its declaration of independence in 1966, was the Board's creating the position of full-time business manager in 1978. Under the leadership of Mary Sommervold, over the next six years the full-time administrative staff increased to four. Of greater significance in the musical growth of the orchestra has been the addition of a full-time string quartet (1978) and a full-time wind quintet (1982). Each now has its own touring schedule throughout the state and region, and each has visited dozens of isolated communities where live classical music never before had been heard.

Throughout most of its existence the orchestra was a department of Augustana, with the college providing the conductor and with ticket sales and small donations paying most of the bills. Now, however, funding comes from nearly all of Sioux Falls's major businesses, several hundred individuals, and grants from such agencies as the NEA, the South Dakota Arts Council, and private foundations.

Over the twenty years since it became independent, the orchestra has seen its audience become more musically sophisticated, even though most of the players are part-time. From a season of four low-priced concerts, the orchestra has gone today to a divided season, with three concerts in a pops series, five in a classical series, seven concerts for young people, seven concerts on tour, and three holiday concerts. In addition, the quartet and quintet offer a six-concert series of chamber music. Present plans are for the orchestra to continue its regular series in the 1,933-seat Coliseum, and in 1984–1985 to add a low-priced mini-series that repeats for seniors and church groups three of the regular classical concerts.

CHRONOLOGY OF MUSIC DIRECTORS: Isa J. Duncan, 1922–1923. Marie Toohey, 1923–1927. Richard J. Guderyahn, 1927–1959. Thruston Johnson, 1959. Leo Kucinski, 1959–1972. George Trautwein, 1972–1976. James MacInnes, 1976–1978. Emmanuel Vardi, 1978–1982. Kenneth Klein, 1983-present.

BIBLIOGRAPHY: Interview with Mary Sommervold, South Dakota Symphony Business Manager. Augustana College *Mirror*, 13 Nov. 1922. Heidi Waleson, "Orchestras and the Local Business Connection," *Symphony Magazine*, April/May 1984.

ACCESS: South Dakota Symphony, 707 East 41st Street, Sioux Falls, SD 57105. (605) 335–7933. Mary Sommervold, Business Manager.

ARTHUR R. HUSEBOE

Tennessee —————————

CHATTANOOGA (426,540)

Chattanooga Symphony Orchestra (Mt)

The Chattanooga Symphony has had a long history of close ties to its community and to educational endeavors. Its current annual season typically comprises nine subscription concerts at the Tivoli Theatre, two performances of the *Nutcracker* with the Eglevsky Ballet and Chattanooga Civic Ballet Company at Memorial Auditorium, a five-concert repeat series in Cleveland, Tennessee, run-out family concerts, four youth concerts, and a tiny tots concert. The CSO also presents free pops concerts in Georgia's Chattanooga-Chickamauga National Military Park on Memorial Day, Independence Day, and Labor Day weekends. These performances are each attended by 10,000 to 25,000 people and are presented under corporate sponsorship.

According to the history of the CSO published by the orchestra, the organization traces its roots to Chattanooga's Cadek Conservatory of Music, which until the death of its founder in 1927 was the city's sole supplier of classical music, through the Cadek Symphony Orchestra. In the early 1930s, Melvin Margolin and Borden Jones (members of the Orchestra Club founded by Cadek) organized the CSO as a community orchestra with educational goals. Rehearsals began at the county courthouse in 1933 under Margolin; Jones took over in 1936. Birmingham Symphony Concertmaster Ottakar Cadek was concertmaster, and two other Cadek family members were also string principals.

A period of artistic and audience growth followed the appointment under a Juilliard Foundation grant in 1937 of Dr. Arthur Plettner as music director. His tenure lasted 12 years.

Community action in the form of a Jaycees fund-raising campaign in the early 1950s was the beginning of the orchestra's professional history. Joseph Hawthorne became full-time music director, Ralph Black was hired as the orchestra's first manager, Jack Henry (who had long-standing ties to both the orchestra and the community) became personnel manager, the concert season was lengthened, and musicians received honoraria. Further growth was achieved under Julius Hegyi (Music Director, 1955–1964) and Charles Gabor (1965–1966). In 1963 the CSO moved its performance site from City High School to the 1,794-seat Tivoli Theatre, which today, though over 60 years old, boasts excellent acoustics and ambience despite some cosmetic flaws that the Symphony hopes to see corrected as part of a general modernization.

The CSO sees its modern period coinciding with the tenure of Dr. Richard Cormier (1967–1983), who led the group through an era of enormous growth to its present active season. Cormier's repertoire, featuring many works of the classical period and the twentieth century—particularly the latter—with less emphasis on the large romantic works, was unusual for an orchestra of the size and character of the CSO. Following his departure at the end of the 1982–1983 season, a two-year conductor search ensued, during which the guest conductors were auditioned and featured in performance. A new music director will be appointed for the 1985–1986 season.

The governing body of the CSO—The Chattanooga Symphony and Opera Association, consisting of invited members—also runs the Chattanooga Opera, with which the CSO shares bylaws and administrative staff; however, the two are funded separately. The CSO budget for 1983–1984 was $575,000, of which 36% was derived from ticket sales, program advertising, and concert fees. In addition to its government grants and corporate and private sponsorships, the CSO also receives funding from the Chattanooga Symphony and Opera Guild. In past seasons the orchestra experienced deficits that were remedied by fund-raising measures and additional support from the Allied Arts of Greater Chattanooga. A great majority of the CSO's musicians are union members. Their youth promises still greater artistic growth. About half are on short contracts, the others being hired on a per-service basis. An Orchestra Committee represents the musicians in negotiations and other matters. Although the CSO does not now maintain chamber ensembles, several chamber groups from within the orchestra personnel perform locally under private auspices.

CHRONOLOGY OF MUSIC DIRECTORS: Melvin Margolin, 1933–1937. Borden Jones, 1936–1937. Dr. Arthur Plettner, 1937–1950. Joseph Hawthorne, 1950–1955. Julius Heygi, 1955–1964. Charles Gabor, 1965–1967. Dr. Richard Cormier, 1967–1983. (Guest conductors, 1983–1985.)

BIBLIOGRAPHY: Dean Corey, CSO General Manager, Correspondence, 1984. "A Half-Century: The Chattanooga Symphony Orchestra," (CSO, n.d.). Philip Hart, *Or-

pheus in the New World (New York: Norton, 1973). Nikki C. Hasden, reviews in *The Chattanooga Times*.

ACCESS: Chattanooga Symphony Orchestra, 8 Patten Parkway, Chattanooga, TN 37402. (615) 267–8583. Dean Corey, General Manager.

ROBERT R. CRAVEN

KNOXVILLE (476,517)

Knoxville Symphony Orchestra (Mt)

The Knoxville Symphony Orchestra traces its origin to the founding of the Philharmonic Orchestra, which presented its first concert on June 2, 1924. The conductor was Bertha Walburn Clark, a well-known local violinist and teacher who wished to provide quality musical events for the community and to give talented local musicians opportunities to perform. The orchestra presented periodic concerts for the next 10 years. In 1935 the name was officially changed to the Knoxville Symphony Orchestra, although it remained a community rather than professional orchestra. The season was formalized at three concerts each year, and the practice of featuring well-known guest artists was begun.

Lamar Stringfield succeeded Clark as conductor of the Symphony in 1946. One year later he relinquished the baton to David Van Vactor, well-known composer and faculty member of the University of Tennessee, who for the next 26 years was to lead the orchestra to a position of musical maturity. It was in this same year, 1947, that the Knoxville Symphony Society was chartered as a non-profit educational organization to encourage all the arts in the community and, primarily, to establish a financial base in support of the orchestra. Early in his tenure Van Vactor initiated educational concerts for students through the 12th grade featuring competitions for performers and composers.

In 1973 Van Vactor was succeeded by Arpad Joo. Joo expanded the orchestra's repertoire by concentrating on larger works of the late nineteenth and early twentieth centuries. Two other milestones marked that same year. One was the change in character of the orchestra from a community ensemble to a fully paid organization. The other was the organization, by the Knoxville Symphony League, of the Knoxville Youth Symphony Orchestra as a training ground for junior and senior high school players.

When Joo left the Symphony in 1978 to become music director of the Calgary Philharmonic, leadership passed to Zoltan Rozsnyai, who left the orchestra at the end of the 1984–1985 season. In 1981 the Symphony engaged, for the first time, a core orchestra of 16 full-time string players. These musicians, who form the nucleus of the Knoxville Symphony Orchestra and the Chamber Orchestra, are employed for a season of 30 weeks each year. This step has provided a dramatic improvement in the artistic quality of the orchestra and has made possible a significant expansion of its services.

The Symphony season features a variety of presentations to the city of Knoxville and the surrounding area. The regular subscription series consists of seven concert pairs by the full orchestra. These have included such soloists as Byron Janis, Eugenia Zukerman, and others. The Knoxville Chamber Orchestra plays a series of five concerts each year, also featuring outstanding soloists. In addition to these performances, the orchestra provides special presentations for the Dogwood Arts Festival and a Knoxville Chamber Orchestra mini-series for nearby Morristown. The orchestra also performs with the Knoxville Opera Company and the Appalachian Ballet Company. The annual free family outdoor concert in the Tennessee Amphitheatre attracts an audience of several thousand to the 1982 World's Fair site.

Among the many educational services of the orchestra are a number of young people's concerts by the full orchestra and 70 in-school lecture demonstrations by string quartets. Rural communities in the surrounding area are served by many runouts. Groups of Symphony players tour the schools to perform, demonstrate their instruments, and meet with players in the school bands. After the schools have been visited, the Symphony provides a free concert for all. This has proven to be of great value, particularly in view of the lack of cultural resources in many nearby areas. The Youth Orchestra is now coached by the KSO's core string players and conducted by its assistant conductor.

The Knoxville Symphony Society, Inc., is governed by a Board of Directors of 60, whose policies are implemented by an 11-person Executive Committee, assisted by a manager and staff. Board membership is rotated so that two-thirds remain active each year. The Knoxville Symphony League, formed in 1952, is a 500-member auxiliary of the Society. The Knoxville Symphony Orchestra Young Professionals, formed in 1983, is a 100-member auxiliary. The annual budget of $675,000 comes from ticket sales, concert fees, government grants, and contributions.

The oldest continuing symphony in the Southeast, the KSO's major goals are to continue improvement in artistic quality, to continue to move toward a full-time orchestra through expansion of the core, to widen its geographic impact, and to expand its financial base in order to support such growth.

CHRONOLOGY OF MUSIC DIRECTORS: Bertha Walburn Clark, 1924–1946. Lamar Stringfield, 1946–1947. David Van Vactor, 1947–1973. Arpad Joo, 1973–1978. Zoltan Rozsnyai, 1978–1985.

BIBLIOGRAPHY: "A Night at the Symphony," *Knoxville Lifestyle*, Dec. 1982.

ACCESS: Knoxville Symphony Orchestra, 618 South Gay Street, Knoxville, TN 37901. (615) 523–1178. Constance Harrison, General Manager.

CHARLES H. BALL

MEMPHIS (913,472)

Memphis Orchestral Society (Rg)

The present Memphis Orchestral Society was founded under the name Memphis Sinfonietta in 1952. Offering, among other commitments, a formal concert series over a nine-month period in the Vincent de Frank and the Dixon-Meyers Halls, it serves a region encompassing approximately 150 miles. The series comprises nine pairs of subscription concerts. In addition, the orchestra presents a series of three pops concerts in the Peabody Hotel, two performances of the *Nutcracker*, weekly school concerts, children's concerts in shopping malls, and chamber concerts at the Dixon Gallery and Gardens.

The MOS has a 42-member Board of Directors that sets policies and engages the music director, who is responsible for all musical affairs, and a general manager who is responsible for all administrative matters. Its annual budget of slightly over $1 million derives from ticket sales, individual and corporate contributions, fund-raising projects of the Women's League, grants, and interest from endowments. A master agreement with the Musicians Union governs the relationship between management and the musicians.

The current repertoire may be considered, for the most part, standard symphonic literature. To date, little contemporary music has been programmed; however, some orchestra members indicate a preference for more venturesome and contemporary programming.

There were several symphonic organizations in Memphis before the Orchestral Society. The earliest, the Philharmonic Orchestral Association (founded around 1895), consisted of about 40 amateur musicians, and existed for nearly 15 years under the direction of Professor William W. Saxby, Jr. A second organization, the Beethoven String Orchestra, was formed under the leadership of Jacob Bloom, who came to Memphis from Cincinnati. By 1909 this group added wind players and took the name Memphis Symphony Orchestra. Prior to disbanding in 1925, it had come under the aegis of the Memphis Park Commission.

Memphis was without an orchestra until 1933, when Joseph Henkel, the last director of the Memphis Symphony Orchestra and then acting dean of the Memphis College of Music, organized and conducted a student orchestra, which in 1934 took the name Memphis Philharmonic Orchestra and comprised some 50 students, amateurs, and professionals. It seems to have ceased functioning by 1937.

Another Memphis Symphony Orchestra, this time under the leadership of Burnet C. Tuthill, presented its first concert in March of 1939, followed by a season of four concerts at the Orpheum Theater. By 1945 it had moved its concerts to the larger Ellis Auditorium and expanded its offerings to include a number of children's concerts. The following season Vincent de

Frank was named assistant conductor and in 1947 replaced Tuthill as principal conductor. This orchestra disbanded due to financial difficulties in April of 1947.

Memphis was again without an orchestra until 1952, when through the efforts of Vincent de Frank and the Young Artists Concert Management, the Memphis Sinfonietta was formed. This organization was the nucleus of the present Memphis Orchestral Society. It began to grow, and by the fall of 1958 its concerts were moved from the Goodwyn Institute (seating capacity approximately 1,000) to the Music Hall of Ellis Auditorium (seating capacity approximately 2,400). In 1960 it acquired its present designation and has continued to function under this name since. Since then the orchestra has seen a gradual increase in the number of concerts offered and the addition of the sub-groups noted here.

The 1983–1984 season was the last under the direction of Vincent de Frank, who is to be succeeded by Alan Balter, formerly associate conductor of the Baltimore Symphony.* Ellis Auditorium, home of the MOS subscription concerts, was renamed the Vincent de Frank Auditorium in honor of the founding director of the Memphis Orchestral Society.

CHRONOLOGY OF MUSIC DIRECTORS: Vincent de Frank, 1952–1983. Alan Balter, 1984-present.

BIBLIOGRAPHY: Kay Feree Myracle and John Whisler, "Music in Memphis," *Memphis, the Mississippi Valley, and the Mid-South*, a collection of typescript essays on file in the Mississippi Valley Collection of the Memphis State University Library, Memphis, Tenn.

ACCESS: Memphis Orchestral Society, Inc., 3100 Walnut Grove Road, Memphis, TN 38111. (901) 324–3627. General Manager, Florence Young.

EFRIM FRUCHTMAN

NASHVILLE (850,505)

Nashville Symphony Orchestra (Rg)

"The Athens of the South," Nashville has long been an educational center with many schools and colleges, many featuring musical instruction, with attendant cultural interests. However, its first local group deserving of the name "symphony" was a semi-professional orchestra of 50 to 65 members called the Nashville Symphony Orchestra, which provided a focus for local pride and support from 1920 to 1932, when it succumbed to the depression.

The founding of the present Nashville Symphony Orchestra was due entirely to the personality and efforts of Walter Sharp, a multitalented lover of the arts. Upon his return from military service, Sharp began to contact all the "right" people (socially, fiscally, politically, and artistically), and, in 1946, he started the Nashville Symphony off on a firm basis, with both social and broad-based popular support, which has endured and increased to the present time.

From a season of six concerts in the early years, the offerings have grown to three performances each of 10 subscription concerts (11 in 1984–1985). The pops concerts have increased so greatly in popularity that two performances each of five concerts are almost sold out. There are numerous special concerts, including five annual Christmas season performances of the *Nutcracker* with the Atlanta, Louisville, Pittsburgh, or Indianapolis Ballet, a fall Symphony outing, the Pied Piper concert, and others, in addition to educational concerts for young people. A fully staged opera, partly financed by a bequest from former conductor Thor Johnson, has been a feature of the regular series in recent years (*Madame Butterfly* in 1981, *Tosca* in 1983, and *La Traviata* in 1984). Mascagni's *Cavalleria Rusticana* and Leoncavallo's *Pagliacci* were scheduled to be performed by the Nashville Symphony in early 1985.

Fairly frequent runouts for concerts in neighboring communities and states have been a feature of the Symphony season for more than a decade. At various times, a wide variety of ensembles from the Symphony have given hundreds of concerts in the schools, in informal as well as formal settings.

Nashville's being a center for the recording industry has brought some fine musicians to the city to play in the recording studios; others have come to play in the Symphony but have taken the first opportunity to get into the more lucrative field of recording. Only members of the core group of the Symphony are on full-time contracts. Any of the Symphony members may play recording dates if they do not conflict with their obligations to the Symphony, and vice versa; but this sort of crossing over obviously has limited possibilities and is bound to be only marginally satisfactory to both orchestra and players.

The opening of the Tennessee Performing Arts Center in the fall of 1980 has given a tremendous impetus to the Nashville Symphony Orchestra, which is not only the focus of the city's cultural life, but also the principal tenant of TPAC's 2,400-seat Andrew Jackson Hall. This handsome hall has generally good acoustics.

The Symphony has been fortunate in its conductors, each having brought qualities that helped it improve and build on the firm foundation of professionalism instilled in the players by William Strickland, the first conductor (1946). Strickland was an organist and a particularly sensitive accompanist. His insistence on high quality in every aspect of the enterprise from the very outset proved of incalculable value to its firm establishment and acceptance in a community of knowledgeable patrons. His hospitality to American music was a welcome feature of his tenure. Most programs contained an American composition, and there were even several commissions and world premieres. He trained the orchestra so well that he was able to offer the entire cycle of Beethoven symphonies in the fourth season and increased the series to nine concerts to accommodate them.

The next conductor, Guy Taylor (1951), was a stimulating program planner and a careful rehearser who never failed to bring a work to an effective climax. He, too, was generous to American composers and scheduled composers who had been invited to Composers Forums at George Peabody College as guest conductors of their own works (Howard Hanson and Vincent Persichetti) or as guest composers (Aaron Copland, Randall Thompson, and Norman Dello Joio). He, in company with most of the other conductors, was hospitable to local composers and performers.

Willis Page (1959) was best with the splashier items of the repertoire and was quite the best conductor of pops concerts the orchestra has ever had. His all-Gershwin, all-Rodgers and Hammerstein, and other single-composer programs drew delighted crowds who were never seen at other Symphony concerts. Harry Newstone, visiting conductor and music director for one season while Page fulfilled a stint of conducting in Tokyo, was a baroque and classical specialist and gave polished performances of this repertoire that were the more welcome for its having been largely neglected by his predecessors.

Thor Johnson (1967) was the most distinguished of the orchestra's leaders, with an unequaled ability to make any group play well in a very short time and a positive genius for training the young people of the Nashville Youth Symphony. It was his pleasure to train them for professional playing, to promote them, when ready, to the Symphony, and to make larger opportunities for them when they were ready to move on. He was also endlessly resourceful in his programming; he always knew just what to play to feature strengths and hide weaknesses when a number of the better players were lost to the recording studios and economic stringencies dictated a reduction in the number of rehearsals for each concert.

Following Johnson's death in 1975, many guest conductors were heard during a season and a half under the musical advisorship of John Nelson, before Michael Charry was engaged as music director. Charry's solid musicianship and intelligence were coupled with valuable leadership in community activities, such as the organization of the Nashville Institute for the Arts and the Music Consortium. His conducting talents have shown most brilliantly in his conducting and production of operas.

After a year of guest conductors, with Kenneth Schermerhorn as musical advisor, Schermerhorn became music director in 1982, and there is much enthusiasm and hopeful planning afoot to expand the Symphony to Major orchestra status through increased performances and the presentation of more challenging works in a wider variety of venues. Orchestra management is also evaluating alternative services, such as family concerts and summer pops concerts that incorporate popular music artists, including some from the Nashville music industry.

A Ford Foundation matching grant made possible the establishment of the Nashville Chamber Orchestra of 16 players within the Symphony during the 1966–1967 season for giving approximately 100 concerts in Middle Tennessee schools under Title III of the Education Act of 1965. The engagement of some highly capable players and the greater amount of playing and practice involved had raised the orchestra's skill to its highest point.

Other ancillary activities of the Symphony have had great importance at various periods. The Nashville Choral Society was organized during the Symphony's first season under the direction of Music Director William Strickland, but Taylor and Page preferred to use the George Peabody College for Teachers choral groups or those from other area schools when the Symphony performed choral works. The discontinuance in 1961 of the annual community *Messiah* performance sponsored by Peabody College for more than 20 years encouraged Page to reactivate the Symphony Chorus to take over this activity. He directed the group at first but eventually turned it over to Charles Nelson, whose successors were Scott Withrow and then Sandra Willetts. The group appears in two of the subscription concerts and one pops concert each season, as well as one or more of the Centennial Park summer concerts, and gives concerts of its own from time to time.

The Nashville Youth Orchestra (later, Symphony) was established in 1947 by Assistant Conductor Andrew Ponder, who conducted it until his death in 1953. A variety of conductors, including the music director at times, succeeded—notably Dan Cassel for a fruitful decade, 1954–1964—until it reached its apogee of effectiveness and ability under Thor Johnson, assisted by Harold Cruthirds. It was then separated from the Symphony, to be administered by the Blair Academy of Music.

The Nashville Symphony Association, the membership of which comprises all who give a minimum of $50 annually to its support, is governed by an elected Board of Directors, one-third of whom are nominated yearly by an appointed Nominating Committee. Artistic matters are in the hands of the music director, and implementation of policy is the responsibility of the executive director, with advice and assistance of the Executive Committee of the Board. The current budget of almost $3.3 million is funded through ticket sales, concert fees, sponsorships by corporations and individuals, government grants, contributions, benefits, investment earnings, contributions of services and in-kind gifts, and most notably, the Women's Symphony Guild, which contributes about $200,000 annually.

Responding to objections that the programs contained too much "unfamiliar" music, the symphony has made a determined effort the past two seasons to feature the familiar. The 1983–1984 programs accordingly offered works of the romantic masters, with the barest nod to the twentieth century in the form of Stravinsky, Prokofiev, Poulenc, Rodrigo, and Corigliano.

RECORDING HISTORY AND SELECTIVE DISCOGRAPHY: All first-night subscription concerts are recorded for broadcast over WPLN-FM the following week. A collection of "Themes from the Great Symphonies" was recorded on the Dot label under Willis Page, but is no longer available.

CHRONOLOGY OF MUSIC DIRECTORS: William Strickland, 1946–1951. Guy Taylor, 1951–1959. Willis Page, 1959–1967. Harry Newstone (Visiting Conductor and Music Director), 1962–1963. Thor Johnson, 1967–1975. (Guest conductors, 1975–1976.) Michael Charry, 1976–1982. (Guest conductors, 1982–1983.) Kenneth Schermerhorn, 1983-present.

BIBLIOGRAPHY: Nashville Symphony Orchestra Archives, including clippings from *The Tennesseean* and the *Nashville Banner*. Louis Nicholas, *Thor Johnson, American Conductor* (Fishcreek, Wis.: The Music Festival Committee of the Peninsula Arts Association, 1982).

ACCESS: Nashville Symphony Association, 208 23rd Avenue North, Nashville, TN 37203. (615) 329–3033. Matthew G. B. Maddin, Executive Director.

LOUIS NICHOLAS

Texas ——————————————————

AMARILLO (173,699)

Amarillo Symphony (Mt)

In 1924 the Philharmonic Club of Amarillo organized a Philharmonic Orchestra consisting of a 12-member women's string ensemble. This marked the beginning of the Amarillo Symphony. A year later the orchestra added wind instruments (and men) to make a 20-piece ensemble, performances of which were given at the Federated Club Rooms located in the old civic auditorium. The orchestra struggled financially during its formative years, especially during the Dust Bowl days, and concert seasons were adjusted accordingly. In 1932 the Amarillo Philharmonic Orchestral Association was formed to govern the activities of the orchestra. At this time the Symphony had 54 members, but it grew to 83 members for the 1934–1935 season. For the most part, though, the size of the orchestra averaged approximately 60 musicians from 1940 through the 1960s. In 1950 the orchestra received its present name: the Amarillo Symphony. Like most orchestras, the Symphony has had its ups and downs, musically and financially, but it managed to stay solvent and has taken great strides, particularly in recent years.

The orchestra made several phonograph recordings during the 1960s and early 1970s, all of which were produced and sold locally. KGNC, a local radio station, aired previews and Symphony performances during the late 1950s and early 1960s. In 1965 several tapes of the orchestra were broadcast as part of the English Sunday Concert Hour series of the U.S. Information Agency's "Voice of America." From 1976 until 1982 performances were videotaped for delayed broadcast over KACV-TV, a public television station operated by Amarillo College. Currently, performances are still being taped for KACV-FM, the college's radio station.

A Board of Directors of 40 members now governs the Symphony, which has an annual operating budget of approximately $500,000. The three major sources of income are season ticket sales, the donor member program, and program advertising. The Amarillo Symphony Guild, a women's auxiliary organized in 1955, has been a strong support group in fund raising and in furthering the Symphony's cultural objectives.

There are two subscription series: a Saturday evening series of seven concerts and a Sunday matinee series of five concerts (the Sunday concerts are repeated performances of the Saturday evening concerts). Usually each concert features a renowned soloist. A concert featuring the combined choirs of the Amarillo Symphony Chorus (directed by George Biffle since 1976) and the choirs of Amarillo College and West Texas State University is given in December, and a pops concert is given in the spring. Additionally, the orchestra presents some 45 educational concerts for students in the Amarillo Independent School District and three Kinder Konzerts for pre-school children. Since 1981 the Symphony has also performed Tchaikovsky's *Nutcracker* annually with the Amarillo-based Lone Star Ballet (Neil Hess, Director). In recent years approximately one-fourth to one-third of each program is devoted to twentieth-century music. There have been several premiere performances of works by area composers; Don Gillis was commissioned to write *Amarillo: A Symphonic Celebration* for the city's Diamond Jubilee in 1962.

On the average, five or six rehearsals precede each subscription concert; the number of musicians will vary from 80 to 95 depending on instrumentation needs. Members of the orchestra receive an honorarium on a per-service basis. All subscription concerts are presented in the Amarillo Civic Center Auditorium, a 2,300-seat hall completed in 1968. Audiences number approximately 2,000 for the Saturday performances and 1,500 for Sunday performances.

Grants from the Don and Sybil Harrington Foundation of Amarillo totalling $1,621,000 to the Symphony and to West Texas State University have endowed the resident Harrington String Quartet formed in 1981. Members of the quartet function as principals in the Symphony and music faculty at WTSU. The quartet has performed extensively throughout the United States.

CHRONOLOGY OF MUSIC DIRECTORS: Grace Hamilton, 1924–1925. Hall Axtell, 1925–1926. Ellis B. Hall, 1926–1934. Christian Thaulow, 1934–1935. T. Duncan Stewart and Edgar Parsons, 1935–1936. Dr. H. L. Robinson, 1936–1938. Murray Meeker, 1938–1939. (Guest conductors, 1939–1940.) Robert Louis Barron, 1940–1947. (Guest conductors, 1947–1948.) A. Clyde Roller, 1948–1962. (Guest conductors, 1962–1963.) Dr. Thomas Hohstadt, 1963–1973. (Guest conductors, 1973–1975.) Thomas Conlin, 1975–1983. (Guest conductors, 1983-present.)

BIBLIOGRAPHY: Mrs. W. Travis Aaron, "The Amarillo Symphony: The First Fifty Years," Manuscript [1974]. *Amarillo Globe-News*. Amarillo Symphony Guild Scrapbooks, in the collection of the Amarillo Public Library.

ACCESS: Amarillo Symphony, 1000 S. Polk, Amarillo, TX 79101. (806) 376–8782. James M. Alfonte, Managing Director.

TED A. DUBOIS

AUSTIN (483,353)

Austin Symphony Orchestra (Rg)

Austin's Symphony orchestra presented its first public concert April 25, 1911. The 28-piece orchestra was conducted by Hans Harthans at the Hancock Opera House. The history of the orchestra, however, extends back to the mid–1890s, when William Besserer, conductor and pianist, led a group of businessmen/musicians that played for gubernatorial inaugurations every two years and also gave public concerts.

Until 1938, Austin's Symphony was a community orchestra. In that year, because of increased community support and interest, a reorganization of the orchestra resulted in the change from a non-official community orchestra to a formal organization presenting regularly scheduled subscription concerts and employing salaried musicians.

Hendrik Buytendorp, formerly of the Royal Orchestra of Holland, was chosen as conductor, and the first formal season of the Austin Symphony Orchestra began with a concert presented on December 20, 1938. The Austin Symphony Orchestra Society, the community support group and governing body of the ASO, drafted their first constitution in 1941. As the ASO grew, it hired its first full-time general manager shortly after World War II.

It was during this period that the Symphony's governing Board persuaded Austin's Mayor Tom Miller to officially recognize the ASO's contribution to the community by giving it support through the City of Austin Parks and Recreation Department. Still another breakthrough followed shortly thereafter, when members of the orchestra achieved professional standing by affiliating with the AFM.

The 1948–1949 season saw the appointment of Ezra Rachlin as music director and conductor. During his 20-year association with the Symphony, Rachlin initiated the student concert series in 1950, included internationally acclaimed guest artists on subscription programs, and founded the annual pops concerts.

By 1970 Maurice Peress, formerly the assistant conductor of the New York Philharmonic* under Leonard Bernstein, was hired as the new conductor, and the season offered five subscription concerts. Peress was followed as conductor after the 1971–1972 season by Lawrence Smith, formerly associated with the Metropolitan Opera's National Company. Smith left after one season and Walter Ducloux, Professor of Music at the University of Texas, stepped in to conduct and arrange for guest conductors. One of the guest conductors was Akira Endo, a former pupil of Ducloux. Endo had formerly held conducting positions with the Long Beach* and Houston* Symphonies and was signed as ASO conductor and music director in April of 1978.

In 1979, the ASO under Akira Endo toured Mexico at the invitation of the Mexican government. Concerts were offered at Oaxtepec and the Palacio de Bellas Artes in Mexico City, and a special concert was given at Chapultepec Castle for President José Lopez Portillo and his family. This marked the first time the ASO had performed outside the United States.

The ASO continues to be a per-service orchestra, today employing 90 musicians for a 32-week season. The regular subscription series consists of 18 concerts with an additional 15 concerts involving the Austin Civic Ballet, the Austin Choral Union, outdoor summer concerts, performances in nearby cities, and Kinder Concerts. The orchestra also performs eight children's concerts each year in cooperation with the Austin Independent School District and the school districts of nearby communities. These concerts reach over 20,000 children every year and serve to emphasize the orchestra's commitment to its young audiences.

The Symphony enjoys the participation of an exceptionally high calibre of musician. Several universities with strong music departments located in and around Austin, as well as a healthy economic growth rate for the region, make many musicians available to the ASO, whom the orchestra alone might not attract. The fact that Austin is the capital of Texas brings a wide range of government leaders and prominent people into contact with ASO activities. Members of the orchestra come from all walks of life and include business persons, university professors, housewives, teachers, university students, and former members of such major symphony orchestras as the Chicago Symphony,* Philadelphia Orchestra,* and many others.

One of the more unusual facets of the ASO cultural and financial structure is a historical restoration known as Symphony Square. Located a short distance from the State Capitol, the four stone buildings, each over 100 years old, have been completely restored and serve as offices for the ASO staff as well as provide facilities for the orchestra's youth programs. A main feature of the square is the 350-seat Walker Creek Amphitheatre, which serves as a forum for all the performing arts; small ensembles from within the ASO are encouraged to perform here. Symphony Square's other buildings contain a restaurant and support facilities for the various ASO volunteer groups. The Symphony Society foresees this project becoming a "living endowment" for the orchestra, and as far as is known to the Symphony, this is the only historical restoration project to directly benefit a symphony orchestra.

The efforts of the ASO to serve the needs of the region as well as to encourage musical involvement have produced an impressive list of activities in addition to those of the orchestra proper. The Classical Sunset Series is the Symphony's contribution to Austin's chamber music activities. In this series outstanding chamber groups are encouraged to perform at Symphony Square and receive assistance from the Texas Commission on the Arts. Building Blocks of the Orchestra is a program designed to acquaint young children with orchestral instruments through in-school visits by small chamber ensembles. Each Wednesday morning during the summer, the ASO sponsors Children's Day at Symphony Square, where children actively participate in all facets of the arts. Back Stage with the Arts is a program providing adults with the opportunity to talk with the conductor and guest soloists before an orchestra rehearsal. The Symphony Preview Luncheon serves the same purpose, except that it offers a wider range of guest speakers and takes place in Symphony Square's restaurant.

All concerts during the regular subscription series, with the exception of the pops concerts, which feature cabaret seating, are presented in the new Performing Arts Center located on the University of Texas campus. This new state-of-the-art hall seats 2,800 and has recently played host to the Chicago Symphony Orchestra.

Sung Kwak, the current conductor of the ASO, has just assumed full-time residence in Austin after a three-year tenure as assistant conductor with the Cleveland Orchestra.* Kwak was born in Seoul, Korea, and studied trumpet and music theory at Kyoung-Hee University. A faculty member of New York's Mannes College of Music, he was also conductor of the City Center Joffrey Ballet. From 1977 to 1980 he served as the Exxon/Arts Endowment Conductor for the Atlanta Symphony.*

The ASO staff consists of eight full-time employees including the general manager. The Symphony Society comprises 95 members from which a Governing Board is chosen. Other community groups directly involved in support of the ASO are the Austin Women's Symphony League (400 members), Knights of the Symphony (a businessman's organization), the Symphony Square Committee, and the Advisory Board made up of prominent people from throughout the state.

The ASO budget is presently $1.2 million, and the orchestra has just received, as of 1984, a change in ASOL classification to Regional orchestra. Funding is derived from the fund drive (25%), ticket sales and fees (42%), income-producing activities, government agencies, school districts, the city of Austin, grants, private and corporate donations, and the NEA.

CHRONOLOGY OF MUSIC DIRECTORS: Dr. Hendrik J. Buytendorp, 1940–1948. Ezra Rachlin, 1948–1969. Andor Toth, 1969–1970. Maurice Peress, 1970–1972. Lawrence Smith, 1972–1973. Walter Ducloux, 1973–1975. Akira Endo, 1975–1980. (Guest conductors, 1980–1982.) Sung Kwak, 1982-present.

BIBLIOGRAPHY: Interviews with ASO General Manager Kenneth K. Caswell, Personnel Manager Anita Marie Killen, Music Director Sung Kwak, and Director of Publicity Ann McCutchan.

ACCESS: Austin Symphony Orchestra Society, Symphony Square, 11th and Red River, Austin, TX 78701. (512) 476–6064. Kenneth K. Caswell, General Manager.

CHARLES R. HURT

CORPUS CHRISTI (326,228)

Corpus Christi Symphony Orchestra (Mt)

The Corpus Christi Symphony Orchestra celebrated its 40th anniversary season during the 1984–1985 season. The actual anniversary occurred on December 10, 1985, exactly 40 years after the first concert given in a 600-seat high school auditorium. Del Mar College, Corpus Christi's two-year community college (with which the Symphony has long been associated), observed its 50th anniversary during the 1984–1985 academic year. Both celebrations began a year early.

Burdette Wolfe was appointed director of instrumental music at the college when its music department began in 1945. With the support of music lovers and professional musicians in the community, he immediately organized the Symphony and began rehearsals for the first concert. He used as many professionals as he could find just after the war, some students, and many *Aushilfe* strings, especially from the University of Texas at Austin. The first concert included the Liszt Piano Concerto in E-flat, with 23-year-old Eunice Podis of Cleveland as soloist; the Overture to *Der Freischütz*; excerpts from the *Nutcracker Suite* and from *Hansel and Gretel*; and pieces by Grieg and Liadov. Wolfe was made chairman of the college music department, a position he held until his retirement in 1965. He conducted the orchestra until 1952.

During the first few seasons, Wolfe made it his practice to obtain big-name soloists (such as Percy Grainger or Yehudi Menuhin) to attract audiences. On their own, the 60 to 65 men and women in the orchestra were playing standard classical and romantic repertoire. With the help of the Community Chorus, also founded in 1945, and with some outside soloists, the orchestra managed to mount three operas in the first four years: *Cavalleria Rusticana*, *The Bartered Bride*, and *La Traviata*.

Upon his resignation, Wolfe was replaced by Frederick Vajda, who remained for two years. Jacques Singer became conductor in 1954 and remained until 1962. Under his direction the orchestra took on a professionalism that it has maintained under Maurice Peress (1962–1975) and under Cornelius Eberhardt, who became conductor in 1975.

Eberhardt began his conducting career as conductor and musical director of the Regensburg Symphony and Opera, where he remained for 10 years. After beginning his tenure with the Corpus Christi orchestra, he was appointed Professor of Opera Conducting at the Munich Hochschule für Musik. He has commuted between Munich and Texas ever since. For more than 10 years, he has also been musical director and principal conductor of the American Institute of Musical Studies in Graz, Austria.

In 1956, during the early part of his tenure, Jacques Singer succeeded in having Litta Kline appointed first manager of the orchestra, a position she has held since that time. She is responsible to an Executive Committee, by whom the chairman of the Board and other officers are elected, and to a Board of Directors. Artistic and programming decisions are the sole responsibility of the conductor/music director, within the budget limitations imposed by the Board of Directors.

The orchestra's $300,000 budget is generated for the most part through ticket sales, the work of an active, separately incorporated Symphony Guild, program advertising, individual gifts and bequests, and grants from foundations and federal, state, and local government agencies. A committee of orchestra members, almost all of whom are members of Local 644, AFM, functions as a grievance body governing working conditions and hours, including overtime, but not basic salaries.

Usually the orchestra includes about 75 players, although this number may be increased to 100 depending on the requirements of the music. The orchestra, after 40 years, is still largely interdependent with the music department of Del Mar College, an unusually large department of 23 full-time and seven part-time teachers. Ten principals and about 30 other players are current teachers or current or past students of the college. The orchestra still imports about 20 string players for each subscription concert.

The orchestra presents seven subscription concerts a season, including one opera, normally the final program. As a chamber orchestra, comprising only the local players (about 55 in number), it also plays two free concerts a year and several youth concerts. Annually the orchestra is joined by the Corpus Christi Chorale (formerly the Community Chorus) under J. Eugene McKinley, for a Christmas season program of excerpts from Handel's *Messiah* sung alternately in Spanish and English. Home concerts are played at the new Bayfront Plaza Auditorium, a 2,500-seat hall that is part of a larger convention center fronting on Corpus Christi Bay on the Gulf of Mexico. Also nearby are museums of art and anthropology and a well-appointed amateur theater.

Over the years, the orchestral repertoire has been heavily traditional and European. Underlying the programming is the apparent assumption that more progressive music would lose a largely conservative and musically unsophisticated audience. The orchestra is the premier cultural asset of the community and serves audiences drawn from the city of Corpus Christi and surrounding towns to a distance of some 50 miles.

CHRONOLOGY OF MUSIC DIRECTORS: C. Burdette Wolfe, 1945–1952. Frederick Vajda, 1952–1954. Jacques Singer, 1954–1962. Maurice Peress, 1962–1975. Cornelius Eberhardt, 1975-present.

BIBLIOGRAPHY: Interviews with CCSO Music Director Cornelius Eberhardt and Manager Litta Kline. Corpus Christi *Caller-Times*. Billie Ferrell Archives in La Retama Public Library, Corpus Christi.

ACCESS: Corpus Christi Symphony Orchestra, P.O. Box 495, Corpus Christi, TX 78403. Litta Kline, Manager.

RALPH THIBODEAU

DALLAS (2,974,805)

Dallas Symphony Orchestra (Mj)

With the appointment of Eduardo Mata as music director of the Dallas Symphony Orchestra in 1977, an emphasis on programming compositions of Latin American composers has become evident. Under the Mexican conductor's baton the orchestra has highlighted performances of such works as the late Alberto Ginastera's Violin Concerto and Carlos Chavez's *Sinfonia di Antigone*, as well as newly commissioned compositions by Robert Xavier Rodriguez. Mata also holds the post of artistic advisor of the National Opera in Mexico, where he directs several operatic performances each season. A Mata innovation in Dallas has been the programming of operas in concert form as a part of the orchestra's subscription series.

The orchestra is committed to performing at least one world premiere per year and several works new to the Dallas Symphony each season. Funded through "Meet the Composer" of New York City, Robert Xavier Rodriguez (born in San Antonio, Texas) has been the orchestra's composer-in-residence since 1982. His *Oktoechos* for eight soloists and large orchestra, the second work written expressly for the Dallas Symphony, was premiered by Mata in Dallas on May 4, 1984. A colorful composer with romantically dramatic (though atonal) inclinations, he has been well accepted by the Dallas audiences.

The Dallas Symphony is located in the heart of the financial center of the Southwest. Approximately 53% of its 1984–1985 budget of $8 million is earned by the orchestra, the remainder coming from private contributions, endowment, support-guild activities, and benefits. The Dallas Independent School District and a number of locally based foundations contribute significant funds in support of children's concerts. The Atlantic Richfield Foundation provides additional funds for ensembles from the orchestra to perform concerts in schools.

The present administrative staff of the orchestra includes 31 persons in addition to Maestro Mata. Kirk Trevor is Exxon/Arts Endowment Resident Conductor of the Symphony, and James Rives-Jones is associate conductor. The orchestra consists of 88 players on a full-time year-round contract.

In its yearly schedule the Dallas Symphony Orchestra presents a split season. Beginning earlier in the fall than most professional orchestras, a short autumn season precedes a hiatus during October, November and December, while the orchestra accompanies the Dallas Opera.

The orchestral season consists of 50 subscription concerts at the 3,420-seat Fair Park Music Hall on Thursday, Friday, and Saturday evenings and Sunday afternoons, six special concerts, 20 youth concerts, 15 free park or sidewalk concerts, and 10 subscription concerts in regional cities. A six-week outdoor summer season entitled "Starfest" is presented on Friday,

Saturday, and Sunday evenings on the grounds of the Park Central. Six "Starfest Discovery" Thursday evening summer concerts feature classical music directed by guest conductors in the newly renovated Majestic Theatre. More than half a million people have attended live performances in each of the Symphony's recent seasons.

In November of 1979 the citizens of Dallas voted $2.25 million for the acquisition of land in the central area of the city for a new concert hall. In 1982 voters approved a bond issue for $28 million, or 60% of the cost of the Symphony's new home. The Dallas Symphony Center will be a long-needed permanent home for the orchestra, a center for many other musical events, and an attractive addition to the new Arts District in downtown Dallas. I. M. Pei, designer of several impressive new buildings in Dallas, is the architect, and Russell Johnson will collaborate on the acoustics of the 2,200-seat auditorium. The new hall should be ready for concerts in 1987.

Much of the following history of the orchestra is derived from a booklet published in 1983 entitled *Dallas Symphony Orchestra*. The founding of the orchestra owes much of its impetus to the German-born violinist-pianist Hans Kreissig. Stranded in the Southwest when the Grau Light Opera Company dissolved while on tour, Kreissig found his way back to Dallas, where he settled as conductor of a German-American singing society, serving as an organist as well as choirmaster. In 1890 he helped organize the Dallas Symphony Club, each of whose 21 members was a violinist.

Ten years later, on May 12, 1900, the Dallas Symphony Orchestra presented its first concert, with Kreissig as conductor and piano soloist. Five of the 40 members were professional musicians. Included on that first program was "Allons donc," composed by Hans Kreissig. The concertmaster of that first ensemble was Walter J. Fried, also a native of Germany. In 1905 Fried took over the leadership of the orchestra, which had now adopted the name of The Beethoven Symphony Orchestra. He led this group six seasons.

Another German violinist followed Fried to the podium: Carl Venth of Cologne. Having played in European orchestras under both Richard Wagner and Giuseppe Verdi, Venth had served as concertmaster of the New York Metropolitan Opera Orchestra and had helped organize the Brooklyn Symphony. When Venth became conductor in 1911 he imported a dozen musicians from New York City to help revitalize the orchestra.

The backgrounds of Kreissig, Fried, and Venth suggest a heavy orientation toward German music, and indeed the early programs show repeated schedulings of Mozart, Beethoven, Brahms, Wagner, and Richard Strauss. Under the pressure of anti-German feeling in the community at the outbreak of World War I and of epidemics of influenza and meningitis, the Symphony was dissolved in 1914. In 1918 Walter Fried again organized an orchestra. He led the new group until his death in 1925.

Then Dr. Paul van Katwijk, Dean of the School of Music at Southern Methodist University of Dallas, assumed leadership. The orchestra expanded both its season and the scope of its programming but remained a largely amateur organization. Van Katwijk led the group in from two to four concerts a year, but interest gradually waned to the point that during the 1937 season no public concerts were presented.

In November of 1937 the Dallas Symphony Society announced the selection of a new conductor for the approaching season. Jacques Singer, a protégé of Leopold Stokowski of Philadelphia,* led the group for the next five years. The tour de force of the 1940–1941 season was a performance of Honegger's *Pacific 231*, the tone poem in which the French composer so vividly captures the sounds and rhythms of a steam engine. Before the Dallas concert, Conductor Singer was photographed hopping onto a cowcatcher to listen for "the locomotive rhythm." The loss of Singer to the American armed forces and the Second World War again silenced the Symphony.

John Rosenfield, arts editor of the *Dallas Morning News*, began working diligently with some of the music lovers of the community for a revival of the orchestra. When this was accomplished in 1945, the declared intention was to create a major professional orchestra, using only highly trained, well-paid musicians.

For conductor the Symphony Board chose Antal Dorati, assigning him power to recruit and import most of the instrumentalists. Dorati held auditions on the East Coast, bringing his players to Texas on the railroad. An annual budget of $500,000 was implemented, and a schedule of 15 subscription concerts, numerous special concerts, children's concerts, tours in the vicinity, and recordings was proposed. Dorati's Hungarian background and his interest in the works of an almost unknown countryman resulted in important performances of Béla Bartók, beginning with Yehudi Menuhin playing Bartók's Violin Concerto No. 2.

On January 8, 1949, the first performance in the Western Hemisphere of Bartók's *Prince Bluebeard's Castle* was broadcast on the National Broadcasting System's Saturday afternoon series, "Orchestras of the Nation." A series of commissions to American composers encouraged the composition of Paul Hindemith's *Sinfonia Serena* in 1946 and Walter Piston's *Symphonic Suite* in 1948. When Dorati left Dallas in 1949 to accept a new post in Minneapolis,* he left behind a mature orchestra that had become an important cultural institution.

That year the Dallas Symphony Orchestra offered its musical directorship to the young associate of the New York Philharmonic.* Walter Hendl led the group for eight seasons, until 1958, except for a leave in 1955, when he took the American Symphony of the Air on a 50-concert tour of the Orient.

Paul Kletzki, the eighth maestro of the orchestra, insisted that the Symphony move its concerts from the Fair Park Auditorium, with 4,400 seats, to the McFarlin Auditorium on the campus of Southern Methodist University, a hall of 2,600 seats. Kletzki conducted in Dallas from 1958 until 1961. The

Symphony has presented its concerts at Music Hall from 1945 to June 1951; at McFarlin Auditorium from September 1951 to June 1956; at Music Hall from September 1956 to June 1961; at McFarlin Auditorium from September 1961 to November 1972; and at Music Hall from December 1972 until the present.

Georg Solti led the Dallas Symphony as "senior conductor," a title of his own devising, during the 1961–1962 season, the same year he became musical director of the Royal Opera at Covent Garden. In 1962, having already served six seasons in Dallas as associate conductor and resident conductor, Donald Johanos succeeded Solti on the podium. The Iowa-born, Eastman-trained Johanos was successful in securing a $2.5 million grant from the Ford Foundation, contingent on the orchestra attracting matching funds. Within a year the Dallas community met the Ford challenge. Johanos continued for eight years until 1970.

Anshel Brusilow, who held the Dallas baton from 1970 until 1973, made a determined effort to reach out for a wider audience. Brusilow led the orchestra in a series of "Dallasound" concerts that featured rock and popular compositions scored for full symphony orchestra.

Max Rudolf was retained as the Symphony's artistic advisor for the 1973–1974 season. At a stormy press conference in January 1974, Rudolf resigned. A series of contract disputes and a distressing financial situation (a debt rumored in the press at $1 million) forced the orchestra to suspend services. Lloyd Haldeman was enticed into becoming manager of the Dallas group in the fall of 1974. He successfully settled the contract disputes with the players, launched massive fund drives that erased the deficits, and was able to persuade civic leaders into more active involvement in the fortunes of the orchestra. Revised performance schedules now included a profitable summer pops series and a 52-week contract for the musicians. Now established on a broader and sounder financial foundation, the orchestra was reformed under the baton of Louis Lane, a native-born Texan from Eagle Pass. He led the group from 1974 until 1977.

Under Eduardo Mata, who became music director in 1977, the group has achieved dramatic increases in attendance, expanded concert schedules, and an active recording schedule. Touring has been an integral part of the orchestra schedule as well. In addition to giving regional concerts, the Symphony traveled to Mexico in 1981 and again in 1982. In October 1981, the orchestra undertook a major tour of the East Coast of the United States and appeared in sold-out concerts in Carnegie Hall in New York, in Washington's Kennedy Center, and in other notable halls. The Dallas Symphony is now formulating plans for a tour of Europe in 1985 to coincide with the organization's 85th anniversary.

RECORDING HISTORY AND SELECTIVE DISCOGRAPHY: The Dallas Symphony's first important recordings were made under Antal Dorati, whose RCA Victor recording of Bartók's Violin Concerto No. 2 with Menuhin won a Grammy Award in

1946. Under Mata, 11 record albums have been produced for the Symphony by RCA and one by Telarc. Nonesuch Records will soon issue the Dallas performance of Rodriguez's *Oktoechos*.

Debussy, *Iberia*; Rimsky-Korsakov, *Capriccio Espagnol* (Mata): Telarc CD–10055. Gershwin, *Cuban Overture, Porgy and Bess: A Symphonic Picture*, and *An American in Paris* (Mata): RCA Victor Red Seal ATC1–4149. Mozart, Piano Concerto No. 20, K. 466 and Piano Concerto No. 22, K. 482 (Emanuel Ax/Mata): RCA Victor Red Seal ARL1–3457. Mussorgsky-Ravel, *Pictures at an Exhibition*; Ravel, *Le tombeau de Couperin* (Mata): RCA Victor Red Seal ARC1–4573. Strauss, *Death and Transfiguration, Don Juan, Dance of the Seven Veils* (Mata): RCA Red Seal ARC1–4353.

CHRONOLOGY OF MUSIC DIRECTORS: Hans Kreissig, 1900–1905. Walter J. Fried, 1905–1911. Carl Venth, 1911–1914. (Operations suspended, 1914–1918.) Walter J. Fried, 1918–1925. Paul van Katwijk, 1925–1937. (Operations suspended, 1937–1938.) Jacques Singer, 1938–1942. (Operations suspended, 1942–1945.) Antal Dorati, 1945–1949. Walter Hendl, 1949–1958. Paul Kletzki, 1958–1961. Georg Solti (Senior Conductor), 1961–1962. Donald Johanos, 1962–1970. Anshel Brusilow, 1970–1973. Max Rudolf, 1973–1974. Louis Lane, 1974–1977. Eduardo Mata, 1977-present.

BIBLIOGRAPHY: Interviews with Dallas Symphony players Dorothea Kelly, Joe Cinquemani, and others. *Dallas Morning News*. *Dallas Symphony Orchestra* (Dallas: [published by a group of business and individual sponsors] 1983). *Dallas Times-Herald*. *New York Times*, 4 Oct. 1981.

ACCESS: Dallas Symphony Orchestra, Music Hall, Fair Park, P.O. Box 26207, Dallas, TX 75226. (214) 565–9100. Leonard Stone, General Manager. Barbara Diles, Public Relations Manager.

JOHN WILLIAM WOLDT

EL PASO (479,899)

El Paso Symphony Orchestra (Mt)

Isolated from its nearest comparable neighbor by 250 miles of desert and cactus, El Paso is a city with a virile and distinctive cultural climate. Just across the international bridge is Juarez, Mexico, with its million-plus residents. Cultural identities have enlaced over the past century to create a significant and unique heritage. The symphonic tradition has also flourished here. Ethnic backgrounds of the player personnel reflect the racial balances throughout the area: roughly 50% Spanish surnames with 50% Anglos and other racial stocks. The Symphony's marketing area draws equally from members of both cultures. Over the years, programming has emphasized the universal appeal of music by targeting these national affinities. In recent years audiences have been growing ever younger, with tremendous ticket sales among teenagers and young adults. Additionally, the Symphony's concerts directed to young audiences reach about 17,000 children annually.

The first performance of an El Paso Symphony Orchestra took place in the Court House Building on December 29, 1893. At that time, El Paso had fewer than 15,000 people, no paved streets, and still an occasional Western shootout. This orchestra gave only two performances, and the attempted revival in 1913–1914 lasted but four concerts. A discernible improvement marked the concerts of the "new" El Paso Symphony Orchestra beginning in 1919. This time, secure financial backing allowed the orchestra to work productively for several years. Then suddenly another orchestra, the El Paso Philharmonic, appeared and soon began diluting the player pool and draining financial resources; both groups died in 1924. The long-term effect of these orchestras, however, was to plant the seeds of a more permanent symphonic tradition. With the third revival in May 1927, the El Paso Symphony Orchestra finally took root and has continued to this day.

In 1931, newspaperman Dorrance Roderick organized and became president of the first Board of the El Paso Symphony Orchestra Association. For the next 50 years, Roderick was the guiding spirit behind the Symphony's administrative and financial endeavors. Many seasons owed their continuance to Roderick's personal contributions.

Originally Board members served for life but in the late 1970s policy changed to allow for no more than two consecutive three-year terms. As a result, unprecedented activity by new members has produced dramatic results. Annual budgets have steadily mounted, putting the orchestra at the top of the ASOL Metropolitan classification; paired concerts are a reality, and varieties of program packages are now offered.

A new, acoustically designed Civic Center complex has replaced the original barnlike arena as the orchestra's permanent home. Pops concerts regularly feature guest artists such as Dave Brubeck, Ella Fitzgerald, Roy Clark, and the Empire Brass Quintet. Major concert artists often appear with the orchestra as well.

Only four people have occupied the position of music director and conductor of the El Paso Symphony since its incorporation in 1931. H. Arthur Brown came to El Paso as a violinist and Juilliard graduate. Increasing repertoire and attendance while charismatically attracting greater numbers of volunteers and patrons, he built the orchestra from almost nothing to an ensemble of over 60 players. He and Rockerick soon had full houses in which to showcase their ever-improving orchestra.

In 1951, Orlando Barera stepped onto the podium of an established organization. Having experience as concertmaster in Kansas City and assistant conductor in Houston,* Barera brought to the orchestra a personal charm noted for its continental flare. His 20-year tenure saw a greater emphasis on individual practice and preparation, a broadening of basic orchestra repertoire, and a drastic increase in the number of famous guest artists. It was during this time that the effects of public school music education were first being appreciated. Into Barera's orchestra of the 1950s and 1960s came many more young players than ever before.

William Kirschke led the orchestra from 1971 through 1974. His association brought to the El Paso Symphony the real beginnings of financial responsibility and organizational streamlining. Works of twentieth-century composers received their first El Paso performances. Kirschke's brief reign also saw new matinee concerts, expanded runouts to area communities and Mexico, and in-service preparation of teachers and students for youth concerts.

A season of guest conductors in 1974–1975 ultimately resulted in the appointment of Abraham Chavez. He brings to El Paso innate and consummate musical conceptions and finesse, which inspire the orchestra to reach beyond normal expectations. Works previously left to major orchestras have become standard repertoire, and artistic quality has risen sharply; permanent orchestra membership is now 85. In 1984, the orchestra experienced and survived a traumatic period of internal conflict concerning artistic policies and personnel from which it emerged with hopes for a renewed period of growth. Immediate plans call for gradual but steady development of a core ensemble, which should be fully operational by 1990.

In a community of high unemployment, the El Paso Symphony, providing low-cost entertainment and artistic rewards, has continued to exist and grow. Most of the musicians have full-time jobs outside the orchestra, with music education occupying much of their time. The El Paso area is exceedingly strong in instrumental music, its resident musicians having been critically acclaimed at state, national, and even international-level competitions. The University of Texas at El Paso has been a key supporter in the development of the arts in El Paso, and many of its faculty have served either on the orchestra Board or on its concert stage. The El Paso and Ysleta Independent School districts have consistently hired instructional faculty who are proficient performers and who have become substantial contributors to the success of the orchestra. Loyalty and dedication have been hallmarks in the history of the El Paso Symphony, numerous players having devoted 25 or more years of service.

CHRONOLOGY OF MUSIC DIRECTORS: H. Arthur Brown, 1931–1951. Orlando Barera, 1951–1971. William Kirschke, 1971–1974. (Guest conductors, 1974–1975.) Abraham Chavez, 1975-present.

BIBLIOGRAPHY: Interviews with El Paso Symphony music directors and personnel. *El Paso Herald Post, El Paso Times*. Neal Weaver is currently writing a complete history of the El Paso Symphony Orchestra.

ACCESS: El Paso Symphony Orchestra, P.O. Box 180, El Paso, Texas. 79942 (915) 532–8707.

                                                                          NEAL M. WEAVER

FORT WORTH (385,100; 2,974,805—Dallas/Fort Worth)

Fort Worth Symphony Orchestra (Rg)

Efforts to establish a symphony orchestra in Fort Worth began as early as 1912. C. D. Lusk, a flutist, was especially prominent in these efforts, as he gathered a small group of instrumentalists for performances that usually took place at his home. Succeeding this group was a somewhat larger ensemble conducted by Carl Venth, a violinist and faculty member of Texas Women's College in Fort Worth. Venth's orchestra performed concerts at the Chamber of Commerce Auditorium on Sunday afternoons. These early efforts were interrupted by World War I, but in 1925 the Fort Worth Symphony Orchestra was organized through the leadership of Brooks Morris, a violin teacher who had been concert master of the pre-war orchestra.

The initial concert of the FWSO was performed on December 11, 1925, before an overflow audience of nearly 4,000 at the First Baptist Church Auditorium. The orchestra, which included C. D. Lusk, was composed of musicians drawn from local schools, theaters, hotels, and restaurants. Soon after, the church burned, and in the following years the FWSO performed at Paschal High School and later at the Northside Coliseum, until the Will Rogers Auditorium was built in 1936. The founder of the FWSO, Brooks Morris, also served as conductor from 1925 to 1943, and during this period the orchestra's season grew to about six concerts per year. Morris received no fixed salary as FWSO conductor, but was given a nominal remuneration whenever the box office receipts were sufficient.

The FWSO disbanded in 1943 because of World War II. Subsequently, the city relied on performances by local college orchestras and visits by the Dallas Symphony Orchestra* to satisfy the public desire for orchestral concerts. Fourteen years passed before several interested citizens, again led by Brooks Morris, were successful in reestablishing the FWSO. In 1957 the Symphony League of Fort Worth was formed to promote and support the growth of the orchestra, and on October 29, 1957, the revitalized FWSO returned to the Will Rogers Auditorium in the first of three concerts scheduled for the 1957–1958 season. The conductor was Robert Hull, Dean of the School of Fine Arts at Texas Christian University.

Hull remained conductor of the FWSO until 1963. But over the next nine years, the orchestra was to have four different resident conductors. In 1963–1964 Rudolf Kruger served as conductor. Kruger, who was the conductor of the Fort Worth Opera Association from 1955 to 1982, shared the FWSO conducting duties in 1964–1965 with Ralph Guenther of the Texas Christian University faculty. Ezra Rachlin was the conductor of the FWSO in 1965–1971; until 1969 he was concurrently conductor of the Austin (Texas) Symphony Orchestra.*

For the 1971–1972 season, Ralph Guenther returned as acting music director of the FWSO. That season, several guest conductors appeared with the orchestra, including John Giordano, who had been the music director of the Youth Orchestra of Greater Forth Worth since 1969. Giordano was appointed music director and conductor of the FWSO beginning with the 1972–1973 season and has continued since.

During Giordano's tenure, the FWSO has undergone many important changes. In 1974 a group of young men and women founded the Symphony Society of Tarrant County to supplement the work of the Symphony League in promoting the growth of the orchestra. The administrative offices of the FWSO moved to Orchestra Hall in 1976. This facility, shared with the Youth Orchestra, contained needed office space and also provided a permanent rehearsal hall.

Of special sigificance for the development of the orchestra was a three-year grant received in 1976 from the Richardson Foundation. With this grant it was possible to create within the FWSO a core of musicians hired on a full-time basis. Besides serving as the core of the orchestra, this group of 32 musicians performed separately under Giordano's direction as the Texas Little Symphony and thus provided Fort Worth with a chamber orchestra to complement the full FWSO. Moreover, the comparatively small size of the Texas Little Symphony made it economically feasible for this ensemble to tour widely, bringing live symphonic music to communities throughout north and central Texas.

The Texas Little Symphony proved enormously successful and continued beyond the period of the original grant. The ensemble was renamed the Fort Worth Chamber Orchestra in 1983 and by that time had been increased to 35 musicians employed full-time for a 34-week season. (Twenty-four of the orchestra's positions were underwritten by major annual contributors.) To bring the FWSO to its full strength of 93 members, musicians in addition to the Chamber Orchestra were hired on a season contract basis.

Annually, the FWSO and Chamber Orchestra perform about 200 concerts to audiences totalling more than 250,000 people. The concerts consist predominantly of works from the standard symphonic and concerto repertoire of the eighteenth, nineteenth, and early twentieth centuries. There are occasional performances of more recent works, however, among which are compositions commissioned for the FWSO or Chamber Orchestra.

The FWSO season includes several subscription series, each featuring well-known guest artists. The full orchestra offers a series of seven pairs of concerts at the Tarrant County Convention Center Theatre, a multipurpose auditorium seating 3,054. The average attendance at these concerts is 1,800. In the same theater, the FWSO offers a pops series of five pairs of concerts with an average attendance of approximately 2,800. The Chamber Orchestra performs a series of six concerts to audiences averaging 450 in the 1,264-seat Landreth Auditorium on the campus of Texas Christian University.

Beyond the subscription series, both the FWSO and the Chamber Orchestra make many other appearances in Fort Worth during the course of a season. These include the young people's concerts (presented at the Will Rogers Auditorium) and concerts given in schools throughout the Fort Worth area. Music education has continued as an important mission of the orchestra from its first concert, when the *Fort Worth Star-Telegram* reported that "the entire balcony was reserved for school children and part of the downstairs sections were turned over to them." Concerts specifically for children have been integral to FWSO seasons since 1926. Other regular performances by the orchestra include the city park series, Oktoberfest, Mayfest, and its participation as resident orchestra for the Van Cliburn Quadrennial International Piano Competition.

The FWSO and Chamber Orchestra also tour extensively, with 20% to 25% of each year's performances given outside of Forth Worth. The Chamber Orchestra tours throughout north and central Texas and appears for a week each summer at the Ruidoso (New Mexico) Summer Festival. The orchestra also undertakes biennial, major tours outside of Texas. In the spring of 1983 the Chamber Orchestra spent 21 days on tour in the People's Republic of China and Hong Kong.

The rapid development of the FWSO during the 1970s necessitated in 1979 the appointment of its first associate conductor—James Simpson Miller, who had been conductor of the Youth Orchestra. He was succeeded in 1984 by George Del Gobbo, who was appointed assistant conductor. Del Gobbo had also been conductor of the Youth Orchestra as well as the Texas Christian University Symphony Orchestra. For the 1984–1985 season, the FWSO conducting staff was further increased with the addition of a principal guest conductor. The choice of Jose-Luis Garcia, who was also conductor and violin soloist with the English Chamber Orchestra (London), was indicative of the FWSO's goal of eventual growth from regional to international prominence.

The 1984–1985 budget of the FWSO was approximately $2.5 million. In addition to the financial support raised through the Symphony League and Symphony Society, sources of funding include ticket sales, corporate grants, foundation grants, underwritten orchestra chairs, and private donations. The FWSO is also one of seven arts organizations that share funds raised by the Arts Council of Fort Worth and Tarrant County. Tours have been funded in part by grants from the Texas Commission on the Arts and the NEA, as well as by stipends from the host communities.

Governance and administration of the FWSO (including the Chamber Orchestra) are carried out by a Board of Directors, the music director, and an executive director with a full-time administrative staff of nine.

CHRONOLOGY OF MUSIC DIRECTORS: Brooks Morris, 1925–1943. (Orchestra inactive, 1943–1957.) Robert Hull, 1957–1963. Rudolf Kruger, 1963–1964. Rudolf Kruger and Ralph Guenther, 1964–1965. Ezra Rachlin, 1965–1971. Ralph Guenther (Acting Music Director), 1971–1972. John Giordano, 1972-present.

BIBLIOGRAPHY: "Boy Musician Will Appear in Concert," *Fort Worth Star-Telegram*, 12 Dec. 1925. Sheri Jan Broyles, ed., *Fanfare* (newsletter of the Fort Worth Symphony Orchestra Association). Sheri Jan Broyles, ed., *Fort Worth Symphony Program Magazine*. Norwood P. Dixon, "The Story of the Fort Worth Symphony" (Report distributed by the Fort Worth Symphony Orchestra, 1980). Brian Howard, "Symphony Innovator Dies at 92," *Fort Worth Star-Telegram*, 15 Sept. 1982. "Initial Symphony Orhcestra [*sic*] Concert Is Well Received," *Fort Worth Star-Telegram*, 12 Dec. 1925. Chester Lane, "Fort Worth to the Great Wall: Bridging a Cultural Chasm," *Symphony Magazine*, Aug./Sept. 1983. "State of the Art Symphony," *Fort Worth Star-Telegram*, 29 Aug. 1982. E. Clyde Whitlock, "Fort Worth Symphony Will Repeat History," *Fort Worth Star-Telegram*, 27 Oct. 1957.

ACCESS: Fort Worth Symphony Orchestra, Orchestra Hall, 4401 Trail Lake Drive, Fort Worth, TX 76109. (817) 921–2676. Ann Koonsman, Executive Director.

CHARLES A. ROECKLE

HOUSTON (2,905,353)

Houston Symphony Orchestra (Mj)

The premier performing arts organization of the Texas Gulf Coast, the Houston Symphony Orchestra has also won acclaim on the national and international levels. It performs more than 172 concerts a year and has a budget of over $7.6 million. More than 350,000 people make up its annual audience.

In addition to the subscription series concerts held in Jones Hall, the Symphony incorporates into its schedule a chamber orchestra series, pops concerts, area concerts, family concerts, free outdoor concerts, a music festival, touring, and recording. Other performing activities include student concerts for more than 30,000 young people a year. There are 13 concerts and the season is divided into three types of programs geared to the specific needs of each age group. Each program is structured to illustrate a particular concept of theme. In 1983–1984, one program used music depicting storms and showed the evolution of the orchestra from the time of Vivaldi to that of Britten. There are also master classes and seminars in conjunction with Rice University and the University of Houston, special concerts for the handicapped and senior citizens, and annual holiday programs such as the Christmas Pops and the New Years Eve Gala. The Symphony also opens Jones Hall to the public for a series of free open rehearsals during the year.

There are two chamber series: the Cathedral series, held in downtown Houston at Christ Church Cathedral, and the Rice series, at Rice University, featuring a contemporary concert led by Music Director Sergiu Comissiona and other concerts led by Concertmaster Ruben Gonzalez and guest artists.

Summer programs include free concerts in Miller Outdoor Theatre and a summer music festival in Jones Hall. The Symphony has toured Mexico, and it appeared at the Festival Casals in San Juan, Puerto Rico, for a week in June 1982. It toured Texas in September 1982 as part of the American Orchestras on Tour sponsored by the Bell Telephone System. The Symphony has also performed at Carnegie Hall in New York City and at the Kennedy Center in Washington, D.C., as part of a six-concert tour of the East Coast. At the beginning of the 1983–1984 concert season, the British Broadcasting Company (BBC) began broadcasting concerts of the orchestra in England.

The only complete published history of the orchestra is Hubert Roussel's *The Houston Symphony Orchestra* (1977), upon which the following account is partially based. In 1912, petroleum was springing up as a resource on the Gulf Coast, and Houston became headquarters for this industry. The city's growing population (by that time Houston had approximately 80,000 people) included a number of professional musicians who played in restaurant and theater orchestras. Several influences encouraged the growth of music in the city. Houston's sizeable German population had an established musical tradition. Prominent touring groups—among them New York's Metropolitan Opera Company and a Gilbert and Sullivan ensemble—had performed in Houston.

A group of influential city leaders felt it was time to start a symphony orchestra. Prominent in this group was a trained musician, Ima Hogg, daughter of former Texas Governor James Hogg. Among the number of touring organizations that performed in Houston during the 1912–1913 season was a Russian symphony orchestra conducted by its concertmaster, Nikolai Sokoloff, who had assumed leadership after its previous conductor, Modest Altschuler, abruptly abandoned it. Finding his orchestra stranded in Houston, Sokoloff offered to make the orchestra a permanent resident of the city in exchange for financial support. While this offer was rejected by the city leaders, it did reinforce their interest in a permanent symphony orchestra. Ima Hogg persuaded others to form the Houston Symphony Association for the purpose of establishing such an orchestra.

The Symphony's development proceeded swiftly. On December 19, 1913, the first of the season's three concerts was performed to a capacity audience under the direction of Conductor Julien Paul Blitz, who was paid the same salary as the members of the orchestra. The Houston Symphony's first season was deemed a success. While the musicians performed only satisfactorily, the public showed its support of the venture. Houston's business community displayed an interest; the Foley Brothers contributed to the guaranty fund, and the Levy Brothers included the Symphony in company advertising.

The Symphony's second season was as successful as its first. Although World War I was now in progress, the anti-German sentiment pervasive in many areas of the country was not much in evidence in Houston. The concerts continued into the third season, and in 1916, Paul Berge succeeded Julien Paul Blitz as conductor. Berge conducted for two years, until April 1918, after which the Houston Symphony suspended operations because so many of its musicians had been drafted into military service. There was still an official symphony society and it met occasionally, largely through the efforts of Ima Hogg. In 1921 Mrs. H. M. Garwood succeeded Hogg as president of the Association.

Until 1931, when the Houston Symphony resumed its concerts, several semi-professional orchestras performed in Houston, including the Houston Philharmonic and the Ellison Van Hoose Little Symphony. Again, Ima Hogg was influential in the Symphony's rebirth, and the Houston Symphony Association signed a contract with the local musicians union and announced a series of concerts at the City Auditorium. An Italian, Uriel Nespoli, conducted the Symphony for one season, but an impasse with the Board concerning Nespoli's apparent incompatibility with the mannerisms of Houston high society, with whom he was expected to hobnob, led to his departure the following year.

From 1932 to 1935 six concerts were performed each season under the direction of Frank St. Leger. During this time, all soloists were local musicians, not guest performers. Born of English parents in India and educated in England, St. Leger was more at home in and more accepted by Houston society than his predecessor. Nevertheless, despite St. Leger's popularity as a conductor and a pianist, the Symphony suffered during his tenure. The Symphony's budget was simply too small to support an orchestra of full-time musicians. Lax discipline, inferior instruments, and personnel gaps were caused or exacerbated by lack of funds. When there were not enough musicians to fill the chairs, players were imported from St. Louis or Chicago. As might be predicted, the concerts during this time were not of extraordinary quality; St. Leger, deemed by some to be the cause of their dissatisfaction, resigned at the end of the third season and accepted a position on the staff of the Metropolitan Opera Company. The Symphony's repertoire comprised mostly standard works during St. Leger's tenure. One of few exceptions was a work by the contemporary American, Leo Sowerby, performed during the 1934–1935 season.

Things soon changed with the arrival of three successive guest conductors engaged for 1935–1936: Vittorio Verse, Alfred Hertz, and Modeste Aloo. Of the three, Hertz left the strongest impression. He demanded the importation of five players—an oboist, an English hornist, two bassoonists, and a principal hornist. Known for his performances of Wagner, whose compositions he scheduled amply in his two programs, Hertz also included Respighi's *Pines of Rome*, composed 11 years earlier. Hertz was an important conductor in the Houston Symphony's history, for he brought it up to a level of playing excellence not achieved in earlier years.

Hertz died not long after his guest conductorship, and the American Ernst Hoffmann was hired as the next conductor. He had been recommended to Houston Symphony President Walter Walne by Serge Koussevitzky in Boston. Hoffman was educated at Harvard University as well as in Germany. In 1924 he was named conductor of the Breslau Opera and Philharmonic Orchestra, and he continued in that capacity until he spoke out against Hitler and the Nazi Party. After a short stint with the Commonwealth Orchestra in Boston, he came to Houston, where he became one of the chief proponents and builders of the Houston Symphony Orchestra.

The orchestra had 74 musicians in the 1937–1938 season, and it gave six concerts that year. In order to achieve a particular sound in the brass choir, Hoffman supplied brass instruments from a German manufacturer at his own expense. During the 1938 season, Hoffman led the orchestra in a production of *Madame Butterfly* and an evening of Shakespeare in music. An orchestral interpretation of *The Tempest*, written by American composer John K. Paine, accompanied several other compositions by Tchaikovsky and Mendelssohn.

A new music hall was built in time for the Symphony's 1938–1939 season, but the hall proved acoustically unsatisfactory, and the Symphony returned to its original home in the City Auditorium the following season. That season coincided with the beginning of World War II. The Symphony nevertheless performed a 10-concert schedule, as well as a concert at Miller Outdoor Theatre in Hermann Park, with the financial support of N. D. Naman. Orchestra audiences were growing. The concert at Miller Outdoor Theatre drew 15,000 people that first season—many of them soldiers in uniform—and even more during the next few seasons.

Despite the loss of a number of musicians to the armed forces, the Symphony's activities and outreach grew during the war years. Touring was active, the capacity of City Auditorium was increased to 4,000, national broadcasts were begun in the Cities Service Radio Program, the first staged opera (Puccini's *Tosca*) was presented, and numerous first Houston performances were offered, including Beethoven's Ninth Symphony as well as compositions by Piston, Gould, and de Falla. During the 1944–1945 season the Symphony performed 72 events, including three staged operas.

Financial management of the Symphony before this time was somewhat unstable. Roy Cullen, a long-time patron of the Houston Symphony, resigned as president and became chairman of the Board. It is not known how much money he contributed to the orchestra, since he often simply wrote a check and handed it to Ernst Hoffman. In 1946 Francis Deering was named the Symphony's first professional orchestra manager. Previously, the duties of manager had been performed by a part-time manager and a small staff. In 1947 Deering resigned because of health problems; at his suggestion Tom Johnson assumed his duties on December 23, 1947. Hoffmann also resigned in 1947.

There followed a season of 12 guest conductors, after which Efrem Kurtz was appointed. Kurtz served from 1948 to 1954; during his tenure he introduced works by Honegger, Bartók, Ives, and many others. He began with an orchestra of 84 members—57 of them new—and he received much enthusiastic support from the city. In 1949–1950 the season was expanded to 20 concerts and the budget to $400,000.

Following a partial season with Ferenc Fricsay as principal conductor (1954–1955), Leopold Stokowski began his tenure as music director in the refurbished Music Hall. He presented the first local performance of *Carmina Burana* by Carl Orff. The Houston Grand Opera Association gave its first performance using members of the Houston Symphony Orchestra. World premieres of Aram Khatchaturian's *Festive Poem* and Heitor Villa-Lobos's Guitar Concerto were given that season. The orchestra appeared on national television for the first time; it performed Alan Hovhaness's *Mysterious Mountain*, commissioned by the conductor. Guest conductors included Max Rudolf, Heitor Villa-Lobos, and Sr. Thomas Beecham. At this time Ima Hogg, President of the Symphony Society, retired and was succeeded by General Maurice Hirsch.

During the 1956–1957 season Stokowski conducted six Beethoven concerts in the Music Hall's acoustical shell, which had been donated by Ima Hogg. Stokowski introduced Berlioz's *L'Enfance du Christ* as well as a concerto by Houston composer William E. Rice. In the following season, the numbers of subscription concerts was increased from 20 to 24. Guest conductors included Heitor Villa-Lobos, Igor Stravinsky, and Walter Susskind. A Houston Contemporary Music Society was formed by Stokowski to play contemporary works, which appeared infrequently on most American symphony orchestra programs. Since Stokowski scheduled more twentieth-century music than his predecessors did, some members of the more conservative music public did not respond favorably.

Stokowski's frustrations increased. In August of 1960 he wrote a letter to Dr. Nicholas Geren, head of the Music Department at Texas Southern University, a school with a predominantly black enrollment, requesting that the men's chorus be used in a forthcoming performance of Arnold Schoenberg's *Gurrelieder*, along with two other men's choruses. The Houston Symphony Association denied his request. Stokowski wrote, according to the *Houston Chronicle* (8 Feb. 1961), "In my opinion, the true reason why the planned performances have been canceled is that some, possibly only a few, persons are opposed to having a colored chorus be a part of the performance," a charge denied by Manager Tom Johnson. Stokowski's tenure as conductor, from 1955 to 1961, benefitted both the orchestra and the musical public. However, when he resigned, Stokowski may have known that negotiations were underway with Sir John Barbirolli to be the next conductor. According to Roussel, who cites various reasons for his leaving, Stokowski had, in a typically theatrical gesture, already announced his "farewell season."

From 1961 to 1967, Barbirolli was principal conductor and later conductor-in-chief. During the 1963–1964 season the orchestra made a post-season tour that included Washington, D.C. and New York City. The year 1965 saw the inauguration of the Nazro Memorial Concerts, a series of subscription concerts endowed by Joseph Mullen.

Jones Hall, the new home of the Houston Symphony, was completed in 1966, and the orchestra gave its opening concert there on October 3 of that year with Barbirolli conducting. Barbirolli divided his time between conducting the Hallé Orchestra in England and the Houston Symphony Orchestra. This proved too strenuous a schedule for him, and in 1967 André Previn replaced him as conductor-in-chief. Sir John Barbirolli was held in high esteem, however, and was made conductor laureate. In his first season, Previn premiered his own Cello Concerto and appeared as a pianist in a jazz combo in a series of pops concerts for young audiences sponsored by Foleys Department Store. In his second season, a young artists competition was sponsored by Pennzoil, and the Moody Foundation funded two annual concerts in Galveston. Although Previn remained with the HSO for only two years, his tenure had included programs with a fair amount of contemporary music.

The American conductor Lawrence Foster began his term as conductor-in-chief in 1971. Notable among compositions performed during that season were Prokofiev's *Alexander Nevsky*, Beethoven's complete music for *Egmont*, and Haydn's *Creation*. Foster continued a tradition of performing contemporary music began by Efrem Kurtz and championed as well by Leopold Stokowski. Compositions performed during his tenure were George Rochberg's Violin Concerto, Michael Tippett's *A Child of Our Time*, Donald Erb's Concerto for Orchestra, and others.

In 1976 a labor dispute delayed the opening of the season until November. Fifteen programs were given that season under seven directors, with Music Director Lawrence Foster conducting seven concerts. Foster's departure in 1978 was followed by a season featuring 14 guest conductors. One, Sergiu Comissiona, was signed in July of 1979 as artistic advisor to the Houston Symphony. In December of 1982 Comissiona signed a four-year contract naming him music director of the orchestra. In his four years Comissiona has been instrumental in renewing the orchestra's recording activities, with four new discs on the Vanguard label, and television activities comprising concerts taped and aired by Bravo Cable Network, QUBE Cable, and most recently by Houston television station KTXH. Regular radio broadcasts, contemporary music series, pops concerts, and chamber orchestra concerts have also been the result of Comissiona's influence. Comissiona inaugurated the indoor Summer Symphony Festival with a Tchaikovsky Festival in 1981 and, in association with a new executive director, Gideon Toeplitz, he took the orchestra (only the second one ever invited) to the Festival Casals in San Juan, Puerto Rico. Comissiona conducted the orchestra on its national tour and presided over the single largest concert organized by the symphony, a performance of Schoenberg's *Gurrelieder*. Leonard Bernstein and

Sergiu Comissiona led the orchestra in its 70th Anniversary Concert, held at Miller Outdoor Theatre in Hermann Park, on June 21, 1983, to an audience of nearly 30,000 people.

RECORDING HISTORY AND SELECTIVE DISCOGRAPHY: The Houston Symphony Orchestra has recorded from the tenure of Efrem Kurtz to the present day. It now has a contract with Centaur Records. Some of the first recordings were for Columbia Records, and others are on Angel/Seraphim, Capitol, CRI, Everest, and Vanguard.

Paul Cooper, Symphony No. 4 (*Landscape*) (Jones): CRI S–347. Debussy, *Nocturnes* and *La Mer* (Comissiona): Vanguard VA–25015. Franck, Symphony in D Minor (Comissiona): Vanguard VA–25016. Woody Herman, *Children of Lima* (Previn): Fantasy 9477. Orff, *Carmina Burana* (Stokowski): Seraphim S–60236. Cole Porter, *Kiss Me Kate* (Kurtz): Columbia ML–2104.

CHRONOLOGY OF MUSIC DIRECTORS: Julien Paul Blitz, 1913–1916. Paul Berge, 1916–1918. (Operations suspended, 1918–1931.) Uriel Nespoli, 1931–1932. Frank St. Leger, 1932–1935. Ernst Hoffmann, 1935–1947. Efrem Kurtz, 1948–1954. Ferenc Fricsay, 1954. Leopold Stokowski, 1955–1961. Sir John Barbirolli, 1961–1967. André Previn, 1967–1969. Antonio de Almeida (Principal Guest Conductor), 1969–1971. Lawrence Foster, 1971–1978. Erich Bergel (Principal Guest Conductor), 1979–1980. Sergiu Comissiona, 1980-present.

BIBLIOGRAPHY: *Houston Chronicle.* "Houston Symphony Society," Binder, HSO, [1984]. Michael Kennedy, *Barbirolli: Conductor Laureate* (London: MacGibbon & Kee, 1971). Paul Robinson, *Stokowski* (New York: Vanguard Press, 1977). Hubert Roussel, *The Houston Symphony Orchestra, 1913–1977* (Austin: University of Texas Press, 1972).

ACCESS: Houston Symphony Orchestra, Jesse H. Jones Hall, 615 Louisiana Street, Houston, TX 77002. (713) 224–4240. Gideon Toeplitz, Executive Director.

JOSEPH B. SCHMOLL

SAN ANTONIO (1,071,954)

San Antonio Symphony (Mj)

The city of San Antonio possesses a unique geographical location and combination of cultures that have contributed to its rich and varied music. European music was first brought by Spanish missionaries who founded Mission San Antonio de Valero (the Alamo) in 1718. Despite war and political upheaval, San Antonio grew culturally during the nineteenth century, largely due to the efforts of new German settlers. The first opera house (1858) and the Beethoven Maennerchor (1867) are examples. By the turn of the century the city boasted a Grand Opera House (1886), the Beethoven Concert Hall (1895), several choirs, chamber music, and a brief orchestra season. Although cultivated music lagged in the 1920s, it rallied by the end of the next decade. The most significant event in this development was the founding of the San Antonio Symphony, an organization soon to be one of the three major symphony orchestras in the state of Texas.

The first performance given by the future San Antonio Symphony took place in the Sunken Garden Theater on June 12, 1939. It was a trial concert, organized and underwritten by Mrs. Pauline Washer Goldsmith. The conductor, immigrant Max Reiter, had given a similar demonstration concert in Waco, Texas, in the spring. Reiter's resoundingly successful San Antonio concert justified Mrs. Goldsmith's developing a group of benefactors to guarantee a short season of concerts starting in the fall of 1939. Thus, the San Antonio Symphony was established with Max Reiter as its first music director. For the four concerts the first season, one-third of the 95 orchestra players had to be brought in from other cities in the Southwest. However, Reiter's ability to engage top soloists helped the orchestra succeed in the first years.

From 1943 to 1945 the city of San Antonio experienced a wartime boom because of its numerous military installations. One result was an enlarged patronage, which helped the Symphony become increasingly successful. In 1943 the lengthy regular season was augmented by an outdoor summer concert series. With the 1943–1944 season the San Antonio Symphony became a fully professional orchestra. The following season's budget topped $100,000, qualifying the orchestra as one of the nation's 19 Major symphony orchestras, and the only one in Texas at the time.

From 1945 to 1950 Reiter gave San Antonio more resourceful programming than it had previously known. World and American premieres were given of works by Antheil, Gillis, Hanson, and Richard Strauss. Noted guest conductors were brought in as well. Stravinsky conducted the orchestra in 1947. Sir Thomas Beecham and Dimitri Mitropoulos were guest conductors during these years and each praised the Symphony's abilities. Beecham characterized it as "among the few leading orchestras of this country," and Mitropoulos went so far as to declare, "This orchestra can compete with any orchestra in this country or Europe."

In December 1950 Max Reiter died unexpectedly of a heart attack, and early the next year Victor Alessandro, Reiter's choice for a successor, was appointed as the new music director. Alessandro, a native Texan, was music director of the Oklahoma City Symphony* and had guest-conducted the San Antonio Symphony on several occasions. He arrived at a difficult time for the Symphony, due to the city's increasing economic recession in the postwar years. Alessandro helped the Symphony ride out its difficulties, partly by improving or expanding certain activities, such as the Symphony's Grand Opera Festival, held annually since 1945. Unsuccessful attempts had been made in the 1940s to hold pops concerts, but in 1954 Alessandro initiated a pops series that was well attended and became a regular part of the orchestra's season.

Since 1943 the San Antonio Symphony had made use of an auxiliary choir. At first the group was used only as an opera chorus, but gradually it grew stronger and was eventually employed in every area of the orchestra's performances. During the 1958–1959 season this choir became formally known as the Mastersingers, an adjunct of the Symphony, but capable also of presenting independent programs of its own.

After nearly six years of planning, the Symphony presented in early 1961 the first Rio Grande Valley International Music Festival. The festival traditionally included one opera. The 1960s also saw the impact of technology on Symphony programming. From 1964 to 1966 several audience preference tests were given and evaluated using data processing equipment. There were mixed results, but the tests yielded valuable information said to have been influential in future programming.

Since its inception the San Antonio Symphony had played its regular concerts in the city's Municipal Auditorium. In 1968 the Theater for the Performing Arts was completed. It had a larger seating capacity and markedly improved acoustics over the Municipal Auditorium. Starting in October 1969 this hall became the permanent home of the Symphony.

Under Victor Alessandro's leadership the orchestra grew not only in size but in stature as well. The Symphony commissioned, premiered (April 1968), and subsequently recorded John Corigliano's Piano Concerto with Hilde Somer as soloist. In June 1969 the Symphony recorded music by Carlos Surinach for the TV documentary, "The Missions of San Antonio." By 1970 the orchestra had made three recordings for the Mercury label. Alessandro's 25-year tenure drew to a close in late 1976, when he retired under doctor's orders. He was immediately named conductor emeritus.

After the Symphony's two-year search for a new music director, François Huybrechts came to San Antonio from the Wichita Symphony.* His conducting style was more flamboyant and his choice of works less orthodox than the city's concertgoers were accustomed to. For example, Stravinsky's *Sacre du Printemps* was performed, and Berg's *Wozzeck* was scheduled for the opera season, although the latter was performed after Huybrechts left San Antonio.

Another search ensued in 1979, and in March 1980 Lawrence Leighton Smith was named the Symphony's new music director. Smith came from a seven-year tenure with the Oregon Symphony,* where he had gained recognition for commissioning and performing new music. He had also conducted numerous major U.S. symphony orchestras and at the Metropolitan Opera.

In San Antonio Smith has combined a knack for innovative programming with a distinctive personal touch. Before each of his programs he offers an informative preview session. Audiences have been responsive to this approach and have more enthusiastically than previously accepted the performance of modern or unusual works. Smith has also challenged the orchestra by stressing large-scale works (by Berlioz and Mahler, for example) and twentieth-century music. Of the 14 classical programs of the 1984–1985 season, nine contained twentieth-century works. Smith has striven to increase the orchestra's size (presently 83 players) and to perfect its sound, which he considers to be characteristically "warm." The results of his efforts have been positive to the point that at the opening of the 1983–1984 season the *San Antonio Express* declared the Symphony to be "the city's artistic cornerstone."

The San Antonio Symphony's regular performance season extends from September through May. The season presently consists of three regular series, several special individual concerts, and a student concert series. The Classical Series over the years has ranged from 14 to 20 programs, most of which are conducted by the music director. These concerts are performed twice: in the Lila M. Cockrell Theater (formerly the Theater for the Performing Arts) and in Laurie Auditorium on the Trinity University campus. The Pops Series consists of approximately eight programs, generally conducted by the orchestra's associate conductor. These informal evenings take place in the Convention Center Banquet Hall, where cabaret-style seating and refreshments contribute to a relaxed atmosphere. A Family Series of three or four programs is performed at the Majestic Theater. These often incorporate striking visual stimuli, such as dance or a multimedia light show. Programs in this series are conducted by either the music director or associate conductor.

As part of a long-standing educational program, the Symphony performs a student concert series in various locations throughout the city. These have been offered since 1944. Most of the student concerts are conducted by the assistant conductor/educational director; however, the music director and associate conductor also take part in this series. Special individual classical concerts are presented at various times and in different locations. Those given during the regular season generally involve guest artists of exceptional reputation or are ballets. Community concerts are also offered, and occasionally a post-season series will be performed, such as the Twilight Series.

The San Antonio Symphony's annual tour of southern Texas is generally held in conjunction with the Rio Grande Valley International Music Festival. Sponsored by the Symphony, the Festival is supported by 11 South Texas cities and is usually more than a week in duration. The Symphony has toured out of state five times in its history. In 1982 the orchestra appeared in the Roundtop Music Festival (Roundtop, Texas). The first foreign tour was made to Monterrey, Mexico in 1958. Tours of Mexico City were made in 1978 and 1980, and the orchestra performed three concerts in Mexico City as part of "Expo San Antonio en Mexico" in 1982.

The San Antonio Symphony began sponsoring a Grand Opera Festival in 1945. Four or five works were performed each season until 1983, when the series had to be discontinued for budgetary reasons. The Grand Opera Festival chiefly featured Italian works (75%) with a few others, including standard German operas. Featured soloists were brought in from the Metropolitan Opera, the Paris Opera, and other celebrated companies. Among the more unusual and ambitious works have been Wagner's *Rienzi* (1977), Berg's *Wozzeck* (1980), and Mussorgsky's *Boris Gudonov* (1980).

Since 1983 a new agency outside the San Antonio Symphony has staged an annual San Antonio Festival, encompassing varied styles and geographic representation. Although opera and ballet have generally been imported, the San Antonio Symphony is the main festival orchestra.

The San Antonio Symphony is governed by a Board of Directors comprising elected members, ex officio members, Regional Council officers, and members of the Advisory Committee. The Symphony office employs 16 full-time persons. Operations are funded from earned income, contributions (including the Annual Fund and substantial gifts from businesses and private donors), and supplemental income (including endowment funds and various fund-raising projects). The Symphony has received grants from the city of San Antonio, the Texas Commission on the Arts, the National Endowment for the Arts, and the Mellon Foundation. The orchestra's annual budget has grown steadily; for the 1983–1984 season it stood at $3.95 million.

San Antonio, the nation's tenth largest city, is still expanding and is giving greater support to the arts than ever before. The Symphony and its music director look forward to the orchestra's 50th anniversary in 1989 and to prospects of initiating compositional commissioning projects on a Pan-American level.

SELECTIVE DISCOGRAPHY: John Corigliano, Piano Concerto (Hilde Somer/Alessandro): Mercury 75118. Joaquin Rodrigo, *Concierto de Aranjuez* and *Concierto Andaluz* (Angel Romero and Los Romeros, guitar soloists/Alessandro): Mercury 75021. Vivaldi, Mandolin Concertos in A and C; Two-Mandolin Concerto (Los Romeros guitar soloists/Alessandro): Mercury 75054.

CHRONOLOGY OF MUSIC DIRECTORS: Max Reiter, 1939–1950. Victor Alessandro, 1951–1976. François Huybrechts, 1978–1979. Lawrence Leighton Smith, 1980-present.

BIBLIOGRAPHY: Interviews with SAS Music Director Lawrence Leighton Smith and Managing Director Carlos Wilson, 1984. Jane L. Berdes, "Remembering the Arts in Alamo City," *Symphony Magazine*, June/July 1983. Jay J. Foraker, "The San Antonio Symphony: Some Problems Solved," *High Fidelity and Musical America*, Mar. 1982. Edward W. Heusinger, *A Chronology of Events in San Antonio* (San Antonio: Standard Printing Co., 1951). Marcia P. Holliman, "The Development of the San Antonio Symphony, 1939–1966," Masters thesis, Trinity University, San Antonio, 1966.

ACCESS: San Antonio Symphony, 109 Lexington, Suite 207, San Antonio, TX 78205. (512) 225–6161. Carlos Wilson, Managing Director. Carolee Scharmen, Director of Marketing and Public Relations.

MICHAEL FINK

Utah

SALT LAKE CITY (936,255—Salt Lake City/Ogden)

Utah Symphony Orchestra (Mj)

Considered by critic Martin Mayer as one of the top 10 symphony orchestras in the United States, the Utah Symphony Orchestra is the premier musical ensemble in the Intermountain West, serving an area of over a quarter million square miles in six states. The 85-member group performs 52 weeks per year, presenting about 250 concerts divided between a regular subscription season in Salt Lake City at the new Symphony Hall, outdoor and benefit performances, a series of concerts in local schools, others in towns scattered throughout the vast region, and on tour. Included in this total are performances by groups whose members consist of USO players, such as Ballet West, the Utah Opera, the Utah Symphony Chamber Orchestra, the Camerata Utah, and smaller impromptu chamber ensembles. The orchestra sponsors the internationally known Gina Bachauer Piano Competition, which it inherited from Brigham Young University in 1981. Winners perform with the USO. The USO also supports the Utah Oratorio Society. The 1984–1985 season is divided into seven series: regular subscription, Summer Pops, Chamber Orchestra, Preview, New Audience, Morning Youth, and a Visiting Orchestra Special (for 1984–1985, the London Philharmonic).

Founded in 1940, the USO is headed by the Utah Symphony Board, which has about 60 members. An Executive Committee of 11 members is responsible for policy development goals and long-range planning. The Utah Symphony Board reviews operational activities, while the Utah Symphony Foundation Board evaluates financial objectives. This Board is responsible for overseeing the artistic and administrative staff. In addition, fund-raising and logistical support is provided by the Utah Symphony Guild, which sponsors a membership drive, receptions, competitions, and symposiums. A professional staff of 16 handles administrative operations under the guidance of the Executive Committee. There are two levels of contracts with the musicians: full-time and a so-called B level (for musicians not playing with the opera and ballet). As of the 1985–1986 season, the two-tier contract levels will be phased out in favor of a single one. Additional musicians may be hired on an individual basis as required by the needs of the orchestra. Salary minimums and working conditions are negotiated with the Musicians' Union, and there are benefits and a retirement plan available. All contracts are negotiated individually.

The USO annual budget has risen from $10,000 in 1940 to about $5 million for 1984–1985, the greatest increase coming in 1976 when the USO expanded its season from 28 to 52 weeks. About 65% of this budget is funded through ticket sales and other orchestra services, with the remainder coming from a wide variety of sources, such as endowments, recordings, government funds, and corporate and private contributions. For example, the Utah State Legislature has supported a series of concerts in public schools throughout the state since 1970, and the former conductor of the USO, Maurice Abravanel, helped originate the formula by which funds from the Ford Foundation were distributed to orchestras in this country, including the USO. In terms of financial support, the USO, having ended 24 of the last 27 seasons in the black, is one of the most financially stable cultural organizations in the United States.

Although the home of the USO is in Salt Lake City, the orchestra has had a large cultural impact on the entire, somewhat sparsely populated Intermountain region of the West. It is primarily a state orchestra, but its musical influence reaches from the Canadian border to northern Arizona. It is the only Major symphony orchestra between Denver and San Franciso. The positive reviews it received while the USO toured Europe and South America have not only brought critical acclaim to the orchestra as a group, but have helped establish Utah as a center of culture. Its musicians function as soloists and teachers, and many, including the conductor and assistant conductor, have achieved considerable reputations outside of the state in separate careers. However, an informal relationship with the University of Utah, whereby many of the principal musicians also served as music faculty, is no longer as strong as formerly, owing to the evolution of the USO into a full-time musical organization.

The USO makes its home in Symphony Hall, a new facility especially designed for its use and located in downtown Salt Lake City in a multipurpose area devoted as well to a convention center and art museum. Prior to 1979, the USO performed both at the University of Utah and in the Mormon Tabernacle. The latter was used for dress rehearsals, concerts, and recordings—the time and space donated by the Mormon Church, which also provided the land upon which the new facility now stands. Symphony Hall, which cost $12 million to build, was designed as part of the Utah Bicentennial complex for the performing arts by Cyril Harris, known for his work on Washington's Kennedy Center and other major halls. Assistance was provided by a local architectural firm. The auditorium has been praised for both its facade and acoustics.

Forerunners of the USO existed as early as the middle of the nineteenth century, when Mormon pioneers arrived in the Salt Lake valley. In 1862, the Salt Lake Theater Orchestra was organized and performed sporadically under the direction of C. J. Thomas. During the next 40 years several attempts were made to establish a permanent orchestra in the Salt Lake basin: the Salt Lake Symphony Orchestra (1888–1908), the Salt Lake Philharmonic (1913–1924), and a second Salt Lake Symphony (1925–1927). In 1936, Reginald Beales was called upon to organize a Works Progress Administration orchestra. This group, which performed regularly up to 1940, formed the core for and was the immediate predecessor of the present USO.

The USO presented its first concert on May 8, 1940, in Kingsbury Hall on the University of Utah campus under the direction of Hans Heniot. The 52-piece ensemble played a program of Handel, Beethoven, Johann Strauss, Jr., Smetana, and Sibelius, and the initial success of the concert was followed by others over the next several years, many of which were conducted by illustrious guest artists like Sir Thomas Beecham and Constantin Bakaleinikoff when Heniot's military duties interfered with his position with the USO. The 1942–1943 season of six concerts included an appearance of the Ballet Russe de Monte Carlo and the USO's first performance with a soloist— pianist Leonard Pennario. Heniot resigned in the fall of 1945, and James Sample, who had conducted the orchestra as a guest, was engaged as interim music director. Sample proposed to the Board that the USO become a permanent professional orchestra, and in the spring of 1946 the Board created a Symphony Progress Fund designed to implement this changeover.

The first permanent professional conductor, Werner Janssen, was hired the following season on a three-year contract. Janssen, a prominent musician with an orchestra of his own (The Janssen Orchestra of New York), intended to increase the USO from 70 to 85 musicians and to extend the concert season to 10 performances. The first concert in the fall of 1946 was held at the Mormon Tabernacle on Temple Square in Salt Lake City, a facility that became the USO's primary home until the building of Symphony Hall in 1979. However, Janssen's efforts met with resistance, and the conductor terminated his contract after only one season.

After a hasty search, the Board, initiating a relationship that was to last 32 years, hired Maurice Abravanel for the 10-concert 1947–1948 season. Born in Greece and a student of Bruno Walter and Kurt Weill, Abravanel was one of the youngest conductors of the Metropolitan Opera in New York. His first contact with the USO was a tenuous one; he considered this orchestra a "temporary" assignment and upon arrival found a group with little funding and no permanent place to rehearse, since the Tabernacle was being used by the Mormon Tabernacle Choir, among others. Nonetheless, he accepted the challenges and soon began a series of improvements that solved a majority of the problems. Abravanel renewed the USO's close association with the University of Utah, which provided practice space, granted the conductor a professorship, and arranged for part-time faculty appointments for the principal players. He began a series of advertising campaigns to increase concert subscriptions and opened the rehearsals to the University community, setting the stage for the extensive educational programs currently an important part of the USO's function as a regional resource. Abravanel also began promoting the USO outside of Utah, achieving national prominence through recordings and concert tours.

The Abravanel years were marked by a number of innovations and the development of the USO into an ASOL Major orchestra. In 1947, during his first year as music director, a broadcast on NBC's "Orchestras of the Nation" won praise from New York critics and allowed Abravanel to negotiate the beginning of a successful recording program. That same year saw the USO and University choruses perform the regional premiere of Beethoven's Ninth Symphony. In fact, the association with the University lasted through the 1950s and resulted in 55 joint performances and 25 recordings.

In terms of repertoire, Abravanel pioneered new ground, first by agreeing to record the heretofore unrecorded Handel oratorios and second by becoming one of the leading proponents of the revival of the music of Gustave Mahler (he recorded the complete Mahler symphonies). The conductor also promoted twentieth-century music in a series of "Contemporary Concerts" that featured works by Varèse, Milhaud, William Schuman, and Ned Rorem. Native Utah composers such as Leroy Robertson also had their works premiered by the USO under Abravanel. International tours were undertaken periodically, the first in 1966 to Greece, Yugoslavia, Austria, Germany, and England. The USO has since played in Latin America in 1971, England in 1975, central and southern Europe in 1977, and Scandinavia in 1981.

In 1979 Abravanel retired owing to health problems, and the 1979–1980 season was designed to test a number of prospective replacements. However, only two months into the season Varujan Kojian, who had had a meteoric rise as assistant conductor of orchestras in Los Angeles, Seattle, and Stockholm and was a protégé of Zubin Mehta, was announced as the USO's new music director. Although Kojian's tenure with the USO was fraught with controversy, his three years with the orchestra resulted in several critically acclaimed recordings and in a revival of interest in contemporary music. No longer confined to separate concerts, works by modern composers were interspersed within the context of the regular subscription series.

Kojian's successor was Joseph Silverstein, concertmaster and assistant conductor of the Boston Symphony Orchestra.* Silverstein continued the trend toward integrating contemporary music into the regular concert series and has been a frequent soloist with the USO in addition to carrying out his normal conducting duties.

RECORDING HISTORY AND SELECTIVE DISCOGRAPHY: The USO's first recording (Handel's *Judas Maccabeus* with the University of Utah choruses) was released in 1952 on the Concert Hall label. Since 1957 the orchestra has recorded with many companies, including Westminster (Handel oratorios and the complete Gershwin), Vanguard (the complete Mahler symphonies), Vox, and Angel. In addition, Columbia has used the USO in the guise of the Columbia Symphony Orchestra on numerous occasions. The USO has recorded 112 discs with 185 titles, three having been nominated for Grammy Awards. Prior to 1979 recordings were made at the Mormon Tabernacle. Since then it has used Symphony Hall. The recorded repertoire ranges from Handel to Varèse and Rorem, with an emphasis on such romantics as Mahler and Berlioz. The USO has recently signed a five-year contract with Pro Arte and has released recordings on the Varese-Sarabande label.

Gershwin, *An American in Paris* (Abravanel): Vanguard C–100177. Grofé, *Grand Canyon Suite* (Abravanel): Angel S–37314. Mahler, Symphony No. 5 in C-sharp Minor (Abravanel): Vanguard 321, 2 (2 records). Mahler, Symphony No. 8 in E-flat Major (*Symphony of a Thousand*) (Abravanel): Vanguard S–276, 7. Leroy Robertson, *Punch and Judy Overture*, with music of Bernstein, Gould, Nelhybel, and Siegmeister (Abravanel): Turnabout 34459.

CHRONOLOGY OF MUSIC DIRECTORS; Hans Heniot, 1940-1945. James Sample, 1945-1946. Werner Janssen, 1946-1947. Maurice Abravanel, 1947-1979. Varujan Kojian, 1979-1983. Joseph Silverstein, 1983-present.

BIBLIOGRAPHY: Maurice Abravanel, "The Utah Story: No Deviltry, Just Good Sense," *High Fidelity*, Aug. 1974. Deane Brown, "Growth and Development of Utah Professional Symphonic Orchestras Prior to 1940," Masters thesis, Brigham Young University, 1959. Herold Gregory, "Utah Symphony Tours Europe," *Music Journal*, 27 (1967). Conrad B. Harrison, "The Utah Symphony Story," manuscript, [n.d.]. Philip Hart, *Orpheus in the New World* (New York: Norton, 1973). Donal Henahan, "Utah Symphony Opens Its New Home," *New York Times*, 17 Sept. 1979. John Holmes, *Conductors on Record* (London: Gollancz, 1982). Clayton Jones, "Salt Lake City: All the Valley is a Stage for a Surplus of Performing Arts," *Christian Science Monitor*, 28 Apr. 1982. Karen Monson, "Salt Lake's Multitalented New Conductor," *Wall Street Journal*, 27 Dec. 1983. "Saints and Sinners," *Time Magazine* (15 Mar. 1976). George Seltzer, *The Professional Symphony Orchestra in the United States* (Metuchen, N.J.: Scarecrow, 1975). Henry Swoboda, ed., *The American Symphony Orchestra* (New York: Basic, 1967). "Twenty Questions about the Utah Symphony Orchestra," Salt Lake City: USO, 1982.

ACCESS: Utah Symphony Orchestra, 123 West South Temple, Salt Lake City, UT 84101. (801) 533–6407. Herold L. Gregory, Executive Director. Lance Gurwell, Publicity Coordinator.

BERTIL H. VAN BOER, JR. and MARGARET LYNN FAST

Vermont ———————————

BURLINGTON (114,070)

Vermont Symphony Orchestra (Mt)

The Vermont Symphony Orchestra is the oldest state-supported orchestra in the United States. Dr. Alan Carter founded the orchestra in 1934 to provide audiences across Vermont access to live concerts of symphonic music and to encourage musical performance and education among the residents of what was and still is one of the most rural states in the country.

Dr. Carter was an innovative music director who from the start programmed many performances of American music. He was able to attract world-class soloists such as Rudolf Serkin, who performed with the orchestra for little or no fee because of their belief in Carter's mission. In 1938 the Vermont State Legislature appropriated $1,000 for the VSO to travel and perform at the 1939 World's Fair. That support has continued uninterrupted since and has grown to an annual level of $45,000, roughly 10% of the $400,000-plus budget. The musicians continue to play an annual concert for the legislators in the rotunda of the state capitol.

The VSO is supported by an unusual system of twelve local Concert Committees that raise funds and present the orchestra across the state. Each Committee chairman sits on the State Board, which is made up of 37 members (25 elected) and which meets six times a year. The organization relies very heavily on these committees to keep it fiscally solvent through ticket sales and individual and business fund-raising and also to take care of concert production in their area. A four-person staff oversees the operation of the orchestra and the committees.

The VSO has grown into a professional orchestra utilizing between 55 and 75 musicians, 47 with a part-time contract and the rest hired on a per-service basis. Over 60% of its musicians reside in Vermont, and the rest travel from as far away as Boston. It is the goal of the organization to attract more players to live and teach in state. The orchestra performs over 20 full concerts annually in theaters, gymnasiums, and opera houses, including a four-concert series in Burlington and a busy summer outdoor pops season at estates, parks, and mountainside resorts. A small, flexible "cafe orchestra" of between 10 and 20 musicians and various chamber ensembles play over 80 concerts annually in town halls, schools, and other locations. These groups provide additional income and exposure for Symphony musicians. The full orchestra gathers to perform on weekends throughout the spring, summer and fall. It tours an average of four programs. Because of the unpredictable weather in the winter and the VSO's dependence on traveling, no performances are scheduled during that season.

The orchestra's second and current music director, Argentinian-born Efrain Guigui, was chosen to succeed Dr. Carter in 1975. He has brought the orchestra through troubled artistic and financial times, which started during the early 1960s as the VSO tried to expand without a strong enough system of financial support. His energy and musical excellence have transformed it into a quality regional ensemble that is performing at its best level ever. Through careful programming (often dictated by the small economy of the state), and with 25% less rehearsal time than other comparable orchestras (typically seven hours of preparation with run-throughs on concert days), he manages to lead exciting performances that are marked by his special gift for communicating musical structure. During the last 10 years of strengthening the VSO, Guigui began by concentrating on repertoire from the late-classical and romantic eras (e.g., Beethoven, Schubert, Tchaikovsky). With the improved playing of the orchestra (the string sections in particular), he has been able to add more delicate pieces from the early classical period, as well as late romantic and contemporary works requiring greater virtuosity. Guest soloists and composers are constantly surprised at the quality of performance that the orchestra achieves, even with so little rehearsal time.

The VSO has spawned two separate organizations still in existence. The Green Mountain String Program, begun in 1963, has trained many young violinists, violists, and cellists—three of whom are now members of the Symphony. The Composers's Conference, a nationally recognized two-week forum for contemporary music, grew out of the Vermont Symphony 40 years ago and is currently in residence at Wellesley College in Massachusetts with Guigui as its music director.

The VSO began broadcasting in the late 1950s with a series of television programs produced by a local station and featuring the orchestra in concert. A statewide radio network of 26 stations broadcast tapes of VSO concerts for nine seasons in the 1960s.

CHRONOLOGY OF MUSIC DIRECTORS: Dr. Alan Carter, 1934–1974. Efrain Guigui, 1974—present.

BIBLIOGRAPHY: Dorothy Canfield Fisher, "Green Mountain Music," *Vermont Life Magazine*, Winter, 1948.

ACCESS: Vermont Symphony Orchestra, 77 College Street, Burlington, VT 05401. (802) 864–5741. Morris Block, Manager.

MORRIS BLOCK

Virginia ————————————————

RICHMOND (632,015)

Richmond Symphony (Rg)

Founded in 1957, the Richmond Symphony is Virginia's largest and most active symphony orchestra. In the 1983–1984 season it or one of its agencies performed 245 public concerts. The Orchestra's activity centers around 16 Masterworks subscription concerts (eight programs performed twice, each on a Saturday and the succeeding Monday evenings). In addition, six Weekend Ovation concerts are presented by the Richmond Sinfonia, a 28-member, full-time professional chamber orchestra. Six Saturday pops concerts by the full Symphony and three morning Symphony Suites by the Sinfonia complete the regular yearly schedule.

The Masterworks and Ovation concerts are performed in the Virginia Center for the Performing Arts (VCPA), a 2,033-seat hall at 600 East Grace Street. The Saturday pops concerts are presented in the 3,700-seat Mosque Auditorium at 6 North Laurel Street, and the Symphony Suites are given at breakfasts in the ballroom of a large hotel. Other concerts are performed at local arts festivals and for civic and business groups on particular occasions. The Sinfonia has played in Bermuda and tours each year to many Virginia cities. The full Symphony has performed in five other Virginia cities and at Wolf Trap (Filene Center) in northern Virginia.

The Richmond Symphony began rehearsing and performing in the VCPA at the start of the 1983–1984 season. Under an arrangement with the autonomous VCPA management, it has rights to the use of the hall for regular rehearsals and for subscription concerts; but at the same time the VCPA management has the freedom to schedule other cultural events.

Although Richmond, with its Mozart Association and Mozart Academy, had been a significant musical center in the period 1880–1900, attempts to establish a symphony orchestra for the city in 1908, 1932, 1933, and 1934 had no lasting success. The present Richmond Symphony had its beginning at a meeting held April 15, 1957, when a group of civic leaders determined that earlier efforts to found an orchestra failed because of too much reliance on out-of-town musicians and on ticket sales without supporting donations. This group subsequently became the Symphony's first Board of Directors, presided over by Brig. Gen. Vincent Meyer. In May 1957, Edgar Schenkman, since 1948 conductor of the Norfolk Symphony, also became conductor of the Richmond Symphony and its first music director. At a meeting on May 16 the Board and Mr. Schenkman approved a $10,000 budget, a projected 60-member orchestra, and a season of three concerts to be held in the Mosque Auditorium.

A Women's Auxiliary (subsequently renamed the Women's Committee) under the leadership of Mrs. Nancy Moran, sold out virtually the whole season's tickets, raising more money than expected. Furthermore, the number of able resident string players interested in joining the orchestra was larger than anticipated.

Outstanding events in the years 1958 to 1970 were the introduction of pops concerts, the beginnings of annual subsidies by city and state governments, the inauguration of out-of-town concerts, a lecture series on coming concerts, a youth orchestra, the start of a chamber orchestra, introduction of light-repertoire matinee concerts, ASOL Metropolitan status, and a $650,000 Ford Foundation grant to be matched by $500,000 raised by the Symphony. By 1969 the orchestra was offering 112 public concerts in and out of the city.

In 1970 Music Director Edgar Schenkman resigned in a public dispute with the Board over policy jurisdiction. After a year of controversy during which several key players resigned and the Symphony's future was in doubt, a Selection Committee appointed by the Board named Jacques Houtmann the Richmond Symphony's second music director. Several changes came under Houtmann's leadership, most notably the establishment of a body of full-time musicians comprising the Richmond Sinfonia, the professional nucleus of the Symphony.

In 1971 the 150-voice Richmond Symphony Chorus was organized by James Erb for a performance of Beethoven's *Missa Solemnis* under Robert Shaw. The Chorus continues to be active in every Symphony season.

Shaw was the Symphony's first guest conductor. Because of Houtmann's own active guest-conducting schedule in and out of the United States, a succession of other guest conductors has led the orchestra since 1971; and since 1970 an assistant conductor has shared Houtmann's conducting responsibilities in Sinfonia concerts, pops and children's concerts, and on special occasions.

A major event in the Symphony's history was the 1983 move into the

Virginia Center for the Performing Arts. Previously most rehearsals had been held elsewhere than in the Mosque Auditorium, where concerts were given. Logistical difficulties, acoustical problems in the Mosque, the obvious advantage of rehearsing regularly in the concert-hall environment, and the desirability of a smaller hall led the Symphony in 1979 to acquire Loew's Theatre, a luxury motion picture house built in 1928. After four years of acoustical studies, fund-raising, and renovations, the old Loew's became the VCPA, the Symphony's permanent home. Subscriptions for 1984–1985 confirm the favorable response of critics and public alike to the new hall's acoustics and to the dual scheduling of the Masterworks series. An arrangement between the Symphony and the autonomous VCPA management also allows the Center the freedom to schedule cultural events other than the Symphony's.

The Richmond Symphony employs 109 persons. Approximately 88 of these are orchestra musicians working under one of two master agreements. The first applies to Sinfonia members, who are on salary for a stated number of weeks (about 300 services). The second agreement applies to some 60 players engaged on a per-service basis. Each group elects an Orchestra Committee to meet regularly with management on current issues, to meet twice yearly with the Board's Personnel Committee, and to meet once a year with the whole Board to discuss long-range plans. Two orchestra members sit on the Board as voting members.

The administrative staff, headed by the general manager, has nine full-time employees as well as six part-time workers. The music director, assistant conductor, chorusmaster and chorus accompanist comprise the artistic staff. The current $1.8 million budget is supplied in the following approximate percentages: ticket sales, 43%; gifts and donations, 22%; government grants, 16%; foundation grants, 8%; endowment income, 7%; other, 2%. Allied organizations with significant influence on Symphony governance, fund-raising, or administration are the Women's Committee, the Virginia Commission for the Arts, the NEA, local corporations, and individual donors.

Music from the nineteenth and early twentieth centuries dominates the Richmond Symphony's programming; baroque, classic and contemporary works are most prominent in the Sinfonia's repertoire. Experimental works appear rarely, world premieres or works commissioned from prominent avant-garde composers scarcely at all. The Symphony recognizes an obligation to play music by Virginia composers, with particular attention to compositions by women.

The Symphony's impact on community cultural life has been strong from the start. In addition to its regular season of four sets of subscription concerts, the orchestra plays for the Richmond Ballet, for a large number of school concerts, and for three annual outdoor festivals. It also serves as the orchestra for selected Richmond and Norfolk performances by the Norfolk-based Virginia Opera Association. The Symphony's string quartet, woodwind quintet, and brass ensemble add to its visibility by concertizing widely in both formal and informal settings.

The Richmond Youth Symphony, founded in 1963 under Edgar Schenkman, is open to qualified players from all of Richmond's public and private schools. Since 1970 it has had its own conductor. Beginning as one orchestra, it has grown into a complex of three: the String Sinfonietta for beginners, the Junior Youth Orchestra, and the Youth Orchestra proper, each led by a Symphony member who is a professional music educator. Youth Orchestra concerts take place in the fall and spring, the spring concert featuring as soloist the winner of a student instrumental competition sponsored by the Women's Committee and judged by the music director and a committee of Symphony players.

Commercial recordings by the Richmond Symphony were released for local sale in 1959 and 1966. Since 1971 concerts have been routinely recorded for archival purposes, and since 1980 selected tapes from each season's concerts have been broadcast on Richmond's WRFK-FM. Audiences for these broadcasts have grown steadily and promise soon to rival, in per capita terms, those of major metropolitan centers.

CHRONOLOGY OF MUSIC DIRECTORS: Edgar Schenkman, 1957–1971. Jacques Houtmann, 1971-present.

BIBLIOGRAPHY: Walter Franklin Masters, Jr., "A History of the Richmond Symphony, Incorporated," B.A. thesis, University of Richmond, 1962. Elaine Susan McCauley, "The Development and Growth of the Richmond Symphony," B.A. thesis, University of Richmond, 1979.

ACCESS: Richmond Symphony, 211 West Franklin Street, Richmond, VA 23220. (804) 788–4717. Richard Thompson, General Manager.

JAMES ERB

Washington ⎯⎯⎯⎯⎯⎯⎯⎯

SEATTLE (1,607,469)

Northwest Chamber Orchestra (Mt)

As the only professional chamber orchestra in the Pacific Northwest, the Northwest Chamber Orchestra of 16 players has a significant local and regional impact. In 1980 the NWCO received an ASCAP Metropolitan Orchestra Award for "adventuresome overall programming of contemporary music," and the orchestra has been ranked nationally as one of the top six orchestras of its type.

Through its 49 performances annually, the NWCO reaches an audience of 280,000, including radio listeners who have been able to hear the Sunday afternoon subscription concerts broadcast live over KING-FM since 1983. In addition to the eight pairs of subscription concerts between September and May to an audience of 8,000, the NWCO travels frequently to disadvantaged adult and children's groups and to cities, often in remote areas. The NWCO players augment their contracts of 100 guaranteed services by teaching privately and in local colleges and universities and by substituting with local orchestras such as the Seattle Symphony.*

The NWCO was founded in 1973 with nine players and a budget of $16,000 by Louis Richmond, then a 30-year old cellist who had played with the National Symphony* and Chamber Symphony of Philadelphia before forming a chamber orchestra at the University of Nevada. In 1970 he joined the faculty of the University of Puget Sound in Tacoma, where he directed their chamber orchestra. Richmond was able to sell his vision of a professional chamber orchestra that would support contemporary composers, especially those residing in the region. The first season alone contained eight world premieres, and before Richmond had completed his six-year stewardship the NWCO had presented 33 Seattle, nine Northwest, four American, and 30 world premieres.

Most prominently represented among the many composers whose works were introduced by Richmond was Alan Hovhaness, a former composer-in-residence with the Seattle Symphony Orchestra who had recently become a Seattle resident. Before the conclusion of the 1979–1980 season the NWCO had presented 19 Hovhaness compositions, including five world premieres, the latest being Symphony No. 31, op. 294 (1977).

Richmond relinquished his position during the summer of 1979. Among the guest conductors the following season was Alun Francis, a horn virtuoso earlier in his career. A Welsh native, Francis at 36 was a veteran of numerous guest conducting engagements and recordings with major orchestras, had served as music director of the Ulster Orchestra, and had conducted the London Symphony Orchestra. Under Francis the NWCO gained world stature, attracted internationally acclaimed soloists, and signed several recording contracts. It moved from the Seattle Concert Theater (400 seats) to its main present location, Kane Hall at the University of Washington (700 seats).

During the Francis years the NWCO has shifted its emphasis from the twentieth century to the baroque era, including an annual *Messiah* in tandem with various local choruses. Nevertheless, local contemporary composers are featured through the recently established Composers' Forum competition, in which the works of four Washington State finalists are performed by the NWCO in a special concert with a second performance of the winning composition at a regular subscription concert the following season.

The NWCO, with a 1984–1985 budget of $434,000, is governed by a Board of Trustees and managed by an executive director. Artistic decisions are determined by the musical director. The trustees as principal fund-raisers are supported by a large volunteer organization known as the Continuo. The NWCO also boasts an impressive 54% return rate on grant applications. But like most musical organizations, the NWCO has had its share of financial difficulties in recent years, which has led to a reduction of recording and touring plans. Particularly disappointing was the decision to decline an invitation to tour the People's Republic of China in 1981. The NWCO is thus prudently confining its touring to local areas until the current deficit (now improving) allows for artistic expansion in the years ahead.

RECORDING HISTORY AND DISCOGRAPHY: The initial recording of the NWCO was made in 1978 by Pandora Records, a Seattle company, and featured the premiere recording of Hovhaness's Symphony No. 38, op. 134. Most recently the NWCO has received a grant to record Shostakovich's Chamber Symphony No. 8, op. 110 in the near future.

Hovhaness, Symphony No. 38 (Hovhaness): Pandora Records Pan 3001. Alan Rawsthorne, Concerto for Clarinet and String Orchestra; Gordon Jacob, Mini-Concerto for Clarinet and String Orchestra; Arnold Cook, Concerto for Clarinet and String Orchestra (Thea King/Francis): Hyperion A66031. *Baroque Christmas Music* (Francis): Hyperion A66028.

CHRONOLOGY OF MUSIC DIRECTORS: Louis Richmond, 1973–1979. Alun Francis, 1980-present.

BIBLIOGRAPHY: Interviews with NWCO administrators, 1984. Esther W. Campbell, *Bagpipes in the Woodwind Section* (Seattle: Seattle Women's Association, 1978). Edward Jablonski, *The Encyclopedia of American Music* (Garden City, N.Y.: Doubleday, 1981).

ACCESS: Northwest Chamber Orchestra, 119 South Main, 2nd Floor, Seattle, WA 98104. (206) 343–0445. Joy Wood, Executive Director.

GEOFFREY BLOCK

Seattle Symphony Orchestra (Mj)

The largest orchestral ensemble in the Pacific Northwest, the 90 members of the Seattle Symphony Orchestra present approximately 90 concerts yearly to a live audience of 200,000. Each season the orchestra offers several subscription categories in the Seattle Opera House from September through early June, including a Masterpiece Series of 14 programs, a Sunday series (formerly known as the Rising Star Series), a family Musical Galaxy Series on Saturday mornings, and a pops series. A summer pops and Mainly Mozart Series follow the regular season at the downtown Fifth Avenue Theatre.

For the ten years preceding the 1983–1984 season, most members of the SSO shared an integrated schedule with the Seattle Opera Association and the Pacific Northwest Ballet for a yearly total of 350 services. Although the contracts are now segregated, the schedules remain coordinated. In 1976 the orchestra adopted the Seattle Symphony Chorale, a volunteer group of 175 auditioned singers, to perform as needed each season. As the parent group for these later-forming organizations, the SSO has had a crucial impact on cultural life in the Pacific Northwest. SSO members also teach privately or in one or more of the universities and colleges in the Puget Sound area and serve regularly as soloists and conductors for local community orchestras.

Educational services include master classes or lecture/demonstrations for music students, pre-concert lectures, and the Musical Galaxy Series. The Washington State Cultural Enrichment Program sponsors the busing of approximately 12,000 students (fifth graders) to the Seattle Opera House (two days of concerts, two concerts each day). In the past some concerts were presented in the schools, and this practice may be renewed in the future.

The SSO, founded in 1903 and incorporated in 1907, is governed by an approximately 70-member Board of Trustees who are served by a general manager and (normally) a music director. Since the sudden death of Music Director Rainier Miedél in March 1983, the post was called "music advisor" and then "principal conductor," and in both cases it has been filled by Gerard Schwarz. Newly available Symphony positions are filled by the music director in concert with a committee of orchestra players.

Funding for the annual $4 million budget comes from ticket sales, an endowment, private and corporate contributions, grants, and special projects. The largest and most prominent fund-raising auxiliary group since 1930, the Seattle Symphony Women's Association (formerly the Women's Committee), has launched each season since 1950 with a fashion show and dinner dance, the Symphoneve. Two additional groups formed in the late 1960s, the Seattle Symphony League and the Symphonics, have donated large amounts of time and money annually to the orchestra. A broader based organization, PONCHO (Patrons of the Northwest Civic, Cultural, and Charitable Organizations), formed in 1963, has been such a strong contributor to the SSO that the annual pops series is now designated the PONCHO Pops.

Not least among the valuable projects of the Seattle Symphony Women's Association was the sponsorship of the first and only major published historical account of the SSO, *Bagpipes in the Woodwind Section*, written by Esther Campbell in 1978 to celebrate the 75th anniversary of the orchestra.

The history of the SSO falls into three distinct phases, each marked by struggle and turbulence as well as reconciliation and artistic growth. Throughout its early years from 1903 to the arrival of Karl Krueger in 1926, the SSO struggled, often unsuccessfully, to establish itself as a continuous professional orchestra. Between Krueger and the abrupt departure of Manuel Rosenthal in 1951, the orchestra experienced a succession of seven conductors, including Sir Thomas Beecham. But it was not until the long reign of Milton Katims (Music Director, 1954–1976) that the SSO established itself as an important orchestra with a sustained period of artistic and fiscal expansion and stability.

Seattle, a town of 133,000 by 1900, had already experienced phenomenal growth since its initial settlement in 1851 and its sparse population of 250 in 1860. The devastating fire of 1889 brought thousands of workers to rebuild the city, and Seattle became the western terminus of the Great Northern Railroad in 1893. Contributing further to the growth and corresponding changes of the newly reconstructed city was the Alaska Gold Rush of 1897. By 1903 Seattle was ready for its first symphony concert.

The event took place on December 29 in the Christensen's 300-seat hall of the Arcade Building, constructed in 1902 on the former site of Seattle's first opera house, which had been destroyed in the 1889 fire. Conducted by a prominent local violinist and conductor, Harry West, the 24 musicians played five works, including Bruch's Violin Concerto, Schubert's *Unfinished* Symphony, and the closing work, Rossini's *William Tell* Overture, to a less-than-capacity audience. West and his orchestra offered a total of three concerts during its first season and five the next. By the third season the orchestra moved to the Grand Opera House (1900), which seated 2,200, until its destruction by fire in 1917. By the fifth season (1907–1908) the Seattle Symphony Society was formed and incorporated with a capital of $40,000.

A new conductor, Michael Kegrize, was hired by the newly formed Society

for its inaugural season of eight concerts. Although eventually a succession
of petty conflicts led to Kegrize's departure at the conclusion of his second
season (in 1909), the SSO within Kegrize's brief tenure had expanded to
46 musicians and 16 concerts per year, begun its intermittent but extended
use of the newly built Moore Theatre, inaugurated the practice of separate
"popular" concerts (later called "pops"), and introduced Seattle audiences
to such major artists as Mischa Elman and Josef Lhevinne. Henry Hadley, a
conductor and prolific composer from New York, would direct the SSO for
the next two seasons. During these years (1909–1911) impressive guest
artists appeared to packed houses, the orchestra grew to 65 musicians, and
the association could afford the services of a business manager.

Despite these successes the SSO concluded the 1910–1911 season with
a $30,000 deficit and sparse pledge money. The poor financial prospects
prompted Hadley to leave Seattle to take a position as conductor of the
newly formed San Francisco Symphony,* a post he would hold until 1915.
Only the efforts of the noted concertmaster John Spargur enabled the orchestra to continue for the next five seasons as the Philharmonic Orchestra.

The difficult financial conditions did not prohibit the Philharmonic under
Spargur from sponsoring internationally acclaimed artists or from introducing children's concerts in 1912. By 1917–1918, the Symphony Society was
reorganized, Spargur and 85 musicians could receive contracts, and the SSO
could reclaim its name. The orchestra moved to Meany Hall on the University of Washington campus for the 1919–1920 season, and the future
appeared bright.

But soon the SSO lost its financial support and professional status and
would not regain either until 1926. During the first part of this interregnum
(1921–1923), Mme. Davenport-Engberg, a Spokane violinist and teacher,
led a largely amateur group of 90 musicians. This organization disbanded
in 1923, and there are no records of further symphony concerts until Karl
Krueger conducted a concert to test the waters for the support of a revitalized symphony organization on May 14, 1926.

A student of Nikisch and the assistant conductor of the Vienna Philharmonic and Vienna Opera under Schalk, Krueger brought to Seattle the
distinction and experience it needed to start its second historical chapter.
A representative season under Krueger consisted of eight regular concerts,
four popular concerts, and four children's concerts. The latter series provided numerous opportunities for young musicians to perform as soloists.
Krueger also gave a series of lectures sponsored by the Extension Services
of the University of Washington in order to prepare adult listeners for the
symphonic repertoire. The tradition of the pre-concert lecture has continued to the present, with introductory lectures for each performance of the
14 Masterpiece Concerts.

In the summer following Krueger's first season, more than 12,000 attended an open air production of *Aida*. By 1929 the SSO had grown from

65 to 83 musicians and performed for an average audience of 1,500, an outstanding sign of Seattle's growing support for live orchestral music. Moreover, under Krueger the SSO was widely considered to be one of the 12 leading American orchestras.

Nevertheless, the effects of the stock market crash prompted a reduction in the 1931–1932 season, audience attendance dropped, and the lack of financial support necessitated a salary reduction for the players. Faced with these difficulties in addition to open conflicts among the board members, Krueger, who would become the founding artistic director of the Kansas City Philharmonic in 1933, resigned from his position with the SSO in December 1931.

Krueger's departure had a sobering effect on the Seattle community, and within a short time it raised enough capital to present a five-concert season in 1932 under Basil Cameron, co-conductor of the San Francisco Symphony since 1930. Eventually Cameron established a season of eight subscription concerts, seven popular concerts, a forerunner of the future Rising Star Series, a Saturday morning children's series, and a Guest Artist Series, a format that has largely remained to the present day. Cameron also introduced a policy of programming a minimum of one modern composition at each concert. Within a few years financial shortages again led to a shortened season and salary reductions, and at the beginning of the 1938–1939 season, Cameron's contract was revoked. For the following three seasons the SSO was directed by Nikolai Sokoloff, the founding director of the Cleveland Orchestra.*

In 1941 one of the world's best-known conductors, Sir Thomas Beecham, arrived for a two-season visit to Seattle before returning to England to establish the Royal Philharmonic. Sir Thomas's arrival precipitated the first sold-out season of the SSO and the first of numerous insulting yet endearing remarks about the Seattle community that, according to Sir Thomas, resided in an "esthetic dustbin." After a season of guest conductors, Carl Bricken, a former composition professor at the University of Chicago, was hired as a permanent conductor; at the time he was one of only three Americans to be leading major U.S. orchestras (along with Alfred Wallenstein of Los Angeles and Seattle's illustrious former conductor, Karl Krueger, now with Detroit). Bricken's four seasons ended unharmoniously with major dissention from the orchestra, many of whom had played only under Sir Thomas, and the 1947–1948 season revealed the surprising merger of the SSO and the Tacoma Philharmonic into the Pacific Northwest Symphony Orchestra, with Bricken and Tacoma's Eugene Linden alternating batons. With Bricken's resignation at the conclusion of the first joint season, Linden would take charge of a crisis-laden organization for the next two years.

The years after Bricken's departure were particularly turbulent ones in SSO history. Personnel problems, including the merger of the two bitterly opposing Seattle symphonic organizations into a restructured SSO, were mainly resolved before Linden's second and final season in 1949–1950. Financial difficulties, however, became so acute that the musicians found it necessary to give up their regular salaries and play only for box office receipts.

Manuel Rosenthal, former director of the French National Radio Orchestra, had recently arrived as composer-in-residence at the University of Puget Sound (then the College of Puget Sound) in Tacoma and was asked to replace Linden for the 1950–1951 season. Despite Rosenthal's artistic successes and the strenuous financial efforts by Symphony fund-raisers, the Seattle public was shocked to discover that their conductor had apparently perjured himself when he had denied the existence of his legal French wife and falsely claimed a legal status with his Seattle companion and was therefore barred re-entrance to the United States. Since the Symphony Board could not secure a new permanent conductor on such short notice, a season of guest conductors was the only solution. That season soon grew to three (1951–1954).

One of the many guests, Milton Katims, who had served as principal violist under Toscanini and the NBC Symphony from 1943 and as guest conductor for 50 nationwide broadcasts with that orchestra, was appointed to his first full season with the SSO in 1954. By the time he stepped down 22 seasons later, only Ormandy's 37 years with the Philadelphia Orchestra* and Steinberg's 25 years with the Pittsburgh Symphony* surpassed Katims's for longevity with a major orchestra. Katims generated unprecedented artistic and financial growth as well as the continuity that had been lacking since the orchestra's inception.

In 1959, the year Katims had distributed in the lobby "courtesy concert cough drops" prior to a performance of the Verdi *Requiem*, season attendance had doubled from 100,000 to 200,000; this figure would more than double again during the 1966–1967 season when the 163 concerts were seen by more than 450,000. Moreover, Katims's first eight seasons ran in the black, and the stable financial climate led to the conversion of the old Civic Auditorium (1928), home of the SSO from 1950 to 1953, into an elegant 3,100-seat hall that would be considered one of the nation's finest. The new Opera House, part of a cultural complex in the Seattle Center, opened in time for the 1962 World's Fair.

With increased services came a higher pay scale, an endowment, a $2 million budget, and funding to produce the SSO's first recordings. The orchestra, bringing live orchestral music to thousands of students and adults gave numerous tours in Washington and had the distinction of becoming the first major American orchestra to visit Alaska. In 1972 the first of two Alaskan tours reached an estimated 90% of that state's population.

Perhaps more significant than the world premieres such as piano concertos by Leon Kirchner and William Bolcolm and works by such renowned Seattle natives as Hovhaness was the impressive total number of works that

Katims introduced to Seattle audiences. By 1959 he had performed Stra-vinsky's *Rite of Spring*, Mahler's Second Symphony, and 73 other works in their Seattle premieres. Other major modern works, such as Poulenc's *La Voix Humaine*, Britten's *War Requiem*, and Berio's *Sinfonia*, were intro-duced within a few years or even months after their world premieres.

Despite these accomplishments, Katims began to lose support from mem-bers of the orchestra, the Seattle critics, and the Board of Trustees. Although he would continue nominally as musical advisor from 1976 to 1979, Katims's long and distinguished career with the SSO was largely terminated at the conclusion of the 1975–1976 season after much partisan and public conflict. His replacement was the German conductor, Rainier Miedél, formerly a cellist with the Stockholm Philharmonic who had served as music director of the Gavelborgs Orchestra in Sweden and assistant conductor of the Bal-timore Symphony.* Miedél led the SSO for seven seasons before his death in March 1983.

Major achievements under Miedél include the adoption of the 175-mem-ber Seattle Chorale (1976) and the SSO's first European tour (1980). Even with a sold-out subscription audience, the SSO was not immune to the labor and financial problems that have plagued American orchestras in recent decades. In 1979 the orchestra members went on strike for 10 weeks, and the orchestra's accumulated deficit by the 1982–1983 season brought the group to its borrowing limit. The Seattle community responded generously, and the orchestra agreed not to seek salary increases for three years. The 1981–1982 deficit of $531,000 was reduced to $75,000 by the end of the 1982–1983 season, and the number of yearly contributors increased from 1,800 in 1982 to 5,200 in 1984. For the 1983–1984 season the SSO acquired the services of Gerard Schwarz, whose activities ranged from being music director of several groups, including the Los Angeles Chamber Orchestra,* to advising festivals such as the Mostly Mozart Festival at New York's Lincoln Center. Schwarz was named principal conductor beginning in the 1984–1985 season.

RECORDING HISTORY AND DISCOGRAPHY: The SSO issued its first recordings in 1964 to commemorate Milton Katims's tenth season. In 1968 the SSO released an RCA recording of Morton Gould's *Venice: An Audiograph for Two Orchestras* and *Vivaldi Gallery*, both of which were commissioned by the SSO and performed earlier that season.

Dohnányi, *Suite in F-Sharp Minor* and *Variations on a Nursery Song* (Bela Siki, piano/Katims): Turnabout 34623. Glière *Red Poppy*; Rimsky-Korsakov *Musical Pictures from Sadko*; Shostakovich *Age of Gold* (Katims): Turnabout 34644.

CHRONOLOGY OF MUSIC DIRECTORS: Harry West, 1903–1907. Michael Kegrize, 1907–1909. Henry Hadley, 1909–1911. John Spargur, 1911–1921. Mme. Davenport-Engberg, 1921–1923. Karl Krueger, 1926–1932. Basil Cameron, 1932–1938. Nikolai Sokoloff, 1938–1941. Sir Thomas Beecham, 1941–1943. Carl Bricken, 1944–1948. Eugene Linden, 1948–1950. Manuel Rosenthal, 1950–1951. (Guest conductors, 1951–

1954.) Milton Katims, 1954–1976. Rainier Miedél, 1976–1983. Gerard Schwarz (Musical Advisor), 1983–1984; (Principal Conductor), 1984-present.

BIBLIOGRAPHY: Interviews with SSO personnel. Esther W. Campbell, *Bagpipes in the Woodwind Section* (Seattle: Seattle Symphony Women's Association, 1978). David Ewen, *Dictators of the Baton* (Chicago: Alliance, 1943). Philip Hart, *Orpheus in the New World* (New York: Norton, 1973). Edward Jablonski, *The Encyclopedia of American Music* (Garden City, N.Y.: Doubleday, 1981). Marianne Lewis, "The Seattle Symphony," *Encore* 3, no. 1 (1983–1984). Harold C. Schonberg, *The Great Conductors* (New York: Simon & Schuster, 1967).

ACCESS: Seattle Symphony Orchestra, 4th Floor, Seattle Center House, 305 Harrison Street, Seattle, WA 98109. (206) 447–4740. Mark Walker, General Manager.

GEOFFREY BLOCK

SPOKANE (341,835)

Spokane Symphony Orchestra (Rg)

The Spokane Symphony Orchestra grew from a series of orchestral organizations that date back to 1909. After faltering starts, performers from local vaudeville theater orchestras joined to form a new Spokane Orchestra headed by Leonard Brill from 1915 until the intervention of World War I. After the war, the orchestra reorganized and began a schedule of as many as 10 concerts a year until inadequate funding caused its demise in 1924. In 1927 the orchestra emerged again and continued until the onset of World War II.

In 1945, community support for such musical activity culminated in the organization of the Spokane Philharmonic Orchestra with Harold Paul Whelan as its first music director. The orchestra's first home was the Masonic Temple Auditorium, but it soon moved to the old Post Theater.

In 1962, the orchestra was incorporated as the Spokane Symphony Society and engaged Donald Thulean as its first music director. Thulean guided the orchestra until his resignation, effective at the end of the 1983–1984 season. During his tenure the orchestra moved to the Fox Theater in 1968, and finally, in 1974, to its present home, the 2,700-seat Spokane Opera House. This hall is centrally located in an area of urban renewal which was renovated for the World's Fair, Expo '74. The parklike surroundings have greatly enhanced the central area of the city—the cultural center of the interior Northwest.

The Spokane Symphony currently has 80 players, including 28 on full-time contracts. The season is 35 weeks (29 weeks of services), during which the orchestra or its full-time nucleus, the Spokane Symphony Touring Orchestra, gives more than 50 concerts. The basic season is 10 classical concerts and five pops concerts. The orchestra performs for opera, either in concert or full production, and ballet. The full-time players are also organized into various smaller chamber ensembles. All these activities are taken to the community to enhance educational and cultural programs throughout the metropolitan area.

The orchestra supports the Spokane Chorale, conducted by Charles Zimmerman. This group combines with the Symphony for large choral-orchestral works while also maintaining a musical life of its own. The orchestra also had an Exxon/Arts/Affiliate Artists' conducting assistant (1982–1983) and participated in the Xerox Affiliate Artists' Pianists Program.

The Spokane Symphony Touring Orchestra has performed in Washington state and northern Idaho as "ambassadors of classical music" to audiences of school children and adults. The Spokane Symphony has begun what may become an annual event, the Musicians' Benefit Marathon Concert, a six-hour concert, featuring various chamber groups as well as the entire orchestra and given in the venerable Davenport Hotel.

These and other activities fulfill the dual function of community service and arts education. Wesley Brustad, the orchestra's executive director, calls it "music on the hoof, not on the shelf" when he describes the impact of the orchestra in the community.

The Spokane Symphony is governed by a Board of Directors whose authority flows to the executive director and the music director/conductor. A delicate balance of authority is maintained between the two positions, as, for example, in the choice of repertoire, which affects ticket sales. The Spokane Symphony budget for the 1983–1984 season was slightly over $1 million and the organization has managed to operate in the black for several seasons. The orchestra's income is generated from ticket sales and contract performances (53%), gifts and contributions (33%), state and federal grants (6%), and the orchestra's endowment (7%). The current endowment holdings exceed $1 million.

The geographical location of Spokane is relatively remote from similar metropolitan centers. The result is that the players are residents of the immediate area. The nucleus of the orchestra does serve in a full-time capacity, but the majority have other careers in a variety of positions including music teaching, popular and jazz music performance, or in non-musical occupations. These players are an artistic catalyst for Spokane, a condition which may not exist in communities where a large percentage of key players are imported for each concert.

The orchestra's repertoire is somewhat eclectic, as is suggested by the inclusion of five pops concerts in the 15-concert series. Music Director Thulean emphasized the ever-present need to balance the old and the new with his comment, "people *really* do want to hear what they think they want to hear." The Spokane repertoire, though, has reflected Thulean's interest in twentieth-century music. He counsels that "one function of music is to tell us things about ourselves that we don't know."

The orchestra has given some 15 first performances during Thulean's tenure, has commissioned *The Image of Man* by Michael Colgrass, and has been instrumental in assisting area composers to receive foundation or government grants for new music. An example is the orchestra's premiere of William Billingsley's work for soprano, speaking chorus, and orchestra, *The Paradox*, which began as an NEA project, but ended as a commissioned performance of a new work. Thulean has commented that in the old days it was somewhat easier to be daring in repertoire. The halls were smaller, the average concert goer was already experienced in concert repertoire and somewhat more tolerant of departures from tradition.

With a solid repertoire of standard works sprinkled with occasional innovation, the Spokane Symphony has also given time to the spectacular and grandiose musical statement. Such concerts include opera in concert and the 1983–1984 performance of William Walton's *Belshazzar's Feast*. These join such earlier fare as Beethoven's Ninth Symphony, Handel's *Messiah*, Britten's *War Requiem*, and Mahler's Eighth Symphony. The latter performance is an example of the orchestra's outreach in the area. The choirs and supplemental instrumentalists came from the University of Idaho and Washington State University. The concert was presented on one of the campuses as well as in Spokane.

The orchestra has been a deciding factor in industrial settlement. An example is the arrival of Hewlett-Packard, whose decision to enter Spokane was enhanced by the presence and quality of the orchestra.

When Donald Thulean announced his resignation as music director at the end of the 1983–1984 season, a conductor search led to a series of guest conductors for 1983–1984. The difficulties in such a procedure were beginning to emerge when the Symphony electrified the musical community by announcing the engagement of the eminent composer/conductor Gunther Schuller in a one-year position as artistic advisor and principal conductor for 1984–1985. Schuller had previously been a guest conductor with the Symphony and was a favorite with the orchestra and audience. In 1984 the symphony announced the selection of its new music director, Bruce Ferder, who will join the orchestra in the 1985–1986 season.

CHRONOLOGY OF MUSIC DIRECTORS: Gottfried Herbst, 1927–1934. George Poinar, 1934–1942. (Operations suspended, 1942–1945.) Harold Paul Whelan, 1945–1961. [Orchestra incorporated, 1962.] Donald Thulean, 1962–1984. Gunther Schuller (Artistic Advisor and Principal Conductor), 1984–1985.

BIBLIOGRAPHY: Interviews with Donald Thulean and SSO Executive Director Wesley Brustad, 1984. Spokane Symphony Orchestra, *Annual Report*, 1982–1983. The Spokane *Spokesman-Review*.

ACCESS: Spokane Symphony Orchestra, The Flour Mill, Suite 203, W. 621 Mallon, Spokane, WA 99201. (509) 326–3126. Wesley O. Brustad, Executive Director.

FLOYD PETERSON

West Virginia _____

CHARLESTON (269,595)

Charleston Symphony Orchestra (Mt)

Founded in 1939 as the Charleston Civic Orchestra under the musical direction of local resident William Wiant and with a total expenditure of less than $5,000 the first year, the Charleston Symphony Orchestra has grown to become a Metropolitan orchestra with a full-time resident conductor, a professional management staff, and a yearly budget approaching $500,000. In particular, two facets of the Charleston Symphony's history afford it a unique place in the development of the orchestra in our society.

The first was a cooperative venture between the Symphony and the local chemical plants, a major area industry, to bring more musicians to the area to play in the community orchestra by providing them with jobs. The industry, particularly Union Carbide, offered to make a concerted effort to search for applicants who met their needs as scientists but who could also play musical instruments. Advertisements were placed in musicians' and engineers' trade papers. The industrial placement idea caught on and was publicized in national magazines; over 1,800 musicians eventually applied, and during the next several years the orchestra made 40 placements of musicians who became part of the community.

Simultaneously with the search for musicians came the second significant development in the organization's history with the appointment of Helen Thompson, a second violinist, as manager. Mrs. Thompson found herself besieged with requests for information about the orchestra's program, thus beginning her involvement on a national level with the American Symphony Orchestra League, then a fledgling organization. In 1950 she was selected as the first full-time executive of ASOL, which maintained its office in Charleston until 1962.

Both developments were the result of the influence of the orchestra's second conductor, Antonio Modarelli, who insisted that the central core of a cultural community is a symphony orchestra whose basic tools must include resident musicians and a manager. Modarelli's influence on the importance of community cultural enrichment as well as the development of "local groups that foster continuous training and participation in the arts" (Thompson, 1952) is still an underlying tenet of the organization's philosophy today.

It follows naturally that music education has been an important value to the organization. The orchestra now performs young people's concerts for over 10,000 students each year, and a Student Enrichment Program developed by the Orchestra's Women's Committee offers outstanding teaching materials and four weeks of classroom musical instruction to students prior to the concerts. The Women's Committee also sponsors a Young Artist Competition, which rotates on a three-year cycle between strings, piano, and voice.

In 1982, with funding from a private foundation, the Symphony was successful in bringing to the community a resident string quartet whose members became the first full-time musicians employed by the CSO. The Charleston String Quartet, comprising the principal string players in the orchestra, presents a series of chamber music concerts and performs many tour concerts throughout the state as well as providing educational services and youth concerts.

The CSO today comprises nearly 80 musicians, about half of whom reside in the local Kanawha Valley area. The remainder, primarily string players, are imported from other areas on a per-service basis, although they are contracted for the entire season. An Orchestra Committee of representativeselected by the musicians serves as a liaison between musicians, management, and the local union.

The organization is governed by a 27-member Board of Directors and administered by a full-time manager and support staff. Funding comes from ticket sales, private and government grants, a community Fund for the Arts supported by local businesses, and from private contributions. A very strong and active Women's Committee also raises a significant amount of money each year through various fund-raising activities.

Annual ticket sales are approximately 2,100 and growing. The orchestra performs at the Municipal Auditorium, which has a seating capacity of 3,500, making it one of the largest halls in the country. In the early 1980s a donation by James Kessler made possible the acquisition of an acoustical shell that has greatly improved the hall's acoustics for symphonic music.

The appointment of Sidney Rothstein as music director and conductor in 1980 brought tremendous artistic growth to the CSO as well as expanded programming and a greater community awareness of the importance of the Symphony. This expansion and artistic growth is continuing under the leadership of the new music director, Thomas Conlin.

The current season includes six subscription concerts and will expand to seven in 1985–1986. In addition, the orchestra performs two pops concerts and four young people's concerts and provides chamber ensembles for other functions on occasion. Plans for next season include an expanded tour program to take the orchestra to other communities in West Virginia, concert broadcasts, the formation of a symphony chorus, and production of an opera—a significant addition in West Virginia, which currently has no resident performing opera company.

A new string development program in the public schools launched in the spring of 1984 and scheduled for expansion the following fall will bring two additional full-time resident string players to the community and will continue the organization's commitment to educational and cultural enrichment.

CHRONOLOGY OF MUSIC DIRECTORS: William Wiant, 1939–1942. Antonio Modarelli, 1942–1954. Geoffrey Hobday, 1954–1961. (Guest conductors, 1962–1963.) Charles Gabor, 1963–1964. Charles Schiff, 1965–1976. Ronald Dishinger, 1977–1979. (Guest conductors, 1970–1980.) Sidney Rothstein, 1980–1984. Thomas B. Conlin, 1984-present.

BIBLIOGRAPHY: Helen M. Thompson, *The Community Symphony Orchestra: How to Organize and Develop It.* (Charleston: ASOL, 1952). Helen M. Thompson, "The Charleston Symphony Story," typescript, 1953.

ACCESS: Charleston Symphony Orchestra, P.O. Box 2292, Charleston, WV 25328. (304) 342–0151. Shirley Furry, General Manager.

SHIRLEY FURRY

WHEELING (185,566)

Wheeling Symphony (Mt)

Founded in 1929, the Wheeling Symphony was the first orchestra established in West Virginia. It has created a substantial cultural impact within the Ohio Valley.

The Symphony Society was founded by Mrs. Eleanor D. Caldwell at a time when Wheeling was a thriving industrial center with a wealthy society demanding artistic activities. Prior to the Society's funding, Mrs. Caldwell had sponsored string quartet concerts in her home; according to her, the "organization of the orchestra was spontaneous, prompted by a love of music and because . . . a larger organization could undertake more comprehensive programs and play for the entertainment of more people." The founding of the orchestra was a fortuitous event, for within the next year the introduction of vitaphone music in the theaters threatened the livelihood of Wheeling's professional musicians. For the first concert by an exclusively string orchestra, Mrs. Caldwell selected an outdoor performance in the newly created Oglebay Park.

The 1934 season signaled the beginning of a new era for the orchestra. Enrico Tambourini, the first conductor, resigned and Antonio Modarelli, conductor of the Pittsburgh Symphony Orchestra,* accepted the conducting post. Under Modarelli's direction the orchestra added more members and became less of a community orchestra, as musicians were brought in from Pittsburgh. Modarelli remained with the Wheeling Symphony until 1947 when he assumed the conducting position with the newly formed Charleston (West Virginia) Symphony Orchestra.* With his departure, the orchestra again turned to Pittsburgh and acquired Henry Mazer, assistant conductor to Fritz Reiner. During Mazer's tenure, guest artists of international stature (for example, Rudolf Serkin, Roberta Peters, and Artur Rubinstein) appeared with the orchestra. In 1960 Henry Aaron, who had been a member of the Metropolitan Opera Orchestra for 20 years, succeeded Henry Mazer; during the next four years, Wheeling experienced large-scale choral presentations. In 1964 the orchestra acquired Robert Kreis, assistant conductor of the Pittsburgh Symphony Orchestra, as its music director. Although the winter concerts consisted of traditional repertoire, the summer concerts were dominated by popular pieces and show tunes. Under Kreis, the orchestra also participated in the production of musicals. Robert Kreis left the Wheeling Symphony in 1972, and following a year of guest conductors, Jeff Holland Cook became the sixth music director. Under the guidance of Cook, a professional trombonist, the orchestra has experienced continued growth artistically and financially. The Wheeling Symphony Orchestra was awarded an ASCAP Award in 1974 for adventurous programming of contemporary music.

The Symphony's six annual subscription concerts, four young people's concerts, and two "Lollipop" concerts are presented in the 2,500-seat Capitol Music Hall, a structure built in 1927–1928, when it was known as the Capitol Theatre and served as a house for silent films and vaudeville shows. The ensemble of 75–80 performers plays to a typical audience of 1,300 per concert. In addition, the orchestra presents one summer concert, "Music under the Stars," in the Oglebay Amphitheater and concerts on occasional tours. The varied repertoire of the orchestra accommodates but also challenges a diverse audience. Most concerts feature a guest artist who also presents a workshop or master class.

The Wheeling Symphony is governed by a 36-member Board of Directors, an Executive Committee of 12, and an administration comprising general manager and secretary-bookkeeper. It functions with a budget of $325,000, funded by charitable and arts grants, private donors and corporate gifts, Auxiliary fund-raisers, the Caldwell Endowment, the Symphony Board Endowment, and earned income.

The orchestra's resident string quartet comprises the only contracted personnel in the ensemble; other musicians are hired on a per-service basis. All capable local people are used before filling positions with other performers; however, many members of the orchestra are faculty or students from nearby colleges and universities or free-lance performers from Pittsburgh.

Four chamber ensembles derive from the larger orchestra: the Appalachian String Quartet, the Caldwell Quartet, Cinque Jouerers (a woodwind quintet), and the Woodlands Brass. The Caldwell Quartet, named for the orchestra's founder, was organized about 35 years ago; its first violinist is Concertmaster Earl Summers, Jr., who has been an orchestra member since its founding. The Appalachian Quartet was founded in 1974 as a trio and expanded in 1977. Its members, orchestra principals, provide string instruction to students in the Ohio and Brooke County Public Schools, and are also adjunct instructors at West Liberty College and Bethany College.

A significant part of the orchestra's activity is the enhancement of the arts in the schools through its educational program. The young people's concerts comprise a set of four presentations on two consecutive days, attended by up to 9,000 third through sixth grade students from about 30 school districts in the tri-state area. In preparation for the concerts, students are instructed through a docent program. Every third year the orchestra presents children's concerts in Marshall County. As part of its 50th anniversary season in 1979, the Wheeling Symphony inaugurated the Ohio Valley Young Musicians' Concerto Competition for Strings, which is open to residents 17–28 years of age who live in West Virginia, Pennsylvania, Ohio, Kentucky, Indiana, or Illinois.

CHRONOLOGY OF MUSIC DIRECTORS: Enrico Tambourini, 1929–1934. Antonio Modarelli, 1934–1947. Henry Mazer, 1947–1960. Henry Aaron, 1960–1964. Robert Kreis, 1964–1972. (Guest conductors, 1972–1973.) Jeff Holland Cook, 1973-present.

BIBLIOGRAPHY: Debbie Kiester, "The Story of WSO's 'Music Under the Stars,' " Wheeling News-Register, 15 June 1983. Francie McPheeters, The Wheeling Symphony Society, Inc.: Fiftieth Anniversary (Wheeling: Wheeling Symphony Society, 1979).

ACCESS: The Wheeling Symphony Society, Inc., Suite 307, Hawley Building, Wheeling, WV 26003 (403) 232–6191. Susan Nelson, General Manager.

HARRY ELZINGA

Wisconsin ————————————————

MADISON (323,545)

Madison Symphony Orchestra (Mt)

Madison, Wisconsin's capital, is noted not only for its unusual terrain (the downtown is a 1.5-mile isthmus between two lakes), but also for a cultural life that is unusually rich for a city its size. The Madison Symphony Orchestra and its affiliated groups are outgrowths of the Madison Civic Music Association, founded in 1925. The MSO is the larger and older of the two professional orchestras in the city (the other group is the Wisconsin Chamber Orchestra, founded in 1960).

Each season the MSO performs seven regular subscription concerts, one pops concert, one youth concert, and at least one fully staged opera. It sponsors the Steenbeck competition through which young performers have a chance to be soloists with the MSO and receive scholarships for advanced training. Since 1980 the MSO has performed in its home, the 2,200-seat Oscar Mayer Theatre of the Madison Civic Center, which was built in 1926 and renovated in 1977–1980. A typical concert draws an audience of about 1,600. Each year six MSO concerts are taped for statewide rebroadcast over the public radio network.

The orchestra's programs generally rely heavily on the nineteenth- and early-twentieth-century repertoire, although some baroque and classical works are performed. The orchestra also features contemporary works. During the 1967–1968 season the MSO performed the world premiere of Gunther Schuller's *Verige d'Eros*, and during the 1974–1975 season the premiere of Alec Wilder's Concerto for Clarinet and Chamber Orchestra was featured. The MSO has also commissioned or performed works by Madison natives Stephen Chatman, Lee Hoiby, and Primous Fountain.

The MSO regularly employs 85 instrumentalists on a per-service basis, many of whom teach in the area and are on the music faculty of the University of Wisconsin (total enrollment 44,000). The orchestra hires additional musicians as it needs them and each year brings in four or five nationally famous soloists. The orchestra has an annual budget of about $300,000. The music director has responsibility for programming, although the general manager and an advisory Board of Directors, orchestra players, and chorus members are also consulted. The Madison Civic Music Association's Board of Directors (which governs the MSO) consists of 17 voting and 15 non-voting members drawn from all segments of the community. The MSO also has a full-time manager. Although the MSO neither applied for nor received any federal or state grants for the 1983–1984 season, it usually does receive some state or federal funds. The income from ticket sales (about 42% of the budget) is supplemented by corporate gifts, private donations, fund-raising by auxiliary groups, and interest on investments.

The orchestra first performed in 1926 and played in a number of locations including the University of Wisconsin Stock Pavilion and the auditorium at the former Central High School, which later became the home of Madison Area Technical College. Since its beginning, the MSO has preserved its close ties to numerous educational institutions in the area. In the past, for example, the conductor has taught at the University of Wisconsin and Madison Area Technical College.

The Madison Symphony Chorus was founded in 1928 and usually performs one or two major choral works each season. In the early 1960s, for example, the chorus and the MSO performed the Midwest premiere of Benjamin Britten's *War Requiem*. More recent offerings included Prokofiev's *Alexander Nevsky* as well as the requiems by Verdi and Mozart. The pops concerts were inaugurated in 1960, and the Civic Opera Guild was founded in 1963. Like the MSO and the Symphony Chorus, the Opera Guild is legally tied to and administered by the tax-exempt Madison Civic Music Association.

CHRONOLOGY OF MUSIC DIRECTORS: Dr. Sigfrid Prager, 1926–1948. Walter Heerman, 1948–1961. Roland Johnson, 1961-present.

BIBLIOGRAPHY: *The Capital Times. The First Fifty Years, 1925–1975: A History of the Madison Civic Music Association* [MCMA, 1975]. *Isthmus* (weekly newspaper). *The Wisconsin State Journal.*

ACCESS: Madison Symphony Orchestra, 211 N. Carroll Street, Madison, WI 53703. (608) 257–3734. Robert Palmer, General Manager.

JACOB STOCKINGER

MILWAUKEE (1,397,143)

Milwaukee Symphony Orchestra (Mj)

In a relatively few years, the Milwaukee Symphony Orchestra achieved what characteristically takes an orchestra decades. Performing in Carnegie

Hall for the first time in 1972, the upstart, 13-year-old Milwaukee Symphony was proclaimed a "great virtuoso orchestra" by *The New Yorker*. Two years later, after a concert at the Kennedy Center, the *Washington Star* exclaimed that the Milwaukee Symphony could stand comparison "with the very best."

Its formative years spent in the shadow of the Chicago Symphony Orchestra*—which had played concerts in Milwaukee since 1891 and still performs a 10-concert Milwaukee series—the Milwaukee Symphony emerged in the 1970s as one of America's eminent ensembles. The orchestra celebrated its 25th anniversary during the 1983–1984 season. It now has a budget of over $5 million, employing 90 players for 46 weeks.

Under the musical direction of conductor-composer Lukas Foss since 1981, it annually plays to a paying audience of over 200,000 persons. It is Wisconsin's only ASOL Major symphony orchestra and the state's largest performing arts institution. As such, it is the largest beneficiary of the Wisconsin Arts Board and of Milwaukee's United Performing Arts Fund.

Governed by a 71-member Board of Directors and a 57-member Corporate Board of Directors, the Milwaukee Symphony is the primary tenant of Milwaukee's Performing Arts Center, which also houses the Milwaukee Repertory Theater, the Milwaukee Ballet, the Florentine Opera Company, and the Milwaukee Chamber Orchestra. Its subscription series at the Performing Arts Center's Uihlein Hall includes 20 classical programs and 10 pops programs. In 1983, the Symphony broke the $1 million ticket sales barrier for the first time.

The Milwaukee Symphony, in cooperation with the Wisconsin Conservatory of Music, sponsors the Wisconsin Conservatory Symphony Chorus, which since its founding in 1976 has been directed by Margaret Hawkins. The Chorus performs in as many as five classical subscription programs each season, sings in the orchestra's holiday performances, and has accompanied the orchestra to Carnegie Hall.

In addition to its subscription series in Milwaukee's Performing Arts Center, the orchestra presents its own series of summer concerts at the Milwaukee County Zoo and performs holiday concerts at Milwaukee's Riverside Theater and in Milwaukee churches. Its educational activities include 25 youth concerts supported by a strong docent program. Since 1967, the orchestra has held a Young Artist Competition for high-school-age instrumentalists, and in 1981 it inaugurated a competition in piano and strings for soloists above the age of 19.

In addition to support from the United Performing Arts Fund, government sources (including the state, the NEA, and Milwaukee County), and its recently raised endowment funds, the orchestra receives support from an active women's league, which has received a number of ASOL awards.

Its Symphony's relative youth notwithstanding, Milwaukee has a symphonic tradition reaching back into the nineteenth century. There were a number of unsuccessful attempts to form an orchestra, starting in 1890 when Arthur Cecil Gordon Weld established a Milwaukee Symphony that lasted only a single season. Weld tried again in 1893, collaborating with Eugen Luening (the father of composer Otto Luening) to form a Milwaukee Philharmonic. That effort also lasted only a season.

The torch was seized in 1901 by William Boeppler, one of the founders of the Wisconsin Conservatory of Music. He also formed a Milwaukee Symphony, but it met the same end as the others and he moved to Chicago in 1903.

Composer Carl Eppert attempted to start a Milwaukee Civic Orchestra in 1922. Eppert was well known as a composer. His symphonies, including his *Traffic* Symphony, were performed by ensembles of the stature of the NBC Orchestra and the Chicago Symphony.* But he was also unsuccessful in forming a permanent Milwaukee orchestra, even if the organization that helped support his efforts, the Milwaukee Civic Music Association, still continues.

Conductor Frank Laird Waller tried again in 1929. His Milwaukee Philharmonic was supported by Herman A. Uihlein, of the family that owned and operated the Schlitz Brewery, and lasted until Uihlein reduced his support in 1933. The Polish-born conductor Jerzy Bojanowski conducted still another Milwaukee Symphony in 1935, and soon afterward the German-born Julius Ehrlich established an ensemble named the Milwaukee Sinfonietta. In 1942 it reincorporated as the Milwaukee Symphony, but despite a certain measure of public support, its last concerts were in 1947.

Yet another Milwaukee Philharmonic was organized in 1951. But even with the endorsement of impresario Arthur Judson, manager of the New York Philharmonic,* it folded before playing a single concert. One of its organizers, Conductor John Anello, persevered, and in 1953, Anello, with the assistance of civic leader Gertrude M. Puelicher and others, incorporated the Milwaukee Pops Orchestra.

It was this orchestra—a pops orchestra that provided an alternative to, rather than competition with, the Chicago Symphony—that finally led directly to the incorporation of a permanent Milwaukee Symphony in 1959. But even the Pops was faced with seemingly overwhelming difficulties. Out of money, the Pops cancelled its 1955 season, and in early 1956 the orchestra was reorganized by a more powerful Board of Directors including Judge Robert W. Landry, Mrs. Herman A. Uihlein, Jr., Puelicher, and others. Enlisting the aid of Mitch Miller and Arthur Fiedler, and modeling the orchestra after Fiedler's Boston Pops,* the new Milwaukee Pops raised $50,000 and attracted 3,000 persons to its reopening concert in the Milwaukee Auditorium in October 1956.

Still, there were problems. Conflicts between Anello and some Board members led to his departure. And by the end of its 1957–1958 season, the orchestra had accumulated a $6,231 deficit. Its business manager resigned and its president stepped down. Nevertheless, this was the moment of the Milwaukee Symphony's birth. Stanley Williams took over as president of the Board. He appointed Robert Zigman as business manager, led a fund drive that successfully erased the Symphony's debt, and presided over the Pops' 1958–1959 season, its most successful season ever. The season's culmination was a performance by Van Cliburn, witnessed by 6,300 persons at the Milwaukee Auditorium. At long last, the time seemed to be right.

"It just seemed ridiculous," Williams said later, "that what was then the 10th largest city in the country didn't have a symphony orchestra." Williams made the case that the Chicago Symphony, because its concerts were always sold out and limited to 10 performances, didn't serve a large segment of the community, including its youth. He and other Board members also believed a symphony would improve the city's cultural life and help attract new companies and employees to Milwaukee.

In the chambers of Judge Landry on April 2, 1959, Williams made the motion to change the Pops' name to the Milwaukee Symphony Orchestra. In selecting a music director, the Board decided to make a clean break with the past, engaging CBS Symphony Conductor Alfredo Antonini as non-resident music director. On a budget of $128,000, the orchestra presented seven concerts, including five pops concerts.

The Milwaukee Symphony's first permanent conductor, Harry John Brown, was appointed in 1960. Brown, who had conducted the Milwaukee Pops when Cliburn performed, had been music director of the Tri-City Symphony Orchestra in Davenport, Iowa. He had also conducted television's "Voice of Firestone" series. He expanded the orchestra's series to eight concerts, including four pops concerts. Only in 1961–1962 did the orchestra finally play more classical subscription concerts (eight) than pops (four). In that same season, it hired a resident ensemble of 16 musicians, including the Symphony's present concertmaster, Edward Mumm. The orchestra's budget was approximately $200,000.

Brown worked tirelessly to gain community support for the orchestra. In his first season alone, he attended 167 cocktail parties, receptions, and/ or speaking engagements. He built the support and the community enthusiasm that enabled the Board to increase the ensemble to 38 musicians by 1961–1963. In 1963–1964, 60 musicians were hired for a 28-week schedule.

With the Milwaukee Symphony in 1966 earning Major status from ASOL, gaining a $1 million Ford Foundation Challenge Grant, growing to a budget size of $500,000, and anticipating construction of its new home (Milwaukee's Performing Arts Center, which opened in 1969), it had embarked on a road toward national recognition.

After Brown resigned in May 1967, the Board looked to Kenneth Schermerhorn, a conductor with the American Ballet Theater and music director of the New Jersey Symphony,* who had made a very positive impression when he guest conducted the orchestra in late 1966. In September of 1967, he was appointed the orchestra's music director, starting with the 1968–1969 season.

Schermerhorn was charged by the Board with establishing a "first-rate, major symphony orchestra." To achieve that goal, he was faced with the unenviable task of weeding out many of the orchestra's weaker players. The ensemble of 84 players Schermerhorn convened at the beginning of the 1969–1970 season included 30 new musicians, among them 22 string players. Not surprisingly, in the 1970 contract negotiations, the musicians inserted a clause into the master agreement limiting Schermerhorn's power to fire. Nevertheless, Schermerhorn's relationship with the musicians was good, and the orchestra's success at its 1972 Carnegie Hall debut seemingly confirmed that he and the orchestra were on the right course. His contract was renewed in 1976 and he projected that the Symphony would increase from 90 to 102 players and from 20 classical programs to 24. He hoped to culminate his Milwaukee tenure with a European tour.

Meanwhile, however, the Board was discovering that a first-rate orchestra required a first-rate budget. Deficits began to grow, and in 1976 the orchestra had to take $100,000 out of the principal of its $2.5 million endowment to help pay for its $2.7 million budget. In the next four years, the budget increased to $4.1 million and the deficit by 1980 was in excess of $1.2 million.

Although he had led the orchestra in eight national tours, Schermerhorn never got his European tour, nor his 102 musicians, nor his 24 classical concerts. He had built a fine, major symphony orchestra in Milwaukee, but he announced that the 1979–1980 season would be his last in Milwaukee.

Among the guest conductors who led the Symphony during Schermerhorn's last few seasons, composer and former Buffalo Philharmonic* conductor Lukas Foss had been especially well received. Negotiations with Foss were begun in May of 1980. Only a few months before the Symphony had hired a new executive director, Robert L. Caulfield, who still maintains that position.

While Schermerhorn was a very demonstrative conductor, inclined toward programming many of the larger-scale, nineteenth-century romantic works, Foss tends toward the unusual. Although he is a strong proponent of American and contemporary music, he has mellowed since his days of programming avant-garde music with the Buffalo Philharmonic. "I used to sort of hit them over the head and they didn't want it," says Foss of his tenure in Buffalo. "Now I have a different approach. Also, I discovered that I love to play old music. To make it come alive is such a rewarding experience for me . . . I think I have really matured." Typically, Foss will program obscure pieces by a well-known composer, juxtapose certain works of certain composers, or base his programs around particular themes. The Milwaukee Symphony's 1984–1985 season included several characteristic Foss programs. Among them was a program combining an overture by Salieri with Mozart's complete *Impresario* (with Foss-composed recitatives), Weill's songspiel *Mahagonny*, and Milhaud's "Le boeuf sur le toit." Another program included Chadwick's *Jubilee*, Herbert's Cello Concerto, and Copland's Symphony No. 3.

Foss has inaugurated an annual American music festival in Milwaukee. In 1983, the festival's second year, it was devoted to the music of Copland, and in 1984 to American sacred music. The music of Leonard Bernstein is scheduled for the 1985 festival. In 1986, Foss will lead the Milwaukee Symphony on its first European tour.

RECORDING HISTORY AND SELECTIVE DISCOGRAPHY: During Foss's tenure, the Symphony made its first recordings for Pro-Arte records (it made its first recording in 1974, Samuel Barber's Symphony No. 1, for Vox with Schermerhorn conducting).

American Festival, works by Copland, Bernstein, Schuman, and Barber (Foss): Pro-Arte PAD–102. Stravinsky, *Symphony of Psalms*; Foss, *Psalms*; Ives, *Psalm 67* (Foss): Pro-Arte PAD–169 (soon to be released).

CHRONOLOGY OF MUSIC DIRECTORS: Alfredo Antonini, 1959–1960. Harry John Brown, 1960–1968. Kenneth Schermerhorn, 1968–1980. Lukas Foss, 1980-present.

BIBLIOGRAPHY: Herbert Kupferberg, "Lucas Foss, Newfound Focus for the Composer/Conductor," *Ovation*, Apr. 1984. *Milwaukee Symphony Orchestra 25th Anniversary: A Series of Articles [by James Chute and Thomas Heinen] from the Milwaukee Journal* (Milwaukee: Milwaukee Journal, 1984). Stephen E. Rubin, "What Do You Say to a Naked Prima Donna," *New York Times*, 31 Mar. 1974. Frederick Winship, "Conductor/Composer Plays Musical Chairs," *Chicago Tribune*, 22 Nov. 1984.

ACCESS: Milwaukee Symphony Orchestra, 212 W. Wisconsin Avenue, Milwaukee, WI 53203. (414) 291–6010. Robert L. Caulfield, Executive Director. Jane Keegan, Public Relations Director.

JAMES CHUTE

Wyoming ————————————

CASPER (71,856)

Casper Symphony Orchestra (Ur)

The history of the Casper Symphony Orchestra dates back sixty years, when a clarinetist brought together some amateur musicians to form a band. This evolved into the Casper Philharmonic, which flourished until World War II. Then, in 1948, Blaine Coolbaugh, music director at Natrona County High School, organized a group of local musicians who became the Casper Civic Symphony Orchestra, Inc.

When Coolbaugh retired in 1959, the Symphony's Board of Directors, together with Casper Junior College, jointly hired a person to serve as faculty member and orchestra conductor. Ernest Hagen, the first to assume this role, brought new impetus to the organization. With an increased budget through community fund-raising, musicians were paid for the first time, and professional musicians were brought in as soloists.

In 1962 Hagen resigned and Edmund Marty took the podium. He introduced the Kinder Konzerts in local schools, as well as a statewide young artist competition, the winner of which receives a cash award and the opportunity to perform with the orchestra at the Kinder Konzerts.

When Marty resigned in mid–1971, Assistant Conductor Rex Eggleston capably held the orchestra together until the advent in 1972 of Curtis Peacock, the current conductor. Peacock has striven to improve the quality of the orchestra through developing and nurturing local talent and has succeeded, through the cooperative efforts of the Board and staff, in implementing a core orchestra concept that now includes three full-time, professional musicians. These efforts were recently recognized when the Casper Symphony Association won the 1984 Governor's Award for the Arts as the Outstanding Civic Organization in the State of Wyoming. This recognition is particularly gratifying, since Casper is an isolated community in the middle of Wyoming, with little access to other professional musical resources.

Natrona County High School's auditorium, with a seating capacity of 1,409, is the orchestra's home for its six-concert subscription series, which is supplemented by an annual tour (funded by the city of Casper) to two different Wyoming communities each year. In 1984–1985 the Symphony's first series of run-out concerts was given at the new, 943-seat Arts Center Theatre in Riverton, Wyoming, 120 miles west of Casper. In all, more than 17,000 people heard the orchestra live in 1983–1984, including more than 6,500 school children. Public radio broadcasts from Laramie reached some 200,000 potential listeners in Wyoming and northern Colorado. The orchestra's commitment to outreach is also manifested in joint concerts with the Wyoming State Choir, a free Labor Day pops concert, in-school chamber ensemble performances, a free student ticket plan, paid performing internships for talented high school and college students, and a special series of adult lectures previewing upcoming concerts.

The orchestra's 30-member Board of Directors, with representation from the staff, Guild, and musicians, sets organizational goals and long-range policy and is responsible for fund-raising projects and for the hiring and firing of the top staff. The 80-member Casper Symphony Guild sells season subscriptions, participates in numerous special fund-raising projects, and provides volunteers for concert support and office assistance. The music director is responsible for artistic decisions including personnel, soloist selection, and repertoire, with advice from orchestra committees.

The projected budget for the 1984–1985 season was just under $200,000, of which about 38% would be earned through revenue and support from the Symphony's operations, the remainder from the Annual Maintenance Fund Drive, grants, and other public and private sources.

The artistic characteristics of the CSO can best be defined by its growing professionalism and broad spectrum of programming, ranging from the baroque to modern eras. In 1984, the Symphony presented the world premiere of *Ode to the Rockies* by Delton L. Hudson, and future plans include the performance of music by other contemporary American composers.

RECORDING HISTORY: There are no commercial recordings, but many archival recordings are available through the Natrona County Public Library.

CHRONOLOGY OF MUSIC DIRECTORS: Blaine Coolbaugh, 1948–1959. Ernest Hagen, 1959–1962. Edmund Marty, 1962–1971. Rex Eggleston, 1971–1972. Curtis Peacock, 1972-present.

BIBLIOGRAPHY: Interview with former CSO General Manager Ken Steiger, 1984. Mrs. Blaine Coolbaugh, personal notes. Mrs. George Knapp, personal notes.

ACCESS: Casper Symphony Orchestra, Inc., P.O. Box 667, Casper, WY 82602. (307) 266–1478. Don Tull, Business Manager.

MRS. GEORGE KNAPP

Chronology of Foundings
for Orchestras Profiled ⎯⎯⎯⎯

The foundings of many of the profiled orchestras involved mergers, false starts, periods of suspended operations, antecedent organizations, and other complexities that defy a tabular format. In some cases, the "founding date" of the orchestra is inevitably a matter of historical interpretation, as may be inferred from the profiles themselves.

Handel and Haydn Society (Boston)	1815
New York Philharmonic	1842
St. Louis Symphony Orchestra	1880
Boston Symphony Orchestra	1881
Detroit Symphony Orchestra	1887
Chicago Symphony Orchestra	1891
Cincinnati Symphony Orchestra	1894
New Haven Symphony Orchestra	1894
Pittsburgh Symphony Orchestra	1895
Oregon Symphony Orchestra	1896
Dallas Symphony Orchestra	1900
Philadelphia Orchestra	1900
Minnesota Orchestra	1903
Seattle Symphony Orchestra	1903
San Francisco Symphony	1911
Houston Symphony Orchestra	1913
Baltimore Symphony Orchestra	1916
Cleveland Orchestra	1918
Los Angeles Philharmonic	1919
Cedar Rapids Symphony	1921
Kalamazoo Symphony Orchestra	1921
Omaha Symphony	1921
New Jersey Symphony Orchestra	1922
South Dakota Symphony	1922

Rochester Philharmonic Orchestra	1923
Amarillo Symphony	1924
Glendale Symphony Orchestra	1924
Honolulu Symphony Orchestra	1924
Knoxville Symphony Orchestra	1924
Fort Worth Symphony Orchestra	1925
Madison Symphony Orchestra	1926
Youngstown Symphony Orchestra	1926
Colorado Springs Symphony	1927
San Diego Symphony Orchestra	1927
Spokane Symphony Orchestra	1927
Long Beach Symphony Orchestra	1928
Pasadena Symphony Orchestra	1928
Tucson Symphony Orchestra	1928
Chautauqua (N.Y.) Symphony Orchestra	1929
Wheeling Symphony	1929
Albany Symphony Orchestra	1930
Indianapolis Symphony Orchestra	1930
El Paso Symphony Orchestra	1931
Fargo-Moorhead Symphony Orchestra	1931
National Symphony Orchestra (Washington, D.C.)	1931
Buffalo Philharmonic Orchestra	1932
Charlotte Symphony Orchestra	1932
Duluth-Superior Symphony Orchestra	1932
New Mexico Symphony Orchestra	1932
North Carolina Symphony	1932
Portland (Maine) Symphony Orchestra	1932
Alabama Symphony Orchestra	1933
Chattanooga Symphony Orchestra	1933
Dayton Philharmonic Orchestra	1933
Oakland Symphony Orchestra	1933
Denver Symphony Orchestra	1934
Vermont Symphony Orchestra	1934
Charleston (W.V.) Symphony Orchestra	1936
New Orleans Symphony Orchestra	1936
Canton Symphony Orchestra	1937
Des Moines Symphony	1937
Louisville Orchestra	1937
Oklahoma Symphony Orchestra	1937
Austin Symphony Orchestra	1938
San Antonio Symphony	1939
Utah Symphony Orchestra	1940
Charleston (S.C.) Symphony	1942
Fort Wayne Philharmonic	1943
Springfield (Mass.) Symphony Orchestra	1943
Toledo Symphony	1943
Atlanta Symphony Orchestra	1944
Jackson Symphony Orchestra	1944

Selected Bibliography ⎯⎯⎯⎯

The Albany Symphony Orchestra: Programming New Music. Washington, D.C.: American Symphony Orchestra League, 1984. Monograph.

Antek, Samuel. *This Was Toscanini*. New York: Vanguard, 1963.

Arian, Edward. *Bach, Beethoven, and Bureaucracy*. University of Alabama Press, 1971.

Baker-Carr, Janet. *Evening at Symphony*. Boston: Houghton-Mifflin, 1977.

Balick, Lillian R. *The Delaware Symphony: Origins and the First Fifty Years*. Wilmington: Delaware Symphony Association, 1984.

Baynham, Edward G. *A History of Pittsburgh Music, 1758–1958*. Pittsburgh: Author, 1970.

Blaukopf, Kurt. *Mahler*. New York: Praeger, 1973.

BMI Orchestral Programs Survey. New York: Broadcast Music, Inc., 1960-Annual.

Bobbitt, Blanche M. *The Glendale Symphony Orchestra, 1924–1980*. Glendale: Glendale Symphony Association, 1980.

Campbell, Esther W. *Bagpipes in the Woodwind Section*. Seattle: Seattle Symphony Women's Association, 1978.

Chasins, Abram. *Leopold Stokowski*. New York: Hawthorn, 1979.

Chotzinoff, Samuel. *Toscanini: An Intimate Portrait*. New York: Knopf, 1956.

Damrosch, Walter, *My Musical Life*. New York: Scribners, 1926.

DeWall, Charles R. *A History of the Dayton Philharmonic Orchestra 1933–1983*. Dayton: DPO, 1983.

Dickson, Harry Ellis. *Arthur Fiedler and the Boston Pops*. Boston: Houghton-Mifflin, 1981.

⎯⎯⎯. *Gentlemen, More Dolce, Please (Second Movement)*. Boston: Beacon Press, 1974.

Estes, David, and Robert Stock. *The San Diego Symphony: Problems of Institution Building*. San Diego State University Institute of Public and Urban Affairs, 1978.

Ewen, David J. *Dictators of the Baton*. Chicago: Alliance, 1943.

————. *The Man with the Baton: The Story of Conductors and Their Orchestras*. New York: Thomas Crowell, 1936.

The First Fifty Years: A History of the Madison Civic Music Association. Madison: MCMA, 1975.

Freed, Richard. *History of the National Symphony Orchestra, 1931–1981*. Washington, D.C.: NSO, n.d.

Furlong, William Barry. *Season with Solti: A Year in the Life of the Chicago Symphony*. New York: Macmillan, 1974.

Grant, Margaret. *America's Symphony Orchestras and How They Are Supported*. New York: Norton, 1940.

Haggin, B. H. *The Toscanini Musicians Knew*. New York: 1967.

Hart, Philip. *Conductors: A New Generation*. New York: Scribners, 1979.

————. *Orpheus In the New World*. New York: Norton, 1973.

Howe, Mark Anthony DeWolfe. *The Boston Symphony Orchestra, 1881–1931*. Boston: Houghton-Mifflin, 1931.

Hurd, Michael, *The Orchestra*. New York: Facts on File, 1980.

Johnson, H. Earle. *Halleluja, Amen!: The Story of the Handel and Haydn Society*. Boston: Bruch Humphries, 1965.

Kennedy, Michael. *Barbirolli: Conductor Laureate*. London: MacGibbon & Kee, 1971.

Kupferberg, Herbert. *Those Fabulous Philadelphians*. New York: Scribner's, 1969.

Leichtentritt, Hugo. *Serge Koussevitzky, the Boston Symphony Orchestra, and the New American Music*. Cambridge: Harvard University Press, 1946.

Leinsdorf, Erich. *Cadenza*. Boston: Houghton-Mifflin, 1976.

Leiter, Robert D. *The Musicians and Petrillo*. New York: Bookman, 1953.

Marsh, Robert C. *The Cleveland Orchestra*. Cleveland: World, 1967.

Matheopoulos, Helena. *Maestro: Encounters with Conductors of Today*. New York: Harper & Row, 1982.

Milwaukee Symphony Orchestra 25th Anniversary: A Series of Articles [by James Chute and Thomas Heinen] from the Milwaukee Journal. Milwaukee: Milwaukee Journal, 1984.

Monteux, Doris. *It's All in the Music: The Life and Work of Pierre Monteux*. New York: Farrar, Straus and Giroux, 1965.

Mueller, John H. *The American Symphony Orchestra: A Social History of Musical Taste*. 1951; reprint, Westport, Conn.: Greenwood Press, 1976.

Mueller, Kate H. *Twenty-Seven Major American Orchestras: A History and Analysis of Their Repertoires, Seasons 1842/3–1967/70*. Bloomington: Indiana University Press, 1973.

Munch, Charles. *I Am a Conductor*. London: Oxford University Press, 1955.

New Schwann Artist Issue. Boston: Schwann Record and Tape Catalogs, 1982.

New Schwann Record and Tape Guide. July, 1984.

Nicholas, Louis. *Thor Johnson, American Conductor*. Fishcreek, Wis.: Penninsula Arts Association, 1982.

Northcutt, John Orlando. *The Story of the Los Angeles Philharmonic Orchestra*. Los Angeles: Southern California Symphony Association, 1963.

Oliver, Daniel. *Stokowski*. New York: Dodd, Mead, 1982.

Otis, Philo Adams. *The Chicago Symphony Orchestra*. Chicago: Clayton F. Summy, 1924.

Previn, André, ed. *Orchestra*. Garden City, N.Y.: Doubleday, 1979.

Raynor, Henry. *The Orchestra*. New York: Scribners, 1978.

Reid, Charles. *John Barbirolli*. New York: Taplinger, 1971.

Roberts, Helen H. and Doris Cousins. *A History of the New Haven Symphony Orchetra Celebrating Its Seventy-Fifth Season, 1894–1969*. New Haven: Yale University Press, 1969.

Robinson, Paul. *Stokowski*. New York: Vanguard, 1977.

Rodzinzki, Helena. *Our Two Lives*. New York: Scribners, 1976.

Roussel, Hubert. *The Houston Symphony Orchestra, 1913–1977*. Austin: University of Texas Press, 1977.

Russell, Charles Edward. *The American Orchestra and Theodore Thomas*. Garden City, N.Y.: Doubleday, Page & Co., 1927.

Schlesinger, Janet. *Challenge to the Urban Orchestra: The Case of the Pittsburgh Symphony*. Pittsburgh: Author, 1971.

Schneider, David. *The San Francisco Symphony: Music, Maestros and Musicians*. Novato, Calif.: Presidio Press, 1983.

Schonberg, Harold C. *The Great Conductors*. New York: Simon & Schuster, 1967.

Schools and Symphony Orchestras: A Summary of Selected Youth Concert Activities. Washington, D.C.: U.S. Department of Health, Education & Walfare, Office of Education, 1971.

Seltzer, George, comp. *The Professional Symphony Orchestra in the United States*. Metuchen, N.J.: Scarecrow Press, 1975.

Shanet, Howard. *Philharmonic: A History of New York's Orchestra*. Garden City, N.Y.: Doubleday, 1975.

Sherman, John K. *Music and Maestros: The Story of the Minneapolis Symphony Orchestra*. Minneapolis: University of Minnesota, 1952.

Shickel, Richard. *The World of Carnegie Hall*. Westport, Conn.: Greenwood Press, 1960.

Smith, Caroline Estes. *The Philharmonic Orchestra of Los Angeles: The First Decade, 1919–1929*. Los Angeles: United Printing, 1930.

Smith, Moses. *Koussevitzky*. New York: Allen, Towne & Heath, 1947.

Snyder, Louis. *Community of Sound: The Boston Symphony and Its World of Players*. Boston: Beacon Press, 1979.

Stoddard, Hope. *Symphony Conductors in the U.S.A.* New York: Crowell, 1957.

Swoboda, Henry, comp. *The American Symphony Orchestra*. New York: Basic Books, 1967.

Wells, Jeanette. *A History of the Music Festival at Chautauqua Institution from 1974–1957*. Washington, D.C.: Catholic University of America Press, 1958.

Wells, Katherine G. *Symphony and Song: The Saint Louis Symphony Orchestra*. St. Louis: Countryman, 1980.

Willis, Thomas. *The Chicago Symphony Orchestra*. Chicago: Rand McNally, 1974.

Wister, Frances. *Twenty-Five Years of the Philadelphia Orchestra, 1900–1925*. 1925; reprint, Freeport, N.Y.: Books for Libraries Press, 1970.

Index ───────────────────────────────

About the Contributors _____

PETER ALEXANDER, Ed. D., is Professor of Music at S.U.N.Y., New Paltz, and heads its Woodwind Quintet. He is also Principal Clarinetist with the Hudson Valley Philharmonic.

DANIEL ALFARO, Ph.D., is Director of Clinical Experiences and Assistant Professor of Music at Metropolitan State College, Denver, and was bassoonist with the Wichita (Kansas) and Denver Symphony Orchestra.

ENRIQUE ALBERTO ARIAS, Ph.D., is Chairman of Doctoral Studies at the American Conservatory in Chicago. A pianist, composer, and musicologist, he has written many articles on the Spanish Renaissance.

DAVID L. AUSTIN, M.A., M.L.S., is Fine Arts Librarian at Wichita State University. He writes articles and reviews for various publications and is an abstractor for *RILM*.

CHARLES H. BALL is Professor of Music Education and Head of the Department of Art and Music Education at the University of Tennessee, Knoxville.

STEPHEN H. BARNES, Ph.D., is Dean of the College of Fine Arts at Eastern New Mexico University. His area of scholarly interest is the sociological and social-psychological foundations of aesthetic education in the United States.

JEAN-PIERRE BARRICELLI, Ph.D., is Professor of Humanities and Comparative Literature at the University of California/Riverside. The author of books and articles on literature and music, a musicologist, composer, and former conductor, he serves as music critic for the Riverside *Press/Enterprise*.

VIOLET C. BEAHAN was for seven years the General Manager/Publicist of the Monterey County (California) Symphony (1970–1976). She has been President and a participating member of the Monterey Peninsula Choral Society.

ROBERT K. BECKWITH, Professor of Music at Bowdoin College, co-founder of the Bowdoin Summer Music School and Festival, is President of Opera New England of Maine and lectures frequently on opera and symphony.

JEANNE MARIE BELFY, Assistant Professor of Music, teaches music history and oboe at Boise State University and is finishing her dissertation on the Commissioning Project of the Louisville Orchestra.

DAVID BEVERIDGE, Ph.D, is Assistant Professor of Musicology at the University of New Orleans. Following graduate work at Berkeley, he taught at Oberlin and Indiana before moving south in 1983.

GEOFFREY H. BLOCK, Ph.D., is Assistant Professor of Music at the University of Puget Sound. An author and composer, he is currently writing a book on American musical theater.

MORRIS BLOCK is the Manager of the Vermont Symphony. Formerly a cellist with the orchestra, he continues to perform with numerous ensembles in northern New England.

FRED BLUMENTHAL, Ph.D., teaches music, writes reviews for the St. Louis *Globe Democrat*, directs a church choir, and sings in two professional choirs in St. Louis.

WILLIAM A. BROWN is Professor of Music at the University of North Florida, Jacksonville. A tenor, he is an internationally recognized concert, opera, and recording artist.

KAY BUCKSBAUM, B.A., is President of the Des Moines Symphony Foundation, Past President of the Des Moines Symphony Association, and has been an active Board member of many organizations in the Des Moines area.

RONALD N. BUKOFF is a musicologist, bassoonist, and Historian of the International Double Reed Society.

THOMAS A. BUMGARDNER, D.M.A., is Professor of Music at the University of Wisconsin-Superior. He is the author of a book on American composer Norman Dello Joio and a Board member of Symphony School of America.

ALLISON CHESTNUT, an English instructor at Louisiana State University and former publicist of the Baton Rouge Symphony, holds an undergraduate degree in music and performs with several professional ensembles.

JAMES CHUTE, M.Mus., is Music Critic of the *Milwaukee Journal* and Organist/Choirmaster at Christ Church, Episcopal, Whitefish Bay. Widely published in major periodicals and a contributor to the *New Grove Dictionary of Music and Musicians in the United States*, he won the 1982 ASCAP Deems Taylor Award for his writing at the *Cincinnati Post*.

JOHN W. CLARK, Ph.D., Assistant Professor of Music History and Theory at Towson State University in Baltimore, is a specialist in twentieth-century American music and is active as a pianist and conductor. He is the author of several articles.

RAYMOND COMSTOCK, Ph.D., is Assistant Professor of Music at the University of Minnesota, Duluth, where he conducts the orchestras and teaches violin and viola.

ROBERT R. CRAVEN, Ph.D., Professor of English, teaches multidisciplinary humanities at New Hampshire College. His earlier publications include works in the areas of bibliography, literature, and philology. He is presently editing a companion volume on major orchestras outside the United States.

RONALD A. CRUTCHER, D.M.A., is Associate Professor of Music at the University of North Carolina at Greensboro. A former Board member and Orchestra Committee Chairman, he is Associate Principal Cello of the Greensboro Symphony Orchestra.

SAM DI BONAVENTURA, D.M.A., Professor of Music at George Mason University, has contributed to professional journals and the *New Grove Dictionaries*. He writes music reviews for the *Baltimore Evening Sun* and is Program Annotator for the Baltimore Symphony and other area ensembles.

GEORGE K. DIEHL, Ph.D., is Professor and Chairman of Fine Arts at La Salle University. He is also a program annotator, author of articles, concert narrator, pianist-accompanist, and classical music radio commentator.

CATHERINE DOWER, Ph.D., Professor of Music at Westfield State College, author of a book and numerous articles, is a Corporator of the Springfield Symphony Orchestra Association and Life Member of the Women's Symphony League.

TED DUBOIS, Ph.D., is Assistant Professor of Music at West Texas State University and is an oboist with the Amarillo Symphony Orchestra.

MARGARETTE F. EBY, Ph.D., is Professor of Music at the University of Michigan-Flint. A former Board member of the Flint Institute of Music, she is also a performer on piano and harpsichord.

SANDRA KEISER EDWARDS is General Manager of the Shreveport Symphony.

HARRY ELZINGA, Ph.D., is Professor of Music at West Virginia University.

JAMES ERB, Ph.D., Professor of Music, University of Richmond (Virginia), directs the Richmond Symphony Chorus. He is also an editor in the new series of Orlando Di Lasso's complete works.

STUART M. ERWIN, Ph.D., is Instructor of Music History at California State University at Long Beach. Twice a Fulbright scholar, he also holds an advanced degree from UCLA in Business and Management.

MICHAEL J. ESSELSTROM, Ed.D., is Professor of Music at Indiana University at South Bend. He is also Music Director and Conductor of the Elkhart County Symphony Orchestra and the Kokomo Symphony Orchestra.

DAVID ESTES is Regional Manager for Tower Records. A former professional horn player, he has authored articles on musicology and arts management.

PATRICIA H. EVANS is the Public Relations Director/League Co-ordinator for the Jackson Symphony Orchestra.

JAMES P. FAIRLEIGH, Ph.D., is Head of the Music Department at Jacksonville State University in Alabama. A pianist and organist, he has also contributed articles to several professional music journals.

MARGARET L. FAST is a Humanities Reference Librarian at the University of Utah in Salt Lake City.

JOHN FERRITTO, Associate Professor of Music and Director of Orchestral Music at Kent State University, is also Music Director/Conductor of the Springfield (Ohio) Symphony and Associate Director of the Blossom Festival School (Music).

MICHAEL FINK, Ph.D., is Associate Professor of Music at The University of Texas at San Antonio. He is Program Annotator for the San Antonio Chamber

Music Society and frequently contributes notes to the San Antonio Symphony as well.

ROGER E. FOLTZ, Ph.D., is Chairman of the Department of Music, University of Nebraska at Omaha, and serves as Program Annotator for the Omaha Symphony.

DONALD H. FOSTER, Ph.D., is Professor of Musicology at the College-Conservatory of Music, University of Cincinnati. He has published articles and editions of music pertaining to eighteenth-century France.

EFRIM FRUCHTMAN, Ph.D., Professor of Music at Memphis State University, is the author of articles in the *New Grove, Acta Musicologica*, and *Studies in Musicology*, and editor of the *Journal of the American Viola da Gamba Society*.

SHIRLEY FURRY is General Manager of the Charleston (West Virginia) Symphony. A piano teacher and past member of the CSO Board, she has been an active worker and advocate for many arts groups in the community.

PETER GANO, Ph.D., Associate Professor of Music History and Chairman of the Music History Division at Ohio State University, has been a member of the Columbus Symphony bass section and the orchestra's Program Annotator.

PAUL GANSON, M.A., is Assistant Principal Bassonist of the Detroit Symphony and President of Orchestra Hall.

LISA GONZALEZ, B.A., M.A., has been employed in management, public relations, finance, and research positions with the La Jolla Chamber Music Society, Eastern Music Festival, American Symphony Orchestra League, Syracuse Symphony, Albany Symphony, and the Philharmonic Orchestra of Florida.

MICHAEL D. GRACE, Ph.D., Chairman of the Music Department at Colorado College, is Director of the Colorado College Conservatory for the Gifted Young American and has served on the Board of Directors of the Colorado Springs Symphony.

FRAN GREENBERG (Mrs. Milton E.), Past President of the Youngstown (Ohio) Symphony Orchestra, does free-lance publicity for local arts groups.

DALE E. HALL, Ph.D., is Assistant Professor of music at the University of Hawaii at Manoa. He is co-authoring a book on the history of the Honolulu Symphony.

JAMES HARPER is a feature writer and music critic for the *St. Petersburg [Florida] Times*. His reviews have won several awards for general excellence in criticism.

FRED HAUPTMAN, M.A., is Assistant Professor of Music at the City College of New York, where he conducts the chorus and orchestra.

JOSEPH R. HERBISON, A. Mus. D., is Director of Music and Performing Arts Education at Hauppauge Public Schools. He is active in government relations for the Music Educators National Conference (MENC) and the New York State School Music Association (NYSSMA).

BETTY E. HIGDON teaches English at Kings River Community College in Reedley, California, and plays second oboe in the Fresno Philharmonic Orchestra.

ARDIS O. HIGGINS (Mrs. Arthur J.), M.M., is an international consultant in music education and the author of books, articles, and music reviews. She is Vice President of the Santa Barbara Symphony Orchestra.

KARL HINTERBICHLER, D.M.A., is Professor of Music at the University of New Mexico. He is Principal Trombonist in the New Mexico Symphony and has had numerous articles, reviews, arrangements, editions, and pedagogical works published.

GERALD R. HOEKSTRA, Ph.D. in Musicology, is Assistant Professor of Music at St. Olaf College in Northfield, Minnesota. He is the author of several journal articles and editions of Renaissance music.

D. KERN HOLOMAN, Ph.D., is Professor and Chairman of Music at the University of California, Davis, where he conducts the University Symphony. He is Chief Program Annotator for the Sacramento Symphony and an authority on the music of Berlioz.

CHARLES R. HURT, Associate Professor of Music (Trombone) at Southwest Texas State University, serves on the staff of the *International Trombone Association Journal* and is Principal Trombonist with the Austin Symphony Orchestra.

ARTHUR R. HUSEBOE, Ph.D., is Professor of English and Humanities Division Chairman at Augustan College. Author of many books and articles, he is a member and former President of the South Dakota Symphony Board.

ALFREDA LOCKE IRWIN is Historian-in-Residence for Chautauqua Institution and is author of *"Three Taps of the Gavel," The Story of Chautauqua*.

ISRAEL J. KATZ, musicologist and former bassoonist, has taught at McGill, Columbia, and the City University of New York. He is a specialist on music of the Mediterranean region.

STEPHEN KELLY, Ph.D., is Associate Professor of Music and Department Co-Chairman at Carleton College. He teaches music history courses, directs an early music ensemble, and plays jazz saxophone.

RICHARD P. KENNELL is Assistant Dean at the Bowling Green State University College of Musical Arts in Bowling Green, Ohio.

CHARLES W. KING, M.S.L.S., is Assistant Music Librarian at the University of Arizona. He is a former school orchestra director and string teacher.

MRS. GEORGE M. KNAPP, a 20-year member and Past President of the Casper Symphony Orchestra's Board of Directors, writes the program notes for all of its concerts.

JOHN W. LAMBERT was educated at the University of North Carolina at Chapel Hill. He is Music Critic for *Spectator Magazine*, a weekly arts newspaper serving Raleigh, Durham, and Chapel Hill.

JOSEPH LITTLE, recipient of the Charlotte Symphony President's Award for his 50 years as flutist with that orchestra, owns a hi-fi shop and is President of the Charlotte Musicians's Association.

NANCY PARKS LOADER is Vice President of Tully Loader Associates Public Relations in Hamden, Connecticut, consultants to the New Haven Symphony Orchestra. She has lectured on public relations at ASOL regional workshops.

REY M. LONGYEAR, Ph.D., Professor of Musicology at the University of Kentucky and former timpanist, is the author of *Schiller and Music* and *Nineteenth-Century Romanticism in Music*, editor of three volumes of Italian symphonies for Garland Press, and has produced over 100 articles and reviews.

JOHN A. MACDONALD, Ph.D., Professor of Music, University of Akron, author and arranger, was formerly Choral Conductor of the Akron Symphony Orchestra (1962–1982) and Assistant Choral Director of the Blossom Festival Chorus (1968–1974).

DAVID MAVES, Composer-in-Residence at The College of Charleston (South Carolina), was timpanist in the Charleston Symphony for eight years. The orchestra performs his works periodically.

DORIS EVANS MCGINTY, Ph.D., is Professor of Musicology and Chairman of the Department of Music at Howard University. She is a former member of the NSO Education and Community Outreach Committee.

ELLIE MEDNICK is Director of Marketing for the Marin Symphony. In the community she is also known for her work as a dancer/choreographer and narrator. She works primarily with children in community, symphony, and high school productions. She has been a "stringer" for National Public Radio.

MARY-THERESE MENNINO is Program Director for Chautauqua Institution, a position that includes managing the Chautauqua Symphony, Opera, Theatre, and Dance Companies. She serves on the Boards of various local and regional arts organizations.

MARTHA D. MINOR, Ph.D., is currently Assistant Professor of Music History and Literature at the University of Northern Iowa.

LINDA V. MOORHOUSE, General Manager of the Canton Symphony Orchestra, is President of the Metropolitan Orchestra Managers Association and a Board member of ASOL and the Organization of Ohio Orchestras.

ROY E. MORGAN, D.H.L., President of Wyoming Valley Broadcasting Company, is Drama, Music, and Art Critic for the *Times Leader*, Wilkes-Barre, Pennsylvania. A former college professor, he has been a broadcaster and writer since 1947.

MYRNA NACHMAN, D.M.A., is Assistant Professor of Music at Nassau Community College (S.U.N.Y.). An active pianist, she has also written articles for *Musical Heritage Review* and the *New Grove Dictionary of Music and Musicians in the United States*.

LOUIS NICHOLAS, M.M., Emeritus Professor of Music, George Peabody College for Teachers, is the former President of the National Association of Teachers of Singing. For 25 years a music critic with *The Nashville Tennessean*, he is also author of *Thor Johnson, American Conductor*.

ELLIE MEINDL O'HAGAN is the Public Relations Coordinator of the Oregon Symphony Association. A native of Chicago, Mrs. O'Hagan lives in Portland, Oregon, with her husband and children.

MARJORIE OREN, trained with the Civic Orchestra of the Chicago Symphony, has been a cellist with the Monterey County (California) Symphony for 20 years. She was Symphony Librarian for 10 years, to 1981–1982.

REV. ARTHUR H. PARÉ, S.J., is Chairman of the Social Studies Department at Bishop Connolly High School, Fall River, Massachusetts. He plays horn in the Fall River Symphony.

ROBERT R. PATTENGALE, Ph.D., is Professor of Music at Moorhead State University, Moorhead, Minnesota. A musicologist whose principal area is eighteenth-century performance practice, he is active with the Fargo-Moorhead Symphony as harpsichordist and Program Annotator.

HELEN SIVE PAXTON is Director of Public Relations of the New Jersey Symphony Orchestra. Author of *Music's Connecticut Yankee* (Atheneum, 1977), a young-adult biography of Charles Ives, she is also a Program Annotator for the Chamber Music Society of Lincoln Center.

GEORGE PERKINS is Associate Professor of Music at Eastern Montana College, where he teaches piano and theory. He was Conductor of the Billings Symphony from 1955 to 1984.

FLOYD PETERSON is Professor of Music at the University of Idaho. He is a clarinetist in solo and chamber music performance and serves on the Boards of various arts associations in the Pacific Northwest.

JAMES PORTER is Professor of Music at the University of California, Los Angeles. He has published widely and has contributed articles on Europe to the *New Grove Dictionary of Music and Musicians*.

WALLACE J. RAVE, Ph.D., is Associate Professor of Music at Arizona State University. His major areas of research are in instrumental music of the seventeenth century and music of the twentieth century.

MORRETTE RIDER, D.Ed., Dean, School of Music, University of Oregon, has conducted more than 600 orchestral concerts throughout the world. He is a member of both the Eugene Symphony's Board and its Artistic Advisory Committee.

CHARLES A. ROECKLE, Ph.D., is Assistant Dean of the College of Fine Arts and a Lecturer in Musicology at the University of Texas at Austin.

BRUCE SAYLOR, composer, is Associate Professor at the Aaron Copland School of Music at Queens College. His works have been commissioned and performed by major soloists and orchestras, and he writes about contemporary music.

ANN M. SCHMIDT, B.A., is the Marketing/Public Relations Assistant of the Oklahoma Symphony Orchestra.

JOSEPH B. SCHMOLL, Ph.D., is Chairman of the Music and Art Departments at Texas Southern University. The author of books and articles, he is also a composer and a horn player.

DAVID SCHNEIDER, a violinist with the San Francisco Symphony for 50 years (1936–1986), is also a retired Lecturer-Professor at San Francisco State University and author of *The San Francisco Symphony: Music, Maestros and Musicians* (Presidio Press, 1984).

GEORGE SELTZER is Emeritus Professor of Music at Miami University. The author of *The Professional Orchestra in the United States* and other books and articles, he has been a member of professional orchestras for over 40 years.

DON W. SIEKER, Ph.D., is Associate Professor of English at New Hampshire College. His interest in the eighteenth century includes keyboard music, particularly that of Scarlatti, Soler, and Mozart.

EUGENE THAMON SIMPSON, Ed.D., is Professor of Music and Director of the Chamber Choir and Choral Union at Glassboro State College. He writes for the *Choral Journal* and *NATS Bulletin*.

CATHERINE PARSONS SMITH, D.M.A., Associate Professor of Music at the University of Nevada Reno and Principal Flute of the Reno Philharmonic, is the author of a biography of the composer Mary Carr Moore.

NORRIS L. STEPHENS, Ph.D., is Music Librarian at the University of Pittsburgh. An organist, carillonneur, and composer, he is also an author of articles and contributor to major encyclopedias.

ANDREW STILLER, Ph.D., is Secretary of the Composers' Alliance of Buffalo and plays woodwinds with the Buffalo New Music Ensemble. He teaches college and is author of *Handbook of Instrumentation*.

ROBERT STOCK, Ph.D., is Associate Professor of Public Administration at San Diego State University. A researcher on tourism and national economic development, he presently is doing work for the Israel Department of Tourism and is researching a political analysis of the Mondale campaign.

JACOB STOCKINGER, Ph.D., is a reporter and arts writer for *The Capital Times* in Madison, Wisconsin, where he also teaches journalism at the University of Wisconsin and pursues his amateur career as a pianist.

RALPH THIBODEAU, M.A., is Professor of Music Literature and Humanities at Del Mar College, Corpus Christi, Texas. He is also Music Critic of the Corpus Christi *Caller-Times*.

DONALD THOMPSON, Ph.D., is Chairman of the University of Puerto Rico Music Department, Music Critic for the *San Juan Star*, and the author of many publications dealing with music in the Caribbean.

DAVID G. TOVEY, Ph.D., Assistant Professor in the Department of Music at Cleveland State University, is also an organist, choral conductor, and member of the Advisory Council for the Musical Arts Association of Cleveland.

VIOLET VAGRAMIAN-NISHANIAN, Ph.D., is Associate Professor of Counterpoint, Form and Analysis, and Music History at Florida International University. The author of journal articles and compositions, she is also a pianist.

BERTIL H. VAN BOER, JR., Ph.D., is Assistant Professor of Musicology at Brigham Young University. He is the author of numerous editions and articles on eighteenth-century music.

RALPH E. VERRASTRO, Ed.D., is Professor of Music and Director of the School of Music at The University of Georgia, Athens, Georgia.

STENNIS WALDON, M.M., A.A.G.O., is Professor of Music at Pasadena City College and is Director of Music for the First Congregational Church of Pasadena, California.

RUTH WATANABE, Ph.D., Professor of Music Bibliography, Archivist, and former Librarian, Eastman School of Music, is Past President of the Music Library Association and Program Annotator for the Rochester Philharmonic Orchestra.

NEAL M. WEAVER, M.M., Principal Flute and Personnel Manager of the El Paso Symphony, is currently writing a complete history of that orchestra.

JOHN WILLIAM WOLDT, Ph.D., Professor of Music at Texas Christian University in Fort Worth, was formerly Principal Horn in the Fort Worth Symphony and the Fort Worth Opera Orchestras.

JOSEPH T. WORK, D.M.A., Professor of Viola and Chairman of the String Area at Western Michigan University, is Principal Viola of the Kalamazoo Symphony.